Praise for Charles Glass's *Americans in Paris*

"[Charles Glass] sketches in the complexities, moral, political, and practical, that assailed American expatriates as Paris moved from the comfort of the 'phony war' to the privations of the real war. . . . Such stories would be interesting in their own right. The extra value that Mr. Glass brings is to insert them seamlessly into the context of international diplomacy and the history of the war."
—*The Economist*

"Glass, a former journalist, has written a lively account of the moral and political quandaries and increasing privations under German occupation. He skillfully uses memoirs, diaries, letters, documents, and official records to draw a picture of expatriates caught in a mesh of deceit, bravery, self-sacrifice, and fear, and places them in the context of diplomacy and the wider war."
—*Pittsburgh Post-Gazette*

"An account of the 2,000 Americans who remained in Paris during the Second World War is rich in intrigue and heroism. . . . For anyone interested in France during this period it is a fascinating treat." —Antony Beevor, *Daily Telegraph* (London)

"Charles Glass has written one of those rare books that makes you laugh and cry, that catches you up in the sweep of history."
—*The Irish Times*

"These fascinating tales reflect the complicated network of choices —passive compromise, outright collaboration, patient retreat, and active resistance—that existed for Americans caught in the German web." —*Booklist*

"Glass's tales . . . illuminate a dark, fascinating period in World War II history." —*Kirkus Reviews*

"Charles Glass's fascinating and absorbing account of American civilians trapped in Paris under the Nazi occupation. . . . He makes us think again about the nature of life in occupied Paris and refreshes what many would consider something of a tired and overworked period of contemporary history. . . . Glass writes with great fluency and verve and evident scholarship and has unearthed facts and figures that both illuminate and perturb."
—*Sunday Times* (London)

"Charles Glass's highly impressive new book tells us of an assortment of U.S. citizens who remained in Paris during the war. Charles Glass describes the various realities with just the right combination of objectivity and compassion; this is a moving and deeply thought-provoking book." —*Sunday Telegraph* (London)

"Provides valuable insight into a little-known theater of that great tragicomic mess which we call the Second World War."
—*Spectator*

"Wartime France comes alive in Charles Glass's new book. . . . A fine piece of historical research, and powerful insight into one of the darkest periods of modern European history."
—*Evening Standard* (London)

"A taut, beguiling narrative." —*The Daily Express* (London)

PENGUIN BOOKS

AMERICANS IN PARIS

Charles Glass has written *Tribes with Flags*, *The Tribes Triumphant*, *Money for Old Rope*, and *The Northern Front*. He was ABC News chief Middle East correspondent from 1983 to 1993 and has covered conflict in the Middle East, Africa, and the Balkans. A regular contributor to *Harper's Magazine* and the *London Review of Books*, he divides his time among Paris, London, and Tuscany.

CHARLES GLASS

Americans in Paris

LIFE AND DEATH
UNDER NAZI OCCUPATION

PENGUIN BOOKS

PENGUIN BOOKS

Published by the Penguin Group
Penguin Group (USA) Inc., 375 Hudson Street, New York, New York 10014, U.S.A.
Penguin Group (Canada), 90 Eglinton Avenue East, Suite 700, Toronto,
Ontario, Canada M4P 2Y3 (a division of Pearson Penguin Canada Inc.)
Penguin Books Ltd, 80 Strand, London WC2R 0RL, England
Penguin Ireland, 25 St Stephen's Green, Dublin 2, Ireland (a division of Penguin Books Ltd)
Penguin Group (Australia), 250 Camberwell Road, Camberwell,
Victoria 3124, Australia (a division of Pearson Australia Group Pty Ltd)
Penguin Books India Pvt Ltd, 11 Community Centre,
Panchsheel Park, New Delhi – 110 017, India
Penguin Group (NZ), 67 Apollo Drive, Rosedale, North Shore 0632,
New Zealand (a division of Pearson New Zealand Ltd)
Penguin Books (South Africa) (Pty) Ltd, 24 Sturdee Avenue,
Rosebank, Johannesburg 2196, South Africa

Penguin Books Ltd, Registered Offices:
80 Strand, London WC2R 0RL, England

First published in Great Britain by HarperPress, an imprint of HarperCollins Publishers Limited 2009
First published in the United States of America by Viking Penguin,
a member of Penguin Group (USA) Inc. 2010
Published in Penguin Books 2011

1   3   5   7   9   10   8   6   4   2

THE LIBRARY OF CONGRESS HAS CATALOGED THE HARDCOVER EDITION AS FOLLOWS:
Glass, Charles, 1951–
Americans in Paris : life and death under Nazi occupation / Charles Glass.
p.   cm.
Originally published : London : Harper, 2009.
Includes bibliographical references and index.
ISBN 978-1-59420-242-1 (hc.)
ISBN 978-0-14-311866-4 (pbk.)
1. Americans—France—Paris—History—20th century.   2. France—History—German
occupation, 1940–1945.   3. Paris (France)—History—1940–1944.   4. Paris (France)—
Intellectual life—20th century.   5. World War, 1939–1945—France—Paris.   I. Title.
DC718.A44G53   2010
944'.3610816092313—dc22   2009039650

Printed in the United States of America
Map illustrations: www.joygosney.co.uk

To the memory and glorious spirit of Charles Glass, Jr.,
my father and unwavering partisan,
born 11 October, 1920, died 2 February, 2008.

CONTENTS

PART SIX: 1944

PART SEVEN: 24–26 August 1944

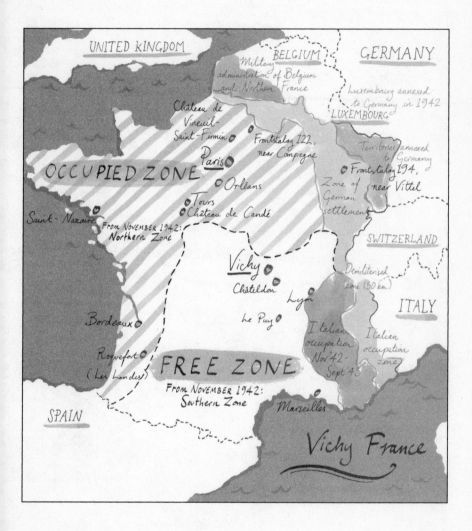

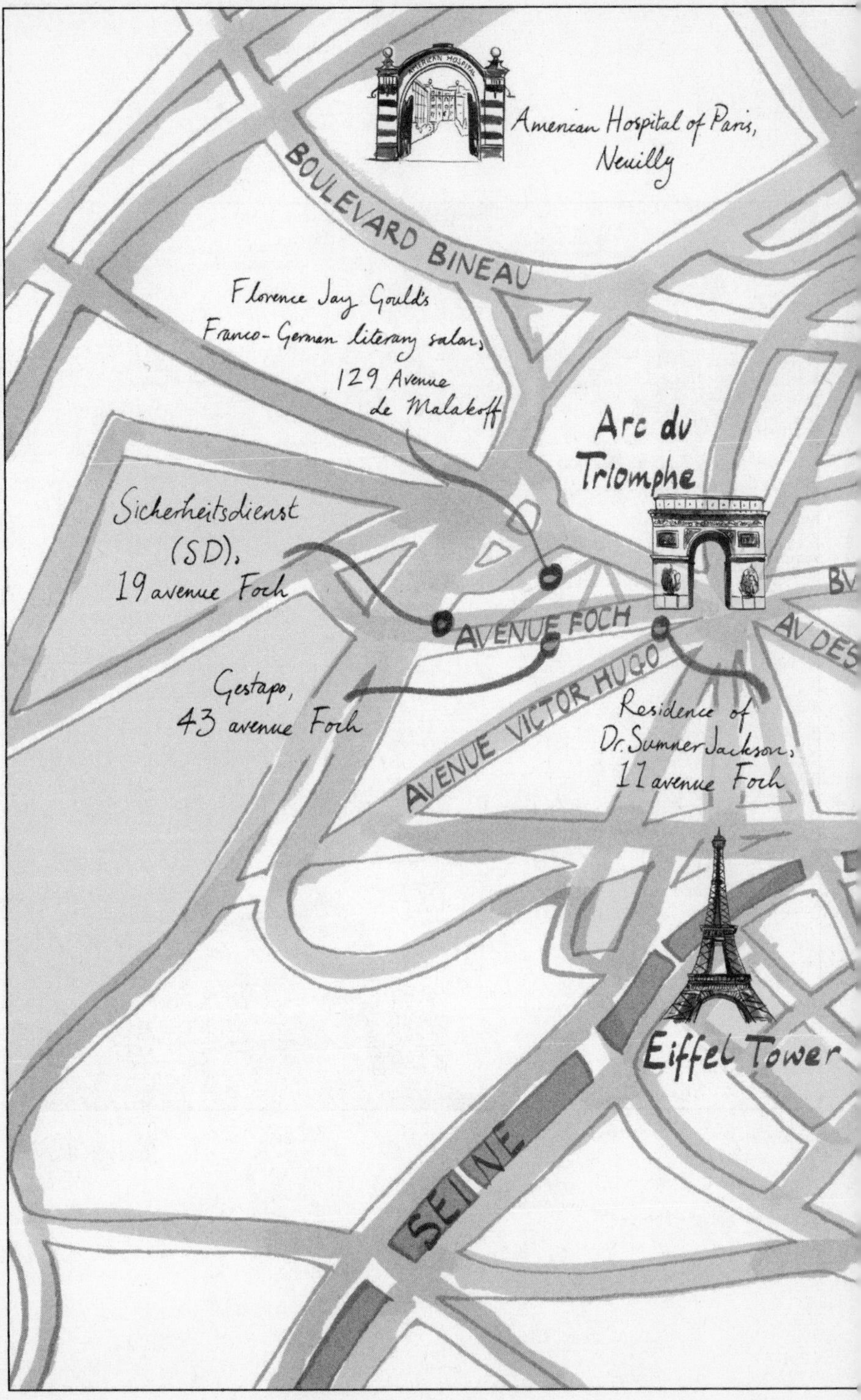

American Hospital of Paris, Neuilly

BOULEVARD BINEAU

Florence Jay Gould's
Franco-German literary salon,
129 Avenue
de Malakoff

Arc du
Triomphe

Sicherheitsdienst
(SD),
19 avenue Foch

AVENUE FOCH

BV

AV DES

Gestapo,
43 avenue Foch

AVENUE VICTOR HUGO

Residence of
Dr. Sumner Jackson,
11 avenue Foch

Eiffel Tower

SEINE

Occupied Paris
1940-1944

American Library in Paris,
9 rue de Teheran

BVD DE CLICHY

Hôtel Crillon,
first German Army HQ in Paris 1940

RUE LA FAYETTE

Hôtel Bristol,
American residence
under diplomatic
protection from
1940 to 1942

AUSSMANN

Hôtel Meurice,
last German Army HQ in Paris 1944

Ritz Hotel where
Charles Bedaux
lived in Paris

-ELYSÉES

PLACE
DE LA
CONCORDE

American Embassy,
2 avenue
Gabriel

BVD SAINT-GERMAIN

Notre
Dame

Residence of René and
Josée de Chambrun,
6 place du Palais Bourbon

Shakespeare & Co,
12 rue
de l'Odéon

Residence of Aldebert
and Clara de Chambrun,
58 rue de Vaugirard

La Maison des
Amis des Livres,
7 rue de l'Odéon

The Monument in
Place Saint-Michel

LIST OF ILLUSTRATIONS

The author and publisher are grateful to the following for permission to reproduce their copyright material. While every effort has been made to trace the owners of copyright material reproduced herein, the publishers would like to apologise for any omissions and will be pleased to incorporate missing acknowledgements in any future editions.

Clara's house. *(In* Shadows Lengthen *by Clara Longworth de Chambrum, Scribner, New York, 1949)*

Pierre Laval leaving the Château de Châteldon. *(©Roger-Viollet/TopFoto)*

Charles Bedaux and his wife, Fern, in South Africa. *(In* The Price of Power *by Jim Christy, Doubleday and Company Inc., New York, 1984)*

Charles and Fern Bedaux. *(©Bettman/CORBIS)*

J. Edgar Hoover. *(MPI/Getty Images)*

Charles Bedaux's country residence, the Château de Candé. *(© Condé Nast Archive/CORBIS)*

Dr Sumner Jackson with his son, Phillip. *(Courtesy of Phillip Jackson)*

SD Major-General Karl Oberg. *(© Rue des Archives/Tal)*

Dr Edmund Gros. *(Courtesy of The American Hospital of Paris)*

Dr Sumner Jackson, Dr Thierry Martel, Dr Edmund Gros and Toquette. *(Courtesy of The American Hospital of Paris)*

The entrance to the American Hospital in Neuilly. *(Time & Life Pictures/Getty Images)*

Drue Leyton. *(Otto Dyar/General Photographic Agency/Getty Images)*

Florence Jay Gould. *(© Fonds Foundation Florence Gould in Florence Gould by Gilles Cornut-Gentille and Phillipe Michel-Thiriet, Mercure de France, Paris, 1989)*

Polly Peabody. *(In* Occupied Territory *by Polly Peabody, The Cresst Press, London, 1941)*

General Otto von Stülpnagel. *(©Roger-Viollet/TopFoto)*

Karl-Heinrich von Stülpnagel. *(akg-images/ullstein bild)*

A German military parade passes the Hôtel de Crillon. *(RDA/Tallandier/Archive Photos/Getty Images)*

Paris under occupation outside the Hôtel Meurice. *(©Roger-Viollet/TopFoto)*

Marshal Pétain, pictured with his cabinet. *(akg-images)*

Marshal Pétain with American Ambassador to Vichy, Admiral William D. Leahy. *(akg-images)*

Shakespeare's *King John. (In* Shadows Lengthen *by Clara Longworth de Chambrum, Scribner, New York, 1949)*

Parisians welcome an Allied tank. *(RDA/Getty Images)*

American flags on the Champs-Elysées. *(Roger Viollet/Getty Images)*

Ernest Hemingway in Sylvia Beach's flat. *(Princeton University Library)*

Phillip "Pete" Jackson. *(Courtesy of Phillip Jackson)*

Charlotte "Toquette" Jackson. *(Courtesy of Phillip Jackson)*

INTRODUCTION

IN THE PLAZA WHERE THE Boulevard Saint-Michel approaches the River Seine, water cascades down stone blocks of a vast monumental tribute to those who endured the four-year German occupation of Paris. The Archangel Michael stands guard above an old memorial that was rededicated after the Second World War, above all, to the civilians killed nearby when the people of Paris finally rose against their oppressors in the summer of 1944. Reading the inscriptions and looking at the stone lions beside the shallow pool, I used to imagine life during the fifty months from 14 June 1940, when the Germans marched proudly into Paris, and 25 August 1944, when they retreated in shame. I wondered how I would have behaved while the Wehrmacht ruled the cultural capital of Europe. Many books and films on the period depicted French behaviour that varied from self-sacrifice and heroism to treason and complicity in genocide. But what would I, as an American, have done? Was it possible to survive until liberation day, 26 August 1944, without compromising or collaborating? Would I have risked my life, or the lives of my family, by fighting for the Resistance? Or would I have waited patiently with the majority of Parisians for the German retreat?

Nearly 30,000 Americans lived in or near Paris before the Second World War. Those who refused to leave were, paraphrasing Dickens, the best and the worst of America. Like the French, some collaborated, others resisted. The Germans forced some into slave labour. At least one was taken back to the United States to face a trial for treason. Americans in Paris under the occupation were among the most eccentric, original and disparate collection of their countrymen anywhere – tested as few others have been before or since. This is their story.

1

When Britain and France declared war on Germany for invading Poland in September 1939, American Ambassador William Bullitt advised United States citizens without vital business to leave France immediately. At least 5,000 ignored him and stayed. While many had professional and family ties to Paris, the majority had a peculiarly American love for the city that had its origins in the debt the young United States owed to the Frenchmen who volunteered with the Marquis de Lafayette to fight for American independence after 1776. The American love affair with Paris, where the United States opened its first diplomatic mission, was shared by Benjamin Franklin, John Adams (whose wife, Abigail, famously said, 'No one leaves Paris without a feeling of *tristesse*'), Thomas Jefferson, Thomas Paine, James Monroe and generations of writers, artists, musicians, diplomats, journalists, socialites and financiers. It was with a certain pride that Walt Whitman wrote, 'I am a real Parisian.' A year or two in Paris was a vital component in the education of any socially acceptable young American.

Where the rich led, poorer painters, writers, singers and vagabonds followed. An African-American soldier expressed this love better than most, as his troopship from France cruised into New York harbour after the First World War. An officer asked him why he was saluting the Statue of Liberty, and he answered, 'Because France gave her to us.' The thousands of Americans who stood with the French during the humiliation of German rule from 1940 to 1944 found their relationships to Paris and America expressed in the famed lyrics of Josephine Baker, the quintessential American Parisian, '*J'ai deux amours, mon pays et Paris*.'('I have two loves, my country and Paris.')

Among the few thousand Americans who remained in Paris throughout the war, four had pronounced reactions to the occupation that represented in relief the experiences of the rest of their countrymen. The French-born, naturalized American millionaire Charles Bedaux did business as he had before the war. If he compromised with the occupier, his rationale was that European industry had to be preserved for the post-war world. Sylvia Beach attempted to keep her English language bookshop, Shakespeare and Company, functioning as it had in the 1920s when it was a beacon for American, British and French writers. She preserved her humanity by defying the Germans in small ways and giving moral support to French friends whose resistance was more open and violent. Clara Longworth de Chambrun, whose brother had been America's Speaker of the House of Representatives and husband to Teddy Roosevelt's daughter Alice, worked tirelessly for the benefit of the readers at the American Library of Paris – even when this meant dealing with German officials. For her, duty lay in holding firm, obeying a Vichy government that she believed was legitimate and waiting for D-Day to deliver France from its agony. Her relationship to the occupying power was complicated by the fact that her Franco-American son, Count René de Chambrun, was married to the daughter of Vichy France's prime minister, Pierre Laval. Her husband, Count Aldebert de Chambrun, was a direct descendant of the Marquis de Lafayette and had been born in Washington, DC. The American Hospital of Paris, which the Germans coveted, was kept out of their hands through the deception and conscientious effort of this American citizen and former general of the French Army. The American Hospital's chief surgeon, Dr Sumner Jackson, took the clearest decision of all: from the first day of the occupation, he resisted. Although he risked his life, and those of his wife and young son, the Yankee physician from Maine never doubted for a moment where duty lay: not in survival, not in cooperation, but in determined resistance to what he saw as the overriding evil of the age.

The Americans in inter-war Paris were young and old, black and white, rich and poor – as diverse a collection of opposed beliefs and backgrounds as in any American metropolis. Among them were communists and fascists, Democrats and Republicans, the apolitical and the apathetic, opportunists and idealists. They were writers, painters, musicians, businessmen, bankers, journalists, clergy, photographers, physicians, lawyers, teachers, diplomats, spies, conmen and gangsters. Until the Germans turned France into a version of their own prison-state, African-Americans, homosexuals, lesbians and bohemians felt freer in Paris than in the socially more repressive United States. German occupation was not enough to send all of them home.

In the spring of 1940, after nine months of the *drôle de guerre* or phony war, normality was returning to Paris. Parisians of all nationalities had become accustomed to war without battles and shared the illusion that the Germans would never penetrate the 'impregnable' Maginot Line. Most, apart from realists like General Charles de Gaulle and Ambassador William Bullitt, did not believe Germany would or could attack France. Restaurants were doing brisk business. Charles Bedaux was throwing lavish parties for European royalty. Josephine Baker reopened on the Champs Elysées with Maurice Chevalier in an extravagant song and dance revue. American Eugene Bullard's Le Duc jazz club in Montmartre attracted sell-out audiences. Americans in the city led enchanted lives, discussing art and love affairs in cafés, some sending their children to the American school and most preparing for summer in the south. Even as the Germans were approaching in late May, the Runyonesque sports columnist of the *Paris Herald Tribune*, Sparrow Robinson, wrote, 'Owing to unsettled conditions, the racing card scheduled for this afternoon at Longchamps has been called off.'

The 'unsettled conditions' referred to the Nazi blitzkrieg that conquered Denmark, Holland and Belgium. Refugees from the occupied countries escaped to France. Belgian cars and horse-drawn carts packed with clothing and furniture were the first omens that France would also fall. German Panzer divisions broke into France through the poorly defended Ardennes forest, beginning the Battle of France that Britain and France would lose in three short weeks. This engagement – a swift, merciless advance by Wehrmacht armour and Luftwaffe air power – suddenly altered the balance of power in Europe. The British Expeditionary Force retreated from Dunkirk, and the Germans captured more than a million French soldiers. The way to Paris lay open to Hitler's armies. Most Parisians, French and foreigners alike, fled the city ahead of the Germans. Escape was a mistake. The Germans bombed refugee columns on the roads, but they did not bomb Paris itself. As fighting raged along the River Meuse, Ambassador Bullitt pleaded with President Franklin Delano Roosevelt to provide the French and the British with aircraft to withstand the German invasion. Roosevelt promised surplus planes for shipment from Canada, but it was too late.

French Premier Paul Reynaud, preparing to flee to Tours with his government, declared Paris an open city and asked Bullitt to persuade the Wehrmacht not to destroy it. Bullitt, a one-time playboy and writer who co-authored with Sigmund Freud a psychological study of President Woodrow Wilson, spent the last nights of May 1940 in his wine cellar to avoid the Luftwaffe bombs. One nearly killed him. Bullitt was as close to France's senior politicians, especially Prime Minister Reynaud, as he was to his old friend Roosevelt. Bullitt was the only ambassador still in Paris when the Germans arrived on 14 June 1940.

At first, Americans shared the French panic that the Germans would treat Paris as they had Warsaw – raping, killing and destroying as they entered. But the Nazis' racist ideology accorded a higher place to the French than it did to the Poles. They did not target Americans, who were allowed to stay and work unhindered. The two most important American organizations, the American Hospital of Paris and the American Library of Paris, were open to Americans and French alike. A few courageous American consuls disobeyed State Department orders by issuing passports and visas to Jewish refugees and establishing safe routes to help them reach North and South America.

The African-Americans who stayed were not as lucky as their white countrymen. After Adolf Hitler's only visit to Paris, on 24 June 1940, the Germans banned concerts by black American musicians. Proclamations published in the *Officiel du Spectacle* set out to eliminate what the Nazis called 'degenerate Jewish-Negro jazz.' A month later, the Germans ordered a census of all foreign nationals in Paris. Black Americans were ordered to report to the police, and the American consulate did not protect them. The famous American jazz trumpeter Arthur Briggs was sent in late June 1940 to a concentration camp at St. Denis, where he formed a classical orchestra with other black musicians from America, Britain and the West Indies. The Germans detained many other African-American performers, including Roberta Dodd Crawford from Chicago. She was a prominent singer, known as Princess Tovalou since her marriage in 1923 to Prince Tovalou of Benin. Another trumpeter, Harry Cooper, was sent to an internment camp. The African-American classical composer and musician Maceo Jefferson escaped Paris – only to be captured outside the city and interned at Frontslag 122. Henry Crowder, whose thirteen year affair with British shipping heiress Nancy Cunard shocked white America more than it did Paris society, was giving a concert in Belgium when the

Nazis invaded. He escaped on the last train to Paris, but the Luftwaffe bombed it. Continuing to his beloved Paris on foot, he was taken by the Germans. Thus, the vibrant African-American community that thrived in the 1920s and 1930s was for the most part absent from Paris during the occupation.

Unlike other African-Americans, Josephine Baker was not interned, thanks to her fame in Paris and abroad. An entertainer who had captivated Paris in the 1920s with her topless *Danse Sauvage*, she was a much-married and much-loved social fixture. Her decision not to abandon France was moral: the Nazis represented an extreme version of the racial hatred she had escaped in the United States. She stayed at her chateau in the country at first and joined the new French Resistance. Her commander was Jacques Abtey, the police officer for whom she had worked spying on Germans in Paris before the war. Miss Baker smuggled documents out of France between the pages of her sheet music and took Resistance leaders disguised as band members to clandestine meetings in Portugal. She made her way to Morocco, where she entertained French and American troops after the North African invasion of November 1942.

The occupation threw up heroes and villains, but more often it produced in the people of Paris a determination to stand fast until the storm passed. In 1940, they did not know who would win the war. They doubted that the United States would give up its cherished neutrality to confront the Nazi menace. Choices were difficult, frequently involving alternatives that were less bad rather than clearly good or evil. When it was all over, the names of the Americans who stayed with their French neighbours for those fifty cruel months are invisibly etched alongside all the others honoured by the monument in the Place Saint-Michel.

PART ONE

———◆◆◆———

14 June 1940

ONE

The American Mayor of Paris

JUST BEFORE MIDNIGHT ON Thursday, 13 June 1940, two men walked out of the American Embassy in Paris into the vast and deserted Place de la Concorde. The French capital's blacked-out streets presented a strange spectacle to Robert Murphy, the embassy's counsellor, and naval attaché Commander Roscoe Hillenkoetter. The government, the army and most of the population had abandoned Paris. Two million people, including the vast majority of the 30,000 Americans that Murphy estimated lived in Paris before the war, had fled in fear of the conquering Wehrmacht. Thousands of victorious German soldiers were poised to occupy the undefended city at dawn. American Ambassador William Christian Bullitt, whom the departing French government had effectively appointed mayor of Paris on 12 June, had assured the Wehrmacht's commanders that Paris was an 'open city'. Open cities waived their right to resist in exchange for a peaceful occupation. Paris had already given up. Twelve hours earlier, at noon, Robert Murphy barely recognized the previously vibrant avenue des Champs-Elysées: 'The only living creatures in sight were three abandoned dogs cavorting beneath the large French flags which still hung at each corner of the great concourse.' On the opposite, Left Bank of the Seine, sheep belonging to refugees from northern France grazed on the Hôpital des Invalides' ceremonial lawns.

Amid the forlorn expanse of the Place de la Concorde, its Egyptian obelisk swaddled in sandbags and its roundabout eerily devoid of traffic, Murphy and Hillenkoetter watched four spectral figures approach

9

out of the darkness. Murphy recognized Chief Rabbi Julien Weill, religious head of Paris's Jewish community. With the *Grand Rabbin* were his wife and two friends. Murphy appreciated their fears. As head consular official for the previous nine years until he became counsellor, Murphy's responsibility had been the well-being of France's American community. When the Germans began their rampage through the north of France in May, American citizens demanded embassy protection. At the same time, fourteen million Belgian, Dutch and French men, women and children took to the road ahead of the Nazis. Knowing of German atrocities in Poland during the Blitzkrieg of 1939, Parisians, especially Jews, were understandably fearful. Murphy reflected, 'We in the embassy felt more sympathy for these victims than we did for a considerable number of Americans who became panic-stricken at the last minute and behaved as if they were particular targets of the Nazis. They had much less reason to become alarmed, since we were not at war.'

Rabbi Weill could have obtained an American visa and gone to New York, where his brother, Professor Felix Weill, taught French and was a United States citizen. Despite Nazi treatment of Jews in Germany and the lands the German Army had occupied since 1938, he had chosen to remain in Paris. Knowing now that the French government itself – including the tough and patriotic Jewish interior minister, Georges Mandel – had fled Paris, the rabbi was reconsidering his decision. Murphy thought that Rabbi Weill had 'very understandable reasons' for changing his mind. The rabbi asked Murphy and Hillenkoetter whether he and his family might find places in an embassy car, with its diplomatic immunity, leaving Paris. It was too late, Murphy said. German Panzer divisions surrounded Paris. The exiled American Ambassador to Poland, Anthony Drexel Biddle, Jr, and Embassy Secretary H. Freeman Matthews had departed with the fleeing French government for Tours and were following it on to Bordeaux. No other diplomats were leaving Paris that night. Nonetheless, Murphy lent the rabbi and his family a car whose chauffeur drove them to the city gates. There, German sentries ordered them to return.

The two Americans continued their promenade. No cafés were open, as some usually were at midnight. No light shone from any window or street lamp. The prostitutes had vanished from their usual posts along the rue Saint-Denis and up in Pigalle. The great nighttime gathering places, the markets of Les Halles and the jazz clubs of Montmartre, were closed. Many of the vibrant American 'Negro' community, like night club owner Ada 'Bricktop' Smith and band leader Benny Carter, had left Paris in the autumn of 1939 or were about to sail on the last America-bound ship from Bordeaux. Even the most celebrated American woman in Paris, 34-year-old chanteuse Josephine Baker, had left – first as a Red Cross nurse aiding the war's refugees, then for the safety of her country chateau. 'The few people who remained in the city were buttoned up in their shuttered homes,' Murphy noted. The only light Murphy could see was arching across the sky north of Paris, each burst of artillery reminding him of a shooting star. Commander Hillenkoetter similarly recalled, 'Contrary to rumors, the night passed quietly, although artillery firing could be seen and heard in the northwest.'

The night sky was at last clear of a week's all-pervasive black smoke including that from the burning files of the French government and British Embassy. Most of the conflagration had come from the Standard Oil Company's petroleum reserves. Standard's man in Paris, William Dewitt Crampton, had set the stocks alight at the request of the French General Staff only after checking with the American Embassy. Robert Murphy, rather than let a full month's supply of petrol fuel German tanks, had told Crampton to go ahead.

Murphy, the red-haired Irish Catholic diplomat from Milwaukee, and Hillenkoetter, a 43-year-old Annapolis graduate from St Louis, returned to the rue de Boissy d'Anglas at the northwest corner of the Place de la Concorde. They heard, coming along the Seine from the east, the gigantic bells in the Cathedral of Notre Dame's spires tolling midnight to herald the new day, 14 June 1940. The embassy's iron gates, opposite the façade of the now-shuttered Hôtel Crillon in its brooding Palladian majesty, opened to admit Murphy and Hillenkoetter. They entered the chancellery, where, along with Ambassador Bullitt and a skeleton staff, they waited for the German army. Theirs was the last walk anyone took through free Paris.

The American community in Paris, the largest in continental Europe, had little to fear from the Germans. The United States stood aloof from the war between Germany and the Allies, and it enjoyed the respect of both sides. Although Ambassador Bullitt had advised American citizens without vital business to leave when France and Britain declared war on Germany in September 1939, about half had elected to stay. The *drôle de guerre*, which the Germans called the *Sitzkrieg* and the British and Americans the 'phoney war', dragged on for the next eight months. Only the occasional air raid drill or the sight of sandbags around the monuments disturbed their routine. In May 1940, the German advance through Holland and Belgium into France was so swift that the Americans who feared life under German occupation fled south from Paris. Three weeks before the city fell, as the French and British armies retreated, *The New York Times*' front page announced, 'Most Americans Staying in Paris': 'The United States Embassy said that of the slightly more than 3,600 Americans in the Paris district on Dec. 31, about 2,500 are still here. They are mostly businessmen and members of their families and newspaper men, more of whom have been arriving recently.'

The journalists were not the only American arrivals. American Field Service ambulances, funded and directed by the indefatigable sister of New York financier J. P. Morgan, Miss Anne Morgan, ferried wounded British and French soldiers to hospitals from the front throughout the Battle of France. As soon as the Wehrmacht invaded neighbouring Belgium on 10 May, hundreds of young American men rushed to France. They swore to defend democracy, just as 17,000 Frenchmen had answered the Marquis de Lafayette's call to fight for American independence. So many Americans attempted to join the French Army during the Battle of France that the French could not accommodate them all. Twenty-seven-year-old Tom McBride of Queens, New York, and twelve aviator colleagues attempted to reconstitute the old Lafayette Escadrille, the squadron of American pilots who fought for France in the Great War. When they reached Paris on 1 May 1940, they were welcomed by General Aldebert de Chambrun, a direct descendant of Lafayette, and the air minister. 'They showed us all over Paris,' McBride said, 'then dropped us cold.' He complained, 'All the Air Minister would say was, "Wait. Wait. Wait."' The French Air Corps commissioned McBride a lieutenant, but he never got the chance to fly against the Luftwaffe. Undeterred, he went to Canada and joined the Royal Canadian Air Force.

American citizens who remained in Paris had little to fear. The embassy issued more than 1,000 red certificates, signed by Third Secretary Tyler Thompson, to indicate which houses and businesses belonged to American citizens and could not, under international law, be touched. The Americans' institutions – the American Hospital in the fashionable western suburb of Neuilly, the American Library in the rue de Téhéran, the American Cathedral on the avenue George-V, the American Church on the Quai d'Orsay, the Rotary Club, the American Chamber of Commerce and many other clubs and charitable societies – were still functioning. The American Church bulletin had announced the previous Sunday, 'The American Church will continue its activities and remain open throughout the days to come. The building will be open daily and the various groups will meet as usual.' The Americans' newspaper, the *Paris Herald Tribune*, went on publishing until 12 June, the last paper sold in Paris before the Germans arrived. The American Ambassador, despite White House and State Department entreaties, refused to leave. 'No American ambassador in Paris has ever run away from anything,' Bullitt cabled President Franklin Delano Roosevelt, 'and that I think is the best tradition we have in the American diplomatic service.' That tradition dated to Gouverneur Morris's decision to stay during the French Revolution. Elihu B. Washburne continued it throughout the German occupation of 1870. In 1914, when Germany's offensive put Paris within range of the Kaiser's artillery, every ambassador except the American, Myron T. Herrick, fled. Bullitt would not to be the first to cut and run.

Born in Philadelphia in January 1891 to a WASP family of rich lawyers and railroad magnates who traced their American ancestors through Patrick Henry and Pocahontas, Bullitt spent much of his youth in Europe. His mother's family, the Horowitzes, was originally German Jewish. The family spoke French at home, and he learned German in Munich. Graduating from Yale in 1912, Bullitt covered the world war in Russia, Germany, Austria and France as a correspondent for the *Philadelphia Public Ledger*. When America entered on the Allied side in 1917, the State Department hired him to conduct research for its intelligence section. President Woodrow Wilson took him to the Paris Peace Conference in 1918 as part of the American commission. Bullitt resigned, along with historian Samuel Eliot Morison and six other diplomats, to protest the terms of the Versailles Treaty. He pointed out to Wilson that the treaty, with its other flaws, left three million Germans under Czech rule and abandoned thirty-six million Chinese in Shantung to Japan. His resignation letter lamented, 'But our government has consented now to deliver the suffering peoples of the world to new oppressions, subjection, and dismemberments – a new century of war.' He predicted, 'This isn't a treaty of peace. I can see at least eleven wars in it.' Political oblivion followed, but he had the funds to enjoy himself in a palace in Istanbul and luxurious apartments in Paris. His only novel, *It's Not Done*, sold 150,000 copies in 1925 – prompting Ernest Hemingway, whose books were not selling as well, to mention him in a letter to F. Scott Fitzgerald in 1927 as 'Bill Bullitt or Bull Billet, a big Jew from Yale and a fellow novel writer'. He married Louise Bryant, whose late husband, John Reed, had died in Russia after documenting its revolution in *Ten Days that Shook the World*. Bullitt and Louise had one child, Anne, and divorced in 1930. When his friend Franklin Delano Roosevelt became president in 1933, he appointed Bullitt America's first ambassador to the Soviet Union. Bullitt's initial enthusiasm for the Russian Revolution collapsed in the face of Stalinist repression.

In 1936, FDR assigned Bullitt to Paris, where the French admired his style. He employed an excellent chef, served only the finest wines, dressed immaculately and flirted in flawless French. Bullitt rented the Château de Vineuil-Saint-Firmin in thoroughbred country at Chantilly, where he entertained France's senior politicians at weekends. Ernest Hemingway, who had left Paris in 1929 but visited during the Spanish Civil War from 1936 to 1939, came out occasionally to shoot clay pigeons. During the week, Bullitt lived with his daughter, Anne, in the embassy residence in avenue d'Iéna. He negotiated vigorously in Europe for American interests, while advocating the French cause in Washington. No foreign ambassador was closer to the French cabinet, many of whom confided personal and state secrets in him. After three years in France, during which the country received persecuted Jewish refugees from Germany and Austria, Bullitt hated Hitler as much as he did Stalin. In March 1940, the German Foreign Office released a 'White Book' of transcripts seized in Warsaw in which Bullitt told the Polish Ambassador to Washington, Count Jerzy Potocki, that 'the French Army is the first line of defense for the United States'. The German press accused Bullitt and Ambassador to Britain Joseph Kennedy, despite Kennedy's reputation for appeasement of Nazi Germany, of 'using all their influence to aggravate the atmosphere of hostility in Europe'. The Nazis regarded Bullitt as the American diplomat most hostile to Germany, and they were probably right. No one fought harder to persuade America to send planes, tanks and other armaments to France. He had even arranged for French pilots secretly to test fly the latest American warplanes.

When the French government left Paris on 10 June, Bullitt telegraphed Secretary of State Cordell Hull: 'This Embassy is the only official organization still functioning in the City of Paris except the Headquarters of the military forces, Governor and the Prefecture of Police.' Italy, seeing that Germany would win, declared war on France and launched an invasion from the south that the outnumbered French repulsed. A few hours later, at the University of Virginia, Roosevelt declared, 'On this tenth day of June 1940, the hand that held the dagger struck it into the back of its neighbor.' He had borrowed the phrase from Bullitt. Gallup published its latest poll the same day: 62 per cent of the American people believed that, if Germany defeated both France and Britain, it would attack America next. The following day, Bullitt cabled Roosevelt: 'I have talked with the Provisional Governor of Paris, who is the single government official remaining, and it may be that at a given moment I, as the only representative of the Diplomatic Corps remaining in Paris, will be obliged in the interest of public safety to take control of the City pending arrival of the German Army ... Reynaud and Mandel just before their departure requested me to do this, if necessary.'

On 12 June, the day that Prime Minister Reynaud and Interior Minister Georges Mandel made him in effect Paris's provisional mayor, Bullitt attended a prayer service at the Cathedral of Notre Dame.

Kneeling in the front pew, he was seen to weep for the city and country he loved.

Secretary of State Hull urged Bullitt to follow the French government to Tours and persuade the French to fight on from their bases in Morocco, Algeria and Tunisia. Bullitt argued that, in the absence of FDR's commitment of American arms, the French would ignore him. He cabled Hull after the service in Notre Dame, 'As I said to you when you telephoned me the night of Sunday the 9th my deepest personal reason for staying in Paris is that whatever I have as a character, good or bad, is based on the fact that since the age of four I have never run away from anything however painful or dangerous when I thought it was my duty to take a stand. If I should leave Paris now I would no longer be myself.' Bullitt was saving Paris. Hull was asking him to save France.

A few hours later, Bullitt wrote a follow-up telegram to Hull: 'I propose to send my Military Attaché and my Naval Attaché to the German General Commanding the forces in the Paris area to explain the situation and return with suggestions of the German command as to methods of facilitating the orderly transition of government.' German forces agreed to enter the city peacefully the next morning, but someone fired on German truce officers near the Porte Saint-Denis in the north of Paris. General Georg von Küchler, the German 10th Army commander who had demolished Rotterdam only a few weeks earlier, responded by ordering an all-out air and artillery assault on Paris. It was scheduled for eight o'clock in the morning, leaving Bullitt only hours to save the city from destruction. His communications, like everyone else's, had been sporadic since the French Army cut Paris's telegraph lines as it withdrew on 11 June. A chance telephone call from the American Embassy in Berne, Switzerland, opened a line for Bullitt to relay a message to Berlin. He urgently requested the Germans to recognize that 'Paris has been declared an open city'. He proposed a parley early the next morning, 14 June, to save lives on both sides and prevent the destruction of Paris. Bullitt wanted to spare Paris the fate of Warsaw the year before, when the Luftwaffe demolished much of the Polish capital and killed 17,000 people.

General von Küchler agreed to try again before bombing the city. However, the French commander of the Paris region, 48-year-old General Henri-Fernand Dentz, refused a German demand to negotiate the transfer of power. His orders, he told the Germans via a radio link through the Prefecture of Police, were to provide security. He was not authorized to hold discussions with the enemy. At 2.25 in the morning, the Germans radioed Dentz: 'Delegates till 5 a.m. German time on the fourteenth at Sarcelles. Comply – otherwise attack ordered on Paris.' (German time was Greenwich Mean Time plus two hours, an hour later than in Paris.) Dentz acquiesced, sending two officers, Major Devouges and Lieutenant Holtzer, to treat with the Germans at Écouen, 12 miles north of Paris. At 5.30 a.m., Paris time, the two sides settled terms for the handover. The French achieved one amendment to the document: withdrawal of a forty-eight-hour non-stop curfew on the grounds that it contradicted the German requirement for public services like water and electricity to function normally. German Major Brink compromised by limiting the curfew from 9 p.m. to dawn. With the document signed, von Küchler cancelled the bombardment of Paris. Bullitt's intervention had spared the City of Light.

Some Germans did not wait for the official capitulation. At 3.40 in the morning, a German soldier on motorcycle sped through the 11th Arrondissement, between the Place de la Nation and the Place de la République. More troops penetrated the city in trucks and armoured cars, followed by large units marching in formation, all spit and polish to impress the Parisians. The first American resident of Paris to see them was most likely Charles Anderson, who lived in Montmartre and rose before sunrise each day to take the Metro train to work. Born in Lebanon, Illinois, in 1861, Anderson ran away from home to join the Barnum Circus when he was 15. He enlisted in the American Army as it was completing the annihilation of the Indian tribes. In 1884, he worked his way by merchant ship from Boston to Europe. When his seaman's pay ran out in France, he volunteered for the French Foreign Legion. Military service took him to the North African desert and, during the Great War, to Paris. On leaving the Legion after the Armistice of November 1918, he became an interpreter at the International Transport Company of Maurice de Brosse. De Brosse, in the frantic days before the Germans arrived, urged Anderson and his French wife, Eugénie Delmar, to leave Paris and come south with him. Nazi racial policies could be harsh on a black American, especially one married to a white woman. Anderson answered, 'No, I'll stay. No need to run.'

M. de Brosse asked Anderson what he would do in German-occupied Paris. When Anderson answered that he would report to work every day as usual, de Brosse pleaded, 'The office will be closed!' Anderson, a patient man who taught chess to young people in the evenings, said, 'That doesn't matter. I'm too old now to change my ways.' De Brosse left, and Anderson stayed. He was almost eighty years old. On the morning of 14 June, Anderson watched German troops occupy an apartment building opposite his seven-room flat in Montmartre. The soldiers were courteous to him, and he was polite in return. The occupation, he decided, would not change his life. And he went to work.

Ambassador Bullitt, fearing a communist revolt in the working class suburbs, had made it a condition of his appointment as acting mayor of Paris that the police and firemen remain at their posts. He had also requested that Washington ship Thompson sub-machine guns to protect the embassy, mainly from the communist uprising that he wrongly predicted. Diplomatic manuals did not dictate protocol for an American ambassador to turn over a foreign capital to a conquering army, so Bullitt improvised. General Bogislav von Studnitz, commander of Germany's 87th Infantry Division who would soon be Provisional Military Governor of a city he had never visited, simplified Bullitt's task by instructing his staff to requisition the Hôtel Crillon at 7.55 that morning. The Crillon was only a dozen yards from the embassy wall. Von Studnitz, noted one French writer, was the type of Prussian officer that generations of Frenchmen thought 'were born with monocles fixed to their eyes'. One of his first acts on entering the city was to put Paris one hour ahead to Berlin time.

Bullitt instructed Counsellor Robert Murphy, military attaché Colonel Horace H. Fuller and naval attaché Commander Roscoe Hillenkoetter to pay a courtesy call on General von Studnitz 'as soon as he appeared to be settled'. When Murphy saw the Swastika rise on the roof of the Crillon, he decided 'the moment had arrived for us to make our call'. Their purpose was to keep Bullitt's promise to Premier Paul Reynaud to ensure a peaceful occupation. When the three Americans left the embassy that warm summer morning, a military convoy passed between them and the Crillon. One car stopped, and a German lieutenant asked in English, 'You are Americans, aren't you?' They nodded. The lieutenant, who said he had lived in the United States, asked, 'Can you tell us where we might find a suitable hotel here?' Murphy laughed. 'The whole city seems to be in your possession. It has hundreds of empty hotels. Take your pick.'

Inside the Crillon's gilt lobby, Murphy saw a French police commissioner amid a throng of Germans. 'You can't imagine what happened,' the man said. He told Murphy, Hillenkoetter and Fuller that a German colonel stopped him earlier that morning and ordered, 'Open that hotel. It will be our headquarters. Take down the French flag from the roof, and replace it with this German flag.' The empty hotel's doors and shutters could not be opened, and the colonel warned, 'If that hotel is not open in fifteen minutes and the French flag is not down, we will shoot it down and shoot you, too!' A locksmith opened the doors in time, but the commissioner was still in a sweat.

'Murphy!' one of the German officers in the Prince of Wales suite upstairs called out. Murphy knew Colonel Weber from his years as US Vice-Consul in Munich. Weber, now von Studnitz's aide-de-camp, welcomed the Americans, wrote Murphy,

as if we were all old friends, ushering us immediately into the drawing room where the general was talking with a dozen staff officers. We had expected to spend only a few minutes with the general, but he had previously ordered champagne from the Crillon's excellent cellars and was in a mood to answer all the questions of our military and naval attachés. The only information we had about the progress of the war was what we had heard from western and Berlin radio broadcasts, which necessarily were confusing. General von Studnitz, who had served as German military attaché in Poland, said he appreciated it was the duty of attachés to gather intelligence for their governments and he was quite willing to inform us fully and frankly.

Von Studnitz gave the attachés a 'clear and concise summary of the military campaign to date' and predicted that 'mopping up operations in France would not require more than another ten days, after which preparations would begin for crossing the channel to England'. Von Studnitz believed the British, without a single army division intact and most of their heavy artillery abandoned at Dunkirk, would not resist. Hillenkoetter asked how the Germans would cross the Channel, but von Studnitz 'brushed aside this question with the comment that all plans were made'. The war, he added, would be over by the end of July, in six weeks. Walking the short distance back to the embassy, Murphy and the two attachés agreed that 'none of us was at all sure he might not be right'.

Commander Hillenkoetter, recalling the same encounter, but without the champagne, wrote that 'although it was only 10.30 a.m., we were offered a glass of what the General said was the very best brandy in the Crillon'. Hillenkoetter reported that von Studnitz was 'most happy to make his call on the Ambassador at 1:30 p.m. as the Ambassador wished – assured us that all American property would be protected, and that we could count on the best of cooperation as far as the German military were concerned'. Von Studnitz invited Hillenkoetter and Fuller to attend the review of the Green Heart Division, the 185th Infantry, which he had once commanded, in the Place de la Concorde at 3.30 that afternoon. The two Americans could think of no polite way to refuse.

For Colonel Horace Fuller, the experience of handing Paris over to the Germans was galling. The 1909 West Point graduate had been briefing American and British journalists daily that the French Army would not hold. 'Colonel Fuller was the only man in Paris who knew what was coming,' Quentin Reynolds, the *Collier's Weekly* correspondent, wrote. 'He advised us to make plans to get out. He told us "off the record" that the French Army wouldn't even bother to defend Paris.' Fuller's astute observations contrasted with the French government spokesman's reply to a question from Virginia Cowles, the attractive American correspondent of Britain's *Sunday Times*, asking whether Paris would be declared an 'open city': 'Never,' he said. 'We're confident that Hitler's mechanized hordes will never get to Paris. But should they come so far, you may tell your countrymen we shall defend every stone, every clod of earth, every lamp-post, every building, for we would rather have our city razed than fall into the hands of the Germans.' Colonel Fuller had fought the Germans in the Great War, when he commanded the US 108th Field Artillery Regiment in the Meuse-Argonne and Ypres-Lys offensives. Clare Boothe, covering the invasion for *Life* magazine, asked Fuller 'what's going to happen':

> His hands trembled. His eyes were quite bloodshot from loss of sleep. He tried to smile, but he couldn't. He said, 'Oh, there's hope of course – the morale of the French – we can deliver 1,000 planes a month soon.' 'Oh,' I said, 'don't talk morale and economics, talk WAR. What do you think?' He said so wearily, 'I don't want to think any more, I want to use my heart. You see, I want them to win so much, so *very* much,' he said. 'I fought with them at Chateau-Thierry in the last war – and oh, they've been Goddamn dumb, but dear Christ I love them.'

Back in his office at the chancellery, Murphy saw German soldiers climbing over the embassy gate: 'They were running a telephone wire across our courtyard to the Crillon Hotel.' To Murphy's shock, the embassy's 'picturesque colored doorman', George Washington Mitchell of North Carolina, was helping them. Mitchell had come to Paris before the Great War as a rider in a cowboy and Indian show. Murphy, who knew Mitchell was married to a German woman and spoke German, demanded to know why he had disobeyed orders not to allow German troops onto embassy premises. Mitchell said the soldiers were from Hamburg, where he knew people, and were 'nice fellas'. Bullitt reacted with fury, not at George Mitchell, but at the Germans. He sent word to von Studnitz to remove the telephone cable at once. Henceforth, any German soldier breaking into the embassy grounds would be shot. The Germans removed the wire, but they posted a sign in front of the embassy that said, '*Amerikanische Botschaft*', 'American Embassy'. It was one of hundreds of signs the Germans affixed all over Paris for their troops and the German civilians, both administrators and tourists, who would arrive in their wake.

Von Studnitz, recalled Hillenkoetter, came to the embassy on time at 1.30 p.m. and spoke with Bullitt for about ten minutes 'of correctness'. An hour later, Hillenkoetter and Fuller accompanied Bullitt for a similar, formal session at the Crillon. At 3.30, as promised, the two uniformed American attachés met General von Studnitz in the Place de la Concorde. With Nazi newsreel cameramen poised to record the military march-past, von Studnitz invited them to join him on the reviewing stand. 'Both Fuller and I could easily see how that would look in newsreels, photos, etc. – two American officers taking a review with a German general. So we hastily, but firmly, declined, saying that we didn't feel worthy to share the General's honor; that it was his division and his glory; and that it would be a shame to deprive him of even a share of the glory.' Fuller and Hillenkoetter diplomatically disappeared into the crowd. Robert Murphy, however, stood uncomfortably beside the German generals as the Green Heart Division goose-stepped across the great square to thumping martial music. When the parade ended and Murphy was walking back to the embassy, he complained to *New York Herald Tribune* correspondent Walter Kerr, 'The general wanted the ambassador, and the ambassador told me to take his place.' From an upper window of the embassy, a young diplomat hired locally in Paris, Keeler Faus, surreptitiously took photographs of the German troops in the Place de la Concorde.

Associated Press correspondent Philip W. Whitcomb, a graduate of Washburn University in Kansas and of Oxford, watched the same parade from the pavement and detected a bizarre normality:

On that day the garbage-men cleaned the streets alongside of German troops as they marched up the Friedland and Wagram Avenues or across the Place de la Concorde. The underground railway men ran their trains, though some carried only Germans on their way through Paris. The telephones worked. The police, under instructions to obey German orders, were all on duty, though on June 14th they were little more than members of the silent throng lining the streets through which the Germans moved.

The triumphalism of the military parades offended even a few Germans. A 33-year-old officer, Count Claus Schenk von Stauffenberg, shared his disgust with General Franz Halder and his staff in Paris. Hitler deserved death for this nihilism, von Stauffenberg said. Although Major General Henning von Tresckow was brave enough to second him, General Halder counselled von Stauffenberg that the German public was unlikely to support a coup at a time of military victory.

Martial parades established themselves as facts of daily life that Parisians soon treated with the indifference they accorded to red lights.

TWO

The Bookseller

As the first German soldiers took control of Paris that morning, Sylvia Beach was waiting in Adrienne Monnier's fourth-storey apartment in the rue de l'Odéon. Adrienne's window commanded a clear view to the north, where the tiny street crossed the tree-shaded boulevard Saint-Germain. A column of German Army trucks and motorcycles appeared, along with troops riding and marching past. Sylvia called it an 'endless procession of motorized forces: tanks and armored cars and helmeted men seated with arms folded ... all a cold grey, and they moved to a steady deafening roar.' For the first time, Sylvia heard the Germans' famous leather jackboots. 'Those boots always made them seem much more enraged than they were,' she wrote. As she and Adrienne watched, 'Tears were streaming down our cheeks. It was an awful experience. Horrible.'

'Miss Beach', as James Joyce called the American from the time they met in 1920, was 53 years old. Adrienne, her longtime collaborator, friend and former lover, was four years younger. For twenty years, the American and the Frenchwoman had presided over a unique and fertile realm of French and English literature. Adrienne called their little kingdom 'Odéonia', for the two bookshops – her French La Maison des Amis des Livres and Sylvia's English Shakespeare and Company – whose plate-glass windows reflected each other across the rue de l'Odéon. James Joyce, who had made Shakespeare and Company his office, called it 'Stratford-on-Odéon'.

24

The modest rue de l'Odéon flowed downhill from the crest of a rise, dominated by the rear of the great Théâtre de l'Odéon, to a round-about, the Carrefour de l'Odéon, and the boulevard Saint-Germain. A canyon of five- and six-storey apartment buildings rose from ground-floor laundries, antique shops, carpet merchants and printers. Adrienne's shop was at Number 7, and she lived on the fourth floor of Number 18. Shakespeare and Company was at Number 12, and Sylvia's flat was in the mezzanine above the shop. The rue de l'Odéon's twin bookshops, where contemporary writers were supported and published, made it the world capital of Franco-American letters. For a week before the Germans seized Paris, French people, as well as refugees from the Low Countries, had trudged up the rue de l'Odéon on their way out of the city. Sylvia and Adrienne watched them bearing the weight of all the possessions they could carry on their backs. While other booksellers and publishers were fleeing, the two women preferred to remain, if only to guard a small light amid what their friend Arthur Koestler called Europe's Nazi 'night'. Sylvia dismissed what many saw as her courage: 'I never left Paris – hadn't the energy to flee, luckily, as nothing happened to us or the other monuments.'

Adrienne had come to Odéonia in 1915, opening her bookshop during the war when rents were low and the city's male booksellers were mostly in the army. From a peasant family in eastern, Alpine France, Adrienne had retained her earthy love of food and all other things sensual. Her father, Clovis, was a postal clerk who sorted mail on trains. An injury he received in a rail accident gave him an insurance settlement that his daughter used to start her business. La Maison des Amis des Livres became more than a bookshop. It was the base for publishing Adrienne's literary journals and a venue for authors' readings and discussions. She had befriended and defended some of France's greatest writers – among them, poets Paul Valéry and Guillaume Apollinaire and novelists André Gide and Jules Romains.

Sylvia Woodbridge Beach arrived a couple of years later. Born in Baltimore in 1887, she had spent two teenage years in Paris from 1902 to 1904, when her father served as Presbyterian clergyman at the American Church on the Quai d'Orsay. From Paris, the family moved to Princeton, New Jersey. The Reverend Sylvester Beach's most prominent parishioner was Virginia-born Democrat Woodrow Wilson, who was president of Princeton University before being elected governor of New Jersey. The Reverend Sylvester Beach officiated at the weddings of both Wilson daughters and, after Wilson's election to the White House in 1912, was known as the 'president's pastor'. Sylvia, who already spoke French fluently, learned Spanish in Madrid and Italian in Florence before returning to Paris during the Great War in 1917. A course in French literature at the Sorbonne led Sylvia to Adrienne Monnier's shop in the rue de l'Odéon in search of a French literary journal. In March 1917, the slender, 5-foot-2-inch wisp of an American met the voluptuous French bookseller. Sylvia was thirty and Adrienne almost twenty-six. They discussed American and French books. Adrienne, who spoke little English, said she loved the works of Benjamin Franklin – albeit in French translation. When she told Sylvia, '*J'aime beaucoup l'Amérique,*' Sylvia answered, '*J'aime beaucoup la France.*' Soon, they loved each other as well.

Alice B. Toklas called Sylvia 'flagstaff' as much for her bony figure as her commitment to flying the banner of American literature on French soil. The American composer Virgil Thompson, who like Aaron Copland and George Antheil came to Paris to study music with Nadia Boulanger, called Sylvia 'angular ... Alice in Wonderland at forty'. Adrienne reminded him of 'a French milkmaid from the eighteenth century'. William Carlos Williams remembered Adrienne in the kitchen, 'That woman loved food, the senses were her meat.' Her dining room was pink, she said, because pink was 'good for the appetite'. Janet Flanner, who moved to Paris in 1922 with her lover Solita Solano and began her *New Yorker* column three years later, was a friend of both Sylvia and Adrienne. She compared 'these two extraordinary women – Mlle. Monnier, buxom as an abbess, placidly picturesque in the costume she had permanently adopted, consisting of a long, full gray skirt, a bright velveteen waistcoat, and a white blouse, and slim, jacketed Sylvia, with her schoolgirl white collar and big colored bowknot, in the style of Colette's Claudine à l'Ecole'.

Adrienne invited Sylvia to readings in her bookshop, where she heard, among many others, Paul Valéry in French Army uniform read his anti-war poem, 'Europe'. When the Great War ended in November 1918, Sylvia went to Serbia to help her sister Holly with relief work for the Red Cross. Six months later, she was back in Paris. Adrienne encouraged her to open a French bookshop, like La Maison des Amis des Livres, in New York or London. Both cities proved impractical because of high rents and small readerships for French literature. Sylvia's fallback was to establish an English language bookshop and lending library in Paris. Adrienne found her space on the ground floor of a building at 8 rue Dupuytren, around the corner from her own shop. With $3,000 sent by her mother, Eleanor Beach, Sylvia opened Shakespeare and Company on 17 November 1919. Above the door hung a pub-like sign of William Shakespeare's head by the French-Polish painter Charles Winzer. When it was stolen, Winzer painted another. The second too disappeared, and Adrienne made one herself to replace it. Sylvia slept at the back of the tiny shop. Without running water but surrounded by the books she loved, she was content.

The first American writer to patronize Shakespeare and Company was the formidable Gertrude Stein, who appeared in the shop on 16 March 1920 with her companion, Alice B. Toklas. Already a figure on the Paris scene, Stein had yet to achieve success in America. Her weekly salon, initiated in 1906, attracted Pablo Picasso and other artists, whose paintings she assiduously collected. In the 1920s, American writers in Paris, including Ernest Hemingway and Sherwood Anderson, sought her invitations. Stein became one of the Shakespeare and Company library's original 'bunnies', as Sylvia called them, from the French word for subscriber, *abonné*. On 12 November 1920, 22-year-old Stephen Vincent Benét became the first young, aspiring American writer to join the library. Sylvia's English competitors were Brentano's bookshop for sales and the American Library of Paris for lending, both Right Bank institutions not favoured by the Left Bank bohemians. Brentano's did not stock books by new writers or sell the experimental literary journals that Sylvia promoted. The blue-stockinged American Library matrons played moral censor, something Sylvia refused to do. When they removed H. L. Mencken's journal, *American Mercury*, from their shelves, poet Ezra Pound, another of Sylvia's American bunnies, wrote, 'DAMN the right bank pigs, anyway.' Shakespeare and Company became the haven of a new generation of writers and publishers. Most of its bunnies were students from the nearby University of Paris who, too poor to buy imported English books, paid the small subscription to borrow them.

In the summer of 1920, Shakespeare and Company reopened in a larger space at 12 rue de l'Odéon, facing Adrienne's shop. Sylvia had two rooms just above Shakespeare and Company, but she did not live in them. She moved in with Adrienne at Number 8 and rented the rooms over the shop to pilgrims, as she called Americans arriving in Paris. Avant-garde American composer George Antheil lived there for several years. He used to climb up the front of the building to enter through a window rather than bother Sylvia by ringing at the shop. At the back, Sylvia kept a stove to brew tea and keep warm in winter. William Shirer, the great American journalist who was then working at the *Paris Tribune*, recalled how he 'loved to browse among the shelves or be invited to tea in the back room, when in winter a fireplace blazed and there was much good talk'. Also at the back were children's books, toys and a little red table. The outline of Odéonia was complete. It comprised the outdoor bookstalls in the arcades of the Théâtre de l'Odéon, the two bookshops, a music store, a library appraiser and, in the boulevard Saint-Germain, the writers' favoured cafés, the Flore and the Deux Magots, and the Alsatian Brasserie Lipp.

Sylvia met James Joyce in July 1920. Joyce had just moved with his wife, Nora Barnacle, and their two children from Trieste. At the time, he was consumed with writing *Ulysses*. Sylvia, who had already read his short stories, later admitted, 'Probably I was strongly attracted to Joyce as well as to his work, but unconsciously. My only love was Adrienne.' When American courts convicted Margaret Anderson and Jane Heap of the *Little Review* for printing 'obscene' sections of Joyce's *Ulysses*, American and British publishers refused to consider the book. Sylvia Beach hated censorship. 'You cannot legislate against human nature,' she said. Although she had never published anything, she came to Joyce's rescue by publishing *Ulysses*. Adrienne's French typesetters printed it, and Sylvia proofread every page. It went on sale in her shop, and she persuaded friends like Ernest Hemingway to smuggle copies into the United States. Her friend Janet Flanner called Sylvia 'the intrepid, unselfish, totally inexperienced and little-moneyed young-lady publisher of "Ulysses" in Paris in 1922'. When the book appeared, Sylvia lost one of her first bunnies, Gertrude Stein. Miss Stein, who hated Joyce, took her custom to the American Library on the Right Bank.

Within six years of opening her shop, Sylvia Beach was called by Eugene Jolas, the American publisher of the Paris literary magazine *transition*, 'probably the best known woman in Paris'. If she had any rival for that honour, it could only have been another American, the beautiful singer-dancer Josephine Baker. Sylvia made Shakespeare and Company the centre of Parisian American literary life. Ernest Hemingway, F. Scott Fitzgerald, Thornton Wilder, John Dos Passos, Elliot Paul, Malcolm Cowley and other expatriate American writers used her combined bookshop-lending library as, in Janet Flanner's words, 'their club, mail drop, meeting house and forum'. Over tea at Shakespeare and Company, the Americans met the Irishman James Joyce and French writers like Louis Aragon and André Breton, as well as one another. It was a time of high living for the Americans, who found Paris cheaper than home and loved the freedom to write without censorship and to drink alcohol without being arrested. Aged 22, Hemingway fell in love, however platonically, with 34-year-old Sylvia the moment they met in 1921. 'She had pretty legs and she was kind, cheerful and interested, and loved to make jokes and gossip,' Hemingway wrote of her in his Paris memoir, *A Moveable Feast*. 'No one that I ever knew was nicer to me.' He made a point of taking her to boxing matches to shake her further from her Protestant clerical upbringing. She became an enthusiast and introduced Hemingway to French writer Jean Prévost, who wrote a book called *The Pleasure of Sport* and matched Hemingway's physicality. The two men sparred in the ring, but Prévost's head was so hard that Hemingway broke a thumb on it. Sylvia adored Hemingway, encouraging the young journalist to publish in Paris's growing number of literary periodicals.

The Twenties bounty turned, for Sylvia as for much of the western world, into Thirties desperation. The dollar's devaluation slashed the incomes of expatriate Americans – impoverished writers, painters and composers most of all. Ernest Hemingway and her other favourites left Paris for the United States. In December 1933, restrictions on drinking and writing that had driven many American writers to France were lifted with the repeal of Prohibition and the American publication of Joyce's *Ulysses*. Judge John Woolsey of the US District Court in New York wrote the landmark decision that *Ulysses*, despite its sexual content, was a 'sincere and honest book'. He famously added, 'His locale was Celtic and his season spring.' This was good news for Joyce, whose book sold 35,000 copies in three months, but it came at a cost to Sylvia. Joyce had convinced her, after her years of subsidizing him and keeping his book in print, to relinquish publishing rights to Random House in New York and the Bodley Head in London. Her health, plagued since childhood by eczema and migraines, suffered. The writer Katherine Anne Porter recalled 'attacks of migraine that stopped her in her tracks'. Lack of business in Depression-era Paris put her deeper into debt. Her family helped when it could – small amounts arriving in their letters from Princeton and California. But the presents were not enough to protect Shakespeare and Company from bankruptcy.

When Sylvia told André Gide in 1935 that the shop might close, he declared, 'But something must be done!' Thanks to Gide and fellow writers Jean Schlumberger and Paul Valéry, something was. They created the Friends of Shakespeare and Company, whose members paid dues for two years to support the shop. Almost all of France's best writers contributed. André Maurois, Jean Paulhan, Jules Romains and Georges Duhamel headed a long list of donors who paid a minimum of $45 a year to attend readings by French and American novelists and poets. The poet Archibald MacLeish sent $75. The largest donation came from Sylvia's childhood friend, Carlotta Welles Briggs, with whom she had spent summers at the Welles's country house near Bourré in the Touraine.

The civil war in Spain brought American writers back to Paris, where they took leave from the battlefront. Ernest Hemingway, John Dos Passos and the English poets W. H. Auden and Stephen Spender became Sylvia's loyal customers. Sylvia persuaded Hemingway to do a reading to raise funds. He agreed on condition that Spender join him on the platform. This was less generosity than stage-fright. He was so nervous that he drank copiously before and during his reading of the short story

'Fathers and Sons'. Faltering at first, he was declaiming like a Shakespearean dramatist by the end. The *Paris Herald Tribune* wrote, 'He was beginning to show grace under pressure.' Hemingway left Europe again when the Republicans lost the war in Spain and the half million Spanish refugees who escaped to France were being interned in camps.

In 1936, with the shop on a more secure footing, Sylvia made her first visit to the United States since coming to Paris in 1917. Her older sister, Holly, followed by younger sister Cyprian and their father, had moved to Altadena, California, where Sylvia saw them for a few weeks. By the time she stopped in Princeton to see childhood friends, severe menstrual bleeding took her to a Connecticut hospital for diagnosis and a hysterectomy. While Sylvia was away from Paris, a young German-Jewish photographer, Gisèle Freund, whom she and Adrienne had encountered two years earlier, supplanted her in Adrienne's affections and apartment. Returning to convalesce in Paris, Sylvia, without demur, moved into the mezzanine rooms above Shakespeare and Company. The three women remained close, usually having lunch together in Adrienne's kitchen.

A year later, after receiving nominations from parliamentarian Edouard Herriot and Henri Hoppenot, a poet in the French diplomatic corps, the French government made Sylvia a Knight of the Legion of Honour. It was the first official recognition she had received of her contribution to Franco-American letters. While she made light of her 'little ribbon gibbon given me by the French', she wore it proudly when occasion demanded.

At the outbreak of war in September 1939, Sylvia's family urged her to return home. But her home was Paris. Friends, though, were leaving. The few American writers there in 1940, like Henry Miller and Robert McAlmon, as well as the photographer Man Ray, were fleeing to the south, where most went on to safer countries. Gisèle Freund waited until the Germans were bombing the industrial suburbs of Paris before she too escaped, first to the south, finally to Argentina. As a German-Jewish refugee, she would have been arrested immediately. By June 1940, Joyce was on his way to Switzerland. Sylvia Beach, Adrienne Monnier and their contracting circle of brave friends awaited the humiliation of their city.

On Monday, 3 June, Adrienne wrote, 'Loud noise of planes roaring over our heads. Raid: 200 planes, numerous victims.' Six days later, she and Sylvia heard German artillery pounding Paris's outskirts. Adrienne's diary entry for the day said, 'We think seriously of putting mattresses in the cellar to sleep on.' Only the day before, a friend warned them that 'Paris will be involved in the battle.' Two days later, the same friend's husband 'let me understand that Paris will not be involved in the battle'. Rumours, compounded by government radio bulletins that lied about the war, were confusing rather than reassuring. Someone warned Adrienne that, if she stayed in Paris, people would assume she welcomed German occupation. By the morning of 12 June, Adrienne was ready to quit: 'Personal longing to leave and go to Rocfoin', the village southwest of Paris where her mother and father had a smallholding. After asking Sylvia to bicycle to Montparnasse station to see whether there were any trains, Adrienne had lunch in her kitchen with her sister, Marie. Marie, whose pet name was Rinette from Marinette, persuaded her to stay, saying that 'we should live such moments here'. Sylvia, meanwhile, urged Ruth Camp, a young Canadian student who worked for her, to escape. Canada, unlike the United States, was at war with Germany, making Ruth subject to detention as an enemy alien. Sylvia despaired that 'she could not be persuaded to leave in spite of my efforts to push her homeward, [and] was still helping me when the Germans swarmed into France'. As the Germans neared Paris, Ruth, in Sylvia's words, 'did try to get away. She was machine-gunned in the ditches, and was later interned in spite of her efforts.' On the 13th, Sylvia had an urge to flee. She went to the American Embassy, where she discovered it was too late.

The anti-Nazi, anti-Soviet, Hungarian-Jewish writer Arthur Koestler had been hiding in Adrienne's apartment. The French authorities had already interned him with other foreigners, many of whom were also anti-Nazis and Jews. The Nazis would take charge of those still stuck in the camps when the occupation began. After Koestler's temporary release, Adrienne took him in. He was reading Stendhal's *Le Rouge et le noir* on her sofa, when a four leaf clover in the book 'fell right between his eyes!' Adrienne kissed the spot and assured him it was an omen that he would be safe. A year later, Koestler wrote discreetly in London, 'I still had some friends. Who these friends were, how they passed me on in turn, hiding me for one night each, and how they succeeded in obtaining for me a travelling permit to Limoges, where a fortnight later I ceased legally to exist, will be an amusing and moving story to tell at a time when the night has gone from Europe and acts of kindness and solidarity no longer count as crimes.' When the Nazi night had passed, he was free to give Adrienne credit without putting her in jeopardy: 'For a few days I remained in hiding, first at the flat of Adrienne Monnier, then at the P.E.N. Club.' The president of International PEN was Sylvia and Adrienne's old friend Jules Romains. The French novelist's anti-Nazi views were known, and he fled Paris for the south in hope of reaching New York with his wife, Lise, the French-American novelist Julien Green and American surgeon Dr Alexander Bruno. Romains said, more in hope than truth, 'It is impossible that France should go fascist.'

On 14 June, Sylvia's and Adrienne's bookshops, like all other businesses in Paris, were closed. Sylvia's premises enjoyed some protection. Two American diplomats, Third Secretary Tyler Thompson and her friend Keeler Faus, had personally affixed red American seals to her apartment and shop to tell the Germans they belonged to a US citizen. But Sylvia and Adrienne's anti-Nazi past made them vulnerable to the occupier. Adrienne, as well as hiding Arthur Koestler, had assisted the brilliant German-Jewish writer Walter Benjamin's escape from Paris to the south of France. (Benjamin was hoping to obtain an American visa from the consulate in Marseilles and travel to the United States via Spain and Portugal. He made an exhausting trek over the Pyrenees, but Spanish police forced him back to Nazi-occupied France. Rather than be sent to a concentration camp, he committed suicide.) Adrienne had also written a long condemnation of Nazi anti-Semitism in her *Gazette des Amis des Livres* in 1938: 'From the day the Jews were emancipated (as you know, it is one of the glories of the French Revolution that they were), they have proved that they could be national elements of the first order.' Sylvia had sold artists' prints in her shop to raise money for Spain's legitimate republican government to fight the Nazi-supported Francisco Franco. She also had many

Jewish friends, including an unpaid voluntary assistant at Shakespeare and Company, Françoise Bernheim.

As the Germans occupied each arrondissement in Paris, someone told Adrienne that they were ordering everyone to remain indoors for forty-eight hours. Wehrmacht loudspeaker vans repeated this message, until it became known the curfew had been amended to begin at 9 p.m. Adrienne waited with Sylvia all morning in her apartment. At noon, they noticed civilians on the streets. In some places, Parisians were accepting gifts of food from German army trucks sent to feed the populace. In others, women flirted with soldiers. One of the better bordellos posted a notice: 'Business as usual from 3 p.m.' A few cafés opened to serve their first uniformed German customers, who were polite and paid for all they ate and drank. Adrienne was disgusted by a common sentiment she overheard: 'What if the Germans are here? At least there will be order.' She prepared lunch for Sylvia in the kitchen where for twenty years the earthy and maternal bookseller had cooked oily peasant dinners for the luminaries of French and American literature. It would be her last lunch before the Germans began requisitioning most of France's food.

After lunch, the husband of Adrienne's sister Rinette, painter Paul-Emile Becat, came to the flat to see her and Sylvia. He told them he had seen 'the procession of the first German battalions this morning at the Place de l'Etoile'. A great phalanx of helmeted Wehrmacht troops marched to a Nazi band, while the Swastika flew over the Arc de Triomphe. At this scene, Parisians had stared sullen and silent, many of them weeping. Adrienne ended her diary of the day, 'In the evening, great depression.' She was not alone.

German forces seized both houses of France's parliament, the Chamber of Deputies over the Seine from the Place de la Concorde and the Senate in the Luxembourg Gardens. They also commandeered the Ministry of Foreign Affairs on the Quai d'Orsay, the Naval Ministry beside the Hôtel Crillon and most other government buildings. Signs were posted in German saying they were under the 'protection' of the German army. Troops set up light cannon and machine guns at the main approaches to the Arc de Triomphe. They replaced French flags with Swastikas on government buildings, monuments, the arcades of the rue de Rivoli and the main hotels. Robert Murphy wrote, 'I was amazed in those first occupation days to discover how thoroughly the Germans had prepared for every phase of military government. It became apparent that they had drafted comprehensive blueprints long in advance to suit whatever conditions they might encounter in conquered countries.'

The only fatal incident occurred at nine in the morning, when a lone French soldier shot at German troops in the southern suburb of Antony. 'The German soldiers responded to the firing, killing the French soldier and a woman,' noted the Paris Prefect of Police, Roger Langeron, in his diary. No Americans were harmed.

The Germans honoured most of the embassy certificates of American property ownership, including one that Bullitt personally issued to a French friend, Marie-Laure de Noailles. Married to an aristocrat, Marie-Laure was the daughter of a Jewish banker. Bullitt's gesture undoubtedly saved her collection of Goyas and other masterpieces from German seizure. Nonetheless, the Nazis requisitioned two American homes near Paris in Versailles. One belonged to James Hazen Hyde, whose house was ransacked by German troops. The other was the villa of the twice-widowed Mrs James Gordon Bennett, in her youth Miss Maud Potter of Philadelphia. Her first husband had been Baron George de Reuter of the news agency his father founded. Five years after his death, she wed the eccentric, 73-year-old owner of the *Paris Herald*. When the Germans occupied her Versailles villa, she stayed in her Paris townhouse in the avenue d'Iéna near the American Ambassador's residence. Other American losses were houses north of Paris belonging to Harlan Page Rowe and Ogden Bishop, both looted during the battles. The Luftwaffe bombed American oil and communications facilities on the northern French coast. Another American loss during the Battle of France was a consignment of 150,000 cigarettes for Ambassador Bullitt. The Germans did not tamper with any other embassy supplies, but a Wehrmacht colonel told French officials in the Paris customs house, 'So these are Bullitt's cigarettes! Well, he won't get them. I used to live in Philadelphia and I never did like Bullitt. Take them away.'

In the evening, Bullitt received a visit at the embassy from Police Prefect Roger Langeron. For the past weeks, the two men had come to know and respect each other. Langeron told the ambassador that the Germans had arrested and were interrogating his chief of general intelligence, Jacques Simon. This violated the assurances given that morning by General von Studnitz, who told Langeron, 'If order is maintained, if you can guarantee the security of my troops, you won't hear a word from me.' Langeron asked for Bullitt's help. The ambassador called Robert Murphy, who went immediately to the Crillon with a message from Bullitt: if Simon were not released, no one would be responsible for security in Paris. Without Langeron's 25,000 policemen, who had remained at Bullitt's request when the French government was planning to remove them, the occupation which had gone smoothly until evening would become a shambles. At 11 p.m., Simon appeared unharmed in Langeron's office on the Ile de la Cité.

THREE

The Countess from Ohio

THE NAZIS REQUISITIONED the best Parisian hotels – not only the Crillon, but the Ritz, Majestic, Raphael and George-V. The American Embassy beat them to the Hôtel Bristol, Ambassador Bullitt having already leased it from proprietor Hippolyte Jammet. The elegant hotel in the rue du Faubourg Saint-Honoré was suitable as an American refuge, because its basement shelter was the only one in Paris with protection against poison gas. The hotel flew the American flag, which the Germans did not remove. One American expatriate, Isadora Duncan's brother Raymond, made the Bristol bar his second home. The Hellenophile Duncan was easy to recognize, invariably dressed in a toga and hand-made sandals. His Left Bank art gallery, the Akademia in rue de Seine, was close enough to the Bristol for him to walk there over the river. Representatives of the American Red Cross, the Rockefeller Foundation and the American ambulance units moved into the Bristol. Anne Morgan also took up residence there, hiding foreign and French Jews under quasi-diplomatic protection until she found ways for them to leave France. Dorothy Reeder, directress of the American Library in the rue de Téhéran, went to the Bristol on the occupation's first day to work for the embassy verifying that the residents were American citizens.

Two days earlier, Miss Reeder had received an unexpected visit from the American Library's first vice-president, Countess Clara Longworth de Chambrun. The two women conferred in the darkness of a library whose windows were obscured in brown paper as a precaution against bombing. The rest of the library's board were preparing to leave France altogether, but Countess de Chambrun was going that afternoon to the country – imperiously informing Miss Reeder that she would return as usual in September. Miss Reeder, the countess recalled, 'promised to remain on the spot and continue to wave the flag of neutrality. Meantime, she appeared to be getting what she termed "quite a kick" out of the position in which she was left as sole guardian of the premises, and with authority to negotiate the most delicate questions with the occupants, certain that the American Embassy would back her decisions.' Miss Reeder herself wrote, 'Was it really Paris whose streets I walked through the 11th, 12th and 13th of June 1940? I do not think so. It was a dead city. Everything was closed, locked and deserted. Even the fall of a pin could be heard.'

Clara Longworth de Chambrun was reluctant to abandon Paris. Her husband's employers, the National City Bank of New York, had a 'theory that, should the enemy enter Paris, certain French directors might be held as hostages and endanger the interests of the establishment'. So, Count Aldebert de Chambrun, the Marquis de Mun and six French employees were ordered to move the bank south of any imaginable German penetration to Le Puy. Clara told Aldebert that he could leave Paris without her. She refused to desert their house at 58 rue de Vaugirard, overlooking the Luxembourg Gardens and the Senate's ornate Palais du Luxembourg, in the 6th Arrondissement. A few dozen yards away was the Théâtre de l'Odéon, where Clara staged plays. Sylvia Beach's Shakespeare and Company was just around the corner. Clara was obstinate: 'My temperamental dislike of retreating from danger when others less capable of facing it remained behind caused me to protest vigorously against this mandate [from the bank to leave].'

Her husband reminded her that she would be alone in Paris. Aldebert himself had to be in Le Puy with the bank. Their only son, René, was in Washington on a mission from the French government at the request of Ambassador Bullitt to persuade President Franklin Roosevelt, a distant cousin by marriage, to send emergency military aid to Britain. Her husband's brothers had also left. Pierre, who as the eldest had inherited their father's title of Marquis de Chambrun in

1891, had gone to his country seat, the Château l'Empery-Carrières, in Lozère. As representative of Lozère in the Senate, he was the only American citizen in the upper house. With him was his wife, Clara's cousin, Margaret Rives Nichols. Aldebert's younger brother, Count Charles, known as Charlie and formerly French Ambassador in Rome, took refuge with relatives in Brittany. 'My husband argued that, if I remained in Paris and saw the hideous swastika replace the tricolor, I would be cut off from everyone and everything I loved except the house itself and a little grave [of her daughter] nearby. I gave in before the inevitable and busied myself with the practical arrangements for that hated flight.'

On 12 June, after her visit to Dorothy Reeder at the American Library, Clara met her husband for a last lunch at home. Their chauffeur having disappeared in the chaos, an American employee of the bank, Mr Hunt, drove the count, the countess with her Japanese dog, Tsouni, on her lap and the Chambruns' house maid out of the city that afternoon. With a million other Parisians, they found themselves in a disorderly procession that disrupted military convoys heading to the front. Their car crawled southwards along National Route Seven to Juvisy. There, where the highway joined regional roads, the traffic halted.

> There were trucks, delivery wagons, military lorries and the whole running equipment of certain factories and aviation centers. Men and women were standing entwined on flatcars, careless of the fact that they could not remain erect for ever – or even at all – when running at normal speed. No question of that now; all proceeded at a footpace, and were stopped completely every three minutes. A lad on a dark brown thoroughbred pushed past our car and, on extricating himself from the mass, galloped off across country.

Further along the road, Clara noticed people setting out picnics. One man and woman in particular caught her eye: 'I recall the silhouettes of a distinguished-looking couple in well-cut clothes seated at a tiny folding-table which formed part of their Rolls-Royce equipment. She was dressed in printed crepe de Chine with silver fox boa; he, in impeccable grey jacket with decorations. His carefully trimmed beard recalled Leopard II.'

Mr Hunt drove them for twenty-five hours on a journey that normally took seven. They had to sleep overnight in the car. On the second night, they reached Vichy, where the Hôtel du Parc gave Aldebert and Clara a room. They were lucky. Most of the other displaced Parisians who survived Luftwaffe strafing on the highways were sleeping rough in barns, on roadsides and in cheaper hotels and inns, several families often crowded into the same room. The rambling, white-porticoed Hôtel du Parc was the best that the spa town had to offer. Its management knew the Chambruns, who had summered there to 'take the waters' since 1926. Their July reservations were simply pushed forward to June. The couple took baths and settled in for their first good sleep in three days.

At four o'clock in the morning, while the Germans were about to occupy Paris, the urgent banging of a gong woke them. The incessant racket worsened when 'an excited servant thundered at our door, and commanded us to dress and pack without delay as all guests must be out of the hotel by five o'clock'. The military staff of General Maxime Weygand, France's new minister of national defence, had requisitioned the hotel. 'We argued, but to no avail,' Countess de Chambrun recalled. The hotel servant 'compromised by giving us a cup of coffee before the start'. Despite their age, their wealth and Aldebert's status as a retired army general, they packed and left the hotel before dawn.

Clara Longworth de Chambrun, a stalwart American matron of 66 years, and her American-born husband did not complain. 'I must say for our personal honor,' she wrote, 'all thought of self was totally forgotten in the magnitude of national disaster. Even my little dog seemed to understand that no attention could be paid to him. Instead of balancing himself on my knees to supervise the chauffeur or admire the landscape, he crept down on the floor of the car and lay between my feet.' They left Vichy for Le Puy, where the National City Bank had arranged lodging for its Paris staff.

This was Clara's third war since she left Cincinnati, Ohio, in 1901. She took it in her stride. Four years before the Battle of France, she had written, 'By birth and education, my life – which began on October 18,

1873, was predestined to adventure, tragedy, romance and mirth.' By the time her third war began in September 1939, she was an accomplished Shakespearean scholar and had written sixteen books, eight each in English and French. These included the memoir of her life to 1935, *Shadows Like Myself*, and *The Making of Nicholas Longworth*, a biography of her brother. Nicholas Longworth III had been a Republican congressman from Cincinnati and was twice Speaker of the House of Representatives. His marriage to President Theodore Roosevelt's daughter, Alice, at the White House was *the* American social event of 1906. Born into a rich and respected Cincinnati pioneer family, Clara Eleanor Longworth was, by her own admission, no beauty. 'Why should any man wish to marry a woman who is not extremely beautiful?' she asked in her first memoir. Clara nonetheless had bountiful chestnut hair that she tied back to reveal a striking face that exuded patrician self-confidence. Her fiercely independent, intellectual temperament had probably made her unsuitable to the Ohio boys who congregated at her family's mansion on Grandin Road. In 1895, her cousin, Margaret Rives Nichols, married a French aristocrat, Pierre de Chambrun. Clara met his younger brother, Count Aldebert, at the same time.

Although the Chambrun brothers had an impeccably French pedigree, they were American twice-over. Aldebert and Charles had been born in Washington, DC, where their father, Adolphe de Chambrun, served as legal counsel to the French Embassy during the administrations of Abraham Lincoln and Andrew Johnson. The Marquis de Chambrun's Washington memoir, *Impressions of Lincoln and the Civil War*, recounted his friendship with President and Mrs Lincoln, who invited him to join them at Ford's Theatre on the night Lincoln would be assassinated. The Chambruns were direct descendants of the Marquis de Lafayette, the French hero of American independence and loyal friend of George Washington. Under an April 1788 act of the Maryland legislature, all of Lafayette's male heirs were automatically citizens of the state and, thus, of the United States. Aldebert's favourite sport, dating to his Washington boyhood, was baseball. Clara said that Aldebert 'never considered the United States, where he was born and passed his early school-boy days, as foreign soil'. She also thought that he looked at moral problems 'from a more American point of view' than she did. Their differences were many: 'Like all his family, he upholds a woman's right to vote; I am firmly and temperamentally against it ... His ultrahumanitarian views condemn the practice of capital punishment while my baser and more practical mind considers that in our present imperfect state of civilization it is a necessary evil.' They wed in 1901, a Cincinnati ceremony presided over by the Episcopal Archbishop of St Paul for the Longworths and the Catholic Archbishop of Ohio for the Chambruns. Aged 27, she was not a young bride for her generation. Aldebert, born in Washington on 23 July 1872, was a year older.

Clara moved with Aldebert to France and tackled French life with the determination that her late eighteenth-century forebears brought to settling the Ohio frontier. She perfected her French, took a doctorate at the Sorbonne and became a figure in the conservative world of the French aristocracy. The couple had a son, René, whose godfather was President William Howard Taft; and a daughter, Suzanne, who died of an accidental electrocution in Paris at the age of 19. In 1910, Aldebert was dispatched to Washington as French military attaché and became with Clara part of what the press called President Taft's 'golf cabinet'. Taft, a jovial and rotund Ohio Republican who had been governor of the Philippines and secretary of war under Theodore Roosevelt, called Aldebert 'Bertie'. The Longworth and Taft families had been friends in Cincinnati, where Taft had taught her brother Nicholas at law school. In 1912, Teddy Roosevelt challenged Taft, his former protégé, for the presidency, splitting the Republican vote and handing the election to Democrat Woodrow Wilson. The Longworths and Chambruns, almost alone in Washington, remained close to both the Roosevelt and the Taft families.

The Chambruns returned to France in time for the Great War in 1914. Aldebert, a career soldier who had worked his way through the ranks to become a colonel, commanded the French 40th Regiment. At Bar-le-Duc during the Battle of Verdun in 1916, his entire unit was cited in dispatches for bravery. The award was presented by Aldebert's former military academy instructor, General Henri-Philippe Pétain. Clara used her privileged position to visit her husband near the front.

When she was forced to return to Paris and feared she might never see him again, she wrote, 'But there is an end to everything, even tears.' Her family's sense of *noblesse oblige* led her to work for French refugees from the Meuse Valley battle zone and her mother to come from Ohio and nurse the wounded at the American Hospital of Paris. When the United States entered the war in April 1917, Aldebert was made French adviser to the commander of the American Expeditionary Force, General John Pershing. Clara preserved three images of the war: 'the appearance of General Pershing on the balcony of the Hotel Crillon, the arrival of the [American] First Division, and the salute to Lafayette at Picpus Cemetery'. It was said that an American officer arrived in Paris, went straight to Lafayette's simple grave at Picpus in the east of the city and announced, '*Nous revoilà, Lafayette!*' This was America's answer to Lafayette's famed '*Nous voilà!*' on reaching the rebellious American colonies 140 years before.

After the war, the Sorbonne awarded Clara, then aged 48, a doctorate in literature. Her interests included staging plays at the Comédie Française and helping to manage the American Library. The library had been established to provide books to doughboys, as the American soldiers were affectionately known, and remained open after they went home. Its members were mainly American residents of Paris and French students studying English. Among Clara's American friends on the library board were its only other female members, Edith Wharton and Anne Morgan. The American Library, like Clara herself, had little contact with the Left Bank 'lost generation' writers who congregated at Sylvia Beach's Shakespeare and Company.

Aldebert was posted to Morocco in 1922, where Clara experienced her second war three years later. 'In the spring of 1925,' she wrote, 'the storm that had been brewing over the Rif broke with full force against the French outposts.' Her husband, promoted to general, helped Maréchal Pétain to crush a war for independence that she called the 'onslaught of more than 50,000 warriors of the fiercest description' and capture their leader, the legendary Abd el-Krim. The French exiled Abd el-Krim to Réunion in the Indian Ocean, and the Chambruns returned to France. The French Academy awarded her its Bordin Prize for her Shakespearean scholarship in 1926, and in 1928 she became a

Chevalier of the Legion of Honour. Aldebert retired from the army as a general in 1933.

Two years later, their son, René, returned from practising law in New York to marry Josée Laval. Her father, Pierre Laval, had served in several French cabinets and had recently been prime minister. At the Laval–Chambrun wedding in Paris on 19 August 1935, the best man was General Pershing. Among the witnesses was René's Aunt Alice Roosevelt Longworth. 'Bunny', as family and friends called the 6-foot, dark-haired René, opened law offices at 52 avenue des Champs-Elysées, where his father's National City Bank maintained its French headquarters. René was the first lawyer admitted to the bars of both New York and France.

Bunny's father-in-law was not from a similar aristocratic background. The mercurial Pierre Laval was born poor in the village of Châteldon. He studied law and defended trade unionists. In 1914, he was elected as a socialist to the lower house of parliament, the Chamber of Deputies. When the party split between socialists and communists in 1920, he became an independent. He eventually bought the chateau in his home village and a flat in the exclusive Villa Saïd off the avenue Foch in Paris. In 1927, he moved to the upper chamber, the Senate, and became Président du Conseil, prime minister, in 1931. *Time* magazine named him its 1931 'Man of the Year'. 'Swarthy as a Greek, this compact little Auvergnat (son of a village butcher in Auvergne, south-central France) was a Senator of no party, an Independent,' *Time* commented. 'The public neither knew that he always wears a white wash tie (cheapest and unfading) nor cared to figure out that his name spells itself backward as well as forward. Addicted to scowling, didactic (he once taught school), possessed of a mellow but unexciting voice, identified with no conspicuous cause or movement, Senator Laval was also too young to be noticeable in France in January 1931.' In October 1931, he became the first French prime minister to visit the United States. His government fell in February 1932, but he served in several more cabinets until the 1936 victory of the leftist Popular Front coalition. Friends said that René's devotion to his father-in-law, who called him affectionately '*lapin*' rather than the English 'Bunny', derived from his passionate love for his wife, Josée. After René and Josée married, the two families became close and socialized regularly in Paris and the countryside.

On the morning of 14 June 1940, when Clara and Aldebert were evicted from the Hôtel du Parc in Vichy, Mr Hunt drove the Chambruns to see the Lavals at the Château de Châteldon. It was only a short detour on their way from Vichy to Le Puy. Pierre Laval was at home with his wife, Jeanne, and their daughter, Josée. The former prime minister immediately gave his in-laws the latest news. Clara wrote, 'There was too much of it, and all bad: the Government was at Tours. They were joined there on June the thirteenth by Winston Churchill, Lord Halifax, Lord Beaverbrook and General Spears – the latter some days later was to spirit away from Bordeaux the recently appointed Under-Secretary of War, Colonel Charles de Gaulle, elevated for the nonce to the rank of Brigadier General *pro tem*.' Clara conceived at this time a hatred of de Gaulle. Her memoirs, while criticizing him as an upstart without compassion for French suffering, omitted his brilliant armoured offensive against the Germans – a rare French success during the debacle of 1940. Laval and the countess dismissed the proposal by de Gaulle and Premier Paul Reynaud to continue the struggle against Germany from the North African colonies as 'a wild scheme of continued military resistance from across the Mediterranean'.

Although Clara favoured an early armistice to spare France the loss of more people, she insisted she was adamantly anti-German. Clara's hostility to Germany dated to her Washington years, when the French and German embassies vied for influence over American opinion. She detested German behaviour during the Great War and believed Germany should have paid its full war reparations to France. She wrote that her son René 'fully shared his parents' anti-German feelings'. René founded the French Information Center in New York before the Second World War to counter 'the scarcely concealed Teutonic propaganda' in the United States. Yet the perceptive American journalist Vincent Sheean detected in Clara a certain sympathy for Nazi objectives in Europe. He met the countess in Paris during the Spanish Civil War and wrote that 'she had referred to Franco's forces as "our army", and had said "we shall soon be in Madrid", and had declared quite flatly that if any of Hitler's officers needed help getting to Spain she would assist them'. Clara did not mention this conversation, or her views on Spain, in her memoirs.

General de Chambrun recalled the stopover at Châteldon: 'There we found M. and Mme. Laval, ready to leave for Bordeaux, where M. Laval believed his presence to be necessary. He questioned me at great length regarding Maréchal Pétain and told me his desire that the Maréchal should be placed at the head of the country, believing that he would be able to keep the upper hand against the enemy.' The Lavals drove to the government's new rest stop at Bordeaux, and the Chambruns resumed their journey to Le Puy.

'The sights on the road were worse than those between Montargis and Vichy,' Clara wrote. 'We caught up with the same groups of trucks from aviation and munition centers but the picnic spirit had quite died down. Youths and maidens were no longer thinking of embracing each other; scowls and curses were the best they had to bestow upon passers-by.' The route via Thiers and La Chaise Dieu took them slowly through the mountains until they saw Le Puy, 'seated apparently on several extinct volcanoes upon whose empty craters rose tall churches'. Lodgings had been arranged nearby at an old castle belonging to the Comtesse de Polignac. There, the household maid told them that

> Madame de Polignac was away for the afternoon but that she had left orders that the accommodations offered should be shown us. Our hearts sank a bit when she told us that every individual connected with the bank had already inspected the château, and after one look had gone on to Le Puy. There was no choice left at present, for that very morning a messenger had come from Mr. Pearce, the manager of the bank, saying that there was not a single bed left vacant in town.

To Clara's question about the castle's gas and electricity, the maid answered, 'No gas, Madame, and just enough electricity to light one bulb in each room. If the river rises there may be more.' They went down two flights of stairs to a massive kitchen cut into solid stone. It was bare, apart from a large, ancient stove. Was there either coal or wood for the stove? 'Unfortunately, no, Madame,' the maid said. 'There is none at all here, and none to be bought in the village either. We have hardly enough fuel for the bakers' oven. We hope to have bread in three days' time. They are grinding the first sacks of flour at the mill below the castle.' To Clara's statement that she had been told the bathroom had hot water, the maid answered, 'There is, if you heat it.'

Mr Hunt soon demonstrated his Yankee ingenuity. 'Having explored the wildest parts of India and Thibet, the Sierras and the Rockies were to him mere child's play,' Clara observed of her erstwhile chauffeur. Hunt drove to the village of Lavoûte-sur-Loire and returned with implements to make a success of the kitchen – pots, pans, kettle and cooking gas. He gathered firewood, turned his hand to preparing dinner and in the gatekeeper's cottage located a radio for them to hear the news. Clara and Aldebert nicknamed him 'Daniel Boone', only to discover that 'he was in fact a true and lineal descendant of our great Kentucky hunter and pioneer'.

On 17 June, the radio informed the Chambrun party that Paul Reynaud had resigned and the new prime minister was their old friend, 84-year-old Maréchal Philippe Pétain. They listened sympathetically to Pétain's broadcast that day, in which he called for an early armistice and an end to the fighting. By then, more than a hundred thousand French soldiers were dead, almost two million had been taken prisoner and many of the others were in flight – hiding their uniforms to disguise themselves as civilians. A few heroic units fought on, while many others had been evacuated from Dunkirk to England. On 18 June, the Chambruns listened to the British Broadcasting Corporation's French language service from London. General Charles de Gaulle, who had only just reached England, assured the few French who could hear him, 'France has lost a battle, but France has not lost the war.'

De Gaulle's 'Appeal of June 18th' calling for resistance to the Nazis infuriated Clara de Chambrun, who denigrated the rebel general. At the same time, the countess promoted her son, 34-year-old René, as a more suitable national hero. It was Count René, after all, who had convinced Ambassador Bullitt at the end of May that Britain would stand fast against German bombardment and invasion. While leaving for England from Dunkirk in May on a mission for the French general staff, Captain René de Chambrun – who had been a reserve officer since studying at the military academy of Saint-Cyr in 1927 – observed the superiority of the Royal Air Force over the Luftwaffe:

And then, just as we were leaving the shores of France, three squadrons of Heinkels, twenty-seven planes in all, converged upon the city [Dunkirk] from three different directions, and, as if they had had some secret rendezvous with the Germans, six small British planes appeared almost at the same moment, flying at very high altitude. The Germans began to pour their bombs just as the British fighters swooped down upon them. The sound of the British engines was unlike any plane I knew, and their guns sounded strange too, but they did the most deadly job of dogfighting I have seen. I counted within a few minutes nineteen trails of smoke as Heinkel after Heinkel dropped and the six little fighters took control of the sky.

Back in Paris, René de Chambrun had convinced Bullitt that the RAF would stop Germany from winning the war. At Bullitt's request, Prime Minister Paul Reynaud dispatched René to Washington to intercede for Britain with his cousin, Franklin Roosevelt.

Clara wrote, 'It is historically interesting to note that his [René's] assurances that England would inevitably win the war were made in New York twenty-four hours before Charles de Gaulle launched his radio broadcast from London.' In Clara's eyes, de Gaulle, who had only just been promoted to one-star general, possessed neither breeding nor compassion:

That any man of military training should have attempted to make hay in the political sunshine of the colossal falsehood FRANCE HAS LOST ONLY A BATTLE NOT A WAR shows how far the speaker had already flown from the grim realities of total disaster in the midst of which we found ourselves. It must be supposed that an officer who seeks shelter far from the tragic situation that he himself has abandoned, who is clothed, fed and financed by a Government [Britain's] which has seldom throughout history manifested affection toward his fatherland, is hardly in a position to judge the conditions from which he himself has escaped.

Clara applauded Pétain's decision to give up a struggle that was bleeding France of its young men. Without the Armistice, she wrote, 'nothing would have been left but capitulation and unconditional surrender. What would then have become of all those who had taken refuge in the ever-dwindling free zone, and of those who laboriously made their way to England, America, or North Africa, had the entire south, east and west been overrun?' She admired her husband's old commander, Maréchal Pétain, as 'the very symbol of integrity and glory' and compared Pierre Laval to Abraham Lincoln. 'Both of them were sometimes called ugly,' she wrote, 'but in the President of the United States as in the great French statesman there was strength and beauty of soul which shone in their eyes and placed them above other mortals.' Her in-law, Laval, had been instrumental in making Pétain premier, but had not himself been included in the cabinet of 17 June. Meanwhile, along with other citizens and expatriates, Clara and Aldebert waited for the Battle of France to end. The humiliating capitulation came on 22 June at Compiègne in the same railway car in which Germany submitted to France in November 1918. At that moment, in Washington, her son, René, was pleading with the Senate Foreign Affairs Committee for America to provide arms for Britain to resist the Nazis. In the forests and hills surrounding Mme de Polignac's riverside castle, Mr Hunt foraged for firewood and food. 'Our three weeks there,' Clara wrote, 'were one long effort merely to keep alive.'

FOUR

All Blood Runs Red

WHILE CLARA AND ALDEBERT WERE HEADING south to avoid the Germans, another American left Paris to find them. Eugene Bullard walked towards the front lines, lugging a knapsack of sausages, crackers, canned food and a two-volume history of the American contingent of the French air corps during the First World War, the Lafayette Escadrille. 'I said good-bye and set out to join the 170th Regiment in holding back the enemy – at least that was what I thought,' Bullard wrote. His march took him to Châlons, about halfway along the 100-mile trek to Épinal in the Moselle Valley, where Bullard believed the French infantry regiment was holding the Germans back. Refugees at Châlons told him the Germans had already captured Épinal. So, he walked back to Paris. At the gates of Paris, Bullard learned that another infantry regiment, the 51st, had engaged the Germans near Orleans. He trudged south to join them.

Bullard, with the heavy pack still on his back, marched 50 miles in twenty-eight hours. He stopped at Chartres, where, as he wrote, 'I had a stroke of luck. I ran into Bob Scanlon, the black boxer and comrade from the Foreign Legion. There were two of us now, together, two friends sharing everything. I did not feel lonely anymore.'

German Stukas dive-bombed Chartres as the two Americans were leaving. 'During the bombardments I threw myself on the ground, and I saw Bob Scanlon do the same thing about twenty feet away,' wrote Bullard. 'A huge shell burst about where he was, leaving a crater with the dead and wounded and bits of human bodies strewn around it. I

thought Bob's must be one of them, for he was nowhere in sight.'
Bullard, unable to find even a shred of Scanlon's clothing, abandoned
the search for his friend. Near the bomb crater, a boy with a paralysed
arm screamed for his mother. The woman, Bullard wrote,

> lay cut in half as if by a guillotine, her hand still clutching a piece of
> chicken. The crippled lad jumped up and down shrieking. He went
> into a convulsion as I tried to comfort him. I put my hand on his
> shoulder to take him with me – where, I don't know – but the poor
> little thing jerked away in terror and his eyes actually crossed and
> uncrossed ... Still crying, I pushed on in the hope of fighting the
> enemy that causes such horrors.

An unusual route had brought Eugene Jacques Bullard from his birth-
place, Columbus, Georgia, in 1895 to the Battle of France in 1940.
His parents were of mixed African-Creek Indian heritage, and his
father had been born a slave at the beginning of the Civil War. When
Eugene was 6 years old, his mother died. His father supported his six
children working as a labourer. When a foreman struck him with an
iron grappling hook, William Bullard made the mistake of fighting
back. A white mob rode out to the family cabin that night to lynch him,
but the terrified children convinced the men their father was away. The
drunken racists swore to return. 'This near lynching of his father,'
wrote one of Bullard's biographers, Craig Lloyd, 'was the traumatic
event that led young Bullard to leave home sometime later.'

Bullard was ten years old when he ran away. At first, he travelled
with a gypsy family and worked with horses. A year later, he stowed
away on a tramp steamer to Hamburg. When the captain discovered
the youngster on board, he gave him £5 and dropped him in Glasgow.
Bullard found odd jobs and, in Manchester, became a professional
boxer. A twenty-round match with Georges Forrest in 1913 brought
him to Paris. After winning the decision, he stayed in Paris as a boxer
and sparring partner. He loved the city. 'There never was any name-
calling like "Nigger",' he wrote in his unpublished memoirs. 'It seemed
to me that the French democracy influenced the minds of both white
and black Americans there and helped us all to act like brothers as

nearly as possible.' Two months after France went to war with Germany in 1914, on Bullard's nineteenth birthday, he repaid the people who had treated him as an equal by joining the French Foreign Legion. Among the Americans in his unit was Bob Scanlon. They were posted to the Somme, where Bullard fought as a machine gunner. He was wounded and commended for bravery. So many Legionnaires were killed in 1914 and 1915 that the survivors were transferred to the 170th Infantry Regiment. For many months from late February 1916, the 170th resisted the German mass offensive that became the Battle of Verdun. In one engagement, Bullard sustained shrapnel wounds to his head. In another, a shell ripped open his leg. He won the Croix de Guerre and was invalided from the army. After six months' recovery in Lyons, he returned to Paris and applied to the French Army's air corps.

Bullard qualified as a pilot in May 1917, winning a bet with a Southern white friend that he could do it. He took advanced combat flight training along with other American volunteers at Avord. The Americans formed what became the Lafayette Escadrille. As each pilot qualified, he was sent into action. But some trainees who started school after Bullard left before he did. A friend confided to Bullard that an American in Paris was pressuring the French to prevent American blacks from flying in the war. Dr Edmund Gros, the director of the American Hospital of Paris, was responsible for the welfare of Americans in the Lafayette Escadrille and the American Ambulance Corps. Bullard had already noticed how Dr Gros distributed the cheques from a fund that wealthy Americans in Paris had established for the American pilots: 'I was always the first in Dr. Gros' office. But the dear doctor would never give me my check until after the whole crowd received theirs and the banks were closed for the day, so I could not cash mine.' When Bullard threatened to write to the Inspector General of the Schools of Aviation about being passed over for a combat assignment, he was finally sent to the front. His comrades in the Escadrille gave him a party to celebrate, and someone confided that 'a certain person in Paris in the Ambulance Corps ... had done everything he could to keep me from becoming the first Negro military flyer for no reason except that he didn't like my color'. The 'certain person', Dr Gros, had failed.

Bullard flew his first combat mission in September 1917 with the motto 'All Blood Runs Red' painted on his plane. He flew more than twenty missions, most over the Verdun front, and had one confirmed downing of a German plane. The squadrons in which he served, the N-93 and N-85, acknowledged his bravery. His plane took bullets from German ground fire and fighter planes, but he always made it back to base. When the American Army Air Corps arrived in France that autumn, the other 266 American pilots in French service became the US 103rd Pursuit Squadron. Bullard was the only pilot excluded. He was also the only black.

Dr Gros took matters further when, using a dispute that Bullard had with a white colonial officer who refused to return his salute, he influenced the French to dismiss him from their air corps. Bullard was reassigned to his old regiment, the 170th Infantry, as a non-combatant for the last ten months of the war. In May 1918, the French government issued scrolls of gratitude to all American pilots who had flown for France. Dr Gros, delegated to make the presentation, gave scrolls to every flyer except Bullard.

Dr Gros was not alone in his opinion that African-Americans should not be sent into battle against white soldiers. US Army commanders prevented troops of the all-black 15th Infantry Regiment from serving at the front with the American Army. The Harlem Hellfighters, as they were called, were put under the command of General Henri Gouraud in the French Fourth Army. The French did not believe in segregated units and were grateful to combatants of any colour. The Hellfighters became the 369th Regiment and spent more time under continuous fire, 191 days, than any other unit of American soldiers. They ceded no ground, and none surrendered. They were the first regiment to reach the River Rhine, and they collectively earned the Croix de Guerre for valour. At war's end, however, General Pershing did not permit them, or their popular regimental band under James Reese Europe, to participate in the Allies' victory march through Paris. Many of the demobilized African-American doughboys, unsurprisingly, stayed in Paris rather than return to the land of Jim Crow and lynching.

The army discharged Bullard in October 1919 at the end of a distinguished tour of duty that included the rare achievement of service in the Foreign Legion, the regular army and the air corps. He had also been awarded the Légion d'Honneur, the Médaille Militaire, Croix de Guerre, Croix du Combattant Volontaire de la Guerre and many other medals for bravery and for his wounds. There was no decoration for being the first black combat pilot and the only African-American to fly for any army in the Great War.

Peacetime proved more eventful for Bullard than war. Back in Paris, he returned to boxing but also took up the drums in one of the increasingly popular jazz bands. Montmartre became home to new jazz ensembles and to the demobilized black American soldiers who elected not to return to the United States. Some had played in James Reese Europe's famous Harlem Hellfighters' orchestra. Bullard became artistic director at Joe Zelli's nightclub in Montmartre after helping the Italian to obtain the first Parisian licence to open after midnight. He booked some of the finest jazz talent in the world to play at Zelli's.

In 1923, Bullard married Marcelle Eugénie Henriette Straumann, daughter of a rich industrialist and his aristocrat wife. To Bullard's delight, the Straumann parents welcomed him into their family. Eugene and Marcelle had three children, a son who died in infancy of pneumonia and two daughters, Jacqueline and Lolita. In 1928, Bullard bought his own Montmartre club, Le Grand Duc, at 52 rue Pigalle. It became the centre of a jazz age scene that drew the likes of the Prince of Wales and Ernest Hemingway to Bullard's champagne-laden table. Bullard hired Ada Smith, whose red hair earned her the name 'Bricktop', to sing. He also gave Langston Hughes, then a struggling young poet, work as a dishwasher. This was an exciting time in Montmartre, when jazz lovers could hear trumpeter Arthur Briggs in one club and celebrated pianist Henry Crowder in another. Eugene Bullard dominated the Parisian scene as impresario, restaurateur and benefactor of Americans in need. Clarinettist Sidney Bechet, who played in the club and became Bullard's friend, wrote:

> If someone needed help, he did more than any Salvation Army could
> with a whole army; and what he wanted to do for himself, he could
> do in a smooth, smart way. He'd made himself the kind of man
> people had a need for. The cabarets, the clubs, the musicaners – when

there was some trouble they couldn't straighten out by themselves, they called on Gene. He was a man you could count on.

Bullard opened another club, L'Escadrille, at 5 rue Fontaine, and a gym, Bullard's Athletic Club, at 15 rue Mansart in Pigalle. Marcelle wanted him to give up his Montmartre life and become a country gentleman. 'Like most American men,' Bullard wrote, 'who aren't sissies, I could not stand the idea of being a gigolo even to my wife. So I told her she could lead the life of a full-time society woman if she liked but to count me out during working hours because I was not going to give up earning my living. Soon we were seeing so little of each other that we decided to part company.' She may have wearied of the occasional scars he carried home from fights in and out of the clubs, as well as of his all-night hours. They divorced in 1935, and he was awarded custody of their two daughters.

In early 1939, a new French intelligence service, created three years earlier within the Ministry of the Interior to monitor the 17,000 Germans in Paris, recruited Bullard as an agent. An *ancien combattant* with an impeccable war record, fluent in French and speaking good German, the nightclub and gymnasium owner was an ideal spy. So many Germans flocked to his gym and club that he was bound to hear something. His police handler, Georges Leplanquais, assigned a 27-year-old Alsatian woman, Cleopatre 'Kitty' Terrier, to work with him. Fluent in German, French and English, she had loyalty that was beyond doubt – the Germans had murdered her father during their wartime occupation of Alsace. Gene and Kitty were a good team. When Germans dropped into Le Grand Duc, Bullard was always nearby.

Of course, they figured, no Negro could be bright enough to understand any language except his own, much less figure out the military importance of whatever they said in German. So, as the Nazis talked together at my tables and I served them, they were not at all careful about discussing military secrets within my hearing. These I promptly passed on to Kitty, who could slip unnoticed out of the bar, if need be, and pass along everything important to headquarters.

French intelligence recruited another prominent African-American, Josephine Baker, who passed along information on German clients at the theatres and nightclubs where she sang. When war came in September 1939, Paris was blacked out at night. This finished the nightclub business in Montmartre, and many of its more famous musical residents – including singer and club owner Ada 'Bricktop' Smith – left. Bullard closed his nightclub and gym. A wealthy American woman, June Jewett James, offered him work as a major domo and a home for his daughters at her chateau in Neuilly. While there, he sent Kitty Terrier any important information he heard from Mrs James's visitors. At one formal party, Bullard wore his full dress army uniform with medals. Among the guests was Dr Edmund Gros, who said, 'Bullard, I didn't know you had the Médaille Militaire.' Bullard shot back, 'I thought you kept all my records just as you keep the scroll issued me by the French government as it was to every member of the Flying Corps.'

When the curfew was relaxed to midnight in February 1940, Bullard went back to Paris and reopened Le Grand Duc. In late May, the Germans launched their blitzkrieg of the Low Countries and cut through France at shocking speed. Kitty Terrier warned him, 'Now, get out of Paris as fast as you can.' Bullard knew that his skin colour would make him a target for Nazis, who were even more race-obsessed than the white 'crackers' he had grown up with in Georgia. They might also discover he was working for French intelligence. The Germans interned African-American jazz musicians, despite their status as neutrals, as they found them in their advance on Paris. Trumpeter Arthur Briggs was sent to a camp at Saint-Denis, where he formed a twenty-five-member classical orchestra. Bullard agreed to leave Paris as Kitty asked, but not to escape the Nazis. He went to fight them, as he had from 1914 to 1918. Bullard asked Kitty to care for his daughters and keep an eye on his apartment. Kitty helped him to pack the food and books he was carrying on his back when he walked from Chartres to Le Mans on 14 June 1940, just as the Germans were occupying Paris.

In Le Mans that hot summer afternoon, Bullard tried to fill his empty canteen with water, but he could not get to the town pump through the crowd fighting for a drink. The next morning, he found the 51st Infantry Regiment in Orleans. The commanding officer greeted him, 'Bullard! Is it really you?' Major Roger Bader had been Bullard's lieutenant in the 170th Regiment at Verdun. Bullard's memoirs recorded the events that followed:

> Major Bader assigned me to a machine gun company and ordered me to install machine guns on the left bank of the Loire River opposite German infantry on the right bank and to take charge of a section. We managed to hold the Germans back until midnight. Then they brought their artillery to within three miles of the city on the right bank. French resistance became non-existent and we were ordered to retreat.
>
> The Germans bombarded Orléans and set it on fire. Thanks be to God, the wind was blowing from east to west. This saved Orléans, and one of the world's finest cathedrals.

The Germans shelled Orleans for two days, occupying Joan of Arc's city on 17 June – when Maréchal Pétain asked Germany for an Armistice. The soldiers of the 51st fought well in retreat, although their high command had already chosen to abandon the struggle. A hundred miles south of Orleans at Le Blanc on 18 June, the regiment took heavy German artillery fire. Bullard was running across the street with a light machine gun, when a shell blast killed eleven of his comrades and injured sixteen more. Bullard was hurled against a wall, smashing vertebrae in his back. Hot shrapnel burned his forehead above the right eye.

Nursing his wounds, Bullard was told by other soldiers that Charles de Gaulle had broadcast an appeal that day from London. 'I, General de Gaulle,' the troops heard him say, 'currently in London, invite the officers and the French soldiers who are located in British territory or who would come there, with their weapons or without their weapons, I invite the engineers and the special workers of armament industries who are located in British territory or who would come there, to put themselves in contact with me. Whatever happens, the flame of the French resistance must not be extinguished and will not be extinguished.'

Bullard wanted to fight on with the regiment or join de Gaulle in London, but he was in no condition to do either.

The 51st Regiment's medical unit was in disarray, so Major Bader, as he testified later, ordered Bullard 'to take advantage of an open route to Bordeaux, to leave my unit, and I gave him, on June 19th, 1940, a safe conduct pass'. Bordeaux was not yet occupied, and the American Hospital of Paris had established a field station on the way to Bordeaux at Angoulême. Bullard walked and hitch-hiked all day and night until he found the hospital. 'By the time I got to Angoulême,' Bullard wrote, 'I was about done with pain ... Wounded men were lying all over the place, on floors and everywhere. Again God was with me. The doctor on duty was an old friend, Dr. H. C. De Vaux, physician to the 170th Regiment when I was in it at Verdun.' De Vaux bandaged him, gave him pain killers and advised him, as a wounded black American who fought for France, to leave the country before the Germans found him. With a canteen of water and 'six boxes of sardines' from Dr Vaux, Bullard began walking again. He slept that night on the side of a road. In the morning, a French soldier took pity on Bullard and gave him his bicycle. 'I made such good time that I decided to bypass Bordeaux and keep on to Biarritz near the Spanish border.'

At four o'clock on the morning of Saturday, 22 June, Bullard cycled up to the American Consulate in Biarritz to apply for a passport. Other Americans were already there, waiting for the consulate to open. Bullard took a place in the queue and lay on the ground to sleep. Consul Roy McWilliams arrived early and saw each American in turn. When Bullard came in dressed as a French soldier, McWilliams said, 'Better get out of that uniform. Forty German officers dined at my hotel last night.' Other Americans waiting behind Bullard asked him to hurry. 'I'm trying to save this soldier from the Germans,' McWilliams admonished them. 'If you can't wait, go away.' He asked if any of them had clothes for Bullard. One man gave him a pair of trousers and another a shirt. A little boy asked his father, 'Daddy, can I give the nigger my beret?'

The man reprimanded his son for saying 'nigger', but Bullard told him, 'Your child only repeated what he hears at home. It would be nicer if you'd teach him to say "colored man".'

McWilliams asked to see Bullard's passport. 'I told him I had never had one. Before the First World War, an American could travel without a passport.' To verify his citizenship, the Consul asked Bullard where he was born. 'Columbus, Georgia, October 9, 1894, sir,' Bullard answered.

'Bullard, what river flows through Columbus?'

'The Chattahoochee, sir.'

'What's the name of the town across the bridge from Columbus?'

'If you turn right, Phenix City. If you turn left, Girard, Alabama.'

'That's good enough for me. I know Columbus. But it's not good enough for Washington. Wait over there.'

Fortunately for Bullard, two prominent members of the American community in Paris, Colonel James V. Sparks and R. Crane Gartz, came to the consulate and vouched for him. McWilliams approved Bullard's passport, but he had no authority to issue it. He told Bullard to go to the consulate in Bordeaux. Bullard cycled there through the night and most of the next morning. Consul Henry Waterman was helpful, advancing him $30 and issuing him a passport. At five o'clock in the evening, as Bullard left the consulate, 'My bicycle had vanished – c'est la guerre – so I did unto someone as someone did unto me and just rode off south on another bike.' He returned to Biarritz. Charlie Levy, a friend from Paris, who was driving ambulance loads of Americans to the Spanish border, offered Bullard a lift. On 12 July, Bullard left Lisbon harbour with more than seven hundred other Americans and their dependants on the liner *Manhattan* bound for New York.

FIVE

Le Millionnaire américain

'WE WANDERED LIKE MANY OTHERS on out-of-the-way roads that we had to take to go from Paris towards Touraine,' Gaston Bedaux recalled of his escape from Paris with his American older brother, Charles. Their destination was the Château de Candé, the fabulous estate that Charles had bought in 1927 and restored with some of the millions he made as an 'efficiency engineer' in America. The Renaissance castle was about 20 miles from Tours, capital of the Touraine region. Charles had been reluctant to leave Paris, until Gaston called from Beauvais, about 50 miles to the north, warning him to flee. Living and working as an engineer for the Department of Bridges and Highways nearer the front lines, Gaston knew that radio reports of French victories were false. But Charles, Gaston wrote, 'didn't want to believe me and called me a pessimist'. When Charles insisted that he had to remain in Paris for an important rendezvous with French Minister of Armaments Raoul Dautry, Gaston informed him that the French government, including Minister Dautry, had already left the capital. As the Germans deployed their forces around Paris, the two brothers, together with Gaston's Beauvais staff, drove southwest to the Loire Valley in cars that Gaston had arranged for such an emergency.

Charles Bedaux's exquisite country house, the Château de Candé, had been converted into the temporary quarters of the American Embassy. Ambassador Bullitt and Counsellor Murphy rented part of the Renaissance castle in September 1939, when the Anglo-French declaration of war on Germany raised the possibility of fighting in

Paris. Bedaux, who granted a lease for the duration of the war to First Secretary Hugh Fullerton, charged the US Treasury only $30 for the initial year's rent and did not cash the cheque. The lease benefited Bedaux as well as the embassy. Under American diplomatic protection, his chateau, unlike those of his French neighbours, could not be requisitioned legally as a billet for German troops and was less likely to be bombed. For the embassy, Candé was an ideal location if Paris became a battle zone: it lay in the southwest, far from Germany's invasion routes of 1870 and 1914, in 1,200 hectares of woods, farm and gardens that could not be easily disturbed. Moreover, Bedaux had equipped the property with modern American conveniences unknown elsewhere in the French countryside: US plumbing fixtures in lavish art deco bathrooms, a $15,000 telephone system for twenty-four-hour international calls and a private golf course. Its vaulted stone cellars, one of which had a fully stocked bar while another stored 40,000 bottles of wine, doubled as air raid shelters. The dining table seated twenty-six, and the servants were managed by an English butler named James. The library, with a balustrade modelled on the choir loft at Chartres Cathedral, had been commissioned by Charles for his American-born wife, Fern. The centrepiece of Charles's bedroom was a Chinese opium bed. A cupboard with fifteenth-century panels provided an elegant hiding place for his most important documents. Fern had a gymnasium boasting the latest exercise equipment. Her dressing room was large enough for the designers Molyneux, Coco Chanel and Elsa Schiaparelli to model their latest fashions for the clothes-conscious Mme Bedaux. An underground passage led to the old hunting lodge, which Bedaux had converted into a billiard room. 'The chateau has one disadvantage,' a United Press report in the *New York Times* noted in 1939. 'The big powder factory, a natural bombing objective, is situated in a wooded valley near the entrance to the estate.'

An embassy secretary, Carroll W. Holmes, was the first to move into Candé in October 1939, while other staff spent weekends. In January 1940, Vice-consul Worthington E. Hagerman joined Holmes. Hagerman, an amateur artist, painted scenes of Candé that he gave to Charles and Fern in gratitude for their hospitality. By early June 1940, with the

French command vowing to defend Paris street by street, more diplomats and their families moved there full time.

When Charles and Gaston Bedaux reached the chateau, American Embassy First Secretary Hugh Fullerton, Third Secretary Ernest Mayer, commercial attaché Leigh Hunt and a large support staff were already installed. Charles Bedaux found himself host, not only to the diplomats, but to Americans escaping from Paris and other parts of France. Under Bedaux's generous stewardship, Candé became an extended country house party for displaced American citizens. Champagne greeted the American *réfugiés de luxe* to the fairy-tale palace with its turrets, towers and tennis courts. The impeccably dressed and urbane Bedaux charmed them all, especially the women.

Fullerton found Bedaux, despite his geniality to the guests, 'greatly depressed by France's military defeat'. Bedaux blamed the collapse on the people of France, rather than its politicians and military officers, for being 'slothful and unbridled and in need of discipline and organization'. Mental depression did not impede Bedaux's characteristic passion to get things done. When German officers inspected the chateau, Bedaux persuaded them to grant exit permits for the Americans who wanted to leave the country. An American diplomat asked Bedaux why he did not obtain an exit visa for himself. Bedaux, who believed that Germany and the US had too much in common to fight each other, said, 'I can be of more use here.' While the Americans enjoyed the chateau's luxury at one remove from the war, French cadets at the nearby Cavalry School in Saumur were bravely covering the French Army's retreat over the River Loire.

Three American journalists – H. R. Knickerbocker of Hearst Newspapers, Ken Downs of the International News Service and Quentin Reynolds of *Collier's* – pitched up at Candé late one night as the French government was leaving Tours. Ken Downs, who had been there in 1937, knew Bedaux's housekeeper. When she came to the gate, he asked her for somewhere to sleep. 'She grumbled that she'd have to get permission from the American Embassy, which occupied the house,' Reynolds wrote. 'She went away and didn't return. We were in no mood to dicker. We'd all had a tough seven days and we wanted a night's sleep. Knick and Downs climbed the iron picket fence and walked the mile and a half to the house. They roused a sleepy and very junior member of the Embassy staff. Reluctantly he came back with them and opened the gate.' The diplomat led them to the stables and gave them some horse blankets. 'We were a bit put out because our relations with the Embassy had been excellent. We had been accustomed to the effusive friendliness of Ambassador Bullitt, the genial companionship of Maynard Barnes, the press attaché, and of Colonel Fuller. Any of them would have said, "Here's the house, boys. Come in, have a drink, and make yourselves at home." But this very junior member was very sleepy and not at all interested.' The journalists woke on the dewy grass at sunrise. Needing petrol for their car, they threw pebbles at the chateau's windows to rouse the diplomats inside. The resourceful Reynolds wrote,

> No one woke. There was of course only one thing to do. We went to the garage and siphoned off a few liters of juice from the Embassy cars which were standing there. We comforted ourselves with the excuse that had Bullitt been there he would have given us all the petrol we needed. Afterwards, in Bordeaux, we met some of the American Embassy lads who told us that the theft of petrol had made the junior members of the staff very angry ... Junior members of an embassy are apt to take themselves more seriously than their bosses.

Candé offered better hospitality to Peter Muir, an American First World War ambulance driver who had recently returned to France as a medical officer with the American Field Service. When a German battalion at the front captured the Lawrenceville and University of Virginia graduate, he and another driver convinced the Germans they were physicians. Taken to Paris, they escaped, begged some civilian clothes and bought a car. On the drive west in search of their missing medical unit, they stopped at Candé.

> There were quite a few people gathered in the magnificent salon for cocktails. The owners, Mr. and Mrs. Bedaux, were there and could not have received us more graciously. The others were embassy attachés and their wives, and two or three refugees. It was a grand

feeling to stand about, drinking cold Martinis and chatting in one's own language among friends and seemingly far away from the war and the Huns. There was only one reminder of the war, and that could be seen through the window down in the valley to the south-west. It was a brown spot covering about five hundred acres of forest, and was an eye-sore. A gunpowder factory had been built there, well hidden by the trees, and the French had blown it up before the arrival of the enemy. Mr. Bedaux told me that he had thought the explosion would cause the Chateau to tumble in ruins, but though it had trembled slightly it had withstood the shock.

Bedaux neglected to add that the explosion from the Ripault factory had killed one of his horses, damaged the ceiling in an art deco bath-room and shattered several windows. The morning after Muir's arrival at Candé, he was unable to start his car. An American diplomat drove him to the nearest highway to hitch a ride. Believing his ambulance team had gone to Bordeaux after his capture, the German-speaking Muir accepted lifts from Wehrmacht soldiers heading that way. He finally found his American comrades in Biarritz and escaped with them over the border to Spain.

Arriving in New York on 18 July aboard the SS *Manhattan* with about seven hundred other Americans, Peter Muir told the *New York Times* that he had seen both sides in the war and was convinced that 'we had better start thinking about the German Army; it is terrific, marvelous, with perfect efficiency'. In *War without Music*, a memoir he wrote and published a few months later, he warned his country-men, 'It was then, and is now, my firm conviction that the Madman of Munich is out to dominate the world, and if England does not stop him, America must.'

The *Manhattan* had also carried a contingent of American First World War veterans of the French army. One of them, Eugene Bullard, was still recovering from the injuries he suffered at Le Mans and recalled his welcome home: 'On our arrival we were met by Jack E. Specter, then a representative of American Legion Post No. 1, Paris, of which I was a member in good standing. Specter announced that he had arranged hotel reservations for our group of refugee legionnaires.

To me, the only Negro, he added, "Bullard, I haven't got any reservation for you. I didn't know you were in the group."' After twenty-seven years in France, the first black combat pilot and veteran of two wars against Germany was reminded why he had not come home before. He reflected, 'For me, that burst of brightness from Miss Liberty's torch was quickly clouded.'

At Charles Bedaux's luxurious Château de Candé, the American party went on. More than a quarter of a million refugees from Belgium, Holland and Paris sought shelter in the surrounding Loire provinces. The German Army was encircling and bombarding the city of Tours, which burned for three days before Wehrmacht troops conquered the gutted city. As the number of Americans at Candé increased to 500, Bedaux housed and fed them in considerable style. To deal with normal health problems, Bedaux requested assistance from the American Hospital at Neuilly. The hospital dispatched a medical team, headed by Dr Sumner Waldron Jackson.

SIX

The Yankee Doctor

BACK IN PARIS, WHILE THE GERMANS were settling in next door to the American Embassy at the Hôtel Crillon, Ambassador Bullitt read a letter from the American Hospital's chief surgeon, Dr Thierry de Martel. On 13 June, de Martel wrote, 'I promised you not to leave Paris. I did not say if I would remain in Paris alive or dead. To remain living in Paris would be a cashable check for our adversaries. If I remain here dead, it is a check without funds to cover it. Adieu. Martel.' A meticulous neurosurgeon, he prepared for the German occupation as for an operation. He woke early on 14 June in his elegant apartment at 18 rue Weber near the Champs-Elysées. After shaving and dressing, he went to his study on the apartment's second storey and lay on a sofa. Hours later, a French colleague from the American Hospital found his body. Beside him lay a strychnine solution syringe. Nearby were two documents. One was a note with instructions that nothing be done to save him. The other was the play *Hernani, ou l'Honneur Castillan*, about the suicide of a Spanish nobleman, open at Victor Hugo's words, 'Since one must be tall to die, I arise.' By the time Bullitt read his letter promising not to desert Paris, 65-year-old Thierry de Martel was dead.

Thierry de Martel was the son of Count Roger de Martel de Janville and Sybille de Mirabeau, who wrote romantic novels under the name Gyp. His mother's books mocked the French aristocratic society of which she was a part, and they denigrated late nineteenth-century Jewish *arrivistes*. Adrienne Monnier thought her books were 'disgust-

66

ingly stupid novels'. Born in 1875, de Martel grew up under the new Third Republic in his family's royalist milieu that believed in the guilt of Captain Alfred Dreyfus, the Jewish officer charged in 1894 with treason, unjustly convicted, imprisoned and later exonerated. During the Great War, Dr de Martel fought, was wounded and received military citations before joining the American Hospital as a surgeon in 1917. Together with Dr Clovis Vincent, he revolutionized brain surgery in France. Their techniques reduced mortality during brain tumour operations from 60 to 16 per cent, and he was made a Commander of the Legion of Honour. His devotion to patients impressed the American Hospital's staff as much as his surgical skills. In 1931, when another physician's neglect of the American poet Pauline Avery Crawford forced him to amputate her infected leg, he came to her bedside in the American Hospital afterwards. 'Do not cry!' he said. 'I have just returned from Italy where I found that all the most beautiful statues in the museums were those that were a little broken. And I thought of you, my little patient!'

On 13 June, the day de Martel wrote to Ambassador Bullitt, Dr Charles Bove made 'one attempt to rouse him from his melancholy ... we were standing on an upper verandah [of the American Hospital] overlooking the gardens that had once been so beautiful and now were disfigured by tents, barracks, and entrances to air raid shelters'. De Martel said he had a plan, and Bove asked what it was. 'No,' de Martel said. 'It's not a very interesting plan.' The American recalled, 'His gaze wandered to the garden. After a moment he turned to me with a puzzled frown. "Those birds out there in the garden – those damn birds – they keep on singing as if nothing has happened."' Bove approached the hospital's director, Dr Edmund Gros, with his concerns about de Martel. 'I know,' Dr Gros said. 'We Americans feel badly enough about this thing. But the French ...' Bove called de Martel that evening, but no one answered.

De Martel had told friends about his son's death in the Great War and his subsequent vow never to speak to any German. The writer Jacques Bernard insisted to Georges Duhamel, whom he had succeeded as editor of the journal *Mercure de France*, that de Martel's son had killed himself, possibly as a result of war trauma: 'There is a kind of reverse heredity, the son's act operating on the father, the same moral defect.' Thomas Kernan, the American editor of *Vogue* magazine in France, believed that de Martel had cancer. De Martel was a complex man, a philanthropist and yet a member of right-wing, anti-German and anti-Jewish political groups like Action Française. But writer André Maurois, born Émile Salomon Wilhelm Herzog in 1885 to Jewish parents who had left Alsace when the Germans occupied it in 1870, detected no anti-Semitism in his friend. Maurois and his wife would learn of de Martel's suicide more than a week afterwards, when their New York-bound Pan American Airlines Dixie Clipper from Lisbon stopped to refuel in the Azores. Reading the news in the American papers, Maurois reflected,

> In him we lost an incomparable friend, and France one of the noblest types she has bred. This surgeon was a great gentleman. He had made fortunes and used them to support free clinics in which he operated on thousands of unfortunates. I know of a case in which he saved from death, by an operation that he alone could perform, a man who had pursued him for years with jealousy and hatred. He had proved on a thousand occasions his physical and moral courage.

Dr Thierry de Martel's suicide was one of fourteen recorded in Paris on 14 June, but it received more coverage than the others when the Parisian press resumed publication four days later. Under the headline, 'Death of Dr de Martel', *Le Matin* reported that one of his relatives, on hearing a false rumour of his death, called the doctor's house. Believing a servant had answered, he asked for the date of the funeral. 'The surgeon, who was at the end of the line, responded, "I don't know yet, but I'll tell you when I'm dead."' The funeral, attended by his medical colleagues, took place on Sunday, 16 June. His loss created havoc at the American Hospital of Paris, where other doctors had depended on his leadership as much as the patients did on his surgical expertise. Direction of war surgery fell to de Martel's colleague and friend, a modest genito-urinary specialist from Maine, Dr Sumner Waldron Jackson.

Dr Jackson was a model of the tall, strong and silent Yankee. Born in Spruce Head on the rocky shore north of Portland, Maine, on 7 October 1885, he stood 6 feet and 1 inch tall. His sky blue eyes contrasted with heavy, dark eyebrows. As a youngster, he had worked on farms and in quarries. His rugged looks and powerful physique marked him as an outdoorsman of the harsh American northeast. A Frenchwoman who fell in love with him remembered him striding out of a lake: 'He wore only a brief bathing slip and at a distance he looked like one of the heroes of a Fenimore Cooper novel.' Having worked his way through Maine's Bowdoin College and Jefferson Medical School in Philadelphia, he served his internship at Massachusetts General Hospital in Boston. His next post was with the Harvard Group of volunteers, well-bred young Americans who joined the British Army in 1916. He arrived in France as a field surgeon in time to treat thousands of casualties thrown up by the Second Battle of the Somme. The five-month engagement inflicted bullet and shrapnel wounds, burned flesh, gangrene, trench fever, gas poisoning and the *gueule cassée* or broken face that left men without jaw, cheek or eye socket. Doctors frequently lacked pain-killers or anaesthetics for major surgery, and the medical use of antibiotics had yet to be discovered. Jackson dealt with all types of wound, and he achieved the respect of his British colleagues for his steady work under impossible circumstances.

A year after Jackson's arrival in France, the United States armed forces joined the Allied cause. Captain Sumner Jackson transferred from the British Army to the American as a lieutenant. One of the few American physicians with modern battlefield surgery experience, he was posted to American Red Cross Hospital Number Two in Paris to treat severely wounded men brought back from the trenches. Jackson met a French Red Cross nurse, Charlotte Sylvie Barrelet de Ricout, and stole a first kiss from her in a linen cupboard. Charlotte had taken up nursing when the war began in 1914. Her lawyer father and her mother were Swiss Protestants, who had settled in France. She loved playing tennis and sailing on a lake near Paris at Enghien-les-Bains, where her family had a holiday house. Jackson called her by her family's pet name, Toquette, and she called him Jack. Jack had just turned 32 when he married 27-year-old Toquette on 19 November

1917. Nine months after the Armistice of November 1918, the couple sailed to the United States.

When Jackson left the army in September 1919, he and his war bride went from Fort Dix to Spruce Head, Maine, the hometown he had left in 1905 for Bowdoin College, medical school and France. The people of Maine were famously hardy and insular. Most of them voted Republican and minded their own business, and few had been as far from home as Europe. Toquette felt unwelcome. Jackson's experiences of France and war had alienated him from his New England roots. Before the icy winter set in, the couple moved to Philadelphia for Jackson to take up a medical practice. Somehow, they did not fit. The infamous Palmer Raids that deported aliens for their political opinions exposed a streak of American xenophobia, and the new prohibition on alcohol seemed silly to a couple used to wine with dinner. Jackson wrote to the director of the American Hospital of Paris, Dr Edmund Gros, to inquire about employment. Dr Gros, who had met Jackson during the war, replied that he would be welcome. However, French law required foreign doctors to obtain a French high school diploma, the *baccalauréat*, and earn a French medical degree. For a 36-year-old physician with his experience it would be difficult to sacrifice four years of his professional life. Dr Gros told him that another American physician who had worked in France during the war, Dr Charles Bove, had taken his *baccalauréat* and was studying at the École de Médecine in Paris. Jackson agreed to do the same. He and Toquette sailed to France in September 1921.

Jackson studied French with a 30-year-old tutor named Clemence Bock. Despite hard work by teacher and student, Jackson failed the philosophy section of the syllabus and thus did not qualify for medical school. The Jacksons went to Algiers, where he could take the examination again under a regime that was said to be somewhat easier. After nine months of study in Algeria, Jackson passed the exams and was admitted to the École de Médecine in Paris. Two years later, he successfully defended his thesis, moved into an apartment at 11 avenue Foch in the expensive 16th Arrondissement and began work as a surgeon and urologist at the American Hospital.

'This hospital is a little bit of the United States right here in Paris, Bove,' Dr Edmund Gros had told Dr Charles Bove a few years before.

When Jackson went to work there in 1925, its leading medical practitioners were Dr Gros and Dr Thierry de Martel. The little hospital that admitted its first patient in 1910 had served the French and American armies in wartime, when medical tents covered its expansive gardens. Its American Ambulance Service became United States Military Hospital Number One, treating American casualties from the battles at Château-Thierry and the Argonne. Since the war and the post-war influx of Americans to Paris, it had outgrown its original confines at the corner of the boulevard du Château and rue du Château in Neuilly. The new Memorial Building, designed by American architect Charles Knight, opened next door on boulevard Victor Hugo in May 1926. Looking like a comfortable seaside hotel, the Memorial Building housed 150 patient beds in a central block with two matching wings. The hospital's charter, signed into American law in January 1913 by President William Howard Taft, required it to offer medical services free to American citizens in France. Wealthy Americans and foreigners, like the kings of Yugoslavia and Spain, paid for private rooms. Indigent Americans were placed in wards. Among Americans without funds was Ernest Hemingway, who came to the hospital at least twice during the 1920s. Dr Bove removed his appendix, after which he began writing *The Sun Also Rises* in a ward bed. Dr Jackson stitched and bandaged Hemingway's head when a skylight in his bathroom fell on it. James Joyce was made an 'honorary American' to receive eye surgery at the hospital in 1923. Scott Fitzgerald's wife, Zelda, came to the hospital in 1926 with gynaecological ailments, and Dr de Martel operated on her. Gertrude Stein, the poet e e cummings and other American writers relied on Dr Jackson and the American Hospital for medical care that, as often as not, was given free of charge.

In January 1928, Charlotte Jackson gave birth to a boy. They named him Phillip. In this family of nicknames, young Phillip became Pete. When the Depression that came to France a few years after it hit the United States forced many Americans out of Paris, the hospital lost patients and cut staff salaries. The board of governors sought donations in the United States, and the Paris branch of Morgan and Company Bank extended an overdraft at reduced interest. 'The permanent American colony in Paris in those days divided quite sharply between those who worked for a living like the newspapermen and those who kept country chateaux and moved between Paris and various spas,' wrote Eric Sevareid, then a reporter at the *Paris Herald* by day and for the United Press at night. During the Spanish Civil War, he remembered, it became an 'impossible task' for Americans wounded in the service of the legitimate Spanish government to 'break into that fortress of snobbery, the American Hospital in Paris'. The official American community in Paris, Sevareid noticed, looked down on those who fought against the Nazis in Spain. They were 'dirty Reds' to some on his own newspaper and to 'Dean [Frederick Warren] Beekman, the sententious head of the most fashionable American church'.

Sumner Jackson belonged to the established American colony of Paris. He lived in the most chic district of the Right Bank, and his family spent weekends in the country. His patients were from European aristocracy and American high society. Dean Beekman, the anti-communist Episcopal firebrand of the faux-Gothic American Cathedral in the avenue George-V, was a friend. Yet Dr Jackson was a dissenter. He and Toquette were both agnostics from Protestant, free-thinking families. They had known war and poverty, and both distrusted Hitler. His entry in *Americans in France: A Directory, 1939–1940* listed the American Legion as his only membership. Most of the other Americans in the Paris version of the *Blue Book* belonged to fraternities, country clubs and alumni associations like the Harvard and Yale clubs. As a member of the hospital's medical committee, Jackson braced the institution for war and took a special interest in his poorer patients.

Soon after the Munich agreement in 1938, the American Hospital's governors offered their facilities to the French government to treat the wounded if war broke out. When war came in September 1939, casualties were far fewer than in the Great War. The hospital took them in, and Jackson operated on wounds similar to those he had seen between 1916 and 1918. Over Christmas 1939, Josephine Baker sang and danced at the American Hospital for injured French troops. The soldiers, in pyjamas and many in wheelchairs, toasted her beside a Christmas tree. The hospital established a temporary centre on the Normandy coast at Entretat. When the Germans invaded France in mid-May 1940 and made swift advances through the north, the facility had to move. The *New York Herald Tribune* reported on 8 June 1940 that the hospital's doctors had already 'selected a building at Angoulême in the Charente, which has been requisitioned to be turned over to the hospital for this purpose by the French government'. The 100-bed field hospital was on the direct Paris–Bordeaux railway line, so the wounded could be moved there without being trapped on roads blocked by refugees. Other temporary American hospitals and dressing stations opened at Châteauroux and in the casino of Fontainebleau, just south of Paris. Dr Jackson, Dr Bove, Dr Morris Sanders and other American surgeons laboured day and night on the growing number of French soldiers whom the Germans had seriously wounded. Most of the casualties came to the hospital in ambulances of the American Ambulance Corps, paid for by donations from American citizens and driven by American volunteers. When French friendly fire hit one ambulance and wounded a French soldier, Jackson had to amputate his leg in darkness. The amputation was nonetheless clean enough for the leg to take a prosthetic. When he was not operating on patients, Jackson took care of anaesthesia for other doctors. It was grinding, bloody labour without any reassurance that the suffering would save France from German conquest.

French General Lannois came to the American Hospital to award the Médaille Militaire, France's highest military decoration, and the Croix de Guerre to a wounded Zouave dispatch bearer named Maurice Longuet. With the general was the soldier's father, whose eye patch marked him as a wounded veteran of the previous war. His 19-year-old son lay in bed, while the general pinned the ribbons on his pyjama shirt. Drs Jackson, Bove, Gros and de Martel watched the informal ceremony. Jackson whispered to Bove, '*Tel père, tel fils,*' such a father, such a son. More sons were brought in every day.

Dr Bove, who operated beside Sumner Jackson, recalled the chaos of the final weeks:

> When the Allies, pushed to the coast, fought a rear-guard engagement at Dunkirk, Paris felt the full impact of things. All city hospitals were crowded with casualties. The nurses were so overwhelmed

with work that additional women volunteered by the hundreds to wash the faces and feet of the wounded. They carried cups of coffee to those who were able to swallow. We surgeons operated until late into the night, cutting away on jagged wounds like butchers in a slaughterhouse. I lived on five or six cups of coffee and a few sandwiches daily ... We rarely stopped before midnight. The agony of the men awaiting their turn in the outer room and begging us to relieve them made it impossible for us to quit. My feet became so sore that I could barely walk, and to attempt to straighten up out of the bent position I had maintained for so many hours over the operating table caused excruciating pain.

This went on for two weeks. Then, as the Nazis approached Paris, the city was virtually cut off; the wounded began pouring down to evacuation centers in the middle and southern parts of France. As the news filtered into Paris that thousands of British and French troops had been evacuated from Dunkirk, the crowds pushed and fought their way into the churches to light candles to their patron saints and to pray that their loved ones had reached England.

The day before the Germans entered Paris, Dr Bove told Sumner and Toquette, 'It's only a matter of a few weeks before Roosevelt brings America in and declares war on Germany. But this time the Boches will have Paris, and if we stay they'll lock us up.' Bove prepared to leave. Dr Gros, in Bove's words, 'seemed to age before our eyes' and was no longer able to work. Sumner considered going, but his wife convinced him that the hospital's French staff would not stay without him. Sumner asked Toquette, who had resumed working as a nurse, to take their son to safety. She and her sister Alice, nicknamed Tat, left Paris with 12-year-old Phillip for the family's lakeside house at Enghien.

With his wife and son no longer in their avenue Foch apartment, Jackson moved into one on the third floor of the hospital. On the last warm June night before Paris fell, he ascended to the roof to smoke a cigar. He could see the fields where French kings hunted before the nineteenth-century bourgeoisie planted suburban villas in Neuilly. Artillery flashes on the horizon made it clear that the Germans were advancing on Paris from the east and north. It would not be long before they reached Neuilly. Jackson's main concern now was to save the hospital from falling into German hands. Wounded French and British soldiers needed the institution, one of the finest in France, as much as the American civilians still in Paris. There were already rumours that the Germans had listed the hospital for requisitioning. Soon, Jackson would face another dilemma. Donald Coster, a young American who had come from Montreal to drive ambulances for the American Ambulance Field Service, asked for a safe haven. There was something curious about Coster. As an American neutral, he had nothing to fear from the Germans. Yet, for some reason, he was hiding in the hospital's basement. If he were caught there, the Germans might seize the hospital and arrest Jackson for helping him. Jackson, 54 years old with a wife and young son to protect, had decided which side he was on. Helping Coster was only the first step along the anti-German road.

By the time the Germans consolidated their hold on Paris, most of the Americans who had vanished in the war's chaos had been accounted for. Some of the American volunteer ambulance drivers, however, were still missing. They had either been killed or captured. Two American charities, the American Ambulance Field Service (AAFS) and Anne Morgan's American Volunteer Ambulance Corps (AVAC), had dispatched drivers, crews and ambulances to France from the early spring of 1940. Americans from all forty-eight states donated a fleet of Chevrolet three-quarter ton trucks with the latest mobile medical facilities. At the end of May, seventy-five American drivers and sixty-six Chevrolets from AVAC and another thirty-eight men and six ambulances from AAFS were at the front. Drivers paid their own expenses and the cost of their equipment. Most were young Ivy Leaguers. One, Robert Montgomery, was a prominent Hollywood actor. When the Germans occupied Denmark on 9 April, the AAFS was attached to the French Tenth Army. Throughout May and June, the Americans went into action to retrieve wounded and evacuate civilians without cars or unable to depart on railway lines bombed by the Luftwaffe. Anne Morgan, although aged 67, led her drivers into the fighting in the Meuse Valley.

One American ambulance driver, 26-year-old Lawrence Jump, was reported dead in May after a German shell struck his ambulance. *Life* magazine declared the Oakland, California, native and Dartmouth graduate the 'first American casualty' of the war. Then, on 24 June, two days after the signing of the Franco-German Armistice at Compiègne, *Life* published a letter from his sister, Cynthia Jump Willett: 'I received a telegram yesterday from the State Department informing me he was in a prison in Weinberg near Stuttgart.' The American Embassy in Berlin arranged his release.

At least two American drivers were wounded, and nine went missing in action. Four of the missing, presumed dead, belonged to the AAFS unit with the French Tenth Army at Beauvais. Their *chef de section* was Peter Muir, the First World War ambulance veteran who would be captured by the Germans and escape to enjoy Charles Bedaux's hospitality at the Château de Candé. The four missing drivers were Muir's immediate subordinate, Donald Quested Coster, a Lawrenceville and Princeton alumnus who had worked in advertising in Montreal, Canada; John Clement of Brookline, Massachusetts; Gregory Wait of Shelburne, Vermont; and George King of Providence, Rhode Island. The last place Muir had seen them was the unit's forward position at Beauvais: 'Coster was in the Colonel's office and spoke to me. He was taking his two cars to Amiens. There had been terrific bombings. The town was in flames. The Germans were coming in. Perhaps we would meet there. Good-by. Good luck. I never heard his voice again in France.'

Muir wrote that 'with the knowledge that the Germans were in one part of the town, if not all of it, Coster was courageously leading his two cars back for a last load of wounded'. Muir waited all night for the men to return and, in the morning, made several attempts to find them. French soldiers outside Amiens stopped him each time for his own safety. 'At noon I gave up Don Coster, Gregory Wait, George King, and John Clement as lost in action, and sent a report in to the Paris office to the effect that they had disappeared while carrying out a dangerous mission under orders from their [French] commanding officer, Colonel Soulier. They had been killed, wounded, or captured on duty.' On 26 May, the *New York Times* reported, 'Lovering Hill, commander of the American Ambulance Field Service, returned to Paris today after an unsuccessful hunt for four missing American ambulance drivers.'

The French government awarded Coster, Wait, King and Clement the Croix de Guerre with a citation that noted they had been killed in action – *mort pour la France.*

Coster and the others had, in fact, found shelter in the cellar of the Hôpital Châteaudun in Amiens. The city was ablaze, and only its cathedral was unscarred. Taking cover below the hospital with 150 doctors, nurses, wounded soldiers, women and children, Coster heard 'exploding shells like punches against your chest'. The shelling stopped, but it was followed by a more ominous sound: heavy boots stamping overhead. Everyone remained quiet while they passed. Cautiously, Coster stepped outside. 'I walked into the courtyard, and there for the first time saw the grey-green soldier's uniform,' he wrote. 'The soldier's rifle was aimed at a line of French prisoners backed against a wall.' Fearing the soldier was about to execute the men, but unable to speak German, Coster held up the Geneva identification card that showed he was a civilian ambulance driver and an American. 'He turned his gun on me, and seemed to be considering whether to squeeze the trigger. But the answer, at least for the moment, was no.'

Fellow driver George King spoke enough German to ask to see an officer. The soldier led them about fifty yards to the main road. 'There,' Coster wrote, 'we were greeted by the most awe inspiring sight I have ever seen.' It was a Wehrmacht mechanized unit speeding into Amiens.

You may have seen photographs of a Panzer column. But you haven't seen the endless stretch of it. You haven't seen its speed – roaring down the road at forty miles an hour. German tanks with officers standing upright in the turrets, sweeping the landscape with binoculars. Mean little whippet tanks. Armored cars with machinegunners peering out through the slits. Motorized anti-aircraft cannon with their barrels pointed upward and crews ready for action. Armored touring cars with ranks of alert soldiers stiffly pointing rifles. Guns of every caliber, on pneumatic tires or caterpillars. Motor boats and rubber rafts mounted on wheels; fire engines; camouflaged trucks loaded with petrol – all ready at the first sign of resistance to disperse across the fields and take up positions of defense or attack. Over-head were reconnaissance planes.

Near where we were standing the French had thrown a pitiful wooden barricade across the road, which the column had mowed down like matchsticks; nothing yet invented by man, you felt with a shock of despair, could possibly withstand this inhuman monster which had already flattened half of Europe.

The German soldier stopped an armoured car and turned the Americans over to its officer, who drove them to his commander. 'The general was a broad-shouldered, tough, six-foot-three mountain of Prussian efficiency,' Coster remembered. 'He listened to us with polite impatience. But either our French or the general's was not too good because he took us for American *doctors* and scribbled an order that we were to be placed in charge of the Châteaudun Hospital, which we were to put in scrupulous order for use as a "German-American" hospital.' Coster and his colleagues spent two nights bringing wounded British soldiers off a battlefield. The scene was horrifying in the darkness, but it was worse at dawn of the second day:

> Under a hot, cloudless sky lay a wide field of high grass, simply covered with the English dead and wounded, and wounded and dead cattle. The British boys had been massacred by the tanks, as they had no artillery, only a few light machine guns to supplement their rifles – about as effective against a tank's armor as a peashooter ... Here, as last night, we didn't find a single dead or wounded German. Out of possibly 300 British, we picked up maybe 25 or 30. The rest had all been killed.

When Coster asked one wounded Englishman what he thought of the Panzer columns, he said, 'Beautiful to watch, but terrible to receive.'

A German soldier mistook Coster, whose ambulance uniform was similar to a British soldier's, for an Englishman and stole his leather gloves. Coster grabbed the gloves back. 'In the fraction of a second, his revolver was pointed at my stomach. I pointed to the American

Field Service band on my arm and explained, *"Amerikanisch"*.' The officer saluted him and walked off. Other German officers complained of the Americans, 'Ah – we never see any of you – on our side.'

On 14 June, the day the Germans occupied Paris, the four American 'doctors' were still working at the Amiens 'German-American' hospital. A Belgian Red Cross delegate and his wife, M. and Mme Alfred Chambon, arrived to visit the wounded. Coster asked if they would take him and his three comrades to Brussels. 'We hurried to the *Kommandant*. At first his answer was definitely no; but we argued so loudly (and lied so convincingly about the pressure that would be applied by the American Consulate in Brussels when they heard of our plight) that at last he relented.' The Chambons drove the four Americans in their small Ford to Brussels, where the American Ambassador placed them 'under the protection of the Embassy'. Wait, King and Clement stayed in Belgium awaiting repatriation to the United States. On 1 July, American diplomat George Kennan, who was visiting from the US Embassy in Berlin, took Coster in his car back to Paris. 'We were stopped three times,' Coster wrote of the drive, 'but Mr. Kennan's pass and his perfect German took us safely through.' Kennan wrote that he had given a lift to 'one of the American ambulance drivers, who was trying to get down to Paris to recover his clothes'. The French peasants along the roads evoked strong sympathy from the two Americans. 'Refugees were laboriously making their way back northwards, in search of their homes,' Kennan recorded in his diary. 'Most were traveling on the great two-wheeled horse-drawn cart of the French peasant, which could accommodate a whole family and many of its belongings.' Kennan noticed a young girl on one of the carts:

Her dress was torn and soiled. She had probably not taken her clothes off, or been able to wash, for days ... All the youth had gone out of her face. There was only a bitterness too deep for complaint, a wondering too intense for questions. What would be her reaction to life after this? Just try to tell her of liberalism and democracy, of progress, of ideals, of tradition, of romantic love; see how far you get ... She saw the complete moral breakdown and degradation of her own people. She saw them fight with each other and stumble over each other in their blind stampede to get away and to save their possessions before the advancing Germans. She saw her own soldiers, routed, demoralized, trying to push their way back through the streams of refugees on the highways. She saw her own people pillaging and looting in a veritable orgy of dissolution as they fled before the advancing enemy ... She saw these French people in all the ugliness of panic, defeat, and demoralization.

In Paris, Kennan dropped Coster and his luggage at the Hôtel Bristol, 'a place of refuge for the remaining Americans'. After making a nostalgic tour and dropping his car at the American Embassy after the ten o'clock curfew, Kennan walked to the Hôtel Bristol. 'At the hotel the ambulance driver and I, feeling much too near the end of the world to think of sleep, cracked out a bottle of rye,' Kennan noted. 'We were joined by our next-door neighbor, a female and no longer entirely young. She was a true product of Parisian America and was accepting her privations with such excellent good humor that she kept us in gales of laughter with the account of her experiences.' The next day, Kennan drove through the city looking up 'friends of friends'. Having known Paris before the war, he thought the German-occupied city looked the same but was no longer itself: 'Was there not some Greek myth about the man who tried to ravish the goddess, only to have her turn to stone when he touched her? That is literally what has happened to Paris. When the Germans came, the soul simply went out of it; and what is left is only stone.'

Coster learned that a French officer had seen his Ambulance Number 20 near Amiens, burned out with four charred corpses beside it. 'This explained why King, Wait, Clement and I had been awarded the Croix de Guerre – posthumously!' Rather than linger at the Bristol or return to his room at Cité Universitaire, Coster went to the American Hospital at Neuilly. There was no indication that he knew Dr Sumner Jackson, but he asked the surgeon for help.

Donald Coster was more than a naïve volunteer. After his graduation from Princeton in 1929, he moved to Montreal, the nearest venue for American diplomats and others to perfect their French. He worked there as an advertising executive, and he had no difficulty leaving the job in 1940 to serve in France. When he arrived in Brussels from Amiens on 14 June, he had the option of awaiting repatriation with his colleagues. Instead, he went to Paris. Coming back to France after the Germans had arrested him once was a gamble. Under international law, as an American he would not have been apprehended. The Nazis could have arrested him only if they suspected him of being a spy. Coster probably returned to Paris to collect – not his clothes – but information on France, German troop strength or the new escape routes through which British and French soldiers were making their way to England. Dr Jackson, having served in the British and American armies in the last war against Germany, was organizing an underground railroad. When Coster found him, Jackson agreed to obtain the papers he would need to cross the border to Spain. Until the false identity documents were ready, Coster stayed out of sight under the American Hospital.

The American Hospital of Paris continued its assistance to the war's victims after Paris fell under Nazi domination. 'The Germans permitted Dr. Jackson to set up a dressing station for the French wounded at Fontainbleau [sic] and to evacuate selected patients to the American Hospital,' wrote Dr Morris Sanders, chief anaesthesiologist at the American Hospital in 1940. Sanders, who called Sumner 'Dr Jack', went on the first ambulance to Fontainebleau with Drs Jackson and Gros, and he took part in surgery on the French wounded there. 'With the Occupation of Paris,' Sanders wrote, 'Dr. Jack worked long hours, gave his blood numerous times and slept in the building, and visited his family only on weekends.'

From the first day of the occupation of Paris, the American Hospital expanded its operations from field hospitals to prison camps, where many of the newly interned soldiers were either ill or wounded. Facilities for prisoners were rudimentary, if only because the Germans were not wholly prepared to deal with almost two million captives. Otto Gresser, the hospital's Swiss superintendent, recalled, 'An impressive line of ambulances packed with bread and other essential products, all run by American and French volunteers, daily left the Hospital for the prisoner camps in the Paris area, some of them went even as far as

Château-Thierry, Chartres and Alençon. From June 15 they visited 250,000 prisoners desperately in need of food.' Dr Sumner Jackson, who worked without rest, did not believe enough was being done for the prisoners. He blamed what he called the 'bullshit bureaucracy of old men', both German and French, for failing to distribute all the American aid intended for the prisoners. The hospital, while providing assistance to demoralized French PoWs, had the most up to date intelligence on the locations, security measures and sizes of all the German camps in the Paris region. Some of the injured prisoners that the ambulances brought to the hospital did not, when they recovered, return to the camps. Dr Jackson made certain that those who walked out of the hospital left no trace for the Germans to follow.

Immediately after the Germans entered Paris, a report prepared by the American Hospital for its US governors in New York concluded, 'Too much praise cannot be given to Dr. Sumner W. Jackson, who has been a member of the attending Staff since 1925 and who accepted the professional supervision of the wounded for the period of the war.'

Dr Thierry de Martel left a nephew, Jacques Tartière, an actor who used the stage name Jacques Terrane. Jacques' wife was a glamorous, long-legged American actress, Drue Leyton. They had met in New York in 1937, while he was visiting his father and his American stepmother. Drue was acting in a Work Projects Administration (WPA) Theatre Project – 'for I had grown weary,' she wrote, 'of the part of the blonde heroine in Charlie Chan mysteries to which I had been confined in Hollywood'. She recalled meeting Jacques, 'He was a good-looking, tall man, twenty-six years old, six years younger than I. He had been educated in England as well as France and spoke English perfectly.' They went together to England, where Drue played in Clifford Odets's *Golden Boy*. They married in London in 1938, the day before Neville Chamberlain and Edouard Daladier ceded Czechoslovakia to Hitler at Munich. When war began in September 1939, Jacques enlisted in the French Army. His weak lungs kept him out of combat, so the army assigned him to liaise with British forces in Brittany. Drue, meanwhile, accepted a theatrical agent's proposal to work for the Ministry of Information at its international Radio

Mondiale. There, she produced programmes that promoted France in America, interviewing the French novelist Colette, the comedienne Mistinguett and American reporters like Dorothy Thompson and Vincent Sheean. Her broadcasts under the name Drue Leyton won the attention of the Nazis. German radio announced in five of its French language broadcasts that, when Germany conquered France, she would be executed.

In late May 1940, 35-year-old Drue Leyton Tartière watched Belgians seeking safety from the Nazis in Paris, 'grandmothers holding dead babies in their arms, women with parts of their faces shot away, and insane women who had lost their children, their husbands, and all reasons for living'. It was then that 'we realized that the so-called "phony" war was over, and that horror had begun in earnest'. Her desire to help contrasted with the response of another American, mining heiress Peggy Guggenheim. She had seen the same refugees dragging their meagre belongings through Paris and admitted later that she felt and did nothing for them. She was buying paintings from artists desperate to leave Paris before the Nazis reached it – acquiring for $250,000 a collection that would be worth over $40 million. When she called uninvited at Picasso's studio, the artist told her, 'Lingerie is on the next floor.' Soon, as the Nazis shelled the outskirts of Paris, Guggenheim fled south. Drue Tartière was not far behind.

At ten in the morning on 11 June, the 'forty-two assorted nationals' of Radio Mondiale left Paris for Tours in a convoy of cars loaded with heavy bags.

> The day was stifling, and there were panic, misery, and anxiety wherever one looked. On the road out of the city people were pushing baby carriages or pulling small carts, others were on loaded bicycles, and some were walking, carrying their children and their valises. Some were moving their families and possessions in wagons drawn by oxen. Farther on, we saw dead bodies on the side of the road, French men, women, and children who had been machine-gunned by German Stukas. Cars were lying in ditches, overturned, and men and women stood near them, weeping.

When they reached Tours more than twenty-four hours later, they had to sleep in a bordello commandeered by police for the radio's staff. 'In Tours, there was even greater panic than in Paris, and no one seemed to know whether the government intended to stay there or go further south.' Drue was astounded to observe Prime Minister Paul Reynaud ignoring British envoys Lord Gort and General Ironside. Although the two Britons were supporting him against his defeatist ministers, Reynaud brushed past them to the car of his mistress, Countess Hélène de Portes. The government then left Tours without informing Radio Mondiale. Early on 13 June, Drue and her international colleagues drove south to Bordeaux in pursuit of France's elusive leaders.

'From the Bordeaux radio station,' Drue recalled, 'we sent out frantic pleas for help for France, and we tried to give people across the Atlantic some picture of the wretchedness of the refugees who were pouring into the temporary capital of France. We described the machine-gunning of these refugees on the clogged roads by low-flying German planes, and we told of the misery of the men and women who were arriving in the atmosphere of panic and confusion which was prevalent in Bordeaux.' An American named Smitty, who had volunteered to fight for France, found himself working as a broadcaster. At one thirty in the morning on 17 June, as the Germans were bombing Bordeaux, he bellowed over the air to the United States, 'Hear that, America, the God-damned sons of bitches are bombing us now!'

By dawn, all had changed. Philippe Pétain, dressed in the gold-braided uniform of a Marshal of France, strode into Radio France's temporary broadcast centre in Bordeaux to deliver an important announcement. At ten o'clock in the morning, the 84-year-old 'hero of Verdun' stepped into the studio, where, Drue observed, 'a boy was arranging the microphone, but he did not do it fast enough to suit the old Marshal. Pétain gave him a kick.' As the new head of government, he announced, 'I say that by the affection of our admirable army ... [and] by the confidence of all the people, I give to France my person to assuage her misfortune ... It is with a broken heart that I tell you today it is necessary to stop fighting. I addressed myself last night to the adversary to ask him if he is ready to seek with me, soldier to soldier, after the actual fighting is over, and with honor, the means of putting an end to hostilities.' Drue was unimpressed. 'I had stood next to him in the small broadcasting studio and had seen no signs of the broken heart he said he had when he told the French people that he had asked the Nazis for peace terms.' Pétain had given up the fight, but Drue Tartière had not.

The scheme that Paul Reynaud and Charles de Gaulle had urged, to fight on from the colonies, did not seem far-fetched to the French people that *New Yorker* correspondent A. J. Liebling met between Tours and Bordeaux. Liebling was driving with fellow American reporters Waverly Root from Mutual Radio and John Elliot of the *New York Herald Tribune* in Root's 'old Citroën with a motor that made a noise like anti-aircraft fire'. They stopped for the night in the house of a garage owner in Barbezieux. Liebling wrote, 'We had our *café au lait* with a professor of the local lycée in the garden of a restaurant the next morning. None of the little people one met, like the *garagiste* and the professor, considered that France might drop out of the war altogether or that Germany might win it. They took it for granted the Government would retain the fleet, go on to North Africa and fight from there. We weren't so sure. The little people hadn't seen the ministers and their mistresses.'

Reynaud's mistress, Countess Hélène de Portes, had long urged capitulation – persuading her lover to appoint the ministers who would finally throw him out of office and end the battle. When Pétain called on France to quit, the Germans held only 10 per cent of the country. France still had its empire and a vast armada. Reynaud, de Gaulle and Churchill were urging the government to move to North Africa and fight on. Many Frenchmen had already gone to Algiers, including Antoine de Saint-Exupéry. The famed aviator and writer recruited forty other pilots, commandeered a plane in Bordeaux and flew to North Africa to continue the struggle. Some French forces were counterattacking, and the Germans were taking heavier casualties than at the beginning of the invasion. But Pétain, Weygand and the rest of the new leadership called an end to the war. Eleven days after Pétain's armistice broadcast, Mme de Portes died in a car accident.

A. J. Liebling and many other Americans went to Lisbon to take the Pan Am Clipper home. The Clipper had limited capacity only, and hundreds of Americans were waiting in Portugal for a flight. Others booked passage on ships that usually called first in South America. The neutral Portuguese capital was filling with Allied and Axis spies, as well as refugees. Liebling was staying at the Grand Hotel do Mont Estoril on 18 June, when the radio in the lobby broadcast a message from London. It was the first time Liebling heard the clear French of Charles de Gaulle: 'The voice spoke of resistance and hope; it was strong and manly. The half-dozen weeping Frenchwomen huddled about the radio cabinet where they had been listening to the bulletins of defeat and surrender ceased for a moment in their sobbing. Someone had spoken for France; Pétain always seemed to speak *against* her, reproachful with the cruelty of the impotent.'

In the hotel bar, an Englishman, who proudly claimed to be a fascist and to support Franco in Spain, declared, 'Within three years all Democrats will be shot or in prison!' Liebling considered knocking out the man's brain 'with an olive pip, adapting the size of the missile to the importance of the target'. Instead, he drank a glass of Vermouth and remembered something that Jack McAuliffe, 'the last bare-knuckle lightweight champion of the world', had told him: 'In Cork, where I was born, there was an old saying: "Once down is no battle."'

PART TWO

1940

SEVEN

Bookshop Row

SYLVIA BEACH AND ADRIENNE MONNIER heard Maréchal Pétain's appeal for an armistice over the radio at lunchtime on Monday, 17 June. Afterwards, they reopened their bookshops until six in the evening. Adrienne sold only one book, appropriately, *Gone with the Wind*. Sylvia's business was little better. Her landlord, who did not want the Germans to requisition his building and would not easily find another tenant, helped by waiving her rent. In her diary that evening, Adrienne wrote, 'Gloomy evening. I feel defeat and that it's going to be fascism.' The next day, Tuesday, her concerns were more personal: 'No meat, no butter, only a bit of pork.' At four o'clock that afternoon, the concierge at Sylvia's apartment and bookshop, Mme Allier, hurried across the street to tell Adrienne something was wrong. Adrienne wrote in her diary,

> Sylvia, who left this morning around 9.00 on bicycle, has not yet come back. Seriously worried. Telephone the American Embassy, tell Mme Allier to go to the police station. Around 6:30 Marthe Lamy arrives on bicycle (she feels her Spanish blood rising), tell her my worry about Sylvia; she telephones the Hôpital Marmottan, where they bring those who are injured in street accidents, and the American Hospital. Around 7.00 Sylvia arrives. She had gone to Carlotta's apartment on the boulevard Suchet, then to the American Embassy. [Carlotta Welles Briggs, Sylvia's childhood friend, had left for the United States and asked Sylvia to guard her Paris apartment.]

Sylvia's safe return at seven o'clock barely diluted Adrienne's depression. Her diary for the day concluded, 'I am resigned to defeat and fascism.' Like most other Parisians on 18 June, she and Sylvia missed General Charles de Gaulle's defiant speech on the BBC's French service.

On Wednesday, more of Paris's cafés and restaurants were opening. Adrienne, who made a long inspection of the city on foot, saw 'Fouquet's open with great style. The Triomphe and various others of lesser importance also open.' Paris acquired an unexpected array of German musical bands. Adrienne heard one at the Rond-Point des Champs-Elysées 'composed chiefly of drums, brass instruments, and Chinese bells. Rather monotonous march.' A little further on her promenade, near the Hôtel Crillon, was 'another orchestra, playing somewhat lighter marches'. In the Place de l'Opéra, the Café de la Paix was 'open with terrace: many Germans at the tables'. She ate lunch at 'the Danish Patisserie, which never shut'. In the evening, she and Sylvia walked in the Luxembourg Gardens 'to see the borders of pink flowers'. When Sylvia asked a woman with a dog whether she made drawings of her pet, she answered, 'No, only when he is dead.' On Thursday, things were better. Sylvia and Adrienne found 'superb escarole and even tarragon and chives' at the market in rue Mouffetard and 'a bit of beef at the butcher's', but no butter or potatoes.

On Sunday, 23 June, the day after Germany and France signed the Armistice at Compiègne, Sylvia and Adrienne took afternoon tea at the apartment of a young American diplomat, Keeler Faus. Adrienne thought his flat was 'ravishing, books in profusion, fine old furniture, etc.'. She observed, 'Feeling of the embassy people, completely isolated, as if on an island, with the German police next to them (quartered in the Ministry of the Navy).' Walking home, the two women saw 'an interminable procession of vans and artillery pieces [on the] boulevard Saint-Germain'. But a 'working class man' there told them, 'The game isn't over; if the English were to beat them, that would give me pleasure, *really*.' The next week set the pattern for their life under occupation: a Sisyphean quest for food that appeared as mysteriously as it vanished from patisseries, greengrocers, butchers and black marketeers. On Friday, 28 June, 'Sylvia goes to Nortier's (she had been told that there would be butter). No butter ... No meat. Almost nothing on the market.' On Sunday: 'Nothing at the market, no meat. Still no butter or potatoes. Ate peas at noon bought yesterday at the Bon Marché; the most tender of the year ... A few raspberries, like yesterday, a little bit mushy.'

Adrienne needed butter for her Savoyard sauces and to make pastry, which Sylvia called 'her great amusement and indoor sport'. But there was never enough. On Tuesday, 2 July, she moaned, 'This morning, saw at Nortier's a queue of more than a hundred people [waiting] to have a quarter [kilogram] of butter.' The monthly soap ration was only 100 grams, and women had to queue for that. Adrienne and Sylvia needed patience even to buy books to sell in their shops. 'We often have to stand in line at the publishers,' Adrienne wrote, 'and most of them give us copies of the good titles one at a time.'

'Parisians who survived the exodus came back,' Sylvia wrote of the early months of occupation, 'and my French friends were delighted to find Shakespeare and Company still open. They fairly stuffed themselves on our books, and I was busier than ever.' Although busy, she was unhappy. Her world had been separated from almost everyone, apart from Adrienne, she loved. James Joyce was in eastern France at Saint-Gérand-le-Puy, awaiting a visa to enter Switzerland. Her oldest friend, Carlotta Welles Briggs, had moved to Altadena, a suburb north of Los Angeles, where Sylvia's father and sisters already lived. The letters Sylvia wrote to them revealed a growing anxiety about her father's health. The Reverend Sylvester Beach at the age of 88 was losing his sight and his hearing, and he was increasingly distracted. In his lucid moments, he fretted for his daughter in occupied Paris.

Sylvia's relations with her father and mother, while close, were troubling. Her mother had warned her, when she was in her early teens, 'never to let a man touch me' and later confessed to Sylvia that she and Sylvester had a 'miserable marriage'. After her three girls grew up, Eleanor Orbison Beach travelled in Europe without her husband. When Sylvia was studying Spanish in Madrid in 1915 and 1916, Mrs Beach lived with her. She also stayed in Paris near Sylvia and her youngest daughter, Cyprian, who were sharing an apartment in the Palais Royal in 1917. The Reverend Sylvester Beach remained at his rectory in Princeton amid occasional rumours that he was philandering. Sylvia had always been passionate about her father. Christened Nancy for her maternal grandmother, she changed her name at an early age to Sylvia, the feminine equivalent of Sylvester. (Eleanor Beach had originally intended to name her second daughter Gladys, inspiring James Joyce to call a character in *Ulysses* 'Gladys Beech'. Sylvia's change of name from that of Eleanor's mother to a version of her father's may have seemed like a declaration of disloyalty.) Sylvia felt the tug of two parents vying for their children's affections within a marriage marred by emotional warfare. Nonetheless, both parents encouraged their daughters to pursue careers and establish independent lives. Of the three girls, only Mary Hollingsworth Morris Beach, called Holly, married. Sylvia was a publisher and bookseller, and her sister Cyprian became an actress. At the time, publishing *Ulysses*, deemed obscene by Puritan America, and appearing in films were scandalous. 'The cinema for my sister and my *Ulysses* publication must have made life difficult for my father,' Sylvia admitted. If Sylvester Beach had qualms about his daughters' work, he never said so.

Sylvia's estrangement from her sister Cyprian was also hard. As youngsters, they had been inseparable. Cyprian's beauty made her a star in French silent films, but no one thought Sylvia was beautiful. Even one of her greatest admirers, the writer Katherine Anne Porter, observed, 'She was not pretty, never had been, never tried to be.' When the two sisters were living in the Palais Royal, an actor in a play next door at the Théâtre du Palais Royal was so besotted with Cyprian that he climbed up to their balcony and went inside to introduce himself. Sylvia was not surprised: 'Cyprian was so beautiful that you couldn't blame a fellow for coming in the window without an invitation.' The actor was not the only one to dote on her. 'Among my sister's admirers was the poet [Louis] Aragon, then active in the Dada movement,' Sylvia wrote. 'After raving about his passion for the momie [mummy] of Cleopatra at a Parisian museum, Aragon told me he had now transferred his admiration to Cyprian. Later, in search of Cyprian, he made frequent visits to my bookshop and sometimes recited for me his Alphabet poem and the one called "La Table".' 'Alphabet' was a monotonous recitation of the alphabet, and 'La Table' endlessly repeated the word 'table'. The poet Léon-Paul Lafargue also declared his love for Cyprian, but she was as indifferent to him as to the fans who recognized her as *Belles Mirettes* (Beautiful Eyes) in a 1917 film serial that was playing in weekly instalments at Paris cinemas.

Sylvia's publication of *Ulysses* in 1922 had made her one of the most famous women in Paris, while Cyprian's film career was fading. In 1923, the two sisters had a mysterious argument over something that they kept secret from everyone else. In January 1923, Cyprian sent a letter to Sylvia that said she was 'miserable' when she was with her and wanted never to see her again. She moved back to the United States, where she looked for movie roles in Hollywood.

An unexpected tragedy further distanced Sylvia from her family. In 1927, French police served Sylvia's 63-year-old mother with an arrest warrant. It seemed Eleanor Beach had been accused three years earlier of shoplifting at the Galéries Lafayette department store. The sum involved was only a few francs, but she had left France without appearing in court. When she received the summons on a subsequent visit to Sylvia, Mrs Beach feared public disgrace. She wrote a long letter protesting her innocence and took an overdose of pills. At five o'clock that evening, she died in the American Hospital of Paris. Sylvia covered up the suicide, permitting her father and sisters to believe the cause of death was a heart attack. If Sylvia suffered the guilt that usually follows the suicide of a loved one, she had to bear it alone.

When the war began in September 1939, the Reverend Sylvester Beach asked Sylvia to come home. On 9 January 1940, she wrote to her sister Holly, who had invited Sylvia to stay in California, 'It's pleasant to think of a visit to the folks, but this is not the right time for such plans unless there is something definite in view for me over there. I would not be allowed to return here and the journey would use up enough money for me to live on a year or two here. And Carlotta has provided a perfectly safe comfortable delightful dwelling I can go to anytime Paris got uncomfortable.' Carlotta Welles Briggs had inherited her father Frank's country house, La Salle du Roc, at Bourré in the Touraine. The house, which Sylvia had known since she and Carlotta were teenagers, was partially built into mountain caves. In an earlier letter to Holly, she had reassured her that 'caves are bombproof'.

Sylvia nonetheless missed her family. 'If only I could see my daddy and the California girls and Carlotta, it wouldn't be at all bad over here,' she wrote to her father on 10 April 1940, 'though today we have heard of another of Hitler's snatches and we wonder what next.' Hitler's 'snatches' of the day before were Norway and Denmark, his prelude to the invasion of France a month later. Sylvia scolded her father for sending another $10 cheque, adding, 'And you know I am getting along in this little war very nicely. You needn't ever worry about me. If for any reason things got difficult I would sail away right back home.' Holly wrote on 20 May that she had read Sylvia's letters aloud to their father, who feared for Sylvia's safety and often sent her small sums of money. 'Of course,' Holly wrote, 'we can't help worrying about you in these terrible days, but we are concerned that the Allies must win and we hope that beautiful Paris may never be threatened. We know you will go down to Carlotta's if necessary.'

Carlotta Welles Briggs wrote regularly to Sylvia, usually enclosing a cheque to help her survive. She reminded her to take some jam from her Paris apartment and to use or give away the clothes her husband Jim had left behind. On 25 August, Carlotta wrote to Sylvia from Altadena that she was 'very glad to read a letter which Cyprian received by diplomatic channels and so to know that you had stuck to your shop and were still, as far as we could tell, all right'. She sent Sylvia money to have her piano moth-proofed by the Steinway dealer. In the same letter, she asked, 'Are you still riding your bicycle around?' Three months into the occupation, everyone in Paris was either riding a bicycle or walking.

Sylvia, from the distance of Paris, had also been commissioned to keep an eye on Carlotta's house at Bourré. A mutual friend, an American named Gertrude de Gallaix, went to La Salle du Roc at the end of the summer with her French husband, Marcel de Gallaix. Marcel was a lawyer who represented some of the wine growers who were resisting German confiscation of their lands. Gertrude wrote a distressing letter to Sylvia on Monday, 2 September. While helping to take honey from the hives near the house, a bee stung her ankle and left her immobile for a few days. She continued, with a cavalier disdain for apostrophes,

But the really unpleasant news is that the Germans are back. We headed here Tuesday morning the 27th – during that heat wave … Friday my husband left here at 7:00 a.m. to return at 8:00 p.m. having spent the day at Blois on business. And that afternoon the soldiers came looking for officers quarters. That was the beginning of our troubles.

Wednesday afternoon they were back again, and Wednesday evening while we were in the garden the officers came!! They were furious at not finding us, so my husband went to the mayors where they threatened to requisition the whole house – and told us we must clean the Welles room at once.

Gertrude's maid from Paris, Maria, and Mme Julia, Carlotta's housekeeper, spent the whole day sweeping and polishing the house for the Germans. With Gertrude, they carried chairs and curtains down from the attic to make two rooms habitable for a captain and lieutenant who were to be quartered there.

The most dangerous time was Friday noon, when the Colonel came himself to see the house – we had guests, so he had the discretion not to come in on the drawing room floor, but he was quite pleased with the Welles room. He told us we didn't need two homes – that we had a domicile in Paris. My husband insisted it was his office – and after showing him the rooms downstairs (he also looked into the drawing room) and learning we were to have officers he did not insist again. But he had come determined to turn us out!!!

Gertrude advised Sylvia to 'be thankful you haven't had to face soldiers and officers again and again as we have here'. In Paris, Sylvia confronted other difficulties. Merely to eat, she and Adrienne became scavengers, chasing the latest rumour of butter, eggs or fresh fruit in one shop or another. Shakespeare and Company no longer received periodicals and books from the United States. The Germans were censoring her favourite authors, including André Gide and Ernest Hemingway. Adrienne had ceased publishing her *Gazette des Amis des Livres*, because most of her authors were either banned by the Germans or could not pass German censorship. The writers who had fled from France or been forced underground were being replaced in the main journals and publishing houses by a clique, including Marcel Jouhandeau and Robert Brasillach, who were either fascists and anti-Semites already or adjusted their philosophies to German *Kulturkampf*. Symbolic of the change was the appointment of one of France's most anti-Semitic authors, Pierre Drieu La Rochelle, to edit André Gide's prestigious *Nouvelle Revue Française*.

Odéonia, whose literary giants had been left-wing and pro-Jewish, was giving way to the salon of Florence Jay Gould. In the American beauty's suite at the Hôtel Bristol, followed by the move to her flat at 129 avenue Malakoff in 1942, collaborationist French writers socialized over champagne with the celebrated German author Ernst Jünger and Propagandastaffel officer Gerhard Heller. The French writer Claude Mauriac wrote in his memoirs of one of Mrs Jay Gould's parties that he was 'stupefied to be shaking hands with one of those [German] officers whose contact I find so repugnant on the metro ... The champagne and the atmosphere of sympathy and youth made everything too easy. I should not have been there.' Florence's friendship with the German Ambassador Otto Abetz was so intimate that he gave her a long-term *Ausweis* to travel freely between Paris and her winter house at Juan les Pins, where her husband Frank was living. Gerhard Heller was charmed by Mrs Gould and was honoured to be welcomed into her 'sanctuary'. He reminisced, 'She was beautiful, great, with chestnut hair; a very attractive woman in her thirties; she had a great knowledge and a great love of literature. She deployed another lure, very important for the period: her table ignored rationing.' One writer, who smuggled an anonymous 'Letter from France' to Cyril Connolly's London magazine, *Horizon*, described the new bookmen of the right:

Among the collaborationists the best known are Jacques Chardonne ... Abel Bonnard – now more commonly known as Abetz Bonnard, a degraded and corrupt academician who has long been a public laughing stock; [Pierre] Drieu La Rochelle, a clever and talented Fascist; Ramon Fernandez, a professional Fascist and drunkard;

Henri Bidou, an able journalist; and Bernard Fay, a professor who
has just been made head of the Bibliothèque Nationale, in place of
[Julien] Cain, and whose first act was to 'lend' Marshal Goering that
institution's great collection of hunting books. [Fay was a friend of
Gertrude Stein and Alice B. Toklas.]

Neither Sylvia nor Adrienne had a place in the collaborators' literary
milieu, and they despised those who did – apart from Jacques Benoist-
Méchin. They had known Benoist-Méchin as a teenage music student,
who played in George Antheil's orchestra when Antheil was living
above Shakespeare and Company. A writer and translator as well as
a musician, war veteran Benoist-Méchin came to Odéonia in 1920.
Adrienne wrote of him in 1926, 'He was there when [Paul] Valéry read
us, in a corner of the bookshop, the pages of *Eupalinos*, which he was
about to hand over to his publisher. One day he showed us, jubilant,
a copy of *Partage du midi* [*Break of Noon*] that he had written by
hand. We saw him translate fragments of *Ulysses* for [Valéry] Larbaud,
who was preparing his lecture on Joyce ... No young man was so much
the son of the house as he was ... I am very proud of our son.' She did
not write what became of that pride in January 1941 when his minis-
terial-level appointment as Vichy's secretary general for relations with
Germany put him in daily touch with the Nazis.

EIGHT

Americans at Vichy

POLLY PEABODY WAS A RAVISHING, 22-year-old 'all-American girl' from East 57th Street in New York. The blonde-haired society beauty spoke perfect French and German, having studied in France, Switzerland and Germany for much of her childhood. Defeating the Nazis became her obsession from the moment the war began in September 1939. Seeking to play a part, she volunteered to drive ambulances in France for Anne Morgan's American Relief Service. Miss Morgan, who had returned to Paris from New York in March 1940 to direct humanitarian operations, rejected Polly's application on the grounds that she was too young. Undeterred, Polly applied to the American-Scandinavian Field Hospital and was accepted for medical work in Finland. 'About that time,' she wrote, 'stories of Finland's gallant resistance were flooding New York.' Stalin's Red Army, allied with Hitler, was invading its neutral neighbour, and the Finns fought hard to defend their independence. 'Finno-hysteria broke out in New York, like a violent rash on a baby's face ... "My deah! you simply MUST come to my little 'do' for the Finns".' The American-Scandinavian Field Hospital's trustees, no doubt recognizing determination when they met it, made her their Assistant Secretary. Polly set sail for Norway in March 1940, one of 'twenty-eight wild Americans' including Hubert Fauntleroy Julian, 'the Black Eagle of Harlem, a negro who claimed he was going to teach the Finns how to fly'. When her ship docked in Norway, the Germans invaded the country – the first stage of an operation leading to the Nazi conquest of Denmark, Holland, Luxembourg,

98

Belgium and France. She escaped to Sweden, Russia and Switzerland. By the time she caught a train over the border to France, it was a German-occupied country.

'At each station,' Polly wrote, 'a huge pile of twisted and rusting metal was dumped beside the tracks. Old bedsteads, pipes, etc. – all intended to make guns for the defence of France.' On one of the many buses she took through the ravaged countryside after her train broke down, she overheard a disheartened French soldier moan, 'Hell, we'll be just as well off under German rule as under our own.' That was too much for Polly Peabody.

> I turned on him like a she-wolf. The discussion grew louder and louder, and pretty soon everyone had joined in on my side. Nobody suspected that I wasn't French until I made my fatal mistake:
> 'I, an American, am more patriotically inclined towards your country than you are …' I shrieked, in a fit of impatience. There was a silence followed by an explosion. This time the positions were reversed. Everyone attacked me.
> 'An American! … if you are patriotic about France as all that, then why didn't you send us some guns instead of a lot of cotton-wool and pills?'

The bus dropped her in Clermont Ferrand, the industrial centre of the French midlands. The government had left only hours before. '"Where is everybody?" I asked, like the ostrich peering over the rumps of other ostriches whose heads were in the sand. But I couldn't find out where the Government had gone to, although everybody seemed pretty sure they had gone somewhere.' In the government's wake, the Germans arrived.

> The people were greatly impressed with the behaviour of the Nazi soldiers. They even bordered on enthusiasm. They had visualized the enemy as monsters who raped little girls and chopped off the ears of little boys and hung them on their belts. They were grate-fully surprised when this did not happen; but they did not stop to think that had the enemy been ordered to turn all the inhabitants of

France into sausage meat, they would have carried out their orders with just as much efficiency.

Polly Peabody was unaware that German soldiers who committed rape or pillage were subject to court martial and execution, a precaution the Wehrmacht had not taken in Poland. The Franco-German Armistice, signed at Compiègne on 22 June, carved France into four zones: the northern coast around Calais, administered from Belgium as a 'forbidden' area; Alsace and Lorraine, incorporated as provinces of the German Reich from which citizens of French origin were expelled; the bulk of France around Paris and down to Bordeaux, officially occupied territory; and the south, free of direct occupation by German troops. Because Clermont Ferrand fell south of the main line of demarcation between the 'Occupied' and 'Free' zones, the Germans withdrew from the city. Polly then noticed that 'the Mayor had not waited until the last Nazi tank was out of sight before he ordered the French flag to be hoisted in the public square. Around it the townspeople quickly gathered and sang the Marseillaise with unrestrained emotion.'

Following the new Pétain government to Vichy, Polly chanced upon a French officer in the lobby of the Hôtel des Ambassadeurs. He had been military attaché in Norway, where they had met two months before. He offered to help her find lodgings, and he introduced her to the dapper Senator Gaston Henry-Haye. Senator Henry-Haye and the officer took Polly out to see 'all the Vichy celebrities' at the fashionable Restaurant Coq d'Or. 'Stepping into the street, whom should I see emerging from a long black limousine, but Ambassador Bullitt? He looked so dashing and neat, just like the hero in the million-dollar picture, compared with all those who ogled him.' Polly settled into 'a questionable, small hotel', which charged her twenty francs a night for a room shared with three other people. She remembered, 'During the first few days in Vichy, I witnessed some of the saddest and most amazing pages of French history.'

Aldebert and Clara de Chambrun, after three weeks of privation at the Polignacs' austere castle near Le Puy, were back in Vichy for their usual summer vacation. In their absence, the town had transformed itself from a bourgeois resort for rich hypochondriacs into the temporary capital of France. Vichy's resident population of 50,000, while used to providing rooms for 40,000 summer visitors, was hosting almost 100,000 refugees, civil servants, soldiers, diplomats, legislators and journalists. All of them were clamouring for places to sleep, wash and eat. Polly Peabody observed 'a French duchess – who for eight nights slept sitting bolt upright in an armchair, because she could not find a room'. Aldebert and Clara had, thanks to a longstanding arrangement with the Hôtel du Parc, their own room. But government officials found themselves running ministries from hotel bathrooms, receiving ambassadors in garrets and sleeping in corridors.

The American Embassy made its ambassadorial residence in a luxurious summer house, Villa Les Adrets at 56 rue Thermal, that it leased from Florence Jay Gould and her husband, Frank. The chancellery was in a doctor's house, the Villa Ica, nearby. Most of the diplomats moved into the fortuitously named Hôtel des Ambassadeurs. Clara's already low opinion of American diplomacy sank further because of what she saw as Counsellor Robert Murphy and his staff's hostility to Maréchal Pétain and Pierre Laval. She wrote, 'They made up their minds first on what tack they had best embark, avoided any information which might be calculated to bring new light on the subject in hand, and were particularly careful not to get mixed up with other than leftist politicians with whom their sympathies obviously lay.'

Ambassador Bullitt had left Paris on 30 June with Carmel Offie, his longtime secretary who had served with him in Moscow, as well as Commander Roscoe Hillenkoetter and Robert Murphy. Riding in their chauffeured convoy were Bullitt's Chantilly neighbours, the Gilroys. Frances Gilroy was an American friend from Bullitt's home town, Philadelphia. Her British husband, Dudley, was a thoroughbred trainer. Bullitt caught up with the government in Clermont Ferrand and lodged in the comfortable Hôtel de Charlannes in the mountains nearby at La Bourboule. By the time he contacted the government again in Vichy, Clara wrote, Bullitt 'seemed to have lost many of his illusions concerning the Popular Front [the leftist coalition that won the last pre-war parliamentary elections, in 1936], and missed no opportunity of getting in closer touch with Pierre Laval, whose feelings toward him were very friendly'. She reserved particular animosity for Third Secretaries Douglas MacArthur, nephew of his namesake, General MacArthur, and H. Freeman Matthews – both of whom believed Laval was too accommodating to Germany. The Americans tended to see Laval as Vichy's villain, although Pétain and most of the new Vichy establishment curried favour with the German occupier as much as Laval did. The British were also critical of Laval, but they were forced to withdraw their diplomats when Pétain broke relations with Britain in July. The diplomatic rupture resulted from a British ultimatum to French warships in the Algerian naval base of Mers-el-Kébir to surrender on 3 July. When the French commanders refused, the Royal Navy sank their ships and killed 1,267 French seamen to avoid the possibility of the ships falling into German hands. Pétain not only cut relations with Britain, he ordered an aerial bombardment of Gibraltar. The United States and about forty other countries kept embassies in Vichy – to the fury of Britain.

On the hot and sunny morning of 9 July, Clara and Aldebert watched the Chamber of Deputies and the Senate convene in the theatre of the Vichy Casino. Other fashionable, well-dressed women joined Clara in the gallery to witness the death of the Third Republic. By 395 votes to three, the lower house abolished the 1875 Constitution. The Senate, urged by Pierre Laval and its president, Jules Jeanneney, voted for abolition 225 votes to one. The dissenter was Aldebert's 75-year-old brother, Pierre, Marquis de Chambrun. He was the Senate's sole American member, who had come from German-occupied Lozère with his wife, Clara's cousin Margaret, to defend the Republic. Despite her brother-in-law's republican convictions, Clara's sympathies lay with Laval and Pétain's project for a new France of order, hierarchy and discipline.

When the next day, 10 July, dawned, Polly Peabody noticed a change of mood in Vichy: 'During that morning, the halls of the big hotels, the streets, the public squares, were full of little groups of agitated men, discussing, arguing, weeping, repudiating blame, while some paced nervously up and down alone, their eyes riveted on the ground.' The people outside wept and argued, and the two houses of parliament met together in the Casino as the Assemblée Nationale. The resolution before them was whether to grant 'full powers to the Government of the Republic under the authority and signature of Maréchal Pétain in order that he may promulgate by one or more acts a new Constitution for the French State'. Short of declaring war, which would require the Assembly's approval, Pétain would be given carte blanche to rule by decree. The morning session was held in secret, although few of the parliamentarians used the opportunity to launch a vigorous opposition to the proposed dictatorship. In a committee meeting that afternoon, Laval inserted language into the resolution that increased Pétain's executive and legislative authority – eradicating the Republic's separation of powers. The Free Zone would be a tyranny, royalist in its prerogatives yet subject to the fiat of the occupier in the north.

In the late afternoon, the National Assembly reconvened in public. Observing from the visitors' gallery were Ambassador Bullitt, Clara de Chambrun, Polly Peabody and the grandes dames of the emerging Vichy elite. Edouard Herriot, president of the Chamber of Deputies, rose to declare that the absence of the legislators most likely to vote against the motion made the exercise a sham. William Bullitt cabled President Roosevelt that Herriot's speech was

> the single example of courage and dignity during the dreary afternoon. He pointed out that the French Government had decided to go to North Africa; that [Edouard] Daladier, [César] Campinchi and others who had boarded the *Massilia* which had been placed at their disposal by the French Government, had done so thinking that the Government was going to North Africa to continue the war, and insisted that they should not be treated as men who had run away. His words made such a deep impression that Laval immediately took the platform and admitted that everything that Herriot said was absolutely true.

Laval added that he, Maréchal Pétain and other patriotic Frenchmen, in contrast, had refused to abandon the sacred soil. The implication was that parliamentarians, like Georges Mandel, who sought to carry on the war from North Africa were deserters. (When the deputies disembarked from the *Massilia* in Casablanca, the Pétain government's representatives arrested them.)

In the early evening, the votes were cast: 509 for Pétain's dictatorial powers against eighty opposed. Bullitt heard a lone voice cry out, '*Vive la République, quand même!*' 'Long live the Republic, just the same!' He noted, 'The last scene of the tragedy of the death of the French Republic was well placed in a theatre.'

Among the eighty dissidents was Pierre de Chambrun, the only senator to vote against abolishing the Constitution the day before. When Maréchal Pétain saw Aldebert de Chambrun, he called to him in the street, 'Say there, Aldebert, your brother voted against my constitution.' De Chambrun replied, 'Yes. You know, he has always been a liberal ... the only one in the family.'

Senator Henry-Haye took Polly to meet Maréchal Pétain, who had been awaiting the result at his usual table in the Hôtel du Parc's Chanteclerc restaurant. 'I was introduced as the young American girl who had travelled through chaotic Europe doing a lot of things and who still wanted to do a little more for France,' Polly wrote. 'The Marshal arose and shook my hand, and said something about admiring American girls because they were so "*débrouillardes*" [resourceful] and, unlike French girls, managed everything by themselves, without any help.' Pétain invited her to sit, and he told her, 'I am going to Versailles in two weeks. This time I have quite made up my mind. I have sent word to the Germans to evacuate the premises.' The 22 June Armistice Agreement permitted the French government to move to Versailles, but Pétain had no force with which to compel the German occupier to evacuate any premises. Perhaps he was bluffing to impress the *débrouillarde* American girl. He even told her that he 'had had his suitcase more or less ready'. Like most of France that summer, Polly was sympathetic to the aged roué: 'Of all the people, young and old, who were present, the Marshal was probably the oldest and yet he looked far younger than many of his juniors ... he struck me as being what, for want of a better expression, I would call a "fine figure of a man", and very alert to the happenings of the moment, that is to say, as many happenings as reached his ears, for I think that a lot was carefully kept from him.'

Maréchal Philippe Pétain had become, at the age of 84, both 'head of state' in the so-called French State that replaced the French Republic and prime minister. His deputy, or vice-president of the council of ministers, was Pierre Laval. The only people, as well as the only Americans, on intimate terms with the two most powerful men of the new Vichy regime were Aldebert and Clara de Chambrun. Pétain was an old friend, who had been Aldebert's military instructor and his commander in the Great War and Morocco. Laval's family and the Chambruns had been close since their children married in 1935. Clara, although enthusiastic about the new leadership, spotted danger in the court forming around Pétain: 'Without suspecting that his entourage was working for its own aggrandizement, the Marshal became in fact their prisoner.' She watched the old soldier being cut off from reality: 'A row of high screens separated the regular habitués of the Hotel du Parc from the Chief of State and the guests whom he daily invited.' Her scepticism did not prevent her from succumbing to the reflected attention. 'What a kowtowing and flattery went on: What glances of envy were darted in our direction when, as he often did, Marshal Pétain came to join us for coffee in our corner!'

William Bullitt, despite his respect for Pétain, preferred not to be accredited to the Vichy government. Roosevelt had asked for Bullitt's help in the 1940 presidential elections, when he would stand for an unprecedented third term. He also dangled in front of his outspoken ambassador the possibility of a cabinet appointment if he won. Bullitt left Vichy for Spain with his secretary, Carmel Offie, and his Chantilly neighbours, the Gilroys. He had issued Dudley Gilroy, a reserve officer in the British Army, an American passport to help him over the Spanish border. The Spaniards were sending British subjects back to France, where they risked internment. As cover, Bullitt listed the Gilroys as his valet and maid. Dudley carried off his part, but the regal Frances aroused suspicion. One Spanish official commented, 'She is not a maid.' Carmel Offie took him aside and said, 'Of course not. Don't you understand that the ambassador has a mistress?' The Spaniard admitted them at once.

In Bullitt's absence, Robert Murphy became chargé d'affaires at Vichy. 'In those first weeks at Vichy,' the red-haired Milwaukeean wrote,

I think most of us felt as if we had been knocked on the head and were slowly recovering our senses. History has rarely, if ever, moved with such dizzy speed as in that summer, and it seemed almost impossible to readjust our thoughts to a Europe dominated by one man, as in the Napoleonic era more than a century before. In this new Alice-in-Wonderland atmosphere, Vichy seemed an appropriate capital for that portion of France, one-third of the country, which the German armistice permitted Frenchmen still to govern. Offices were located in gambling casinos, music halls, and tourist hotels designed to lighten the hours of health-seekers. The Hotel du Parc, long popular with fashionable invalids, became the seat of government. All of us felt absurdly isolated in this inbred community, making our diplomatic rounds in this artificial, gaudy, improvised political center which nobody expected to serve this purpose for long.

Washington maintained diplomatic relations with the Vichy government. At the same time, Roosevelt circumvented America's 1939 Neutrality Act by sending weapons to Britain. Murphy and his small staff worked late into the night, doing political and consular work. He set out to 'sell' the American position of pro-British neutrality to Pétain and Laval. 'The old soldier and the suave lawyer-politician,' Murphy wrote of the head of state and his vice-premier, 'had almost nothing in common except their conviction that Germany had won the war and that Frenchmen must somehow adapt themselves to this fact.' He recalled his first meeting with Pétain in July 1940:

The Marshal was then eighty-four years old and in his eyes I was only a young diplomat substituting for an ambassador, so he smiled at me indulgently. Then, in his cool, clear, rather formal French, he said that continuance of the war would have been insanity, and that France would have been completely destroyed, since neither France nor Britain should have gone into a war for which they were wholly unprepared. With some emotion he declared that France could not afford again to have a million of its sons killed ... Each time I talked with Pétain he expressed in some way his friendly feeling for the

United States, implying that it was only his affection for our country that made him tolerate my rather unwelcome arguments.

Count René de Chambrun arrived in Vichy on 19 August. Clara had not seen her only son for more than two months. A frontline soldier during the Battle of France, René had served as a lieutenant on the Maginot Line. The high command promoted him to captain and assigned him as liaison officer to the British forces at the front. His brief mission to England convinced him that Britain would hold if America provided aid. At Ambassador Bullitt's suggestion, Prime Minister Paul Reynaud posted René to Washington as a temporary military attaché to persuade President Franklin Roosevelt to send weapons to Britain. René spent two months in America, seeing Roosevelt, his cabinet, the Senate Foreign Relations Committee, the press and Republican isolationists like his Aunt Alice Roosevelt Longworth and Ohio Senator Robert Taft. On returning to France via Spain, René went first to Châteldon to see his wife, Josée. The next day, at Vichy's Hôtel du Parc, he told Clara and Aldebert what he had accomplished in the land of their births.

It was an impressive story. On 12 June, two days before Paris fell, René's Yankee Clipper touched down in the water off Long Island's La Guardia Field. A Pan Am employee handed René an urgent message from Marguerite Lehand, FDR's longtime private secretary and, unknown to René, sometime mistress of Ambassador Bullitt. It asked him to call President Roosevelt as soon as he reached his hotel, the old Ritz, in Manhattan. When he called, 'Missy' Lehand told him, 'The president wants to see you as soon as possible.' René turned up at the White House the next day to be greeted by the president, 'Happy to receive you, cousin!' Roosevelt asked, 'Are you going to win this war?' René answered, 'That depends very much on you.' Later, FDR welcomed him to the presidential yacht, the converted 165-foot Coast Guard cutter *Potomac*. Also on board were financier Averell Harriman, who was advising Roosevelt on foreign affairs despite his business interests in Germany, and Commerce Secretary Harry Hopkins. René wrote later to a friend about the cruise: 'Radiograms reporting the advance of the German army through France kept coming in and when it was about 7 p.m. the President was informed that the German army had crossed the Loire. He turned towards me and said, with deep feeling in his voice: "René, the show is over" and then, after a silence of a few seconds, he added, "I really think Britain will be unable to hold out."'

René repeated what he had told Bullitt at the embassy in Paris: 'I maintain that Britain, entrenched in her island, is invincible, thanks to her fleet, her fighter force, which is becoming the best in the world, a good antiaircraft defense, which must be reinforced immediately, and ground forces, which have been miraculously rescued.' Roosevelt, a sagacious politician whose private views already accorded with René's, needed less persuading than René imagined. He had already arranged for 3,100 planes purchased by France but embargoed under the Neutrality Act to be sent via Canada to Britain.

Running for his third term as president, Roosevelt had pledged not to send American boys to die in Europe. Yet he was trying to help the British to stop the Germans and their threat to American interests in the western hemisphere. FDR saw in his young Franco-American cousin an ally who could lobby for the additional arms that Britain needed without seeming too close to the administration. FDR wrote a list of twenty-two influential Americans that René needed to persuade. They included Secretary of State Cordell Hull, House Speaker Sam Rayburn, Treasury Secretary Henry Morgenthau Jr. and *New York Daily News* publisher Joe Patterson. When Missy Lehand suggested René meet important women, FDR added a twenty-third name, his wife Eleanor's. René saw Mrs Roosevelt, who was also his cousin, the next day. He toured the United States, using family members, like his Aunt Alice, who was as powerful within the conservative wing of the Republican Party as his cousin Eleanor was among New Deal Democrats. Alice, Teddy Roosevelt's only daughter and René's 'favorite aunt on both sides of the Atlantic', arranged an important dinner with Senate Republican leader Robert Taft and Joe Patterson. René undoubtedly knew that his mother disliked Aunt Alice. Clara had sided with her brother, Congressman Nicholas Longworth, in his many marital disputes with his wife, who was notoriously temperamental. Alice had once caught her husband in flagrante with her closest friend, Cissy

Patterson. Although the flamboyant and red-headed Cissy was Joe's sister, she went to work for his national newspaper rival, William Randolph Hearst, as editor of the *Washington Herald*. Whenever she could, Cissy published malicious gossip about Alice. René may have been aware of the tortuous background, but the dinner was business. He convinced both Taft and Joe Patterson not to oppose FDR's proposed increase in military spending. Producing more American weapons would make some available to Britain.

At public meetings, René was usually introduced as Lafayette's descendant and the nephew of the late House Speaker, Nicholas Longworth – links that emphasized his American origins. That René's campaign worked was borne out by Roosevelt's release to Britain of tanks, anti-aircraft guns and machine guns that had been ordered by France and embargoed since the beginning of the war. Lord Lothian, Britain's ambassador to Washington with whom René had breakfasted regularly there, wrote to the young captain on 9 August, 'You have been able, almost alone, to change official public opinion in favour of my country ... For all of this, I want to assure you that Great Britain will never forget anything that you have done for her during her days of misfortune and distress.'

René maintained what contact he could from the United States, via telegram and occasional telephone calls, with his parents and his wife, Josée, in France. Aware of food shortages and the millions of refugees in the Vichy zone, he asked Roosevelt to send humanitarian aid to southern France. On 14 July, the president said he might do it, 'if Bullitt agrees'. When William Bullitt arrived from Lisbon on 20 July, René was waiting for him at La Guardia Field. Bullitt endorsed his scheme to send food to France. On 1 August in Washington, René repeated his request to Roosevelt. The president wanted assurances that Germany would not seize the American food. René pointed out that the German army would not cross the line of demarcation to seize powdered milk, when its forces were concentrated in the north to invade Britain. FDR agreed to provide assistance on two conditions: Maréchal Philippe Pétain must cease his government's anti-British propaganda and declare publicly to the American reporters in Vichy that he supported America's increased defence expenditure and its democratic ideals.

Back in New York, Henry Luce, founder and owner of *Time* and *Life* magazines, invited René to lunch and an editorial staff meeting. René was already a friend of Luce and his glamorous wife, the playwright Clare Boothe, whom he had guided around the Maginot Line the previous May. *Time* had given favourable publicity to René, noting on 24 June that Roosevelt had returned from his cruise with de Chambrun on the *Potomac* 'refreshed and ready to act within the limits of his great powers. Some of them he used forthwith – to wave U.S. planes across the Canadian border'. Luce asked René a favour: would he meet *Time*'s 33-year-old editor, Frank Norris, and photographer Ed Riley 'by chance' on the Pan Am Dixie Clipper to Lisbon and ease their way across Portugal and Spain to Vichy? Luce told René he wanted *Time* to be first with a story out of the Free Zone, perhaps choosing to forget that a dozen American newspaper correspondents were already there.

When René arrived in Vichy with the two *Time* men, Clara was proud of her son and his achievements in the United States. She did not have to tell him what everyone in France knew: that his father-in-law, Pierre Laval, believed that Britain would lose the war and France must find a place, albeit secondary, in the new German Europe. If René de Chambrun and Pierre Laval argued about their differing conceptions of the outcome of the war, neither René nor Clara spoke of it. Nonetheless, Clara persisted in her belief that René, rather than Charles de Gaulle, who had been condemned to death in August for desertion by a Vichy court martial, was the man to save France.

After seeing his parents at the Hôtel du Parc, René met his father's old commander, Maréchal Pétain, to deliver Roosevelt's message. Pétain agreed to the president's conditions for supplying powdered milk and other necessities to France. His foreign minister, Paul Baudoin, was immediately instructed to suspend his verbal attacks on Great Britain. At five o'clock that evening, Pétain gave the press conference Roosevelt had asked for. Correspondents from the United Press, *New York Herald Tribune*, *New York Times*, *Baltimore Sun* and *Chicago Daily News* recorded Pétain's words: 'France will remain firmly attached to the ideal that she shares with the great American democracy, an ideal based on respect for individual rights, devotion to family and the fatherland, love of justice and humanity.' Satisfied that

Pétain had done all Roosevelt asked, René returned to the United States on 31 August with his wife, Josée, bearing a letter from Pétain to the president.

René's plans unravelled as soon as he reached New York, where Missy Lehand told him over the telephone not to come to Washington. Harry Hopkins, one of Roosevelt's closest advisers in the cabinet, was on his way to New York to meet him for dinner that night. Hopkins was candid: 'The president has had to give up the plan of shipping condensed milk. Churchill telephoned him insisting that we maintain the blockade [of France].'

René de Chambrun, whom the president declined to meet again, felt betrayed. Arrayed against him were, in addition to the British, many French émigrés in the United States like Eve Curie who believed that aid to any part of German-occupied Europe would only help the Nazis. Yet René persevered, campaigning across the country and seeking private assistance from Anne Morgan and the Quakers. Henry Luce's *Time* magazine wrote, 'René de Chambrun, a captain of French infantry, is a wiry little man of 33, with the late Nick Longworth for an uncle, a profitable knowledge of the law, both French and American, a host of important connections, a taste for driving too fast in an automobile and an inborn capacity for landing out of any catastrophe on his feet.' The praise was for the book he had just published, *I Saw France Fall: Will She Rise Again?*, whose royalties he donated to a charity for French prisoners of war.

When Clara learned of Roosevelt's change of mind, she took her son's side:

Like his mother, the fact that a President of the United States, after all that passed between them, is false to his promise, does not turn him from his purpose when once it is settled. Consequently, after the terrible shock of such a disappointment he said little, but set about getting relief for France from other than government sources. He obtained all that was possible from the Red Cross and ex-President [Herbert] Hoover. The two ships which were sent over to Marseilles (where they arrived safely) did as much as two ships can to attenuate suffering.

René's circumvention of Britain's blockade of France attracted the attention of the British Embassy in Washington. Forgotten was Lord Lothian's praise for René's help to Britain in its most difficult hour. The embassy sent a cable to the Foreign Office in London recommending that René and Josée be denied transit visas for Bermuda, where the Pan Am Dixie Clipper stopped on its way across the Atlantic. (On René's first return to France from New York in August, he had carried an introduction from Lord Lothian asking the Governor of Bermuda to offer him full hospitality.) An embassy officer named Mr Butler wrote on 14 November of René, 'He is a plausible anti-British talker and the Passport Control Officer agrees that he and his wife be granted visas for the outward journey [to France], and his return [to the United States], if possible, be impeded. He possesses United States citizenship as well as French, but difficulties may be put in the way of him using a United States Passport on return.' A handwritten note in the margin signed 'MS' added that 'we don't like the Chambruns'.

NINE

Back to Paris

POLLY PEABODY TIRED OF VICHY IN MID-AUGUST and obtained
a pass to drive to Paris. 'It was late afternoon when we reached the
Gates of Paris,' she recalled. 'We rolled into the Capital which had
become a vast garrison. Millions of black boots stomped noisily along
the stone pavements, the Swastika fluttered from building fronts, road
signs in German characters were pinned on the street corners. A cloud
of sadness hung over the city.' She stayed in a borrowed flat on the
Left Bank, where the concierge was wary until she ascertained that the
blonde Polly was not German. The concierge told her that she and her
friends, despite German prohibitions, listened to BBC radio transmis-
sions from London. It was not the only defiance the young American
detected. On the terrace of Fouquet's restaurant near the Arc de Triomphe, where 'sword-scarred, bemedalled' German officers feasted, she
saw a drunken old Parisienne watching the Nazis from the sidewalk.
The woman 'put both fists on her hips and yelled out: "*Eh bien, moi
je vous dis MERDE!*" ["All right, me, I say to you SHIT!"] The waiters bumped into each other trying to conceal their amusement, while
I and the few French people present laughed heartily into our napkins.'
Polly observed, 'This was my introduction to the spirit of resistance
which existed in the occupied zone.' It was a contrast to what she had
seen in her last six weeks at Vichy, although hardly representative of
all Paris.

France's internal frontiers deprived Clara and Aldebert de Chambrun of news from Paris for the first weeks of the occupation. Train service soon resumed between Paris and Vichy, at least for those privileged to possess a German travel permit, the much-coveted *Ausweis*. Vicomte de Poncins arrived from Paris to tell Clara that Luftwaffe chief Hermann Goering had seized the Senate building, the Palais du Luxembourg, opposite her house at 58 rue de Vaugirard, for his headquarters. Empty flats in the rue de Vaugirard became billets for his officers. The vicomte comforted her with the assurance that her housekeeper, Mlle d'Ambléon, 'continued to hold the fort' at Number 58. Clara wrote, 'My old lady, though frightened out of her wits, showed energy and character by insisting that the premises were not empty and that the proprietors would be back before the first of September. "We shall see on September the first if what you say is true," the German officer said significantly.'

The threat determined Aldebert and Clara to return to Paris. 'Our cure was finished,' she wrote of their six weeks in the spa town. On 1 September, they drove home. When Clara entered the city through the Porte d'Orléans, 'a German official handed out an order to present our car for requisition within forty-eight hours. It was our first indication that what we possessed was not really our own.' She was relieved to discover the Germans were not, as rumoured, capturing and killing dogs like her darling Tsouni, who was buried beneath her skirts. At Vichy, she had heard rumours about the new German Paris: 'The use of the sidewalks was reserved for the *Wehrmacht*; citizens were kicked off the street and French passengers booted in the subway. Curfew was tolled at seven o'clock. Loiterers after that hour were imprisoned. All household linen had been requisitioned for German service. There was a constant interchange of shots across the Champs Elysées, etc. ... etc.' On the contrary, she discovered, the Germans in the early months of the occupation were cultivating both the French and the neutrals, especially the Americans. German soldiers behaved well and left policing of the capital to French Prefect Roger Langeron and his 25,000 gendarmes. What annoyed Clara more than German behaviour was the symbolism.

During those first days after our return to Paris what hit me hardest was an aspect which I could not have foreseen. Supersensitive as I have always been to visual impressions, the horrible and hideous symbols of German domination made the city I loved hateful. Gigantic banners filled the streets and were unescapable. They did not float over the housetops and towers like the flags of civilized nations so that one had to raise the eye to see them, but hung in the direct line of vision, suspended like huge carpets waiting to be beaten. Sometimes they veiled several stories of an unofficial building. Each time I crossed the threshold, or even looked forth from my balcony, it was like receiving a blow between the eyes and a stab which reached the heart.

Clara did not brood long over the Swastikas. When Aldebert surrendered their car to the Germans, she accustomed herself to long walks and to the novel experience of riding the Metro. She took a bus over the Seine to the American Library, where she was still on the board of trustees, in the rue de Téhèran. The library had yet to reopen, but its appearance had altered for the better. The brown paper pasted on the windows against bomb-shattered glass had been removed, as had the anti-fire sandbags blocking the doorways on the top floor. The US Embassy seal guaranteed that it was American property, safe in law from German seizure. Two flags, American and French, still hung over the ornate doorway. The building housed about 100,000 books, mostly in stacks at the back where desks and chairs beside French windows faced a small garden. An ornate staircase led to the periodicals reading room and the office of the directress, Miss Dorothy Reeder. On this, the countess's first visit since her return to Paris, she found Miss Reeder at her desk. Behind the directress hung a large aerial photograph of Washington, DC, where Miss Reeder had trained and worked in the Library of Congress for six years before coming to the American Library of Paris in 1929. Miss Reeder was a popular librarian, whom the American writer Marion Dix had described to American radio listeners the previous February as 'young, attractive and full of pep – with, at the same time, that quality of friendly but efficient leadership which has made a smoothly running machine as well as a useful organization of the library'. Dix thought the librarian had 'a grand sense of humor, as well as good sense'.

Miss Reeder told Clara about her work for the American Embassy at the Hôtel Bristol since 14 June. For two and a half months, she had been living in the hotel and had 'pasted U.S. seals on U.S. and British property, helped take over the British Consul General's office and tried to console those left stranded ... My job was to check to see that only American passports were admitted and to inform all others they could not live there.' Miss Reeder was either unaware of or ignored the non-American Jews whom Anne Morgan had smuggled into the hotel for their safety. Of her employment by the embassy, she insisted, 'This in no way interrupted or interfered in my work at the Library.' She added that she regularly carried books from the library to the Bristol so the Americans there would have something to read. Some were too old to walk to the library, and reading filled the long curfew hours that confined the Americans to the hotel at first from 9 p.m., later relaxed to eleven and finally to midnight.

Soon after the Armistice of 22 June, four members of the library's staff came back to Paris. They had taken refuge at Angoulême, where they assisted the emergency American Hospital facility. The library remained closed all summer, but Miss Reeder allowed subscribers who rang the bell to borrow and return books. The staff, meanwhile, wrapped books that the American Red Cross, YMCA and Quakers delivered to British prisoners of war in German camps. Some French prisoners wrote to the library requesting English books. 'It is a funny point that the Germans would allow requests of this kind to come through,' Miss Reeder noted, 'but would not allow us to fulfill them.' Only French books could go to French soldiers. The occupation meant that the supply of new publications in English from Britain and America stopped, but Miss Reeder declined German offers to order them through Berlin.

German officials paid regular calls on the library. Miss Reeder recalled that they always spoke French, because she knew no German and they did not like to use English. She told Clara about one ominous visit from the German *Bibliotheksschütz* (Library Protector), 'a stiff Prussian-looking officer with full authority to do as he deemed proper in regard to the administration of such centers of intellectual activity, whether in Holland, Belgium, or French occupied territory'. She told Clara that the official in full-dress Nazi uniform made her afraid. But, several minutes into his inspection of the library, she recognized him as the director of the Berlin Library, Dr Hermann Fuchs. They had met at international library conferences before the war and 'held each other in high esteem, so everything went very smoothly from that moment'. Dr Fuchs praised the library, stating nothing in Europe compared with it. He assured her that it could reopen on two conditions. 'You will necessarily be bound by the rules imposed on the Bibliothèque Nationale,' he said, referring to the French National Library, 'where certain persons may not enter and certain books may not circulate.' 'Certain persons' were Jews, and 'certain books' were those on the so-called 'Bernhard List' of publications that the Nazis had already banned in Germany and the other occupied territories.

Dorothy Reeder asked whether the banned books had to be burned, as they were in Germany. 'No, my dear young lady,' he assured her. 'What a question between professional librarians! People like us do not destroy books! I said they must not circulate!' Works by Ernest Hemingway, Sinclair Lewis and the journalists William Shirer and H. R. Knickerbocker, along with ten volumes in French, were removed from the shelves and held in Miss Reeder's office, taking a total of forty books from the stock of 100,000 out of circulation. The American Library fared better than the libraries of the Alliance Israelite and the Freemasons, both of whose entire collections were seized and sent to Germany 'for purposes of study'. The Germans destroyed the Polish Library.

'No Jews are allowed in the Library by the Nazi police regulations,' Miss Reeder complained to the countess. 'Some of them are our best subscribers, and I don't see how we can permit them now to take out their books.' Clara was not troubled. In her brisk, Yankee manner, she dismissed the problem.

My simple solution recalled the old story of Mahomet and the mountain. I fear it hurt her feelings. I went on: 'I possess a pair of feet, so do [staff members] Boris [Netchaeff] and Peter. I am ready and willing to carry books to those subscribers who are cut off from them by any such ruling, and feel sure that every member of the staff would be happy to do the same.'

Would that all of our difficulties could have been so easily arranged?

On 18 September, the American Library reopened. The New York board of directors sent a telegram: 'GREETINGS BEST WISHES DR. GROS CONGRATULATIONS COMTESSE CHAMBRUN REEDER ON REOPENING LIBRARY.' In a letter to the Rockefeller Foundation dated 19 September, Miss Reeder wrote, 'We are now open to the public between 2 and 5 every afternoon. During the morning, we try to take care of the necessary work which cannot be done when dealing with the public. We still take care of books to the prisoners of war as best we can. We are a staff of four including myself. I do hope this arrangement will continue and that we shall be able to carry on.' Most of the active subscribers were now French. 'Few people came to the Library, as a matter of fact,' Dorothy Reeder wrote, 'in the first day or two, but as soon as word got round that we were open, there was a rush, which has been growing in size ever since.' Within a month, the Library had lent 1,500 books.

In September, the Germans introduced food rationing at a mere 1,300 calories a day, about half what an adult needed to survive. The concierge began cooking for staff in the Library. Miss Reeder remarked, 'It is enough to say that the first day she gave us fried chicken, so you can imagine our joyfulness. The only bad part is that we are all gaining weight.'

Clara had the 'rare opportunity of sending a letter out of the zone where we are now living' to Edward Alleyne Sumner in New York on 26 September, eight days after the Library reopened. Sumner had been the Library's third vice-president. Before his departure from Paris with his wife Ernestine in June, he had lent cars from his American Radiator Company to evacuate staff, particularly the British and Canadians who would be interned, from Paris to Angoulême. In New York, he became chairman of the executive committee with responsibility for the library's survival in the most difficult moment of its existence.

Clara wrote to him on her personal writing paper with '58, rue de Vaugirard, VIe' printed at the top. The typed letter reached Sumner's New York office on 29 October 1940.

> I want particularly that you know what remarkable work Miss Reeder has done during these troublous times. There has never been a day when she has not been at her post at the Library, more than that, except for about twelve days, our institution has been open and accessible to all those who really needed it. For the last week, we have been and shall continue to be open to the public. What I most particularly want to say is this: we on the spot are the only possible judges of what can and must be done; without flattering Miss Reeder or myself, I may say that we are both people of intelligence and are extremely well advised ['extremely well advised' is underlined in black ink]. What is done here has been, and will be, the right thing to do, and if you can persuade those who are interested over there to realize this, we shall succeed in keeping the American Library in Paris going and maintain its spirit alive until better times. I am afraid that you will be much shocked upon seeing our president who will whortly [sic] arrive in New York, if not already there. He has had what I fear will prove a knock out blow in all these happenings.

The president of the American Library was Dr Edmund Gros, who was also director of the American Hospital. Directing the two primary American institutions in Paris, at the same time operating on war wounded alongside his surgical colleagues, had taken a toll on a man of seventy years. Dorothy Reeder wrote on 19 September, 'Dr. Gros has been quite ill and plans to go to the States.' By the time he left Paris later that month, he had suffered an emotional and physical breakdown. With his departure, the library fell to the charge of Dorothy Reeder and the hospital to Dr Sumner Jackson. Clara worked with Miss Reeder at the library, and Aldebert de Chambrun, for years on the hospital's board of trustees, assisted Dr Jackson. Edward Sumner found Clara's letter reassuring, as he did the earlier one from Miss Reeder, and he circulated both to the other trustees. He sought library funding from the Rockefeller Foundation and the Carnegie Institute. Without financial support, Dorothy Reeder's and Clara de Chambrun's hard work would not be enough to preserve the American Library.

TEN

In Love with Love

AT THE CHÂTEAU DE CANDÉ among his diplomatic and unofficial guests, Charles Eugene Bedaux seemed an unlikely dean of the American community in Paris. Three years before welcoming the embassy and hundreds of displaced Americans into his home, he had left New York in disgrace. *Time* derided him as 'a Mephistophelean little Franco-American efficiency expert'. The description was accurate. 'Mephistophelean' Bedaux had charmed his way to a vast fortune by teaching American industrial barons how to earn more money without extra expense. 'Little' Bedaux then weighed only 112 pounds and was 5 foot 7½ inches tall. 'He reminded himself of Napoleon, because, among other things, both of them were short,' wrote the *New Yorker*'s Janet Flanner, who met and interviewed him before the German invasion. 'Franco-American' Bedaux was born in France in 1886 and became an American citizen in 1917. As *Time* noted, he was an expert in industrial efficiency, having refined Charles Winslow Taylor's late nineteenth-century time and motion techniques to extract the maximum from workers. Bedaux's life, the *Chicago Daily Tribune* commented, was 'a real Horatio Alger story of a poor boy climbing to riches'. Associates called him 'Charles-the-Man'.

Charles Eugene Bedaux, third of four children of a railway engineer and a seamstress, grew up near Paris at Charenton-le-Pont. Leaving school early, he broke away from his family to hawk for business at the cabarets-cum-brothels of Montmartre in the north of Paris. When a woman shot and killed Bedaux's employer, a pimp named Henri

Ledoux, he left France on a cattle boat for New York. Arriving aged 19 in 1906, he took a variety of low-paid jobs, including bottle washer in a saloon and sandhog, lugging sacks of earth, on the Hudson River Tunnel. That lasted a month, until the bends or exhaustion drove him above ground. He taught French at Berlitz in Philadelphia and took odd jobs all over the Midwest, Oklahoma and Colorado. In 1908, he applied for US citizenship and voted, he said later, in the presidential election for Republican William Howard Taft. Also in 1908, he took a job at the Mallinckrodt Chemical Works in St Louis, Missouri, and married a local beauty queen, Blanche de Kressier Allen. A year later, they had a son, whom he named Charles Emile after his father.

At Mallinckrodt, Bedaux said later, he had a revelation: 'I soon found that engineers had assigned units of measurement to power of all sorts – fuel, water, electrical. Why, I wondered, couldn't a wholly scientific and mathematical measurement of manpower be ascertained?' He devised this measurement himself and called it the 'B', for Bedaux, unit – sixty units of labour per hour, based on the average worker's output, above which workers should receive extra pay. An Italian industrial engineer, A. M. Morrini, recruited Bedaux as interpreter on a trip to Europe with a group of consultants who were marketing the older Taylor efficiency system. When the Great War began in 1914, Bedaux was in France with Blanche and Charles Emile. He enlisted in the French Foreign Legion and, after an accident crushed his foot, he was discharged without seeing battle. Back in the United States, Bedaux founded his own company to advise on industrial efficiency. American labour unions would soon condemn the 'Bedaux System' as a 'speed-up' process that treated workingmen like machines to be measured and exploited to the maximum. Bedaux called it the 'proper use of manpower for faster output with fewer men'. This was the era of streamlining, when Italian futurists and American industrialists alike were casting away the extraneous, the decorative and the unnecessary – in favour of undiminished speed and efficiency. In 1936, Charlie Chaplin would mock such industrial regimentation in his classic film *Modern Times*. Its villain was a manager called 'Mr Billows', a Bedaux-like efficiency demon and inventor of the 'Billows Feeding Machine' that force-fed workers on the assembly line to save time on lunch-breaks.

Bedaux's mission, he explained to his engineers, transcended mere business: 'Let us be the missionary. It is no longer our part to coax a man to install this or that efficiency method on the strength that it will save him money. Let us make him understand that he must do it if he loves his business, if he loves his home, if he loves his workers, if he loves his flag.' With this spiel, the Charles Bedaux Company signed Campbell's Soup, Gillette, Eastman Kodak, DuPont and Goodrich Rubber. Workers did not share their employers' benevolent view of Bedaux. The American Federation of Labor claimed that his system, 'stripped of its pseudo-technical verbiage, is nothing more than a method of forcing the last ounce of effort out of workers at the smallest possible cost in wages'. John L. Lewis's rival Committee, later Congress, of Industrial Organizations called it 'the most completely exhausting, inhuman "efficiency" system ever invented'. At a textile plant in Rhode Island and other factories, workers went on strike when management imposed his recommendations. With labour discontent and employer satisfaction, Bedaux's fortunes increased.

The newly rich Bedaux jettisoned beauty queen Blanche Allen for socialite Fern Lombard. At 5 feet 11 inches, Fern stood 3½ inches taller than Bedaux. She was also several rungs higher on the social ladder. A native of Grand Rapids, Michigan, and a Christian Scientist, she was the child of a rich industrialist, belonged to the socially pretentious Daughters of the American Revolution and introduced Charles to millionaires with whom he now had a personal, rather than purely business, connection. Among them was 'Colonel' Archibald Rogers, whose property in upstate New York adjoined the Hyde Park estate of Franklin Delano Roosevelt, then assistant secretary of the navy. Charles married Fern in 1917, the year he gained full US citizenship and the United States declared war on Germany. The next year, his first Charles Bedaux Company opened in Cleveland, Ohio. His ex-wife married another millionaire and moved to California with Charles Junior, whom Bedaux rarely saw during his childhood.

Charles and Fern moved to New York in 1920, living in suites that they furnished at the Plaza Hotel and then the Ritz. They also bought a large apartment on Fifth Avenue with a view over Central Park. His first offices were downtown at 17 Battery Place. Wherever he had a long-term consultancy, Bedaux rented a grand house nearby. He claimed later to have lived in twenty-four of the then forty-eight American states. He leased an estate in Marblehead, north of Boston, from the Crowninshield family, one of whom, Frank, edited *Vanity Fair*. The Paris-born Boston Brahmin Frank drew Bedaux into a fashionable and literary world that included Ernest Hemingway, Babe Ruth, financier Bernard Baruch, drama critic Alexander Woollcott and the beautiful playwright Clare Boothe. Bedaux became a figure in the speakeasies and nightclubs of Prohibition-era New York, where he indulged his erotic appetites. He kept an apartment in Greenwich Village for a succession of mistresses. Fern came to accept his infidelities so thoroughly that she brought women to him and occasionally took part in their trysts. 'Men, women, children, and animals all found Bedaux attractive,' wrote Janet Flanner, who thought he had a 'worldly, boldly battered face, dominated by his fine, dark eyes.' Bedaux, using his wavy brown hair to good effect, exuded Gallic charm, dressed in the finest flannel suits that his tailor could stitch and suavely smoked fifty cigarettes a day.

In 1924, Bedaux founded the Washington-Lafayette Institute to improve relations between the United States and France. He brought business and political contacts onto the board. Two members of President Calvin Coolidge's cabinet, Commerce Secretary Herbert Hoover and Postmaster General Harry New, belonged, as did the former commander of American forces in France, General John 'Black Jack' Pershing. The institute worked out of Bedaux's company premises on Battery Place, until he moved his offices uptown to an oak-panelled storey of the new and more glamorous Chrysler Building.

The Bedauxs, who had no children together, thrived on adventure. No journey was too exhausting or too expensive, and every trip was a new honeymoon. On tyres made by his client Goodrich, they drove across the African continent, east to west, then the full length from the Cape to Cairo, pausing in Southern Rhodesia to inspect mines at their owners' request. They sailed a schooner across the South Pacific, rode ponies into Tibet and made the first long-distance car journey from the mountains of British Columbia through uncharted brush to Alaska. Much of their route provided the basis for the Alcan Highway that later linked Alaska to the state of Washington. Bedaux loved inventing – patenting a crêpe-soled shoe, data-storage on film to replace paper and several children's games.

Bedaux's business empire expanded beyond the United States – to Britain in 1926, then to France, Germany, Italy, Sweden and Holland. In a speech to American businessmen, he reflected on the expansion of commerce beyond national borders: 'A man loves his country. He makes laws for the glory of his flag. He traces the outline of a national ideal he would like to live up to, but his stomach, his need for trade are essentially international. He is a patriot, and a sincere one, but when his money is concerned, he blissfully commits treason.'

Within ten years, Bedaux's nineteen offices around the world were advising 500 companies in the United States, 225 in Britain, 144 in France, forty-nine in Italy and thirty-nine in Germany. The seizure without compensation of his German company in 1934, a year after Adolf Hitler assumed power, led Bedaux to ingratiate himself with the Nazi hierarchy. He used Austrian friends, the brothers Count Friedrich and Count Joseph von Ledebur, to contact the Nazi leadership. The young counts and their four other brothers were well connected, their grandfather having been a finance minister under the Austrian Emperor Franz Joseph. Friedrich met Bedaux at the Ambassador Hotel in Los Angeles in 1929, two years after his wedding to Iris Tree, an English actress and daughter of Sir Herbert Beerbohm Tree. Later in 1929, he travelled with Bedaux through Spain and France and arranged for his fishing trip in the South Pacific. He also took charge of the native bearers and equipment for Bedaux's African crossings. His brother Joseph ran a land agency in Vienna and was married to Gladys Olcutt of Boston. Of the six brothers, only Joseph was pro-Nazi. Bedaux made Joseph his Berlin agent to contact the appropriate Nazi officials to reverse the company's nationalization.

For two frustrating years, Bedaux negotiated with the Germans. He approached a German banker, Dr Emil Georg von Stauss, whom the Nazis had placed in charge of nationalized firms including Lufthansa and Mercedes. Through him, Bedaux became intimate with a sculptress favoured by the Nazi leadership, Annie Hoefken-Hempel. Bedaux commissioned her to make busts of himself and Fern at 5,000 Marks, about $2,000, apiece in June 1935. Next came his sponsorship of an exhibition of her work in Paris where busts of Hitler, Goering and Bedaux were displayed alongside her sculpted nudes. Frau Annie introduced Bedaux to Labour Front director Dr Robert Ley, Hitler adjutant Captain Fritz Wiedemann and Dr Hjalmar Schacht. Schacht, in addition to being her lover, was minister of economic affairs and head of the German central bank, the Reichsbank. Although the acquaintances blossomed, the Germans did not give Bedaux back his company.

In 1937, Bedaux hosted an event at Château de Candé that opened doors in Germany while closing others in America. It began with a letter from Fern's old friend, Katherine Rogers. Katherine was married to Herman Livingstone Rogers, son of Franklin Roosevelt's upstate New York neighbour Archibald Rogers. Herman Rogers and his brother Edmund had accompanied Bedaux on his British Columbia expeditions. By 1937, Herman and Katherine were living on the French Riviera that American millionaires like Gerald and Sarah Murphy and Frank and Florence Jay Gould had already made fashionable. Theirs was the privileged world that F. Scott Fitzgerald depicted in *Tender is the Night*. That winter season, the Rogers's Villa Lou Vieu near Cannes became a refuge for Mrs Wallis Warfield Simpson. Wallis was 'that woman', the twice-wed American divorcée for whom England's King Edward VIII abdicated his throne in December 1936. She and Katherine Rogers, herself divorced before she married Herman, had been friends since 1916. At Villa Lou Vieu, while reporters camped at the front gate, Wallis awaited her final decree of divorce from British shipping heir Ernest Simpson. Protocol imposed by Buckingham Palace did not permit Mrs Simpson and the former monarch, now the Duke of Windsor, to meet while she was Simpson's lawful wife. The duke was waiting in Austria at the Schloss Enzesfeld of Baron Eugene de Rothschild and his American wife, the former Kitty Spottswood.

In the letter that Katherine Rogers sent to Fern Bedaux in early 1937, she asked Fern to invite Wallis to the Château de Candé. Its 1,200 walled hectares were more secluded and discreet than her beach villa near Cannes. Fern and Charles agreed, and Wallis moved with the Rogers to Candé in early March. Bedaux told a journalist, 'My wife and I believe that when two people sacrifice so much for love they are entitled to the admiration and the utmost consideration of those who still believe in this ideal.' He explained to another that, although he did not know Wallis Simpson, 'my wife and I are still in love with love'.

He was probably telling the truth. Fern and Charles displayed profound affection for each other twenty years into their marriage. His many affairs had not reduced Fern's ardour for him, and he told friends that life without her was unimaginable. She had learned tennis, golf and shooting to an expert level to please him. Every year, his birthday was 'the most precious day of the year' to her. To outsiders, their marriage was inexplicable. One of Fern's friends told Janet Flanner, 'She was so much finer than he, and so perfectly trained, that when you saw the Bedauxs together, it was like watching a thoroughbred paraded on a lead by her squat groom.' Charles's brother Gaston wrote that Fern surrounded Charles with 'unceasing affection' and 'knew how to help him with her judgement and her fine psychology'.

The Duke of Windsor joined Charles and Fern at Candé in April, when Mrs Simpson's divorce decree absolute was granted. With the permission of the British government, but with no members of the royal family present, Edward and Wallis were married at the Château de Candé on 3 June 1937. Among the sixteen witnesses to the civil and religious ceremonies, along with Herman and Katherine Rogers and Winston Churchill's son Randolph, were Charles and Fern Bedaux. Bedaux's wedding present was an Annie Hoefken-Hempel statuette entitled *L'Amour*.

In the meantime, Bedaux and the duke developed a friendship, as Bedaux saw it, between 'the ex-sandhog and the ex-king'. They played golf together at Candé during the day and had long talks at night. They shared an interest, from however lofty a distance, in the lives of working people. Bedaux made his living studying work practices, and the duke had earned a reputation in Britain as the Prince of Wales with sympathy for Welsh coal miners. Friedrich von Ledebur, who met the Windsors at Candé, believed that the duke was the first to kindle Bedaux's interest in politics. Until then, his only concerns had been business and sport. The duke desired to see how the working classes lived in Hitler's new Germany. Could Bedaux, with his industrial and political contacts in Berlin, arrange a tour? Bedaux suggested that the duke expand his inspection to include the United States and other parts of Europe. He approached Robert Murphy at the American Embassy in Paris and Dr Robert Ley in Germany on the duke's behalf. Subsequently, the duke met Fritz Wiedemann, one of Hitler's three adjutants, in Bedaux's permanent suite at the Paris Ritz to settle details of the German visit.

The semi-royal tour of Germany began in Berlin on 11 October 1937 and lasted twelve days. Although the duke visited industrial plants using the Bedaux system, his procession through Hitler's Germany was primarily a triumph for Nazi propaganda. Photographs of the duke and duchess with Hitler, Hermann Goering and Joseph Goebbels were published around the world. Bedaux, who had not accompanied the Windsors to Germany, laid the ground for a month-long American tour to begin in November. Bedaux asked IBM head Thomas J. Watson to sponsor the Windsors in his role as chairman of the International Chamber of Commerce, and Watson accepted. (Watson had enjoyed a private meeting with Adolf Hitler the previous June, after which he attended a Nazi rally. The German government was IBM's second largest client.)

Cruising into New York on 1 November, Bedaux faced uniform hostility to the Windsor tour from American labour, the press and the State Department. Workers' unions in Wallis Simpson's home town, Baltimore, led the national campaign against a couple who had just been entertained by the Nazis. One Baltimore labour leader, Joseph P. McCurdy, accused the Duchess of Windsor of not having shown, as a young woman in Baltimore, 'the slightest concern nor sympathy for the problems of labor or the poor and needy'.

The prime target of labour venom was the Windsors' sponsor, Charles Bedaux. Some of Bedaux's American clients cancelled their contracts to shield themselves from the bad publicity. A few engineers resigned from the Bedaux Company, and his board of directors demanded that he dissociate himself from the firm that bore his name. Stunned by the reaction to what he imagined would be a public relations coup for himself and the Duke of Windsor, he agreed to yield control, but not ownership, of his American companies. His successor was Albert Ramond, another French-born American, whom Bedaux had hired. Bedaux retained non-voting shares and gave his power of attorney to his loyal secretary, Isabella Cameron. At the same time, the State Department announced, at Britain's request, it would deny royal protocol to the Duchess of Windsor. The battering of Bedaux did not let up. The Internal Revenue Service issued him an income tax demand, and a former mistress lodged a suit against him for breach of promise. The multiple humiliations forced Charles and Fern to slink through a side entrance of the Plaza Hotel to avoid the journalists and the ex-mistress, drive to Canada and sail to France from Montreal. The Windsors, who were waiting in Paris with trunks packed to board the *Cherbourg* for New York, cancelled.

Bedaux suffered what was undoubtedly a nervous breakdown, diagnosed as arterial thrombosis, and spent months convalescing in a Bavarian hospital. The threat to his health was sufficient to break his heavy smoking habit of the previous thirty years. The treatment led to a dependence on sleeping pills – mainly a German-manufactured barbiturate, Medinal.

Germany, regarding Bedaux as a close friend of an ex-king whom it was cultivating, offered to return his company if he donated $20,000 for reinvestment and $30,000 'penetration money' to Dr Robert Ley's Labour Front. Payment of this barely masked bribe worked, up to a point. The Nazis restored the company, but they withheld royalties on his consultancies. Six months later, they took the company back, again without compensation.

When France and Britain declared war on Germany on 3 September 1939, Bedaux announced he would not make profits from the conflict. His promise may have had more publicity than practical effect. The French assigned him to study and improve their inefficient production of arms during the eight-month *drôle de guerre*, or phoney war, that preceded the German invasion of May 1940. As he had done with American clients like the Ford Motor Company, Bedaux analysed French ordnance production to reduce inefficiency, rationalize the supply of raw materials, increase labour productivity and deliver finished products without delay. The factories under Bedaux's direction more than doubled their arms output. To the French, his methods were impeccably

American and might have helped their army had they been implemented over years rather than months. Bedaux went to Britain, where he urged the military to pool resources with France and to standardize equipment to fight effectively with the French army on the battlefield. The British, who distrusted him over his involvement with the Windsors, ignored him. French Armaments Minister Raoul Dautry, himself an industrialist, sent Bedaux to Francisco Franco's Spain to obtain steel for the manufacture of French weapons. The French Ambassador in Madrid, Maréchal Henri-Philippe Pétain, who had known Bedaux since 1926, afforded him introductions to Spanish politicians and businessmen. When Bedaux discovered that Spain lacked sufficient coal to fire its steel furnaces to meet French demand, he travelled to French Algeria to see whether the Kenadsa coal mines could make up the shortfall. On 7 June 1940, he flew back to Paris from Kenadsa to persuade Armaments Minister Dautry to make coal deliveries to Spain a government priority. With Spanish steel, France could produce the weapons it needed to match the Germans. But, by the time he was due to see Dautry on 12 June, the French army barely existed. That was when his brother, Gaston, called and persuaded him to leave Paris.

The Charles Bedaux who returned to the Château de Candé in June 1940 as host of France's American community had redeemed his reputation after the Windsor affair. The embassy, in leasing Candé and granting him diplomatic status, had effectively given him US government approval. And the French government had shown its trust by assigning him to enhance France's fighting capacity. His standing with the German occupiers had yet to be measured.

At the end of June, German officers invaded the Château de Candé and requisitioned it for the Wehrmacht. Charles Bedaux's diplomatic protection and his neutrality as an American citizen did not save his chateau from becoming, like many others, a German barracks. Maynard Barnes and other embassy personnel retired to Paris. German officers replaced the Americans in the main bedrooms and at the dining table. Charles and Fern displayed the same hospitality to their new guests as they had to the old.

From the beginning of the Armistice, Bedaux organized local businesses, civil servants and labourers to rebuild the battle-damaged and fire-ravaged city of Tours and its nearby factories with assistance from the American Red Cross. Bedaux oversaw much of the work himself with Marcel Grolleau, a former lumberjack whom he had hired in 1927 after seeing him at work in a forest near Candé. Grolleau, 22 when he met Bedaux, had since become a Bedaux engineer and, unbeknownst to Bedaux, was active in the nascent resistance to German occupation. German privations impeded reconstruction. Not only did the Germans seize heavy equipment, they took most of France's petrol supply for their army. Bedaux and Grolleau turned wood from the forests of the Loire Valley into charcoal for *gazogene* to run cars and machinery. *Gazogene*, less efficient and smokier than petrol, fuelled the few French cars that the Germans allowed on the roads.

Bedaux in the late summer went to Paris, where he discovered that the German Stadtkommissar's Office of Locations had seized the Hôtel Ritz on the Place Vendôme. Having lost their permanent suite to the Germans, Charles and Fern were reduced to a smaller hotel nearby. Most of its other guests were German officers. The German army also evicted Bedaux company engineers from their homes in Paris to make room for soldiers. A few of the engineers went to Candé, and others moved with their families into Bedaux's offices at 39 avenue de Friedland, between the Arc de Triomphe and rue du Faubourg Saint Honoré. Bedaux had once again to placate the Nazis, this time to reclaim his employees' houses.

Early in September, Bedaux chanced upon his old friend and former employee, the Austrian Count Joseph von Ledebur, in his hotel. Ledebur, now a Wehrmacht Rittmeister, or cavalry captain, had served in Poland. In the more desirable posting of Paris, he was delighted to see Bedaux. Bedaux was close to Joseph and his younger brother, Friedrich, although they were not on good terms with each other. Friedrich had condemned Joseph for wearing a Nazi emblem on his lapel in 1939. Bedaux arranged for Friedrich, who was avoiding military conscription by the Wehrmacht, to escape from Germany that August. In Berlin a week before Hitler's invasion of Poland, Bedaux had given Friedrich false identity documents and a car to go to Holland. Friedrich said later that Bedaux was with him in Amsterdam. The Bedaux Company's Dutch headquarters provided him with extra large clothes – the gangly Friedrich was 6 foot 9 – for his disguise as a sailor. Alexandra Ter Hart, who managed the Bedaux office, drove him to Rotterdam harbour, where he signed on as an ordinary seaman on a ship bound for the United States. An excellent horseman and polo player, Friedrich took jobs in California, where he had lived intermittently since 1928, on ranches and training horses for Hollywood movies. Bedaux, who flew to Paris on one of the last civilian planes from Berlin before war was declared, said that he regarded Friedrich von Ledebur as more of a son than his own son.

Meeting again in newly occupied Paris, Bedaux and Joseph rekindled a friendship redolent of possible benefits to them both. After Bedaux related his woes about his engineers' confiscated homes, Ledebur arranged for Bedaux to see Heinrich Otto Abetz, Germany's Francophile 'ambassador' to France. (Under the Armistice, France and Germany had no formal diplomatic relations in advance of a full peace treaty. Abetz was married to a French former secretary of pro-Nazi journalist Jean Luchaire, Suzanne de Brockere. He functioned as ambassador in the old German Embassy, the Hôtel de Beauharnais, at 79 rue de Lille in the 7th Arrondissement. His opposite number was General Léon de la Laurencie, 'Delegate General of the French Government in the Occupied Territories', ostensibly Vichy's 'ambassador' to the Germans in Paris.) Abetz had last seen Bedaux in 1939, when he arranged an interview for him with Foreign Minister Joachim von Ribbentrop concerning Bedaux's unpaid consultancy fees. Bedaux now found Abetz willing but unable to help in an occupied Paris governed by the military. The ambassador had little choice but to refer Bedaux to the army, which showed no interest in his problem. Bedaux refused to give up. Marcel Grolleau recalled this time in his employer's life: 'Bedaux was more dynamic than ever under this pressure. He worked non-stop to see that all engineers and associates were taken care of. Much of his time was taken with protecting the interests of Jewish clients.'

The Bedauxs, despite losing their Ritz suite, maintained an active social life among German officials and the upper class French who had no qualms about mixing with the conquerors. The theatres, music halls and restaurants of Paris entertained the old rich, the rising collaborationist elite, newly wealthy black marketeers and Germans from the army and civil service. Jean Patou, working from the eighteenth-century Parisian palace where the Duc de Talleyrand had kept one of his mistresses, went on making dresses for Fern Bedaux and other rich matrons as he had before the occupation. For those with a financial buffer against the hunger that German rationing had imposed on most Parisians in September 1940, the dinner parties went on and on. Occupation restrictions did not affect the Bedauxs or most of their friends. They exchanged invitations to country weekends, lunched at Maxim's and dined at La Tour d'Argent. Charles and Fern were regulars at the house of leading collaborationist Fernand de Brinon, whose Jewish stepson, Bernard Ullmann, recalled, 'This millionaire, French natural-ized American, boasted of having free access to Hermann Goering.' Among the *beau monde* French couples who hosted the Bedauxs were André Dubonnet, a First World War French flying ace, race car driver and alcohol heir, and his American wife, Ruth. During a dinner party at Dubonnet's in late September, Bedaux met the wife of François Dupré, owner of Paris's George V, Regina and Plaza Athenée hotels. Ferevies Dupré, when Bedaux mentioned the problem of his staff's houses, introduced him to a German official named Dr Franz Medicus. As assistant director of the Department of Administrative Economy with the military rank of general, Medicus controlled property, includ-ing that of Parisian Jews, seized by the Nazis. He invited Bedaux to dinner in the Majestic, the Nazi-requisitioned hotel where he lived.

The friendship that developed between Bedaux and Medicus made Medicus one of the three closest people in Bedaux's life – the others being his wife, Fern, and Friedrich von Ledebur. Both men had Ameri-can connections: Bedaux as a US citizen, Medicus as son of a father with such affectionate memories of living in the United States that he gave his son the middle names 'Horace Greeley'. Despite Medicus's involvement in drafting the anti-Jewish Nuremberg laws of 1935 and in transferring French-Jewish businesses to Aryan ownership, Bedaux saw the Nazi functionary as a civilized scholar. Medicus had degrees in medicine and law and punctuated his French, English and German conversations with Latin and Greek aphorisms. He photographed France's cathedrals in his spare time for a book he was writing. Bedaux excused Medicus for disposing of property stolen from Jews: 'He is a man drafted and has to obey orders or die.' Not everyone accepted Medicus's self-portrayal as a gentleman-scholar forced to serve the Nazi cause. Even Pierre Laval, who became cordial with Ambassador Otto Abetz and other German officials, wrote in his diary, 'During this preliminary period [autumn 1940] the Germans with whom I came into contact said nothing to which I could take offence, if I except General Medicus who reminded me that we had been beaten.'

After his first, jovial dinner in the lavish dining room of the Hôtel Majestic with Charles Bedaux, unconstrained by German rationing regulations, Medicus agreed to give Bedaux's engineers back their houses. In return, Bedaux employed German army clerks in his avenue de Friedland offices. The Germans would thus have access to information on all of Bedaux's clients, among whom were France's most important industrial enterprises. Medicus supplied Bedaux with petrol ration tickets and 'WH' licence plates reserved for Germans, a cut above the 'SP', *Service Publique*, insignia granted to certain French doctors, actresses popular with the German high command and important allies of the occupation. Since 16 June, two days after the German arrival in Paris, all other cars had been requisitioned or otherwise banned from the streets of Paris. His dinner with Medicus at the Majestic committed Bedaux to work as much for Germany as for France. He convinced himself he was doing nothing wrong. To be safe, he kept Robert Murphy and other American diplomats informed of his activities.

It was not long before the Germans gave the Château de Candé back to Bedaux. American Embassy staff moved in again, and German officers stayed at weekends. The chateau became a salon for Germans, Americans and French, who mingled under crystal chandeliers with drinks served by footmen in livery. Dr Franz Medicus was a regular weekend guest. So was the Comtesse de Brinon, wife of Comte Fernand de Brinon. Before the war, de Brinon had written pro-Hitler propaganda in the French press and sent intelligence to Berlin while simultaneously accepting subsidies from Parisian Jewish bankers Rothschild and Lazard. De Brinon and Abetz had been colleagues in a pre-war Nazi-front organization, the *Comité Franco-Allemand*. The

Germans declared de Brinon's Jewish wife, Lisette, whose name at birth was Jeanne Louise Rachel Franck, an 'honorary Aryan'. This attractive divorcée, whose first husband had been a wealthy Jewish banker named Claude Ullmann, had her first marriage annulled and converted to Catholicism to marry de Brinon. Her sons, Pierre-Jérôme and Bernard Ullmann, were not accorded Aryan status. Bedaux gave Pierre-Jérôme work under a false name to avoid Nazi scrutiny, while the younger Bernard remained with his mother. De Brinon himself found it inconvenient to be seen with his Jewish wife, although he maintained contact with her through Bedaux and other friends. (His wife's absence afforded him more time with his secretary and mistress, Simone Mittre.) For her part, Lisette de Brinon socialized as comfortably with the Germans as she did with Robert Murphy of the American Embassy. Before the war, her circle of acquaintances included the Jewish socialist ex-prime minister Léon Blum and the anti-Semitic writer Pierre Drieu La Rochelle. Much of the French collaborationist set, who doted on their German masters, found a home at Candé. Charles Bedaux navigated among his French, German and American guests with less interest in their politics than in keeping their champagne glasses full and his eye open to business opportunities.

ELEVEN

A French Prisoner with the Americans

ON 6 JULY 1940, AN AMERICAN AMBULANCE brought two wounded French prisoners to Neuilly from the Hôpital Foch in Suresnes, which the Germans had just requisitioned. One of the two casualties was André Guillon, classified as dying from wounds he received fighting on 6 June at Beauvais. Guillon noticed, as he was wheeled into the Memorial Building, 'the flowers, the walkways, winding through impeccable lawns, the very beautiful trees, an oasis of calm and silence, and yet something troubled us the moment we entered this magnificent hospital ... the coldness of our welcome'. He soon realized that what he took for indifference was 'neutrality that we quickly understood and that was absolutely necessary'. Another aspect of the hospital made a stronger impression: 'There were no sentries at the door and no one controlled the entrances or the exits of the hospital.' The Germans, however, had established their Neuilly headquarters, the Kommandatur, opposite the hospital's main gate.

One of the first patients Guillon met in his ward was a Jewish officer he called Captain M., who told him, 'Because I'm Jewish, someone [a German officer] refused to accept my word of honour as a French officer. Now, morally, I must try to escape.' He asked Guillon what he should do. Guillon advised him to flee. 'That, moreover, is what he did.' As Guillon observed, Captain M. was not the only one. Dr Sumner Jackson, far from discouraging escape, looked the other way and falsified hospital records to say the men were terminally ill or had died.

Neither Guillon nor any of the other French prisoners saw Donald Coster, the American ambulance driver, in his basement hideout. Some time in mid-July, Sumner Jackson brought him documents to cross the Line of Demarcation and the Spanish border. Then, like Captain M., Coster disappeared from the hospital. When he reached Lisbon, his fellow drivers George King and Gregory Wait were waiting for him. They said that their fourth colleague, John Clement, had gone to Switzerland to work for the Red Cross. Coster returned to the United States. Writing about his experiences in the *Reader's Digest*, he did not say why he went back to Paris from Belgium or that Sumner Jackson had helped him. Later, it was revealed that Coster was in the American consular service.

Sumner Jackson examined André Guillon's wounds, which were not healing. Guillon wrote, 'I remember Dr Jackson, who advised me to use sun therapy to reabsorb my wounds which were extensive and infected with a green pus bacillus. I went out every day to expose myself to the sun on the terraces of the hospital.' Little by little, the wounds dried and healed.

During his time at the hospital, Guillon grew fond of Elisabeth Comte, who was sometimes called 'Head Nurse' but was listed on the hospital register as 'assistant to the director'. Guillon observed two types of nurses, professionals and volunteers. Many of the latter were 'daughters of Paris high society'. The rest were Swiss, American, Australian, Norwegian, Austrian and White Russian. 'This ethnic group in particular ... very much sympathized with the wounded, maybe a little too much for the Administration. There were flirtations, even marriages. We came to know the many varieties of caviar and vodka!'

Guillon appears not to have done much flirting himself, probably because his fiancée was visiting him. He got to know one French nurse who had worked in a leprosy colony in Madagascar and another who had been a race car driver. Two Canadian sisters, who were only 18 and 16, worked long hours as nurses and tended to his wounds. They had moved to France in 1939 to study the organ with the virtuoso organist of Saint-Sulpice Church, Marcel Dupré. The Germans had interned them in a concentration camp with other enemy aliens, but they escaped to the hospital.

'The nurses imposed a regime that was as strict as it was necessary,' Guillon commented. They ordered him to rest, but he was unable to lie still in bed every day.

> I went out regularly in Paris. The attraction of liberty was that it helped me regain my strength. I found myself on the boulevard des Filles du Calvaire, when I felt I was going to faint. I managed despite this to go down into the Metro and transfer at La République (never had the wait seemed so long). Two hours later, I was in the American Hospital and my room where I climbed into bed. My neighbour alerted Mademoiselle L. [an Austrian nurse] about my catastrophic trip: my wounds were suppurating, my temperature passed 39° ...! Sententiously, Mademoiselle L. told me, 'You're not going out to Paris again.' Next day, my temperature went down. Eight days later, I went out again to Paris, but I was more careful!

Although the hospital tried to keep Germans out, Guillon came across a German physician observing procedures in the orthopaedic centre. He was Professor Schacht of the Berlin Faculty of Medicine, brother of former Reichsbank chief Hjalmar Schacht, who had been Charles Bedaux's contact in Berlin. Hospital records ignored Professor Schacht's visit as well as the treatment given to a German medical officer in June. He had broken a leg while working during the Battle of France with refugees near an American medical team. 'He was taken to the American Hospital, where he spends his time praising the institution,' the *New York Times* reported on 29 June. 'He hates to think of leaving.'

TWELVE

American Grandees

WHILE CLARA DE CHAMBRUN assumed greater responsibility for preserving the American Library, her husband found himself tasked with saving the other major American institution, the American Hospital in Neuilly. Aldebert served on the hospital's board of governors, whose members were were the grandees of American Paris. The president was Nelson Dean Jay, who had come to Paris during the Great War as an aide to General John Pershing. He had stayed on to work with J. P. Morgan's Paris bank, Morgan & Cie, expanding its business from a convenience for expatriate American depositors into a major corporate investment house. Dean Jay and his wife, Anne Augustine, lived at 58 avenue Foch, just down the street from Dr Sumner Jackson. The couple entertained most of the prominent Americans, like Charles Lindbergh, IBM chairman Thomas Watson and Allen Dulles of the law firm Sullivan and Cromwell, who came to Paris between the wars. The managing governor and first vice-president was Edward B. Close. The popular 'Eddie' Close owed his fortune to his ex-father-in-law, General Foods founder Charles William Post. Mr Post had been so fond of Close that he left him a vast inheritance despite his divorce from Post's daughter, Marjorie, in 1919. The board's secretary was William DeWitt Crampton, John D. Rockefeller's man in France, officially vice-president of Standard Française des Pétroles. Like the other members of the board, he lived in the lavish 16th Arrondissement on the Right Bank, at 23 rue Raynouard. A 1914 Columbia graduate, he had been awarded the Distinguished Service

Order by the British and become a Chevalier of France's Legion of Honour during the Great War. Crampton belonged to the gentlemen's Travellers' Club on the avenue Champs-Elysées, not far from his office at number 82. He and his wife, the former Maude Evelyn Billin, golfed at the Chantilly and Le Touquet golf clubs. It was Crampton who, just before the Germans entered Paris, had obtained Robert Murphy's approval to torch Standard's oil reserves. Other board members were treasurer Bernard S. Carter, lawyer Max Shoop, Laurence Hills, J. S. Wright and General Aldebert de Chambrun.

The occupation did not interrupt the board's monthly meetings. On 26 July, most of the board appeared for the 6 p.m. conference at 25 avenue des Champs-Elysées. Count de Chambrun was in Le Puy, but Dr Edmund L. Gros, the hospital's chief of staff, attended 'by invitation'. 'At present,' the minutes noted, 'we have approximately 125 serious fracture cases in the Hospital, most of which will take several months to recover.' The first item of business was to order a plaque in memory of Dr Thierry de Martel. The governors voted to pay salaries of 5,000 French francs monthly to Miss Elisabeth Comte, assistant to the director, and Mr Otto Gresser, chief superintendent. The Count de Chambrun had praised the two Swiss nationals for their 'intelligence, courage and exceptional devotion'. The board also recommended that the managing governor 'should endeavor to slow down our gratuitous activities vis-à-vis soldiers and an endeavor should be made to reduce our expenses in connection with this work, the principal reason being that we at the present time cannot see ahead nor formulate any definite financial program for the future due to conditions brought about by the present situation'.

In August, Dr Sumner Jackson's wife and son, Toquette and Phillip, returned to Paris from the lake house at Enghien. Sumner wanted them back to protect their empty apartment in the avenue Foch from requisitioning by the Germans. Even with a red US Embassy seal, the Jacksons' apartment in the avenue Foch was vulnerable if no one lived in it. The Nazis had already taken houses in the avenue Foch for the Gestapo and Sicherheitsdienst, the party's secret police known as the SD. At the same time, Sumner asked Toquette's sister Alice, nicknamed Tat, to remain at Enghien to protect the vacation house from seizure.

Dr Jackson continued to sleep at the hospital in case of emergencies. He tried to get home at weekends, and Toquette and Phillip visited him in Neuilly.

Like most other Parisians, the Jacksons made the transition from driving cars to riding bicycles. Jackson ordered an extra large bike, because he was too tall for those made for the average Frenchman. The family cycled everywhere, even an hour away to Enghien. While visiting the lake in the late summer, Sumner and young Phillip cut firewood to be ready for winter.

The board of governors met again in September amid the uncertainty of an occupation that was making new rules every week, closing theatres and allowing some to reopen with German licences, changing the hours of curfew, gradually tightening the restrictions on Jews and permitting different German bureaus to set conflicting policies. The board had urgently to decide how the hospital would manage if the governors were forced to leave France. More than 2,500 American civilians and many French and British prisoners of war depended on the facility. The governors unanimously approved a motion that 'in the event of prolonged illness, absence or inability to act for any other reason of Mr. Edward B. Close, Aldebert de Chambrun be and hereby is appointed Managing Governor ad interim in the place and stead of Mr. Close, with the same powers as those now held by Mr. Close'. Eddie Close told the board that Wayne C. Taylor of the American Red Cross had asked him to increase the number of beds for military use to 200, effectively adding fifty beds for French and British war casualties. The board 'unanimously carried' a resolution to make the 200 beds available and 'not to call upon the Red Cross for financial assistance at this time'. Fortunately for the hospital, the American Society for French Medical and Civilian Aid, a fund-raising committee that Bullitt had asked Winthrop Aldrich of the Chase National Bank to establish in New York at the beginning of the war, had already transferred $40,000 to cover running costs. The last item of business was to commission a report for a fee of 7,500 francs from a Mr Sage on the hospital's performance during the Battle of France, the 'War History Report'.

When the meeting ended at 6.45 p.m., General de Chambrun went back to the business of keeping the hospital open and free of German control. A veteran of the First World War, he still called the Germans 'Boches'. Despite the policy of collaboration adopted by his in-law, Pierre Laval, Aldebert vowed never to give a bed to a Boche soldier.

Aldebert de Chambrun, Sumner Jackson, Otto Gresser, Elisabeth Comte and the rest of the staff improvised so that the hospital could function without many of the necessities the Germans had either requisitioned or prohibited. The Germans did not seize the American Hospital's ambulances, and the governors voted to donate six or seven of the fleet of ten to 'services or municipal organizations where they could be utilized in the best interest of the parties concerned'. Without petrol, ambulances had to be converted to run on *gazogene*. The remaining ambulances were vital, not only for transporting patients, but for bringing food from farms around Paris to feed 500 people a day. 'The Winter 1940–1941 was exceptionally cold,' Otto Gresser remembered, 'and no fuel oil was available. The Boiler-Room had to be converted to be heated with coal of very bad quality. The hospital cars were run with charcoal. Contracts were drawn up with farmers for supply of potatoes and other vegetables and fruits and sometimes beef was hidden in the car and covered with salad.'

Dr Jackson challenged Gresser one day about the food shortages. 'Look here,' he said, 'we have so many patients and so little meat and it's absolutely insufficient. If we can't do any better, some patients are going to have malnutrition.' Gresser asked a butcher he knew to send the hospital more meat. A week later, when Gresser came to work, he saw a large German car parked in the courtyard. 'Then I noticed,' the superintendent recalled, 'that they were unloading three hundred kilos [of beef] into the storeroom. I immediately called the butcher and asked what the devil was going on since there were Germans at the hospital delivering meat. And he answered, "Well, these are not Germans, these are French volunteers in German uniforms having joined the German Army and they brought it in a German car from out in the country. You don't risk anything."' Nonetheless, Gresser was worried, especially with the German Kommandatur only a few hundred yards away.

The next day, German officials paid a visit to the hospital and demanded to see Mr Gresser. 'They asked me if I had seen a German car at the hospital with such and such a number, and I replied that I never took note of car numbers.' When they asked how much meat was in the kitchen, Gresser admitted only to the legal limit of 60 kilograms. 'After more questions,' Gresser said later,

> they wanted to talk to the Chief Cook to verify my story. Trying to act calm and not cause suspicion, I offered them seats in the lobby and slowly left to go to the kitchen where at this exact moment they were in the process of taking care of the three hundred kilos of meat. I said, 'Throw that meat out in the garden. I don't want to see it. And you go up and tell the Germans you have sixty kilos and you are not responsible for the purchasing of the meat supply.' The Chief Cook answered the Germans' questions. They seemed satisfied, said they would make a report and left.

Fearing he would be arrested, Gresser returned to the hospital with a suitcase of clothes and other essentials he would need in prison. He told General de Chambrun about the hidden meat and the German inspection. 'Now look here, Gresser,' the general said, 'we've been talking about this for nearly a half hour, and nothing has happened. All is fine. Why do you worry?' Gresser was not arrested.

With no gas for cooking in the kitchen, the chef boiled vegetables in cauldrons over open fires in the courtyard. Surgical instruments and hospital linen were sterilized in boiling water over wood fires. Part of the garage was converted into a pigsty to raise six piglets at a time. Keeping pigs was prohibited by the Germans, as was most hunting of wild game. When the pigs matured, the cook slaughtered them and made a feast for staff and patients alike.

THIRTEEN

Polly's Paris

Soon after her arrival in Paris from Vichy, Polly Peabody volunteered to drive ambulances for the American Hospital. She and a young American colleague named Jean moved into a flat in Passy near the Trocadéro on the Right Bank. Off-duty, the two women shared a bicycle – Jean driving with Polly on the handlebars: 'Thus we sailed down the Champs Elysées, with my skirts flying high, and feeling very much like the daring young man on his flying trapeze; some Frenchmen stooping for a better view screamed out, "O! *les belles cuisses*," ruining completely the little balance I had so painfully managed to maintain.' The American girls, though working hard for the American Hospital, adapted exuberantly to life under occupation. Like other Parisian women deprived of hosiery, they dyed their legs the colour of nylon stockings with a line at the top where garters should have begun. Daringly, they tied little British and French flags from Chanel around their necks. One evening, Polly and Jean gate-crashed a *Nur für Deutsch Gesellschaft* (German Community Only) nightclub by following two German officers inside.

The room was full of uniforms: the majority of the men sat in pairs or small groups; some of them had girls with them – the lowest form of Paris tarts – and they looked bored – almost as bored as their companions. I noticed that the conversation flowed like glue between the Germans and their ladies. There were scenes occasionally, when the Nazis treated them roughly, and I once saw a pink-haired blonde retaliate with a resounding smack across the flabby fat face of the Prussian who was with her.

The waiters, while serving the cheapest champagne to the Germans, charged for the most expensive. The sommelier whispered to Polly that he could not bear to see his better vintages sliding down the throats of 'beer-drinkers'. As one evening came to an end, Polly recalled, 'The curfew hour was heralded by the blowing of a siren, and police cars with loud-speakers travelled through the streets, warning the population that there was only a quarter of an hour to go before bed-time. Then, as soon as the French had been safely removed, the Germans would take over. They would sit at tables which the waiters hastily finished clearing, and order wine: (I saw one squirting soda-water into a glass of claret).'

In September, Polly saw posters that forbad Germans from dancing. An officer explained, 'We cannot dance while so many of our brave men are being shot down over England.' In one night alone, Polly heard, the British had downed ninety-two German planes. The Luftwaffe, as René de Chambrun had predicted in June to Ambassador Bullitt and President Roosevelt, was losing mastery of the air to the RAF. The invasion of Britain, nonetheless, remained Hitler's objective. One German told Polly that his army was ready to sacrifice 300,000 men to conquer Britain. As the months wore on and German air losses outstripped Britain's, Polly noted, 'A new hope sprang up and even the most hard-bitten sceptics began to pin their faith on England.'

The Germans assigned soldiers to accompany the American ambulances that Polly, Jean and other volunteers drove to the prisoner of war camps. 'At the camps,' Polly wrote, 'they insisted on distributing the goods, and would not tolerate any American supervision.' To Polly, German interference in American humanitarian work meant only one thing: 'The truth is that they were longing to get rid of the Americans residing in Paris. Too many stories were leaking out, told to the Press by Americans returning to the States. They were also accusing many of us of aiding the British prisoners to escape.' The accusation, although Polly may not have known, was true. Some of the culprits worked alongside her at the American Hospital. 'In any event, we were destined to become increasingly unpopular as Uncle Sam took bigger and better steps to assist England in the fight for freedom.'

Polly drove her ambulance in mid-September to a hospital for wounded prisoners at Rouen, near Paris. A physician there said that hospitalized French soldiers who were well enough had been taken to a train three days before, part of the German programme to transfer 1.58 million French prisoners of war to camps in Germany. When two French officers leaned out of one train to take a last breath of French air, a sentry shouted at them in German. The doctor thought that 'they either hadn't heard or hadn't understood, for the two officers went right on looking, and talking to each other. The sentry addressed them again; still nothing happened. He then picked up his rifle and shot them both through the head.' One was killed instantly, and the other died in the hospital an hour before Polly arrived.

The American Volunteer Ambulance Corps, forced out of service by German meddling, let most of its volunteer drivers go. 'With no more work to do,' Polly wrote, 'I began thinking of packing my bags, but I couldn't quite adjust myself to the thought of leaving the country, knowing it might be years before I was able to return.' She was young and had enough money to live, so she stayed. 'The first of October,' she noted, 'found the schools opened. The streets and the "Metros" were crowded with children carrying their satchels full of copy-books and sharpened pencils. Most of the children had been removed from the Capital at the outbreak of war, and had only just returned. Their funny little faces were serious and composed: they too reflected the tragedy of defeat.' Many Parisians remained traumatized by the German bombing of the refugee columns the previous June. In the Gare de l'Est, Polly saw a distracted woman clutching a blue flannel bundle. When a railway official approached her, she said, 'You can't have him.' The woman was sobbing. 'I have buried four of them. Four of them along the road ... this is my youngest and my last ... nobody shall take him from me!' When the official looked inside the blanket, it was empty.

Sanctions against Jews in Paris became the norm. From 15 September, the Germans prohibited all Jews, as well as Africans and Algerians, who had fled Paris during the invasion from returning to their homes. The property and safe deposit boxes of the absentees were then seized. Polly witnessed a savage assault by French youths, who smashed the windows of Jewish-owned shops on the Champs-Elysées. Another American eyewitness to the pogrom, French *Vogue* editor Thomas Kernan, recalled, 'One day in September, 1940, I happened to be standing on the balcony of my office in the Champs-Elysées, talking with one of my colleagues, when we heard shouting up toward the Etoile. A yellow roadster sped down the almost deserted avenue at 50 miles an hour, with a vaguely uniformed young man standing up in the tonneau yelling, "*A bas les Juifs!*" ("Down with the Jews!").' Kernan watched uniformed thugs hurling bricks through each window the roadster passed. 'Before my startled eyes, the great windows of Cedric, Vanina, Annabel, Brunswick, Marie-Louise, Toutmain – a million francs worth of plate glass – fell into shards on the pavement. Most, if not all, of these shops were owned by Jews, and had been reopened by their faithful French employees, who stood trembling and weeping in the aisles.' Kernan saw the perpetrators strut into the headquarters at 36 avenue des Champs-Elysées of the fascist *Front Jeune*, Youth Front. Its members, in Kernan's words, were 'pimply-faced youths of fifteen or sixteen years, of the Montmartre gutter type'. The police pretended not to notice, but a German officer coming out of the Claridge Hotel grabbed one of the brick-throwers. The youth handed the German a card. Kernan wrote, 'What it said I do not know, but I saw the officer glance at it and then promptly release the prisoner.'

Kernan felt that 'Paris had no stomach for this sort of vicious vandalism.' The Nazi-controlled Paris dailies portrayed the attacks as 'spontaneous outbursts of indignation by the populace against their Jewish exploiters'. (Most Parisians called their newspapers 'the German press in the French language'.) Kernan detected the opposite: 'The following days, behind boarded up windows, Toutmain and Annabel were filled with more customers than these shops had served for many months, customers they had never had before.'

The anti-Semitism fostered by both the occupation authorities and the regime in Vichy repelled Polly. She wrote, 'The newspaper *France au Travail*, which – like all Paris papers – was under German control

– suggested that the Jews should be isolated on some island, such as Australia, Madagascar or England, where they could establish their own government.' Anti-Semitic demagogues like Jacques Doriot, a former communist turned fascist, staged rallies at which they condemned Jews and blamed them for France's defeat. Polly saw 'No-Jews-Allowed' notices in restaurants. Jewish businesses that failed to display 'Jewish Enterprise' signs were subject to fines and confiscation. American Jews, including Gertrude Stein and Alice B. Toklas, who had left Paris before the occupation remained in the so-called Free Zone, where the Vichy government – to maintain cordial relations with Washington – did not discriminate against them as it did European Jews.

On 6 October, an American newspaper correspondent took Polly on an excursion that let her forget, for a moment, what Paris had become. The reporter had borrowed 'a crazy little buggy' with 'four wheels, a steering gear and two sets of pedals; it was puce colour, and so small that instead of getting into it, we put it on like an apron. With a large American flag waving out of each door of the contraption, we pedalled frantically around Paris, alternately bringing one knee up under our chin, stretching out the other.' Traffic police laughed, and 'pedestrians hooted and grinned and when on the Avenue de l'Opéra we got caught in the middle of a convoy of large trucks full of Nazi troops, there was pandemonium. The officers and soldiers stared wide-eyed at the Stars and Stripes, and the ridiculous vehicle, containing two crazy Americans, and for once they laughed too.'

Polly and the journalist, falling in with the German convoy, circled the Arc de Triomphe. A lone French workman was pedalling a three-wheel cycle beside a Wehrmacht touring car. 'Twice the grey car was stopped by red lights, and each time the man on the bicycle passed it. At the third light the car drew up at the kerb: the officer jumped out and halted the Frenchman, who was coasting along quite happily. He roared at him in broken French, accusing him of lacking in respect towards his superior, by passing him twice on the wrong side.' The officer ordered his driver to take the air out of the cyclist's tyres. 'Crowds gathered to watch the ludicrous picture of the infuriated officer, the silent Frenchman and the soldier on his hands and knees unscrewing the caps of three pairs of tyres.' The Germans drove off, leaving the Frenchman to refill his tyres. A mile ahead, the cyclist came upon the Nazi car again with its hood up and a soldier trying to repair the engine. 'The cyclist rode past once more, this time with a faint smile on his lips.'

FOURTEEN

Rugged Individualists

CHARLES BEDAUX REVEALED COMPLEX, contradictory facets of character from the moment the occupation began. Having no political loyalties, he openly conducted business with and for the German occupier. 'The Germans were the only ones left in Paris to do business with,' Bedaux explained. Janet Flanner later wrote, 'This is probably the best and briefest definition of collaborationism yet put on record.' Yet Bedaux endangered his wealth and his life to protect Jewish friends, employees and clients. He convinced the Germans that his Jewish secretary in France was a Christian. She worked for him throughout the occupation. He did the same for Alexandra Ter Hart, the manager of his Amsterdam international headquarters, who had helped Friedrich von Ledebur to escape via Rotterdam in 1939. Married to a Dutch decorator, the former Alexandra Lubowski was both Polish and Jewish. Bedaux also helped to save three textile firms that belonged to Jewish friends, Vogel, Schraft and Blin et Blin, from Nazi confiscation by putting the companies in his name. Their share certificates were hidden at Candé to be returned to their original owners when the occupation ended. To most Americans and others in France, German occupation was a source of shame, irritation and anguish. To Bedaux, it was an opportunity.

In October 1940, German Ambassador Otto Abetz provided Bedaux with an *Ausweis*, or pass, to cross the demarcation line between France's Occupied Zone and the Free Zone. Bedaux's mission was to consult Maréchal Henri-Philippe Pétain about reviving his scheme to increase coal production at Algeria's Kenadsa coal mines –

no longer for Spanish mills to produce steel for France to fight Germany, but to fuel trains in North Africa. The old Maréchal received Bedaux at his Hôtel du Parc headquarters in Vichy. They discussed various Bedaux projects, and Pétain granted his request to study the Kenadsa mines' operation and evaluate the quality of the coal. Bedaux left Vichy to inspect mineshafts in the northern Sahara.

On 21 October, Clara and Aldebert de Chambrun had lunch in Paris with Pierre Laval. Laval, already Pétain's vice-premier, had just been named foreign minister as well. Their children, René de Chambrun and Josée Laval, were in Boston seeking American aid for children and refugees in the Free Zone. Laval told Clara and Aldebert that Abetz had just invited him to meet a senior German official: 'He must be speaking of [Foreign Minister Joachim] von Ribbentrop, I believe. He is somewhere in the offing, and, it seems, has more influence with Hitler than anyone else.' The next day, Abetz told Laval he was taking him to meet, as he had suspected, Ribbentrop. A German car drove the two men out of Paris, past Rambouillet, to the Loire Valley. It was then that Abetz admitted to Laval that he would see, in addition to Ribbentrop, Hitler himself. Laval blurted out, '*Sans blague?*' 'No joke?' They went to a nondescript village, Montoire-sur-Loire, chosen for its proximity to a tunnel in which the Führer's private train, the *Amerika*, could hide in the event of RAF bombing. Hitler and Ribbentrop, who received Laval in the train's dining car, invited him to return in two days with Maréchal Pétain for the first post-defeat summit between the German and French leaders.

In the meantime, Hitler had a rendezvous with the Spanish dictator, General Francisco Franco, at Hendaye in French Basque country beside the Spanish frontier. Franco, who had taken power with German military assistance in the Spanish Civil War only the year before, resisted Hitler's demand that he repay the debt by joining the war against Britain. The Spaniard's prevarication scuttled German plans to send troops through Spain to conquer the British Mediterranean fortress at Gibraltar. Hitler responded by denying Franco, who had occupied Tangier on the day the Germans entered Paris, permission to occupy other parts of French Morocco. Franco left Hitler in a bad mood to receive Pétain and Pierre Laval on 24 October back in Montoire.

On the *Amerika*, Hitler asked Pétain, stung by the British attack on the French fleet at Mers-el-Kébir in July, to declare war on Britain. Pétain said he was not yet in a position to go that far in cooperating with Germany, but he asked for a peace treaty so that 'the two million French prisoners of war may return to their families as soon as possible'. Like Franco, Pétain would not commit his country to war against Britain. But he would not resume the fight against Germany either. His goal was to keep France's fleet and colonies out of both Allied and Axis control, while cooperating with the Germans to obtain a gentler occupation. After the meeting, Pétain broadcast a speech that introduced the notion of 'collaboration': 'This collaboration must be sincere. It must exclude all idea of aggression. It must carry with it a patient and confident effort ... Follow me. Trust in eternal France.' At the same time, he sent a message to Winston Churchill, via the Portuguese Ambassador in order to conceal its contents from Pierre Laval, that Vichy's collaboration with Germany would not be military.

Charles Bedaux returned from North Africa a few days later to hear first-hand from Laval what had transpired at Montoire. Gaston Bedaux, who attended dinner in Paris with his brother and Laval, wrote, 'I was placed to the right of the President [Laval retained the title 'President', having been President of the Council of Ministers, or prime minister, several times before 1936], my brother was at his left.' Laval recounted at length that evening details of his meeting at Montoire. Laval, who had kept 'careful notes' of the meetings on 22 and 24 October, told the Bedaux brothers of 'his differences with the Maréchal and the efforts he made to save the French in explaining to the Germans what one meant by collaboration. He also told us particularly how he succeeded in taking out of German hands some Frenchmen who, in the course of a football match, had mistreated their German neighbours after a conversation purely about sports.'

Laval did not seem to understand that, whether or not he cajoled Germany into minor concessions, much of French, as well as American, public opinion perceived him as a German puppet. 'Laval was happy with the success that he achieved in this affair in declaring that collaboration was not subordination,' Gaston Bedaux recalled, adding Laval's view 'that it was necessary to live together and it was not necessary for one blindly to obey the other. The partner had to understand that to collaborate did not mean to exclude contradiction, discussion and even dispute.' Laval, who was proud of his skill as an orator, assured the Bedauxs, 'So long as I have my vocal cords, I'll get out of trouble.' Charles Bedaux was bored by Laval's exposition of the politics of collaboration. When Laval criticized Vichy's recent decision to reduce civil servants' salaries, Charles the efficiency engineer came to life. He argued that only increased productivity would achieve both higher salaries and a reduction in the cost of living. Gaston took from the dinner the impression of Laval as 'a lively intelligence and a man who sought to perform a difficult task'. He was also a valuable ally for Bedaux in the Vichy administration.

Charles Bedaux left Paris again, with German permission, for The Hague to apply for a Dutch patent on a new method of analysing industrial productivity. At this time, according to Bedaux's biographer Jim Christy, a Bedaux engineer named Gartner colluded with the Germans and Albert Ramond, who had replaced Bedaux as director of his American companies in 1937, to deprive Bedaux of his Netherlands interests. The Germans seized the Bedaux companies' global headquarters in Amsterdam as 'enemy' property. When Bedaux heard of the confiscation a few days later in Paris, he informed the Nazis that, as an American, he was not an enemy of the Reich but a neutral. The Germans kept the headquarters anyway, declaring it 'alien' property, also subject to confiscation.

Sylvia Beach and Adrienne Monnier had a few compensations for the hardships of life under the Germans. One was a reading by Paul Valéry of his unfinished masterpiece, '*Mon Faust (Ebauches)*', 'My Faust (Sketches)' in the rue de l'Odéon. 'With unconcealed pride,' Adrienne Monnier wrote, 'I shall say here that the poet gave a reading of it to us – to Sylvia, my sister Marie, and myself, in September 1940; I shall even say our own ears were the first to hear it'. Valéry's words and voice captivated the women. Adrienne observed that Lust, 'the feminine character of the play', was 'an ingenuous intellectual. She is a spirited, a lively spirited girl, very free with her master ... There are many girls and women like Lust, there are many of them in France. This capacity for being smitten with genius and loving to serve it is certainly a trait of the women of our country, even if the genius inhabits an ugly or aged being'. She may have meant herself in relation to Valéry or, equally, Sylvia to James Joyce.

Sylvia was increasingly distraught for the Joyce family, who had been delayed for months without visas on the Swiss border in Haute Savoie. Joyce's daughter, Lucia, was mentally disturbed, and he placed her in a French asylum. Sylvia had dedicated much of her adult life to Joyce as his publisher, secretary and factotum, but she could not help him now. Nor could she do anything for her aged father in California. She relayed assistance from her old friend, Carlotta Welles Briggs, to people in Paris. Carlotta sent her a cheque for 2,000 francs in October 1940: 600 for Sylvia to give to 'old Rose', whose pension had not been paid; and another six hundred for 'Rigollet', an old man who lived in the alley behind Carlotta's flat in Paris. (She told Sylvia to keep the remaining 800 francs for herself, one instance among many in which Carlotta aided her impoverished childhood friend.) Carlotta wrote to Sylvia from California on 2 November asking her to visit an Armenian woman named Mme Barseghian at 22 avenue Paul Appell near Montparnasse. Mme Barseghian was losing her eyesight, and her only son was in the army. 'In case she is still there a little call from you would cheer her up no end. Give her my love in case you find her.'

On 13 November, Holly Beach Dennis wrote to Sylvia, who was then taking a break at Carlotta's house, La Salle du Roc, near Bourré. Because she had not received any reply to her recent letters, she wondered whether Sylvia was receiving her mail. Postal services between the United States and France were slow and unreliable. All letters were subject to German censorship in France and to British censorship en route through Bermuda. 'I told you,' Holly wrote, 'that Father's mind being somewhat bewildered, due to age, Cyprian has put him in an attractive "Rest Home" on Rosemead Boulevard, near Pasadena, where he is well taken care of ... Father is such a wonderful person and I believe he is as happy now in his imaginings as he was when his mind was quite clear.' Holly, meanwhile, had moved with her husband, Frederic Dennis, and their adopted son, Freddie, back to Princeton. Sylvester, blind, deaf and senile, received visits from Carlotta

Welles Briggs and his daughter Cyprian, both of whom lived nearby. Cyprian wrote to her sister in Paris, 'The greatest blessing is that he has forgotten there is a war in Europe, and thinks of you only as you were before.' By the time Sylvia read the letters that told her of Sylvester's confinement, he was dead. Cyprian wrote again, just after their father died on 16 November, to assure Sylvia that he lived 'happily till the very end, and that end couldn't have been more merciful'.

The injured French soldier André Guillon had been in the American Hospital for two months, when a new patient moved into his room. Captain A., an Alsatian prisoner of war with two wounds in his leg, had been a German language instructor at the French military academy, Saint-Cyr. To pass the time, Guillon studied German under his tutelage.

He told me between lessons that he had had permission in 1938 to spend a year as a 'businessman' in Munich. I didn't understand immediately what he was alluding to. He then gave me some information about lodgings he had in the centre of Paris ... lodgings where we could meet if I liked when he left the American Hospital. His legs, practically smashed to pieces at the beginning of October, were completely healed by the 25th. And on the 30th, he disappeared. Miracle of the Intelligence Services ...

During the winter, Guillon had little chance of taking sun therapy, but he walked along the corridors and outside to the terrace to strengthen his legs. At five o'clock one evening, 'I found myself on the terrace admiring the dome of Sacré-Coeur in Montmartre, twinkling in the rays of the setting sun, and I dreamed of mosques in African lands.' He encountered a new arrival at the hospital, a Royal Air Force pilot whose plane had been shot down over France. The British officer had lost the sight in both eyes. 'Blind, he wandered slowly in his blue, slate-grey uniform along the paths of the hospital without saying a word.' Soon, the officer was gone.

How the Americans succeeded in getting him to England, I cannot say. I believe there were two stages, of which one was Vichy. But the thing I am sure of is that during eighty days, everyone in the hospital spoke only of this question and the way in which the American ambulance had tricked the Germans at the Line of Demarcation, of his arrival at Vichy and, two or three days later, not more, the completion of his trip in England. How the Germans knew nothing of this story astounded me. The blind man, isn't he perhaps someone who does not want to see?

The officer's escape in an American ambulance revealed the extent to which other hospital employees were aiding Sumner Jackson in the Resistance. They did this despite the ever-present prospect of torture and the firing squad.

Another gravely wounded French soldier told Guillon that, in addition to his war injuries, he had gonorrhoea. 'The American doctor who took care of him with sulfa drugs at a very high dosage, trying the lot on everything, accomplished an exploit in healing. We learned that three weeks after he left the hospital, he was in London.' The American doctor was undoubtedly the hospital's genito-urinary specialist, Sumner Jackson.

On Friday, 11 October, General of the Army Charles Huntziger, who had signed the Armistice for France in June and was now minister of war at Vichy, presented the hospital with the Order of Merit and the Croix de Guerre for services to the wounded during the Battle of France. Sumner Jackson, Elisabeth Comte and Edward Close were cited by name. 'Operating by day and by night,' the citation read, 'the hospital took care of an almost interminable number of wounded and undoubtedly saved a great number of lives. In direct contact with the enemy, and working in an enemy-occupied zone, the hospital continued with unflagging dedication not only to care for the wounded but also to bring aid to the prisoners.' General Huntziger and his wife stayed for lunch, and the patients were given champagne for the occasion.

Lunch, dinner and walks broke up André Guillon's otherwise tedious days. After six o'clock, there was nothing to do. He read books, including three that the hospital's American staff recommended for him to understand their country: *Gone with the Wind*, *Babbitt* and a treatise on the American economy by French academic and now head of the Bibliothèque Nationale, Bernard Fay. 'I read them,' Guillon wrote. 'I don't know if I know the United States any better.' He played chess and poker with the other soldiers. Occasionally, there was entertainment. An actor named Victor Boucher and the singer Marianne Oswald, who reminded him of Edith Piaf, came to the hospital. Miss Thierry, a nurse of French ancestry from Boston, gave them a violin concert in the library. 'She had the grace to visit every room afterwards to play a little for those who were too injured to get up and join the rest of us at the concert. Neutral? The Americans? Oh, no. "Miss Thierry's gesture shows us better".'

At the end of November, the French patients celebrated the birthday of one of their comrades: 'He was alone. He had lost his wife in the bombardment, and he was in bed with two broken legs. We obtained from outside a cake and a bottle of champagne. And we met in his room at seven o'clock.' As they began the party, they were joined by a young Russian nurse whom Guillon referred to as Mademoiselle S. (She was probably a surgical nurse named Mlle Svetchine.) After finishing the cake and champagne, they played poker. By midnight, Mlle S. had lost all her money. One of the wounded soldiers suggested a way for her to win it back. 'You undress,' he said. 'With each article of clothing you take off, we'll place a bet for you.' She lost hand after hand. By twelve-thirty, she had no clothes left. Guillon thought the girl was perhaps not as used to champagne as the Frenchmen were, because she accepted their suggestion to go back to her room nude as she was. 'There was obviously a "black-out", and Mademoiselle S. lived only two hundred metres from the hospital and at that hour she wouldn't come across anyone.' She ran home through the dark without a stitch or a mishap.

The hospital attracted medical staff with no obvious medical expertise. One of these was Mademoiselle D. 'A very beautiful girl,' Guillon thought, 'she nonetheless did not win our sympathy because we were wounded and she certainly knew absolutely nothing about the nursing profession.' Three weeks later, Guillon read in the German-sponsored Paris press a communiqué from the *Feldkommandatur* of Grossparis that a young American woman, who turned out to be Mademoiselle D., had been expelled for abusing her privileges on 'neutral territory'. Guillon took this to mean she was 'conducting anti-German activities'. Mademoiselle D. was probably Elizabeth Deegan, a clerk in the American Embassy who was arrested by the Germans on 1 December. Because the US Consulate was representing British interests in France, Elizabeth Deegan had visited British prisoners at the German prison in the rue du Cherche Midi and at the American Hospital. The Nazis held and questioned her at Cherche Midi. Before the Germans finally allowed her to be deported under pressure from the State Department, the Paris press alleged that her crime was 'conniving at the escape of British officers'.

FIFTEEN

Germany's Confidential American Agent

IN PARIS, CHARLES BEDAUX became more closely involved with Otto Abetz and Pierre Laval over what *Time* magazine would call 'the affair of the dead eaglet'. On 12 December, Abetz delivered Laval an invitation for Maréchal Pétain. Adolf Hitler was asking Pétain to join him in a ceremony to inter the ashes of Napoleon's son, the Duke of Reichstadt, in his father's crypt in the Hôpital des Invalides. Simultaneously, the Germans issued an official announcement of the Führer's gift to France. *L'Aiglon*, or 'the little eagle', as the French affectionately called the younger Bonaparte, had been buried in Vienna's Capuchin church at his death in 1832. Hitler himself would accompany the remains on the train to Paris in two days, the hundredth anniversary of the return of Napoleon's body from St Helena. The Germans intended their public relations extravaganza to demonstrate the benefits of collaboration. The return of the little eagle's remains drew Charles Bedaux into a political web whose strands led from Berlin to Vichy and Paris for control of France.

Laval warned Abetz that Pétain's age and the December weather might prevent his attendance, but he called Vichy anyway to urge the Maréchal to accept. An official there declined on Pétain's behalf, so Laval drove early the next morning to Vichy with his daughter Josée to invite him in person. Josée Laval de Chambrun, who had just left her husband, Comte René de Chambrun, in the United States, noted ominously in her diary that the day was Friday the thirteenth. Laval claimed that Pétain met him that afternoon and agreed to attend the interment service in Paris. At five o'clock, Laval presided at a short meeting of the cabinet in the Hôtel du Parc. Afterwards, someone informed him that the cabinet would meet again at eight o'clock. 'I had scarcely entered the Council Room when the Marshal came in ... He said, "I wish each minister to hand in his resignation."' When they obeyed, Pétain accepted the resignations of only Laval and one other minister. Laval argued with Pétain. Pétain accused Laval of not pressing the Germans to allow him to move the government from Vichy to the Paris suburb of Versailles, traditional seat of French kings. (The Pétain government was responsible for police, roads and the rest of the civil infrastructure in both the Occupied and Free Zones. It also commanded the colonies, which at the time comprised 10 per cent of the world's landmass. Vichy had begun as a temporary capital that Pétain longed to leave.) When Laval denied keeping Pétain from Versailles, the Maréchal walked out.

A special unit of Vichy police, the *Groupe de Protection*, arrested Laval and took him to his modest chateau at Châteldon, 13 miles from Vichy. Fifty policemen held him, his wife and daughter under house arrest. At the Hôtel du Parc that evening, Fernand de Brinon tried to leave his room. But a policeman pointed a revolver at him and ordered him back inside. At Châteldon, police cut Laval's telephone line.

Vichy's 13 December coup d'état amused Charles de Gaulle in London. The Free French leader dismissed it as 'a palace revolution that expelled the Grand Vizier'. Washington accepted the result quietly, but with satisfaction.

Pétain announced his decision to dispense with Laval's services 'for reasons of internal policy' over French radio the next day. He sent Hitler a letter that arrived early on Saturday morning, 14 December, informing him of Laval's dismissal and arrest. Pétain, while thanking Hitler for returning the Duke of Reichstadt's ashes, declined his invitation to the interment. Hitler exploded, cancelled his trip to Paris and threatened to invade Vichy's Free Zone immediately. 'This is a heavy defeat for Ribbentrop and his Abetz,' Ulrich von Hassell, a former German Ambassador to Italy and anti-Nazi conspirator in the Foreign

Ministry, wrote in his diary. 'Even if we now force them to take Laval back into the Cabinet the situation has shifted much to Germany's disadvantage. Hitler has ordered preparations for occupying all of France.' Hitler accepted Ribbentrop's advice to send Otto Abetz to Vichy to see Pétain and free Laval, before resorting to an expensive invasion.

On Sunday, 15 December, Abetz presided at the delayed midnight service for the Duke of Reichstadt without either Hitler or Pétain in attendance. Unimpressed Parisians, freezing that winter, said they preferred coal to ashes. The ceremony was so tawdry that some of the German-supported Paris newspapers did not report it. Abetz sped early in the morning to Vichy and demanded Laval's immediate release. At two o'clock, Laval was brought from Châteldon to Vichy to see Pétain, who apologized for his arrest but refused to reinstate him. A few hours later, Josée de Chambrun and her mother heard motorcycles at the head of a German Embassy convoy bringing Pierre Laval back to the Château de Châteldon. 'I saw for the first time the Germans,' Josée wrote in her diary, 'their initiative perhaps [saving] the life of my father.' To her, these Germans were 'intelligent and pleasant'. Quoting 'a great writer', she switched to English: 'The people from Auvergne never forget; children remember those who hurt their fathers and they don't forget those who give them help or relief in days of stress.' She added in French, 'I'll never forget, but what great sadness.' Laval, free but out of office, went straight to Paris, 'where he is safe'.

Josée sent a telegram from the post office in Vichy to her husband René in the United States: STAY AMERICA STOP NO REASON TO WORRY EXCEPT FOR THE COUNTRY STOP ALL LOVE. René de Chambrun's morale was already low, because his second mission to the United States was failing. His cousin, Franklin Roosevelt, did not return his calls and refused to provide US government humanitarian aid to the Free Zone. Few American officials accepted René's contention that his father-in-law was not pro-German. In New York, René wrote, 'I spent the saddest Christmas of my life.'

Laval's removal cost Charles Bedaux his most effective contact in the Vichy administration. Worse came the next day, 15 December, when Bedaux's friend Count Joseph von Ledebur was recalled by the army from Paris to Germany. The allies he could call on were disappearing. He needed small favours, like German identity cards to travel to Vichy and North Africa, and larger ones, especially the return of his international company's assets in German-occupied Amsterdam. His relations with Ambassador Abetz remained cordial, so he went the next day, 16 December, to the German Embassy. Discovering that Abetz was out, Bedaux dropped in on Fernand de Brinon, who had just escaped from the Vichy putschists. De Brinon, preoccupied with his political survival, asked Bedaux to wait a day. They could talk in the morning while driving to Vichy.

On Tuesday morning, 17 December, the two men, with de Brinon's chauffeur and bodyguards, crossed the line of demarcation from the Occupied to the Free Zone. De Brinon, without explaining himself to Bedaux, was using him as a shield. The Pétain associates who hated him as much as they did Laval may have wanted him dead. But they were unlikely to risk antagonizing Washington by killing an American citizen beside him. In Vichy, de Brinon called on Maréchal Pétain to propose himself for a cabinet post. He also saw his Jewish wife, Lisette, who was in Vichy at the time.

While de Brinon conferred with Pétain, Bedaux met various Vichy officials to discuss projects in France and North Africa. His final meeting was with Robert Murphy at the American Embassy in the Villa Ica. For the past week, Murphy had been reporting to Secretary of State Cordell Hull and President Roosevelt on the machinations at Vichy. The interior minister, Marcel Peyrouton, had informed Murphy in advance of his intention to arrest Laval. It undoubtedly met with American approval. Murphy wrote later, 'We played no concealed part in Laval's overthrow there in 1940, although we did emphasize in all our talks with Pétain's ministers, including Laval himself, that the American Government was convinced that its interests demanded the defeat of Nazi Germany.' Laval's dismissal made it easier for the secretary general of Vichy's Foreign Office, Charles Rochas, to issue Murphy a permit to tour North and West Africa that Laval's faction had been delaying. Bedaux and Murphy, already acquainted from Paris and the Château de Candé, discussed Murphy's coming mission to French Africa. President Roosevelt had asked Murphy to assess the need for American aid to the region. Murphy did not tell Bedaux about his other objective: to place twelve spies in North Africa undercover as US consuls. Their nominal task as 'food control officers' would be to certify that American aid went to the inhabitants, not to Germany. Bedaux was sufficiently informed on the Algerian and Moroccan economies to brief Murphy.

That night, Fernand de Brinon drove Bedaux back to Paris. They arrived at Bedaux's hotel at about three o'clock in the morning. 'Now, you can put aside your gun,' de Brinon said. Bedaux did not carry a gun. De Brinon, whose bodyguards were armed, seemed surprised. According to Bedaux, he said, 'You are worth a thousand men.' Vichy announced later on 18 December that de Brinon would succeed General de la Laurencie as delegate general of the French government in the Occupied Zone, Vichy 'ambassador' in Paris with ministerial status in the government. Abetz had personally demanded de la Laurencie's removal after the general, as part of the anti-Laval coup, had arrested the pro-Nazi French politician Marcel Déat in Paris. (Déat headed one of two political parties, the Rassemblement National Populaire, permitted by the Germans in the Occupied Zone.) Forcing Pétain to accept an obvious German puppet like de Brinon as de la Laurencie's successor was part of Germany's retribution for Laval's dismissal. Other punishments were to rename Vichy's 'Free Zone' the 'Unoccupied Zone'; to restrict further the food supplies in Paris; and to renege on promises to release some of the French prisoners in Germany. If collaboration had benefits, non-cooperation incurred costs. Abetz made Pétain accept a directorate under Admiral Jean-François Darlan, then naval minister, to advise the cabinet and, incidentally, keep an eye on the Vichy government for Abetz. The new regime at Vichy sought to collaborate with the Germans just as Laval had. For Charles Bedaux, the elevation of de Brinon partly compensated for the loss of Laval.

When Abetz returned to Paris, Charles Bedaux met him at the German Embassy in the Hôtel de Beauharnais. (When the anti-Nazi diplomat Ulrich von Hassell visited Paris at the time, he wrote in his diary, 'The beautiful palace seems dishonoured by the present incumbents.') Despite the chill of the Paris winter, Abetz invited Bedaux outside for a walk in the Hôtel de Beauharnais's magnificent garden courtyard. This may have been to avoid the devices with which Hermann Goering's *Forschungsamt*, Research Office, listened to the conversations of most second-rank German officials, many of whom were pursuing contradictory policies in France and other occupied territories. As they strolled around the frosty grass, Abetz confided to Bedaux that Laval's arrest had been 'frivolous'. Abetz was impatient with French politicians and mentioned that even Laval, despite his charm, was superficial. Bedaux, who had a professional obsession with order, said Laval was 'an artist with a horror of orderliness'. Laval had once said to Bedaux, 'I like to look at you and see an example of what I wouldn't be for anything on earth.' Bedaux took the remark as a compliment.

As the two men circled the garden, Abetz said he was considering a scheme to please Hitler and undermine Vichy. Bedaux was part of the plan. Still out of earshot of the embassy's hidden microphones, Abetz told Bedaux he knew of his intention to meet General Maxime Weygand at the Kenadsa mines on his coming trip to North Africa. Weygand, who had been Pétain's minister of defence in the emergency cabinet of 10 July 1940, had been exiled to Algiers as military governor-general because his strict adherence to the Armistice Agreement annoyed the Germans and the collaborationists. Would Abetz ask the general to succeed Pétain as head of a new French government in Paris? Bedaux thought it was a joke, because Weygand hated Germany. Abetz explained, 'We would rather have in France at the head of the government a freely spoken enemy whom we respect than a collaborator whom we don't know.' Bedaux agreed to carry Abetz's offer to Weygand, his first political mission for the Germans. Abetz, at the same time, promised more support, including heavy machinery, to Bedaux's coal mining operation at Kenadsa. Abetz did not mention that Kenadsa's coal might fuel the North African railways for eventual use by the Wehrmacht.

On 23 December, the German occupation forces in Paris executed 23-year-old Jacques Bonsergent 'for an act of violence against a member of the German Army'. The violence was a minor scuffle between some German soldiers and young Frenchmen, all of whom but Bonsergent ran away. On the order of the military commander in France, General Otto von Stülpnagel, Bonsergent became the first Frenchman executed by the Germans in Paris.

As a gesture to win Parisian goodwill, the German command extended the curfew on Christmas Eve from 11 p.m. to 3 a.m. Cafés and restaurants were permitted to remain open until 2.30 a.m., serving food and drink to the Parisians who could afford to pay. The Germans had seized over 90 per cent of the forty million tons of coal France required, as well as the barges used to transport it along canals to the Seine, depriving the capital of fuel. The city's inhabitants, including about 2,000 Americans, endured the coldest winter in fifty years without enough coal to heat their homes.

In New York, Jerome Kern and Oscar Hammerstein released the hit song of the Christmas season, 'The Last Time I Saw Paris'. It was the first number the duo, composers of Broadway musicals like *Show Boat*, had written to stand on its own. Kate Smith sang the lyrics over national radio, reminding some Americans of their relatives cut off in Paris:

> *The last time I saw Paris, her heart was warm and gay.*
> *No matter how they change her, I'll remember her that way.*

PART THREE

1941

SIXTEEN

The Coldest Winter

ON A FROZEN NEW YEAR'S MORNING, a train left the Gare de Lyon in Paris for Marseilles. Among the passengers entrusted by the German occupiers with an *Ausweis* to cross the line into the Vichy zone was Charles Bedaux. Having left Fern at home with their guests in the Château de Candé, he planned to take a short flight from Marseilles to Algiers and drive over the Atlas Mountains to Kenadsa on Sahara's northern fringe. His rendezvous with General Maxime Weygand, military governor general of French North Africa, had the stated purpose of discussing coal production. But Bedaux had a secret agenda: to relay German Ambassador Otto Abetz's offer to place Weygand at the head of a pro-German government in Paris.

The train moved slowly south amid the heavy snows of a treacherous French winter, until it stopped suddenly in bleak countryside north of the Provençal town of Avignon. Thick, packed snow blocked the line. With the train immobilized, Charles Bedaux could not remain passive. He trudged through snow drifts to a farmhouse, telephoned for horse-drawn wagons, and hired men to find provisions for the passengers and the train staff. The delivery of food and other supplies continued for eight days, with Bedaux arranging logistics as he had on the trail in British Columbia. 'Charles was amused by this little adventure,' his brother Gaston remembered. When the snow was cleared from the line, the train reversed north to Lyons. Bedaux flew to Marseilles, but technical problems delayed his flight to Algiers another day. Bedaux reached Algiers by chartered plane on 10 January 1941.

General Weygand, who had already left Kenadsa, sent a message asking Bedaux to visit him in Rabat, capital of Morocco.

General Maxime Weygand had been a hero of the Great War and was one of the officers with Maréchal Ferdinand Foch in the train at Compiègne when France and Germany signed the Armistice Agreement of 1918. Twenty-two years later, as the French and British armies were retreating from the German front, Prime Minister Paul Reynaud recalled Weygand to replace General Gamelin as commander of the French armed forces. Weygand, after declaring Paris an 'open city' in June 1940, joined the defeatist camp in Reynaud's cabinet, along with Maréchal Pétain, in seeking an immediate armistice with Germany. Pétain made him minister of national defence in his July 1940 cabinet. In September, he was reassigned to North Africa as Vichy's delegate general and armed forces commander. Pétain's instructions were to keep the region out of the hands of the British, the Germans and General Charles de Gaulle. In the meantime, all three courted Weygand. De Gaulle asked him to attack the Italians in Libya from French bases in Tunisia while the British launched an offensive in the east from Egypt. Expelling Italy from Libya would remove the Axis from North Africa, thus securing the entire southern Mediterranean for the Allies. Weygand refused.

When Bedaux met Weygand in Rabat, he delivered Abetz's proposal. Would the general preside over a new French government in Paris? 'I consider this a great compliment,' Weygand told Bedaux, 'but the Germans cannot fool me with great compliments. I have one superior. I could not ask for a better one: Maréchal Pétain. I will ask for his orders.' Weygand informed Pétain at once. Charles Bedaux's role as messenger did not endear him to Pétain, who may already have suspected his friendships with Pierre Laval and Fernand de Brinon.

Robert Murphy, in North Africa ostensibly to assess the area's humanitarian needs, cabled Secretary of State Cordell Hull, 'Weygand and his associates are laying the foundation for substantial military action against Germany and Italy.' Perhaps Weygand's dislike of the Germans swept Murphy along, but the general did nothing to challenge the German military. Murphy, meanwhile, reached a humanitarian accord with Weygand that released frozen French funds in the United States for France to purchase civilian provisions for North Africa. The Murphy–Weygand agreement allowed the United States to install American vice-consuls in French North Africa, who would certify that no American aid went to Germany and, secretly, send military intelligence to Washington. 'To demonstrate his confidence in the United States Government,' Murphy wrote, 'General Weygand made an unprecedented concession: our consular staffs, including the twelve new "vice-consuls," would be permitted to use secret codes and to employ couriers carrying locked pouches, a privilege usually restricted to diplomatic missions and not extended in wartime to consular offices in French North Africa.'

In Algiers, Murphy saw Bedaux several times, and in February they called together on Weygand. Bedaux's presence may not have been an asset. Weygand called Bedaux a bandit, because his bill to the French government for installing the Bedaux system at Kenadsa was exorbitant. Bedaux kept Murphy informed of his work at the coal mines, but it seems he did not tell him of Abetz's proposal to Weygand. Murphy referred to it neither in his messages to the State Department nor in his memoirs, *Diplomat among Warriors*. When Bedaux told Abetz that Weygand had declined his proposal to replace Pétain, Germany ordered Pétain to dismiss Weygand. If he did not, the Germans would occupy the Unoccupied Zone. Weygand's loyalty to Pétain earned him dismissal by Pétain. He retired to his farm in the south of France. Soon afterwards, the Germans arrested him.

Bedaux returned to Paris to brief Dr Franz Medicus on Kenadsa. Medicus agreed to push the military to release more heavy machines to augment the mines' coal production. It was as much in Germany's interest as France's to produce coal for the trains of French North Africa. With Medicus's support, the Germans handed over more than $200,000 worth of compressors, diggers and other equipment. Bedaux needed thousands of workers to build a new rail line and mine the extra coal, and the Nazis helped with that as well. To supplement Berber and African labourers in the Sahara, the Germans sent Polish and Czech prisoners of war. From Spanish Sahara, Franco contributed Loyalist prisoners who had fought against him in the Civil War. Bedaux was about to go beyond speeding up low-paid workers in American factories to using slave labour in one of the hottest terrains on earth.

In January 1941, Sylvia Beach received news of the man to whom she had given attention and love for most of her adult life, James Joyce. With his wife and son, he had finally crossed the Swiss border and settled in Zurich on 17 December 1940. Although safe after six months' waiting to exit France, Joyce was consumed with worry. He had left his daughter in a French asylum, and he was short of money. The hostile critical reception of his recently published book, *Finnegans Wake*, preoccupied him. His health, never robust, deteriorated. After emergency surgery for an ulcer and peritonitis on 13 January, the author of *Ulysses* died. To Sylvia, the loss combined with the death of her father in California two months earlier to send her into depression. Her dearest friends, Adrienne Monnier and Françoise Bernheim, offered some consolation. But the deaths of those she loved outside France hurt more than anything in her own precarious existence in occupied Paris. It was a cruel winter.

Although some Americans were leaving France in early 1941, René de Chambrun was returning. He had completed his second and final wartime journey to the land of his parents' birth. But his mission was only half accomplished. On his first visit, he had persuaded Franklin Roosevelt to send arms to Britain. On his second, however, cousin Franklin rebuffed his request for American government food shipments to hungry French and refugees in the Vichy zone. René left New York dejected and, after a rough thirteen-day sea crossing, arrived in Lisbon. On 6 February, Josée was waiting for him just over the Spanish border in Toulouse. They spent the night together before flying to the Laval chateau at Châteldon. Josée noted in her diary that René brought her presents from America: 'Bunny gave me a lovely little dress, a sweater, a magnificent golden cigarette case and some cigarettes.' Two days later, the couple went to Paris to see Clara and Aldebert. The next few days' lunches and dinners were spent in the new Paris with German Ambassador Otto Abetz and his French wife, embassy counsellor Ernst Achenbach and his American bride, German consul-general Rudolph

Schleier, Luftwaffe General Hanesse and famed French actress Arletty. For a soldier who resisted the German invasion and a lobbyist who opposed the Germans in the United States, René adapted quickly to the new order that his father-in-law and wife were introducing him to.

The American Hospital's board of governors' meeting in Aldebert de Chambrun's offices on the Champs-Elysées on 13 February 1941 officially appointed Dr Sumner Jackson *Médecin Chef* (Chief Physician) *ad interim* to replace Dr Edmund Gros, who was too ill to return to Paris from the United States. At the time, the hospital was caring for seventy French soldiers, twenty-five British patients and sixty 'needy French children'. Dr Jackson and Aldebert de Chambrun worked together to keep a patient in every bed so that the Germans would have no excuse to take over the institution. A month later, Edward B. Close reported to the board: 'Another hospital year, and probably the most difficult in the history of The American Hospital of Paris, has again come to an end.' He stated that the number of patient days over the previous year came to 38,952 for wounded French soldiers and 14,103 for civilians. He added, 'I report with great pleasure that we were able, during the year, to care for all American citizens who applied for treatment in our Out-Patient Department or for admission, and that those, who were not able to pay, were treated absolutely free.'

SEVENTEEN

Time to Go?

IN APRIL 1941, Aldebert and Clara de Chambrun invited the ranking American diplomat in Paris, Maynard Barnes, to lunch at 58 rue de Vaugirard. Barnes had been chargé d'affaires in Paris and at the Château de Candé since Ambassador Bullitt's departure a year earlier. The Chambruns had regarded him as a friend for some years, and they believed he understood France better than his colleagues. In Vichy, Bullitt's successor as US Ambassador to France, Admiral William D. Leahy, thought Barnes 'had a higher opinion of Laval than prevailed generally'. Over the modest, rationed lunch, Barnes told Clara and Aldebert that the United States would undoubtedly declare war on Germany. 'Please tell her not to delay much longer,' General de Chambrun admonished the diplomat. Clara shared her husband's view that America must, at last, fight for the Allied cause. This was a change from her conviction in October 1939 on a visit to the United States for the publication of her *History of Cincinnati*, when she told the *Cincinnati Times-Star*, 'Why should the United States even consider getting in the war? The question should be decided purely on the grounds of American trade and American rights ... As for the allies wanting America to enter the war, they already have more men to feed than they need to maintain what can only be a deadlock.' After the Germans broke the deadlock in the spring of 1940, the occupation of France made American intervention acceptable to Clara. At lunch, she pressed Barnes on American intentions. 'Do not worry,' he told her. 'We will be there even if England is beaten. We cannot afford, after the war, to see our trade cut off from Greece, Italy, Spain, France, Austria, Germany, Belgium, Holland, and the Scandinavian Peninsula.' Barnes, who was preparing to close the Paris embassy under orders from the Germans, asked whether the Chambruns wanted to send anything with him to the United States. Aldebert entrusted him with two Purdey shotguns that had been made for him in London. If the Germans found them hidden in the linen cupboard, he and Clara would be sent to prison.

While America remained neutral, Clara wrote, 'Extreme politeness was still the rule towards citizens of a country that Hitler hoped would stay out of active warfare.' She added, 'A considerable number of American businessmen remained and continued to work under these new conditions ... American residents contributed generously to the "Secours National [National Aid]," organized by the Marshal [Pétain], and which helped almost miraculously to keep up the morale of the unfortunate, and to give material help everywhere.'

On 14 April, considering the possibility of a changed American status in France, the American Hospital in Paris asked Count Aldebert de Chambrun to become its director. Although an American citizen, General de Chambrun was also French and, more importantly, connected to the upper reaches of French society and politics that the hospital might have to call upon to survive. Clara lamented that 14 April became the day 'my husband and I were obliged to separate'. She wrote, 'As he seldom does things by halves, he felt that, to begin with at least, he must take up his residence in the hospital building, learn the ropes and become acquainted with his large staff.' On 15 April, the hospital's medical board, including Dr Sumner Jackson, voted unanimously to appoint General de Chambrun president. But, like the American Library, the hospital needed a legal mechanism to spare it from German seizure if the United States and Germany broke relations. Aldebert adopted 'the same formula that proved so efficacious in the case of the American Library'. That is, he turned it over to a French organization, the French Red Cross. Officially, the American Hospital became the *Centre d'Hospitalisation pour Blessés de Guerre Libérés*, the Hospitalization Centre for Liberated War Wounded. General de Chambrun's policy was to provide medical care to anyone – American civilians, Belgian refugees, wounded British and French soldiers – except Germans.

As 1941 progressed, the United States sent more and more supplies to Britain. In March, Congress passed the Lend Lease Act to exchange British bases in the western hemisphere for surplus American destroyers. This made the United States, if not a combatant, at least a partisan in the struggle against the Nazis. A German U-boat sank the American merchantman *Robin Moor* on 21 May 1941 off Brazil. President Roosevelt condemned the attack as an 'act of piracy'. The following October, Nazi submarines torpedoed the American merchant ship *Kearney* and sank the US Navy destroyer *Reuben James* off the coast of Iceland. A hundred American sailors from the *Reuben James* died in frozen waters, giving rise to Woody Guthrie's song with its refrain, 'Tell me what were their names?/Did you have a friend on the good *Reuben James*?' Another folk song popular in the United States demanded, 'What are we waitin' on?'

> *When I think of the men and the ships going down*
> *While the Russians fight on across the dawn*
> *There's London in ruins and Paris in chains*
> *Good people, what are we waitin' on?*
> *Good people, what are we waitin' on?*

In this atmosphere, many Americans in Paris realized that their neutrality would not last much longer. Some decided to leave of their own accord, while others were persuaded by family and employers that remaining would be dangerous. On 5 May 1941, Edward A. Sumner informed the Rockefeller Foundation that 'a cable was sent to Miss Dorothy Reeder, Directress of the Library, recommending her immediate return to the United States, and a cable to the Comtesse de Chambrun, First Vice President, authorizing her to employ a non-American substitute for Miss Reeder. Whether Miss Reeder will be willing to accept this recommendation of the Board of Trustees remains to develop.' Dorothy Reeder did not want to leave, but she accepted the board's advice. In mid-May, she obtained permits to cross the Spanish border and booked a berth on a ship from Lisbon to the United States. Clara wrote, 'When our popular directress Miss Reeder departed, after a whirl of cocktail parties and as much cheer as bunches of souvenirs could give, she left on the desk which was to become mine, a card solemnly delegating me to fill her place together with the verbal encouragement: "Of course you will never be able to keep open."'

Clara, ignoring the board's recommendation that she find a non-American to run the library, decided to take on the job herself: 'Accordingly, here I was, obliged to add to my duties of directing the Library, a position for which no previous training fitted me. What I did possess though was long human experience, a sense of justice, perhaps not too frequent among my sex, and a sense of humor capable of carrying me over very rough ground.' Clara 'wangled' coal from unnamed suppliers, undoubtedly black marketeers, when other establishments were freezing. Nonetheless, there were times when the library lacked enough coal to heat the whole building and the staff worked in 'overcoats, mufflers and gloves'. When the Germans attempted to conscript male employees to work in Germany, she wrote stern letters stating that 'the individual designated was absolutely indispensible [sic] to the proper functioning of the Library'. Her appeals worked, even for Russian Boris Netchaeff after Germany invaded its former Soviet ally in June 1941.

As directress of the library, Clara became acquainted with one of the ugliest aspects of the occupation: *la dénonciation*. The German authorities were inundated with correspondence, often anonymous, from Parisians denouncing their fellow citizens as Jews, communists, Freemasons, black marketeers and *résistants*. Earning anyone's animosity could lead to denunciation and, thus, arrest. One day, a woman who was upset at having to wait in a long check-out queue at the library threatened to denounce 'our long-suffering librarian', Boris Netchaeff. Clara lost her temper. 'Take back your subscription and never darken our doors again,' she ordered. The woman began crying and, in what Clara called 'the greatest tribute ever given us in wartime', said, 'I cannot get along without the books I find here.' Clara told her, 'In that case, you may come back, apologize to Boris and take out your book.' The woman apologized.

When Maynard Barnes closed the American Embassy on 7 May, he entrusted the keys and the flag to Mme Simone Blanchard. The Frenchwoman, who had been housekeeper at the embassy since 1928, hid the Stars and Stripes to await the Americans' return. Barnes drove south to Vichy with Edward B. Close, managing governor of the American Hospital. After reporting to Ambassador Leahy, who had a low regard for him, he returned to Washington. Close sailed to the United States from Portugal, leaving the American Hospital's administration in the hands of Aldebert de Chambrun and its medical staff to Dr Sumner Jackson.

'After the departure of the Chargé d'Affaires,' Clara wrote, 'we bade adieu to almost all our American friends ... Most of the few that did not take that opportunity of leaving, remained to the bitter end – among them was John Robinson, head of the Coudert firm who stayed on because his wife was too seriously ill to be moved. His presence was a real asset as he managed to do so much for the relief of numerous families unable for different reasons to abandon the country.' No Americans in Paris knew it, but even their embassy in Vichy had prepared two emergency escape routes for its diplomats. One was by sea from a Mediterranean port, and the other was overland to Spain. The embassy had 'accumulated and buried in tins in concealed places along the roads enough gas to drive in our own cars over either route'.

Many Americans had no option other than to remain. The poet Pauline Avery Crawford, who had a prosthetic leg, could not make the arduous journey by land to Lisbon, point of embarkation for America-bound passenger ships and the Pan American Clipper aeroplanes. Charles Bedaux was too involved in his business schemes to return to the United States, where his company had not been under his control since the ill-fated Windsor affair of 1937. Sylvia Beach had not considered abandoning Paris or Adrienne Monnier since the first day of occupation, when the two booksellers had briefly contemplated escaping to the countryside. And Dr Sumner Jackson, whose wife and son were French, was responsible for the American Hospital's surgery department and for a growing Resistance network. The American community in Paris dwindled by the spring of 1941 to 2,000 men, women and children – no longer protected by an embassy in the city, but served by their own hospital, library, churches and charitable societies. If America and Germany went to war, most would be subject to internment. For a few, like Dr Jackson, the stakes were higher.

EIGHTEEN

New Perils in Paris

RENÉ DE CHAMBRUN BECAME CLOSER to Pierre Laval following his father-in-law's expulsion from office on 13 December 1940. Laval was spending more time with his family, including the Chambruns, in Paris. He let them know of his dissatisfaction with his successor, Admiral Jean-François Darlan. In May 1941, Darlan had gone to Berchtesgaden, where he acquiesced to Hitler's request for the use of French air bases in Syria against the British in Iraq. The British responded by occupying, with the Free French, Syria and Lebanon. Laval asked René to help him publicize his disapproval of Darlan's concessions to Hitler. René obliged enthusiastically. With the Paris press unlikely to publish criticism of Darlan, René called his friend, the American correspondent Ralph Heinzen of the United Press. 'I traveled to Vichy to get him,' René wrote. In his exclusive interview in Paris with Heinzen on 25 May, Laval 'stressed how greatly the policy of collaboration, as he understood it, differed from Darlan's policy of surrender – though he did not name Darlan directly'. Clara exhibited no misgivings over her son becoming, in effect, Laval's press secretary.

On 3 June 1941, Dr Jackson wrote to Edward B. Close in New York, 'I have just received word stating that I have not enough money in my account with the Chase Bank to pay the premium on my War Risk Insurance ($417) due July 1st. ... Would you mind having the dollars due me from the Hospital deposited to my credit at the Chase Bank N.Y.? ... apparently something has gone haywire with some of my holdings, so I shall rely on you to get this arranged for me.' Close immediately ordered the transfer of the money, confirming it at the end of July by letter through the Morgan Bank at Le Puy in the Unoccupied Zone.

Keeping his War Risk Insurance up to date was characteristic of the canny Maine native. His salary was only $150 a month, plus room and board at the hospital. If the worst happened to him, only an insurance policy would rescue his wife and son from penury. There was not much war risk in Paris, where the fight had ended on 14 June 1940 before it began. But for those who abetted prisoner escapes, the risk of death never abated. Dr Jackson was, so far, lucky. None of his fugitives had been captured, and no one had implicated him in anything. The Germans were either unable to check which prisoners failed to return to their camps from the hospital or accepted Dr Jackson's assurances they were dead. He kept his work secret even from his wife, Toquette, and his son, Phillip. In the meantime, he and Toquette enlisted in a separate Resistance operation from their flat in the avenue Foch. It assisted escapees, but its main objective was to convey military intelligence to London.

Communications between occupied France and the United States were censored and extremely difficult, but General de Chambrun kept the board in New York informed of important matters by censored transatlantic telegram. On 18 June, he cabled board president Nelson Dean Jay via RCA Radiogram in New York: 'JAY MORGAN BANK WALL STREET NEWYORK HOSPITAL RUNNING SMOOTHLY MAY DEFICIT SIXTY THOUSAND INCLUDING TWENTYFIVE THOUSAND FOR PERMANENT IMPROVEMENTS INFORM EDDY – CHUMBRAN [sic].' On 20 June, a letter from William Nelson Cromwell of New York's Sullivan and Cromwell law partnership to Dean Jay noted that 'practically all of the Board of Directors have, under existing conditions, departed from Paris and are temporarily residing in this city [New York] or elsewhere'. It was becoming impossible for governors in New York to administer a hospital in Paris, and all responsibility was devolving on General de Chambrun.

Via a Morgan & Cie internal cable on 9 July, de Chambrun told Dean Jay, 'June deficit francs 20,000 owing legal salary increase. Clara grateful remittance for library. Arrangement with [French] Information Center gives complete assurance protection. Inform [Max] Shoop.' The telegram arrived in Jay's office the next day, 10 July, two days before Max Shoop was scheduled to take the Pan Am Clipper to Lisbon. Shoop, as chairman of the hospital's legal committee, wrote to Jay on 10 July, 'Since the hospital has a registered office here [New York], and since most of the governors and officers are here, the corporation can be considered as being in the United States.' The US corporation would not be able to send financial support to the hospital if the United States and Germany went to war. That task would be assumed by René de Chambrun's French Information Centre in Paris.

Max Shoop was heading back to Europe to work for the American Red Cross. Covertly, he was employed as an agent of America's fledgling wartime intelligence bureau, the Coordinator for Information. Its London chief was Allen Dulles, one of Shoop's law partners at Sullivan and Cromwell. Dulles hated the Nazis so much that he had persuaded the firm in 1935, over the objections of his brother and senior partner, John Foster Dulles, to close Sullivan and Cromwell's Berlin office. America was not a belligerent, but gathering intelligence on German-occupied Europe seemed sensible for a country whose policies in Europe and the Far East were making its combat role in the Second World War all but inevitable.

On Wednesday, 27 August 1941, at seven in the evening, Clara and Aldebert were at home in the rue de Vaugirard when their telephone rang. It was an urgent call from the Versailles hospital. Their in-law, Pierre Laval, had been shot and was in a critical condition. A car came to the house a few minutes later to take the general and the countess to his bedside. 'His breathing was very difficult and prevented him from speaking clearly,' Aldebert remembered. 'The bullet had penetrated very deeply between his lung and his heart.' Clara had been fond of Laval since their first encounter before their children's wedding in 1935. 'He always paid me the courtesy of speaking in my presence as though I were a member of his family,' she said, 'and the very strong admiration I came to feel for him before my son married his daughter soon changed into respectfully sincere affection.' Now, Laval might be dying. He had taken, not one bullet, but two, from a 6.35 mm pistol. One hit his shoulder, and the other came within an inch of his heart. The culprit was one of the *résistants* of whom Clara already disapproved. This trespass on her family's safety made her even more critical of the violence that the Germans called 'terrorism'.

René de Chambrun joined his mother and father at the hospital. His wife, Josée, was at home with her mother in Châteldon. At 10 p.m., passing through a throng of journalists and Laval supporters, René was admitted to his father-in-law's room as the former prime minister asked his physician, Dr Barragué, for the telephone. 'The car has left for Châteldon,' he whispered to his wife, Jeanne. 'See you tomorrow. Kiss Josée.' To Aldebert, he said, 'I don't know how I'm getting on, but above all tell them that no harm must come to the man who shot me. He is young … He was certainly not the one responsible.'

The young man who had attempted to assassinate Laval a few hours earlier was Paul Colette, a militiaman in the collaborationist Legion of French Volunteers Against Bolshevism. *Time* magazine called him 'a tough 21-year-old patriot from Calvados, the applejack section of Normandy'. On the eve of the Legion's departure for the Russian front, Colette was one of many recruits at the Borgnies-Debordes barracks in Versailles. At about 5 p.m., Laval arrived to review the military parade. *Time* reported, 'When Paul Colette's rank swung past the reviewers, he simply stepped out of line, pulled out his German gun and let Laval have it over the heart and [pro-German journalist and politician Marcel] Déat have it in the arm and belly. The colonel of the barracks and another Legionnaire got hit too.' The Germans captured Colette immediately and accused him of being a communist, until he admitted he was a Free French supporter of General Charles de Gaulle. Suspecting the loyalty of other volunteers, the Germans cancelled the Legion's deployment to the Soviet Union.

Josée de Chambrun heard the news from Ralph Heinzen, the United Press correspondent and family friend in Vichy, at 8.30 p.m., an hour and a half before her father called. The car Laval sent drove her and her mother throughout the night. They reached 6-bis Place du Palais Bourbon, René and Josée's magnificent house behind the Chambre des

Députés, at ten the next morning. Aldebert, Clara and René took them immediately to the hospital, where Laval's recovery was proceeding slowly. He had a high temperature, and the family worried he might not survive. By late Saturday night, though, Jeanne Laval decided that, as Josée wrote in her diary, 'Papa is saved.' His health improved rapidly, and René de Chambrun felt confident enough to spend Monday at the horse races. Josée stayed away. 'I had taken a vow not to return there for a year.' It may have been her trade with God for her father's life. René, meanwhile, won a lot of money.

By the time Laval was well enough to leave Paris on 30 September and convalesce at home in Châteldon, the Laval and Chambrun families had become more intimate than ever. The association was costing Clara her reputation at home in America, but her first loyalties had always been to her family and to her obligations as she saw them. Her duty was to make life under occupation bearable for the readers at the American Library, the only public institution in German-occupied Europe where books in English circulated freely. She had helped to make the library 'a haven for French historians, philosophers, journalists and students'. That, she believed, was a more meaningful defiance of dictatorship than assassinations and bombings. Others saw it, not as defiance, but as collaboration.

On Memorial Day, 30 May, Paris's dwindling American community gathered in the American Cathedral on the rue George-V to remember their dead of the previous world war. Colonel Bentley Mott and the cathedral's organist, Lawrence K. Whipp, led the service. Afterwards, they trudged through the rain to lay wreaths at the Chapel of American War Heroes in the Suresnes cemetery above the city. When the United States armed its merchant marine fleet and introduced a peacetime draft in September 1941 for the first time in its history, no Americans in Paris could doubt their country was preparing for war.

In French North Africa, Robert Murphy was installing a network of spies under cover as consular officers nominally monitoring US food shipments. The American consular service lacked personnel qualified in intelligence, so Murphy had turned to 'General William J. ("Wild Bill") Donovan, Medal of Honor winner hero of Rainbow Division of

World War I fame'. Donovan was creating America's first peacetime overseas intelligence agency independent of the army and navy, first called the Coordinator for Information (COI). Donovan hived off a part of the COI, called it the Office of Strategic Services (OSS) and took the best agents with him. Murphy wrote, 'We surely were glad to welcome his representatives, being ourselves rank amateurs in the Intelligence field.' One of the twelve vice-consuls – or 'twelve apostles', as Murphy referred to them – dispatched to North Africa was Donald Coster, the ambulance driver whom Sumner Jackson had helped to escape from France in 1940.

The American Ambassador to France at Vichy, Admiral William Leahy, favoured the shipment of aid to North Africa of 'staples primarily intended for the Arabs, who were susceptible to German propaganda'. He disapproved of some of the spying that went with it. 'I did not know either Donovan or the O.S.S,' he wrote. 'Some of his agents were not entirely innocent of making trouble for the Embassy.' He was surprised that a lawyer from Chicago, Thomas G. Cassidy, was appointed as assistant naval attaché: 'I soon found he did not know which end of a boat went first and wondered what kind of officers the Navy was commissioning. Some time later I learned he was a secret O.S.S. agent planted in the American Embassy. Cassidy was a very good spy – capable and discreet.'

In November, Congress repealed the Neutrality Act of 1939 that most Americans had believed would keep them out of the war. The United States was, in President Roosevelt's words, the 'arsenal of democracy' against the Axis dictatorships. Although their embassy in Paris had closed in May, more than two thousand American citizens remained in the City of Light to endure with the French the privations of occupation. Some hoped America would stay out of the war so that they would not be arrested as enemy aliens. The rest longed for the American army to liberate them from German rule.

United Press correspondent Ralph Heinzen came to Paris from Vichy in September 1941 to write about the American Library, where he 'found both the reading and reference rooms crowded chiefly with French scholars. The files are intact, but since the armistice there has been a complete interruption of mails and no recent American books or magazines are available.' Heinzen noted that Clara had taken over the library on Dorothy Reeder's departure and enjoyed 'an exceptional position in European letters'. Heinzen may have been encouraged to write the article by his friend René de Chambrun. 'Gift books are distributed to prison camps and military hospitals,' he wrote. 'A special circulating library takes care of the reading needs of the British civilians interned in concentration camps at Besançon and Vittel.'

Heinzen also visited the American Hospital, writing that 'General de Chambrun slept in the hospital to protect that property until its status under occupation was definitely established.' He inspected one floor dedicated to military wounded. Of the civilian patients, there were equal numbers of Americans, French and British. He noted that Sumner Jackson had become chief of the medical staff following the departure of Dr Gros. 'Since General de Chambrun has assumed the management of the hospital, there has not been a vacant bed,' he wrote, discreetly avoiding the observation that the general and Dr Jackson kept the hospital full to deny the Germans a foothold they could use to assume complete control.

Aldebert and Clara de Chambrun directed the two leading American institutions in France, because the boards of both had fled to the United States. If Germany and the United States went to war, the Chambruns could not guarantee that their meticulous legal and financial planning would protect the hospital or the library. Rarely had the fate of an entire American community in wartime rested in the hands of two members of the same family. Clara and Aldebert waited to discover whether they could save the hospital, the library and the staffs of both on the day that American citizenship became anathema to the Nazi occupiers of Paris.

Many Americans had run out of money after more than a year under occupation, since the US Treasury had restricted the transfer of funds to German-occupied territory. A few turned for help to the American Hospital. On 6 November 1941, General de Chambrun sent a memorandum to Nelson Dean Jay and Edward B. Close that made it clear the hospital would live up to the purpose for which it had been founded in 1909: 'We have already been obliged to accept in the Hospital five American destitutes and it is my intention to do all I can for this category which may increase and which may become a heavy burden if nothing is done to help the countrymen which will necessarily be left over here either on account of their age or family obligations.'

De Chambrun's memo noted that shortages, which were affecting all of Paris, had become acute at the hospital. Everything from heating oil to bandages was in short supply. There were 250 patients, many still suffering the wounds of war, and the same number of staff, some of whom remained all night to work or to be on call for emergencies. While operating expenses were not in deficit, Aldebert noted the lack of 'stocks of all kind, especially linen, decreasing and no possibility of replacement'. He counselled that 'it seems advisable to stock in America linen which will be necessary in the Hospital in two or three years and which will be impossible to find in France after the war: linen for drawsheets, aprons, bath towels, face towels, kitchen towels, roller towels, cotton flannels for binders, Operating Room draping material (preferably blue), bed spreads, cotton tussor [silk] for beige curtains, kitchen aprons, blue gingham'. An order for American bedspreads that had been sent on the ship *Georgios Patamianos* in May did not arrive. General de Chambrun urged Jay and Close to send another shipment. By the time they could have done so, it was too late.

NINETEEN

Utopia in Les Landes

WHEN THE NEW YORK STOCK MARKET CRASHED in October 1929, Charles Bedaux concluded that the principles he had used successfully on the shop floor should be applied to the economy as a whole. This conception was not another money-making scheme by an immigrant huckster. It was, he insisted, the only way to save mankind from cyclical crashes, mass unemployment and war. The efficiency engineer for industry conceived an efficiency theory for society. To replace the political and economic ideologies of his time – communism, capitalism, fascism and Nazism – he devised his own 'ism', 'equivalism'. Although Bedaux himself never clearly formulated or wrote down the basis of his theory, he defined equivalism as 'capitalism in communism'. He described it to his son, Charles Emile, as 'Distribution of products pro-rata of the contribution of each, while assuring a decent living from the cradle to the grave.' (Charles Emile, having graduated in engineering from Yale University, had come to France in 1939 to work for his father.) The bank failures that followed the Great Crash convinced Bedaux that money was fraud, not unlike Proudhon's anarchist concept of property as theft. Bedaux asserted that history offered no examples of a stable currency. Underwriting money with gold and other precious metals had not prevented devaluations that deprived working people of the wealth they had earned. Even gold coins were debased, he said, by rulers who mixed them with alloy or clipped their size. His solution was to make the medium of exchange a unit of human energy – calibrated as the Bex, a slightly more sophisticated 'B' unit for measuring assembly line work that added a factor for mental labour. Under equivalism, no one would earn less than sixty Bex per hour – the minimum for a worker and his family to maintain an average living. With no more dollars, pounds or francs, producers and consumers would exchange goods and services measured in units of work. Bedaux would eliminate the 'parasite' class of landlords, speculators, agents and traders, who produced nothing, took most of the wealth and were a drag on economic efficiency.

In 1939, Bedaux had proposed that Germany, short of gold reserves, be the first state to back its currency with the Bex. He met Joachim von Ribbentrop at his Salzburg villa, with Joseph von Ledebur and Otto Abetz, in August 1939. Ribbentrop accepted Bedaux's claim that human energy was a more reliable monetary medium than the gold used by the democracies of the West. He hinted that Germany might adopt some version of the Bex to back the Reichsmark. While the two men waxed on about economics, a secretary interrupted their conversation with an urgent message. Ribbentrop read it and exclaimed, in one of history's understatements, 'This may change everything!' The interview ended abruptly.

Bedaux went from Salzburg to Berlin to see Hjalmar Schacht, whom he had met in 1937 as minister of economic affairs and head of the Reichsbank. Hitler had since dismissed Schacht for criticizing *Kristallnacht*, the night of 10 November 1938, when thousands of Jewish synagogues, shops and houses were destroyed and Jews viciously attacked in Germany. Schacht declined Bedaux's invitation to lunch and suggested instead that they meet for dinner in a well-known Berlin restaurant. At dinner, Bedaux told Schacht of his discussions with Ribbentrop on backing the Reichsmark with the Bex. Schacht gave Bedaux a sobering response: 'Monsieur, are you an engineer, an economist or a fool? If von Ribbentrop could lay hands on the gold you Americans have in Fort Knox, Germany's money would rest on that gold and not on your silly unit of human energy.' As Schacht continued what became a tirade, Berlin's chief of police entered the restaurant and arrested him. It turned out the regime had forbidden him to speak to foreigners and to appear in public. By the time Schacht was released from house arrest three days later, Bedaux was back in France.

There, he read why Ribbentrop had left him without explanation. He had flown to Moscow to sign the Ribbentrop–Molotov Pact, whose secret provisions called for dividing Poland between the Nazi and Soviet dictatorships.

On 1 September, as Germany and the Soviet Union invaded Poland, Bedaux told his engineers in Lyons, 'This war will not be like the others, whole populations will be exterminated. And when it is over the same social problems will still be there, the very ones that these horrible criminals had exploited to push people to kill each other.' His goal, he said, was to preserve something from the conflagration to rebuild the post-war world.

The first French official Bedaux converted to equivalism was Maréchal Philippe Pétain. When Bedaux saw him at Vichy in October 1940 about the Kenadsa mines, Pétain seemed unexpectedly responsive to Bedaux's theory. Bedaux recalled, 'He understood nothing whatever about equivalism, but he gave me a very good lecture on it. He takes your words and he amplifies very well without understanding.' Bedaux asked for authorization to experiment on the town of Roquefort in the Department of Les Landes. It was a town Bedaux visited before the war, when he advised its paper mill, the Société des Papeteries de Roquefort. Pétain agreed that Bedaux could proceed, but only with the inhabitants' consent. Bedaux told him he already had it.

Roquefort lay inland from the Atlantic coast between Spain and Bordeaux, about ninety miles north of Bayonne. The Franco-German demarcation line between Occupied and Unoccupied France cut through the town. Bedaux said it had 'a complete cycle in a small sphere', where 2,200 inhabitants worked in forestry, agriculture, sheep herding and small industry. There were also artisans and a few artists. Bedaux and his engineers went to Roquefort in March 1941. The engineers lived in the village, and Bedaux rented a comfortable villa nearby in Lencouacq.

Bedaux undertook the project with his usual thoroughness, assigning efficiency experts to study all aspects of Roquefort's production and consumption. They examined income distribution, trade, labour efficiency and housing. They replaced woodsmen's shacks with modern dwellings. Bedaux himself worked at the paper mill, which was selling mainly to the German occupier. One day, when he and chief engineer Marcel Grolleau argued about the running of the plant, Bedaux shouted abuse at him. Grolleau quit. Bedaux returned to Candé at the weekend and called Grolleau to apologize. They resumed work at Roquefort, but Bedaux left the project's minutiae to Grolleau and the other engineers.

Grolleau, an experienced Touraine *forestier* before he met Bedaux, chopped swathes through the pine forests to create firebreaks. The wood supplied the mill, and he replenished it with fast-growing leucanea pines. The Bedaux model accomplished some of its objectives. Roquefort achieved full employment, the paper mill was working to capacity, the forest became sustainable and the town supplied its own fuel. Practical methods of running the factory and forest maintenance may have had more impact than equivalist theory.

Observers that the Germans sent to Roquefort made no criticisms of Bedaux's methods, but they complained Vichy had made a mistake in assigning the venture to an American. American citizenship, until now an asset in Nazi-occupied France, was about to become a liability.

Charles Bedaux worked most of August on France's planned Trans-Sahara railway, an old imperial goal that by the beginning of the war extended a mere 40 miles from the Algerian port of Nemours to the Moroccan border. Bedaux connected the line to another stretch that had been built in 1931 for manganese mines in the desert at Boufra. His efforts throughout the late summer to patch together a Sahara rail network achieved little. There were difficulties as well at the Kenadsa mines, where he failed to increase coal production. He went to Algiers and paid another visit to Robert Murphy at the US Consulate.

Bedaux was becoming one of Murphy's more useful sources on French politics. Murphy reported to Washington that Bedaux told him that Admiral Jean-François Darlan, whom Pétain had promoted to vice-premier in February, was 'sold lock, stock and barrel to the Germans, that his policy has been based on a belief in the ultimate German victory, but that at present he is extremely uneasy that he may be backing the wrong horse ... He said that of French public men today

General Weygand impressed him as about the only prominent one who had character to keep his word.' Bedaux also thought that his friend Pierre Laval would not soon return to office under Pétain. While receiving political intelligence and analysis from Bedaux, Murphy did not reciprocate with American support for schemes in Vichy-controlled territories that might be useful to Germany.

On 29 September 1941, Bedaux saw Robert Murphy again in Algeria. This time, Murphy asked him to meet him at 'the little nine-hole golf course near Algiers, a perfect place for security-proof discussions'. Like Abetz in Paris, Murphy may have been avoiding the bugging devices that the war had introduced to most diplomatic missions. Murphy warned Bedaux that his work at Kenadsa might be curtailed, explaining that by January 1942 'the roster of participants in the war, and the situation in North Africa, will have changed'. On the same day, the American Embassy in Vichy cabled the secretary of state about Bedaux, who 'let it be known that he is cooperating on friendly terms with the Nazis in developing the trans-Saharan railway. His particular interest pertains to the neighborhood of Colomb-Béchar, which is a mining center. Several months ago, he stated rather boastfully that he was closely connected with Abetz and other Nazis in the Paris region, and he also stated that in his opinion (and with some satisfaction) that the war would be won by Germany.'

TWENTY

To Resist, to Collaborate or to Endure

IN PARIS, SOME OF THE WOMEN AND MEN Sylvia Beach loved most were risking their lives to protest or resist the occupation. 'There were a few Nazi sympathizers in Paris, called "collabos",' she wrote, 'but they were the exception. Everybody we knew was for resistance.' One of them was the daughter of her friends Henri and Hélène Hoppenot. Henri Hoppenot was the French diplomat who had arranged, at Adrienne's request, documents for Arthur Koestler to escape from Paris in 1940. He was also an author and librettist, while Hélène was an accomplished photographer. Their teenage daughter, Violaine, had been a subscriber at Shakespeare and Company's lending library for years. Sylvia had written to her own father on 27 February 1940 about her 'young friend Violaine who was named after [Paul] Claudel's play "La Jeune Fille Violaine" and prefers politics to poetry'. Claudel, a favorite in Odéonia, was Violaine's godfather. Encouraged by Sylvia, Violaine Hoppenot had been admitted to do postgraduate study in America. But her preference for politics over poetry took her into the Resistance, carrying messages on her bicycle past the German troops in Paris and distributing banned literature. Another friend, the writer Jean Prévost, had left Paris to become a Resistance fighter in the mountains of eastern France.

Sylvia and Adrienne's friend and supporter, 69-year-old Paul Valéry, was publicly at odds with the Nazis. When the philosopher Henri

Bergson died on 4 January 1941, Valéry bravely delivered the eulogy. He praised his Jewish friend and Nobel Laureate at the Académie Française on 9 January in full view of collaborators who would report his words to the Germans. He said of Bergson, 'He was the pride of our company.' Born in France in 1859, Bergson was the son of an Anglo-Irish mother and a father who was Polish, Jewish and a musician. When Vichy offered to make Bergson one of the 'special' Jews whose cultural and scientific accomplishments exempted them from discriminatory laws, he declined. Arthur Koestler admired him, and the Nazis hated him. Valéry said Bergson was a 'very pure, truly superior figure of the thinking man, and perhaps one of the last men who had exclusively, profoundly and exceptionally thought, in an epoch when the world goes on thinking less and less'.

Sylvia, who had supported the Nazis' enemies in Spain, neither cooperated with nor appeased the occupiers. She consorted with intellectual opponents of the Nazis like Valéry and *résistants* like Violaine Hoppenot and Jean Prévost. At Shakespeare and Company, she refused to dismiss her Jewish volunteer assistant, 27-year-old Françoise Bernheim. Bernheim was taking a degree in Sanskrit until the University of Paris acquiesced to German pressure to expel its Jewish students. A sympathetic professor allowed Françoise to continue her studies clandestinely.

Françoise and Sylvia politely served Germans who came to Shakespeare and Company in search of English books. Some of the browsers were from the Gestapo. 'I wasn't on good terms with these Germans,' Sylvia said. 'But they came to my shop before we closed and asked to look at my theatrical books. And I showed them all Gordon Craig's books. Then I said, "You know, it's a disgrace for you to have imprisoned Gordon Craig and his wife and little child." And they said, "Oh, we'll get him out."' The son of famed English actress Ellen Terry, Edward Gordon Craig was a respected actor and theatre critic. Shakespeare and Company had sold his theatrical magazine, *Mask*, until it ceased publication in 1929. The Germans had interned him, although he was nearly seventy, along with the other British subjects in France at the beginning of the occupation. The Gestapo men returned to the bookshop with another officer, who told Sylvia to prepare a report on the Craigs that verified they were not Jewish and bring it to Gestapo headquarters. Sylvia complied, and the Gestapo officer promised her the Craigs would be freed by Christmas.

Sylvia and Adrienne closed their shops for the summer holidays. Adrienne joined her family in their thatched cottage near the village of Rocfoin north of Chartres, and Sylvia went to La Salle du Roc. On 14 August 1941, she wrote from Bourré to Carlotta Welles Briggs in California, 'While Rome burns, and everything else, I think you can't do better than play the fiddle. Meanwhile I am a war profiteer. That's plain enough, what with all my holidays in your beautiful place.' She was pleased that a neighbour named Baptiste was supplying her with fresh vegetables for which she did not have to queue for hours. 'It is cool and windy and sometimes rainy here but the flowers in the border are as gay as can be and you know how the fountain and the green-lawn and the trees are swell at this time of year – and at all times.' Alone in the country, Sylvia catalogued Carlotta's books. Country life had minor inconveniences: 'There's a magpie in the village who is going to be for someone's dinner if it doesn't stop flying into rooms and steal-ing anything it can lay its hands on. Trinkets or a whole cheese, the coiffeuse says, disappear in the magpie's secret cache.' The corn was growing well, 'but there are no lima beans this year'. Sylvia's First World War expertise from working the land as a Volontaire Agricole served her well with the flowers and vegetables on Carlotta's land. In the same letter, she sent sad news of the Armenian friend Carlotta had asked her to visit in November 1940: 'Your friend Mme Barseghian died on May 19th. Her son is a prisoner. The neighbors told me all about them. An operation on her eyes was unsuccessful.' She wrote that Marcel and Gertrude de Gallaix, who were also using the house, would return 'soon after the 15th when I shall be going back to town'. The two German officers assigned to live in the house in 1940 must have left by the time of Sylvia's stay, because her letters did not refer to them.

Eleven days later, Sylvia returned to Carlotta's house near Bourré. On 25 August, she wrote to Adrienne Monnier,

Food is missing completely in this countryside – not a chicken nor eggs nor butter nor cheese nor rabbits ... But I have been to all my

relations here to prostrate myself to have a chicken, a duck, a goose
with no result ... One may give me some eggs to be crushed on the
trip to Paris with the mob I'll find on the trains at the end of the
month.

I hope that you have taken your vacation and that you are rested
like me. You need it after all the months of exhaustion and privation to stand another winter of the kind that awaits us ... Until Saturday night at 8 o'clock, I kiss you, Sylvia.

Back in Paris, Sylvia saw more of her friend Sarah Watson. Born in
South Carolina in 1885, Miss Watson had lived in France since 1918
and was directress of the students' hostel for girls in Paris, the Foyer
International des Etudiantes, in the boulevard Saint-Michel. She and
Sylvia met occasionally for lunch in the hostel's cafeteria. Their views
on the Nazis were identical. Miss Watson wrote home, in words that
might have come from almost any American in occupied Paris, 'If only
America can wake up before it is too late, if she can realize this is not
just another war – it is a new religion that is conquering the world.'

The last letter that Sylvia's sisters received from her was sent in June
1941. A parcel of clothing that they sent her never arrived, because
the British were seizing packages sent from the United States to France.
Holly posted a letter to Sylvia in September, but it 'was returned to me
unopened'. George Antheil, Ernest Hemingway, Archibald MacLeish
and other friends from her Golden Age in the 1920s wrote to her as
well, but their letters came back. Paris was increasingly closed off, and
Sylvia was closed off with it.

In the summer of 1941, Charles Bedaux was working on his equivalism project at Roquefort in Les Landes. His *Ausweis* from Otto Abetz
allowed him to return to the Occupied Zone for weekends with Fern
at the Chateau de Candé. At one of Candé's lavish dinner parties, a
German guest mentioned that the Luftwaffe planned to bomb the
British petroleum refinery at Abadan. This information troubled
Bedaux, who had studied the refinery on the Iranian shore of the
Persian Gulf for its owners, Britain's Anglo-Iranian Oil Company, in
1937. In July 1939, he had advised Anglo-Iranian's chairman, Lord

Cadman, in London to protect the oil refinery from bombardment. Abadan, a prime asset in war and peace, was the world's largest refinery with production of twelve million tons of fuel a year. Much of the oil came by pipeline from British-owned fields in Iraq. Petrol and lubricants from Abadan were vital to the British war machine in Iraq, Transjordan, Palestine and Egypt. Without it, Britain's tanks and warplanes could neither deter the indigenous populations from seeking independence nor face the German threat.

To the German high command, denying petrol to Britain's Middle East forces made military sense. A pro-German faction of the Iraqi officer corps under politician Rashid Ali al-Gailani had just seized power in Baghdad and sought German support against the British occupier. Syria and Lebanon were in the hands of French officers loyal to the Vichy regime, and Admiral Darlan granted the Germans access to Syrian airfields within range of Abadan. An air raid was as feasible as the recent Italian attack from Libya on Britain's smaller refinery at Haifa in Palestine. Bedaux argued strongly against destroying Abadan and asked the Germans to take a long-term view of Abadan's possibilities. His solution for Germany was not to destroy Abadan, but to capture it.

His theory was simple. If German troops invaded Iraq from Vichy Syria to support the anti-British coup, they could move on Iran and take Abadan for themselves. Bedaux's rationale for saving Abadan, he said, had less to do with the war than the peace: 'I advanced the philosophy of first thinking that to prevent it was continental logic. My idea was that Continental Europe would rebuild after the war only as fast as continental oil could be supplied, and that with its twelve million tons a year, Abadan was the heart of continental oil, continental gasoline.' He revived the scheme he had presented to Lord Cadman in 1939 to protect the refinery and its Iraqi pipeline by filling them with liquid sand. The Germans, whose experience of Bedauxizing some of their factories had been positive, listened. They discussed it with him in the summer and invited him in November 1941 for planning sessions in Berlin with Albert Speer, the minister of armaments and munitions. With technical experts, Bedaux and Speer went over plans to save Abadan for Germany. Bedaux had already worked it out.

Grains manufactured from sandstone, rather than harder natural desert sand, could be liquidized and fed into the pipes to absorb the shock of bombardment. He convinced Speer the operation could be accomplished in three days. When the refinery was finally safe from bombing, workers would need only three weeks to remove the sand. Bedaux later justified his collaboration with the Germans over Abadan: 'My idea was that in introducing in their minds the idea of preserving, I would remove from their minds the idea of destroying.' The delay made an Abadan attack less likely, because in the meantime Britain had removed the military junta in Iraq and forced the Vichy French out of Syria and Lebanon.

There were reports that Bedaux offered to sabotage Abadan *for* the Germans by filling the refinery with sand to render it unworkable. Such an operation would have denied Britain the petrol it needed to confront General Erwin Rommel's *Afrikakorps* in Italian Libya. No sabotage took place. Bedaux claimed that no one in Berlin would see him about the Abadan project. His invitation had come through German lawyer Alois Westrick, whom Bedaux had known from pre-war soirées at the American Embassy in Berlin. On arrival, Bedaux checked into Berlin's Hotel Adlon at his own expense. While Westrick kept him waiting, Bedaux saw an engineer from his old German company. The man told him that productivity in the German firms he advised had dropped by a third since the war began, which he attributed to low morale among the workers. Dr Emil Georg von Stauss, the banker in charge of nationalized companies whom Bedaux had met in 1937, invited him to his country house for a weekend. Back in Berlin, the German Production Ministry asked for his recommendations for the Bor copper mines in Yugoslavia. Bedaux said that the German Bedaux company, which the Germans owned, could deal with it. 'What about French Bedaux?' an official asked him. Bedaux became evasive, but promised to look into it. Janet Flanner wrote that Bedaux had 'pepped up' copper production at Bor for the Nazis, an accusation he denied.

In Berlin, Bedaux took up the cause of his old friend, Count Joseph von Ledebur. After Germany's invasion of the Soviet Union on 22 June 1941, von Ledebur had been sent to the Russian front. Bedaux used what leverage he had with German officialdom to persuade them that Ledebur was more important to the successful running of the French occupation than as one of thousands of captains in the Russian theatre of operations. Bargaining his expertise for Ledebur's freedom, he appeared to wield some influence. But, as with his other requests to the Nazis, he was advised to wait.

On 21 November, Bedaux entertained the wife and daughter of Dr Franz Medicus to tea at the Adlon. Mrs Medicus, unlike her husband in Paris, was indiscreet enough to criticize the Nazis. She insisted to Bedaux that Germany must not be allowed to win the war. He left Berlin four days later. Back in France, he told Pierre Laval, 'Many people in Germany who were in the know, now after the first retreat on the Russian front, not only didn't think Germany would win the war but opposed it because victory meant perpetuation of Nazi rule.' Laval disagreed, and Bedaux claimed to have answered, 'You will be sorry.'

Although Bedaux insisted Abadan had not been on the agenda during his three weeks in the German capital, the US government opened a file on its expatriate citizen-entrepreneur. His activities came under the scrutiny of several American government agencies, including the Treasury, State Department and the Office of Naval Intelligence. Federal Bureau of Investigation Director J. Edgar Hoover took a personal interest in Bedaux's activities.

Florence Jay Gould arrived late for her weekly salon of German and French writers in her suite at the Hôtel Bristol, where many Americans were still living under the nominal protection of the US Embassy. When one of her guests asked what had delayed her, the society beauty declared, 'The Paris stock market has just crashed. I think it's a bad sign: America is going to enter the war.' Outside her circle of German and collaborationist *littérateurs*, the prospect of American entering the war to defeat the Nazis was not at all unwelcome.

Charles Bedaux had regularly briefed both Counsellor Robert Murphy and First Secretary S. Pinckney Tuck at the American Embassy in Vichy. 'Kippy' Tuck's telegram of 24 September 1941, in which he wrote that Bedaux 'let it be known that he is cooperating on friendly terms with the Nazis', was already part of an expanding file. Adding to the dossier was testimony from Charles and Fern's friends Herman and Katherine Rogers, at whose request he had invited Wallis Simpson and the Duke of Windsor to Candé in 1937. The Rogers were in Portugal in August 1941 to book passage home to the United States. A State Department official met them 'by chance' in Lisbon on 15 August, but he waited three months, until 24 November, to send a memorandum to his superiors. (It may not have been until then that he learned of Washington's interest in Bedaux.) Katherine Rogers denounced Bedaux to the diplomat: 'Mrs. Rogers stated that she had definite information that Mr. Bedaux was using his talents on behalf of the Germans in acquiring for the account of certain German individuals and for himself large properties in and about Paris, and that he traveled about without apparent restrictions and with all indications that he was *persona grata* to the German occupying forces.' This was an unexpected turn in the friendship between the Bedaux and Rogers families. Herman Rogers had crossed British Columbia with Bedaux, Katherine had been a close friend of Fern's and both couples had been witnesses at the Duke and Duchess of Windsor's wedding. Now, the Rogers were denouncing him to the American government as a Nazi collaborator.

The American official who sent this memorandum recalled meeting Bedaux in 1939 'in Rome, Italy, negotiating a contract with the Italian Government and [he] was introduced to attachés of our Embassy by the local representative of the Chase National Bank, Mr. Carlo Ruggieri, who entertained extensively for him'. The official offered 'to elaborate this memorandum if it is found to be of interest'. Of Bedaux, he added, 'He is a man of tremendous energy and apparent ability in his field of work.'

Bedaux was unaware of the interest he had aroused in Washington. From Candé on 6 December 1941, he wrote a two-page, single-spaced, typed letter to the American Consul General in Lisbon, Worthington E. Hagerman. Hagerman, while posted to France in 1940, had been the second of many diplomats to take up residence at Candé and had given Bedaux his drawings of the chateau. Bedaux's letter to him concerned his income tax obligations. The tone was cordial, between two men who appeared to be on good terms. He wrote,

Dear Mr. Hagerman,

On my return from a series of journeys that have kept me away from August 15th to November 30th (Africa, Belgium, Holland and Germany), I find your letter of November 24th. In it I see a deep preoccupation in the minds of you and Mr. [Hugh] Fullerton regarding our fate and your strong desire to see us set rightly [sic].

This preoccupation of both of you is the result of friendship born during the one year when we gave our home of Candé to the United States government for the Embassy. My wife and I are deeply touched by it ...

In 1937 the Treasury Department inquired into our tax position regarding income from sources outside of the United States. As our business is centered in Amsterdam, Holland, and as I have always believed and still do that our entire income is the product of our work and therefore earned income I invited the Treasury Dept., Mr. B. Wait, to order an examination of our books in Amsterdam. This was in December, 1937.

This was done. I was very ill in a hospital of Munich at the time, but in spite of the doctors [sic] orders I received the examiner Mr. Francis T. Smith on two occasions and answered his questions to the best of my ability.

Later, charges for back taxes were made by the Treasury Department. I met them by continuing to contend that in our type of work all our income can only be earned.

Bedaux offered to put his case before the 'highest court in the land'. He wrote that he had ordered his income from most sources to be set aside to pay the tax demand if he lost the case. He mentioned that the Germans had seized his five companies in Amsterdam, the core of his international business. They were being run by a German engineer 'whose health and faculties do not permit energetic management.' In France and Belgium, though, his companies were not confiscated. They 'are doing more business now than they ever did in peace time, this in spite of the defeat of the two countries above named. To this I have added the North African business opened by me during the year. This is a further proof that our income resulting from our work is earned.' His energies on his recent Berlin trip were directed to replacing the manager in Holland, and he believed that he 'will succeed fairly soon. It will enable me to meet our American tax obligations in full under the conditions described above.'

The letter noted that Hagerman had been urging Bedaux to return to the United States or risk losing his American citizenship. Bedaux responded that his citizenship could not be taken away for two reasons:

I have not yet been abroad for a full five years, the date being November 1st, 1942.

I am making a protracted stay abroad to serve an interest vital to the United States, namely the payment of income taxes the nature and amount of which have not yet been determined, taxes that cannot be paid unless I secure an alteration of the confiscatory measures that have been taken against me by Germany. Further I intend when the whole situation has been settled permanently to reside in the United States.

If my interpretation of the two above points is not correct I wish the American Government to know that I would rather lose my citizenship to fight for it later on than to place myself in the position where I would be unable, probably for all times, to meet my tax obligations.

He pointed out that his wife's citizenship 'cannot be seriously challenged'. Fern, born in the United States, had American ancestors dating back to 1630. He added that his son, Charles Emile, had been born in the United States and could not be deprived of his citizenship. Charles Emile was with him in France, he wrote, working 'in a remote village of occupied France, la Haye Descartes'. His son did not know until 4

December that the US consuls had left the Occupied Zone. 'He wishes to return to the United States and asks your advice on how he should proceed.'

Bedaux wrote the letter on Saturday, 6 December 1941. On Sunday the 7th, he and Fern set out on the road to Roquefort. She was going to stay with him at his rented villa in Lencouacq to see his utopian experiment in 'equivalism' at work. They stopped for the night in Bordeaux, which, like Candé, was in the Occupied Zone. They went to Les Landes, where Bedaux mailed the letter to Hagerman. On Sunday morning, when Bedaux mailed the letter, the Empire of Japan bombed the American fleet at Pearl Harbor. What President Roosevelt would shortly call the 'day that will live in infamy' was about to transform Americans in Paris from protected neutrals into enemies of the Third Reich. Even if Bedaux had obeyed Hagerman's request to return home to the United States, it was now – as for the rest of the Americans in occupied France – too late.

TWENTY-ONE

Enemy Aliens

GERMANY DECLARED WAR ON THE UNITED STATES on 11 December 1941, four days after the Japanese bombed Pearl Harbor. The Germans ordered all American citizens in the Occupied Zone to register with the nearest German Kommandatur by 6 p.m. on 17 December. As the deadline passed, the Nazis arrested 340 American men under the age of 60. Among them were the American Cathedral's organist, Lawrence K. Whipp, and Dr Morris Sanders of the American Hospital. Dr Sumner Jackson, although liable to internment at age 56, 'was permitted to remain at liberty'. Ninety-five of the internees were Jewish, whose American citizenship was respected by the Germans. The men were installed at Besançon in crude wooden shacks without heat or plumbing. Like the British internees in 1940, they were soon moved to better quarters at Frontstalag 122 near Compiègne. Compiègne, where Germany and France had signed the Armistices of 1918 and 1940, lay in a forest 50 miles north of Paris. Frontstalag 122, also called the Royallieu Camp, had been the barracks of a Moroccan Spahi regiment. It had heat, running water and kitchens. The Germans divided the camp into sections for enemy aliens, political prisoners, Africans, gypsies, Freemasons and European Jews.

The first American to be released was Gething C. Miller, a friend of René de Chambrun and the lawyer who had represented the defendants in the Teapot Dome oil scandal of the 1920s. 'He came to tell me all the requirements of his compatriots who needed practically everything,' René recalled. 'Josée visited the managers of two or three Paris

Department Stores and was able to buy a great amount of supplies which had been concealed from the French public and the Germans and these we had delivered to the camp in Compiègne through the Red Cross.'

The Germans held the Americans while they determined how Washington treated Axis citizens in the United States. Charles Bedaux was not interned, but the Germans put him and Fern under house arrest at the Château de Candé. They cancelled his 'equivalism' experiment at Roquefort, and they seized his company files and other assets in France and the Netherlands. His friends in the German administration, Dr Franz Medicus and Ambassador Otto Abetz, were powerless to protect him. One week after the Nazis interned the 340 Americans, they deported the last American journalists in Paris, Edward Haffell of the *New York Herald Tribune*, Louis Harl of the International News Service and Philip Whitcomb of the Associated Press, to southern Germany. There, the reporters were interned with other American correspondents to await repatriation to the United States. The Germans did not disturb the rest of the Americans in Paris.

A distinguished, 70-year-old English gentleman walked into Shakespeare and Company on 17 December, ten days after Pearl Harbor and the final day for Americans to register at the Kommandatur. Sylvia Beach had known him since 1920 and had sold his books and magazines. The sudden appearance of Edward Gordon Craig, who had been an actor and director before he became a writer, could not have been more welcome. Sylvia had last seen him before his internment with his wife, their child and the rest of the British community in June 1940. Her persistence with the Gestapo brought his release, as the Gestapo officer had promised her, before Christmas. Craig was grateful and gave her a copy of Enid Rose's *Gordon Craig and the Theatre: A Record and an Interpretation* that he signed 'to Sylvia from E.G.C. December 17th, 1941'. The German who kept his promise to release the Craigs sent them coal for the fireplace in their hotel room, as well as winter clothing and a Christmas tree. Not all Germans were as obliging.

'My German customers were always rare, but of course after I was classified as "the enemy," they stopped coming altogether – until a last outstanding visit ended the series,' Sylvia wrote in her memoir. 'A high-ranking German officer, who had got out of a huge grey military car, stopped to look at a copy of *Finnegans Wake* that was in the window.' The officer came into the shop and said to Sylvia in fluent English, 'I want that copy of *Finnegans Wake* you've got in the window.' She recalled the encounter in an interview: '"Well," I said, "that's the only copy left in Paris, and you can't have it ... You don't understand that anyhow. You don't know Joyce." And he said, "But we admire James Joyce very much in Germany." He was very angry, and he went out and got into his great car, his great military car, surrounded with other fellows in helmets and drove away.'

At Christmas, Sylvia was unable to communicate with her family in the United States. For friends in Paris, she made a list of Christmas presents: chocolates, which rationing had turned into luxuries, for Adrienne and her assistant, an aspiring young writer named Maurice Saillet, as well as to Adrienne's mother and Paul Valéry's wife, Jeannie Gobillard. Françoise Bernheim, the 29-year-old Jewish volunteer at Shakespeare and Company, received from Sylvia a bound copy of *Ulysses*. Then, just after Christmas, the Wehrmacht officer who had demanded Sylvia's only copy of *Finnegans Wake* returned.

He came back again in about ten days, and he said, 'Your copy of *Finnegans Wake* is gone from the window. What did you do with it?' I said, 'I've put it away. It's for me.' He was so furious. He said, 'Well, you know, we're coming this afternoon to confiscate all your goods.' I said, 'Very well. Do so.' And he said, 'Now, will you sell *Finnegans Wake*?' And I said, 'Not at all. Come along.' So, he disappeared in a rage, booming down the street. The only people who had cars in Paris were the Germans. I immediately had everything removed from my shop. In about two hours, there wasn't a book left in it, not only *Finnegans Wake* but everything else disappeared. And the concierge [Mme Allier] told me to put everything in an empty apartment in that house. So, we piled up the stairs with all these things in clothes baskets. All my friends came rushing to the rescue, all my French friends, the ones who were left. And we hid everything upstairs.

Josephine Baker, the quintessential American Parisian, spy for French intelligence and anti-Nazi *résistante*.

William C. Bullitt, United States Ambassador to France 1936–1940. He pleaded with his friend, President Franklin Roosevelt, to save France.

Roosevelt, Marguerite LeHand and William C. Bullitt, July 22, 1940. "Missy" LeHand was Bullitt's sometime mistress, and FDR was disappointed that Bullitt did not marry her.

Myrsine and Helene Moschos and Sylvia Beach next to Ernest Hemingway, outside Shakespeare and Co. at 12 rue de l'Odéon for Sylvia's birthday party in March 1928.

(*Left to right*) James Joyce, Sylvia Beach and Adrienne Monnier in Shakespeare and Co., 1938.

Sylvia Beach in Shakespeare
and Co., May 1941, during
the Battle of France.

Sylvia Beach decorates the bookshop's
window, May 1941.

Adrienne Monnier in La Maison des
Amis des Livres.

Countess Clara Longworth de Chambrun (*far right*) in the American Library in Paris.

Clara fought to keep the library open throughout the occupation.

Photo Associated Press

AMERICAN LIBRARY IN PARIS

9, Rue de Téhéran (8°)

Tel. : Carnot 28 - 10   (Open daily 1.30 to 7 p.m.)

Accessible by Metros : **Miromesnil-Villiers**
Autobus : **AB, AH, AS,** B, S, U, D, 15, 16, 17, 28, 33, 36, 37, 38

ALL READING ROOMS ARE FREE

An information card for the American Library.

René de Chambrun, an American citizen and the first lawyer admitted to the bar in both France and New York, with Josée Laval at the time of their engagement in 1935.

Clara's house at the corner of the Luxembourg Gardens. The small villa it overlooks is heavily fortified by the Luftwaffe.

Pierre Laval (*third from left*) leaving the Château de Châteldon, 1942. Josée de Chambrum, his daughter, and her husband René are either side of him.

Charles Bedaux and his wife, Fern, South Africa, 1939.

Charles and Fern Bedaux.

J. Edgar Hoover, Director of the FBI who took an interest in Bedaux's activities from late 1941. The FBI also investigated René de Chambrun.

Charles Bedaux's country residence, the Château de Candé, in 1937, the year it hosted the wedding of the Duke of Windsor and Wallis Simpson.

Clockwise from top left

Dr Sumner Jackson with his son,
Phillip ("Pete"), in the garden of
their avenue Foch apartment,
c.1930.

SD Major-General Karl Oberg
was responsible for tracking down
members of the Resistance in Paris,
including Dr Jackson.

Dr Edmund Gros, the director of
the American Hospital of Paris.

Dr Sumner Jackson (*centre*), Dr Thierry Martel (*in profile just in front of him*), Dr Edmund Gros (*fourth from the left*) and Charlotte "Toquette" Jackson (*third nurse from the right*). This photo was taken in the garden of the American Hospital at Neuilly just before the German occupation of Paris.

The entrance to the American Hospital in Neuilly, c.1930.

Left Drue Leyton, the glamorous American actress whose broadcasts on Radio Mondiale made her a target for the Nazis.

Below left Florence Jay Gould, who hosted a weekly salon of German and French writers in her suite at the Hôtel Bristol and at her avenue Malakoff apartment.

Below Polly Peabody's author photo from her 1941 book *Occupied Territory*.

Left General Otto von Stülpnagel, German military commander of France, 1939.

Right Karl-Heinrich von Stülpnagel, c.1940. Otto's cousin and successor in France. He believed that killing hostages both violated the soldier's code and failed to intimidate the Resistance.

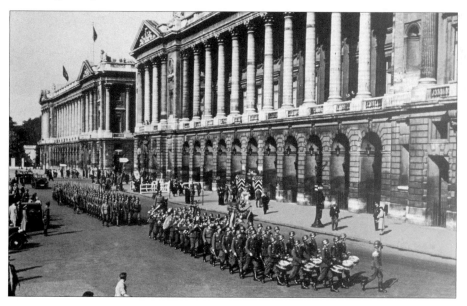

A German military parade passes the Hôtel de Crillon (*left*) and the French Naval Ministry (*right*) on the Place de la Concorde in Paris, 1940. The American Embassy is just beyond the Crillon.

Paris under occupation outside the Hôtel Meurice, the last German HQ in the city.

Marshal Pétain (*centre in dark suit*), pictured with his cabinet, the day after he succeeded French premier Paul Reynaud, 17 June 1940. Also pictured are Pierre Laval (*with papers to the left of Pétain*) and Defence Minister Maxime Weygand (*in uniform to the right of Pétain*).

Marshal Pétain (*left*) with American Ambassador to Vichy, Admiral William D. Leahy, February 1941.

Shakespeare's *King John*, translated by Clara Longworth de Chambrun, opened at the Théâtre de l'Odéon on 3 May 1943 to good reviews.

Parisians welcome an Allied tank
during the Liberation of Paris,
26 August, 1944.

American flags on the
Champs-Elysées,
August 29, 1944.

Ernest Hemingway in Sylvia Beach's flat following the liberation of Paris, 1944.

Phillip "Pete" Jackson in the uniform of the Royal Ambulance Corps, soon after he escaped death on the *SS Thielbek*.

Charlotte "Toquette" Jackson, June 1945, in Sweden following her release from Ravensbrück concentration camp where she had become disabled from starvation and exhaustion.

When the Germans came that afternoon, I peered out the windows. They were all shuttered up. I had the name Shakespeare and Company painted off the front by the house painters, who lived in the house. And the carpenters took down the shelves even. Everything was removed. And the shutters were up. The Germans must have come and saw nothing, nothing left at all. And I retired upstairs.

The entire contents of Shakespeare and Company were stored on the fourth floor, where no one could find them. Sylvia hid the rarest documents, including James Joyce's original manuscripts, at Adrienne's. Adrienne wrote in 'A Letter to Friends in the Free Zone', published in February 1942, 'You ask me how Sylvia Beach is doing. She is still in Paris, which she never left. She had to shut her bookshop a few days ago. Now that she has leisure she is going to start her memoirs.'

Shakespeare and Company had been Sylvia's life for twenty-two years. The occupation had now taken it away, as it had contact with her family and her friends outside France. 'After escaping from what I feared more than emprisonment [sic]: the confiscation of the Shakespeare and Company library ... I settled down in the little rooms above my former bookshop to wait for whatever might happen.'

In 1941, the American Library and the American Hospital celebrated their first Christmas without the protection granted to neutrals in German-ruled Grossparis. The library's staff together with wives, children, aunts and cousins exchanged presents in the rue de Téhèran beside a modest Christmas tree. Boris Netchaeff, the flamboyant White Russian who had worked at the library for almost twenty years, boiled up hot rum punch and mulled wine. The fireplace smouldered with the aroma of roasted chestnuts. A basket of oranges appeared, somehow smuggled up from the Vichy zone. General de Chambrun and some of the hospital's personnel came along to help the library's smaller staff enjoy the occasion. Netchaeff obliged Aldebert by telling him fabulous tales of the Russian czars and their courts. Clara thought the party 'succeeded in stirring up enough gaiety to forget our pains, troubles and anxieties for a brief while'.

One of their anxieties was whether the library, which had grown out of the collection of books donated to the doughboys of the American Expeditionary Force in France in 1917 and 1918, would survive at all. The American Library of Paris held the largest collection of English books on the European continent, and it promoted democracy through American literature. As soon as the United States and Germany were at war, the Rockefeller Foundation in New York withdrew its funding to the library 'under prevailing conditions'. When Edward A. Sumner read the Rockefeller decision, he wrote to its board that 'the Library is being operated by its First Vice President of American birth and, we are confident, without interference from either the German or French authorities ... I personally would rather recognize and confirm this action than have the Library closed or its book collection expropriated or seized.' He asked the foundation to 'keep an open mind on the efforts we are making to keep the Library operating as an independent American institution'. The Carnegie Endowment cancelled its subsidy as well, fearing the library 'might become a tool of the German Occupation Forces or of the collaboration'. Communication with Clara in Paris had become almost impossible since the United States declared war on Germany, but Sumner and the board trusted her to keep it open and to protect its valuable collection. Clara was assisted in her task by the French Information Centre's grant of 600,000 French francs to tide the library over the following three years.

The Christmas celebrations at the American Hospital in Neuilly were far more elaborate than those at the library. Clara recorded a repast unknown to most Parisians, who were losing weight on the starvation diet caused by rationing:

The hospital feast took the chef and his satellites months to prepare. Under the Germans' very noses, clandestine pigs were raised and fattened, and the menu always included ham, bacon and sausage. The songs ran the musical gamut from 'My Old Kentucky Home' to 'My Country, 'Tis of Thee.' The entire staff, who were present, included French, Swiss, Danes, Swedes, and Russians, but on that particular evening all were typical Americans.

Clara recalled that 'we encouraged one another by saying "this time it really is the last; next Christmas we shall be free"'. The hospital auctioned the chef's hand-written Christmas menus to benefit wounded British and French soldiers, whom the hospital cared for under agreements with their two governments. Vichy paid the hospital directly for French servicemen, and the British Embassy in Spain reimbursed the hospital via American banks. The Germans approved the arrangement, one instance in which enemies cooperated while their armies savaged each other on the battlefield. The hospital usually cared for about one hundred French and thirty to forty British casualties at a time. When the soldiers' wounds healed, most of them could look forward only to German prison camps, Oflags for the officers and Stalags for the men. A fortunate minority disappeared via the underground railway to Britain, sent secretly in civilian clothes by Dr Jackson. He accomplished this 'under the Germans' very noses', as well as the nose of General de Chambrun.

PART FOUR

1942

TWENTY-TWO

First Round-up

IN MID-JANUARY, THE GERMANS relaxed the requirement for the Americans in Occupied France to report weekly to the German military. Instead, they could go to the local French police. The American Legation in Switzerland notified the State Department in February that, while a few hundred American men were being held in camps, 'no women yet interned, men over sixty and needing medical care liberated and Americans form separate group from other foreigners'. The Swiss Consulate, representing American interests in Paris, relayed a message from the German authorities to the American Legation in Berne that the internments 'should be considered exclusively as a provisional measure and that each case will be examined separately'.

'The German authorities eased restrictions on 340 American hostages held at Compiègne,' United Press reported from Vichy on 29 January 1942, 'and indicated some physicians needed in American hospitals in Paris may be released if the hostage quota is maintained by internment of other Americans in their places, it was learned today.' The dispatch added that the Germans, who allowed the men to keep radios and receive family visits, had improved conditions 'to insure good treatment of German nationals in the United States'.

Mme Edmond Gillet, director of social services for the French Red Cross, was the first official to send a full report on Frontstalag 122 to the American Embassy in Vichy. On 27 January, she wrote to diplomat S. Pinckney Tuck, requesting that he 'consider this information confidential, in other words to use it only in so far as concerns the assistance to be given to the Americans'. Frontstalag 122 was not one camp, but several. Mme Gillet listed Sector A for 1,200 French communists and other political internees, 300 Russians and sixty Yugoslavs. The Americans were in Sector B with other civilians whose countries were at war with Germany. Sector C was for 1,200 Jews, who had been 'arrested in Paris [and] were interned in the camp as a measure of retaliation. They are subject to particularly harsh treatment.' She added, 'They are not allowed to receive packages, letters or visits. But, among the interned Americans are a few Jews who are allowed to benefit from the treatment granted to Americans. This creates a very delicate situation.'

The Germans, who directed the camp from the *Militärbefehlshaber in Frankreich* (Military Governor in France) Headquarters at the Hôtel Majestic in Paris, informed Mme Gillet that the Americans were given 'preferential treatment'. They, unlike the other prisoners, were allowed to receive two family visits, two letters and three postcards each month and parcels of food from the Red Cross. 'At the same time,' she wrote, 'the French Red Cross, in cooperation with the American Hospital and the American Library, made a shipment of books, armchairs, tables, chairs and various other articles for the creation of a Camp Recreation Center.' Clara Longworth de Chambrun opened a branch of the American Library in the camp, and one of the prisoners was made camp librarian. The French Red Cross was assiduous in providing care to the Americans, shipping them 'three tons of sanitary products and foodstuffs' in the first week.

Vichy was not at war with the United States, and the two governments retained diplomatic relations. No Americans were interned in the Unoccupied Zone. French police in Paris did not assist the Germans, as they had with the Jews, in incarcerating American citizens. The Vichy authorities extended the licences of the three American banks still doing business in France, Chase Bank, J. P. Morgan and Guaranty Trust. The Germans allowed them to keep branches staffed by French employees in Paris. Chase had already appointed Carlos Niedermann, who was Swiss, to replace its American manager in Paris in February 1941. In 1942, its Parisian deposits, including those of German nationals, increased despite the war between

Germany and the United States. Meanwhile, the American Club, American Express and the American private schools in Paris closed. 'Institutions such as the American Hospital and the American Library,' the *New York Times* reported from Vichy on 29 January, 'operated by foundations and open to the French as well as Americans, have not been confiscated, although the Germans hesitated a long time before abandoning claims to the hospital, which is one of the most modern and best equipped in Europe.' The American Chamber of Commerce stayed open to protect American businesses under the direction of acting secretary George Verité.

Mme Gillet of the French Red Cross contacted General de Chambrun at the American Hospital, and he donated medical supplies to Frontstalag 122. The hospital had no linen or blankets to spare, but it sent medical teams to the camp. Some internees were brought to Neuilly for treatment. Otto Gresser recalled, 'These patients were not at all eager to get well very fast. As soon as they were cured, we had to promise the Germans that they had to return to the civilian camps until the war was over.' Jackson and Gresser put some of the internees on a prolonged 'unwell' list in a ward for the elderly. This kept beds full and internees out of the detention camps. Many of the 340 men interned in January were released within a few weeks. Dr Morris Sanders was not released until the end of April, when he was allowed to resume work at the American Hospital.

Apart from auditing the American Hospital's annual accounts, there was 'no other interference by the German authorities'. This left Otto Gresser free to scavenge necessary but contraband supplies and allowed Sumner Jackson to hide the British, and later American, flyers whose planes had been downed in France. The escape network was becoming more sophisticated, as the Resistance developed skills in forging papers, keeping safe houses, crossing the Line of Demarcation and deceiving the Germans. Routes that took Allied soldiers to safety also served to deliver photographs of German military installations and other intelligence to London. The Germans penetrated some of the networks and arrested their members. By the spring of 1942, they had not captured any Allied soldiers, whether escaped prisoners or downed airmen, on routes that began in the American Hospital of

Paris. When the men reached England, they told their commanders about a patriot named Sumner Waldron Jackson.

With fewer Americans in Paris and most French prisoners of war in Germany, Aldebert de Chambrun sought new ways to fill the hospital with non-German patients. A proposal came in January 1942 from Dr Alexis Carrel, a Nobel Prize-winning French physician who had conducted research in America in 1906 at the then-new Rockefeller Institute. Carrel was a friend and mentor of Charles Lindbergh, who had moved to Paris for a time after the kidnapping and murder of his baby son in New Jersey in 1932. The two men had designed a blood profusion pump that allowed human organs to survive outside the body, an early aid to organ transplants. *Time* magazine had pictured the two with their pump on its cover of 13 June 1938. Carrel's medical talent was undisputed, but his views on race and eugenics mirrored the Nazis'. His *L'Homme, cet inconnu* (*Man, This Unknown*) in 1935 recommended that the criminally insane and other undesirables 'should be humanely and economically disposed of in small euthanistic institutions supplied with gases'. Carrel had no objections to Nazi euthanasia of 'defectives', but attacking France was another matter. From the beginning of the war in 1939 to the fall of France, Dr Carrel took an active part in the struggle against Germany, directing the French army's Commission for Oxygen Therapy. He warned Lindbergh, who fronted the largest anti-war movement in the United States, American First, 'It's the Nazis who are destroying western civilization. It's the Nazis!'

Dr Carrel requested the use of a laboratory in the American Hospital for his French Institute for the Study of Human Problems to research workplace injuries and establish standard first aid treatments. Its goal of sending injured men back to work quickly and efficiently would have appealed to Charles Bedaux. De Chambrun accepted Carrel's proposal and approached the French state railway company, Société Nationale des Chemins de Fer, to send its workers to the American Hospital. In March, the hospital designated forty beds for SNCF labourers suffering industrial accidents or wounded in trains bombed by the Allies or sabotaged by the Resistance. 'From this time on our 250 beds were nearly always occupied,' de Chambrun wrote.

Occupied beds meant no space for German troops and independence for the hospital. Dr Jackson cared for many of the *cheminots*, railwaymen, who were among the first groups of workers to organize resistance to the occupation.

Along with the other Americans in Paris, Sylvia Beach reported each week to her local police station. 'There were so few Americans [in the 6th Arrondissement] that our names were in a sort of scrapbook that was always getting mislaid,' she wrote. 'I used to find it for the Commissaire. Opposite my name and antecedents was the notation: "has no horse". I could never find out why.' From then on, 'the Gestapo kept track of me, and they'd come to see me all the time'.

In January 1942, freezing weather proved more of a problem than the time-consuming search for food. Adrienne wrote, 'Hardest to put up with, we are all of the same opinion, is the cold. In the bookshop, where I have had a wood stove installed, it is livable, but my apartment, like those of most people, is glacial; I can neither read nor write.' Sylvia, in her solitary flat above the now-empty bookshop, was finding winter equally bleak: 'I shared the strange occupied life of my French friends, without heat and food dwindling. Electricity was limited, we gave up any ration of coal for a little gas an hour at noon, finally none at all as we combined rations with whoever cooked a meal at noon. I took my lunch at Adrienne's. I had a quarter of a litre of milk a day as I didn't eat meat, and extra macaroni.' Women were not given rations for tobacco, as men were, and there was no longer any chocolate, sugar or coffee for anyone – except on the black market. Contraband coffee cost $8 a pound, eggs $2 a dozen, chickens $5 each and cigarettes about $2 a pack – almost ten times their pre-war prices. 'An average bottle of wine, which before the war cost 8 or 10 cents, now costs 60 cents,' reported the *New York Times* in April 1942. When Adrienne realized one day that she had no cooking fat left, Sylvia watched her burst into tears.

Sylvia, Adrienne and the other women of Paris coped with privation and German decrees, but they did not give up everything. 'Even the electricity restrictions did not prevent women from going to the hairdresser,' wrote Ninetta Jucker, an Englishwoman who remained in

Paris throughout the occupation and had many American friends, 'though we often had to come away with damp heads.' Night was the worst time. Mrs Jucker recalled, 'After eight o'clock the centre of the city was almost deserted, and though many people risked boarding the last train for the pleasure of a few hours' "escape" at the theatre or cinema – never have places of entertainment been so full as they were during the Occupation – as soon as the little crowd dispersed from the entrance to the metro, the city recovered its deathly silence, broken only by the occasional tramp of nailed boots.' She and many other Parisians lived in dread of *la botte allemande*, the German boot:

> No one who has not lived in German-occupied territory can fully realize all that was conveyed by the sound of those five pairs of booted and perfectly synchronized feet: *La patrouille allemande* [the German patrol]. Ein, zwei, drei. Halt! They never moved but to command. Even the sentries gave each other an almost impercept-ible whistle in order to be sure of synchronizing as they marched back and forth from their boxes. There were other night sounds peculiar to the Occupation. Rifle shots; the sudden pepper of a machine-gun – or could it be the firing squad? – the rush past of a powerful car (someone being swept away by the Gestapo perhaps).

After two months of house arrest, which in the opulent Château de Candé's 1,200 hectares would not have been intolerable, Charles and Fern Bedaux were told they could travel again. They immediately requested permission to return to the United States. France must have seemed less attractive than before, now that their country was at war with Germany and their influence with German and Vichy officials had proved inadequate to prevent their detention. The Germans denied the request, given Charles's knowledge of their military and industrial production. Moreover, Nazi officials suspected Fern's adherence to the Christian Science Church, which they rightly accused of involvement with British military intelligence. A condition of their release was that one of them must remain in France at all times, effectively as hostage for the return of the other. Bedaux immediately took advantage of his liberty to lobby for restoration of the property and files that the

Germans had seized from him as an enemy alien after Pearl Harbor. At just the right moment, an ally emerged within the German administration.

In February 1942, Rittmeister Joseph von Ledebur, Bedaux's friend and former employee, returned to Paris. It seemed that Bedaux's appeals had succeeded in saving Ledebur from further combat in the Soviet Union. The timing of his deployment to France, as well as his appointment as a custodian of enemy property, could not have worked more to Bedaux's advantage. Colluding with Bedaux's other close friend in the German administration, Dr Franz Medicus, Ledebur arranged for German officers to accompany Bedaux to Holland to reclaim the International Bedaux Company's files on more than two hundred of the most important industrial concerns in German-occupied Europe. Charles returned to Paris with all his dossiers and with his Amsterdam office manager, Alexandra Ter Hart. The former Miss Lebowski feared denunciation in Holland as a Jew. Bedaux gave her a false Aryan identity to work for him in Paris, where no one knew her or her family history.

As an American citizen, Bedaux was no longer permitted to run a company in any of the lands of the Third Reich. His brother Gaston, with his French citizenship, could. He wrote later that Charles was not permitted to sign contracts with belligerent powers: 'I was therefore authorized by the Minister of Public Works to administer my brother's company.' Charles made Gaston promise to return the company to him at the end of the war and, if anything happened to Charles, to provide for Fern.

Gaston was not surprised that Charles's first concern was his wife's welfare. He recalled a conversation with his brother, when 'Charles told me one day, at the beginning of the war, that if he were separated by events from Fern or if his wife disappeared he would have no reason to live.' With no company responsibilities, Charles was free to pursue a scheme that had been germinating in his imagination for more than a year. 'In 1941,' Gaston wrote, 'he adopted the idea of the pipeline.' The 'pipeline' was to be a bridge between the French territories in black Africa and those in the Arab north. Its functions were to carry water from the fertile areas of Algeria into the desert and to funnel food oil in the opposite direction from the Niger Valley over the inhospitable Sahara to the Mediterranean. Dual-use efficiency appealed to his engineer's instincts. The Trans-Sahara Railway, on which he had already been working, would run beside the pipeline. The railway and pipeline companies, both to be owned by the French state, would share the costs. Bedaux would assume an interest in the peanut oil refineries he planned to construct on the River Niger. The refineries would have a ready market in a Europe starved of edible oils. Gaston commented, 'This idea crystallized one day in his soul, and he became obsessed with it.' The Trans-Sahara Pipeline was undoubtedly Charles Bedaux's most ambitious undertaking, which, if realized, would make him the French Cecil Rhodes.

Gaston was involved from the beginning, as he wrote,

One day, my brother declared firmly, 'It's necessary to put flowing water in the Sahara,' and he exposed me, slowly, patiently, as was his habit, to the solution he envisaged, and for which common mortals tended to take him for a fool. Not only, he explained to me, was it necessary to create this aqueduct to bring the water needed on the future Trans-Saharan [Railway], but also that this pipe must permit simultaneously the provision of oil in Africa and France, given that the Niger basin must furnish the necessary peanuts, that we must establish at the beginning of the operation the refineries and that the oil and the water perfectly use the same channel.

Fearing his brother's dream may not have corresponded to reality, Gaston invited 'the most qualified' engineer in France, Monsieur Rouelle, to speak with Charles. Rouelle, Gaston's colleague at the Department of Highways and Dams in Beauvais, listened to the elder Bedaux expound his proposal. Charles, an accomplished salesman more than anything else, specified the pipeline's measurements, distances between pumping stations and materials that could withstand the desert heat. Rouelle left to study the project in detail. Gaston wrote, 'My friend returned to see me fifteen days later. "It's fantastic," he told me, smiling, "but you know your brother is no fool at all. I've done the calculations. And I find them as sensible as he does. He's right. It's possible. All that remains is to set the means for its realization.'"

Bedaux faced two immediate challenges. The first was to persuade Vichy and the Germans to commit money, material, labour and the permits necessary for regular travel between France and French Africa. The second was to organize an accurate survey of the pipeline's route. The reconnaissance mission was the kind of adventure across deserts and through jungles that Bedaux relished, but this would be his first without Fern. To guarantee he would not escape, she had to remain at Candé. An old friend from past transcontinental treks, however, would be welcome. Charles sent an invitation to the Austrian whom he had said was more like a son to him than his son, Friedrich von Ledebur. Ledebur had organized his previous African expeditions, taking care of the rifles and managing the many native porters. Needing him again, Bedaux wrote to Ledebur on 23 March. The letter was enclosed in an envelope, postmarked Lisbon, to his New York secretary, Mrs Isabella Waite. He wrote,

> My dear Frederic,
>
> It is time that you should return and work by my side. If you need it, get the necessary money from Mrs. Waite. Come any way you can, but come alone. With some good luck your brother Joseph will be working with me in a few weeks. I want you to return while there is still time for the peace of your Soul.
>
> Working with me for a just cause I can promise you that you will have nothing to fear from anyone. You have our deepest affection.
>
> Charles
>
> Mrs. Waite. See to it that he does come back.
>
> C. E. B.

Frederic, as Friedrich called himself in the United States, was living with wealthy friends in southern California. He and the actress Iris Tree had recently divorced. A ranch outside Burlingame, near San

Francisco, occasionally employed him to care for its horses. He spent part of each year in New York, sleeping in reduced rate servants' quarters at the Gladstone Hotel on East 52nd Street. If the offer of another adventure with Charles Bedaux tempted the penniless aristocrat, he managed to resist. Bedaux's allusion to his brother Joseph, with whom he had had a falling out in 1939 over Joseph's dedication to the Nazis, may have deterred him. The FBI read the letter before Frederic did, and its forensics laboratory determined it had been 'written on a typewriter with Continental Pica Type ... of German manufacture'. Frederic did not write back.

America's entry into the war made no immediate impression on the French. American soldiers were not invading France, and no American planes were bombing the Germans. Having lost much of its fleet at Pearl Harbor and training an inexperienced army to fight in both the Asian and European theatres of the global war, the United States needed time. In early February 1942, the Royal Air Force dropped three million leaflets over occupied France stamped with three Victory Vs, one each in red, white and blue. The pamphlets quoted Franklin Roosevelt's goals for America's first year of war: to produce 185,000 planes, 120,000 tanks and eighteen million tons of shipping, quantities of arms unprecedented in the history of warfare. Roosevelt's words were designed to encourage all peoples under Axis occupation: 'Our overwhelming superiority in armament must be adequate to put weapons of war into the hands of those men in the conquered nations who stand ready to seize the first opportunity to revolt against their German and Japanese oppressors and against the traitors in their own ranks, known by the already famous name of Quislings. As we get guns to the patriots in those lands, they too will fire shots "heard round the world".' Roosevelt was promising to help the partisans in German-occupied Europe to liberate themselves. Slowly and cautiously, the French were listening. But convincing the majority that resistance was not hopeless called for more than American leaflets dropped from British planes. The French had to know that, as in 1917, the Yanks really were coming.

The RAF opened its air offensive against occupied Paris on the night of 3 March 1942, when 200 bombers demolished factories in the suburbs. Bombs weighing 2,000 pounds hit the plants, some of which supplied the Nazis with weaponry, and killed 400 people. Maréchal Pétain called the bombardment 'a national catastrophe'. When Vichy Ambassador Gaston Henry-Haye protested to Washington, Under-Secretary of State Sumner Welles called it 'an entirely legitimate bombing'. Despite Allied attacks on French soil, Washington and Vichy preserved their diplomatic relations. *Life* magazine offered a succinct explanation: 'The U.S. is polite because Vichy owns some very strategic colonies and a vital fleet. Vichy is polite because the U.S. may win the war and Vichy may lose the rest of her empire.' Vichy politesse extended to American citizens in the Unoccupied Zone, who were still not interned like some of their compatriots in Paris.

TWENTY-THREE

The Vichy Web

THE AMERICAN LAW FIRM SULLIVAN AND CROMWELL, the world's largest, closed its Paris offices. This left American lawyer François Monahan unable to practise. Like his friend René de Chambrun, Monahan had dual American–French citizenship and belonged to the New York Bar Association. But he was not licensed to plead in the French courts. To speed up the process to qualify, he sought help from René. René explained the origin of their friendship: 'His father-in-law, Captain [Charles] de Marenches, had been an aid to my father, then Colonel de Chambrun. The two together, from 1917 on, directed the liaison between Pétain and Pershing, the commanders of the French and the American armies.' Charles de Marenches, like Aldebert de Chambrun, was married to an American. Together, they wrote a book, *The History of the American Army during the European Conflict*, with the cooperation of Pershing and Pétain. Alexandre de Marenches, François Monahan's brother-in-law, supplied the American Hospital at Aldebert's request with vegetables from his land near Paris. Monahan was on the board of governors at the American Hospital of Paris and occasionally served as its secretary. An official at the Palais de Justice had suggested his admission to the French bar would be accelerated if he inserted in his file a copy of his father-in-law and General de Chambrun's book, signed by Maréchal Pétain. The bureaucrats would take the hint. Monahan asked René to obtain Pétain's signature. René had avoided Pétain since the Maréchal dismissed and arrested Pierre Laval on 13 December 1940, so he took the book to Dr Bernard Ménétral, Pétain's physician and adviser, in Vichy.

At the Hôtel du Parc, René walked up the stairs to avoid Maréchal Pétain in the lift. Dr Ménétral's office was next to the Maréchal's, but René slipped in without difficulty and explained what he wanted. Ménétral agreed to ask Pétain to sign the book for Monahan. As René was about to leave, Pétain came in. Surprised to see his old friend's son, he said, '*Tiens, c'est toi, Bunnie!*' He took Bunny into his office and said, 'Sit down in this chair, a little closer, so I can hear better. How is Josée? How are your parents?' He asked, 'Is your father-in-law still angry with me?'

René explained that Laval was less angry about his arrest on 13 December than about the harm he believed the Maréchal had done to France. It was Laval's contention that, when he was dismissed, the Germans were about to make major concessions: the release of 150,000 French prisoners of war, a huge reduction in French payments to cover Germany's occupation costs and the restoration of the northern provinces, then governed by a German *gauleiter* from Belgium, to French administration. Pétain, according to de Chambrun, blamed his subordinates for Laval's arrest in 1940. He added, 'Laval knew how to talk to the Boches, how to gain time. Darlan is a good sailor, but on land he can't cope.'

As de Chambrun said goodbye, Pétain asked, 'Do you think that in spite of everything that's happened, your father-in-law would consent to come back and help me?' René thought he might, but he warned Pétain that two people would do anything to prevent Laval's return to politics: his wife and his daughter.

René left with a burden heavier than the signed copy of a book for François Monahan. He had become the intermediary between Pétain and Laval. It was not a role he had sought, he claimed, but no one was better placed: family friend of Pétain, devoted son-in-law of Laval. In Paris the next day, he received a telephone call from Dr Bernard Ménétral. The Maréchal wanted René to fix a meeting with Laval as soon as possible. The rendezvous had to remain secret to avoid arousing the suspicions of the current prime minister, Admiral Darlan, and the American Embassy, which had repeatedly expressed its antipathy to

Laval. René returned to Vichy and, with Ménétral, went to the forest of Randan to mark a spot at the crossing of two bridle paths. Pétain and Laval would meet there, supposedly by chance, the next day.

'My father-in-law and I arrived at 4.25,' René wrote. 'A little later, we saw the marshal's car. As he was getting out, I leaned toward my father-in-law and told him what Josée had asked me to say, "Don't give in. Remember December thirteenth."' Pétain and Laval went into the woods without eavesdroppers so that the old Maréchal could ask him to return as prime minister. Despite the secrecy, the American Ambassador, Admiral William Leahy, learned of the meeting within twenty-four hours: 'Ralph Heinzen, of the United Press, told us on March 26 that Laval had had a secret conference with Pétain near Vichy. That same day M. de Chalvron, one of our friends in the Foreign Ministry, reported that he was certain that Laval would be returned and that contact had already been established through Laval's son-in-law, René de Chambrun.' Leahy informed President Roosevelt, who sent Leahy a message for Pétain that America would cease all cooperation with Vichy if Laval were restored.

Admiral Darlan, desperate to remain in office, showed FDR's cable to the Germans. His ploy failed. Hitler now saw the premiership of France as a contest between himself and Roosevelt. He ordered Pétain to choose: America and Darlan or Germany and Laval. Discussions dragged on among Pétain, Laval and Darlan over who would have which post and on what terms. Every detail was reported to Berlin and Washington.

On 1 April 1942, Josée Laval de Chambrun celebrated her thirty-first birthday by driving out from Paris to the Château de Candé to play golf and ping-pong with Charles and Fern Bedaux. Charles and Fern were masterful golfers. Having Laval's daughter to visit helped to cement their friendship with her father. Laval, after all, would be useful if he became prime minister again. Josée bumped into Hans Jürgen Soehring, the German officer who was living with her actress friend, Arletty. In the evening, René joined Josée at the chateau for dinner with the Bedauxs and other friends. René and Josée drove from Candé at midnight to the Villa Argizagita near Biarritz, where Aldebert and

Clara de Chambrun were waiting for them. On Sunday, amid the splendour of the Pyrenees, they celebrated Easter together. Clara did not record whether René confided in her the degree to which he had become involved in Vichy politics or that Laval was about to return to office. As an admirer of Laval, she would have approved anything her son did to bring him back. When the Easter festivities ended, both Chambrun families returned to Paris.

In Paris, Josée became embroiled in another kind of Franco-German dispute. Arletty and her German lover, Soehring, were squabbling. Arletty sought Josée's advice, and Soehring called to accuse her of stirring up trouble between them. On 8 April, René went to Châteldon by train with Josée, François Monahan and Monahan's brother-in-law, Alexandre de Marenches. On board, they met Ernst Achenbach, counsellor at the German Embassy, and the pro-German journalist Jean Luchaire. If René was not a collaborator, the company he was keeping left little room for another interpretation.

On 13 April, Pétain made his choice: Laval and Hitler over Darlan and Roosevelt. Six days later, Laval became prime minister with Darlan in the government as military chief. Including Darlan was not sufficient to placate Roosevelt, who reacted immediately. He recalled Admiral Leahy from Vichy, and the US navy disarmed the French fleet in France's Caribbean colonies. The United States blamed René de Chambrun for instigating Laval's coup, but he pleaded that his involvement had come by chance while trying to help François Monahan. Like his mother, René was guided more by family and friendship than politics.

The Americans were not the only ones displeased to see Laval back in office. Josée had begged her father not to serve under Pétain, whom she had hated since the 13 December affair. Jeanne-Eugénie-Elizabeth Laval, Pierre's wife, was even more adamant. When German Ambassador Otto Abetz arrived at Châteldon to congratulate Laval, Jeanne Laval refused to welcome him or to accept flowers from his French wife, Suzanne. 'I don't want to see Germans in my house,' she told her husband, as she went on making jam in the kitchen.

In the summer of 1942, Germany appointed a new *Militärbefehlshaber in Frankreich*, 56-year-old career soldier and First World

War veteran General Karl Heinrich von Stülpnagel, to replace his cousin, General Otto von Stülpnagel. Otto had implemented Hitler's policy of shooting hostages in retaliation for Resistance attacks. His successor, who had been involved in an aborted but undiscovered conspiracy to depose Hitler in 1939, believed that killing hostages both violated the soldier's code and failed to intimidate the Resistance. In fact, martyrdom attracted more people into its ranks. But Karl Heinrich von Stülpnagel was deprived of the powers his cousin had to police Occupied France. They went instead to Major-General Karl Oberg of the Sicherheitsdienst, the Nazi Party's security agency known as the SD. The SD tracked down the Reich's enemies, and the Gestapo took action against them. The 45-year-old Oberg looked like the archetype of Hollywood's evil Nazi: shaved head, rimless glasses, black uniform and pug face. Born in Hamburg, Oberg joined the SS in 1931, two years before Hitler became chancellor of Germany. Now, he was in Paris as *Höherer SS und Polizeiführer*, Higher SS and Police Leader, to take over policing of the Occupied Zone from the Wehrmacht. Oberg was the protégé of Reinhard Heydrich, tasked with emulating the vicious policies that Heydrich was instituting in Czechoslovakia. The Gestapo chief, Colonel Helmut Knocken, fell under his command, as did the Criminal Police (Kripo), the SS and the SD. Oberg commanded 10,000 German military and political policemen, and he had the support of ten times that many French police who took their orders from Vichy. He had two missions: to send Jews from France to die in Poland and to destroy the French Resistance. He ordered what became known as *la rafle du Vel d'Hiv*, the round-up of the Vélodrome d'Hiver, on 16 July. The Germans dragged 13,000 Jews without French citizenship from their homes in Paris to the bicycle stadium where the French government had interned unwanted foreigners like Arthur Koestler in 1940. Among those held there without proper sanitation or sufficient food and water were 4,000 children. When the hierarchy of the Catholic Church appealed to Laval on their behalf, Laval answered, 'They all must go.' The Vélodrome d'Hiver was a transit point from which the helpless Jewish men, women and children were taken to Drancy, herded onto trains and sent to death camps in Poland.

Oberg's vicious treatment of Jews was nearly matched by the ferocity of his campaign against the Resistance. On 10 July 1942, he declared, in addition to *résistants* themselves, he would punish their families. To intimidate 'saboteurs and troublemakers', he announced, 'One. All close male relatives in ascending line, including brothers-in-law and cousins of the age of eighteen, will be shot. Two. All similarly related females will be sentenced to hard labor. Three. All children of men and women affected by these measures, who are under the age of seventeen, will be put in reform schools.' Oberg hunted down assassins who were shooting German soldiers in the streets and Metro stations of Paris as well as *résistants* who were killing German soldiers and mutilating their bodies in the countryside. His network of French informers spied on and denounced their countrymen. His agents tortured everyone they suspected of possessing information on Allied pilots escaping to England. Executioners worked full-time shooting *résistants* and hostages in the prison at Mont Valérian and outdoors beside the waterfall in the Bois de Boulogne. It did not take long for Oberg to earn the sobriquet 'Butcher of Paris'.

Summer should have led to relief of some kind. Instead, the Germans made life worse. On 1 June, the German military government decreed that all Jews must wear the *étoile jaune*, a yellow Star of David, sewn onto their outer garments. Within days, some of the estimated 110,000 Jews still in Paris bravely demonstrated against the order. Jewish war veterans wore their military decorations beside the yellow stars, and, to the irritation of the German police, 'let it be known that they were proud to be wearing their national emblem'. Gaullists, communists and *Zazous*, young Parisians with a counter-cultural affinity for American jazz music and long hair, sported yellow flowers, yellow handkerchiefs and paper stars in solidarity. Such sympathizers were a brave minority. The star had a practical purpose: it identified Jews who violated General Karl Oberg's order prohibiting them from entering restaurants, cafés, theatres, cinemas, music halls, markets, swimming pools, beaches, museums, libraries, historic monuments, race tracks and parks.

Sylvia Beach, always sensitive to the hurts of others, felt the indignity inflicted on her Jewish friends. Her assistant, Françoise Bernheim, who had remained close to Sylvia after the shop closed, was also forced to wear the star. Displaying it brought derisive stares, and occasional attacks, from anti-Semites. Not displaying it meant arrest. Sylvia wrote that

as I went about with Françoise, I shared with her some of the special restrictions on Jews – though not the large yellow Star of David that she wore on her coat or dress. We went about on bicycles, the only form of transportation. We could not enter public places such as theatres, cinemas, cafés, concert halls or sit down on park benches or even those in the streets. Once, we tried taking our lunch to a shady square. Sitting on the ground beside a bench, we hurriedly ate our hard-boiled eggs and swallowed the tea in our thermos flasks, looking around furtively as we did so. It was not an experience we cared to repeat.

When Sylvia, Françoise and an American artist friend, Katherine Dudley, attended a lecture by Paul Valéry at the College de France, a sympathetic usher hid Françoise's overcoat with its Star of David so she could come inside.

Sylvia and a small group of friends walked through the Latin Quarter with Valéry after his lecture at the College de France. They passed the Rive Gauche, a German propaganda bookshop in what had been the Café d'Harcourt. Police guards were stationed outside to prevent students from smashing its plate-glass windows, as they had when it first opened. When Valéry saw the books of his mentor, Stéphane Mallarmé, on display to promote National Socialism, he was outraged. Sylvia wrote,

'They dare ...' he yelled, waving his umbrella, regardless of disapproving glances from passing uniforms. It looked as if the windows of the 'Rive Gauche' were going to catch it again, and our master would be whirled away in a 'salad basket' [police van] and deported at any minute. Luckily, at that moment, a lot of determined-looking policemen came between us and the offending sight, and we dragged Valéry away, still muttering.

Sylvia visited Valéry at home in the 16th Arrondissement, within sight of the Arc de Triomphe. An air attack by the RAF began just as Sylvia and the Valéry family sat down to lunch. The old poet leaped from his chair and ran to the window to watch the bombardment. His younger son explained to Sylvia, 'Papa adores these raids.'

Of the 340 Americans interned at Compiègne in January, only 173 remained in June. The rest had been repatriated in exchange for Germans in the United States or allowed to return to their homes in Paris. Another sixty-six internees in the camp were from the American countries of Cuba, Haiti, the Dominican Republic, San Salvador, Costa Rica, Panama and Nicaragua. A Red Cross delegation visited the camp on 16 June and reported, 'The morale in the camp is excellent.' Of seven barracks, three were specifically for US citizens. 'The brick barracks are all of one model,' the Red Cross wrote, 'each one contains seven large rooms of fourteen beds and six smaller rooms of two or three beds.' Of the food, the inspectors found, 'American cooks handle the preparation of the meals and the spokesmen declare that they are very well prepared. The spokesmen check on the provisions from the standpoint of quality and quantity. In our opinion the food distributed corresponds to the basic rations.' Clothing, however, was 'not in good condition'. Some of the internees had been arrested in January without time to pack, and they were unable to obtain any clothes apart from those they arrived in: 'Many of them are denuded of everything and do not have the means to buy clothes for themselves; and their families do not either (rationing of cloth, etc.); they do not have enough underclothing and would be very glad if they were aided to obtain some. They do not all have leather shoes, about ten per cent wear wooden shoes.' Washing facilities were adequate. 'From the hygienic point of view this camp allows nothing to be desired,' the Red Cross noted. It added that medical care under the Cuban chief physician, Dr Soler, was 'excellent'.

A camp inspection on 13 April noted, 'There are no air raid precautions, and the latter do not seem to be necessary, as the camp is situated away from any dangerous zone.' Then, on 24 June, United Press monitored a German radio broadcast that announced, 'British planes last night dropped bombs on an internment camp near Compiègne, northeast of Paris, killing three persons and wounding one.' The *New York Times* confused matters with a report one month later that 'four Americans were killed and sixteen wounded when a plane, apparently in difficulties, jettisoned bombs on an internment camp at Compiègne, northeast of Paris on June 21'. Leland Harrison, the US Minister in Berne, Switzerland, raised the possibility that 'German planes, in reprisal for the escapes of interned Americans according to an unsubstantiated street rumor in Paris, which was reported to Consul Squire at Geneva, bombed the American internment camp at Compiègne.' Harrison asked whether the incident had 'been officially reported by the RAF'. The street rumour turned out to be false. The Red Cross confirmed that the camp was bombed during the night between 23 and 24 June by a 'foreign airplane which dropped a total of seven bombs', killing two Filipinos and a Cuban. One American was wounded.

'Since that occurrence,' the Red Cross concluded, 'the morale of the internees has fallen a great deal and several dozens now announce that they will imitate the Americans mentioned above who will be able to leave the camp to go back to America by way of Lisbon.' Until the bombing, many of the American internees had been reluctant to leave their families, homes and businesses in France. Bombardment by their own side changed their minds. A Red Cross visit of 25 July found, 'Some of the internees are living in fear of a new bombing of Compiègne ... The German authorities offered to transfer the whole Camp to some other place, but the internees declared that they preferred to stay here near Paris where they can see their friends and relatives.' The inspector added, 'The general impression of this Camp is still a good one.'

Although conditions at the Compiègne camp were superior to the usual run of German prisons, its resources were about to be stretched to breaking point. Seven barracks might comfortably accommodate 249 inmates, but they would not easily provide beds for another one thousand American men. But, in September 1942, the camp's commanders were ordered to find space for new arrivals.

To American diplomats in Vichy, the iron grille in the Hôtel du Parc between the offices of Maréchal Pétain and his new prime minister, Pierre Laval, symbolized their mutual distrust. René de Chambrun carried messages between them when their own aides would not suffice. Almost as soon as Laval was sworn in, René asked his father-in-law to appoint a new representative to the *Commissariat Général des Prisonniers de Guerre Rapatriés* (General Commission for Repatriated Prisoners of War). His nominee was André Masson, whom René trusted to convince freed prisoners to support collaboration with the Germans. Prisoners were coming home and condemning their German captors for mistreatment and using them as slave labourers. Although their comments were not published in the collaborationist press, word spread. If more returning prisoners supported collaboration, René reasoned, the Germans would set more free. In June, Laval appointed Masson.

René's concern for French prisoners dated to the capture of his Maginot Line comrades in June 1940. His 1940 book, *I Saw France Fall*, whose royalties went to a prisoners' charity, had been dedicated to three prisoner friends. The continued absence of 1.58 million able-bodied men was crippling France, whose wives were without husbands, children without fathers and land without farmers. One in every seven adult males was in a German prison camp. In seeking to ameliorate the suffering of prisoners and their families, René mired himself more deeply in Vichy's politics of intrigue and collaboration.

Laval reached an accord with the Germans that went into effect in June 1942 as the *relève*, or relief, scheme that sent three Frenchmen to work in Germany for each French prisoner freed. As so often with instances of German–French collaboration, Germany was the real beneficiary. The three to one ratio of workers to freed prisoners was in Germany's favour. Sending French workers, who were more skilled than east European slave labour, to Germany was a boon to German industry. What was more, releasing French prisoners or converting them into voluntary workers relieved German soldiers for front-line duty. When 221,000 French prisoners became voluntary workers under the *relève*, 30,000 German guards were transferred to combat units. But thousands of young Frenchmen went into hiding to avoid the forced labour or, with little to lose, joined the Resistance.

Life magazine, owned by René de Chambrun's friend Henry Luce, launched the first salvo of an American press campaign against French collaborators. On 24 August 1942, *Life* published a 'Black List' of 'the Frenchmen condemned by the underground for collaborating with the Germans'. Not surprisingly, prominent pro-Nazi propagandists like Jacques Doriot and Marcel Déat made *Life*'s roll of shame, as did Maréchal Pétain and Pierre Laval. The list included actors Sacha Guitry and Maurice Chevalier and comedienne Mistinguett. Unexpectedly, one alleged collaborator was 'René de Chambrun, son-in-law of Laval'. The Luce–Chambrun friendship ended.

A regular visitor to Vichy that summer was Charles Bedaux, who called frequently at the American Embassy in the Villa Ica. In a five-page memorandum to the secretary of state sent on 25 July 1942, S. Pinckney Tuck relayed Bedaux's analysis of the power struggle between the German army and the SS. Bedaux recommended Pierre Laval as a mediator between the United States and anti-Nazi Germans seeking a compromise peace. 'Kippy' Tuck's final paragraph analysed Bedaux's character:

> My estimate of Charles Bedaux, who proved an interesting and intel-ligent visitor, is the following: I believe this astonishing person can be classified as mentally unmoral. He apparently lacks the tradition and background which should make him realize that there is anything wrong, as an American citizen, in his open association with our declared enemies. He considers himself as a person gifted with unusual qualifications and that his refusal to accept financial remu-neration for his services to mankind justifies the international char-acter of his activities ... One thing is certain about Bedaux and that is, naive as his philosophy may appear, he is apparently completely sincere in his beliefs.

'Germany had been at war with the United States for six whole months before I first received a visit from Nazi authority,' Clara de Chambrun wrote. 'I was working in my office when a voice with strong Teutonic accent inquired over the telephone whether the direc-tress was there. On answering affirmatively, I was informed that Dr

Fuchs would call in twenty minutes.' It was June 1942. Dr Hermann Fuchs was the *Bibliotheksschütz* or 'protector' of libraries in German-occupied Europe, who had established a modus vivendi with Dorothy Reeder in 1940. True to his word, he arrived at the American Library twenty minutes after his call to Clara. Clara found herself 'confronted by an officer with the stiffest back and most piercing spectacles I ever remember to have encountered'. Dr Fuchs was looking for Dorothy Reeder. When Clara explained that Miss Reeder had left Paris, Dr Fuchs confessed his disappointment: 'I guaranteed that Miss Reeder should never be molested come what might; therefore, she ought to have remained at her post.' This was followed by 'a very full interrogation' of Clara, whose answers and credentials satisfied him. The interview concluded with his promise to Clara to deal with any difficulties she might have with other occupation agencies, indicating that Germany's different bureaus were not always in agreement. She was to call him immediately if there were problems. He said, 'I gave my word that this Library should be maintained open during the war. I am glad that you feel able to assume its responsibilities. You have but to continue in the same way as your predecessor and subscribe to the same rules.' The rules were that the library was forbidden to sell any of its books or furniture, to raise the salaries of its staff and, though Dr Fuchs neglected to restate it, to admit Jews. By the time he reassured Clara that the library would remain 'quite independent', however, Jews were so restricted in Paris that they could go to few public places at all.

Just after the Nazis ordered Jews in the Occupied Zone to wear the yellow star sewn conspicuously onto their outer clothing, Clara recognized a man and a woman whom, on her June 1940 flight from Paris, she had seen picnicking beside the road, 'seated at a tiny folding-table which formed part of their Rolls-Royce equipment'. The gentleman with the neatly trimmed beard and his elegant wife were back in Paris. Clara wrote, 'I met them walking down one of the streets near the American Library. The man was still well-dressed but wore a yellow star; to his credit, he wore it jauntily.' The library staff still delivered books to the houses of its remaining Jewish readers, whose numbers decreased with the deportations to concentration camps.

While observing the letter of Dr Fuchs's rules, Clara contrived to violate their spirit: 'Without actually raising salaries, I arranged to have the staff admitted to a free canteen in the neighboring building and instituted an "off the ledger" system of gifts at Christmas and Easter, and bonuses which made living possible.' In the meantime, Clara managed the library with a light hand, noting that 'my small staff whose quality made up for its quantity did better without me. So instead of exhibiting my technical incompetence in the cataloguing department or at the distributing desk, I remained in my office, made regular rounds of the building, and kept myself in readiness to give help in case it was requested.' Her free time was devoted to writing a new book on William Shakespeare's life and works, to be published in English as *Shakespeare Rediscovered*. When Aldebert was not sleeping at the American Hospital, he and Clara went to plays. Their usual venue was the Théâtre de l'Odéon, 'which being a few blocks from the house was easy of access, and allowed us, even in case of an alert, sufficient time to return to our own home without being shepherded into an *abri* [shelter]. But occasionally we were tempted to Montparnasse, where the show was always worth seeing, and even to the Français [Comédie Française] which is more difficult of access.'

To reach the Comédie Française near the Louvre, Clara and Aldebert took the subway across the Seine. Clara was unlikely to have stood up when the train pulled into the George-V Metro station, as many other Parisians did in defiant tribute to the late British monarch. Clara had little patience with meaningless acts of resistance and none at all for direct assaults on the Germans. When Clara and Aldebert were exiting the Barbès Metro station one evening, she recalled, 'There was a deafening noise, whether of a pistol or a hand-grenade I could not tell: then the sound of running feet.' Suddenly, German military police ordered, 'Hands up!' Clara, Aldebert and the other passengers were led single file to two police examiners. The 69-year-old matron was frisked 'from throat to ankle' for firearms, an indignity she endured with her usual sangfroid.

What had happened? A young officer belonging to the German Navy had been killed by a shot fired from behind by a self-styled patriot who took to his heels and escaped, but meanwhile every individual passenger in the station had to be passed through the police sieve and if any suspicious objects were found they were certain of arrest and imprisonment. What was much more grave, following their customs of reprisal against which Vichy never failed to protest until finally the Germans renounced its practice, at least twenty Frenchmen were put to death for a crime with which they had nothing to do.

This was the first assassination in occupied Paris of a German, a naval cadet named Moser, on 21 August 1941. The culprit, 21-year-old communist Pierre Fabien, was later captured by the Gestapo on suspicion of other offences and escaped. In response to such attacks, hostages – communists, Jews, Freemasons, captured *résistants* or anyone held in a police station for violating the midnight curfew – were shot. On 20 October 1941, the Nazis executed fifty hostages in response to the killing of one lieutenant colonel. An anonymous American in Paris wrote to *The Nation* in New York about the reaction to the knifing of a German officer in the Bastille Metro station: 'Everyone on the platform and on the train was arrested. A certain number of them were allowed to see their families. They were optimistic and said they would be home soon. They were executed the next day.' After the killing of a German soldier on 1 March 1942, the commander of Grossparis, General Ernst von Schaumburg, ordered the execution of twenty Jews and communists – with twenty more to follow if the culprits were not captured. Five months later, Schaumburg was himself the object of an assassination attempt when a 17-year-old Jewish communist, Marcel Rayman, threw a bomb into his car. More hostages were murdered in response.

Clara, characteristically, blamed the Resistance rather than the Germans for the executions. The attacks led the Germans, in Clara's words, to come down 'harder and harder upon all those who were known to be connected with England and the United States'. While Dr Fuchs's assurances to the American Library were honoured, the American Hospital came in for scrutiny. Clara wrote, 'Général de Chambrun received visit after visit from German medical officers of high rank with no other object in view than to take over the whole establishment for the use of their army. Every time, he pointed out that it was full to overflowing, and that it would not be large enough for them.' In his obstinate refusal to admit German patients or to allow the Nazis a role in running the American Hospital, Aldebert was inadvertently assisting Dr Jackson to perform work for the Resistance that Clara abhorred.

In Princeton, New Jersey, Holly Beach Dennis began receiving unexpected letters from France. The authors claimed to be friends of her sister Sylvia. One letter, dated 27 August 1942, been posted from Orange in the Vaucluse. It said, 'I am a friend of your sister Sylvia who asked me to tell you she was very well and not in need of anything, has enough to eat and is in all respects all right.' It invited Holly to write to Sylvia at: 'Mlle. F. Bernheim, c/o Mme. Cohen, Hotel des Princes, Orange, Vaucluse.' The writer of the letter added, 'I have been helping her in the shop a little this winter and enjoyed it.' Holly, who had not received Sylvia's letters for many months, did not know that Shakespeare and Company had closed in December. Another letter from Marseilles from an Alexis Roger Roubin said, 'Dear Madame, I have had the pleasure to see, some days ago, your sister, Miss Sylvia Beach, whom I've met often in Paris.' The writer urged Holly to write to her at an address he gave in Marseilles. Holly was understandably suspicious, particularly because Sylvia did not spend time in either Orange or Marseilles. Rather than reply, she sent the letters to the State Department. Had Sylvia known someone was writing to Holly in this way, she would have been certain that the German security services were attempting to incriminate her. The coincidence that all three names – Bernheim, Cohen and Roubin – were Jewish pointed to Gestapo entrapment.

TWENTY-FOUR

The Second Round-up

SUMNER JACKSON HAD A PREMONITION that the Germans would take him in. On a weekend break at Enghien in early September 1942, he told his son, Phillip, that he expected the 'Boches' to lock up Americans like himself to trade for Germans detained in the United States. A few weeks later, Brazil, which had declared war on the Axis after the United States did, interned German citizens within its borders. The German authorities in Paris responded on Thursday morning, 24 September, by rounding up 1,400 American citizens.

Dr Jackson's bags were packed when the Germans swept through Paris that Thursday morning. Luckily, no escaped prisoners or British airmen were in sight at the American Hospital when the German troops arrived. Dr Jackson was examining a patient, but the soldiers ordered him to come with them immediately. Hospital staff, seeing the Germans leading their beloved 'Dr Jack' out of the hospital, mobbed him with presents. 'Before leaving,' Jackson later told Clemence Bock, his friend and former French tutor, 'I was given food packages, a few good bottles, and I stuffed it all in my pockets. I really didn't know what to do with it all.' He was driven to a police station, where, 'I ran into friends. We all had tags hung around our necks. They made me sign my name, and then we were shipped to the Gare du Nord, where I had the good fortune to come across a worker who had been one of my patients.' The worker would have been one of the SNCF employees on Dr Carrel's research and treatment programme. 'He was good enough to tell Toquette where I was.' The internees' next stop was the camp for British men at Saint-Denis, on the northern outskirts of Paris. It was lunchtime, 'and the English were getting aid packages from the King and Queen. So we had an hour and a half lunch that was better than we had at the hospital and at home. I also bought a pair of suspenders, the kind I never found in the Paris shops. And a reamer to clean out my pipe.' The men were taken by train to Compiègne. Clemence Bock recorded Jackson's words: 'That evening we were at Compiègne, the food was far inferior to the Saint Denis camp, but friends surrounded me and they gave me a small room with a small rug. Nearby was a camp where Jews were held.'

Some of the other internees were sons of American doughboys, Teddies, who had abandoned their mothers when they went home in 1918. Although legally American, many spoke no English and few had visited the United States. Some chose American citizenship over French solely to avoid French military conscription. They had little in common with the American-born captives, and there was occasional hostility between the two groups.

Sumner met Americans he knew. Some had been his patients at the hospital. One was the architect who designed the American Hospital's Memorial Building, Charles Knight. Another was the organist of the American Cathedral, Lawrence K. Whipp. Whipp had been in the camp, where he gave occasional organ concerts, since the first round-up in January. In another barracks were Charles Bedaux and his son, Charles Emile.

While Dr Jackson had been ready with his baggage for internment, the 5 a.m. knock on the door of his Ritz Hotel suite came as a shock to Charles Bedaux. Bedaux, who usually slept with the aid of sleeping pills, opened his door to Gestapo officers who informed him he was under arrest. He produced documents, including a *cadre de mission* issued by Pierre Laval on 25 August, to show that he was directing a German-approved project in French Africa. They left him and Fern to sleep. Less than an hour later, more Germans arrived with an order to take Mrs Bedaux. Again, Charles brought out the papers to prove that he was in favour with high-ranking German officials. Again, the Gestapo withdrew.

Instead of going back to sleep, Bedaux drove across the Seine to the Hôtel Lutetia to confer with friendly Wehrmacht officers. They knew of no order for his arrest, but they promised to make inquiries. Bedaux returned to the Ritz to await word. Later, the officers arrived to tell him that, because all Americans were being interned, they could not help him. The Gestapo took Bedaux and his son to a German police station near the avenue Foch and locked them into the lavatory along with fifteen other American men. The degradation of confinement in a police lavatory worried Bedaux less than what might be happening to Fern. The Germans had taken her as well, and he did not know where she was. He waited with his son and countrymen all day in the lavatory, until at nightfall a bus transported them to the camp for British internees at Saint-Denis. The French driver of the bus, Charles Junior recalled, thoughtfully drove a long route via Paris's more beautiful monuments. The driver told young Bedaux he wanted them to have a last look at the city.

The next day, the Americans at Saint-Denis were put on a train to Compiègne, where Charles and his son were strip-searched and given a medical examination. Bedaux father and son settled into Barracks 13, either for the duration of hostilities or until Charles's influence produced their release. In the evenings, Charles Junior played Monopoly with other internees on a board he made. Charles Senior made up his mind to help obtain the release of other prisoners, mainly those in poor health or who were young. Among the names on a list he compiled, he told Charles Emile, was Dr Sumner Jackson. Bedaux liked Jackson, whose medical unit had ministered to the Americans at the Château de Candé in 1940.

On 28 September, the French Foreign Ministry in Vichy confirmed to the American Embassy that the Americans had been seized. The embassy cabled the Secretary of State the same day: 'On the grounds of reprisals for alleged arrests of Germans in the United States on September 24, about one thousand Americans (men) and four hundred American women were arrested in Paris ... The men arrested were sent to St. Denis. They will be eventually sent to Compiègne where other Americans are now interned. Americans over 65 years of age and children under sixteen have not been taken.' The embassy said it had previously sent 'circular letters urging the Americans to go home'. Some had ignored the letters, while family, professional or personal commitments made it impossible for the others to leave.

Frontstalag 122's Section B, an American internment camp since the previous January, had improved with regular Red Cross visits and the efforts of long-term inmates to make it habitable. Donald Lowrie of the Young Men's Christian Association (YMCA), which shared with the Red Cross the privilege of access to camps during the war, visited Frontstalag 122 in October, shortly after the latest influx of internees. His inspection report stated,

The new arrivals have been well received and rapidly accustomed themselves to the camp. There are among them several talented artists who are improving the evening entertainments and the concerts. With regard to the food there is nothing to be desired. They [the internees] even use the word 'perfect' when discussing this matter. As for the heating there are enough stoves and the supply of coal is the envy of the local Parisians. All the foregoing obviously has an influence on the general morale, but that also is very good. We have never found in a camp such a pleasant atmosphere.

Two other YMCA officials, Auguste Senaud and Hemming Andermo, heard from the internees' representatives 'that there was a fine spirit in the camp, that the new arrivals had quickly adapted themselves to the conditions, and that there was no lack of food'. Their report continued,

The kitchen was 'excellent.' They received sufficient Red Cross parcels and were able to devide [sic] them up amongst themselves regularly. In the Canteen fruit and vegetables are available. The German authorities of the camp had now permitted to serve warm drinks to the relatives of the interned men on visiting days. This was received with great satisfaction as the camp is 3 km distant from the railway station, and in bad weather the visitors need something to restore them after the long walk.

One of the earliest visitors was Gaston Bedaux, who obtained the permission of the Feldkommandatur in Beauvais to visit the camp during Charles's first week there. He brought bedclothes and what he called some 'pitiful food' for his two relatives. He recalled,

> The visit was passionate. They would not let us be alone, a guard was present. We met in one of the barracks of the famous camp, which comprised a patrol-way and observation towers with armed sentries and guard dogs with restless characters.
>
> Charles was as cool and cheerful as usual despite the bizarre uniform in which he had been ridiculously dressed, and he had the audacity in front of everyone to criticize the organization of the camp and to give very wise advice in the calmest tone and the most persuasive way to the chief guard who was watching him, emphasizing that the terrible hygiene of the camp was repugnant to men from the New World.
>
> Charles had two ideas in his mind: to free his wife whose situation he did not exactly know and to attend to the common conditions [in the camp].

Gaston attempted to assure his brother that the Germans would not treat Americans harshly, while about two million Germans in the United States might suffer as a result. 'My brother,' Gaston wrote, 'spoke to me of his future African expedition, which worried me even more. I tried, by teasing him, to make him abandon the project that really seemed to me impossible under the circumstances.' He enumerated the obstacles: obtaining permits to travel, overcoming the red tape and acquiring equipment and materials to build a pipeline across the Sahara. But Charles was adamant that he would succeed. He already had Laval's *cadre de mission* authorizing him to 'undertake a study of the means for the improvement of the manufacture of oil in French West Africa and the transport of oil to Metropolitan France'. Dr Franz Medicus was hopeful that the Wehrmacht would provide steel and construction equipment. Gaston counselled his older brother, 'You are comfortably lodged at Compiègne. You have soldiers to guard you, dogs that do the rounds for you all night, no one dreams of robbing you, and I who have kept your accounts for a long time notice that this is the first time you've made some economies.' Charles laughed. Gaston, knowing his brother would return to the pipeline as soon as he was released, feared no good would come of it.

The camp commander permitted Dr Sumner Jackson to offer medical care to African colonial troops of the French army in an adjoining camp. The Germans' treatment of the black, mostly French West African, soldiers disgusted him. He witnessed guards beating an African soldier and forcing him to drink urine from a chamber pot used by the whole barracks. Jackson was not allowed into Sector C, the Jewish camp, where he correctly surmised conditions were worse.

'The Boches continued to annoy me with their paperwork,' Jackson told Clemence Bock. 'I had to sign and re-sign their papers. I've never written my name so often.' The Germans never asked him whether he had helped British or French soldiers to escape to England, apparently suspecting nothing about his work for the Allies. Negotiations for the release or repatriation of some of the Americans were taking place in Paris and Vichy, while the internees awaited news of their fate. On Jackson's behalf, General Aldebert de Chambrun lobbied powerful friends in the French administration. Jackson lingered in the camp for a week, until General de Chambrun 'came to get me in a Red Cross car with a chauffeur. He handed me copies of press clippings. We were famous!'

'Several Americans Released in France', ran the headline in the *New York Times* on 3 October, 'Dr. Jackson of Hospital at Neuilly Is Among Those Freed.' Fame was unwelcome to Sumner Jackson. He had every reason to avoid drawing attention to the hospital, while Allied soldiers waited there to rejoin their units in England.

With Dr Jackson's release, General Karl Oberg unknowingly forfeited a key operative in one of the largest escape networks in occupied Paris. It would not have been difficult to put Dr Jackson under surveillance. He lived in a street with bureaus of both the Nazi Party's Sicherheitsdienst (SD) at 19 avenue Foch and the Gestapo at Number 43. The American Hospital where Jackson worked was directly opposite the Germans' Neuilly Kommandatur. In failing to notice the physician's importance, the 'Butcher of Paris' missed an opportunity to shut down an important Allied escape route. But Jackson, rather than count himself lucky and avoid suspicion, looked for means to do more, not less, to resist. He sent ambulances to bring seriously ill Jews from the transit camps to the American Hospital. Tragically, when the patients recovered, the Germans sent them to their deaths.

Sumner and Toquette joined one of the many Resistance groups under the umbrella of Charles de Gaulle's Free French in London. Through trusted friends, they had contacted the Goélette-Frégate network established in 1941 by Georges Combeau, code-named Chaloupe. Combeau worked for Maurice Duclos, one of de Gaulle's staff officers whose *nom de guerre* was Saint-Jacques. Goélette-Frégate included many railway labourers, who for the most part supported active resistance to the Nazis, at Issoudun in Berry. Their primary objective was to send intelligence to de Gaulle and the Allies in London. The Jacksons' apartment in avenue Foch became one of their mail drops. A courier using the code name Verdier (Greenfinch) picked up and stored papers there. This work was perhaps more dangerous than aiding the escape of soldiers. At the hospital, people came and went without question. Bringing *résistants* and compromising documents into their apartment exposed Sumner and Toquette to denunciation from watchful eyes in a quarter of Paris filled with *Pétainist* Frenchmen and Nazi intelligence offices.

Charles Bedaux, meanwhile, turned down a German offer of release. He insisted on a renewed French commitment to support the construction of his consummate ambition: the Trans-Sahara Pipeline. Without it, he would remain with his son in Frontstalag 122.

TWENTY-FIVE

'Inturned'

GERMAN POLICE CONTINUED TO CALL on Sylvia Beach in her isolated mezzanine apartment above the shell of Shakespeare and Company. She remembered that 'the Gestapo would come and they'd say, "You have a Jewish girl – you had – in the bookshop. And you have a black mark against you." I said, "Okay, okay." And they said, "We'll come for you, you know." I always said okay to them. One day, they did come.' On 24 September 1942, Sylvia was out. A rumour that honey was available somewhere near the Church of the Madeleine sent Sylvia off on her bicycle to 'queue up for an hour or two, and perhaps come away without filling your can'. After waiting two hours for the precious honey, she cycled home to see Mme Allier, her concierge, weeping. She told Sylvia 'that "they" had come for me and I was to get ready at once'. She put away her honey, and 'they' arrived in a large military truck. The first internment of American women in Paris was underway.

'I must pack up only what I could carry,' Sylvia wrote. 'I thought as winter was coming and we might be taken to a cold German camp, woollies were the best: and flustered, with the soldier with a kind of dinnerplate hanging from his neck watching me as I dressed and hurrying me (schnel mächen), I put into my rucksack the woollies and by mistake two bibles and 2 complete Shakespeares as the most condensed portable reading.' Adrienne came down to say goodbye. Mme Allier continued crying, and the coal man opposite 'was for some reason in tears as well'. The commotion in the rue de l'Odéon brought out the

246

neighbours, residents and shopkeepers alike, who 'gathered as close as possible around the truck that I climbed into'.

The German truck was already carrying other American women. The first Sylvia recognized was her old friend Katherine Dudley, 'dressed as though for a vernissage, very smart, and in her usual good spirits'. Katherine was one of the four glamorous Dudley sisters, daughters of a well-connected Chicago gynaecologist, who had come to Europe before the First World War. The eldest, Helen, was a poet and had for a time been the mistress of Bertrand Russell. Dorothy Dudley, who had once been engaged to John Dos Passos, was a writer and the mother of painter Anne Harvey. Caroline Dudley had been instrumental in bringing the *Revue Nègre*, featuring a young Josephine Baker and jazz clarinettist Sydney Bechet, to Paris in 1925. With her husband, Joseph Delteil, she wrote some of the pieces for the *Revue* that astounded Paris and added to the allure of black American jazz among fashionable Parisians. Katherine was an accomplished painter, known mainly for her portraits. She was taking care of Gertrude Stein and Alice B. Toklas's Paris apartment in the rue Christine, near her own at 13 rue de Seine. Stein and Toklas were living at their country house in Bilignin in the Vichy Zone, where Americans were not being interned.

The truck trundled through Paris from the house of one American woman to another. Each time the Germans failed to find anyone, the women cheered loudly. 'After they had rounded up any American women to be found,' Sylvia wrote, 'we went on a long truckride but shut in as we were couldn't see where on earth they were to deliver us.' The Germans deposited the women at the northern edge of Paris in a place Sylvia 'knew in better days as the Zoo', the Jardin d'Acclimatation in the Bois de Boulogne. There, 350 American women were herded into the monkey house in which 'we were the only monkeys'.

The Swiss Consulate in Paris, acting for the United States, prepared a report on the internments for the American Legation in Berne:

The arrests began Thursday morning September 24, 1942 and ended on the evening of September 26. In the meantime each woman was examined not only from a medical point of view but also regarding her identity. Certain ones were immediately released due to their poor health.

Upon arrival of each bus the French Red Cross distributed gratuitously chocolate, biscuits and English books for the travel.

Sylvia received presents from friends who came to the zoo. The Germans allowed the women to take walks 'in a minute garden where, over the distant hedge we could see any friends who cared to come and have a try at making themselves heard and at hearing our voices in unison calling loudly for that something in the top bureau drawer etc.'.

Drue Tartière, the American former actress and wife of Dr Thierry de Martel's nephew, Jacques Terrane, had been picked up on 24 September from her house 20 miles south of Paris in Barbizon. Drue had left Radio Mondiale and become active in the Resistance, hiding Allied flyers in her house. She had rented a second house in the countryside as a rendezvous for *résistants* and a hiding place for British weapons and agents. She thought the Germans had arrested her as a *résistante* and feared that she might betray her comrades under torture. During two uncomfortable nights in German police custody with a 64-year-old American neighbour, Marion Greenough, she came to realize that she was being interned merely as an enemy alien. When she and Miss Greenough arrived in the Bois de Boulogne on 26 September, Drue wrote, 'A crowd was gathered around the large glass-enclosed structure as our bus drew up to the big door of the Jardin d'Acclimatation. People outside the glass windows along the terrace were trying anxiously to catch glimpses of their loved ones within.' Outside, rain poured on the old men, women and children desperate to know what would happen to their imprisoned mothers and wives. A report by the YMCA noted, 'On Sunday visitors were not allowed, but friends soon discovered that by paying five francs admission to the Zoo they could reach a place where they could see and talk with the American women through a double row of gratings with German guards in between. Everyone considered it a great joke that they could pay admission to see their friends in the Zoo.'

In a make-shift dormitory on the second floor of the monkey house, Drue enjoyed a reunion with old friends. 'The first person I ran into was Gladys Delmass, who had worked at the Paris Mondiale radio station after war broke out,' Drue wrote. 'She was a very bright girl from Hartford, Connecticut, educated at Vassar and Cambridge, England, where she had become an authority on Elizabethan literature.' Gladys was married to a Frenchman, Jean Delmass, who worked for the Vichy government. Drue saw another friend, the sculptress Elsa Blanchard, whose family she had known in Pasadena, California. She was introduced to Sarah Watson, directress of the Paris student hostel, the Foyer International des Etudiantes, 'short and round, with the pink skin of a baby, snow-white hair, and a kindly, illuminating smile'. Drue thought her 'soft South Carolina accent added to her charm, and her attractions were enhanced by a lively wit and keen intelligence'. With Miss Watson was another directress of the hostel, Mary Dickson. Sarah Watson introduced Drue to Sylvia Beach, whom she knew by reputation as the 'proprietor of the famous bookshop in the Rue de l'Odéon, Shakespeare and Company, and publisher and friend of James Joyce'. Sylvia, although she did not mention the fact in her own account of being, as she spelled it, 'Inturned', was wearing the ribbon of the Légion d'Honneur that she had been awarded in 1938.

Sylvia was pleased to meet 'our lovely Drue Tartière' and to see again 'our genius sculptress' Mabel Gardner 'in a long cloak, her golden hair like the angels in the Italian pictures'. Drue called Mabel Gardner the 'sculptress who had lived in Montparnasse for many years' and saw her as 'a middle aged woman who looked somewhat untidy, but was perfectly serene and had a detached, mystic air'. Sylvia introduced Drue to Katherine Dudley, 'friend of my friend "Baron" Molet and of Picasso'. Through Katherine, Drue met 'Noel Murphy, a tall, blond, middle-aged woman who looked like a Viking. She had studied lieder in Germany and sang in concerts in Paris. Mrs. Murphy had won the Croix de Guerre in 1940 for her work in evacuating refugees under shellfire.' After meeting many old and new friends in the monkey house, Drue noticed an incongruous sight.

My attention was drawn to a woman who was sitting on the edge of a cot with an ermine wrap around her feet. She was passing around a five-pound box of chocolates to her friends. I learned that she was Mrs. Charles Bedaux, at whose château the Duke of Windsor married Mrs. Simpson. Mrs. Bedaux said in a very loud voice that she did not expect to be with us long, and that she was waiting for Otto Abetz, the Nazi fifth columnist in France before the war and the new Nazi Ambassador in France, to come and get her and her sister released.

Sylvia was surprised to see, as more and more women arrived, American nuns from convents all over the Occupied Zone. The community of American women in France, Sylvia wrote, was an extraordinary mélange: 'There were Americans coming from every kind of milieu – a number of artists as it was Paris, a number of French war-brides of American soldiers from World War I, some teachers, some whores, some dancers, a milliner or two, a poet or two, a lady who lived at the Ritz, the wife of Bedaux the spy and quite a few crazy women whose case was not improved by capture.'

Sarah Watson was, in Sylvia's words, 'busy trying to make us all as comfortable as though in her pleasant hostel, which was with only these cots around the walls, close together, and as we discovered soon when it rained, water dripping from a leak in the roof on our faces'. The conditions affected some of the women more than others. 'Sick women were lying on their cots, moaning,' Drue wrote. 'Nervous and anxious wives and mothers were walking up and down restlessly. Everybody was crammed together in this uncomfortable room, where puddles of rain had gathered from leaks in the glass roof.' Worse, Nazi guards lurking in the bathroom 'did not seem at all embarrassed at the duty of watching us'. Many of the women, including Sylvia and Drue, had doctors' letters certifying that internment would damage their health.

After a dinner of 'soup, meat loaf, and potatoes and German black bread', the women retired to their dormitories. Some of them cried, until, as Drue noted, 'this wailing gave way to a cacophony of snores'. In the darkness, leaking rainwater drenched Drue's feet. German soldiers with flashlights stomped into the room to count the women. A few screamed, and one blurted, 'Don't look now. I've got a man in my bed.' Drue wrote, 'When the Germans had counted methodically up to a number, like forty-four, some of the women would shout, "sixty-four," and get them so mixed up that they had to start all over again. The soldiers yelled roughly, "Sei still!" but it did no good. The women roared with laughter at them.' Sylvia remembered, 'All night long, they would flash the lights in our faces. To count us. They went around counting us, and we were never the same number. And they found this a great bore.'

In the early morning, soldiers woke the women and went to the gallery above the dormitory to watch them get dressed. Not every woman, Drue commented, was embarrassed.

As they were putting on their girdles and stockings, the women resented this intrusion and shouted remarks at the Nazis. One of them, who wore a big pink hat and a silver-fox cape and had henna-dyed hair, let down the front of her slip, bared her heavy breasts and dashed eau de cologne under her armpits. Putting her hands on her hips, she shouted up at the Nazis, 'I do hope you're enjoying yourselves!' They retired hastily.

Some of the women were released quickly because of ill-health or age. Miss Greenough, who would be over the 65-year age limit in two weeks, was permitted to return home. Fern Bedaux was freed for other reasons. Drue watched as a 'group of French collaborationists, obviously personages high in treachery, arrived with an important German in uniform. They were very respectful to Mrs. Bedaux, helped her pack her things, and out she swept while the rest of us were enraged at this exhibition of the power of social and political influence.' United Press reported from Vichy a few days later, 'Mrs. Charles Bedaux, who was arrested at the castle she and her husband provided for the honeymoon of the Duke and Duchess of Windsor, has been released but her French-born husband is still interned at St.-Denis.'

On Monday morning, 28 September, the Germans took 292 of the American women from the monkey house to buses just outside the zoo. They gave each one 'a sausage, a small piece of cheese and a loaf of bread'. Among this group of Americans were Drue Tartière, Gladys

Delmass and sculptresses Elsa Blanchard and Mabel Gardner. While they waited to board their bus, a nurse screamed, 'My God, Drue, you still in this country!' It was Ruth Dubonnet, American wife of André Dubonnet, the former First World War aviator and friend of Charles Bedaux and Aldebert de Chambrun. Ruth, who looked 'very chic in her Red Cross uniform', shouted again, 'What are you doing here?' Then, even louder, she demanded, 'Is it true what I've heard about Jacques being killed?' Drue shuddered and shouted back, 'No, I don't think so, that's the first I've heard of it.'

Drue knew that her husband, Jacques Tartière, was dead. Since the fall of France, when Jacques escaped to London to join Charles de Gaulle, Drue had denied all knowledge of his whereabouts. She told the police in Barbizon that she was waiting for his return, possibly from a prisoner of war camp, and let them believe she had a lover. This gave Drue a reason to remain in France that the police would accept. It also removed suspicion from Jean Fraysse, the putative boyfriend, when he stayed at her house in Barbizon to pass messages to his agents. Fraysse, Drue's former director at Radio Mondiale, had enlisted Drue in one of the earliest Resistance networks. Taking part in the Resistance was her way to support her husband and his country. Jacques was killed fighting for the Free French in 1941, when the British captured Syria and Lebanon from Vichy. Drue told no one of his death, lest the Germans investigate the widow of a Gaullist officer. To continue working effectively as a *résistante*, the former Hollywood actress posed as a harmless wife abandoned by a roaming French husband.

At the Paris zoo on the morning of 28 September, Drue feared that Ruth Dubonnet's chance remark, if overheard by the Germans, would endanger Jean Fraysse and the rest of his network. No one else appeared to hear, but Drue was not reassured when Ruth, whom she now saw as a collaborator, said, 'I'm going to get you out of this, don't worry.'

Drue asked the French driver of her bus to send a letter to one of her accomplices in Barbizon. The driver, who said he was ashamed to be driving for the Germans, hid her letter and promised to mail it. He recognized Mabel Gardner, his neighbour in Montparnasse, and offered to convey messages for her. Mabel recited a list of greetings for the cobbler, his daughter, the cheese seller and the rest of the neighbourhood. The driver told Drue that Mabel was 'much loved in our quarter'. As the buses pulled out, the French husband of the other sculptress, Elsa Blanchard, arrived. He was in tears. Elsa smiled at him, but, when he was out of sight, 'she broke down and wept'. The transfer of the Americans would take place at the small Pantin station, a less conspicuous venue than one of the mainline terminals. Nonetheless, the secret got out. Students from the Foyer International des Etudiantes somehow learned that their directress, Sarah Watson, would be there and were waiting when the buses drove up. The Germans would not allow the girls near, so they screamed goodbye to Sarah over the railway tracks.

Sylvia recalled being driven 'to a remote railway station, where a train of miserable third class cars were awaiting us. Our destination was not mentioned. The cars were sealed up, we started on a journey lasting all day and into the middle of the night.'

Drue, Gladys Delmass, Elsa Blanchard and five other women shared a compartment in a filthy third-class carriage that had not been cleaned from its last load of prisoners. The train headed east, reaching Nancy that night in the midst of Allied bombing. The German guards locked the American women into the train and ran for shelter. When the raid ended, German Red Cross nurses distributed hot coffee to the soldiers. The Americans asked for some, but the nurses 'took pleasure in throwing the dregs from the empty cups in our faces'. One German soldier gave Drue water from his canteen. In the morning, the train arrived in Vittel.

Vittel was a luxurious spa town in the Vosges Mountains in eastern France. An enterprising lawyer from Rodez, Louis Bouloumié, had transformed the village into a resort with lavish hotels, casino and thermal baths shortly after he bought its Fountain of Gérémoy in 1854. The bounty of hotel rooms had made it an ideal locale for interning British women in France in 1940. The camp was a large fenced-in area where most of Vittel's hotels were grouped around a beautiful park. Only barbed wire in the storm-fences and Nazi flags signalled that Vittel was a prison rather than a resort. Red Cross inspections in 1940 and 1941 reported that Frontstalag 194 at Vittel was the best German camp in Europe, although most other camps were so horrible that comparison was meaningless. Inmates lived in hotels. They did their own cooking and ate in their rooms. They received mail, monthly visitors and packages of food from their families and the Red Cross.

The new internees, apart from a few invalids who were taken in ambulances, walked from the train station through Vittel to Frontstalag 194. 'As we marched along,' Drue wrote, 'weary and dispirited, the Englishwomen who had been interned since 1940 hung out of the windows of the hotels where they were quartered and gave us a wild reception. They cheered, shouted greetings to us, and sang.' Like Drue, Sylvia remembered that the British internees 'cheered us as we arrived. We were to join them in what, thanks to their genius for colonizing, was a model internment camp.'

The somewhat squalid Hôtel Central was being renovated for the Americans, but it was not ready. The Swiss Consul explained in a report for the US State Department, 'The haste with which the arrests were made did not permit the authorities to prepare a building where the Americans might be placed upon their arrival.' Until the Hôtel Central was ready, the British women had to make room for their American allies. 'While awaiting the opening of the Hôtel Central the director of the camp placed the new arrivals in the Grand Hotel where they were temporarily assigned to the large rooms already occupied by two or three British internees,' wrote the Swiss Consul. 'Additional beds were placed in these rooms so that altogether four persons were accommodated. Each of these rooms had a private toilet and bath ... Everywhere the conditions of sanitation and ventilation were perfect.'

Frontstalag 194 already housed 1,123 women, mostly British, and 282 mainly older men, who had been released from the Saint-Denis camp to be with their wives. Married couples stayed in the Hôtel des Sources, and most of the British women lived in the five-storey belle époque Grand Hotel. Not all of the British women were pleased to share space and, for the first week, their Red Cross packages with the Americans.

The fresh arrivals had to deposit their money with the Germans, who allowed them to keep 600 francs each and to draw another 600 francs monthly from their accounts. Drue hid an extra 3,000 francs and her medical certificate in a shoe. As soon as she could, she approached the camp's commandant, whom she described as 'a short, stocky German with a pleasant face'. Captain Otto Landhauser was in fact an Austrian, who had been a physical education and singing teacher before the war. Drue asked him whether she and her group of friends – 'Elsa Blanchard, Katherine Dudley, Princess Murat, Gladys Delmass and Noel Murphy' – could share a room. Land-hauser and his assistant, an officer named Damasky who had lived in Canada for fifteen years and spoke English fluently, 'agreed at once'. German officers inspected the women's luggage for 'paper, envelopes, flashlights, which were forbidden for fear of signaling to planes, and reading matter, which was returned after examination by censors'. Drue said to the Gestapo officer going through her suit-case,

'There's nothing in there that would interest you. Why bother?'

He looked up at me and smiled. 'Gee, why the hell didn't you go home?' he asked.

'How do you happen to speak English like that?' I asked.

'I worked in a sugar factory in Yonkers until the war started,' he said. 'Do you know Yonkers?'

Although a Gestapo officer, he planned to return to Yonkers as soon as the war ended. After the suitcases had been cleared, Senegalese men, probably prisoners of war, carried them into the hotel for the women. Drue and her companions found their room, where two Englishwomen were waiting for them with a pot of tea. One was an old friend of hers and her husband's, Mary Walker. Mary had been suspected of work-ing for British intelligence, and the Germans had held her for four months in solitary confinement at the Santé Prison in Paris. 'She looked terribly broken in health and was obviously still suffering from the nervous shock resulting from her experience.' The living quarters were better than anything Drue had expected: 'Our big room had a balcony overlooking the Vittel *parc* and a valley of the Vosges. It was fine, rolling country, but fog often settled in the valleys and made the

255

weather miserable. There were tennis courts, a bowling green, and even a maypole, and some of the women had brought along tennis rackets or managed to get some sent to them.'

Sylvia's migraine headaches earned her a place in the hospital, which was run by English nuns, on the first night. Her friend Sarah Watson joined her. Sylvia 'fixed up a kind of supper for us both on an electric plate'. The nuns let Sylvia serve breakfast to the other patients. Among them were two charwomen, 'who were very pleased at having their breakfast in bed'. Another woman, also named Sylvia, had lived in the Ritz and did not regard breakfast in bed as anything less than her due. Sylvia called her 'the Giraff'. This lanky *grande dame* had brought all of her jewellery, including a pearl necklace that she asked Sylvia to fasten around her neck when she delivered the breakfast tray. The 'Giraff' wore 'dainty nightgowns, so sheer that the German doctor was shocked to see her so plainly through them'. Medical care was excellent, under the direction of a German, Dr von Weber, with five other physicians, four French and one Scottish.

Dr Donald Lowrie, the YMCA representative in Geneva, reported on 29 October 1942, a month after the American women had been installed at Vittel,

> All the previous reports we have had from Vittel and conversations with women here who had escaped from there give a picture of a camp which has practically all the features of a regular resort which Vittel is – space in the summer for tennis and other games, besides extensive parks, all open to the use of the internees. To be sure there is barbed wire around all this and it is actually an internment camp where the inmates, as Paris tries to point out, enjoy many comforts which those in liberty do not have.

Sylvia Beach, Drue Tartière and most of the other American women, despite living in a de luxe prison with better food and amenities than they had at home, wanted to leave. Sylvia, who was already feeling cut off in Paris, missed Adrienne and the rue de l'Odéon. Drue was desperate to resume her work for the Resistance in Barbizon, her only reason for staying in France. Like many others in the camp, Sylvia and Drue used medical certificates from their physicians to make a case for release.

When the Americans' Red Cross packages finally arrived, Drue was delighted with her box of 'tea, coffee, butter, marmalade, canned meats, puddings, and cigarettes. It was like receiving a fine Christmas present to get one of these boxes with things which had been unobtainable in occupied France, and it was wonderful to smoke English cigarettes again.' Her maid in Barbizon, Nadine, sent 'a dozen eggs, a few potatoes, some apples and other fruits'. Sylvia 'fattened up considerably on their contents: in fact we were far better off than were our friends at home who were continuing to do without condensed milk, sugar, coffee, prunes, chocolate and cigarettes, which we indulged in at our camp'. The women also bartered the contents of their care packages for soap and other luxuries.

Sylvia compared the British favourably with her countrywomen: 'We American internees were not much respected by our gaolers. They were accustomed to the English women who were serious people and not frivolous and lighthearted as most of us were. They had established themselves in the Grand Hotel, where they worked on their tea in a spirit of cooperation and discipline, keeping the Germans busy with their demands.' The Englishwomen prepared meals for one another, 'each with the name of the internee and the hour it was to be cooked and when to be taken off the stove'. Teatime was busiest. 'The lift going up and down full of women with trays, with teapots and bread and butter and cakes: murmurs in sweet English voices, "*have* you had your tea? *are* you going to have your tea? ..." They were all provided with teapots and cups and saucers and whatever else might be lacking in the camp.'

Ninetta Jucker in Paris heard from a few of the American women released from Vittel that relations between the Americans and the British were not as cordial as they should have been between Allies:

> For the first few weeks they were billeted on the Englishwomen who were obliged to make room for them, and did so, I regret to say, with a very ill grace, though the Germans told them maliciously that they were to stage a reception for their Allies. They were no better pleased at having to share their Red Cross packages with the Americans until

these received their own, so that although the English camp was very much larger, more comfortable and better organized than the one assigned to the United States citizens, it seems that the American women met with such cavalier treatment at the hands of the British that they were very thankful finally to be removed to a hotel of their own. Some of them however revenged themselves later by stealing the produce from the British vegetable gardens while their owners were at lunch.

Drue Tartière observed that 'antagonisms cropped up between some of the Englishwomen and some of the Americans, and the English were particularly incensed when one American woman was taken away from Vittel in a beautiful private car, allegedly sent for her by [Spanish dictator Francisco] Franco'. Before she left, this woman gave a banquet in a local hotel for Nazi officers. 'The Englishwomen hissed her and were only prevented from stoning the car as it drove out of the barbed-wire enclosure by the presence of German guards.'

Sylvia wrote to Adrienne to thank her for sending some ink and to ask her to thank Françoise Bernheim for mailing a package of 'beautiful fruit ... Kiss her for me.' Although she and Sarah Watson had a room 'with a pretty view from the window', she pleaded, 'Set me free as soon as possible by papa 2.2.' 'Papa 2.2' was her name for Gordon Craig, whom she had helped out of internment almost a year before. She may have been hoping that the Gestapo contact who had released Craig and provided him with basics to get through Christmas would use his influence again. She added that she was saving cigarettes and chocolates to give to Adrienne and Maurice Saillet, her assistant in the bookshop, when they came to visit.

Adrienne and Saillet turned up at Vittel to see Sylvia. A German guard, assigned to observe their meeting, pretended not to notice when Sylvia passed Adrienne food from her Red Cross package: 'A can of condensed milk rolled on the floor – right under the table at which the officer was seated,' Sylvia wrote. As she left the camp, Adrienne used her cloak to conceal Sylvia's delicacies that were unobtainable in Paris.

In October 1942, Dr Edmund Gros died at home in West Chester,

Pennsylvania. He was 73. His obituary in the *New York Times* lauded his work for the Lafayette Escadrille in April 1916, when he had recruited pilots for the French Army's American flying squadron from his house in the rue du Bois de Boulogne. When the American Expeditionary Force arrived in France, the Escadrille was transferred to the US army as its 103rd Pursuit Squadron. Gros's long career encompassed directorships of the American Hospital and Library between the wars. His tireless service for both institutions during May and June 1940 undoubtedly hastened his death. He had left France in the autumn of 1940 a broken man. The realization that the Germans, whom he had opposed in two wars, had at last conquered France may have added to his depression. Nelson Dean Jay and Edward B. Close sent a telegram to Gros's widow on behalf of the hospital: 'There is no one who did more for the American Hospital than he and he will be greatly missed by all his many friends and colleagues.' Eugene Bullard, who took a job as a longshoreman at the US Navy Yard in Staten Island after his arrival from France in 1940, remembered Dr Gros differently. To Bullard, he was the white man who tried to prevent qualified black Americans like himself from flying for either the French or American armies.

In September 1941, Bullard had written to the US army asking whether he needed American government permission to join the 'English, Canadian or Free French Army of General Charles de Gaulle'. Bullard, aged 46, was deemed too old to enlist in the American army. So, he appointed himself recruiting agent for de Gaulle among African-Americans. He urged young black pilots to join de Gaulle's air force. Unlike America's first black air unit being formed at Tuskegee, the Free French squadrons were fully integrated.

Bullard stayed close to the French-speaking community in New York and probably had more in common with them than with his American neighbours in Harlem. His daughters, with the help of former Ambassador William Bullitt, were brought to New York in 1941. After their arrival, Bullard checked into New York's French hospital for the injury his back suffered in the artillery blast at Le Mans. He was exhausted from the war, his flight from France, his loss of status and the shock of living once again in a segregated society. But there was good news: one of his visitors at the hospital was the old Foreign Legion comrade he had given up for dead at Chartres in June 1940, Bob Scanlon. Scanlon told Gene he had been wounded and could not find Bullard in the mêlée after the shell hit. He too had made it safely home and missed their good life in France.

Before an American Legion reunion in New York, Bullard received an anonymous letter: 'Your extended sojourn abroad has perhaps made you forget that in the States white and colored people do not mix at social functions. It would be to your advantage not to attend the dinner on Monday night or to join in any social activities of Paris Post No. 1 in the future.' Bullard, who had never backed down from a fight in war or peace, went anyway. His old friends, many of whom had contributed towards the cost of his daughters' fare to America, welcomed him.

TWENTY-SIX

Uniting Africa

WHEN THE VICHY GOVERNMENT reconfirmed its commitment to the Trans-Saharan Pipeline, Charles Bedaux left the internment camp at Compiègne. Sumner Jackson had left a week earlier, and more 'special cases' were allowed to return to their homes in Paris. Charles Junior was released several days after his father. In the meantime, Bedaux lobbied the Germans to obtain transportation, fuel, building materials and heavy machinery for the African pipeline. 'The German authorities were not particularly impressed,' Gaston Bedaux wrote, 'but Charles was so persuasive, so seductive, that he made his point.' It happened at a meeting, where Gaston observed his brother 'at a green baize table surrounded by Frenchmen in civilian clothes and Germans in uniform. The French nodded, and the Germans said nothing. All of a sudden, my brother looked more severe than before and, turning towards the Germans, said to them, "Messieurs, you are the victors. That is a great responsibility."' The Germans, Gaston recalled, looked thoughtful and finally granted him an *Ausweis* and 'the required raw materials'. Dr Franz Medicus's Department of Administrative Economy set aside 15,000 litres of fuel, 140 kilograms of lubricants and 350 litres of oil for an expedition to survey the route. The supplies would await Bedaux at Casablanca. In addition, he would take thirty engineers and surveyors, a fleet of American trucks, Ford tractors and 200 labourers. He confidently predicted to Gaston that the pipeline would supply peanut oil to France at an annual rate of 200,000 tons within a year.

Gaston asked Charles whether he was afraid of tackling a job, difficult even in peacetime, that could be impossible during a war. 'But that's why I'm going there,' Charles answered. To Gaston, his brother's motives were humanitarian, removing the Sahara 'as a barrier to human progress'. More cynically, Janet Flanner wrote, 'This peanut scheme was the pinnacle in the fantasy, intelligence, and possible treason of Bedaux's business career, since it might actually have squeezed hundreds of thousands of tons of fat a year out of his projected Niger Valley peanut plantations for our enemies, the fat-hungry Herrenvolk, masters of the Continent.' The project stood to increase Charles's considerable fortune. He subscribed 2.5 million francs to a four million franc bond issue, the rest coming from French banks. His Syndicat d'Études du Continent Africain pour le Transport des Huiles Africaines would build and operate peanut refineries in the interior of Niger that would have a captive market for peanut oil in carbohydrate-starved France and, undoubtedly, in Germany. His enterprise would compete with French peanut planters along Africa's west coast and, given its lower delivery costs, probably put them out of business.

A few weeks after his release from internment, Bedaux had everything in place for his expedition to map out the pipeline route. Although Friedrich von Ledebur had declined to join the survey, there was no shortage of volunteers for the desert and jungle adventure. Bedaux prepared to leave for Algiers in late October with the blessings of his friends in the Nazi administration. On 23 October, Dr Franz Medicus wrote to him, 'When I put myself in your situation today, there can be but one thought in your mind: the welfare of your Fern during your absence. Go in perfect tranquility! Only look ahead of you, concentrate your attention on your great mission. Soldiers cannot fight with trouble behind them ... We who are staying behind form a ring of steel around Fern.' Four days later, Bedaux left Fern at Candé and flew to Marseilles, where he changed planes. Bedaux landed at Algiers' Maison Blanche airfield on the same day, 27 October. A torrid desert wind drove sand into the eyes of his son, Charles Emile, and a dozen assistants waiting to welcome his father to Algeria. They stayed at Algiers' most fashionable hotel, the art deco Aletti beside the port.

One of the first people Bedaux sought out was Robert Murphy, US Embassy counsellor in France and President Roosevelt's special representative in North Africa. Murphy had recently returned from Washington, where FDR assigned him to General Eisenhower's staff as political officer for Operation Torch, the impending Anglo-American invasion of French North Africa. It was unusual for State Department personnel to serve on an American military staff, but Roosevelt wanted to afford General Eisenhower the counsel of a diplomat who knew the politics of French Africa. Murphy's transfer from the State Department to the military remained confidential, even to his colleagues. If the posting of FDR's chief North Africa specialist to the Supreme Allied Commander's staff became known, Germany would draw the obvious conclusion that the United States planned to invade, not continental Europe, but French Africa. On 15 September, Roosevelt sent Murphy from Washington, disguised in a US army uniform as 'Lieutenant-Colonel McGowan', for a secret rendezvous in Great Britain with Eisenhower.

When Murphy's plane landed at Prestwick, Scotland, on 16 September, his cover was almost blown. In the air terminal, a familiar voice called out, 'Why, Bob! What are you doing here?' Donald Coster, the former ambulance driver who escaped from France in 1940 thanks to Sumner Jackson, was one of Murphy's vice-consuls supervising American aid deliveries in Morocco while sending intelligence to the Office for Strategic Services (OSS). Murphy did not get the chance to ask Coster why he was not in North Africa, where he would soon be needed: 'The bewildered man suddenly found himself being rushed off under arrest, and he was kept incommunicado ... Coster's innocent error was that he almost betrayed my presence in England, which was supposed to be top secret.' For the next day and night without interruption, Murphy conferred with Eisenhower's staff of American and British officers at the general's country retreat, Telegraph Cottage, near London at Kingston-upon-Thames.

The question confronting General Eisenhower was: would the French army of 125,000 regular soldiers and 200,000 reservists in Africa resist an Anglo-American landing along a 1,200 mile front from Tunis to Casablanca? If they did, it would mean death for thousands of Americans in their first big engagement of the European war. If they cooperated, the divisions would be intact to take on Rommel's Afrikakorps in Libya from the west while the British attacked from Egypt. Murphy, who spent most of the previous year in North Africa gathering intelligence with the assistance of his twelve 'vice-consuls', knew which French officers and civilian officials were pro-Allied. Persuading the rest not to resist an invasion of the French Empire would be a delicate and crucial exercise. To Murphy's surprise, Ike's staff knew almost nothing about North Africa. The general asked whether his soldiers would need warm underwear, and Murphy explained that the Atlas Mountains froze in winter. Politics were more complicated than logistics: 'I explained how seriously French officers took their oath of fidelity to Marshal Pétain and how they feared that Americans would underestimate the strength needed to establish themselves in Africa. I explained that these factors indicated we might encounter French resistance in several places.' The military planners, American and British, 'were unanimous in their insistence that surprise was of the essence'. That meant Murphy could not tell his allies in North Africa the date of the proposed invasion, which would limit their ability to help.

Murphy's return to Algiers on 16 October began a period of meticulous planning for an invasion whose date he dared not reveal. The Allies promised to drop arms for Resistance units to use if the French Army opposed the landings. Murphy established clandestine communications to Eisenhower's temporary headquarters in Gibraltar from hidden radio transmitters. Contacts were being made with prospective French leaders, especially General Henri Honoré Giraud. In April 1942, Giraud had escaped from a German prison, as he had done in the First World War, and gone underground in the Vichy zone under Pétain's protection. Murphy thought this national hero might be more acceptable to French officers in North Africa than General de Gaulle, whom many regarded as a traitor for rejecting the Armistice of 1940. Murphy was also courting Admiral Darlan, the anti-British commander of Vichy's army and navy, who had come to Algiers to see his son. Alain Darlan, stationed there in the army, had just contracted poliomyelitis. President Roosevelt, whose own polio made him sympathetic, offered young Darlan medical care at Warm Springs, Georgia. Murphy believed the gesture would make the admiral amenable to the American cause.

Murphy, despite working round the clock for the invasion, found time for several meetings with Charles Bedaux. The first was on Murphy's forty-eighth birthday, 28 October, the day after Bedaux's arrival. Murphy's three-page, single-space cable of 30 October to the secretary of state made clear that Bedaux was surprisingly candid about his plans. Bedaux described 'the harsh treatment of the male internees in the early days at the camp in Compiègne'. He claimed to have asked the Germans to transfer the Americans to more comfortable dormitories at University City in Paris, where American volunteer ambulance drivers had stayed in 1940. Nothing came of his suggestion, but Bedaux was demonstrating that he had tried to help his countrymen under occupation. How had Bedaux himself been permitted to leave the camp? Murphy wrote, 'Mr. Bedaux's release, he states, was granted on the basis that he is charged by the French Government to perform a mission in French Africa and it was in that connection that he called upon me in Algiers. He said that he convinced General [Karl Heinrich] von Stülpnagel, in command of the German forces in occupied France, of the necessity of permitting France to build a strong French Africa.'

German support for the scheme included the allocation of 55,000 tons of steel at a time when the Wehrmacht was short of metal to manufacture weapons. Germany lent Bedaux 240 workers, who had been constructing the Trans-Saharan Railway. Most of them were prisoners of war or anti-Franco Spaniards and effectively slave labour. The Trans-Saharan Railway, Bedaux told Murphy, 'had been definitely abandoned because of the enormous expense involved and the current lack of material and equipment'. The pipeline project was more important and would have a greater economic impact. Murphy's memo continued, 'According to this plan, the culture of peanuts in French West Africa is to be entirely reorganized and the center of the industry transferred from Dakar to Ouagadougou in the Ivory Coast, and the vast and fertile area in the bend of the Niger river, including parts of the Ivory Coast, French Soudan [sic] and the Niger colony, are to be exploited on a vast scale.'

Robert Murphy did not tell Bedaux anything about the impending invasion or that one of his 'Group of Five' allied agents was Jacques Lemaigre-Dubreuil. The French industrialist was Murphy's link to General Giraud, and he carried messages back and forth across the Mediterranean between the two men. He was called alternately by *Time* magazine 'a leading member of France's financial aristocracy' and 'sleek Jacques Lemaigre-Dubreuil, big time oilman, banker and part owner of the prewar pro-Fascist *Paris Jour*'. He had married Simone Lesieur, whose family owned the peanut oil company Huiles Lesieur. Through her inheritance, her husband was a peanut oil magnate with refineries on the West African coast. Bedaux's pipeline would move the peanut oil industry inland, sending the oil more quickly and cheaply than Lesieur could from Dakar. Murphy saw Bedaux and Lemaigre-Dubreuil frequently in early November, but he did not indicate in his memoirs or his cables to Washington whether he told either about the other. Nor did he warn Bedaux that his dealings with the Nazis might be illegal.

Bedaux, in a display of innocence or boasting, provided Murphy with photostats of his German-issued *Ausweis* of 1 October 1942, a letter from Fernand de Brinon supporting the pipeline and his *cadre de mission* from Laval. Murphy forwarded all three to the State Department. A few days after this interview, Bedaux invited Murphy and American Consul General Felix Cole to the Hôtel Aletti for lunch with his engineers and project managers. Among those who discussed the pipeline with the diplomats were Fernand de Brinon's Jewish stepson, Pierre-Jérôme Ullmann, Charles Emile Bedaux, purser Georges Rimailho, a former French African military governor named Colonel Pivain and Albert Giran, until recently an official of the Trans-Saharan Railway. They explained that the survey was divided into two groups: one from Marrakesh to the River Niger along the proposed pipeline route, the other into the Sahara to study the best means of conveying water to the men who would build the line. Murphy did not, in any of his correspondence to the State Department, indicate that he attempted to dissuade Bedaux from the endeavour.

Bedaux had the impression that French and American officials supported him. 'Here opinions are divided as to our real purpose,'

Bedaux wrote to Fern, who was waiting for him at Candé, 'but it seems to become clear that a pipeline is so logical to wipe out the Sahara as an obstacle that Algiers should now commit suicide for not having thought of it forty years earlier – it takes time for all babies to learn to walk.' He also cabled his New York secretary, Isabella Waite, 'I am on the right side. Doing good work. Why isn't Ledebur here?' Although his son was with him, he and the boy he had hardly known as a child were still not close. Frederic Ledebur remained the son he wished he had, and he wanted him on his greatest adventure.

Murphy saw Bedaux again on 5 November. Bedaux passed along a message from the French director of Port Etienne in Mauretania that he would welcome the arrival of the American fleet in West Africa. He also gave him marine charts of the coast around Port Etienne, which could be of use to American ships. If Vichy and the Germans had known Bedaux provided Murphy with this intelligence, they could legitimately have accused him of spying for the United States.

In France, Gaston awaited news of his brother: 'The last word we received from him was a telegram that protested against the late supply of certain deliveries.' Bedaux, with his son and his engineers, finalized the plans in his suite at the Hôtel Aletti. They set the start date of their Saharan expedition for 15 November.

TWENTY-SEVEN

Americans Go to War

DRUE TARTIÈRE WAS RECEIVING HELP from the Vittel camp gynae-cologist, a Jewish physician named Dr Jean Lévy, in convincing the Germans that she had ovarian cancer and needed treatment in Paris. Dr Lévy had been reluctant at first, telling Drue, 'You must realize the position they have me in, with my old father locked up, and the rest of my family potential hostages.' As Dr Lévy fell in with her plan, he gave her drugs to increase haemorrhaging. Heavy bleeding would help to convince the other doctors she was gravely ill. While examining her in the presence of his Scottish assistant, Dr Monteith, he said, 'Very bad, very bad.' The key was to persuade the camp's chief physician, Dr von Weber, that she was not faking. 'He's a brute,' Dr Lévy explained, 'a regular Prussian, but he knows absolutely nothing about a woman's insides and he asked for my diagnosis.' When von Weber examined Drue, she wrote, 'He treated me politely, but he treated Dr. Lévy, because he was a Jew, as if he were some kind of reptile. It was hard to keep my temper in his presence, but I did, for I would lose everything if I lost that.' They told von Weber that Drue needed X-ray treatments, which were not available in the camp. But von Weber wanted to operate and insisted she remain for more observation.

Jean Fraysse, Drue's friend and Resistance commander, came all the way across France from Barbizon to visit her at Vittel. Tired from a long journey that he made without papers and in constant danger of arrest, Fraysse sobbed when he saw how ill Drue looked. In the visitors' room, which was part of the censor's office at the edge of

Frontstalag 194, he demanded of a German officer, 'What have you done with this woman?' The officer was Captain Landhauser's deputy, Damasky, whom Drue called 'the blond German who had been polite to us when we entered the camp'. Damasky had not known until that moment that Drue was ill. He asked her, 'Is this your sweetheart?' When she said he was, Damasky offered to leave them alone for twenty minutes, adding, 'But you must pass no notes to each other.' When they were alone, Drue begged Jean to stop crying. He must not give the Germans the satisfaction of seeing his grief. 'He blamed himself for getting me into this situation by permitting me to remain in France,' Drue wrote. He told her that all the 'good people' in Barbizon, by which he meant those who hated the Nazis, missed her. Many friends were pleading for her release. Georges Hilaire, secretary general for administration in Pierre Laval's cabinet, had written to the Gestapo in Paris to assure them that Drue was not involved in politics. Jean had asked Serge Lifar, the Russian ballet choreographer popular with the Germans, to appeal to Marshal Goering for her. Another friend had contacted Count Joseph von Ledebur, a friend of Charles Bedaux's, to expedite Drue's release. Jean urged Drue to feign illness so convincingly that she would be hospitalized. Just then, Damasky returned and asked Jean whether he had a pass to be in Vittel.

Jean admitted that he didn't. 'I can understand,' Damasky said, 'what one will do when one is in love.' Damasky did not arrest Jean and allowed him to leave the camp. Drue, walking back to her hotel, stopped beside a tree and wept. An Englishwoman put her arms around Drue and said, 'Darlin', it's awfully nice to have someone who loves you enough to come to see you. You shouldn't be sad about that. He's a very handsome man.'

The camp dentist, Dr Rolland, who was related to some of Drue's friends in Barbizon, was trying to convince von Weber to send her to Paris. If that failed, he said, the superior of hospital sisters, Mother Mary de la Providence, would take her out of Vittel in a nun's habit. Sylvia Beach had already noticed that most of the English nuns were working with the Resistance. Dr Rolland called Dr Lévy, who advised Drue, 'Have a *crise* this afternoon in your room, and I will have you brought over to the hospital, but be very careful. I am told that some of the women in your room are Nazi sympathizers.' He probably meant Noel Murphy and Gladys Delmass, who moved in collaborationist circles in Paris. Drue feigned her *crise* and was admitted to the hospital. Instead of pills to stop bleeding, she took tablets to increase it, imperilling her health. Sylvia Beach and Sarah Watson, who were still living in the hospital, made frequent visits to her bedside. Drue felt guilty for causing her friends so much worry, but she could not tell them the truth. She lay there for a week, growing steadily more frail. Then, one of the nuns rushed into her room and said, 'I must get rid of your ash tray and cigarettes, it's that Prussian brute, and he's due on the floor today.' They heard Dr von Weber's heavy boots in the corridor.

> Von Weber came into my room. I had no make-up on, my hair was hanging down, and I looked as wan and pathetic as possible. Dr. Lévy and Dr. Pigache, who accompanied von Weber on his rounds, stood at the foot of my bed, while the German sat down beside me and took my hand.
> 'I hear, *ma fille*,' he said, 'that things do not go well.'
> I left my hand in his and said, 'No, not at all well, Herr Doktor.'
> 'I still say you should have an operation,' he insisted.

Drue said she would recover with X-ray therapy from her doctor in Paris. Ever the actress, she 'squeezed a few tears'. Von Weber ordered the sister to bring him rubber gloves and Vaseline. 'I was thoroughly scared now and loathed the idea of his touching me,' Drue wrote. 'I had a *crise* and put on a scene like a virgin. Dr. Lévy came around to the side of my bed and said, "Don't be frightened, the Herr Doktor is merely going to examine you, and it will be over very quickly."' Von Weber conducted the examination, kicking Dr Lévy out of his way, but Drue was bleeding too much for him to make a diagnosis. Sylvia Beach and Sarah Watson feared she might die. Drue wrote, 'Dr. Lévy was worried, not only about me, but about his family, of whom he had had no news. He took to walking up and down the corridors of the hospital most of the night, the sisters told me, and they were afraid he would lose his sanity.'

As winter set in, some of Drue's friends from the Hôtel Central made regular visits to see her and to enjoy the central heating their rooms lacked. One was Noel Murphy. When Dr Lévy saw her in Drue's room, he left. Noel said, 'I think it's a disgrace to have you, an American woman, taken care of by that Jew! I loathe the man!' To protect herself and Dr Lévy, Drue did not respond.

On 8 November, Dr Rolland ran into Drue's room. 'The Americans have landed in North Africa!' He beamed. Sylvia Beach and Sarah Watson rushed in as well, and they held a small celebration. Outside in the corridor, Dr Lévy was singing.

Just before midnight on 7 November, the BBC broadcast a message to North Africa, '*Allo Robert, Franklin arrivé.*' In Algiers, Robert Murphy understood. Franklin Roosevelt was at last committing the American army to battle. 'So, for two hours before American forces were supposed to enter Algiers,' Murphy wrote, 'I signaled full speed ahead for our local operation. Our resistance groups began to seize key points in Algiers, taking over quietly and with little opposition.' Of the 540 young men who seized Algiers' government that night, 450 were Algerian and French Jews. A. J. Liebling, the *New Yorker* correspondent who met the *résistants* afterwards, wrote that they 'seized the telegraph office, the municipal power plant, the Préfecture of Police, and other nerve centres, and arrested the ranking army officers who were not in on the plot and Admiral Darlan himself'. After the American invasion force missed its 1 a.m. deadline to enter Algiers, Vichy soldiers took back the buildings held by the *résistants*. 'The troops outnumbered them and had artillery,' Liebling wrote. 'After a resistance during which several of their number had been killed, the pro-Allied civilians had surrendered. They had held Darlan for four hours, and it is easy to understand how much their attack had served to distract attention from our landing.' But where, the pro-Allied French wondered, had the Americans landed?

Charles Bedaux was in a deep sleep at the Hôtel Aletti. His Medinal tablets, combined with noise-blocking wax in his ears, left him impervious to events. His third-floor suite had been commandeered that day by a Wehrmacht general on the Armistice Commission, forcing Bedaux into a room on the second floor that he had to share with a German named Captain Wurmann. Charles Emile recalled knocking on his father's door to inform him of the invasion. He and his father went up to room 305, where Pierre-Jérôme Ullmann and Georges Rimailho were staying, for a better view. Before dawn, a hotel waiter saw Charles Bedaux drinking brandy on the balcony with Captain Wurmann, while tracer bullets passed overhead. The French Resistance passed on a report to the Americans about Bedaux's valedictory drink with the German officer.

Vichy French troops arrested not only the agents who had seized government buildings, but Murphy himself. 'By that time,' Murphy remembered, 'I was experiencing grave doubts, owing to the non-appearance of American soldiers or any word from the "vice consuls" posted on the assigned beaches to receive our troops and guide them into the city.' The Royal Navy, blaming navigational errors, had landed the troops at the wrong beaches. This delayed American entry into Algiers by thirteen hours, when Admiral Darlan agreed to a ceasefire. Murphy suspected the diversion had been deliberate, because the British distrusted the French Resistance units whom Murphy had informed of the landing sites.

Nothing about Operation Torch had gone according to plan. General Giraud, whom Murphy was relying on to persuade his fellow officers not to resist, was still in Gibraltar with Eisenhower. A British destroyer steamed into the port of Algiers, accidentally blowing up petrol reservoirs, and retreated without disembarking any American troops. The British failed to deliver the weapons Murphy had promised the Resistance. One of the OSS vice-consuls, Donald Coster, was under arrest in Scotland, and the other eleven waited uselessly on the landing beaches as guides for troops who never arrived at the assigned rendezvous points. Yet Operation Torch, which Murphy admitted had been 'a partial bluff', worked. 'Only a few hours after the first American and British troops hit the beaches near Algiers,' Murphy wrote, 'two of the highest-ranking French officers in Africa had personally arranged a local ceasefire, and this had been imposed almost without incident. They also had tentatively promised to arrange similar ceasefires throughout French Africa.'

With Algeria and Morocco in American hands, the politicking began among French officers – Generals de Gaulle and Giraud and Admiral Darlan – for control of the liberated French territory. The crucial consideration for the French was that they retain sovereignty in North Africa, which ruled out an American military government. The Americans lacked local expertise and had no personnel who spoke Arabic or Berber and only a few who knew French. The administration continued as before, with Vichy officials governing the Arab and Berber inhabitants. Commerce resumed, and Charles Bedaux saw no reason to abandon the pipeline. It would be just as useful to the Free French and the Americans as it would have been to Vichy and the Germans. When the battle ended, the first thing Bedaux did was to lobby Robert Murphy to give his scheme the full support of the American government.

The Allied invasion of Algeria and Morocco was not the only good news that Drue Tartière received in her Vittel hospital bed on 8 November. Later that afternoon, Dr von Weber told her, 'I am sending word to Berlin that I think it advisable you be sent to Paris.' He would discharge her in three or four weeks. 'Aren't you happy?' 'Not especially,' she said. When he asked her why not, she responded, 'Well, I am sorry for you, because now you are kaput.'

> Dr. Lévy and Dr. Pigache, who were standing at the foot of the bed, looked as if they would collapse. The red-haired English sister giggled. Von Weber looked at me in surprise and answered, 'That's where you make a big mistake. This war has just reached its normal plane, and it can go on now for five years.'

When von Weber left, the red-haired nun said, 'Five years, the old fool.' Dr Lévy reprimanded Drue for taunting the Prussian and reminded her, 'He is a very dangerous man.' Lévy protected Drue, putting blood-soaked rags in her bed before von Weber's visits.

A few nights later, Drue and the other patients in the hospital heard the thunder of engines streaking across the sky. When the internees realized that RAF bomber squadrons were flying over Vittel on their way to targets in Germany, they turned on all the lights in their hotels, waved to the planes overhead and cheered wildly. From the British women's rooms came the strident singing of 'God Save the King'. Prison guards shouted and fired into the air to make the women turn out the lights and be quiet. The English and American internees hurled pots and pans down at the Germans while cheering the bombardiers. In the hospital's corridor, Dr Monteith danced a Highland fling with Mother Mary de la Providence. Dr Lévy was also celebrating, until he saw Drue rushing around in her nightgown. He ordered her back to bed. If Dr von Weber saw her on her feet, she would never get to Paris. Finally, the Germans turned off the electricity, and the women went to bed. But, at one o'clock in the morning, the planes cruised overhead on their way home. The women celebrated again. 'We were sadder now, though,' Drue wrote, 'for we were wondering how many of the planes were missing.'

The camp commandant, Captain Landhauser, cut the women's rations, denied them electricity and revoked their visitors' privileges.

TWENTY-EIGHT

Murphy Forgets a Friend

IN VICHY, THE NORTH AFRICA INVASION astounded American diplomats as much as it did the Pétain regime. Keeler Faus, a junior member of the US Embassy staff, wrote in his diary for 8 November that a colleague 'knocked on my door at 7.45 to tell me that Mr. [Tyler] Thompson wanted me to come to the Embassy at once – for the Americans invaded North Africa – Algeria and Morocco – before dawn this morning'. Thompson told him that embassy Chargé d'Affaires S. Pinckney Tuck had just delivered a message from Roosevelt to Pétain, who declared that the French Empire would defend itself against the American aggressors. Faus was assigned to obtain as much petrol as he could, so that the diplomats could escape when Vichy severed relations with the United States. 'The cops in the streets gave me big smiles,' Faus wrote, 'one or two took off their caps, several stopped me to shake hands to congratulate me.' Thirty-two-year-old Faus, who had been western Maryland clay court champion before joining the foreign service, went to the Tennis Club after lunch and played two sets. In the evening, he went out again 'not knowing whether we might not meet the Germans somewhere on the way. Rumor had it that they were driving south. No incidents.'

Although Pétain had ordered French forces in Africa to oppose the Allied invasion, he refused a German directive to declare war on the Allies. Pierre Laval went to Germany to see Hitler, who demanded the use of French air bases in Tunisia and at Constantine in eastern Algeria. When Laval declined, German troops in the Occupied Zone invaded Vichy France and disarmed the French troops who had been permitted under the Armistice of 1940 to retain light weapons. 'The night before the Germans came down and occupied the southern zone,' Françoise de Boissieu, a Jewish *résistante* hiding near Vichy, said, 'Ruth Thompson, wife of one of the American diplomats [Tyler Thompson], came by bike to tell us we had to leave at once. If not, she warned us, we would be among the first arrested.' Although due to give birth in a few weeks, Françoise and her Catholic husband fled immediately and took refuge in the house of friends in Paris.

The American Embassy's staff did not depart, despite their elaborate preparations. The Germans rolled into Vichy on 11 November and seized the embassy. Tyler Thompson, in an interview years later with author Adam Nossiter, recalled that the Germans ransacked the Villa Ica while 'one goon had a machine gun pointed in my stomach, which is not the way diplomats are supposed to earn their living'. When Keeler Faus tried to enter the building, he noted in his diary that evening, 'a German stuck the point of his submachine gun in my stomach and asked me what I wanted'. The French sent Thompson, Faus, Douglas MacArthur and the rest of the diplomats with their families to be interned in the town of Lourdes. The French lodged them in a hotel of the same name as the one they inhabited in Vichy, the Ambassadeurs. They had the run of the town, provided they went out with a French inspector of police, and were able to play tennis and touch football. Interned in other hotels were American journalists and Red Cross personnel. With the rupture of diplomatic relations between Washington and Vichy, American citizens in France no longer had an embassy to represent them.

Germany's abrupt occupation of southern France, combined with Italy's seizure of Corsica and the Côte d'Azur around Nice and Menton, made French officers in Algeria and Morocco more hostile to Germany. Pétain was now physically, as he had been politically, a hostage of the Nazis. The French officers' loyalty to him had become meaningless, making their conversion to the Allied cause easier. Eisenhower capitalized on French support to combat the Germans, Italians and diehard Vichyites in Tunisia.

To Charles Bedaux, the replacement of Vichy administration in Africa with American occupation did not mean a change of plan. He pursued the Americans for his pipeline, as he had once charmed Franz Medicus and Pierre Laval in pursuit of the same goal. Felix Cole, US Consul General in Algiers since 1938, received Bedaux on 11 November. The efficiency engineer was as persuasive as ever, arguing that the Americans had the opportunity to prove to the French that they would 'not retard French Africa in its development but on the contrary that they are ready to accelerate the rhythm of its progress towards complete unity by aiding in the construction of a pipeline for water and fuel [as] a link between Africa and North Africa'. Consul General Cole's cables to Washington did not indicate that he encouraged Bedaux, but Bedaux told friends in Algiers that Cole was interested in his project. Either Cole said something to give Bedaux hope, or his salesman's bravado made him believe Cole had. In any event, he went on planning his expedition.

During a Luftwaffe raid over liberated Algiers one evening, Bedaux spoke to a group of American reporters on the balcony adjoining his at the Hôtel Aletti. When journalist John MacVane realized the man speaking to him was the famous Charles Bedaux, he asked why the efficiency engineer was in Algeria. Bedaux answered, 'I am carrying out an industrial mission for the Vichy government. A big communications plan in Morocco. I was caught here by the invasion of our American troops.' In MacVane's book, *War and Diplomacy in North Africa*, his publishers removed the section on Bedaux over his objections, in which MacVane wrote, 'He did not seem happy at the arrival of "our American troops." "All my plans are now upset," he said. "Naturally I am going to see Admiral Darlan and the American authorities about the possibility of carrying through the scheme anyway."' MacVane distrusted Bedaux: 'His voice dripped with cordiality but no one who saw those hard, shifting eyes behind the heavy spectacles would have trusted him on sight.' The next night, during another German raid, MacVane was hosting Americans from the 'political-warfare section'. Bedaux invited the men to watch the spectacle from his balcony. 'I tipped off the political warriors as to who he was and we went out on the balcony,' MacVane wrote. One of the Americans was Edmond

Taylor, a former *Chicago Tribune* correspondent in Paris who had signed on with the Office of Strategic Services.

Bedaux needed American approval to cross US army lines with his long truck convoy. He wrote to Robert Murphy on 17 November, congratulating him on 'work well done' and declaring that he was 'ready to place myself at your disposal as soon as the French Government cancels the Mission Order I have'. With French officers ignoring orders from Vichy to fight the Americans, it was unclear why Bedaux was waiting for Vichy to cancel his. When American forces requisitioned the Hôtel Aletti, Bedaux and his son found an auberge not far from Algiers at 'Ain Koussa. From there, he tried to contact Murphy. One letter to the diplomat, written the day his survey mission should have begun, 15 November, argued that the pipeline was in America's interests: 'Carrying through the study of the laying of a pipeline for water and fuel across the Sahara would be a fine opportunity for the United States to show to the world that French Africa far from suffering from the occupation can reasonably hope to receive from America the first practical link between its northern and central sections. At the present exchange the whole project would cost only sixteen million dollars.' Bedaux ended on a personal note, 'Will you remember August 1939 when we gave you Candé as an annex to the Embassy and realize that in my desire to be usefully active today I ask your help.'

Murphy came under strong criticism in the press and among the Free French for leaving Vichy officials in office, appointing former Vichy Interior Minister Marcel Peyrouton as governor general and allowing the *résistants* who had obeyed his orders on 7 November to be arrested. Many of his Jewish agents, including Dr Henri Aboulker, were imprisoned by the very men they had detained on Murphy's orders. When Pierre-Jérôme Ullmann, the Jewish stepson of Fernand de Brinon, learned that many of Murphy's Jewish agents had been taken into custody, he left Bedaux's employ and went south to British territory.

When Dr Aboulker and the colleagues who seized Algiers for the Americans were finally released, the aged doctor told A. J. Liebling, 'It is almost impossible for one of us to see Murphy. He shuns us like a case of an extremely contagious disease.' Murphy, in the aftermath of the invasion, was also ignoring his former host and frequent source, Charles Eugene Bedaux. Bedaux's letters to Murphy went unanswered.

The New York Metropolitan Opera opened its thirty-eighth season at the beginning of December with a lavish production of Gaetano Donizetti's *Daughter of the Regiment*. The French-born soprano Lily Pons, wearing a demure white gown and revolutionary stocking hat, waved what *Life* magazine called 'the Fighting French Cross of Lorraine instead of the Tricolor while the entire company renders the *Marseillaise*'. The Cross of Lorraine was the symbol used by Charles de Gaulle and the Free French in homage to the Lorrainers, who had endured German occupation from 1870 to emerge once again as free Frenchmen in 1918. The rousing anthem, which was not in Donizetti's original, may have convinced some of the audience that, with American help, France would be freed of German troops as Lorraine was in 1918.

TWENTY-NINE

Alone at Vittel

ON 10 DECEMBER, Dr von Weber informed Drue Tartière that she could leave Vittel the next day. Dr Lévy took her aside and asked her to visit his mother in Paris. Drue thanked him for all his help, which he had offered at the risk of his life. 'His eyes filled with tears,' she wrote, 'and he went out.' Noel Murphy and Sarah Watson were released with her. Collaborationist friends in Paris had obtained Mrs Murphy's release, while Sarah Watson's patron had been the rector of the University of Paris, to which her American girls hostel was attached. A Hungarian priest with connections at Vichy may also have interceded for her. The three American women travelled under German guard on the overnight train from Nancy to Paris.

The departure of Sarah Watson and Drue Tartière left Sylvia Beach on her own in the hospital. Nights grew lonelier, and the German censor had still not returned her copies of the complete works of William Shakespeare. She read her bible. She wrote letters, most of which never arrived. And, as she wrote to Adrienne, she had *'migraines toujours'*.

'Suddenly, on Christmas Eve, we were told that all Americans were to move to the hotel reserved for us,' Sylvia wrote. The move was not much of a Christmas present.

Ours [the Hôtel Central] was carefully picked as very rundown, though it had been good in its days, apparently. It was a shabby, dirty old building, with plumbing out of order: the room I was to share with the other Sylvia, the Giraff, had dirty water over the floor which one of my fellow prisoners, the Princess Murat, was mopping up into a goldedged chamber pot with 'Grand Hotel' emblazoned on it. In the middle of the room, a large rathole. The kind of room in which my librarian friend said 'you slit your wrists.' ... The bathroom, I discovered, had no water, and the tub was for some reason full of mud.

The 'Giraff' was released before she could share the room with Sylvia. Sylvia believed that the woman's husband, a French colonel, had arranged it. Maurice Saillet sent Sylvia a Christmas hamper of treats from himself and Adrienne that Sylvia thought was '*magnifique*'. Adrienne's sister, Rinette, sent her home-made gingerbread. Sylvia's thankyou letter for the presents to Adrienne ended, '*Dis à notre ami tu dors.*' *Tu dors*, you sleep, was her play on the name of their friend Tudor Wilkinson, an aged American millionaire from St Louis, Missouri, who was doing his best to obtain Sylvia's release. A former thoroughbred owner, he had given up racing when he decided the fences were harming his animals. Wilkinson had amassed an art collection that included Joshua Reynolds's portrait of George Washington and some of the finest Holbeins in private hands. Hermann Goering knew of Wilkinson's paintings and, on a pre-war visit to Paris, stopped by his flat at 18 quai d'Orléans on the Ile Saint-Louis to see them. Although this acquaintance gave him access to Goering and his minions, the American was no collaborator. Behind the carved mantelpiece of his lavish apartment overlooking the Seine was a cache of short-wave radios and weapons for the Resistance. His wife, Kathleen Marie Rose, had been the most famous dancer in the Ziegfeld Follies under her stage-name, Dolores Rose. She was also helping the Resistance and the downed Allied airmen whom Drue Tartière brought to her. Wilkinson had assured Adrienne in November that Sylvia would be released within a few weeks. Sylvia, however, remained interned, to Adrienne's disappointment.

Christmas at Vittel was nonetheless merry. The Dramatic Society's 150 members staged plays, and internees watched a series of films in the 1,000-seat camp auditorium: *The Corsican Brothers*, *Fort Dolores*, *Stage Door* and *If I Were Boss*. Midnight Mass was held on Christmas Eve in three different chapels for Catholics and Protestants, and on Christmas Day the women held a big party for the children. On New Year's Eve, there was a 'Fancy Dress Ball'.

When Sylvia moved out of the hospital to lodge with the main body of American internees in the Hôtel Central, she threw herself into work as camp postmistress. She sorted and delivered letters, much as she used to collect mail and put it in cubby holes at Shakespeare and Company for her writer friends. 'Every day I went over to the Grand Hotel where the mail was deposited, and brought ours in a pouch to the hotel where we lived,' Sylvia wrote. 'Some of the internees were rather unreasonable and when I was unable to produce a letter for them accused me of keeping it back.' Organizing the kitchen in the new location was more difficult: 'There were no utensils to cook our miserable soup in nor to make our acorn coffee in.' Nor was there any china, as in the Grand Hotel. The task of making the kitchen function was assigned to 'a young, pretty woman with high heels and a long cigarette holder: to my surprise [sic], she took hold of the kitchen problem which was serious when we were suddenly installed in our hotel … This blonde girl made such a row that the articles we needed were finally provided. Every day at noon we filed up for the soup – hot water with a hint of potatoes, cabbage and little else – and the bowls were to contain enough for supper as well as lunch.' Only Mabel Gardner, the Montparnasse sculptress with the golden hair, liked the prison food. All she took from the Red Cross packages was cigarettes. She happily spent her time carving firewood into voluptuous statues.

THIRTY

The Bedaux Dossier

IN ALGIERS, EDMOND TAYLOR, the former *Chicago Tribune* correspondent, was working for the OSS and the US army's Psychological Warfare Branch. His memoirs, *Awakening from History*, contain his account of the decisive role he played in Charles Bedaux's life:

> From acquaintances in the *Deuxième Bureau* [French military intelligence], responsible at the time for counterespionage activities in Algeria, I had learned that Bedaux had been stranded in Algiers while on an economic mission to West Africa on behalf of the German High Command in France. Since he was a naturalized U.S. citizen – though a Frenchman in every other respect – there appeared to be a prima facie case of treason against him. The *Deuxième Bureau* professed to be mildly surprised that the American authorities were uninterested in the matter. Its own interest, however, was no more than tepid, mainly, I gathered, because Bedaux was a frequent dinner guest at tables of several influential and politically conservative French hostesses who were currently launching the post-invasion social season in Algiers; several of my superiors on Gen. Eisenhower's staff, it was intimated, were on occasion his fellow guests. That, as far as I was concerned, made Bedaux a convenient symbol of the unwholesome political promiscuities and of the collusion between defeatism and resistance that the Murphy-Darlan accords had inevitably encouraged ... Without looking deeper into the affair, I made up my mind to have him put behind bars, and eventually, by

283

grossly misrepresenting the French feelings about him to the Americans, and the American attitude to the French, thus making each side feel its good faith was being questioned by the other, I succeeded.

Taylor's memoirs made no mention of the fact that he met Bedaux with journalist John MacVane at the Hôtel Aletti two weeks earlier during a Luftwaffe attack.

On 5 December, a French officer of the Brigade of Surveillance drove to Bedaux's hotel and announced, 'I'm very sorry, Mr Bedaux, but you and your son will have to come with me.' The Bedauxs were under arrest. The French locked them up in a police station overnight and took them to the Italian Club, which had been converted into a filthy and overcrowded prison. The Bedauxs were crammed into a makeshift cell with twenty other inmates, who had shared an open lavatory in a corner. Charles Bedaux, lord of the Château de Candé, slept on a hard concrete floor beside his cellmates from all corners of French Africa and waited for charges to be brought against him.

Eisenhower's confidant and aide, Commander Harry C. Butcher, wrote in his diary for 8 December 1942, 'Charles Bedaux, the stretch-out promoter with whom American labor leaders raised hell when he was discovered as the advance man for the Prince of Wales and the Duchess' visit to US, has been arrested here by the French on charges of being a Nazi agent ... They have photostats of certain letters appointing him as an industrial agent by the Germans ... may be hung.' The photostatic evidence had been given by Bedaux himself to Robert Murphy. Murphy did not reveal who gave it to the French.

The press did not report Bedaux's arrest, although journalists in Algiers who learned of it attempted to. 'I tried to broadcast the story,' John MacVane wrote. 'The censor stopped it. After submitting the story every day for ten days, I brought it up at an open conference with a high American authority. He said that not all the evidence had been collected and it was thought better not to break the story just yet. Other reporters then tried to write the story but could not get it passed.'

The affairs of Charles Bedaux had been under scrutiny in the United States for some time, however, before Edmond Taylor came upon

Bedaux in Algiers. Percy E. Foxworth, the FBI's assistant director in New York, was running the investigation into the case of Charles Eugene Bedaux. It had begun for him in February 1942 when he received a register of suspected Axis sympathizers in the United States from the Office of Naval Intelligence. The suspects were to be investigated and, if judged security threats, detained without trial. On 18 February, Foxworth forwarded the names of the 'German, Italian, French, Spanish and miscellaneous suspected sympathizers to be considered for custodial detention' to FBI Director J. Edgar Hoover. One of the 'miscellaneous' was 'Bedaux, Charles Eugen [sic]'. Bedaux's name – or variants of it, including Henri Bidaux – had been circulating in the intelligence community since September 1941, when the State Department received the cable from Vichy in which Bedaux disclosed his intention to develop the trans-Saharan Railway and gave his opinion that Germany would win the war.

The cable also said that Bedaux had asked the embassy for a copy of John Steinbeck's *The Grapes of Wrath*, adding the accusation that 'he was perhaps trying to magnify the social problems which face the United States'. (Or he may have wanted to read a book that the Nazis had banned in Paris.) The case against Bedaux gained momentum in November 1941, when the American Consulate in Lisbon reported the allegations of Fern's old friend, Katherine Rogers, about Bedaux's work for the Germans. Additional information originated with Bedaux himself during his many candid conversations with American diplomats in Vichy and Algiers. Everything he told Robert Murphy and his colleagues ended up in cables to Washington, where his activities excited increasing suspicion.

In April 1942, Percy Foxworth thought he could close the Bedaux file. He wrote to Hoover from the New York office that, as Bedaux was not in the United States, 'no further action is being taken relative to this matter'. However, on 4 May, S. Pinckney Tuck, American chargé d'affaires in Vichy, wrote to the secretary of state, 'Mr. Charles Bedaux, who is now in the United States, remains on the best of terms with Marshal Goering.' Bedaux was not in the United States, but in France. Tuck saw him there shortly after he sent the cable. Nor was it likely Bedaux was 'on the best of terms' with Goering. When Bedaux had bragged that he knew the Luftwaffe chief, he was probably bluffing. The Bedaux file stayed open and grew thicker. Worthington E. Hagerman, Consul General in Lisbon, relayed a denunciation of Bedaux from Russell M. Porter, an American who had left Paris on his way to the United States. Porter told Hagerman that Charles and Fern lived at the Ritz, 'where they frequented German officers, many such being regular clients of the hotel'. Hagerman, who had lived at the Château de Candé in 1940 and was on amicable terms with Bedaux, added his own observation about Charles's brother, Gaston: 'Mr. Bedaux's brother, of whom I do not know the first name, had the reputation of being a Gestapo agent.'

On 10 July 1942, J. Edgar Hoover sent Percy Foxworth an urgent directive: 'I desire that an appropriate investigation be instituted to ascertain the present whereabouts of Charles Eugene Bedaux, and whether he is engaged in any activity inimical to the interests of the United States.' Foxworth devoted more and more man-hours to the investigation of 'Bedaux, Charles E. – Espionage – G[erman]'. All letters from Charles Bedaux to the United States were subjected to censorship. Bedaux's friend, Frederic Ledebur, and his secretary, Isabella Waite, were also put on the Watch List for varying periods so the FBI could read their mail to assess their involvement with Bedaux. Foxworth read with interest Bedaux's letter to Frederic Ledebur, inviting him to join the North African expedition. Hoover wrote to the New York office on 1 August 1942, asking to know where 'Fred' Ledebur was. He added, 'It is also requested that the identity and activities of Mrs. Waite be ascertained inasmuch as she may be acting as a mail drop for enemy agents.'

While Frenchmen were denouncing one another to the Germans and to Vichy, it seemed Americans were imitating them. Not only was Gaston Bedaux falsely accused by an American diplomat of working for the Gestapo, wild charges about Frederic Ledebur and Isabella Waite were stacking up in the FBI's files. The Bureau's San Francisco office wrote of Ledebur, who hated the Nazis so much he had cut relations with his brother Joseph, 'He is reported by the person who has his greatest confidence to be definitely pro-German, to have made numerous inquiries regarding ship production of the West Coast, to be interested in plane production, and to carry at all times a moving picture camera equipped with telescopic lenses.' The New York office added, 'Fred Ledebur is alleged to have Nazi propaganda in his automobile.' Percy Foxworth echoed Hoover's allegation that Isabella Waite was providing 'a mail drop for enemy agents in this country'.

On 16 October, matters took a more ominous turn for Bedaux. Assistant Attorney General Wendell Berge wrote to J. Edgar Hoover, 'Will you please forward to the Criminal Division all data so furnished (by State Department) and any other matter you may have in your files pertaining to the subject [Bedaux].' The FBI sent the Criminal Division a register of gossip, innuendo, rumour and, also, facts on Charles Eugene Bedaux and those closest to him. No firm evidence of treason had emerged by the time he was arrested on 5 December 1942. In fact, the case appeared so weak that the French police released him and his son on 29 December. Satisfied he had been exonerated, Bedaux – supremely confident as usual – remained in Algiers to begin his desert mission in the New Year.

PART FIVE

1943

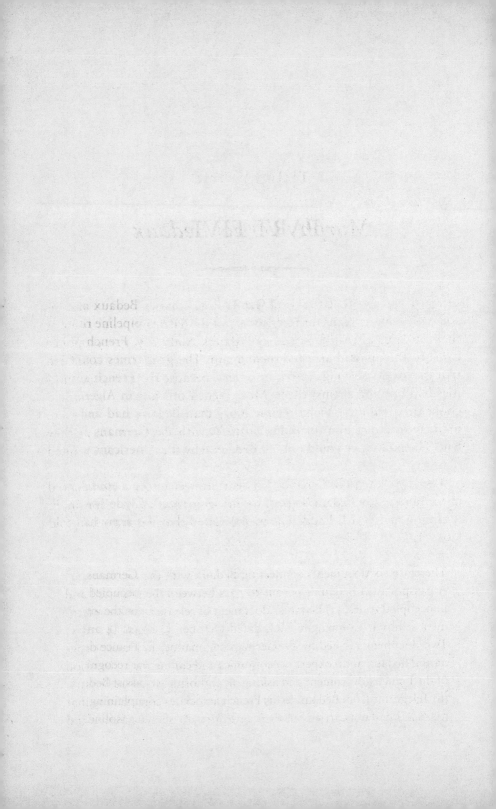

THIRTY-ONE

Murphy versus Bedaux

ON THE MORNING OF 2 JANUARY 1943, Charles Bedaux and his son were making plans for their survey of the Sahara pipeline route at their auberge in 'Ain Koussa near Algiers. Suddenly, French police came to the inn and arrested them again. The gendarmes confessed that they were obeying American orders, because the French authorities had nothing against them. Most French officials in Algeria had cooperated with the Vichy regime more than Bedaux had and were unlikely to indict him for doing business with the Germans as they had. The policemen could not tell Bedaux why the Americans wanted him.

Two days later, FBI Director J. Edgar Hoover wrote a confidential memorandum on Bedaux's arrest for his senior staff, Clyde Tolson, E. A. Tamm and D. M. Ladd. The memo stated that the army had told Hoover:

There are six documents connecting Bedaux with the Germans: (1) A passport. (2) Bedaux's permit to pass between the occupied and unoccupied zones. (3) Bedaux's document of release from the internment camp at Compaigne [sic], dated October 1, 1942. (4 and 5) Two documents issued by the German commander in France designating Bedaux as an expert in economics and calling for recognition of the French government and asking all authorities to assist Bedaux. (6) Telegrams from Bedaux to his French associates complaining that the Nazis had not carried out their agreement to obtain gasoline and tires for him. General Eisenhower does not consider it advisable for political reasons to hold the trial in North Africa.

At 3.15 that afternoon, senior Justice Department, FBI and army intelligence officials discussed Bedaux in Washington in US Attorney General Francis Biddle's office. Colonel Pierce of Army G-2 said that he would 'inquire of General Eisenhower whether it was agreeable for a representative of the FBI to proceed at once by plane to North Africa for the purpose of getting [an] investigative report upon which appropriate prosecution could be initiated ... It had been indicated by General Eisenhower that he did not want to try these two men in Africa because of the peculiar local situation.'

The French held the two Bedauxs for five days, until American Military Police arrived to take charge of the pair. The MPs incarcerated them in a shed at one of their posts in Algiers. When Bedaux protested at the appalling conditions, the MPs moved them to a base just outside Algiers. According to Gaston Bedaux, father and son were 'lodged comfortably in a villa near El Biar', the diplomatic quarter overlooking Algiers.

On 10 January, the army informed the FBI that Eisenhower 'requested an FBI agent be sent to Algiers'. Assistant director Percy Foxworth and agent Harold E. Haberfeld were summoned to Washington to receive yellow fever injections and instructions for their journey to Algiers. Foxworth, who had led the investigation of Bedaux in the United States, would at last have the opportunity to question the man whose life he had painstakingly dissected for the past year. FBI Agent D. M. Ladd wrote to Hoover on 10 January that he had asked the War Department for its complete file on Charles Bedaux. Bureaucratic competitiveness asserted itself, as Ladd wrote to Hoover:

I have had photostatic copies made of the entire file, unbeknownst to the War Department, and a photostatic copy of this file is attached here for your information. It will be noted that the top serial is a radiogram from General Eisenhower which briefly outlines the information available concerning the subject Bedaux. *It does not appear that there is much of an espionage case* from the facts set forth in this wire, which contains nothing beyond definite dates. (Author's italics.)

Two days later the FBI's Percy Foxworth and Harold Haberfeld reported to the Pentagon for military briefings on their impending trip to North Africa. The War Department gave them an appointment for yellow fever vaccinations the next morning in the Pentagon dispensary. Foxworth appeared uneasy about the journey. G. O. Burton, an FBI agent who drove the two men to the War Department, wrote that day that 'Mr. Foxworth attempted to secure from the Colonel information about the trip such as type of plane to be used.' Burton took Foxworth and Haberfeld the next morning to the Pentagon for their inoculations and then to Gravelly Point Airport for a 10.50 a.m. flight to Miami, Florida, in a four-engine Douglas Aircraft military transport. From Miami, they would go to Natal, Brazil, to fly to one of the nearest points in Africa to the western hemisphere, either Accra or Dakar, and on to Algiers. Because military transports flew only in daylight, the two FBI men were not scheduled to see Charles Bedaux in North Africa for five days.

While agents Foxworth and Haberfeld were heading to Miami, the State Department at last disclosed Charles Bedaux's arrest to the press. 'Charles E. Bedaux, friend of the Duke and Duchess of Windsor, has been arrested on charges of trading with the enemy,' the *New York Times* reported on its front page the next morning. 'Secretary of State Cordell Hull said today he had been informed of the arrest but had no details.' Cordell Hull's claim of ignorance would not stand even a cursory scrutiny of the voluminous correspondence that he and his department had exchanged on Charles Bedaux for the previous two years. The FBI was dismayed that the State Department had leaked Bedaux's arrest to the press, D. M. Ladd calling it in a memorandum 'quite disappointing'. Someone, probably in the State Department, told the *New York Times* and *Time* magazine that Bedaux had gone to North Africa to corner the orange crop, but no press report mentioned his pipeline. Bedaux, held incommunicado in Algeria, was not permitted to see journalists and tell his story.

The *New York Times* interviewed Albert Ramond, who had taken control of Bedaux's American company in 1937. Ramond explained that his former boss was 'a man who loves danger for the sheer pleasure of seeing whether he can get out of it'. Ramond defended Bedaux: 'He was a good American, naturalized twenty years ago, and he had always a soft spot for his native France. I cannot conceive his selling out to the enemy.'

Gaston Bedaux recalled that the press in Paris also reported Charles's arrest, but dropped the story 'for a long time'. Information about his brother was difficult to obtain. 'Communications between Africa and us was [sic] totally interrupted,' he wrote. Fern, who had heard nothing from Charles since his first arrest, was effectively a hostage at Candé against her husband's return. All she knew by mid-January was that the Americans were holding him.

Although the State Department informed the press that Bedaux stood accused of 'trading with the enemy' with a maximum penalty of 'ten years' imprisonment, a $10,000 fine and forfeiture of property used in the offense', no one told Bedaux of what he was accused. He and his son could not prepare a defence until they knew what the charges were. They gradually adapted to US Army routine. They ate in the soldiers' canteen and shared their bathroom. When the MPs got to know Bedaux better, they stopped posting an armed guard outside his door.

Confinement was forcing father and son into an unaccustomed intimacy. Until now, they were almost strangers. Waiting in the desert, they had time to discover why they never liked each other.

Percy Foxworth and Harold Haberfeld of the FBI did not reach Algiers to see Charles Bedaux as planned on 18 January. Foxworth had been right to show concern about the 'type of plane to be used'. Soon after their military aircraft took off from the airfield at Natal, Brazil, for the eastward crossing of the Atlantic, it crashed. Everyone on board died. The FBI sent two other operatives to Algeria, but they did not have Foxworth's long experience investigating the exploits of Charles Eugene Bedaux.

The loss of the two FBI men's lives apparently tormented Bedaux. His brother Gaston wrote that Charles Junior told him of the 'sadness and disheartenment of his father. He was distressed that his own life had caused the death of two men.'

Charles Eugene and Charles Emile Bedaux had been cooped up together before – for two weeks at the Compiègne internment camp in September 1942 and more recently in Algiers. Theirs was an unusual distinction, that of having been prisoners of the Germans, French and Americans. In Compiègne and Algiers, they shared quarters with other prisoners. Now, they had only each other in the villa outside El Biar guarded by American Military Police. Circumstances were forcing father and son into the intimacy that they had avoided all of 33-year-old Charles's life. There was little alternative but to speak more meaningfully than they had before. The father thought they might as well tell each other their life stories. After all, they were almost strangers.

For Charles Junior, the monologue could not have been easy. He had once viewed his father in heroic mould, as most other little boys do. His earliest memory was of flying above the French countryside in a two-seater aeroplane piloted by his father. That had been in the spring of 1914, when flying was a novelty, France was enjoying its final days of peace and Charles Emile was four. France and Germany went to war in August, and Charles Senior volunteered as an American for the French Foreign Legion. Charles Junior's mother, Blanche, took their son home to Grand Rapids, Michigan. Thus began the first of many separations from his father.

Charles Senior was discharged in December 1914, without seeing action, after an accidental injury to his foot. He came home to Michigan, and the family took a rest on Michigan's northern peninsula amid the wild Indian country of woods and rivers that Hemingway wrote about from his own childhood. Back in Grand Rapids, while his father grew rich and began to make himself famous as a businessman-engineer, young Charles's world dissolved. Charles Senior's affair in 1916 with his secretary, a young woman named Kathryn Glarum, caused tension at home. Blanche somehow convinced the mistress that they were both victims of her husband's licentiousness, and both women left Bedaux. Blanche embarked on a tour of the Orient, taking young Charles and

Kathryn with her. Aged seven, the boy would not see his father for six years.

In Japan, Blanche learned that Kathryn was communicating with her husband and sent the girl back to the United States. Continuing her eastern voyage with young Charles, Blanche met an American millionaire named Alfred Bagnall. Bagnall was, as Bedaux then aspired to be, a millionaire. Like Bedaux, he worked as an engineer – not of efficiency, but of electricity. He brought Thomas Alva Edison's electric lighting to the Orient, first to the streets of American-occupied Manila, then to Japan. Sixty-year-old Bagnall was a philanthropist, whose charitable donations were often unsought and anonymous. When 27-year-old Blanche's divorce became final, they married and moved with Charles Junior to Bagnall's ranch in Orange County, California.

In the prison villa at El Biar, the son must have told his father about his education at the Harvard School on Venice Boulevard in Los Angeles, growing up in California during Prohibition and other aspects of his life about which the older man knew nothing. His first post-divorce meeting with his father took place in 1922, when, aged 13, the boy went to New York. It was a stiff, formal encounter in his father's suite at the Ritz, and it did nothing to bring the absent father and abandoned son closer. The glamorous stepmother, Fern Lombard, was in the room the whole time. A few questions and answers were all the boy recalled of the meeting.

In 1929, aged 20, Charles Emile returned to New York to see his father again. He had finished school and was contemplating university, although he was already older than usual for entrance. On this occasion, his father received him in his office on the sixty-third floor of the Chrysler Building. Charles sat through two business meetings, one with IBM chief Thomas Watson, before his father took him out to lunch. As in 1922, the session was uncomfortable. Yet, some of his early admiration for his father must have lingered, because the young man said he wanted to study engineering. He hoped to enter Harvard, but his father said Yale would be better. The son went to Yale.

The long discussion at El Biar, over days and nights between meals with the MPs, would have tried any father and son – especially two with mutual resentments. But it was leading to an understanding of a kind. Charles Emile enlightened his father about Albert Ramond, his former employee who had taken control of the American Bedaux company in 1937. It seemed that Ramond's wife had attempted to seduce young Charles in the summer of 1930, while they were together in the Ramonds' country house in north Michigan. He turned her down, more from youthful panic than moral qualm, because she was nearly ten years older than he was. The spurned woman told her husband that the youth had made a play for her. Enraged, Albert Ramond confronted the boy and swore revenge against his family. The revenge came in 1937, when he seized control of Bedaux's company.

When Charles Senior's turn came, he took even longer to regale his son with the adventure that had, until then, been his life. From sandhog to multimillionaire, semi-literate Montmartre street tout to friend of kings and presidents, he had enjoyed a life that was nothing if not eventful. There had been countless lovers, year-long safaris, financial achievements and scandals, his passion for Fern, exploring British Columbia for a safe route to Alaska, all leading to what should have been his greatest accomplishment and adventure: uniting the two halves of Africa with a pipeline across the Sahara. His regret at not having seen more of his son was mitigated by a belief that Blanche had taught the boy to hate him as she did.

On Wednesday evenings at El Biar, Charles Senior withdrew from his son. He said that Fern, a devout Christian Scientist, would be praying then and he wanted to share the moment with her. It was obvious to the son that his father missed her. Towards the end of Charles Senior's days-long narrative, he told his son that his Austrian friend in Paris, Count Joseph von Ledebur, was part of Germany's anti-Nazi underground. Charles Junior later told his father's biographer, Jim Christy, that his father concluded, 'It is better that you don't know what I have done to deceive the Germans. Just remember the words *Schwarze Kapelle*. I shall say no more.' *Schwarze Kapelle*, German for Black Orchestra, meant nothing to the son. He told Christy that the exchange of life histories helped him to understand his father. But he still did not like him.

THIRTY-TWO

Sylvia's War

SYLVIA BEACH'S FRIENDS IN PARIS and Vichy lobbied the Nazis for her liberty. Adrienne wrote to Tudor Wilkinson on 20 January 1943 to remind him of his pledge that Sylvia would be home by Christmas. He responded the next day, 'After receiving your letter this morning, I telephoned the Authorities and they were like me very surprised that Miss Beach has not been freed. But I have been assured that the order has been given for her liberation.' The 'Authorities', presumably the German police command, blamed red tape in Vittel for the delay. Still, nothing happened.

On the same day that Tudor Wilkinson wrote to Adrienne, Vittel received a fresh contingent of internees. If the American women in the camp were desperate to get out, the arrivals from Poland were grateful to be allowed in. Nominally American citizens, most had never seen the United States. The Nazis had taken them from the Warsaw Ghetto, where they confined and terrorized the city's Jewish population, because they held US passports by right of birth, marriage or family connection. One of them, Gutta Eizenzweig, wrote of her arrival at Vittel, 'I stood there in shock, for we had suddenly crossed the divide from hell to paradise.' Eighteen-year-old Miriam Wattenberg, whose mother had been born in the United States but moved to Poland as a child, was one whose US passport brought her to Vittel that winter morning. Her mother Anglicized the children's names to make them sound more American, and Miriam Wattenberg became Mary Berg. The teenager wrote in her diary that the Germans did not tell her, her mother and sister where they were going. They and other US passport holders had been in a camp at Pawiak, where she wrote, 'While we are waiting here we can see transports of people being sent out of the Pawiak to the Oswiecim camp. Is that where the Nazis intend to send us, too?' By then, young Mary had seen 300,000 people marched off to Oswiecim, the Polish town that the Germans called Auschwitz. It was only when the train taking her from Pawiak headed west that she realized her family's destination was not to be the infamous death camp. Crossing the frontier into France and seeing Vittel for the first time, the sensitive and thoughtful teenager wrote, 'Not a trace of the snow that covered Warsaw. Here everything is sunny and spring is in the air.'

After five days in the camp, Mary Berg met 'a number of American nuns, handsome young girls'. Mary, whose English was fluent, told them she had come from Poland. They asked whether she had received Red Cross parcels there.

When I told them that for six months I had been starving in prison, some of them gave me chocolate tablets. Then they asked me to wait a moment while they went back to their rooms. Soon they rushed out again, their hands full of canned food and sweets. I did not dare bite into the chocolate tablet I held in my hand. One of the sisters, seeing my confusion, broke off a piece and put it into my mouth. It was the first chocolate I had had in four years.

Mary met Dr Jean Lévy, who had done so much for Drue Tartière and other women at Vittel. 'His wife and child are in a camp near Paris, whence transports are constantly sent to Poland,' she wrote. 'He keeps asking us whether all that is said about Treblinka is true. He refuses to believe that people are killed there by the thousands with poison gas and steam.' She was pleased to discover the camp had a Resistance movement and a secret radio: 'It seems that the Germans suspect something of the kind, for yesterday they searched the hotel, but they could not find the radio. It is said that while the Germans carried on their search someone was walking in the park carrying the radio in a suitcase.'

Some of the American internees became pregnant. A YMCA inspector observed after a visit on 8 February 1943, 'A problem which concerns the International Red Cross more than us was laid before us: How are the necessary layettes to be secured for the 21 babies expected in the next few months?' More than layettes, some of the women needed husbands. Sylvia wrote that German soldiers respected expectant mothers so much that they found the fathers and told them to marry the women. 'Resistance was overcome and weddings with the bride in white veil and orange blossoms almost like in peacetime,' Sylvia wrote. Some of the brides, though, 'were pale as they had suffered considerably with nausea'.

Sylvia Beach was desperate to leave Vittel as her sixth month of captivity began in February 1943. The camp, however comfortable, meant the denial of the companionship, mainly of Adrienne Monnier, and freedom she needed to survive. Mary Berg, coming from Poland, discovered freedom in Frontstalag 194. 'There is no more wonderful feeling than freedom,' she wrote in her diary for 24 February 1943. 'In Vittel I have a taste of it for the first time in three years. Although I can see the barbed wire and the Nazi guards a few steps away, I feel myself under the protection of the American flag.' Yet the protection of her mother's flag and passport did not stop her mind from roaming back to Warsaw. 'The internees try to make the time pass by organizing all sorts of entertainments, dramatic circles, sports clubs, education groups, etc. But we do not share in all these games. My thoughts are constantly in Warsaw. What is happening there?' In March, the Germans moved the Polish Americans into the Hôtel Nouvel, where the Berg family's rooms 'were pleasant and clean'. In the hotel, Mary observed the American and English women: 'The relations between them are not of the best, for the English are rather snobbish.' On 29 March, the Germans sent all the American males who had been allowed to stay with their wives at Vittel back to Compiègne. Mary wrote, 'The Nazis gave the ridiculous excuse that German war prisoners are being badly treated in America. The camp authorities exempted from this order only Mr. D., who was recently operated on and is still in the hospital, Rabbi R., as a clergyman, and the [Brazilian] consul and his son. It is very lonely here without the men.'

Sylvia's detention allowed her to write to her sister, Holly Beach Dennis, via the Red Cross. A letter that she sent to Holly in October 1942 arrived only in March 1943. Neither Holly's reply nor a package of clothing she sent reached Sylvia at Vittel. In the early spring, Sylvia learned that her release might be imminent: 'Various friends at home who were on sufficiently good terms with the Enemy were continually working on our problem.' Sylvia placed her hopes in Tudor Wilkinson. Adrienne, on the other hand, had lost faith in Wilkinson's promises. She appealed to Jacques Benoist-Méchin, the early devotee of their bookshops who had been first to translate parts of *Ulysses* into French. As a minister for police in the Vichy government, he had helped the Germans to round up Jews, Freemasons and *résistants*. Adrienne's beliefs were in direct opposition to everything Benoist-Méchin represented, but under the occupation friends made compromises to help friends.

In March, the camp loudspeaker called Sylvia Beach's name. She was told she could leave Vittel at once. Mabel Gardner helped her pack, and she went to the commandant's office to obtain her release papers. When she told the officer in charge that she had no money to pay for the train to Paris, he threw her documents into the waste basket. Mary Dickson from the Paris students' hostel lent her money for the ticket, and the officer retrieved Sylvia's papers. A soldier was ordered to escort her out of the camp. Sylvia, who had been craving her freedom, nonetheless took no satisfaction from it: 'And what if my dear dear friends left behind in the camp were not released? This thought spoiled all the pleasure of release for me.'

Occupied Paris in the spring of 1943 was a harder place to live than the camp at Vittel. Although Sylvia could walk or cycle anywhere in the city, she was afraid of being interned again at any moment. 'I came back to Paris and hid for fear they'd think I was well enough to go back,' she said. Rather than move into her flat, where the Germans could find her, she took the advice of friends to 'disappear'. She wrote, 'Miss Sarah Watson undertook to hide me in her Foyer des Etudiantes (Students' Hostel) at 93 boulevard Saint-Michel. I lived happily in the little kitchen at the top of the house with Miss Watson and her assistant, Madame Marcelle Fournier.' She enjoyed student life for the first time in twenty-five years, taking lunch with Sarah Watson and the girls in the cafeteria and using the hostel's library. Best of all was that 'nobody let on that I was there'.

Every day, Sylvia made secret visits to Adrienne in the rue de l'Odéon. In Adrienne's shop, she read the first copies of the underground Editions de Minuit. Jean Bruller, Yvonne Paraf and Yvonne Desvignes had begun publishing the Midnight Editions' books shortly after Pearl Harbor with 5,000 francs donated by a Paris doctor. The first was Bruller's war classic, *Le Silence de la mer*, which he wrote using the nom de plume 'Vercors'. Vercors was the region where, even then, their friend and Hemingway's old sparring partner, Jean Prévost, was fighting in eastern France. Many of her and Adrienne's other friends were writing for the series under pen names. 'François la Colère' was in reality Louis Aragon, the poet who had fallen in love with Cyprian Beach twenty years earlier. 'Forez' was François Mauriac. 'Mortagne' was Claude Morgan, editor of the underground newspaper, *Libération*; 'Jean Noir' was the poet Jean Cassou. Bruller also published John Steinbeck's *The Moon is Down* in French. Sylvia's friend, the poet Paul Eluard, was, she wrote, 'active in bringing out and hawking about in the bookshops the Midnight Editions and other clandestine publications and dodging the Gestapo. He was obliged to sleep in a different place every night.' Copies were sent through the post and passed from reader to reader. Every hand-bound copy was inscribed, '*Ce volume, publié aux dépens de quelques lettrés patriotes, a été achevé d'imprimer sous l'oppression à Paris.*' ('This book, published with the aid of certain literary patriots, has been printed under the oppression in Paris.') One of the writers working on Midnight Editions, the poet Jean Paulhan, was arrested and spent months in solitary confinement. He later told Sylvia he kept his sanity by reciting to himself every poem he could remember. Adrienne took a risk merely reading the volumes, but she went further and hid copies in La Maison des Amis des Livres.

If the literary *résistants* were winning a battle to keep the culture of free France alive, other battles were being lost. Sylvia learned after her return from Vittel that her close friend and former assistant, Françoise Bernheim, had been arrested in one of the *rafles*, round-ups, of Jewish people in Paris. The Germans took her to Drancy and put her on the train for Oswiecim. By then, having heard from the Polish Jewish women at Vittel, Sylvia knew what happened to prisoners at Auschwitz. Another love of her life had been taken from her.

To complicate matters, she had to thank one of those responsible for turning women like Françoise Bernheim over to the Germans, Jacques Benoist-Méchin, for her own liberty. Adrienne confided in a letter to her assistant, Maurice Saillet, on 30 March, 'Sylvia has been to see Benoist-Méchin (it seems that it's really him who set her free, through an SS general). He was very kind, very affectionate and [he] promised to release her again if she is taken.' Nowhere in Sylvia's letters or memoirs did she refer to a courtesy call that she must have found distasteful.

When Drue Tartière asked Sylvia to visit some of the American flyers she was hiding at friends' apartments in Paris, Sylvia seized the chance. She and sculptress Elsa Blanchard went with Drue to see 'the boys' and 'to keep them from getting too bored'. The young Americans would have been delighted to hear her stories about Ernest Hemingway, John Dos Passos and the other 'lost generation' writers Sylvia had known in the 1920s. She gave them some of the clothes that Jim Briggs, Carlotta's husband, had left in their Paris flat with instructions for her to use them as she thought best. Sylvia's friend, Sarah Watson, brought the aviators meat from the refrigerator at her students' hostel. These American women welcomed the chance to do something for the young men whose bravery was bringing their own liberation closer.

THIRTY-THREE

German Agents?

THE WALT WHITMAN SOCIETY of Long Island called on Congress in March 1943 to revoke René de Chambrun's American citizenship. The *New York Times* reported on 7 March, 'The society charged that Count de Chambrun was "the chief instrument of the pending movement to expel a percentage of the Jews in France and responsible for the establishment, now under way, of Nazi-ized ghettos".' Although the accusation was far-fetched, it related to another instance of de Chambrun attempting to use his influence at Vichy. A former Jesuit priest, Abbé Joseph de Catry, had asked René for an introduction to Maréchal Pétain. Chambrun arranged for de Catry to meet Pétain's secretary, André Lavagne. The ex-priest was promoting what he called 'Christian anti-Judaism' to 'restore the dignity of Judaism and to effect its concentration in a Jewish state'. For a time, Vichy considered this as a possible way around Catholic and American opposition to its collaboration with the Nazis in deporting Jews to Poland. Joseph de Catry had a Jewish ally, Kadmi Cohen, whom the Germans had released under suspicious circumstances in late 1941 from internment at the Compiègne camp. Cohen, a Revisionist or right-wing Zionist, made an appeal to the Germans similar to that made by mainstream Zionist leaders, like Chaim Weizmann, to the British: that Germany sponsor a Jewish State in Palestine, Transjordan and the Sinai peninsula that would defend German interests. De Catry's 'Masada' programme required the Germans to expel the British from the Middle East, something Rommel's Afrikakorps had failed to do at El Alamein in November 1942. André Lavagne thought the plan 'could lift the very black cloud that hangs over [France] because of an excessively violent antisemitic policy'. When the Catholic hierarchy disowned de Catry, Pétain's advisers lost faith in the scheme. So did the Germans, who eventually killed Kadmi Cohen at Auschwitz.

Suspicion of René de Chambrun grew in Allied circles. In July 1943, Britain's Ministry of Economic Warfare, in a secret memo to the British Embassy in Buenos Aires, accused de Chambrun of 'organizing a series of holding companies in order to conceal transactions carried out on behalf of the Germans, the object of which is to place looted property in security. Pierre Laval, himself, is the brains behind the scheme.' No evidence emerged to prove the charge, but a careful watch was nonetheless kept on de Chambrun and his friend, fellow Franco-American lawyer François Monahan. Someone began supplying the American press with allegations about René de Chambrun designed to embarrass his family in Ohio, as well as his cousins, the Roosevelts.

Charles Bedaux was the subject of investigation and negotiation, not only in Washington, but in France. Although his arrest made headlines in the German-supported Paris press for only a day, both Vichy and the German occupiers had a residual interest in the millionaire. His name came up when François Monahan went to Lourdes in December 1942 to see the American diplomats interned at the Hôtel des Ambassadeurs. United Press correspondent Ralph Heinzen, who was interned with his wife at another hotel in Lourdes, believed that Monahan was representing Pierre Laval in an effort to reopen a Vichy–Washington channel after the break in relations. Monahan thought that Bedaux might act as an intermediary between Laval, who naively hoped to negotiate peace between Germany and the Allies, and Robert Murphy in Algiers.

André Enfière, a secret member of Charles de Gaulle's Committee of National Resistance, chanced upon a German interest in Bedaux while he was in Paris seeking the release from Vichy custody of the president of the Chamber of Deputies, Edouard Herriot. Herriot's defiant speech at Vichy in July 1940 had been praised by American Ambassador William Bullitt as 'the single example of courage and dignity during the dreary afternoon'. Herriot had subsequently been arrested for condemning Maréchal Pétain's award of the Legion of Honour in August 1942 to the pro-Nazi Legion of French Volunteers Against Bolshevism. Pétain, who had little regard for parliament or its members, confined Herriot in various locations, including Vittel and Nancy, far from his home in Breteil. Herriot was an old man, whose health suffered from the moves. Enfière's concern for his well-being was combined with his respect for a man who represented the Third Republic. In his and de Gaulle's view, the Republic's abolition in July 1940 was illegitimate because it had been coerced by Nazi bayonets. To ameliorate Herriot's condition and have him available to reconvene parliament when the Germans left, Enfière, to his distaste, negotiated with Vichy politicians Georges Bonnet and Pierre Laval.

It became clear that the Germans had the final word regarding Herriot, so Enfière appealed to Charles Bedaux's friend in the Hôtel Majestic, Dr Franz Medicus. Medicus, whom Enfière believed was anti-Nazi, confessed he was powerless to do anything and advised him to approach the Gestapo in avenue Foch. Despite the fear with which all Frenchmen not in Nazi pay had of the Gestapo, Enfière went to them several times on Herriot's behalf. But it was not until he contacted Dr Keller at the German Embassy that progress seemed possible.

Dr Keller worked in an undefined role at the embassy, described merely as 'observer', possibly reporting to Admiral Wilhelm Canaris's military intelligence agency, the Abwehr. His alcohol-induced indiscretions were known even to the American Embassy in Vichy, which received a report on him from a Brazilian diplomat in 1942. Keller, in a drunken outburst at a party in Paris, revealed, 'The Germans are going to eliminate General Weygand from Africa because he was conspiring with the United States against German interests. As soon as the military situation in Russia is stabilized, pressure will be applied to France for use of the Africa bases, with a guarantee of French sovereignty in the African colonies if permission to use the bases is conceded and a threat to take the colonies if the request is not granted.' Keller's gaffe gave weight to those in Washington who favoured invading French North Africa before the Germans did. Keller was nothing if not a loose cannon, but he somehow retained his job. Enfière disliked him from their first meeting. He wrote, 'Dr Keller was a repulsive personality, while giving the appearance of an honest man, cunning, restless, ambitious, fanatic, without being a Nazi officially (so he pretended), a lecher who without shame used the most repugnant means to satisfy his lewd desires on women who wanted to save a husband or a son who had been arrested.'

Enfière used 'flattery and alcohol' on Keller, who arranged the transfer of Herriot and his wife from Nancy to the suburbs of Paris. But Herriot's physician insisted that the only cure for his patient was rest at home in Breteil. Keller was willing to accede to the doctor's wishes on one condition: 'Dr Keller let me know that one could obtain the return of Herriot to Breteil in exchange for a person in the hands of the Allies, a person to whom the German police seemed to attach extraordinary importance and to me was totally unexpected. He proposed the engineer Charles Bedaux … Keller's remark astonished me.' Keller added, 'This man is essential to us. Have him released, and we'll give you Herriot back.'

Knowing the Americans would not release Bedaux, Enfière had no power to make a trade. But Keller's unexpected request made him curious about the American millionaire:

I must admit that I had underestimated Mr Bedaux's importance in world affairs. Gladstone is said to have told a young Member of Parliament, 'The truly powerful of this world are not necessarily those the public knows.' Was this Mr Bedaux such a man?

All of a sudden, Keller informed me the Bedaux affair faced other obstacles that he had, at first, remained silent about. An amazing amount of the finest French cognac loosened his tongue. I got information on internal struggles among the police, the German army and the diplomatic corps. If I understood correctly, it would seem the diplomatic staff and the moderate factions of both the police and the army (the factions who took it for granted that the war was lost and therefore tried to find a compromise peace) wanted at all cost to have the safety of this Bedaux. Those in favour of all-out war could not have cared less about leaving him with the enemy, if only because, thanks to his connections, he would have been able to initiate conversations likely to hasten the war's end.

Enfière at that time could do nothing more for Herriot, who was returned to Nancy. Nor could he help Charles Bedaux. In captivity, Bedaux was unaware that the German peace camp had interceded for him. Enfière resumed his activities as agent Lamballe, reporting to Allen Dulles of the OSS, who favoured talking to anti-Nazi Germans about overthrowing Hitler and making peace, and Charles de Gaulle, who did not. Roosevelt and Churchill had settled the policy at their Casablanca summit in January 1943: the Allies demanded nothing less than Germany's 'unconditional surrender'.

While Charles Bedaux reminisced with his son in Algeria, the one he wished he had had, Frederic Ledebur, was being tailed by the FBI in California and New York. FBI agents there interviewed everyone who knew him, and they kept a close watch on his activities, opened his mail and reported regularly on him to J. Edgar Hoover. Many of the sources the FBI relied upon, as it delved deeper into Ledebur's affairs, contradicted previous denunciations of him as a pro-Nazi immigrant taking pictures of West Coast naval bases. An FBI intelligence report of 8 April 1943 concluded, 'No indication subject engaging in espionage or distributing Nazi propaganda.' One source helpfully suggested that 'he still wants U.S. citizenship in order to join U.S. Army'. Nonetheless, the FBI had its doubts about Lebedur: 'Acquaintances characterize subject as improvident, lazy, immoral individual.'

Interest in Bedaux reached the highest levels of American and British intelligence. A working committee meeting in New York of the Hemisphere Intelligence Conference, which grouped together senior American and British spymasters, discussed Bedaux at length on 24 March 1943. It suggested that 'Watchdog', one of their most important spies in Germany, be contacted about Bedaux. The minutes of the monthly meeting listed two questions for Watchdog. The first concerned a new type of ship locater that the German navy had reportedly installed in the conning towers of its U-boats. The committee wanted to know if Watchdog, on a recent trip to the Canadian coast aboard a U-boat, noticed anyone stationed in the submarine's conning tower. The second question was, 'Did Watchdog, who was in North Africa at the same time as Charles Bedaux, know or hear of him there? As both Bedaux and Watchdog were allegedly associated with the German Armistice Commission, it was thought that Watchdog might produce additional evidence of Bedaux's security activities at that time.' Bedaux had no connection to the Armistice Commission, but a general from the commission had displaced him from his room at the Hôtel Aletti on the night of the invasion. He may have been the same Armistice Commission officer who was captured by the American army and placed in a prisoner of war camp in Trinidad, Colorado. The FBI interrogated the German in September 1943 on the case of 'Charles Eugene Bedaux; – (Mission Bedaux); Trading with the enemy'. The FBI was nothing if not thorough in its pursuit of evidence in the Bedaux case. The main problem was that none of Bedaux's friends in the United States, including Frederic Ledebur, had seen him since the United States and Germany went to war in December 1941.

THIRTY-FOUR

A Hospital at War

On 4 April 1943, Dr Sumner Jackson watched well over a hundred American B-17 bombers, the famous ten-man Flying Fortresses, bomb Paris in daylight for the first time. The roof of the American Hospital afforded a clear view of the planes unleashing tons of high explosives on an island nearby in the River Seine. Their target was the Renault car factory, which manufactured tanks and other armoured vehicles for the Wehrmacht. German Focke-Wulf 190 fighter planes, scrambling only after the raid had begun at 2.16 p.m., pursued the bombers and clashed with their British fighter escorts. The spectacle encouraged Dr Jackson and the other physicians and nurses who had been longing for the United States to fight in France with more than words. France would not be freed immediately, they knew, but the American liberation of the skies had begun.

The heavens above Neuilly that spring afternoon saw the drama of bombardments, dogfights and crews leaping from their planes in parachutes to avoid being burned alive. Below, the Renault plant was on fire. The Luftwaffe shot down at least four of the B-17s and just as many fighter escorts. The air war was beginning to cost the Americans, as it had the British for two years, thousands of planes and crewmen. It was also magnifying the danger to Dr Jackson and the other *résistants* who were dedicated to saving the Allied survivors. Americans, British, Canadians, Australians, New Zealanders, South Africans and free Poles and Czechs were parachuting onto French soil in greater numbers. Some were captured immediately, but others were found by sympathetic Frenchmen who handed them over to clandestine organizations. Many waited in the homes of French and American friends of the Resistance or at the American Hospital for the false documents, civilian clothes and guides they needed to undertake the perilous route back to England. Most spoke no French, and they were vulnerable to capture if the wrong person asked them a question. The pilots, navigators, bombardiers and radio engineers with their valuable training and combat experience were assets the Allies could not afford to lose. For the Resistance, including Sumner Jackson, returning them to fight the Nazis was worth the risk of torture and execution.

The Germans used the air raids to rouse French fear of America's long-term intentions. 'German propaganda was falling upon willing ears in France,' Ninetta Jucker, the Englishwoman who was not interned because she had a young child, remembered. 'We were told that the air raids were intended to destroy French industry so that the "Yankees" should find no competition here after the war; while the "systematic" destruction of French cities would create vast markets for American industry when the time came to build them.'

In 1943, the lack of food in Paris had, in General de Chambrun's words, 'reached its crucial point'. The hospital had to feed 500 staff and patients, who desperately needed a sufficient calorie intake to guarantee their recovery, as well as fifty unpaid volunteers and a group of elderly Englishmen in a hostel. Ninetta Jucker wrote that the house for old Englishmen beside the American Hospital had been a retreat for old women before the war. The Germans requisitioned it and left it empty, until the American wife of a pro-Vichy French diplomat managed to have the house reopened as a hostel in the spring of 1943. Its inhabitants paid no rent, but contributed the small sum of thirty francs a day for three meals at the American Hospital. The hostel somehow came under the supervision of a retired British general. 'He was suffering from a combination of sex, religious and persecution mania,' Ninetta Jucker wrote. When the general forced some elderly Englishwomen to move out of the hostel, Mrs Jucker complained on their behalf. 'There used to be women here,' the general told her, 'but I had to get rid of them. Couldn't do with women around. Females, you know.' When Ninetta complained to the Red Cross, the general was soon 'deprived of his powers'. The hospital, though, had to feed the elderly British subjects along with everyone else – more than six hundred people daily – when France was nearly starving.

'The problem was solved,' Clara de Chambrun wrote, 'by making large farming contracts for regular supplies. Three departments collaborated in this effort: Comte de Caraman and M. Hincelin in Seine-et-Oise, M. André Dubonnet in Seine-et-Marne, and Alexandre de Marenches in the Eure lent their acres to furnish vegetables and fruits.' Otto Gresser recalled that the lawns and flowers that had made the grounds of the hospital so congenial to patients like André Guillon in 1940 were dug up and replaced with furrows of tomatoes, beans, carrots and potatoes. Gresser himself was buying as much food as he could on the black market and from the wholesale food outlets at Les Halles, where the vendors knew him as the hard-bargaining 'Ferdinand'.

Allied air raids around Neuilly raised the fear that the hospital might be cut from its water supply. 'So,' Gresser said, 'we did some digging in the hospital grounds and after about fifteen meters down we found unlimited quantities of water. In fact, it was an underground Seine.' The well was easier to hide than the increasing number of Allied flyers in the hospital.

René Rocher, the French dramatist whom the Théâtre de l'Odéon had just appointed as its director, invited Clara to translate Shakespeare's *The Life and Death of King John*. Rocher had already produced and acted in many Shakespearean plays, but *King John* had yet to appear on a French stage. Clara, as translator of *Hamlet* and author of many Shakespearean studies in French, was an obvious choice. She, however, declined. '*The Life and Death of King John* was no favorite of mine, and I did not see that it held any elements of success at the theater.' When Rocher somehow convinced Clara to attempt an original translation, she spent months going over the text and thinking about the play's meaning. Once she began, she completed the translation in three weeks. *King John* had obvious advantages, she came to see, for a wartime Paris audience: 'The play is short, demanded no cuts, and could be produced even during the brief playing-time which was allowed, for curtains had to be down and lights extinguished by ten-fifty.' For four weeks, Clara attended rehearsals. This led to an amusing exchange with one of the actors. When Rocher instructed him to begin reading his part aloud, the actor asked, 'How can we begin? We don't understand how the lines should be read.' The actor demanded to see the author. Clara, from the stalls, said he was not there. 'Why the devil isn't he here? Does he think he can get us all out and not take the trouble to come himself?' Clara replied, 'I am afraid you will have to excuse the author as he has been dead for more than three hundred years.'

King John opened on 3 May 1943 to good reviews, including praise for Clara's 'miracle of translation'. In the first night's full house were Clara's son, René, and his wife, Josée. They had dinner with Pierre Laval afterwards. A week later, someone hurled a grenade at German soldiers outside the Théâtre de l'Odéon. The show, however, went on.

THIRTY-FIVE

The Adolescent Spy

GERMAN U-BOATS TRAWLED THE NORTH ATLANTIC, sinking American troop carriers and merchant ships delivering vital supplies to Britain. Allied aircraft could not bomb them underwater, but they could attack the bases where submarines returned for maintenance on the Bay of Biscay at Lorient and Saint-Nazaire. Of the two, Lorient was larger, but Saint-Nazaire with its sixty-two torpedo workshops and twenty-one submarine pens was better protected. A picturesque town on the northern bank of the Loire estuary, Saint-Nazaire endured regular bombing missions by the Royal Air Force and a suicidal raid by British commandos on 28 March 1942. Although the raiders did considerable damage, almost all of them were killed or captured. The result of their sacrifice, in which five won Victoria Crosses for gallantry, was that the Germans reinforced the work bays with ten feet of solid concrete. During one raid on 28 February 1943, the American Eighth Air Force destroyed half of the town of Saint-Nazaire but lost six Flying Fortresses with all their crews. The *New York Times* called Saint-Nazaire 'the toughest target of the American and British Air Forces'. German air defences took a large toll of British and American bombers, and Allied intelligence could not tell what effect their bombs made on German naval operations. Aerial photographs taken from the bombers were often obscured by cloud cover and revealed only the damage to the surface of the concrete over the submarine pens. They did not show how deep the bombs went or the exact dispositions of the German anti-aircraft guns. Meanwhile, the U-boats continued cruising out to sea from Saint-Nazaire to disrupt supplies to American troops in Britain and North Africa.

By the summer of 1943, the Allies needed reliable information from Saint-Nazaire more than ever. General Charles de Gaulle's French Committee of National Liberation instructed the Resistance in France to get it. This delicate mission was given to a 38-year-old former gendarme named Paul Kinderfreund. His code name was 'R' for Renaudot, a common French name. R, the operational chief in Paris of the Goélette-Frégate network, needed someone to enter Saint-Nazaire through the German security cordon, take the photographs and smuggle the film to a developer without being detected. Access to Saint-Nazaire was restricted to its inhabitants, workers at the port, *cheminots* on the trains that served the town and German troops. Saint-Nazaire lay within the Forbidden Zone, where Germany was constructing its Atlantic Wall against Allied invasion. Anyone caught there with a camera would be shot for espionage. An agent could not simply blend into the local population, because almost everyone in Saint-Nazaire had fled to the countryside for safety from the air raids.

R went to Nantes, upriver from Saint-Nazaire but outside the Forbidden Zone. It was as close as he dared travel to investigate the feasibility of the mission. In Nantes, he contacted another Resistance operative code-named Dorsal. This bicycle shop owner told R how Saint-Nazaire was protected by anti-aircraft batteries and Luftwaffe fighter squadrons. To get into the town, a visitor needed a special *Ausweis* from the Germans. Although few people were permitted, the Germans allowed students to visit the seaside town on school holidays. R's solution was to send a schoolchild.

In Paris, R went to see Sumner and Toquette Jackson. They had worked with his Goélette network for more than a year and were used to unusual requests. But the proposal R put to them was startling even to these veteran *résistants*: R wanted to borrow their son. Until then, his parents had shielded 15-year-old Phillip from danger and had once reprimanded him for painting anti-German graffiti. The boy was unaware that Allied airmen took shelter in the hospital and that his avenue Foch home was a Resistance mail drop. Whenever Resistance members met at the Jacksons' home, Phillip was sent to his Aunt Tat at Enghien. His parents had taken every precaution to protect the boy. Yet, when R told them that London needed Phillip's help in Saint-Nazaire, Sumner and Toquette agreed.

R's plan was to smuggle Phillip into the port town with a camera, but he would first need a safe place to stay. Toquette remembered an old friend from Saint-Nazaire, Marcelle Le Bagousse. Marcelle and her husband, a railway *cheminot*, had moved from Saint-Nazaire to the countryside nearby at Pontchâteau to avoid Allied bombs. Their farmhouse was just outside the Forbidden Zone, and Phillip knew the family already. He would be welcome there, but he would still have to get into the port town and back again with the photographs. R arranged for Verdier, the Goélette courier whom they knew from his visits to collect and drop off Resistance messages, to accompany Phillip on the train to Nantes.

Phillip and Verdier left early in the morning by train from the Montparnasse station with sandwiches, a container of wine mixed with water and a forged *Ausweis*. When they arrived in Nantes, they went to the house of agent Dorsal. Dorsal gave the boy a Kodak box camera, a simple device with a fixed lens, to hide in his lunch bag. Phillip then rode in the backseat of Dorsal's old Citroën, while Verdier sat in front holding a machine pistol in case the Germans stopped them. It was, Phillip recalled, a dramatic, fast drive on a dangerous road. The two men dropped him at the train station in Pontchâteau, where Mme Le Bagousse met him and took him to their farm. Phillip gave M. and Mme Le Bagousse the presents his mother had wrapped for them: salami, a bottle of claret and some gabardine cloth. To their teenaged daughter, Erika, he presented a copy of La Fontaine's *Fables*.

While Phillip was unpacking, M. Le Bagousse saw his camera and immediately seized it. Possession of a camera so close to Saint-Nazaire could get them all shot. He hid it somewhere in the house. Deprived of his camera, Phillip had no idea how to complete his mission. He could not tell the truth to his hosts, who might send him straight back to Paris. The family gave the boy lunch. Afterwards, Erika took him on the train to Saint-Nazaire with her father's railway worker's pass clearing them through the German security checks. For an afternoon, they were two kids wandering around the old port town and enjoying the remaining sights of Erika's old neighbourhood. They went into the main church of Saint-Nazaire and climbed its belfry. Beside the mostly ruined town lay the docks, which had made Saint-Nazaire a shipbuilding centre in the nineteenth century, the submarine repair base and the anti-aircraft defences. In the harbour, tantalizingly for camera-less Phillip, was a U-boat. Dejected, he went with Erika on the train back to Pontchâteau.

Phillip went to bed feeling he had failed his first test as a *résistant*. He was about to sleep, when Erika slipped silently into his room and gave him the camera. The two youngsters spent the rest of the night together, but Phillip did not tell her why he needed the camera. The next day, she took him back to Saint-Nazaire. They revisited the church, again climbing the stairs to the top. He snapped one picture after another, until the roll ran out. If the Germans had seen him photographing their installations, they would have executed him on the spot. Phillip and Erika went back down and walked unobserved to the train station. At Erika's house, Phillip removed the exposed film. Erika replaced the camera in her father's hiding place. All Phillip had to do next was get the film to Paris.

The courier, Verdier, met him again in Pontchâteau and rode beside him on the Paris train. They cleared the German checkpoints and arrived safely at the Gare de Montparnasse. There, R met them and retrieved the film to send the priceless photographs to London. Phillip was now the third member of the Jackson family to be a fully fledged partisan in *la Résistance*.

THIRTY-SIX

Clara under Suspicion

KING JOHN WAS STILL PLAYING at the Odéon in late June, when a 'new and peculiar sort of reader' appeared at the American Library. These fake readers did not speak to Clara, but they asked about her and 'looked darkly at any member of staff they chanced to encounter'. Clearly, German undercover agents were taking a renewed interest in the library. Had she or one of the staff been denounced? Hilda Frikart, the secretary whose sister, Florence, Clara had saved from execution almost three years earlier, told her one morning in late June 1943 that Dr Hermann Fuchs had telephoned. He apologized for not being able to call on her and asked whether the countess would come to his office near the Hôtel Majestic before business hours. Clara went the next morning with Hilda Frikart to see Dr Fuchs. Aldebert waited across the street, 'in case we did, or did not, come out'.

When Clara and Hilda walked into the office, Dr Fuchs pointedly remained seated at his desk. He warned Clara to speak only the truth. Before he could ask anything, she defended her management of the library. Her duty, she stated, was 'to safeguard the institution and avoid trouble by any so-called "resistance"'. Dr Fuchs said someone had accused her of circulating anti-Hitler propaganda. As Clara knew from her involvement with Hilda's sister in 1940, the Nazis could impose the death penalty for that offence. Dr Fuchs said that magazines from the library with certain caricatures outlined in red ink were in circulation. 'Certain caricatures' were comic illustrations of Adolf Hitler in a pre-war issue of Henry Luce's *Fortune* magazine.

Clara said that periodicals were not permitted outside the reading room. 'If they have been circulated, it must be by Germans who carry them off. They have been particularly attached to the magazine room of late. I assure you, Dr. Fuchs, I am neither knave enough nor fool enough to betray the institution I have promised to safeguard.' Fuchs, uncomfortable during the encounter, warned her not to show any periodicals to Germans without a card issued by himself. The next matter, he said, was more serious. Someone had denounced Countess de Chambrun for conspiring with Dr Karl Epting, director of the German Institute in Paris, to keep the library open by fraud. It appeared Dr Epting, who socialized with her son and his wife and had attended two performances of *King John* at the Odéon, was under suspicion.

Clara was confident she had nothing to fear. Dr Epting had merely sent students to the library two years before. The library, she said, remained open under the agreement Dr Fuchs himself had reached with Dorothy Reeder in 1940. The German ambassador, Otto Abetz, had given his approval to that arrangement and to the subsequent affiliation with the French Information Centre before Dr Epting had seen the library. Dr Fuchs drew a long breath and said, 'Madame, I am very happy for you. It would have been for me a most disagreeable duty to make an unsatisfactory report. I will not conceal that I am also *very happy for myself*.' Clara realized that his fate was somehow linked to hers. If the library violated occupation regulations, he would be responsible.

To avoid further German attention in the short-term, Clara closed the library for the summer holidays on Bastille Day, 14 July, rather than wait until August. That night, the Gestapo called at the home of the senior librarian, Boris Netchaeff. He and his wife, a Russian princess, were playing bridge with friends when the Germans broke into their flat and ordered them to raise their hands. As Netchaeff was about to comply, they shot him. One bullet pierced his lung. Eventually, he was taken to the German-commandeered Hôpital de la Pitié. General de Chambrun rushed to the Pitié to request Boris's transfer to Neuilly for treatment by an American doctor, but the police were adamant that Boris would remain under arrest. Worse, the Gestapo planned to deport him to Germany. As a Russian under Gestapo suspicion, he would probably not return. Clara went to Dr Fuchs to hold him to his promise of responsibility for the library and its employees. If the evidence against the Russian proved false, Fuchs said, he would make sure that the Gestapo released him to the American Hospital. All he needed from Clara was a written report on Boris Netchaeff.

After three years under German rule, Clara had anticipated his request for a report. She had one ready, leaving him no excuse for delay. Dr Fuchs read it and pledged to effect Boris's release within the week. The countess and the *Bibliotheksschütz* then had one of the more curious exchanges of the occupation. He reminded her that, at their previous meeting, he had asked her to tell the truth. Now, he was asking her not to respond if it would embarrass her. He asked, 'Did you ever hear of a man called Aldebert de Chambrun?' Clara, suppressing a laugh, confessed that she did not know *everything* about the Comte de Chambrun. After all, they had been married for only forty-two years. Dr Fuchs explained that the Bibliothèque Nationale had in its catalogue a two-volume life of Aldebert de Chambrun by Richard Wagner. Did the countess know why the great composer would have written a book about her husband? Again, she managed not to laugh. It seemed that Uncle Aldebert de Chambrun, for whom her husband had been named, had had a passion for Wagner's music and had often visited Bayreuth. The senior Aldebert wrote a book about Wagner, not the other way round. Perhaps, she suggested, the cataloguers had accidentally reversed the names of subject and author. 'I was beginning to think something of that kind must have occurred, but my searchers would not admit having been mistaken,' Dr Fuchs said. Four days later, Boris Netchaeff was safe in a bed at the American Hospital.

Paris had nothing to celebrate on 14 July 1943, the 154th anniversary of the storming of the Bastille with its now-hollow promises of liberty, fraternity and equality. But, in New York, expatriate French men and women danced in the street on the evening before France's national day. They roped off 44th Street between Second and Third Avenues and declared it 'a little bit of Paris in Old New York'. Lampposts were festooned with American and French flags, and refreshments were served from a large tent in the middle of 44th Street. A sign labelled 'French territory' advised, 'New Yorkers – Don't believe all you hear – There was a France – There is a France – There will always be a France – ALWAYS.' The actors Marlene Dietrich and Jean Gabin took part. New Yorkers and overseas Parisians danced congas, rhumbas, waltzes and the 'Beer Barrel Polka' on the cobbled ground. At a minute before midnight, a French sailor took the microphone and asked for silence. A young woman wearing red shoes and blue slacks played the accordion, and the Frenchman called on the crowd to join in singing *La Marseillaise*. Even hard-bitten American New Yorkers sang along. At the last refrain, the French sailor said, 'Ladies and gentlemen, we owe this celebration to the generosity and hospitality of our American allies and our American hosts. *Vive l'Amérique!*'

That holiday morning in Paris, Phillip Jackson cycled through deserted streets past German sentries in the avenue Foch and around the Arc de Triomphe to the American Hospital in Neuilly. Phillip was carrying eggs from the family's maid, Louise, for his father. At the hospital where he had been born fifteen years earlier, a British woman patient had posted a poem on the hospital bulletin board to honour a physician on whom she clearly had a crush:

> Portrait of an American:
> We all agree he's a perfect dear
> Altho at times he inspires fear
> And we quake when he draws near
> Oh, so severe!
> But those eyes so stern and steel blue
> Can gleam with laughter, too
> And life takes on a brighter hue
> When he smiles at you.

Sumner was operating on a patient, so the boy went up to the roof to wait. The summer morning was tranquil, until German anti-aircraft batteries suddenly erupted with fire. American Flying Fortresses roared towards the air base at Le Bourget and dropped their payloads. Like his father from the same roof on 4 April, Phillip watched the Luftwaffe and the American Eighth Air Force duelling in the sky. Bombs fell, air gunners fired at one another, planes screamed in flames to the ground and parachutes snapped open. To the 15-year-old, the sight was unforgettable, almost hypnotic. Then his father appeared on the roof. Wearing a white, blood-spattered surgeon's gown, Sumner Jackson shouted, 'Damn, Pete! Get the hell out of here. Shrapnel's flying all around.' In the distance, American airmen were burying their parachutes and running for cover.

Before Sumner left the hospital that afternoon, he modestly removed the British woman's poem from the board. He and Phillip then bicycled with Toquette to their house on the lake at Enghien to spend the rest of the holiday with Toquette's sister, Tat. When Phillip recounted the story of the air battle he had seen, his mother ordered him to stay off the hospital's roof. This seemed strange to a boy whose parents let him risk his life to photograph German naval installations at Saint-Nazaire. That was war. To be injured by falling ack-ack was unnecessary voyeurism.

The Jacksons' lives were increasingly threatened. Toquette told Sumner that General Karl Oberg was paying 50,000 francs to anyone who led his agents to an Allied flyer in hiding. Those assisting the airmen would be shot. Someone had already taken the money, and one British airman disappeared. The informer responsible was himself murdered by the Resistance. One Resistance cell, she said, had been penetrated by Oberg's men. Theirs could be next.

When the family weekend was over, Dr Jackson cycled back to work at the hospital. More airmen needed help to reach England, and more patients were brought from the internment camps. It was business as usual. On the bulletin board, to Sumner's irritation, someone had pinned back the English patient's poem praising her 'perfect dear', Dr Jack.

A month after Phillip Jackson watched the 331st Squadron of the American Eighth Air Force from the hospital's roof, a crewman from one of the downed Flying Fortresses suddenly appeared at the American Hospital. Gladys Marchal, a British woman working for the Resistance, delivered the 19-year-old tail-gunner to Dr Sumner Jackson. The airman's civilian clothes did not fit, and he did not look or speak French. Joe Manos was a half-Greek, half-Polish American from New York City, who, like Jackson, stood just over six feet tall. Joe had been on the run for a month, since that 14 July morning when Phillip Jackson saw his plane shot down. Two of Joe's crewmates had been killed inside the B-17. Joe had parachuted from 16,000 feet with seven others onto a field of sugar beet near Le Bourget. Cut off from the other seven, he wandered along a country road. Two Frenchmen spotted him and warned that a German soldier was cycling past. Joe hid in the brush, until the two men returned with a car, covered him in firewood and took him to a safe house. By the time Gladys Marchal brought Joe to the hospital, he had been in three safe houses waiting for the Resistance to bring him false travel documents. Somehow, though, the *résistants* could not obtain the papers he needed.

Joe appealed to Dr Jackson for help. Jackson took him into his office, which Joe remembered as 'a nice place, well furnished. A citation framed on the wall caught my eye and I believe it was the French Legion of Honor.' After giving Joe a thorough physical examination, Jackson asked Elisabeth Comte to lodge the airman in one of the rooms for patients. 'Everything, bed and linens were spotlessly white,' Joe wrote later. When they could not find a safe house for him, the Jacksons invited Joe to their apartment at 11 avenue Foch. They had taken the precaution of asking Toquette's sister, Tat, to keep Phillip at Enghien for a few days. 'I suppose my mother thought that at fifteen, being with an American B-17 gunner was a bit too much for me,' Phillip told his father's biographer, Hal Vaughan, years later. 'I think my father brought Joe to the apartment on the back of his bike.' Even without Phillip there, Joe's presence was a hazard. A neighbour might denounce them to the Nazi SD secret police, whose bureau was just down the road at Number 19, or to the Gestapo at Number 43. Sumner knew the danger of mixing different Resistance networks. The American Hospital was part of one, and Goélette-Frégate was another. Sumner had kept them separate to avoid the possibility of a captured *résistant* revealing under torture the secrets of *both*. Toquette fed Joe on their meagre rations, and she contacted the escape networks to get him out of Paris before the Germans found him.

Gilbert Asselin of another Resistance group, Libération, was the man Toquette decided could provide Joe with false papers and a safe route to Spain. When she asked Asselin to take responsibility for Joe, the Frenchman did not hesitate. He moved him into the flat of his mistress, Lise Russ. Joe spent long, dull hours there, waiting to go outside again. At any moment, he knew, a neighbour might guess he was there and inform the police to claim Oberg's reward. The Germans were searching everywhere for Joe and the rest of his B-17 crew, arresting French men and women whom they suspected of assisting them. After three weeks, everything was ready. Asselin presented Joe with well-forged documents and delivered him to another safe house near Sainte-Foy-la-Grande. From there, Joe was taken to Toulouse in southwest France to wait for an escort to lead him over the border to Spain. In late October, along with RAF Squadron Leader Frank Griffiths, he was taken across the Pyrenees. Spain did not automatically mean freedom. Spanish police arrested Joe and Griffiths in Barcelona, where a German officer was allowed to interrogate them. For more than a month, they were moved with other Allied airmen from prison to prison. At the end of November, the Spaniards released them to the British Consul and allowed them to cross the border to Gibraltar. Back in England, Joe gave a full account to US military intelligence of his escape route and the help he had received from Sumner and Toquette Jackson.

THIRTY-SEVEN

Calumnies

IN THE AUTUMN OF 1943, the war appeared to turn in the Allies' favour. The British, American and Free French had secured North Africa and the Middle East. The Anglo-American invasion of Italy from Tunisia led to a new Italian government that switched sides and declared war on Germany on 13 October. Five days later, Countess Clara Longworth de Chambrun marked rather than celebrated her seventieth birthday. The matriarch remained vigorous, working daily at the library, helping its staff to endure occupation and completing her book on Shakespeare. Her son and his wife lived as if nothing had changed. In September, they had gone with Seymour Weller, the American manager of the Château Haut-Brion vineyards in Bordeaux, to watch the harvest and sample one of the world's finest wines. René rarely missed a horse race at Longchamp, and Josée was a regular buyer of dresses from Elsa Schiaparelli. In Paris, the couple attended the premiere of Jean Delannoy's film *L'Éternel retour* and, with the actress Arletty, opening night at the Comédie Française of Paul Claudel's *Soulier de satin*.

Clara, struggling to keep the American Library open, bore her son's vilification in the American press with characteristic stoicism. Friends in Cincinnati were reading that her family in France had somehow become traitors – a stain on a patriotic American family and on Lafayette's descendants. Moreover, the Gaullists in London let it be known that there would be scores to settle with those who collaborated with the occupier. First on the list for retribution was Pierre Laval. His son-in-law was not far behind.

The American press campaign against René de Chambrun intensified in November and December 1943, when the *New York Herald Tribune* published three front-page 'exposés'. 'Count de Chambrun in His Role of U.S. Citizen,' the first headline trumpeted on 28 November. The paper called his dual citizenship 'nebulous', although both his parents were American-born and he had demonstrated his right to American citizenship in court when the New York Bar Association admitted him in 1930. 'At present he is attached to Fernand de Brinon, Vichy's Ambassador to Paris, former public relations counsel of Nazi Germany in New York,' journalist Paul Wohl wrote, without naming his source. René was an unofficial adviser to Laval, but he did not work for de Brinon. In the next article, 'Laval's Fortune Reported Safe in U.S.', Paul Wohl claimed that Laval's money was 'brought to America in a diplomatic valise in September 1940, by his son-in-law and personal assistant, Count René de Chambrun, when he visited the United States for the second time after the French defeat with his wife, Countess José [sic] Laval de Chambrun'. No proof was offered that Laval had ever sent money to the United States. René admitted that he had taken cash the other way, from Americans like John Jay and Mrs Seton Porter, to friends in France.

Wohl's articles accused René and Josée of engaging in 'anti-British propaganda' in the United States, although it was René who had campaigned for the United States to send weapons to Britain. The assault on his character extended to his family. Wohl wrote that Aldebert de Chambrun and his brother, Charles, were 'shrewd opportunists'. He did not mention that the third brother, Pierre, had been the only senator to vote against capitulation in July 1940 and that Pierre's daughter, Marthe de Chambrun Ruspoli, had been arrested by the Gestapo in 1941 for providing civilian clothes to escaping Allied soldiers. Clara was upbraided as well, because 'she did not leave Paris in June, 1940'. The final proof of disloyalty was, 'The Paris building of the National City Bank of New York, of which General Aldebert is the nominal head, now houses Marshal Goering's staff. It was one of the first buildings turned over to the Nazis.' Two floors of the building had been requisitioned, not by Marshal Goering, but by Joseph Goebbels's Propagandastaffel. Its tenants, including the National City

Bank and René's law firm, were not consulted. (Goering's Paris head-quarters were in the Palais de Luxembourg opposite Clara and Alde-bert's house in the rue de Vaugirard.) The most likely source of the disinformation was British intelligence, which had clashed with René over food supplies to southern France. Although the charges against René de Chambrun and his family in Paris were for the most part fabri-cations, they were beginning to stick.

The FBI had heard in January that one of the Bedauxs, Charles or his son, had cabled relatives 'giving his best wishes and so forth'. At the FBI's request, the army sent a wire from Washington to Algiers 'instructing that they be kept strictly incommunicado and also that the guards be carefully checked'. In October, Fern Bedaux wrote at least three letters to her husband. It is not clear from the FBI files whether he received them or how she sent them. There was no mail between occupied France and North Africa, but Fern may – as her husband had done in the past – have sent letters with friends to be mailed from neutral Portugal. The US army's Adjutant General's office intercepted them and translated them from French into English for the Depart-ment of Justice. The first, dated 4 October, said,

> My own Charles darling, Now three or four weeks since I have news from you, but my heart tells me that all continues well. I long and live for the day I shall have a word direct.
> ... Do you remember my apprehension the day you left – nearly a year ago now. For days before it was like a black cloud. Something told me I must keep you or go along – We will pass through it – the cloud will lift one day. This test of strength and courage, strength-ens and hardens character. Somehow I feel we didn't need it – So it can only be preparing us for greater and better things after. My own darling sweetheart your last letter & photograph never leave me. Never forget for one instant day and night that you are my whole world. I long for you. Kiss Junior for me.

The second dwelt on business, which she appeared to be monitoring for her husband. Gaston was doing good work, and Candé had an 'excellent new overseer' named Guy. 'I travel at will between Paris and Candé,' she wrote. 'My life is very simple – I always see the same persons – the real friends – Joseph [possibly Joseph von Ledebur] is traveling a lot.' At the top of her third letter, dated 28 October, she wrote, 'Sunday, your birthday was a sacred holy day for me. I feel your nearness.' The letter began: 'My own precious darling, I am told that you have had another letter. How I wish they could all arrive – and one day I will have a few words from you.' It continued:

> You may have heard (as all the Radios announced it) that Monday morning Oct. 18th there was a big explosion at the Ripault [gunpowder factory that the French had blown up in 1940]. The last engineers had left at 9.30. The accident was at 11.00. There is considerable damage at Candé but nothing that cannot be repaired with time. No one was hurt. I had a few cuts and bruises but only on the body. They are all finished and in order again – and I am ready to return to Paris ...
>
> My sweetheart darling – you are with me every minute. You must know and feel it. You were never more close – and I never loved more deeply and completely than now. With our strength and courage we have marvelous, beautiful days ahead. I live and always will live for you.

If Charles wrote back, using the same clandestine route Fern's letters had taken, the letters did not survive.

The case against Bedaux was gaining momentum in Washington, mainly on the basis of the documents and statements he provided. On 30 November, after the FBI failed to unearth evidence against Charles Junior, he was allowed to leave detention at El Biar. He immediately enlisted in the US army. Because of his command of languages and knowledge of continental Europe, the army assigned him to its intelligence branch, G-2. He went back to El Biar to bid farewell to his father before he took up his first posting in Oran. The older man's parting words were, 'Goodbye, good luck, be kind.' Separation had been a recurring motif in the relationship between father and son, but Charles Junior felt this would be the last. His father stayed on in the villa under the surveillance of the MPs. Two weeks later, just before Christmas, a US army colonel escorted him to the airport. With his Trans-Sahara Pipeline reduced to a dream, Charles Bedaux was going home.

The army delivered Bedaux to Miami on 23 December. At 6 a.m., an hour after his plane landed, he was released and given $2,300 in cash that had been taken from him at the time of his arrest. He went to a hotel, but the Immigration and Naturalization Service found him there and arrested him soon afterwards. INS patrolmen took him to the Immigration Detention Center at 525 North East 30th Street in what had been an opulent beach house near Biscayne Bay. Bedaux was lodged in the former chauffeur's apartment above the garage, the latest of his many prisons. He had been in custody without charges for more than a year.

When he was first arrested on 5 December 1942, Bedaux had in his possession what Janet Flanner called 'an invaluable, meticulous source of information on himself, for it had always been his custom to carry with him a small library of private papers and a whole gallery of photographs of his family and his interesting friends'. The FBI, after examining the files, gave the full list to Miss Flanner. She recorded that, in addition to the Vichy and German documents that Bedaux had copied for Robert Murphy, there were

> code telegrams; business telegrams; tender love letters from his wife; carbon copies of letters from the Nazi High Command; carbons of inconsequential letters to Admiral Darlan; photostats of Bedaux's family birth certificates for two generations back; photographs of Otto Abetz's children in peasant costume; an envelope marked 'Edward,' containing the Candé snapshots of the Duchess of Windsor and the Duke mowing the lawn ... notes about important luncheon appointments for the previous year; a bicycle license; a letter from the Snowflake *Herald*, of Snowflake, Arizona; clippings from the *Journal-American*; a red leather box containing pen points; a green leather folder containing nothing; and a package of Medinal sleeping tablets.

The French Brigade of Surveillance had returned his effects to him when they let him go on 29 December 1942. Bedaux apparently did not re-examine them before he gave them to the US army Judge Advocate's office on 17 January 1943 for safekeeping. The three weeks the French held the papers would have been long enough for someone to remove – or to insert – documents without his knowledge. When he arrived in Miami on 23 December, the weapons that could destroy him were waiting.

At Christmas 1943, the usual festivities were held at the American Library and Hospital. Those who had been to the three previous Christmas celebrations recalled their resolutions of those years: 'This time it really is the last; next Christmas we shall be free.' At the library, Boris Netchaeff had recovered sufficiently from his wound to brew his traditional Christmas rum punch. The chef at the hospital once again slaughtered and roasted the pigs he had been hiding from the Germans. The celebration was melancholy, if only because the occupation, far from abating, was becoming more oppressive. Food, coal, soap, clothing and shoes were in short supply. The Germans, with Pierre Laval's assistance, were drafting more French workers for labour details in Germany. They were also executing more hostages as Resistance attacks on their troops increased. Jews, already suffering brutal discrimination and the yellow star emblem, were sent with Vichy's cooperation in greater numbers to the Nazi death camps in Poland. Clara and Aldebert, who kept the two main American institutions in occupied France functioning while their names were sullied in the American press, exhibited a brave front to the doctors, nurses and patients gathered for their fourth Christmas under occupation. When Christmas dinner ended, they left the hospital to reach the avenue de Vaugirard before curfew.

Coming home from the western suburb of Neuilly by public transportation was not an easy affair for the revelers. Having been tempted to linger, we almost broke our shins in feverish efforts to catch the last metro, terrified by the apprehension that if we lost it we must pass the night in the guardhouse ... I remember that once we were almost at the corner of the rue Cassette, and only three short blocks from the house, when a uniform accosted us. The streets were quite empty. It was dreadfully cold and hard to see that a man was standing under the blued streetlamp. Were we in for arrest? Not that time. He thrust into my hand a paper with the address of one of the hotels reserved for German troops. He was lost and visibly frightened, but evidently thought that a lady might be less dangerous than a man. I could make out only the words *bitte* and *wo ist*, but responded, *da*, for the hotel was just around the corner. He must have been an old-fashioned German taken among the last conscriptions, for he murmured feelingly the worn-out formula, 'I kiss your hands, highborn dame.' This was the sole occasion when, moved by the Christmas spirit, I gave aid or comfort to one of our foes.

Clara's closest friends and some of her family were giving more than directions to a lost soldier on Christmas Eve.

Charles Bedaux wrote a letter to his New York office on Monday, 27 December. Marked for the attention of US Bedaux Company chief Albert Ramond, lawyer Judge George Link, Jr, and his secretary, Mrs Isabella Cameron Waite, the letter was their first indication that Bedaux was in the United States. Bedaux wrote that he was a prisoner in Miami's Immigration Detention Center, and he needed help. He asked for sleeping pills. He preferred the Medinal tablets that he took in France, but Luminal – though 'somewhat injurious' – would do. Without the pills, he could not sleep. His other, perhaps more urgent, request was for a lawyer.

PART SIX

1944

THIRTY-EIGHT

The Trial of Citizen Bedaux

ISABELLA CAMERON WAITE HURRIED to Miami on New Year's Day in answer to Charles Bedaux's urgent appeal. The loyal Mrs Waite had come at her own expense, because the Treasury had blocked all of her employer's American accounts. An FBI informant had described her as an 'extremely straightforward person, pro-British and pro-American ... she is an ardent church attendant and would not stand for any nonsense'. Bedaux had hired Isabella Waite as his secretary after her first husband, a drunk who failed to support their two children, left her. It is not clear how intimate Isabella and Charles were. When he left the United States in 1937, he assigned her his power of attorney and trusted her to set her own salary. She married John A. Waite, a salesman and First World War veteran, two years later.

She arrived in Miami the day after his Immigration and Naturalization Service hearing adjourned without a verdict. The stated purpose of the four-day inquiry had been to determine whether Charles Bedaux was still an American citizen. Bedaux's US passport had expired on 27 February 1942 and it had not been renewed. But Bedaux, despite having told his brother Gaston in April 1939 that he was thinking of restoring his French citizenship, had never renounced his American nationality. Nor had he been convicted of a crime for which it could be revoked. Mrs Waite, seeing Bedaux for the first time since his flight from the Windsor American tour scandal in 1937, noticed how much he had aged. His year behind bars, the separation from his wife and what seemed to him the blatant injustice of his arrest had robbed him of the old bravado. And his insomnia left him exhausted. Bedaux confided to her his worries, most of which were for Fern. The first thing Mrs Waite did for him was to deliver a comfortable chair, an ice box and a stove to his chauffeur's flat above the garage in the grounds of the Immigration Detention Center.

Mrs Waite wrote a letter that evening to Albert Ramond, the man who had taken control of the Bedaux Company in 1937: 'I will be here until citizenship difficulties are straightened out ... *I have* the medicine. You and Link get the lawyer please ... He is eating his heart out with worry about Fern. She is held hostage in France. Most *important* is that he knows you are standing by – so a short line to him will perhaps heal some of the wounds the Gestapo, etc., etc., etc., have made.' Ramond contacted officials in Washington, who advised him not to visit Bedaux. Even after Bedaux called him on 4 January, Ramond avoided phoning or seeing him. His sole objective was to distance the company named for Charles Bedaux from the man himself.

John L. Burling, assistant to the Justice Department's administrator of foreign travel control, had chaired the hearing in Miami's Border Patrol Station. Bedaux represented himself, because his letter asking Mrs Waite and Albert Ramond for legal help arrived in New York after the hearings began. (The government apparently did not allow him to make a telephone call, nor did it inform the press that Bedaux was in the country.) The interrogations about his citizenship and his activities in German-occupied Europe and North Africa wearied, but did not unsettle, him. Burling asked if Bedaux understood the potential usefulness of the Trans-Saharan Railway, the aborted project on which Bedaux had worked, to the German army. Bedaux answered that the railway, even if the French had not cancelled it because of the high cost, would have been completed only when the war was over. Moreover, Germany's contribution of 60,000 tons of steel to his peanut oil pipeline deprived the Wehrmacht of raw materials for tanks and other weapons of war. At one stage, Bedaux asked Burling, 'What assurance do I have that in speaking all the truth I do not endanger innocent people?' The 'innocent people' were his wife, brother and friends in occupied France. As the four-day hearing proceeded, Bedaux, despite his lack of sleep, was getting the better of Burling. Janet Flanner thought Bedaux's candid responses might have harmed his case, but 'he showed an ebullience, a charm, and a mixture of plausibility and candor which, coupled with his foreign-movie-star accent, might momentarily have panicked an American jury'.

Burling confronted Bedaux with a document that had been among the papers brought from North Africa along with his damning *Ausweis* from Otto Abetz and his *cadre de mission* from Pierre Laval. It was a German form with spaces for responses to questions about the Allies' military plans in Africa, aeroplane arrivals and departures, shipping information on the port of Dakar and General de Gaulle's signals codes. The paper, nestled among his many letters, passes and photographs, seemed to prove that he was not only trading with the enemy, but spying as well. Bedaux replied that he knew nothing of the document, insisting it must have been slipped into his briefcase during the three weeks that the French were in possession of it. If he had realized what the document was, he said, he would 'have been insane not to destroy it' when the briefcase was back in his possession.

On 18 January, J. Edgar Hoover cabled the FBI's special agent in charge, San Francisco, 'that [Frederic] Ledebur be interviewed before Bedaux's attorney communicates with him regarding his connections with Bedaux and his knowledge of the activities of his brother Joseph'. Hoover had good intuition, or Mrs Waite and the Washington attorney she hired for Bedaux, Edmund Jones, were under FBI surveillance. Two days after the director instructed his field office to question Ledebur, Mrs Waite sent the Austrian a telegram: 'OUR WASHINGTON ATTORNEY WILL SOON ARRANGE FOR YOUR COMING EAST SO YOU WILL BE AVAILABLE'. Ledebur was interviewed by FBI agents in Ventura, California, the day Mrs Waite sent the cable. He received it the next day, 21 January. The FBI questioned him again on 25 January in its Los Angeles office, when he was allowed to bring records to assist his memory. In both interviews, the Austrian gave details of his long association with Bedaux from their first meeting in Los Angeles in 1929 to their last in Amsterdam in 1939. He 'denied any un-American activities' and insisted it would have been impossible for him to film naval installations because he 'had no idea how to operate a motion picture camera'. His loathing for his brother

Joseph, who had not only been a Nazi but had betrayed his aristocratic heritage by working in trade, was a recurring theme of his answers. The FBI's report stated that 'in the event BEDAUX is a Nazi collaborator, he [Lebebur] wants nothing whatsoever to do with him'. The FBI report did not disclose what its agents told Ledebur about Charles Bedaux, but the count declined to go to Miami and testify for the man who had long regarded him as 'more of a son to me than my own son'.

Deserted by his colleague Ramond and his friend Ledebur, Bedaux turned to his family. On 22 January, he wrote to his brother Gaston, 'I received your short card asking for news. I couldn't write before. I can today. I don't have your card with me, my papers are at the censor's, but I think you wrote last February, I think so, that makes nearly a year and we are ageing at a crazy speed.'

He asked how Gaston's son, François, was doing at the Polytechnic and whether 'François should keep an eye open to succeeding you one day in running all of the Bedaux businesses'. The letter made clear that his reconciliation with his own son, Charles Emile, had not gone so far that he would bequeath his companies to him. He suggested that Fern make the Château de Candé self-supporting by turning it into a conference centre. The letter closed with a fraternal farewell: 'It was always my intention to live to see the years and the centuries, but it's war, and an accident can always happen. With a long lease [on Candé], the formalities would be easier for Fern. I live only for the day when I'll join her as well as you and your family. Your affectionate brother, Charles.'

Bedaux's lodgings above the garage were locked at night, but guards allowed him outside during the day to sunbathe on the grass and take walks. During one of his exercise periods, he told Patrolman Joseph Swank, 'Well, one of these days, Charles E. Bedaux will be dead and buried and then the Bedaux case will be a closed file, won't it?' Mrs Waite stayed in Miami to be near him. Edmund Jones, his new lawyer from Washington, tried to prepare his defence without knowing what the charges were. In the meantime, Charles Bedaux waited for his second hearing to begin on Valentine's Day.

On 14 February, the second hearing on the citizenship of Charles Eugene Bedaux convened at the Border Patrol Station in Miami. Unlike the first, which had taken four days, this one was brief. It began at eight in the morning and would adjourn in time for lunch. Presiding officer John L. Burling announced that the Immigration and Naturalization Service had determined that Charles Bedaux was indeed an American citizen entitled to remain in the United States. After delivering the verdict, Burling reverted to his other job, that of prosecutor for the Department of Justice. In that capacity, he officially charged Charles Bedaux, US citizen, with 'treason against the United States'. The penalty for treason, as Bedaux knew, was death.

In his flat above the garage that evening, Bedaux conferred with his lawyer, Edmund Jones, for about an hour. At ten o'clock, he said good night to his guards and went to bed. In the morning at eleven o'clock, Mrs Waite and Edmund Jones came to visit him. Unusually for a man who began his days early, Bedaux was still asleep. Mrs Waite went into his bedroom to wake him, but he could not be roused. His eyes stayed closed, and his tongue was enlarged. But he was breathing. On the bedside table lay a letter addressed to Isabella Waite:

> Dear Friend,
>
> I cannot defend my good name now without endangering those I love.
>
> After the war my beloved wife and my son will prove that I am a good, honest, deserving American. I want you to give her this letter as a token of my undying love.
>
> Give my thanks to all those who have faith in me.
>
> To you dear friend my eternal gratitude for your absolute faith and devotion.
>
> I kept the Luminal the authorities gave me.
>
> Charles Bedaux

The Associated Press reported from Miami on 17 February that Charles Bedaux 'is seriously ill at the Jackson Memorial Hospital'. The unsourced story continued, 'Bedaux has been in technical custody here since late December, when he arrived by army plane from North Africa where he had been arrested on a charge of trading with the enemy. When he arrived in the United States, he was held for not having a passport.' On 18 February, when the story appeared in the newspapers, Charles Bedaux died.

THIRTY-NINE

The Underground Railway

ON 9 FEBRUARY 1944, MAX SHOOP, a governor of the American
Hospital and chairman of its legal committee, sent a cable from Geneva
to hospital president Nelson Dean Jay in Washington:

> Just have news of American Hospital, January 12th letter to Thavoz
> [sic] [Miss M. Thevoz, former chief nurse, had returned home to
> Switzerland after the German invasion] that Hospital full, 1st floor
> occupied French soldier patients, next 2 reserved civilians, 4th floor
> west terrace built into few patients rooms, food problem difficult
> but same old Chef also still there, Bergeret chief Jackson come [sic],
> not one window yet broken.

Nelson Dean Jay wrote to another governor on 14 February that he
did not 'understand Shoop's reference to Dr Jackson although it is a
relief to know he is still there'. In a second letter to Allen the same day,
he added, 'Please say that none of us can make out the reference to
Jackson but from the message we assume he is at the Hospital which
is good news for we were afraid he had been interned.' The board
attributed the confusing 'Jackson come' to a corruption in the radio
cable, but Shoop may have been deliberately enigmatic. He was working undercover in Geneva for his old law partner at Sullivan and
Cromwell, Allen Dulles. Dulles was the Office of Strategic Services'
chief in Berne, Switzerland, responsible for coordinating American
operations with the French Resistance and gathering intelligence on

the German military's order of battle in France. After fifteen months in Switzerland as OSS Agent 284 with the code name 'Mike', Shoop could not have been unaware of Dr Jackson's role in the Resistance.

In Paris, the Jacksons' existence was becoming more precarious. Their health suffered from lack of nutrition, and Sumner contracted pneumonia. He wrote to a French friend in the United States, a former surgical nurse named Elizabeth Ravina, 'about starvation and the family's dire need of clothing'. Clemence Bock's diary recorded, 'He was drawn and careworn and went about in an old army sweater with a hole that showed his elbow when he took off his long surgical coat. He went back and forth to Neuilly on a bicycle.' All he had to keep warm while cycling through rain and snow that winter were an old flying helmet and some fur gloves.

At the American Hospital, Otto Gresser came to see Jackson's clandestine activities as routine: 'He from time to time hid one or two airborne American or British soldiers who had been shot down but weren't killed. He would hide and take care of them. Of course, it was very serious. This continued for a long time and I remember very well in full war there were two British soldiers in the corridor of the Hospital.' Although some of the hospital staff knew that Jackson was aiding the underground escape network, no one appeared to have denounced him to the Germans. If General de Chambrun had any suspicions, he kept them to himself. But, by the spring of 1944, too many people knew the secret.

The danger to American and British airmen did not cease when they left the American Hospital or any of their other refuges in Paris. They had to make their way, accompanied by men and women whom they did not know and with whom they often could not speak a common language, from one town, one village, one safe house to another, until they reached the Spanish border. The frontier region beside Spain lay in the Forbidden Zone, where controls were more rigorous than anywhere else. German troops with hunting dogs patrolled the Pyrenees mountain passes through which the airmen had to walk, sometimes for days, to reach neutral Spain. In April 1944, Sumner Jackson, Drue Tartière and other American and French civilians were dispatching more Allied air crews to the underground railway, but they did not know – or want to know, in case they were interrogated – what happened when the men left Paris.

One of the few Americans to see the network first-hand was Alice-Leone Moats, the *New York Herald Tribune*'s correspondent in Madrid. In late April 1944, contacts in the French Resistance took her over the mountains on foot and donkey into occupied France with the same guides who were taking Allied airmen out. She discovered that the Resistance operations chief along the border was a French customs police captain whom his colleagues called 'Monsieur Frontière'. His colleagues were the smugglers he would have arrested in peacetime. 'Nothing, of course, could have been more incongruous than a customs guard working hand in glove with smugglers,' Moats wrote. 'Monsieur Frontière' had pockets filled with French identity cards and gave one to her 'that someone with very poor eyesight might possibly have mistaken for a picture of me. It described me as a *"Marchande de fri-volité."*'

The customs captain took her to Pau, where she saw her first German soldier. 'I stopped short, staring at him,' she wrote. 'He wore a grayish green uniform that looked as though it might have been taken off a dead man. His blouse was open at the collar to display a red, weather-beaten neck. All the German soldiers I saw went without shirts, and their clothes were invariably of bad quality. Only their boots were good.' In Pau, she met two remarkable women, whom she identified only as Jane and Rosemary. Jane was English, and Rosemary was an American married to a Frenchman. Both 'were directly connected only with the section of the Underground which made the arrangements for the Allied flyers to escape'. They told her that, in Paris alone, 500 airmen were waiting to leave.

Usually the men traveled in groups of four with a Frenchman or -woman acting as convoy. When a foursome left Paris, word would be sent ahead. That was where Rosemary and Jane came into the picture. Their job was to find somewhere to put the flyers up in Pau and see that they got out as quickly as possible. Getting quarters for them was the real problem. Jane's flat was too small and too centrally located to be of any use. Rosemary's house was out of the question ... her husband knew nothing about her connection with the Underground.

Rosemary took Alice-Leone to a small hotel, 'run by two extraordinary old maids', where American airmen were hiding in the attic. 'Not daring to knock,' Miss Moats recalled, 'we just opened the door. Three men lying in bed sat up, eyes popping with terror. "It's all right," Rosemary said. "We're Americans."' The 'boys', as she called them, were wary, because police had raided the hotel that morning. They had not moved from the attic since. The women gave them Lucky Strike cigarettes.

'Gee,' one of the boys exclaimed. 'I didn't even know they made these things any more! We've been rolling our own ever since we've been in this country. None of us is very good at it' ... We asked them if they had had any narrow escapes. One, a snub-nosed kid from Texas, answered, 'Well, at Toulouse there were police at the station asking everybody for identification papers. We just showed them our American cards, and they handed them right back without batting an eyelash. They were French, of course. Still, it was a terrible moment. I don't like these French trains. I tell you, I'd rather go on ten bombing missions over Berlin than to take that train ride from Paris to Toulouse again.'

Jane and Rosemary told Alice-Leone about a downed fighter pilot named Carlow, whom they suspected of being a German spy. When Carlow arrived in Pau, he told Jane he had flown 100 missions. 'To begin with,' Rosemary explained, 'they're never supposed to go on more than twenty-five, and although I've passed about seventy flyers, I've never had one who had been on more than thirteen missions.' Carlow was the first airman who claimed to have flown a fighter plane. All the others had been on bombers, usually B-17s. Having been out of the United States for many years and uncertain of contemporary American slang, Rosemary asked Alice-Leone to talk to Carlow to determine if he really were an American. If not, he would be killed that night.

Carlow came to Jane's flat wearing rough, peasant clothes and a Basque beret. His height and Nordic good looks increased the three women's suspicions that he was a German agent. In the guise of light conversation, they questioned him. 'His accent, as he spoke, was unmistakably New England,' Alice-Leone wrote. 'I wasn't surprised when he told me that he came from Maine. He named a small town that I had never heard of. That didn't make any difference, because I figured that only a person who had lived in Maine a long time could have that accent.' She mimed 'All right' to Rosemary, who relaxed. The Resistance would not have to execute Carlow. His 100 flying missions still troubled the women. Alice-Leone told him, 'But America only got into the war in 1941.' Carlow explained, 'I was with the Eagle Squadron.' The Eagles were Americans who volunteered for the RAF before the United States declared war. It turned out that Alice-Leone knew many of Carlow's Eagle Squadron comrades. 'It was safe,' the women decided, 'to let him leave that night.'

Rosemary prepared Carlow for his trek to Spain. She gave him ration tickets to buy bread and told him to return those he didn't use to his mountain guide. A newspaper that she carefully folded into his pocket would identify him to the escort who would meet him at the bus station. Carlow was to follow Rosemary out of the flat thirty seconds after she left. Rosemary went outside and down the stairs. Carlow put his Basque beret back on his head. Alice-Leone and Jane shook his hand and wished him a safe journey. 'The last we saw of him he was walking nonchalantly through the gate of the courtyard.' Later, they heard Rosemary's wood-soled shoes skipping up the steps. 'She came in, hair flying and eyes shining, and flung herself on the bench in front of the fireplace. We wanted to know if the boys had left safely. "Oh, yes," she answered. Then she cried, "Oh, Jane, just think – he really was a fighter pilot! He's the best one we've ever had. We've never had a fighter pilot before!"'

While Carlow trekked west to Spain, Alice-Leone Moats wanted to go in the other direction, to Paris. Not many Americans dared take that chance, but she was after a scoop: the first eyewitness report from occupied Paris by an American journalist since the last three American reporters were expelled in January 1942. Her Resistance contact told her, 'You will always be followed by someone of our organization, so if you are picked up by the Gestapo we will know it immediately. We will also know exactly where you've been taken and that same night the Maquis will storm the building and get you out.' His promise was not reassuring. Nor were his last words: 'Once they have grilled you with no success, they'll certainly shoot you. As an American with false French papers, you will, of course, count as a spy.' She went anyway.

In February 1944, Drue Tartière, who had no telephone at home, received a call at the garage near her house in Barbizon outside Paris. The caller was Josée Laval de Chambrun. Drue, more involved than ever in operations to rescue Allied aviators, was uneasy listening to the high-pitched voice of a woman she did not know. She was aware, though, that Josée was Pierre Laval's daughter. 'We need an American woman who can broadcast in English, and you have been recommended to me,' Josée said. 'I know you Americans in France need money these days, and I think I can get you 60,000 francs a month.' Drue had concealed her stage name, Drue Leyton, for four years, lest the Germans keep their 1940 promise to put to death the American woman who had maligned them in broadcasts to the United States. Who, she wondered, had told Josée Laval de Chambrun that she was a broadcaster? 'I'm sure you have me confused with someone else,' she said. 'I know nothing about broadcasting, and besides I have been very ill and cannot possibly do a job.' Drue Leyton of Radio Mondiale had disappeared in June 1940, and Drue Tartière had no intention of resurrecting her. Luckily, Josée believed her. Drue walked back across the road to her house, where an American airman from Georgia, Mickey Coles, was hiding. Josée did not call again.

FORTY

Conspiracies

SPECULATION ABOUT THE LIFE and apparent suicide of Charles Bedaux abounded in the months after his death. The *New York Times* wrote, 'Charles E. Bedaux was one of a half-dozen or so figures who moved strangely in this generation behind the mantles of monarchy and the tyranny of totalitarian rule as well as on the back stairs of democratic government; and became legendary even before his death as the Mystery Man of international intrigue.' The government's refusal to release his suicide note added to the speculation. All that John L. Burling, the immigration official and federal prosecutor, disclosed in a statement released to the press was that Bedaux had been ordered to face a grand jury to 'consider whether he should be indicted for treason and for communicating with the enemy'. He stated that the 'sleeping pills had been issued to him from time to time when he complained of sleeplessness, and it is now clear that he had been hoarding them.'

In March, Edwin A. Lahey expressed his doubts about Bedaux in the then-liberal *New Republic*:

> Bedaux submitted a list of names of people who he said would testify favorably as to his character, his integrity and his complete loyalty to the United States. Many of these names are in 'Who's Who in America.' Some are the names of executives of large corporations which either have German holdings or have been named defendants in government suits against international cartels whose machinations

with the Nazis did so much to stymie our own preparedness for war. At least one person is widely known in politics. Another is an important financier. Another is a big steel producer, with mills in Germany.

An editorial in *The Nation* took the plot further: Bedaux had either been killed or was permitted to kill himself in order to protect powerful friends. It claimed that the FBI agents who visited him in Algiers had questioned French intelligence about the validity of its evidence:

They subjected investigators of the *Deuxième Bureau* to a severe interrogation, attempted to get them to withdraw the charges against Bedaux, accused them of 'planting' the [German] questionnaire, and finally of being in the pay 'of some agency of the American government controlled by Communists.'

This is a very extraordinary way of hunting down traitors and one, we think, which would bear further investigation. But so would a number of other questions connected with the last months of Charles Bedaux. Why, for instance, was he removed from French custody? On what grounds was he given the benefit of American citizenship and saved from a French military court? ... Finally, why, when he was in detention, was he permitted to accumulate sufficient luminal to enable him to choose his own time of exit?

The Nation thought Bedaux's important friends 'probably heard the news cheerfully. If they sighed at all, it was a sigh of relief.' On this view, Bedaux's fortuitous demise avoided a trial at which American business collaboration with the Nazis would be made public. Another view, held by Bedaux's family, was that he killed himself to avoid a trial that would reveal his anti-Nazi actions and associations – revelations for which the Gestapo would punish Fern Bedaux.

When Gaston Bedaux learned of his brother's death, he chose at first not to believe it: 'I had been so used to the resourceful imagination of my brother. I thought he could have had the audacity to make this announcement public so his wife in France, as well as his engineers and his friends, would not be disturbed by the Germans because he had returned to America, Germany's enemy.' Gaston, who believed his brother was in league with Germans seeking to overthrow Hitler, came to see the suicide as a heroic act to protect Fern.

Edmond Taylor, the former journalist and OSS agent in Algiers who admitted having ordered Bedaux's arrest, wrote afterwards, 'Perhaps I would not have been so ruthlessly vindictive, nor have resorted to such shoddy methods, if I had not still been haunted by the nightmare of a shadowy yet tightly organized international conspiracy working for a compromise peace.'

Hugh Fullerton, one of the American diplomats who came to know Bedaux at the Château de Candé in 1940, wrote, 'Had Charles waited, he would have been cleared of all charges.' Fullerton may have been correct regarding the accusation of treason. Article Three, Section Three, of the US Constitution states: 'Treason against the United States shall consist only in levying War against them, or in adhering to their Enemies, giving them Aid and Comfort. No Person shall be accused of Treason unless on the Testimony of two Witnesses to the same overt Act, or on Confession in open Court.' Circumstantial evidence in a treason trial would have been insufficient for a conviction. Bedaux was unlikely to make a confession, and there were no witnesses in the United States to any acts that might have been treasonable. On the charge of trading with the enemy, Bedaux had already convicted himself.

FORTY-ONE

Springtime in Paris

MARY BERG, HER MOTHER AND SISTER had been living in the camp at Vittel since early 1943. In August that year, Mary's father arrived with other men from the concentration camp at Tittmoning. At last, the family was reunited. They waited to go to America before they, like other Jews at Vittel whose American passports the Germans arbitrarily ceased to recognize, were shipped to Auschwitz. Even in the luxurious surroundings of the Vittel resort, Auschwitz hung over them.

On 1 March 1944, 160 internees at Vittel were told that they would be exchanged for Germans detained in the United States. The Bergs were among them. They were sent in a train to Biarritz, near the Spanish border, where Mary saw the arrival of German internees. 'They have come from America to be exchanged for us,' she wrote. 'All of us actually pitied these Germans.' The Germans were going into the inferno. Mary and her family were heading to a land untouched by war and death camps. On 15 March, from the deck of the Swedish-American cruise ship *Gripsholm*, the Bergs at last saw the Statue of Liberty.

On board the *Gripsholm* as it docked at Pier F in Jersey City were 559 US citizens and 103 Latin Americans, all repatriated under the exchange with Germany. Among them were thirty-five wounded American soldiers, 160 internees from Vittel and the American diplomats from Vichy, who had been interned by the French at Lourdes and then by the Germans at Baden-Baden. Douglas MacArthur, the embassy's third secretary, told reporters, 'It's swell to be back – but not half as fine as it will be to get back to work at the job.' A former Vittel internee, a medical student named Helen Landis, said the Nazis had kicked out five of her teeth when they caught her attempting to reach Spain in June 1943. The ship was 'boarded by an official party of several hundred, including the State Department, Army and Navy intelligence officers, agents of the Federal Bureau of Investigation and customs and immigration inspectors'. Those whose papers were not in order were taken to Ellis Island for investigation to make certain they were not German spies.

One passenger was a former fashion writer for the *New York Times*, Kathleen Cannel. She had been in Paris throughout the occupation and had left it only two weeks earlier. Her eyewitness account of life in the city was the first the newspaper had published from a staff member in four years. She said that Parisians were eating less food than ever and many were malnourished or anaemic. Electricity shortages closed the Metro for most of the day and all night. When it did run, its carriages were so crowded that 'the sardine box is spacious and deliciously perfumed by comparison'. Many civilians on the Metro 'have their clothes torn off, children are trampled under foot, aged persons are thrown out of the cars and fist fights are so common no one even turns his head to see what the row is about'. Neighbours were denouncing one another, and patriots were murdering collaborationists and black marketeers. 'In spite of all this sound and the fury,' she said, 'Paris is deceptively calm. Avenging bullets echo deep below the surface of daily life. Though there is little bread there are plenty of circuses. People escape from the galling irritation of perpetual difficulties into the realm of art. Theatres and talkies are crowded even in winter when the halls are unheated. The Grand Opera is sold out both for opera and ballet half an hour after the opening of the box office.'

Miss Cannel did not say why she left Paris after having stayed for so long. But she gave the impression that the city was afraid of what would happen to hasten the liberation: 'The Paris air is more highly charged with menace than at any time since the French Revolution. Invasion, civil war, siege, famine, prison – whatever form the future may take – Parisians are minutely expecting the deadliest phase of the war.'

King John opened for a second season at the Théâtre de l'Odéon in the spring of 1944, when the Allies were bombing the industrial suburbs of Paris. Occasionally, air raid sirens interrupted the play and forced the audience into underground shelters. At the same time, rumours of what Clara de Chambrun called the Allies' 'eagerly expected landing' somewhere on the coast of northern France were giving hope to the increasingly oppressed people of Paris. One short passage in the play that had gone unremarked in 1943 suddenly resonated with the spectators. In Act Four, a Messenger declared to King John,

> Never such a power
> For any foreign preparation
> Was levied in the body of a land.
> The copy of your speed is learn'd by them;
> For when you should be told they do prepare,
> The tidings come that they are all arrived.

The audience reacted with frenzied cheers and applause. Clara worried: 'Each time the enthusiasm grew louder. We feared the Germans would hear of it and close the theater. To cut out the passage would have been a moral lowering of the flag; strangely enough, it sufficed to warn the actor who spoke the lines not to stress them but to deliver his message in a conversational tone. Thenceforth expression of approval went on more moderately until the last day.' By this time, 'foreign preparation' to liberate France was ready. Clara and her son were not.

The spring of 1944 added aerial hazards to the hardship of occupation on the ground. From March, when the winter weather abated, Allied bombing of German-occupied Europe intensified. 'Life in Paris,' wrote Clara, 'which had become almost untenable, grew steadily more difficult and dangerous owing to the heavy bombardments from the sky by the R.A.F. and the American Air Forces. We took it for the prelude of the dreamed-of landing, and during the month of March as a necessary evil from which the hoped-for good would spring.'

While the Allies concentrated bombing sorties on the Pas-de-Calais to convince the Germans it was the invasion point, they did not spare the industrial outskirts of Paris. The targets were factories making munitions for the Wehrmacht, and the bombs often exploded in working class neighbourhoods nearby. 'Those who listened, as most people did, to the British radio on April the twenty-first, learned that eight thousand planes had poured down fifteen thousand tons of bombs over Europe,' Clara wrote.

> We could not then estimate what proportion of these was destined for us. But when midnight struck, the alarms showed that the different workmen's centers, St. Denis, St. Ouen, La Courneuve, Noisy-le-Sec, Bobigny, the market gardens of Romainville and Athis-Mons, had been subjected to a furious bombardment which cost almost two thousand lives in these regions which lie in the immediate vicinity of Paris. Eleven large shell holes were counted in close proximity to the Sacré-Coeur Basilica at Montmartre. In the fashionable residence section of the sixteenth Arrondissement, the building containing the reserve stock of the Croix-Rouge was destroyed.

Clara watched relief teams speeding to 'the fallen houses, burning buildings, flooded cellars, and ruptured waterpipes in the unending effort to find the dead, transport the wounded, and lodge the homeless'. Among the dead were two American friends, Miss Lewandowska and Mrs Mygatt. René arranged the funeral for Mrs Mygatt, 'as he did for all my fellow-countrymen and -women, in the crypt of the American Cathedral under the Stars and Stripes'.

The BBC warned people to evacuate ahead of the raids, but Clara thought the advice was useless. Most Parisians had nowhere to go. Food ration coupons were invalid outside the neighbourhoods where they were issued, so those who left risked starvation. And, as in 1940 when the Germans were advancing on Paris, escape could be more dangerous than staying home: 'It was an ironical consolation to be told to leap on a train when you knew at the same time that all trains and locomotives would also be destroyed. The Germans, rich in trucks and gasoline, were practically independent of rail transportation; that is why the large death toll was borne by French civilians.'

Clara did not go to La Chapelle, near Montmartre, to see the worst of the destruction. Another American, Alice-Leone Moats, did. The gutsy Madrid correspondent of the *New York Herald Tribune*, following her perilous border crossing and meetings with American airmen in Pau, was in Paris in late April and early May. Her fluent French and German allowed her to speak at length with French collaborators and *résistants*, as well as German officers and soldiers. She hired a horse-drawn cart to take her up the hill to La Chapelle.

> The quarter presented a gruesome sight. On every street there were houses that had been destroyed. Very little seemed to have been done to clear up the debris. Digging was still going on to get bodies out of the cellars. I overheard a woman saying, 'The cries and moans stopped yesterday. I guess they're all dead now.' Just then a corpse was carted out. The men doing the work were slow and obviously not trained for the job ...
>
> Men and women and children stood about watching the proceedings. The faces all showed the same dazed look of suffering. I spoke to several of them to find out how they felt about the raids. I got the same answer as in Biarritz: 'We can forgive the raids if they are to some purpose, if they really are a preparation for the invasion.'
>
> A man in overalls said, 'The Allies have sent out warnings that everyone is to move away from the vicinity of railways and factories. But what are you to do if you work in a railway or a factory? Move to the Ritz? A man has to have his home near his work.'

When Alice-Leone asked a dry cleaner whether the people of the quarter supported the Allies, he answered, 'People in this quarter, Madame, don't advertise their political opinions.'

Neither the bombardments nor German retaliation for the increasing number of Resistance attacks prevented the Paris *beau monde* from enjoying life. Alice-Leone observed them at Maxim's, where she and a companion lunched on pâté de foie gras, boeuf à la mode, salad and wild strawberries with a bottle of Nuit Saint-Georges 1934. Maxim's was a favourite of René and Josée de Chambrun. Josée still bought her dresses from the salons of fashion houses Rochas and Schiaparelli, whose seasonal shows and access to scarce cloths were not interrupted by the occupation. On 9 April, she and René spent the day at the Auteil races where René won 260,000 francs. In celebratory mood, they went with Pierre, Duc de Brissac, to the Théâtre de La Michodière to see Jean Anouilh's *Le Voyageur sans bagages*. The next night, René's luck brought him 240,000 francs at poker. It was a time of French theatrical revival for a public desperate for entertainment and diversion. Paris saw 400 productions under the occupation, including new plays by Albert Camus, Jean-Paul Sartre, Jean Cocteau and Jean Anouilh. American Florence Jay Gould's salon for German and French writers was thriving in her avenue Malakoff apartment. Jean Cocteau, who enjoyed Florence's hospitality, also attended parties at Baron Robert de Rothschild's palace that had been confiscated by a German general. The butler told Cocteau, 'I am not unhappy working for the Baron, I mean the General, since he receives the same people as the Baron used to.' For such people, the Allied bombardment of France might as well have been taking place in China.

Josée de Chambrun, one of the most social women in Paris, worried about an Allied victory. She told her father one evening, 'We will be hanged because of the Milice.' The Milice of Joseph Darnand had since January 1943 been Vichy's Gestapo, black-shirted thugs who were every bit as ruthless and unpopular as their German exemplars. Pierre Laval replied that she would understand politics if she did not spend so much time at fashion shows. Her mother tried to calm things by saying, 'That's just like little Josée, her charities on one side and her coquetry on the other.'

Pierre Laval convinced the Germans to permit Maréchal Pétain to visit Paris and honour the city's recent war dead, including the 565 killed in La Chapelle. 'Moreover,' Clara enthused, 'they even consented to order their troops to remain forty-eight hours in barracks, and officers were told to keep off the streets. For once, Paris should be left exclusively to Parisians, and the Marshal would not even see a German uniform during his sojourn. These measures were kept so secret that we all went to sleep in Paris on the twenty-fifth of April totally unaware of what was to happen.' At seven o'clock the next morning, Clara received a telephone call from her daughter-in-law, Josée. She relayed the news: Maréchal Pétain was already in Paris with her father to attend a Solemn Requiem Mass at the Cathedral of Notre Dame. The service was taking place in a few hours. Clara dressed quickly and walked through the morning mist from the rue de Vaugirard to Notre Dame, a distance of about a mile. The cramped streets were filling with crowds, as word spread that the Maréchal was in Paris. When Clara reached the open square before the Cathedral, the German sentries who had been there for four years were gone. In their place was a phalanx of French gendarmes. Horse-drawn hearses carried the coffins of the bombing victims, draped in French tricolour palls, into the square. Clara recalled: 'I hesitated a moment as to whether it was more thrilling to wait outside and see the arrival, or to secure an adequate and comfortable observation post. I decided on the latter solution; luckily, too, for I found a seat in the eighth row of the center aisle. Slowly a half hour slipped away and the Cathedral filled gradually. Silence reigned, broken occasionally by the low strains of the organ.'

Clara's excitement was unbounded when Philippe Pétain, in Marshal of France uniform, led a procession into the church with Pierre Laval just behind. Even after four years of Vichy's collaboration with the Nazis, its cooperation in sending a million Frenchmen to forced labour in Germany and its assistance to the Germans in deporting Jews to their deaths, Clara nurtured a belief in the two men she had known and admired since long before the occupation. In her eyes, they were heroic defenders of France, who had remained as 'shields' between the German oppressors and a defenceless populace. To most other Americans, especially in Paris, they were traitors to France and enemies of the United States.

Marching with the Maréchal and his prime minister were the Catholic hierarchy, led by the Cardinal Archbishop of Paris, Monsignor Emmanuel Suchard. Families of the dead stood beside the caskets. The choir sang, and Archbishop Suchard said the Solemn Requiem Mass in Latin. The drama's mixture of religious and polit-ical moved Clara to write, 'During this ceremony, by far the most impressive I have ever witnessed in Notre Dame and one in which the feeling of hope triumphant was so strangely and paradoxically mingled with the mourning sacrificial ceremony for the victims without whom victory has never been achieved, every one felt and repressed the strong desire to show in some way the heartfelt greeting silently offered by the Chief of State.' When the Mass ended, Pétain went to the Hôtel de Ville nearby and mounted its balcony. For the first time during the occupation, the French flag was flying atop the main gable of Paris's city hall. Below the 88-year-old Chief of State, thousands of Parisians were cheering. If critics saw Pétain's first appearance in occupied Paris as a cynical ploy to demonstrate his popularity to the Americans and the Free French, Clara did not. As a loyal American, she yearned for an Allied victory, but her memoirs betray no comprehension of the reasons the victors would not share her enthusiasm for Vichy's collaborators.

The clamour from the Hôtel de Ville attracted Alice-Leone Moats, who followed the throng to its source. 'I imagine that since no one knew the Marshal was coming to Paris,' she wrote, 'a couple of hundred people were undoubtedly planted to attract the rest of the crowd. But the ovation was completely spontaneous.' Moats thought most people had been drawn by the sight of the French flag and the singing of *La Marseillaise*, both *verboten* under German rule. German war losses in the East and the impending Allied invasion of France were, she observed, emboldening the Parisians. The next day, she heard music in the street and

tracked it down to a ragged old man who was working hard on a wheezy concertina. At first I couldn't believe my ears, but as I listened I recognized the unmistakable strains of 'The Marseillaise'. Playing the national anthem was absolutely forbidden, and yet he seemed to be getting away with it. No French person passed him without giving him some money. Similar old men were to be found in most of the metro stations, picking up a few francs by playing either 'The Marseillaise,' 'God Save the King,' or Sousa marches.

FORTY-TWO

The Maquis to Arms!

IN THE SPRING OF 1944, Dr Sumner Jackson and other *résistants* were sending more airmen and escaped prisoners back to Britain to fight the coming battle. American, British and Free French agents parachuted secretly into France to mobilize and train the Resistance for what the US army's Plan Neptune called 'wide-spread guerrilla activity by small bands of lightly armed Frenchmen operating in the enemy's back areas'. In the countryside, diverse groups of communists, socialists, royalists, Catholics and petty criminals were fighting in the maquis. Maquis is a Corsican word, originally from the Italian *macchia*, meaning bush or scrubland. In Corsica, those who hid in the maquis were outlaws. In France, the *maquis* or *maquisards* called themselves patriots. To Vichy and the Germans, they were *terroristes*. Their operations included sabotaging rail lines, assassinating suspected collaborators, attacking German troops and, on occasion, mutilating their corpses. Whatever their politics or their methods, which were often brutal, they were being absorbed into the strategy of the Supreme Allied Commander, General Dwight D. Eisenhower, to drive the Germans from France. They were the Allies' fifth column behind German lines.

In common with many other members of the Resistance, Sumner and Toquette Jackson were helping to satisfy London's growing appetite for information. In advance of a hazardous invasion, providing data on the enemy's forces contributed more to the war effort than minor attacks on German outposts. Winston Churchill, Charles de Gaulle and General

Eisenhower pressed the Resistance for more and better intelligence on German air and coastal defences, train timetables, supply lines, weapons depots, fuel dumps and air bases. An urgent priority was to find Hitler's 'secret weapon'. The first inkling the Allies had of it came in a telegram from the Office of Strategic Services' man in Berne, Allen Dulles, on 5 February 1943: 'From German sources he considers reliable, [OSS Agent] 490 [German industrialist Walter Bovari] reports that the Germans are producing a secret weapon whose exact nature was not disclosed to him with the exception that [it] is a flying contraption in the form of an aerial torpedo.' Soon to be known as the V-1 rocket, this bomb could fly over the English Channel without risking a single German pilot or the Luftwaffe's diminishing arsenal of aeroplanes. Its ½ ton warheads would kill thousands of civilians in Britain while the Allies were sending their forces into France. If targeted on the English port at Southampton, where the Allies planned to assemble the invasion force, there would be no D-Day.

On 17 August 1943, French *résistant* Michel Hollard smuggled plans for the V-1 across the border to British and American intelligence in Switzerland. Passing details of the secret weapon to the Allies earned Hollard, who established and directed the Agir network, arrest and torture by the Germans. The drawings he supplied enabled the British to bomb a factory at Peenemünde, Germany, on 17–18 August 1943. The raid delayed the V-1's production, but it did not stop it. The Allies needed to know more about the bomb, where it was being manufactured and the locations of its launch sites. The invasion could not go ahead while thousands of ½ ton bombs, against which Britain had few defences, threatened to destroy London and disrupt the embarkation at Southampton. This required the work of many agents, all of whom endangered their lives.

Help came from an unexpected source: an officer in the German army. Twenty-nine-year-old Erich Posch-Pastor von Camperfeld had a long record of resistance to Hitler. During the Anschluss in 1938, his Austrian regiment fought to prevent Nazi annexation of their country. His punishment was a year at the Dachau concentration camp. On his release, he was taken into the German army. When Germany invaded Russia in 1941, he was wounded on the Russian front. The army transferred him to France in February 1942 to oversee an armaments factory near the Atlantic coast at Niort. He managed to slow down the monthly production of bomb fuses from 13,000 to about 1,000. While in Niort, Posch-Pastor discussed politics with his landlady, Mme Missant. She was a Goélette-Frégate agent, who told Paris operations chief Renaudot, R, about the dissident Austrian. It was R who had sent Phillip Jackson to photograph Germany's U-boat base at Saint-Nazaire in the summer of 1943. He enlisted Posch-Pastor into the Goélette-Frégate network in October 1943 as Resistance agent CLAYREC RJ4570.

Posch-Pastor adopted the alias Etienne Paul Provost, perhaps to avoid altering the initials E.P.P. embroidered on his dress shirts. A cousin of his worked in the Wehrmacht's munitions department in Paris, and he persuaded him to hand over technical drawings of the V-1 rockets and their locations. It turned out the Germans were building dozens of launch sites along the northern French coast, identical structures with long ramps, loading bays and storage sheds. Posch-Pastor could not rely on the normal mail drops in Paris to send the documents to London. The information was too important to leave anywhere, including the Jacksons' apartment in avenue Foch, which might be under Gestapo surveillance. Posch-Pastor was instructed to deposit the V-1 plans in a public place where the comings and goings of large numbers of people would not attract attention. The American Hospital in Neuilly fitted the description. Posch-Pastor, using his Etienne Paul Provost alias, went to the hospital in December 1943 and introduced himself to Dr Sumner Jackson. Without saying what he had in his possession, he left the papers in Jackson's office. The V-1 plans were passed to a series of couriers and cut-outs, taking a circuitous route north to Brest, on to a priest in the village of Lannils and, finally, to a safe house on the English Channel. There, British sailors and airmen were waiting for a Special Operations Executive boat to carry them home. The boat crossed the Channel in darkness just after Christmas 1943 and delivered the V-1 plans to England. The Allies repeatedly bombed the V-1 sites marked on Posch-Pastor's maps, significantly reducing the rocket's threat to the invasion.

Alice-Leone Moats was given a rare interview with three Resistance leaders in a small Left Bank apartment, 'which smelled strongly of cabbage'. One was a lawyer, one a professor and the third a writer. She was not told their names. 'The lawyer was quite extraordinary looking,' she wrote. 'He had a very young, strong face topped with a thick head of white hair. His skin was as white as paper and his eyes were such a light shade of gray that they made scarcely any contrast with his face. I felt a cold shiver down my spine when I first saw him; there was something uncanny about him, an air of sadness and weariness such as I had never seen before. I thought, he's been hunted.' The Germans were offering a reward of four million francs for his capture. Her Resistance contact assured her that the three middle-aged men 'were more adventurous and fool-hardy than any young hotheads he knew'. She asked them whether Charles de Gaulle would take over France when the liberation came. 'We all admire what he did in 1940,' the writer said. 'He was the one who came to the fore and raised the tricolor in the name of freedom. That can never be forgotten, but it doesn't necessarily mean that he is the right man for France in peacetime. Even the greatest army officers seldom make good statesmen. It doesn't follow that because a man is a genius on the battlefield, he will be a genius on the floor of parliament.'

What, she wondered, did younger *résistants* want after the war? 'They will want a big share in the country they helped liberate,' the lawyer said. 'When it's refused them, as it no doubt will be for practical reasons, they will, of course, turn to communism.' Her last question was about the propaganda that the Allies sent daily into France by radio and on leaflets dropped from the sky. The lawyer responded wearily that 'the only propaganda that gets results is a victory'.

That night, Alice-Leone Moats left Paris on the train to Toulouse. On 5 May, she was back at the border for her return hike into the Spanish mountains. She reached Madrid on 8 May and the next day filed the first American journalist's story from Paris in two and a half years. But the Spanish censor blocked it. She went to the Foreign Ministry, where four Spanish diplomats politely explained that, while they admired her courage, they could not allow her to send her report from Spain. The Germans would object. She offered to file the story from Lisbon, and they agreed that would be the perfect solution. While she waited for a Portuguese visa, a British Embassy military attaché invited her to brief him on the pilots' escape routes and what might be done to improve them. The American Embassy was not interested. When she reached Lisbon and sent her stories to both the *New York Herald Tribune* and *Collier's Weekly*, the US Embassy there demanded the right to censor a broadcast she was about to make for CBS Radio. It also confiscated her American passport. Exhausted by her dangerous journey to Occupied France, the long treks over the Pyrenees and her battle with her own embassy, Alice-Leone Moats took the Pan Am Clipper home to New York. In the book she wrote immediately on her return, she called her last chapter, 'It Was Worth It'.

FORTY-THREE

Résistants *Unmasked*

GENERAL KARL OBERG intensified the hunt for the networks sending information to the Allies. If losing the secret plans for the V-1 was a defeat for German intelligence, the Gestapo had successes to offset it. Oberg's agents had captured Jean Moulin, the incorruptible leader of Charles de Gaulle's Mouvements Unis de la Résistance. In June 1943, Moulin was betrayed, tortured and executed. Oberg had decapitated not one Resistance network, but the umbrella under which almost every network was fighting. Immediately after Moulin's capture, the OSS was forced to order that 'all general meetings even among [Resistance] section groups should be forbidden'. German penetration was disrupting the Resistance and reducing its usefulness to the Allies. A month after Moulin's execution, the Germans broke up the Oaktree escape network that had delivered 175 downed airmen to England. Another of Oberg's achievements came in early May 1944, when his men captured three active *résistants* in Paris, the Englishwoman Gladys Marchal, Gilbert Asselin and his mistress, Lise Russ. All three belonged to the Libération network and had helped the Jacksons in the escape of American tail-gunner Joe Manos the year before. The Gestapo tortured and interrogated them, although no record of what they said survived. A day later, the Germans released Gladys Marchal. Renaudot and the Jacksons remained free, but the Goélette-Frégate network had been compromised. Life was clearly becoming too dangerous for the Jacksons to use their flat for Resistance meetings or as a mail drop. But they continued to do both. A simple code alerted couriers and other Goélette-Frégate visitors: if the curtains were arranged in a certain way, come in; if not, stay away.

General Oberg's security services and their allies in the French Milice placed many *résistants* under surveillance. The Milice, established by Pétain's Decree Number 63 of January 1943 and commanded by First World War hero turned fascist Joseph Darnand, was composed solely of volunteers born in France of French parents. Jews, North Africans and Freemasons were excluded. Most of its 45,000 members were street toughs, although a few were conscientious fascists who wanted to mould France in the image of Hitler's Germany. The *miliciens* knew their society better than the Germans, and they could eavesdrop on fellow Frenchmen more easily than German soldiers. Vichy and the Germans gave the *miliciens* licence to arrest, torture and kill. Not long after the Gestapo arrested Marchal, Asselin and Russ, the Milice raided a Goélette-Frégate cell at La Bourboule in the mountains near Vichy and discovered 'compromising letters addressed to Mrs. Jackson'. Whether the Milice passed along this information to General Oberg is unclear, but the *miliciens* took it upon themselves to please their Nazi masters by taking care of the Goélette-Frégate network.

Hints that something was wrong multiplied in the spring of 1944. An anonymous letter to Clemence Bock, who had tutored Sumner for his French exams in 1921 and been an intimate friend of both Sumner and Toquette ever since, advised her to stop visiting the people she knew in the avenue Foch. A local policeman warned Sumner, 'Look out, sir, you're being watched.' In what the French called *la guerre des ombres*, the war of shadows, between the underground and German counter-intelligence, no one was certain who was telling the truth and who was denouncing whom. As for warnings, Sumner ignored them.

The daily routine of treating American civilians from Paris and the internment camps, as well as the railway *cheminots* and Allied prisoners of war, was in its way reassuring to Dr Jackson. General de Chambrun had managed to keep the hospital open without, so far, admitting German patients. Elisabeth Comte and Otto Gresser, the two efficient and able Swiss managers of the hospital, made certain the patients were fed and their rooms comfortable. No one believed liberation was far off, not even the Germans over the road in the Neuilly Kommandatur. All Dr Jackson had to do was to keep safe at work until Paris was free. Then, he and General de Chambrun could turn the hospital over to the American army.

On the morning of 24 May, Dr Jackson was doing his usual rounds of patients at the American Hospital, when two French 'policemen' in Milice black shirts and berets suddenly entered the hospital looking for him. The Milice agents forced him into their car and drove full-speed to the avenue Foch, where both the Gestapo and the Sicherheitsdienst had bureaus. But they did not stop at either. They took Dr Jackson to the corner of avenue Foch and rue Traktir, his own house. Inside, other *miliciens* were holding his wife and son at gunpoint. Black-shirted gunmen took the family outside to the garden, while the others ransacked the apartment. Toquette could not tell Sumner that she had already disposed of the incriminating documents in the house. When the Milice officers were distracted, she had given her Resistance papers to her maid, Louise, to take away on a household errand.

At lunchtime, the Jacksons invited the *miliciens* to eat with them. Afterwards, Sumner and the Milice commander smoked cigars in the garden. Phillip used the opportunity to arrange the curtains onto the side street, rue Traktir, to indicate to anyone from Goélette-Frégate that a meeting scheduled for that evening was cancelled. The Jacksons were not allowed to use the telephone and remained under Milice guard all night.

The Milice roused the family early in the morning and crammed them into the back of a police Citroën. They headed into the country-side south of Paris and did not stop until they reached Vichy. The *miliciens* deposited Phillip at their headquarters in the Petit Casino. They took Sumner and Toquette onto another interrogation centre in the Château des Brosses. This mid-nineteenth-century folly had two great turrets and a double exterior staircase up to the main door. Sumner and Toquette were led inside and taken upstairs, where they were locked in separate rooms for the night. The *miliciens* kept them apart until the next evening, when they permitted them to have dinner together on a terrace outside. The treatment of the doctor and his wife was strangely courteous. They were even allowed to speak English, something they took advantage of to agree what to say under interrogation.

Toquette wrote, 'We were all arrested on May 25th [the day they were taken from Paris], not because we were Americans, but because we were working for the underground liberation movements, what we call the "Resistance", we were therefore political prisoners and much worse off than regular prisoners of war.'

After two nights at the Château des Brosses, Sumner and Toquette were taken back to Vichy and locked up in the Petit Casino. The Milice headquarters in the casino had evolved into a centre of secret confinement, interrogation and torture. The Vichy government had also authorized the Milice to hold trials and execute defendants. The Milice put Sumner in a cell on the first second floor with his son, and they installed Toquette alone on the one above. Phillip had spent the three previous days without food in the chateau's dungeon, fearful, hungry and occasionally hysterical. The 16-year-old boy was under intense strain, but his father's arrival was comforting. Then, the interrogations began. The Milice questioned the Jacksons separately, a standard police tactic to uncover contradictions and lies. Toquette managed to send a letter to her sister, Tat, on Wednesday, 31 May, which referred to two previous letters she had written. 'Today is the day Pete should have taken his examinations for the Baccalaureate,' she wrote, 'and I haven't seen him since Friday.' She complained that she had not been able to change her clothes or wash since she left Paris six days earlier, but she was relieved to be wearing a tartan skirt 'that doesn't get crumpled and a gray sweater, flexible and comfortable.' She asked her sister to tell Elisabeth Comte at the American Hospital where they were and to deal with various household matters. She added, 'My courage is being tested to the extreme not so much for me as for Pete and also for Jack; if I knew that he was free my particular fate would be less painful.'

On 6 June, the Allies assaulted the Normandy coast and fought one of history's greatest battles for a foothold in France. Many of the young airmen flying over the beaches, as well as some of the soldiers fighting on the ground, made it to D-Day only because Dr Sumner Jackson had helped them to escape from France. They had been spared prison, but Jackson had not. Sumner, Toquette and Pete Jackson, enduring Milice interrogation in the Petit Casino, were unaware that the liberation they longed for was underway. The Milice turned them over to the Gestapo on 7 June, twenty-four hours after the invasion. 'We had spent 8 days at the Militia (in the cellars) at Vichy, then 16 days at the Gestapo, also at Vichy, the Militia having handed us over to the Germans, being unable to settle the affair,' Phillip Jackson wrote later to friends. The Milice may have been seeking to dissociate themselves from the Jacksons' arrest after the sudden appearance of the American army in France. The victorious Americans would hold them responsible for the Jacksons. It is also possible that the Germans, learning of the Jacksons' role in an espionage ring, seized them from the Milice in order to learn the names of their co-conspirators. The Gestapo transferred the family to the Hôtel du Portugal, another notorious torture chamber in Vichy. To hide their victims' cries from neighbours in the boulevard des États-Unis, the Gestapo played loud music day and night. Phillip Jackson wrote,

> We were then separated, my father and myself in different cells, where, however, we were able to communicate. My mother [was] in another building.
>
> We were not badly treated, that is to say, we were not beaten by the French inspectors of the Gestapo who assured us we should shortly be released. (I have learnt to know them better, by now.)

Phillip stayed in a cell with three other men. His daily ration of three small pieces of bread and a flat plate of 'so-called soup' barely sustained him, and the boy lost weight. He later gave an interview to his father's biographer, Hal Vaughan, about the Gestapo prison:

> As I was an American citizen they treated my family and me decently during questioning, which in my case was extremely summary. I told them I knew nothing and I was informed I should be released in a very short time. The man who questioned me was a French inspector of the Gestapo whose name or nickname was Nerou ... The jailers were uniformed members of the German SD: *Sicherheitsdienst* ... I knew and spoke to people, particularly those in my cell, who were whipped and tortured during questioning, and I saw a jailer whip

one of my fellow prisoners about 25 times in my cell. I was also whipped by jailers if I was not standing to attention or for any minor pretext ... One man in my cell, a Frenchman whose name I have forgotten, he came from Clermont-Ferrand, told me he had been whipped and beaten by ... Nerou. I saw evidence of this beating, as the man's back was covered with different colors and bleeding.

Inquiries by the American Hospital, the American Legation in Berne, the Red Cross and the Swiss Consulate in Vichy were turning up only fragmentary details of the Jacksons' incarceration. Vichy made the search for the Jackson family more difficult by repeatedly lying to the Swiss Consul, insisting it knew nothing. But American diplomats had received accurate information on 6 June, when Toquette's brother in Switzerland 'informed U.S. Legation his sister, her husband and son had been arrested on May 26, 1944 by the French authorities and transferred to Vichy.' Misinformation was clouding the original, reliable report. Leland Harrison, the US Minister in Berne, sent a telegram to Secretary of State Cordell Hull on 13 July 1944, saying that 'Swiss Legation Vichy reports it has been informed by Secretariat Mainain [sic] Ordre that inquiry made of French Milice Vichy and Paris reveal Americans mentioned arrested by German police and not (repeat not) taken Vichy.' A later State Department cable reported, 'On June 27, 1944, the Swiss Legation in Vichy reported that the Secrétariat d'Etat du Maintien de l'Ordre advised that the Jackson family had been arrested by the German authorities and that, to its knowledge, it had never been taken to Vichy.' Vichy simply lied to the Swiss, no doubt fearing after the D-Day landings the consequences of mistreating American citizens. Since January 1944, Vichy's secretary for the maintenance of order was Joseph Darnand, founder and chief of the Milice. Darnand, whose own men had arrested the Jacksons, covered up his actions by diverting suspicion to the Germans to whom he had transferred their custody. The State Department turned to other sources, and more evidence emerged. 'At the same time, however,' the State Department reported, 'a letter received by a member of the family in Paris from young [Phillip] Jackson confirmed that the Jacksons had been arrested by the French "Milice"; taken to Vichy; then to Château des Brosses, the headquarters of the "Milice"; and turned over to the Gestapo in Vichy.'

No cables in Allen Dulles's OSS files from Berne show that he or his agent Max Shoop, who was a governor of the American Hospital, either knew of or took any interest in the Jacksons at this time. The OSS was preoccupied with Resistance support for the Allies during the battle for France. The Wehrmacht and the Allied armies were capturing thousands of each other's soldiers, and demands for information about prisoners overwhelmed the Swiss Consulate and the Red Cross. The Jacksons were now a humanitarian issue, and the OSS's priority was to gather intelligence and organize the Resistance to win the war.

Two weeks after the Allies landed, Pierre Laval declared, 'We are not in the war.' But the war was in France. The Wehrmacht was forcing the Allies to fight hard for every acre of French ground they conquered. In Paris, freshly painted black and white signs with the words *Zür Normandie Front* pointed north where troops headed to stop the Allied invasion of the German-occupied continent. The Resistance did its part, blowing up trains, tracks and bridges to disrupt Wehrmacht supply lines. But, to Parisians, the American and British armies were taking too long.

'The star of hope was now far above the horizon,' Clara de Chambrun wrote. 'The troops of General Eisenhower had obtained firmfooting in Normandy; we knew that the British were on the march towards Rouen while the American contingents were taking an oblique line which skirted Paris in a southerly direction. But progress was slow, and they still seemed desperately far away.' Neither Clara nor the other inhabitants of the French capital were aware that capturing Paris was not part of General Eisenhower's strategy. Ike planned to chase the German army from France and defeat it in Germany as rapidly as possible, leaving Paris's German garrison to surrender later. He needed all his resources, especially fuel for his armoured divisions, to do it. Occupying Paris and feeding its two million inhabitants would only divert the Allied armies from their goal.

Paris, as its supply lines were cut, experienced more hunger and greater danger than at any time during the occupation. The railways and roads out of the city were either cut or blocked by Wehrmacht transports, and the majority of Parisians who normally spent August in the country or by the sea were confined to the city. The Metro stopped running from eleven in the morning until three o'clock every afternoon to conserve electricity. Without electricity and cooking fuel, people made fires with paper balls to boil water and to fry what little food there was. With no meat or vegetables coming in from the countryside, the city became a farm. People grew vegetables in their gardens and on their roofs. Many kept chickens, ducks and rabbits on balconies and in cupboards. The smoke that covered the city when the Germans advanced on it in June 1940 returned. Then, the French government had burned its files and its oil reserves. Now, it was the Germans' turn.

To the leaders of the Resistance movement that Clara disparaged, Paris had only one option: to liberate itself.

FORTY-FOUR

Via Dolorosa

IN MID-JUNE, AFTER INTERROGATING Sumner, Toquette and Phillip Jackson, the Gestapo sent the family on a circuitous journey that would be hard to follow. Phillip wrote,

> One fine day, I can hardly call it day, as there was no light and no air in my cell, where I remained shut up for 14 days, only getting out once – then we were transferred to the German military prison at Moulins. During the journey I sat next to my father, in the same bus and we saw my mother who traveled in another bus. Once arrived at Moulins, my mother and ourselves were enclosed in the prison, an old medieval dungeon, where we had to go up 118 steps to our cell. My father and I were in the same cell, my mother in another part of the building. We remained 21 days at Moulins, conditions not too bad, but we suffered from hunger. Examined once more, my father, my mother and myself, this time by a German of the Gestapo. Declarations nil from my father and for myself – for my mother I do not know.

Through the Swiss, the State Department learned that the Jacksons 'finally had been sent by the Germans to the Prison in Moulins'. The Americans asked the Swiss where Moulins was, and Leland Harrison cabled their reply to Washington in August: 'Inquiry of Swiss Foreign Office reveals nothing (repeat nothing) in files indicates exact location Moulins ... Further inquiry impossible as all (repeat all) communication cut.'

On 22 June, Toquette wrote to her sister, 'I saw my son and my husband the other day during an inspection. They are together and that makes me happy.' At seven in the morning on 7 July, father and son were handcuffed together and moved again. Toquette was left behind at Moulins. Phillip recalled, 'Journey by bus, rather trying, without water, in a burning sun. We had left Moulins at 7 a.m. and reached Compiègne the next day at 3 a.m. We were handcuffed from the start at Moulins till the arrival the next day at Compiègne.' Sumner had been imprisoned in Compiègne before, in September 1942, as an internee. When he and Phillip arrived, the American and other enemy alien internees had been moved. The Compiègne camp, now a holding pen for political prisoners, retained some of the privileges of its first years. Phillip noted that there were 'Red Cross parcels – no work; the only trouble was vermin, fleas lice en masses'.

As in 1942, Jackson's stay at Compiègne lasted only a week. In 1942, that seemed a long time. In 1944, it was too short. This time, General de Chambrun did not know where Dr Jackson was and did not drive there to take him home. On 15 July, which Phillip called 'a fatal day', he and his father were force-marched with about 2,000 other political prisoners to the train station 'where we are pushed into cattle wagons for Germany'. Groups of sixty men at a time were packed into the hot and airless cattle wagons. Each man was issued one piece of bread and a sausage for what would be a three-day journey across France and Germany. The prisoners had no room to lie down and very little water. One psychotic guard fired into one of the cattle wagons, killing a prisoner. Seventeen men escaped, and the Germans shoved the other forty-three from their cattle wagon into one that already had sixty men in it. 'We were escorted by German gendarmes in French uniforms, incredibly brutal,' Phillip wrote.

Our convoy was to go to Dachau but, on July 18th, we arrive at Neuengamme, 30 kms. South of Hamburg, in the curve of the River Elbe. There we are horsewhipped out of our carriages, by the S.S., and marched to the camp, guarded by S.S. men with machine guns under their arms and dogs on leach [sic]. At the camp, we are packed into two gigantic cellars, then taken out into small groups to the shower room where rings, false teeth, orthopedic belts are taken from us, after our heads have been shaved.

The men's bare bodies were inspected by guards. Each prisoner was given old and tattered clothes, 'not fit for a beggar to wear', and wooden shoes. Sumner was prisoner Number 36,462, his new identity stamped on canvas strips sewn into his jacket and trousers. Phillip was Number 36,461. Sumner Jackson and his teenage son became American slaves of the Third Reich. It was 18 July, the day that the Allied armies finally broke out of Normandy on their way to Paris.

FORTY-FIVE

Schwarze Kapelle

AT FOUR THIRTY ON THE AFTERNOON OF 20 July, selected German Army officers in Paris received coded news from the *Wolfsschanze*, Wolf's Lair, Adolf Hitler's fortified headquarters near Rastenburg in East Prussia. They passed the word among themselves: 'Hitler's dead. Perhaps Himmler and Goering too. It was a terrible explosion.' A bomb had been placed beside Hitler at a staff meeting in his fortified compound. The culprit was a young Wehrmacht colonel, Count Claus Schenk von Stauffenberg. Von Stauffenberg, who had taken offence at the triumphant and nihilistic parades of Nazi power when Paris fell in June 1940, told his colleagues then that Hitler should be killed. Four years later, Stauffenberg attempted the deed himself. Hearing the thunderous detonation of his bomb-laden briefcase as he drove away from the Wolf's Lair, he passed word to his co-conspirators in Paris that his assassination had succeeded.

General Karl Heinrich von Stülpnagel, *Militärbefehlshaber in Frankreich* (Military Governor in France), gave orders for the arrest of the Gestapo, SS and SD in Paris. The Wehrmacht in France was supporting the installation of Colonel-General Ludwig Beck as Germany's new head of state. Beck planned to make an offer of peace to the Allies. Unfortunately for the conspirators, Hitler survived the explosion. The Gestapo officers the army held under arrest in Paris turned around and arrested their jailers later that night. Stauffenberg was executed immediately after his assassination attempt, and most of his comrades were soon hanged with wire nooses or committed suicide.

Stülpnagel was ordered back to Germany, and he attempted to kill himself. When he recovered in August, he too was put to death.

Stülpnagel had been an acquaintance of Charles Bedaux, providing the engineer with authorization and supplies for his African pipeline. Other Bedaux friends in the German administration had also been involved in the coup. One was Dr Franz Medicus, who fled when it failed. Another, Joseph von Ledebur, escaped across the border to Spain and onto Argentina. Oddly, Dr Keller, the psychotic Nazi who had proposed to André Enfière that Bedaux should mediate between Germany and the Allies, had also been involved in the plot and had to leave France. Medicus and Keller had been attached to the Abwehr, Admiral Wilhelm Canaris's military intelligence branch. Abwehr plotters against Hitler included Canaris himself, Lutheran Pastor Dietrich Bonhoeffer and Bonhoeffer's brother-in-law, Hans Dohnanyi. All three were arrested, tortured and sent to concentration camps for subsequent execution.

It was only after the failure of the 20 July plot that Charles Bedaux's son, Charles Emile, now serving in the US army, learned that the band of anti-Hitler conspirators were called the *Schwarze Kapelle*, the Black Orchestra. During their intimate conversations at El Biar in 1943, his father had said to him gravely, 'It is better that you don't know what I have done to deceive the Germans. Just remember the words *Schwarze Kapelle*. I shall say no more.' That may have been what Edmond Taylor of the OSS meant when he wrote that he arrested Charles Bedaux in Algiers to halt 'the nightmare of a shadowy yet tightly organized international conspiracy working for a compromise peace'.

FORTY-SIX

Slaves of the Reich

ONE OF THE PRISONERS AT NEUENGAMME when Sumner and Phillip Jackson arrived was Michel Hollard, the head of France's Agir Resistance network. Hollard had done more than anyone else to tell the Allies the secrets of the V-1 rocket. The Gestapo captured him and subjected him to the *baignoire*, a torture that would later be called 'water-boarding', in which he was forced backwards into a bath of water and held under for varying periods. His repeated half-hour sessions, dunked and dragged up from the water, left him vomiting and sick. He did not betray the other members of his network, and he was transferred to the Fresnes prison in Paris and then to Compiègne. The SS took him to Neuengamme, where he became prisoner Number 33,948, in early June 1944. Sumner and Phillip met Hollard shortly after their arrival. Hollard told his biographer of 'a remarkable American called Jackson, formerly a doctor at the American Hospital at Neuilly'. Jackson, like Hollard, had helped the Allies to eliminate much of the V-1 threat when he passed along the plans that Erich Posch-Pastor had brought to his office. The American and French *résistants* became friends, surviving twelve-hour days at hard labour in the Walther small arms factory.

'Nobody knew why they had been deported and Jackson never talked about it,' author George Martelli wrote, with help from Hollard himself, in *The Man Who Saved London*.

A man of sixty [in fact, fifty-eight], very upright, with white hair, strong features, and a stern, almost hard expression, he appeared as a person of great energy and forceful character. He was extremely reserved in manner and this and the dignity with which he supported [i.e., stood] the camp life immediately aroused the sympathy of Michel, with whom he soon established a tacit understanding. During their weekly meetings few words were exchanged and those only of a strictly practical use.

To survive Neuengamme was almost impossible. Polish, Russian, Danish, French and other prisoners were worked to death, and many were murdered. For the slightest infraction, men were hanged in the camp square. The Nazis secretly hanged many more in a row of cells from ropes permanently attached to rings in the ceilings. As at Auschwitz, a crematorium disposed of the bodies.

Jackson told Michel Hollard of his desperation to let his family in America know that he and Phillip were alive. Hollard smuggled a post-card out of the camp to his sister in Switzerland. She wrote to Jackson's sister, Freda Swensen, a nurse living in Belmont, Massachusetts. When Freda read the letter, she notified the American government. The United States was certain at last that Dr Jackson was alive. But the American army was a long way from Neuengamme.

In early August, another friend of Sylvia Beach's died. The writer Jean Prévost, whom she and Adrienne had nurtured as a youthful author in the 1920s, had joined the Resistance early in 1943. Not content with being an *écrivain résistant*, circulating illicit pamphlets, the writer whose head was so hard that Hemingway had broken his thumb on it became a fighter in the Vercors. Using the *nom de guerre* Capitaine Goderville, he commanded *maquisards* in ambushes on German positions. Three days after the Allies invaded France, his unit mobilized to confront German troops throughout the hilly region in eastern France. Prévost and his band fought hard in the forests for six weeks. Then, at seven in the morning on 1 August, they were ambushed and killed. It was another hard loss for Sylvia, whose consolation was that another friend in the Resistance, Violaine Hoppenot, was still alive.

FORTY-SEVEN

One Family Now

As THE ALLIES SURROUNDED PARIS and the Germans prepared to defend it to the end, the Laval and de Chambrun families withdrew into a tight family orbit. Aldebert and Clara found themselves in a unique position to observe the Vichy regime's final political man-oeuvres. They turned up at the prime minister's official residence at the Hôtel Matignon for their usual family dinner on the night of 12 August. Pierre Laval himself was unexpectedly absent. He called his wife from Maréville, a town near Nancy. When Jeanne Laval hung up, she explained to Clara, Aldebert, René and Josée that her husband had just freed Edouard Herriot, the president of the Chamber of Deputies, and his wife from German captivity. Ambassador Otto Abetz and Foreign Minister Ribbentrop had approved the release. Laval's old adversary Herriot was the parliamentarian whom Dr Keller at the German Embassy had offered to exchange for the release of Charles Bedaux. Laval was bringing Herriot to Paris to reconvene the National Assembly. His purpose was to ensure a legal transfer of authority from parliament to Charles de Gaulle and to avert a civil war between collaborators and *résistants*. Clara remembered that, when the dinner ended, 'we all went home happy, and learned next day all had gone well'.

Laval appeared to have the assent, not only of the German Foreign Office, but of the United States. He was secretly dealing with Amer-ica's Office of Strategic Services chief in Switzerland, Allen Dulles, through André Enfière. Enfière, as a senior member of Charles de

Gaulle's Committee of National Resistance, had been attempting to obtain Herriot's release for almost a year. He met Dulles in Berne on 15 July 1944 on behalf of Herriot. Enfière, whose American intelligence code name was Lamballe, told Dulles, 'Kindly make it clear that regardless whether Herriot is alive or dead, I carry with me the backing of his supporters for the reinstitution of a democratic and parliamentary republic.' Dulles reported that, while Enfière supported de Gaulle, he and his colleagues 'desire to have genuine republicans surrounding de Gaulle'. Enfière informed Laval on 6 August that President Roosevelt would not oppose a provisional Herriot government. Roosevelt, who would never recognize Laval, had misgivings about Charles de Gaulle and had been looking in vain for alternative French leaders. With a deniable hint of Allied endorsement, Laval went ahead in the hope that a peaceful transition from Pétain to de Gaulle would imply de Gaulle's recognition of Vichy. De Gaulle, however, had never recognized Vichy or the abrogation in July 1940 of the 1875 Constitution. Laval intended to present the Allies and de Gaulle with a fait accompli that they could hardly reject without disavowing France's last elected parliament. He had not reckoned, though, with Paris collaborationists Marcel Déat and Fernand de Brinon, who informed the SS chief in Paris, General Karl Oberg, of the machinations. Oberg's chief, Heinrich Himmler, opposed transferring power to anyone and intended to keep the Vichy puppet government intact – even in exile.

On the morning of 13 August, Laval deposited the Herriots at the Prefecture of the Seine in a wing of Paris's Hôtel de Ville. Members of parliament began arriving at the Hôtel Matignon to endorse Laval's scheme. Laval also sought and received the approval of the eighty mayors of the Paris region, the local prefects and chiefs of police. Preparations to convene the National Assembly with the members who had not joined de Gaulle or were unable to reach Paris went smoothly until the night of 16 August. That evening, the last German civilians were departing with all the wine, radio sets, rugs, haute couture dresses and even bidets that they could carry home in their convoys. Laval was having dinner with Jeanne, Josée and René at the Matignon, when he received a call from the Hôtel de Ville. The Gestapo had just arrested Herriot. Laval went straight there to protest that confining Herriot 'constituted the gravest offence against me'. He called Ambassador Abetz to come to the Hôtel de Ville. When told Himmler himself had ordered Herriot's arrest, Abetz was at a loss to justify the confusion in Germany's command structure since the 20 July attempt on Hitler's life. He and the Foreign Ministry, like the army, had lost influence to the SS, SD and Gestapo. Herriot and his wife remained at the Hôtel de Ville.

On the morning of 17 August, Abetz took the Herriots to the German Embassy and then, at twelve thirty, to the Hôtel Matignon for lunch with the Lavals and René de Chambrun. Before the guests ate, Laval recorded, 'A notice of arrest was served on me.' René de Chambrun recalled Abetz's first words to Laval: 'President Herriot and you are prisoners in the Matignon. President Herriot will be transferred, after lunch, to the Prefecture of the Seine. You will leave with the government in the evening, in the direction of the east.' Lunch went ahead in the grand dining room. Liveried servants poured vintage wines from the prime minister's cellars for Abetz, the Herriots, the Lavals and René and Josée de Chambrun. Josée remembered:

It was a marvelous summer day in that handsome old Hôtel Matignon, with its windows wide open on one of the most beautiful gardens in the world ... The lunch was good. Everyone tried to cover up the anxiousness of the situation with pretended lightness. Abetz began by asking if it was true that, in Lyons, Herriot's city, there was a statue dedicated to a 'good German'? Madame Herriot then told us of the statue of a rich German merchant of the sixteenth century who had showered the city with good works.

Unwilling to endure more false cordiality, Herriot objected to his arrest. He had come to Paris in good faith and with German assurances to preside over the National Assembly. Now, he was being linked to the Vichy government, whose actions he had always opposed. He demanded not to be sent to Germany. 'Abetz looked very much embarrassed,' Josée recalled, 'as he had just received orders to the contrary and had so notified Herriot before the luncheon.' While the conversation proceeded, more armed Gestapo guards surrounded the Hôtel

Matignon. Jeanne Laval appealed to Abetz, 'Mr. Ambassador, this departure, under these conditions, is an outrage. See for yourself the painful situation it puts us all in.' Herriot interjected, 'Please, listen to her, Mr. Ambassador. This is the voice of France.' Jeanne Laval said it was significant that her husband and Herriot, old political opponents, had come together. 'You cannot condone an action that would make it appear as if my husband had instigated unscrupulous tactics resulting in Monsieur Herriot's being forced to undergo the same fate as ours, under duress.' The lunch party lingered till after four o'clock, making small talk, in Josée's words, 'anecdotes and reminiscences – the Duke of Windsor, Anthony Eden, the League of Nations, the Ethiopian crisis, etc.'. At four thirty, Abetz took the Herriots back to the Hôtel de Ville under arrest.

René followed his wife and her father upstairs to the Lavals' apartment. Josée, near tears, told her father, 'I'll go alone with you.' When René heard his wife offer to accompany him to Germany, he said, 'I'll go too.' Laval gave René what he called a 'heavy look', and Josée backed down. '*Alors,*' she said, 'I'll stay in Paris.'

René and Josée returned home to the Place du Palais Bourbon, but René went out again on the pretext of bringing Herriot some cigars and books. It was five thirty when he drove up to the Hôtel de Ville. The Prefect of the Seine led him past Gestapo guards to Herriot's quarters. René offered the old man an escape route. He whispered, 'There is a side exit that is not watched, and I propose, with the prefect's agreement, that you escape with me through the sewers. I will hide you in Passy in a little flat that an American let me have in case of need.' The American was his friend Seymour Weller, who ran Bordeaux's famed Château Haut-Brion vineyards and had avoided German internment through various ruses to remain in Paris. While René waited for an answer, Herriot 'alternately raised and lowered his right and left hands, as if weighing the pros and cons'. Coming to a decision, he said to René in a low voice, 'I must follow my fate.' He then embraced René, who left disappointed.

When all her guests had left the long lunch, Jeanne Laval called Clara de Chambrun. Pierre, she said, had been arrested and was about to be deported. She refused to be separated from her husband and would accompany him to Germany. 'I hurried to Matignon,' Clara wrote, 'where I found her, as always in moments of calamity, in complete possession of her presence of mind and will, and of that extraordinary psychic power of divination which is almost like second sight.' Jeanne Laval worried about the children, René and Josée. When the Resistance came into the open, it would keep its promise to deal with collaborators. She urged Clara, 'They must get to the country and work with their hands, for Josée cannot live and *think* without her father and without me. We three have always formed one unity.' Clara recalled, 'She knew that I would never see her husband again and begged me to ask the General to come from the hospital that night to say farewell.'

Clara left through the courtyard, passing a throng of prefects, presidents of municipal councils, chiefs of police and mayors of the Paris region, who had come to see Laval. Laval issued them a letter requesting their support for two prefects, René Bouffet and Amédée Bussière, 'in whose hands I am placing the fate of Paris'. Clara waited at home in the rue de Vaugirard for Aldebert. He arrived from Neuilly just after nine o'clock, and they went together to the Hôtel Matignon. 'The German police were already on the spot and were arresting all the cabinet members,' Clara wrote. 'Under the cover of darkness and confusion Laval recommended to two of them to disappear and hide themselves, which they accomplished to the fury of the police, who assumed a very threatening aspect towards the President. With his characteristic form of humor he said, "I don't see why you complain to me. I am the aggrieved one. I told them to bring me back two cartons of cigarettes and they have gone off with my change."'

The three Chambruns waited in the gravel forecourt of the Matignon with Josée. Upstairs, where the only light in blacked-out Paris shone weakly from rows of candles, Laval said farewell to a few friends and fellow politicians. He came down holding his cane and wearing his familiar white tie and dark hat. René watched his father-in-law kiss Josée goodbye as he got into a sleek black Hotchkiss car. A moment later, Laval opened the car door, stepped onto the running board and rushed back to Josée. Giving her another kiss, he said, '*Toi, encore une fois*' ('You, one more time'). The palace's iron gate opened, and the Lavals disappeared into the night. Now, the Chambruns would have to save themselves.

The occupation was ending ignominiously for Count René de Chambrun, who had bound his destiny to Pierre Laval's. Only later would he admit the possibility of a different life. If he had married an American he loved before he met Josée, he would not have collaborated with Laval. To Josée's biographer, Yves Pourcher, he confided, 'I was in love with the daughter of the chief of the Federal Reserve Bank, who was originally Jewish and German. I would not have been happy, because she was so oriented to art, to music. Not me, apart from *do-re-me-fa-so*. And in Cincinnati they [the Longworth family] were anti-German and anti-Jewish.' He did not tell Pourcher the name of the woman, whom he had met when he lived in New York between 1930 and 1934. The Federal Reserve chief at the time was Eugene Meyer. Meyer, son of a German-speaking immigrant from Alsace, was the Reserve's first Jewish head since its founding in 1913. Meyer had two daughters, Katharine and Florence. In 1930, his younger daughter, Katharine, was thirteen, and the elder, Florence, was nineteen. Florence Meyer was undoubtedly René's first, albeit secret, love. René explained to Pourcher that the Longworths' objections to her were 'strictly American', in that Cincinnati's large German community had opposed his Uncle Nicholas Longworth in elections. There was also an aversion in conservative, Christian circles to what were called 'mixed marriages'. If René had married Florence Meyer, the Free French, American and British forces approaching Paris would be celebrating Bunny de Chambrun as the soldier who persuaded his cousin Franklin Roosevelt not to abandon Britain in 1940. Instead, all three reviled him as a collaborator and confidant of the despised Pierre Laval.

After the Gestapo left the Hôtel Matignon with Pierre and Jeanne Laval, René and Josée returned to their magnificent duplex apartment at 6-bis Place du Palais Bourbon. A hundred yards from their front door, German troops in the Chamber of Deputies were digging in and erecting bunkers to defend themselves from the Allies and the Resistance. René reflected that only Laval's harsh look had prevented Josée and himself from ending up imprisoned at Sigmaringen castle in Germany with Maréchal Pétain, Laval and most of the Vichy regime.

Paris would soon be no safer: 'We had risked spending the last days of the occupation in a German prison, and being transferred at the liberation to a French prison. We had to disappear quickly, which is what we did, the next day, in going to seek refuge in the rue d'Andigné at the house of our American friend, Seymour Weller.' René had envisioned Weller's flat as a hiding place for Edouard Herriot, but things happened so quickly that he took it for himself and Josée. While Parisians prepared to welcome their American, British and Free French liberators, the younger Chambruns went underground.

Free French forces landed in the south of France on 15 August, moving north to join the Anglo-American invaders and the French Second Armoured Divison on their way south from Normandy. One of General Jean de Lattre de Tassigny's officers in the First French Army was an American. William Christian Bullitt, the last American ambassador to Paris, had spent the previous four years in the United States. President Roosevelt denied him a cabinet post but persuaded him to run, unsuccessfully, as a Democrat for mayor of Philadelphia. When 53-year-old Bullitt asked Secretary of War Henry Stimson for a commission in the American army to fight the Nazis, Stimson turned him down. Charles de Gaulle cabled Bullitt from Algiers on 25 May as the Allies were preparing to invade France: 'Come now! Good and dear American friend. Our ranks are open to you. You will return with us to wounded Paris. Together we will see your star-spangled banners mingled with our tricolors.' De Gaulle commissioned him as the French equivalent of major, *commandant*, in the Free French army.

Bullitt accompanied the First French Army, which he called 'the only French Army', as it captured Marseilles and Toulon. His admiration of General de Lattre, a First World War hero who went into battle wielding his grandfather's Napoleonic era sabre, was unbounded. He wrote to his brother, Orville, 'He goes into the front line constantly with your humble brother along.' In the midst of battle, bon vivant Bullitt appreciated Lattre's 'superb' chef and found time to buy 'a lot of the best wines in Burgundy'. He wanted only two things: to see free Paris again and to defeat the Nazis, whom he had condemned as enemies of America when most Americans wanted to stay on the sidelines.

FORTY-EIGHT

The Paris Front

THE PARTING AT THE HÔTEL MATIGNON had been painful for
Clara, who loved both Jeanne and Pierre Laval. She feared she would
never see them again, and she had no idea when René and Josée could
emerge from hiding. That night, she faced an even more difficult separation, from Aldebert. She wrote, 'Heartbroken as I was, and feeling
the true gravity of what had happened to us and to the country, life
had to go on with thought for the morrow. I was obliged to seek
courage where best I could find it, for I could no longer rely on my
husband's reserve stock of optimism. His presence at the hospital was
essential, and my own duty was clearly at home.' The American Hospital needed all of 72-year-old General de Chambrun's energies if it were
to remain, in its final hours under occupation, as free of Germans as
it had been throughout his stewardship. Just as importantly, his duty
was to save it from becoming a battle ground between the Resistance
and the German garrison beside the hospital. The loss of the commanding presence of Dr Sumner Jackson made his task all the more difficult. The general worked day and night, helping the hospital to
function amid shortages caused by fighting on the roads into Paris and
overseeing the treatment of civilian and Resistance wounded. His
round-the-clock presence there left Clara alone in the rue de Vaugirard, which was about to face a crisis of its own.

From her balcony, Clara saw over the hedges and iron fence of the
Luxembourg Gardens into what had become a Luftwaffe fortress:

Inside the gardens, there is a small two-storied villa – perquisite of one of the city engineers taken over by the German air service – and heavily fortified. On the side of the house they had built out a broad-roofed terrace on which they had placed a battery of automatic cannon and machine guns commanding the entire row of windows. At the crossroads dominated by this improvised fortress, the *Wehrmacht* (after mid-August) had erected a sort of wooden redoubt, lined by a triple row of heavy sandbags, with room enough inside for a large armor-plated tank and its crew to take shelter.

The Luxembourg's defences threatened Clara's 'respectable-looking quarter', but more ominous were the preparations that Clara could not see. The Germans were laying tons of dynamite beneath the Palais de Luxembourg so that, when the order came, they would destroy the seventeenth-century palace with its Senate chamber and its fabulous collection of paintings. General Dietrich von Choltitz, whom Hitler had personally named commander of Grossparis on 7 August, had instructed army engineers to set demolition charges throughout Paris. 'Whatever happens,' General Alfred Jodl, the army's chief of operations, reminded von Choltitz, 'the Führer expects you to carry out the widest destruction possible in the area assigned to your command.' Von Choltitz ordered explosives to be planted under every bridge, electricity station and water-pumping plant as well as the most famous monuments. Marked for destruction were the Eiffel Tower, the Louvre, the Hôpital des Invalides with Napoleon's tomb and the Palais du Luxembourg. Blowing up the palace would take Clara's house and much of the rue de Vaugirard with it. The explosion would not spare the apartments of Sylvia Beach and Adrienne Monnier close by in the rue de l'Odéon.

'Going to and fro was getting too unpleasant,' Sylvia wrote of her daily walks from Sarah Watson's student hostel to Adrienne's flat. With the sudden eruption of street violence in August, the Germans had more important concerns than arresting Sylvia Beach. So, she moved back into her flat in the rue de l'Odéon. German troops patrolled the streets with more fear and hostility than they had before the Normandy landings. 'In the mornings, towards 11 o'clock,' Sylvia wrote, 'the Nazis sallied forth from the Luxembourg with their tanks and went down the Boulevard Saint Michel, shooting here and there. Rather disagreeable for those of us who were lined up at the bakery at the bread hour.'

A straight line of only 500 yards separated Sylvia Beach's apartment from Clara de Chambrun's house. For four years of occupation, the two American women had shared the Sixth Arrondissement and a love of books. Yet they inhabited different worlds. Clara, 70 years of age and friend of men she believed had shielded France from the worst of German occupation, distrusted the mobs that were forming to take over Paris when the Germans left. They were, in her eyes, 'wartime profiteers', 'ruffians' and 'urchins.' Sylvia, 57 and a friend of *résistants* and Jews murdered by the Nazis, saw the same militants as heroes. Negotiating the moral maze of occupation, even Sylvia had thanked a Vichy police minister, Jacques Benoist-Méchin, for her release from internment in 1943. And Clara, whatever her sympathy for Vichy, looked forward to the arrival of the American army and never doubted her loyalty to her native and adopted lands. The Countess from Cincinnati and the publisher from Princeton represented, as well as differing French reactions to occupation, opposing American conceptions of right and wrong. To Sylvia, liberty came first. Clara believed liberty was impossible without order.

Clara and Sylvia watched the same armed men and women erecting roadblocks in their Sixth Arrondissement, not that they saw them in the same way. Clara wrote, 'Amateurish barricades sprang up at about every six or ten blocks, which embarrassed regular traffic, but which meant nothing to a tank.' The same barricades symbolized defiance and courage to Sylvia:

> The children engaged in our defence piled up furniture, stoves, dustbins, and so on at the foot of the rue de l'Odéon, and behind these barricades youths with F.F.I. [*Forces Françaises de l'Intérieure*] armbands and a strange assortment of old-fashioned weapons aimed at the Germans stationed on the steps of the theatre at the top of the street. These [German] soldiers were rather dangerous, but the boys in the Resistance were fearless and they played an important part in the Liberation of Paris.

In the midst of the random shooting in late August, Sylvia received heartening news:

> We heard that 'they' were leaving us, and we joined a jolly crowd of Parisians walking down the Boulevard Saint Michel singing and waving w.c. brushes. We were feeling very joyful and liberated. But 'they' happened to be leaving at the same moment, pouring down the street with the remnants of their motorized forces. 'They' didn't like the celebration, lost their tempers, and began machine-gunning crowds on the pavements. Like everybody else, Adrienne and I lay flat on our bellies and edged over to the nearest doorway. When the shooting stopped and we got up, we saw blood on the pavements and Red Cross stretchers picking up the casualties.

The jubilation along the boulevard Saint-Michel came too soon. The German units leaving Paris were on their way to engage the Allies north and west of the city. Paris remained a German fortress, and its inhabitants were still prisoners.

Neuilly-sur-Seine was one of the quietest suburbs of Paris. Unlike the working-class districts north of the city, the bourgeois western region lacked communist partisans. Few of its citizens attacked German troops. The American Hospital in Neuilly had been unmolested by the German garrison at its Kommandatur headquarters facing the hospital's main gate in the avenue Victor Hugo. The area commander, an Austrian colonel named Bernhuber, had at his disposal a thousand combat troops with six large and twelve small cannon, five tanks and about eighty trucks. In addition, he told General de Chambrun, his men had machine guns and an unlimited supply of ammunition. The tanks were usually stationed at the traffic roundabouts to command the wide boulevards. Their strength was sufficient, the Germans believed, to keep order in tranquil Neuilly.

Violence had come in the late spring and early summer, when the Allies bombed Neuilly's Renault factory. The plant, not far from the American Hospital, was manufacturing military vehicles for the German army. No bombs touched the hospital with its large Red Cross on the roof. When Germans parked their military vehicles near the hospital's main gate for protection, General de Chambrun went to Colonel Bernhuber and said, officer to officer, 'I ask you to consider that the flag of the Red Cross protects the hospital, not the cars of the Wehrmacht.' Colonel Bernhuber immediately ordered the vehicles moved away from the hospital.

On the morning of 19 August, about sixty-five *résistants* of the communist Francs Tireurs et Partisans (FTP) disrupted Neuilly's complacency. They captured two German soldiers in a café, dragged them to the town hall and raised the French flag to proclaim the liberation. Barricading themselves inside with the municipality's staff, the partisans wrapped cloths saying *Vivre libre ou mourir* (Live free or die) around their arms. They did not wait long for the Germans. A truck carrying a Wehrmacht officer and six soldiers roared up to the entrance. The officer ordered the partisans to surrender. The FTP's local commander, 65-year-old André Caillette, responded, 'Surrender yourself. This is the army of Liberation.' Shooting erupted. When it ended, all seven Germans lay dead. They were quickly replaced by a larger detachment with three tanks. Machine guns blasted, and tank shells pierced the building. In the midst of the combat, someone telephoned the town hall with the joyous news that the Americans had just liberated the cathedral city of Chartres. The partisans stopped firing long enough to sing *La Marseillaise*, quickly joined by residents of the surrounding houses. For three more hours, fighting could be heard at the American Hospital and in the rest of Neuilly. The *résistants* lost a dozen men. Another forty fighters and town hall employees were wounded. Most of the survivors escaped through a sewer that led from the town hall basement. Those left behind were taken to Mont Valerian prison, notorious for its executions of more than 4,000 French hostages and *résistants*.

The Germans erected a large *Stüztpunkt* on Neuilly's avenue de Madrid to guard access to the town hall, the Kommandatur and the American Hospital. The bunker was 'a fortress capable of withstanding a siege,' René de Chambrun wrote, based on his father's reminiscences: 'This strongpoint was under the command of a fanatic officer, Major Goetz, who had ordered his tanks to fire on the town hall.'

Major Goetz's unit was not under Colonel Bernhuber's command. It reported directly to General von Choltitz.

The German wounded needed emergency treatment. For the first time during the occupation, the Germans requested admission to the American Hospital. 'It is impossible for me to evacuate about forty of our wounded from the Kommandatur,' Colonel Bernhuber said to General de Chambrun. 'Would you be able to receive them?' Aldebert agreed at once, and the German casualties were brought in on stretchers. Because the hospital's rooms were full, the Germans had to be lodged in the corridors. Otherwise, the staff cared for them just as they did for the French. René de Chambrun wrote, 'Strange spectacle that, in this corner of American earth, my father achieved a miracle: sleeping side by side were French and German soldiers, seriously ill Americans and English, bourgeois Parisians and railway workers from the suburbs who had been wounded in the bombardments of the train yards.' The French and German soldiers were not quite side by side. General de Chambrun had taken the precaution of installing the soldiers in separate wings, Germans in the east, French in the west. It turned out to be a wise decision. While on her regular rounds, Elisabeth Comte uncovered rifles and bullets under the Germans' stretchers and pillows. She went at once to General de Chambrun: 'General, the Germans have arms and ammunition.' The general informed Colonel Bernhuber, who, once again, behaved correctly. He ordered his men to turn over their arms to Otto Gresser, the hospital superintendent. Their cache included thirty grenades and 2,000 rounds of ammunition that Gresser stowed away.

Having recaptured the town hall, Germans patrolled the darkened streets of Neuilly. Apart from an occasional sniper shot at a passing Panzer, the suburb went quiet. Neuilly for the moment was pacified, but the uprising was spreading to the rest of Paris.

The Paris police, who in accord with Vichy policy had collaborated with German authority for four years, followed the example of the Neuilly *résistants* later that day. They suddenly declared a strike and barricaded themselves in the Prefecture of Police. That was the cue for thousands of Parisians to set up makeshift roadblocks, snipe at German troops and attack German positions. It was a dangerous gamble. Left to themselves, the *résistants* could not hold out long against the Wehrmacht.

Rising early again on 20 August, Clara de Chambrun noticed more changes to her 'respectable-looking quarter'. The area around the Luxembourg Gardens had been invaded by 'many persons of extremely rough appearance in the streets; dark-browed youths with sleeveless undershirts, a considerable portion of Algerians from the Parisian outskirts, and a large sprinkling from red Spain. They were not in the least warlike, merely camp followers and wartime profiteers to whom the strike of the Parisian police, ordered the night before, presented a favorable position for taking anything that came handy.' She observed events from a balcony that might be struck by machine-gun fire at any moment. A German Panzer patrolling the streets suddenly found itself face to face with a woman in a scarlet skirt, who was pedalling her bicycle directly towards it. Clara had seen the woman before: 'I recognized her as one of the communist functionaries at our neighboring branch post office and high placed in the C.G.T. [*Confédération Générale du Travail*]. On coming level with the tank she leaped from her wheel, fished from her very *décolleté* bosom a small pistol on a chain, fired two or three shots into the tires of the tank, which being solid were not damaged, then scuttled around the corner on her bike and found shelter inside the *porte-cochère* of number 4 rue Guynemer.' The woman escaped, but Clara's house did not.

German machine gunners on the terrace in the Luxembourg Gardens reacted by spraying fire at the buildings opposite. Clara's house took bullets from ground to roof, shattering every window in between. While she and a few guests crouched on the floor, the fusillade smashed up her home. When the shooting stopped, Clara saw what looked like smoke, but turned out to be plaster dust, rising from her library shelves. One bullet 'had traversed six volumes and remained so deeply buried in the wall behind that we never have been able to find it'.

Outside, the tank continued its patrol, and an officer ordered French workmen to demolish a roadblock. They ripped it down, and he told the crowd, 'Anyone can take the wood.' It took only a few minutes for people to grab all the firewood they could carry, leaving a pile of sand where the barricade had been.

Clara had promised 'the children', René and Josée, to protect their apartment in the Place du Palais Bourbon, 'to see whether all was going well, to inquire if their domestic needed anything and if a high morale was being maintained'. That meant walking a couple of miles each way, past one German *Stützpunkt*, strongpoint, after another and through the Resistance barricades that had been erected all over Paris. To impress guards sporting French tricolour scarves and Gaullist Crosses of Lorraine at the roadblocks, Clara wore the ribbons and medals that she had been awarded over the years: 'a jewel-studded cross of the Legion of Honor and the *palmes académiques* offered me by the town of Fez'. She also wore a social work medal and 'the blue-ribboned insignia of the Society of Colonial Dames'. She pinned them to her breast in a distinguished row, like a general: 'I must say they looked very smart on a black Creed tailor-made suit.' She marched from the rue de Vaugirard to the boulevard Raspail without hindrance, but at the rue de Grenelle a crowd of armed youngsters stopped her. Imperiously, she told their leader, 'My young friend, here it is I who command.' Undoubtedly stunned by the 70-year-old countess's hauteur, he let her through. Soon, though, Clara found herself in the midst of a fire-fight, with bullets coming 'more or less from every direction'. She made it to René and Josée's house, where Elie Ruel, the cook, assured her that all was well. She walked back, 'arrived safely at home not having been asked even to "show cause" at the three barricades made principally of kitchen chairs and tables'. Young *résistants* facing Wehrmacht tanks were too prudent to confront a determined American matron in a Creed tailor-made suit with a chest full of medals.

FORTY-NINE

Tout Mourir

THE NAZIS HAD SENT TOQUETTE JACKSON from Moulins to Romainville, near Paris, on 2 August. At Romainville, the Germans were holding 550 female political prisoners. Toquette was one of three American citizens in the camp. The others were Lucienne Dixon, originally French and married to an American engineer, and Virginia d'Albert-Lake. Born Virginia Roush in Dayton, Ohio, in 1909, she spent her childhood in St Petersburg, Florida. She married a Frenchman and moved to Paris in 1937. In 1943, she and her husband joined the Comet Resistance network, which had the twin distinctions of facilitating more Allied escapes and surviving longer than any other network. She had been arrested by the Feldgendarmerie in June, just after D-Day, while escorting South African airmen through the countryside. The Germans interrogated her at Fresnes prison in Paris and moved her to Romainville with most of the other women political prisoners. The Swedish Consul General Raoul Nordling was frantically attempting to obtain the release of all the women, as well as that of Jewish prisoners at Drancy, from General Dietrich von Choltitz. Von Choltitz and the regular army exerted little influence with the SS and Gestapo, especially after the failed 20 July plot.

Romainville was one of the camps that the Red Cross was permitted to visit, and conditions were better than Toquette had experienced in Vichy and Moulins. Toquette's sister, Tat, was allowed to enter the camp on 10 August to spend half an hour with her. Toquette was unable to tell her what had become of Sumner and Phillip after their confinement at Moulins, where she last saw them. With each passing day, the women prisoners listened for news of the Allied advance that would set them free. One French *résistante*, Yvonne Baratte, wrote on 14 August, the eve of the Feast of the Assumption, 'I am full of hope. They will not have time to take us from here.' The Abbot of Lilas was scheduled to say Mass for the women in the morning. But a German guard, who reminded prisoner Maisie Renault of an orangutan with 'his gigantic size, his immense arms and his powerful hands that seemed always to want to crush someone', woke the women early. He shouted, '*Nicht Messe ... Morgen, Alles transport Deutschland, tous mourir ... tous mourir.*' This mixture of German and French meant, 'No Mass ... Morning, all [to be] transported to Germany, all to die ... all to die.' The women were herded onto buses. Virginia d'Albert-Lake slipped some letters to the French driver, who told her,

> 'Since this morning, I have driven prisoners without stopping from Fresnes and Cherche-Midi to the station at Pantin.'
> 'You mean they are evacuating all the prisons in Paris?'
> 'Yes,' the driver answered.
> She asked, 'And the Allies ... are they advancing?'
> 'Yes. They are at Rambouillet.'

As Toquette Jackson, Virginia d'Albert-Lake and hundreds of other women who had fought hard to liberate France rode in buses through Paris, they knew that the city would soon be free. From the pavements, people who had not resisted looked up, in shame, at the captives. Virginia wrote, 'They pitied us. As I looked at them, the same thought went round and round in my consciousness: "These people will soon see the liberation of Paris. I'm going to miss the day of which I have dreamed for nearly five years and which was to be the greatest in my life."' The Germans took the women to the station at Pantin, where Sylvia Beach and the other American women internees had boarded the train to Vittel in September 1942. This train was not bound for a relatively comfortable mountain resort. Its destination was Germany.

The trains taking the prisoners to Germany were late, so the Germans ordered the women to stand in the hot sun. One of the women, knowing what lay in store for her in Germany, called out to some passers-by, 'Hello, down there ... Listen to me.' They stopped, and she went on, 'All the prisoners and the prisoners from Romainville are leaving ... Warn the Resistance ... Stop the train ... You hear me? Stop the train.' A woman passer-by waved a white handkerchief to signal that she understood. When the trains arrived, the Germans rushed the prisoners, more than 2,000 women and men, into crowded, airless carriages. Amid the wartime confusion, the train moved slowly east towards Nancy. It stopped in a tunnel near Nanteuil-sur-Marne for two hours, while the prisoners in the sealed carriages were nearly asphyxiated. The train could go no further, because the RAF had bombed a bridge a week earlier and the line was impassable. The SS guards marched the deportees out of the train into a field, where they were assembled in military columns. One woman tried to run away, but guards tracked her down and beat her severely.

They walked about five miles through fields to the town of Nanteuil-Saâcy, whose inhabitants called out to the prisoners, '*Bon courage!*' and '*Vive la France!*' Strangely, a contingent of Red Cross personnel was waiting at the train station with boiled potatoes and milk for the prisoners. A few hours later, they boarded a goods train. The train trundled slowly east for four days, until it reached the outskirts of Weimar. There, the SS separated the male from female prisoners. The women were taken off the train at Ravensbrück Konzentrationslager, built in 1939 to house slave labour for the Texled textile and leather factory and the Siemens armaments plant. The date was 21 August.

As soon as they entered the camp, the prisoners were forced to strip completely. The guards wrapped their clothes in brown paper, as if they would be returned one day. Each woman was forced to undergo a gynaecological examination for contraband, with no gesture towards hygiene. Most of the women, including Toquette Jackson, had their heads shaved. Virginia d'Albert-Lake was one of the lucky few whose hair was left. They were then issued camp uniforms – baggy trousers without belt, a pyjama shirt and a loose robe. Veteran prisoners warned the new arrivals not to drink the water, which was infected with typhoid. It would be better, they said, to drink the foul-tasting but boiled ersatz coffee. Their daily ration, apart from a quarter litre of pseudo-coffee, consisted of a half litre of soup made from swede and beetroot, 30 grams of margarine and a slice of bread. It was insufficient even for women who were not doing manual labour; the diet could not sustain women doing manual labour through twelve-hour days in factories. Ravensbrück was not a death camp, where prisoners were gassed or shot en masse. It was a place where the Third Reich's enemies were made to die by starvation, overwork and disease. The prisoners from Romainville were sent into quarantine for two weeks, while they pleaded for any news at all from France. Maisie Renault remembered, 'With a sort of devotion, they repeated, "Soon, France [will be] liberated".' Paris was nearly free, thanks in part to women like Toquette Jackson, Virginia d'Albert-Lake and Maisie Renault. They, who had done the most to set Paris free, faced, not liberation, but slavery.

South of Paris at Rambouillet, Charles de Gaulle pondered how ferociously the Germans would crush the uprising and defend Paris from the Allies. His French Second Armoured Division commander, General Jacques Leclerc, was ready that morning of 24 August to invade Paris and save the insurgents. Leclerc's real name was Philippe François Marie Leclerc, Vicomte de Hautecloque. He had adopted the *nom de guerre* 'Leclerc', when he joined de Gaulle in England in 1940, to protect his wife and six children in France. It did not work for long. The Vichy authorities discovered his identity, seized his chateau and evicted his family. Leclerc had fought in West and North Africa, leading his division of French and African soldiers across the Sahara to connect with the British Eighth Army for the Tunisia campaign, and also in Italy.

As commander of the French Second Armoured Division, whose tanks had just liberated Alençon and Argentan in Normandy with General George Patton's Third Army, Leclerc had been assigned to lead the first Allied force into the city. It was a tarnished honour. The United States had made certain that Leclerc's division expelled all its African colonial troops before it left Algeria via England for France. General Walter Bedell-Smith, Eisenhower's Chief of Staff, had advised, 'It is highly desirable that the [French] division should be composed of white personnel, which points to the second armored division, which has only one quarter native troops and is the only French division which could be made 100 per cent white.' Most French units had large numbers of African troops, but the American racism that had prevented Eugene Bullard from transferring from the French to the American army in the First World War had not vanished in the Second. The American armed forces segregated their units by race, and they expected the same of the French. De Gaulle was proud of the African soldiers, who had fought honourably for France and suffered bestial treatment as prisoners of the Nazis. Although he saw no reason to exclude them from the liberation of Paris, he acceded to pressure from his stronger ally. Only white soldiers, French and Republican Spaniards, came with Leclerc to liberate Paris.

Clara de Chambrun rose at six o'clock on 24 August. The French police who usually guarded the Palais du Luxembourg were gone, and her sedate quarter had given way to insurrection: 'This guerrilla warfare was directed against small enemy detachments, isolated trucks and motor cars.' The skirmishes irritated Clara as much as they did the Germans. At nine o'clock, a friend called to urge her to leave at once. The caller 'was credibly informed that in an hour the Senate buildings would be blown up and that our whole house was sure to go with it. The same warning came again from another source, but left me unmoved.' The warnings were genuine.

By the time Clara looked out of her window again, German troops were barricading themselves into the Senate and digging tank trenches in the gardens for Panzers of the Fifth Sicherregiment. The tanks were well positioned to fire on any armed Frenchmen coming their way. General Dietrich von Choltitz was delaying execution of Hitler's order to destroy Paris. He needed a ceasefire to calm the popular uprising, negotiate with the striking policemen and free his troops to fight the Allies. While he parleyed with the Resistance through Sweden's courageous consul general, Raoul Nordling, the SS unit at the Palais du Luxembourg argued for the immediate destruction of the palace and a fight to the death against the partisans. On the lawns nearby, German firing squads ordered French prisoners to dig their own graves before executing them. Cornered and fearful, the German army, despite von

Choltitz's caution, became more menacing than at any other time during the four-year occupation.

Clara did not know that, in a school a few streets away, veteran and newly recruited *résistants* with captured German weapons were planning to attack the Palais du Luxembourg. Their leader, 25-year-old Pierre Fabien, was one of those whose actions, in his case assassinating a German naval cadet at the Barbès Metro station in 1941, had been strongly condemned by Clara. Their assault would give the SS a pretext to blast the explosives under the building. With the clash looming, most of the rue de Vaugirard's residents evacuated. Clara would not budge. From her balcony vantage, she kept a detached lookout on *résistants* and German soldiers below. The whole neighbourhood might be destroyed at any moment. But Clara's only fear was for Aldebert, who rang to tell her that a battle was raging in Neuilly at the gates of the American Hospital.

While Clara was apprehensive about the stand-off below her window, Sylvia Beach was thrilled to learn that *résistants* were liberating one Parisian quarter after another. She received an unexpected visit from the painter Paul-Emile Becat, husband of Adrienne's sister Rinette: 'He came on his bicycle, which was ornamented with a little French flag.' Becat arrived in time to see the Germans destroy the old Hôtel Corneille near Sylvia's flat. 'The Germans had used it as offices,' Sylvia wrote, 'and, when they left, they destroyed it, with all their papers.' Sylvia had been fond of the Corneille, because James Joyce had lived there, 'and, before Joyce, Yeats and Synge'. Becat said he had come to offer congratulations on the liberation of Paris. Seeing the hotel on fire and the skirmishing near the Luxembourg Gardens, he realized his congratulations would have to wait. He left, carrying his bicycle, through a maze of cellars under the houses.

When General Aldebert de Chambrun called Clara at two o'clock, he was in his office at the American Hospital. The Resistance, which had lost its first battle at Neuilly Town Hall on 19August, had returned to destroy or capture the German Kommandatur a few hundred yards from the hospital. Aldebert described the scene to Clara, 'Cannon is roaring. Leclerc or the Americans can't be very far away, but the trouble is the Germans have organized a veritable fortified camp and have posted big guns in all the avenues leading towards us. They seem to possess quantities of machine guns and wherever you look you can see boche soldiers. It would be pretty sad if they eliminated the hospital.' Aldebert explained later, 'The hospital found itself in the middle of the skirmish line and was equally endangered on both sides. After repeated colloquy with the German commander he became convinced that further resistance would only entail much bloodshed and the destruction of the hospital.' Colonel Bernhuber needed the hospital for German wounded, and fighting while the Germans were about to surrender Paris had become senseless to him. At nine o'clock in the morning, he went into the Memorial Building of the hospital and found General de Chambrun. Without preamble, he announced, 'I am, General, an officer of the German Army, but I am neither a Nazi nor even a German. I am an Austrian, and, since this war is nearly lost, I am ready to capitulate. But the soldier that you are will understand, I am sure, that I refuse to deliver my men and myself to a gang of snipers. I ask to meet a French officer or an American officer to offer my surrender.' (Clara recalled her husband telling her, 'I asked why he did not surrender. "What? To this mob ... I still have strong enough means of defense not to capitulate to such a rabble."') General de Chambrun promised to contact the American or French command, but he had no direct means of communication with either. He would have to go out and find them somewhere beyond the city limits of Paris. Colonel Bernhuber provided him with a laissez-passer to help him through the German checkpoints.

General de Chambrun left the hospital. His route took him past the battle in the avenue Victor Hugo towards the southwest, where the Allies were rumoured to be advancing. After crossing the German lines with Bernhuber's laissez-passer, Aldebert found an American advance unit about twenty-five miles from Neuilly. The American colonel in charge contacted his commanding officer to ask who could accept Colonel Bernhuber's surrender. After a short telephone call, he turned to General de Chambrun and said, 'The French have to receive the surrender, because a French division – Leclerc's, I believe – is going to be the first to enter the capital.' The task now was to find Leclerc. If Aldebert did not contact him soon, the hospital would be destroyed.

General de Chambrun had dealt at the hospital with a man he knew only as 'Monsieur Jean', a chief in de Gaulle's underground Forces Françaises de l'Intérieur (FFI). At three o'clock, when Aldebert returned to the hospital, he got in touch with Monsieur Jean and asked him to find Leclerc. Then, he called Clara. The battle outside had not abated. 'More wounded have been brought in,' he told her, 'and the cannon sounds much nearer.' Hearing the explosions down the line, Clara commented, 'I did not need the telephone to tell me that.' Soon, Monsieur Jean called General de Chambrun to relay a message from Leclerc's Second Armoured Division headquarters. Aldebert was to inform Colonel Bernhuber that Leclerc would send one or two tanks in the morning to the traffic roundabout where the boulevard Inkermann crossed the avenue Victor Hugo, a few hundred yards from the hospital. A German officer should 'carry a white flag to confirm the surrender without conditions by Colonel Bernhuber and the troops under his command'.

Bernhuber accepted the terms, but no one had the power to stop the fighting until he surrendered in the morning. In the hospital, doctors operated all night on the battle's most severely wounded victims and prayed they could hold out until the shooting stopped.

While battle raged outside the hospital, Clara saw a few tanks of General Jacques Leclerc's French Second Armoured Division rolling past the rue de Vaugirard on their way to the Hôtel de Ville. Clara had known Leclerc by his real name, Philippe de Hautecloque, and as the cousin of her old friend Henry de Castries. However much Clara disliked Leclerc's commander de Gaulle, she was relieved to see the arrival of his regular force under a professional, Saint-Cyr-trained soldier, who also happened to be, like her husband, an aristocrat. Leclerc, she believed, could control the *résistants* who remained, to her, so much riff-raff.

A small vanguard of Leclerc's tanks reached the square of the Hotel de Ville during the night, and ecstatic crowds assumed Paris had been liberated. Although the Germans still controlled 85 per cent of the city, *résistants* who captured the radio station broadcast an appeal to the churches to ring their bells to proclaim the liberation. The Left Bank churches responded immediately. Then, at twenty-two minutes past eleven, 13-ton 'Emmanuel', the largest of Notre Dame's bells, rang out in F-sharp so loud it could be heard at least five miles away – for the first time since Robert Murphy heard the bells at midnight on 14 June 1940. Nearby, in the Hôtel Meurice, Paris commander General von Choltitz was speaking to Berlin. Holding the phone to the window, he told General Alfred Jodl, who had been ordering him again to destroy Paris, 'What you hear is announcing that Paris is going to be liberated and Germany without doubt has lost the war.' Outside, Parisians sang *La Marseillaise*. Celebration by the 'Resistance of the Eleventh Hour', as the real *résistants* derisively called the majority who declared their opposition to the Germans only that night when the bells pealed, was premature. The bulk of Leclerc's Second Armoured Division had yet to arrive, and the Americans, who had the only force strong enough to defeat the Germans in battle, were massing for an assault in the morning.

The sound of the bells reached all the way to Neuilly. As Otto Gresser recalled, he, Aldebert de Chambrun, Elisabeth Comte, the other nurses and doctors 'went to the roof of the hospital, we heard all the Paris bells ringing in the churches to celebrate the victory, while we were still surrounded by German troops with guns and tanks'. This was the roof where, for four years, Dr Sumner Jackson had gone to look at the night sky and enjoy a cigar. A year earlier on the same spot, he and his son Phillip had watched American and German warplanes duelling for control of the Paris skies. All that General de Chambrun knew for certain was that Jackson, his wife and his son had been missing since 24 May. There were many rumours: they had been arrested by the Gestapo, detained by the Milice, interned as Americans, tortured as *résistants*, deported, lost, killed. General de Chambrun had approached the Red Cross, which usually had access to internees and prisoners of war. The American Legation in Berne was informed, and the Swiss Consulate asked the Germans for information. Aldebert appealed to his friends in the Vichy government, but Laval's arrest and departure on 17 August had closed that avenue. On 19 August, even

General Karl Oberg, whose secret police knew where the Jacksons were, had fled Paris. The one member of the hospital's staff who had done more than any other to hasten the liberation was not on the roof to witness it.

On schedule, a command car and a tank from Leclerc's Second Armoured Division appeared near the American Hospital at nine thirty on the morning of 25 August. Austrian Colonel Bernhuber, carrying a white flag of surrender, walked cautiously to the boulevard Inkermann–avenue Victor Hugo roundabout. A French officer accepted his capitulation, and Bernhuber ordered his men, 'Stack arms.' The battle of Neuilly, however, was not quite over.

The 'fanatic' Major Goetz and his men refused to abandon their *Stützpunkt* without direct orders from General von Choltitz. The French tank fired on their bunker, setting their trucks ablaze. Before Goetz and his men were burned alive, they laid down their arms and surrendered. The American Hospital of Paris was saved.

Supplies for the hospital had run short. To find food for more than five hundred staff and patients, Otto Gresser drove out in a hospital car into almost-liberated Paris. He recalled that 'we met within three hours German, French, American and British troops and again German troops when returning to the hospital'. Gresser, whose resourcefulness had kept the hospital well victualled for four years and was revered in the food markets of Les Halles as the buyer 'Ferdinand', brought back enough for the hospital's personnel to survive until the American army brought fresh provisions. In the meantime, Gresser managed to save the rifles, thirty grenades and 2,000 rounds of ammunition that he had taken from the German patients in the hospital. When more units of Leclerc's Second Armoured Division arrived, he proudly donated them to the French army. General de Chambrun was not as fortunate with the weapons and military vehicles of Colonel Bernhuber's unit: they were pillaged by the Resistance.

Secretary of State Cordell Hull sent an urgent telegram to the American Minister in Switzerland, Leland Harrison, on 25 August. 'Telegraph exact location Moulin [sic] and request Swiss to report urgently latest known whereabouts of Jackson family.' The Americans were out of date, Sumner and Phillip Jackson having been sent from Moulins to Neuengamme concentration camp a month earlier. The State Department put together what information on Sumner, Phillip and Toquette that it could from a variety of sources. Minister Harrison informed Cordell Hull on 28 August that all three Jacksons might have been moved to Germany 'as hostages'. Hull fired back instructions that the Swiss insist, on America's behalf, that the Germans reveal their whereabouts. The Germans did not respond.

PART SEVEN

24–26 August 1944

FIFTY

Liberating the Rooftops

'IT WAS SATURDAY THE 26TH, the day of the assassination attempt on General de Gaulle,' Adrienne Monnier, who spent that morning with her sister, Rinette, and Sylvia Beach, remembered. 'We had left the house with the intention of going to Notre-Dame, but the gunfire caught us in the Boulevard du Palais and obliged us to turn around and go back the way we came.' That morning, Charles de Gaulle had relit the flame at the Tomb of the Unknown Soldier under the Arc de Triomphe which had been extinguished in June 1940 and marched with Leclerc's Second Armoured Division to symbolize the resumption of French sovereignty. He went to a traditional Te Deum of thanksgiving at the Cathedral of Notre Dame, where he attracted a crowd similar to the one that had welcomed Maréchal Pétain only four months earlier. As he walked towards the cathedral's open Door of the Final Judgement, gunmen started shooting. The general stood erect, while most of those around him hit the ground. Firing continued inside the church, where the congregation dived under chairs. De Gaulle strode in and took his seat.

The wild shooting, whose source was never determined, stopped Adrienne, Rinette and Sylvia from reaching the cathedral. 'The way back,' Adrienne remembered, 'was punctuated by splendid bursts of fire from the rooftops.' When they reached Adrienne's flat, it was impossible for them to tell from her window which snipers were German and which *résistants*. The three women waited indoors for the shooting to stop. Suddenly, in the afternoon, they heard a voice in the street calling, 'Sylvia! Sylvia!' It was Maurice Saillet, the young writer who worked downstairs in Adrienne's bookshop. Cupping his hands around his mouth, he bellowed, 'Sylvia! Hemingway is here!'

Sylvia ran down the stairs and rushed outside. For Sylvia and Adrienne, the most glorious moment of the war had arrived. Sylvia wrote, 'I flew downstairs; we met with a crash; he picked me up and swung me around and kissed me while people on the street and in the windows cheered.' Adrienne watched the scene from above: 'Sylvia ran down the stairs four at a time and my sister and I saw little Sylvia down below, leaping into and lifted up by two Michelangelesque arms, her legs beating the air. I went downstairs myself. Ah, yes, it was Hemingway, more a giant than ever, bareheaded, in shirtsleeves, a caveman with a shrewd and studious look behind his placid eyeglasses.'

With Hemingway were four jeeps and sixteen irregular fighters, French and American, whom he called the 'Hem Division'. Hemingway had returned to France after the first waves of the Allied invasion as a correspondent for *Collier's* magazine. On the way from Brittany to Paris, he collected a small Resistance band that did some fighting. 'War correspondents are forbidden to command troops,' he admitted, 'and I had simply conducted these guerrilla fighters to the infantry command post in order that they might give information.' His ragbag comrades took part in the liberation of Rambouillet, but the real prize for him was the city where he became a writer, the Paris of his *Moveable Feast*. The day before reaching the rue de l'Odéon, he stared at Paris in the distance and reflected, 'I couldn't say anything more then because I had a funny choke in my throat and I had to clean my glasses because there now, below us, gray and always beautiful, was the city I love best in all the world.'

Up and down the rue de l'Odéon, the eccentric and unshaved Franco-American warriors attracted admiring attention. Hemingway introduced Sylvia and Adrienne to his bodyguard, a French *maquisard* named Marceau. 'For the moment, hardly in a hurry to put down their arms, they had come to purge the Rue de l'Odéon of its snipers on the roofs,' Adrienne wrote. 'They had already climbed to the top of several suspect houses, which the onlookers vied with one another to point out to them; but really they had not yet found anything.'

Adrienne approached Hemingway's freedom fighters and 'invited them to come and drink the wine I had kept for them, like every good, self-respecting French person'. They declined, saying that other Parisians had given them too much to drink already. Hemingway, Marceau and a young American went with Sylvia and Adrienne up to the flat. The rest of the 'Hem Division' kept watch outside.

'We went up to Adrienne's apartment and sat Hemingway down,' Sylvia wrote. 'He was in battledress, grimy and bloody.' She noticed 'his clanking machine guns', undoubtedly the first ever in the apartment. Hemingway, as playful as the hungry young writer he had been at Shakespeare and Company twenty years earlier, teased Adrienne. Adrienne recalled the exchange,

> Hadn't I, Adrienne, during those years of the Occupation, been brought to the point of collaborating a little? In which case he offered to draw me out of all possible danger. (Obviously, he must have thought, that fat gourmande couldn't endure the rationing; she must have weakened.) I seriously examined my conscience. No, I swear I had not 'collaborated.' He drew Sylvia off to a corner and repeated the question to her: 'Are you sure, Sylvia, that Adrienne did not collaborate and that she does not need a little help?' – 'Not at all,' Sylvia answered. 'If she collaborated, it was with us, the Americans.' Hemingway seemed to show some regret at not being able to be the knight errant – a slight regret that flickered across his good face as it became serene again.

Sylvia and Adrienne offered to give Hemingway anything he needed. 'He asked Adrienne for a piece of soap, and she gave him her last cake,' Sylvia remembered. Adrienne confessed, 'I gave him, without hesitating too much, my last piece. (Let's be frank, it was the next to the last.)' Hemingway took the much-needed soap and asked what he could do for them. 'Liberate us. Liberate us,' they said. Sylvia wrote that 'the enemy was still firing from the roof. And the Resistance was firing also from the roofs, and this shooting was going on all the time, day and night. And especially on Adrienne Monnier's roof.' Hemingway called his comrades from the street. 'He brought his men up, and they all went up on the roof. And we heard a great deal of shooting going on for a few minutes. Then the shooting stopped forever.'

When Hemingway brought his men back to the flat, Sylvia and Adrienne invited them to stay for a drink. 'Oh, no,' the author of *For Whom the Bell Tolls* said. 'I have to liberate the cellar of the Ritz.' The Hem Division trundled downstairs, jumped into their jeeps and roared out of the rue de l'Odéon. Having liberated Odéonia, they intended to do the same for the finest wines that the Ritz's Swiss manager had kept from the Germans. Sylvia stayed with Adrienne in the rue de l'Odéon and waited for her other American 'bunnies' to come back to Paris.

At the American Embassy on the Place de la Concorde, housekeeper Simone Blanchard had everything ready. Thanks to electrician Georges Rivière and mechanic Paul Feneyrol, the telephones and electricity were in working order. The corridors and offices were as clean as they had been when Ambassador William Bullitt left in 1940. Waiting for the Americans to reclaim the property, Mme Blanchard took from a hiding place something that diplomat Maynard Barnes had entrusted to her when he closed the embassy in 1942. When the new ambassador arrived, she would give to him the Stars and Stripes to fly once again over the embassy.

FIFTY-ONE

Libération, *not Liberation*

ONE AMERICAN WHO HAD REMAINED at his post for four years of occupation watched the Allied armies march down the Champs-Elysées. Charles Anderson, now 83 years old, stood tall in his purple uniform with gold braid. On his chest hung pale ribbons of French military service. He had once worn the American uniform, when it was blue and the army was fighting Indians. The American veteran of the US and French armies had made France his home for fifty-six years. He spoke French as well as he did English. For the past four years, despite the German occupation, he had gone every workday to his empty office in the De Brosse International Transport Company and read the newspapers. Each month, his employer had sent his salary cheque by mail from the south of France.

The Allied armies started their march at the flame above the Tomb of the Unknown Soldier, alight for the first time since 1940, and paraded along the Champs-Elysées to the Place de la Concorde. The soldiers' route was identical to that of the victorious Germans in June 1940. Tears were shed, as in 1940, but in happiness rather than humiliation. All of Paris joyously cheered the saviours. Military bands played *La Marseillaise*, 'God Save the King' and the 'Star Spangled Banner'. Charles Anderson watched the faces of the young Americans, who had liberated Paris and were on their way to free the rest of France and to occupy Germany. They were sixty years younger than he was, but it was not their youth he noticed. It was their white faces. He was looking, among the thousands of bright Americans under their steel helmets, for Negro soldiers. He did not see one in the American ranks. It was as it had been in 1918, when General Pershing banned the all-black Harlem Hellfighters from the First World War's victory pageant. Anderson folded his newspaper and walked home with the slow dignity of an old soldier to the French wife who loved him. Paris had been liberated. America would take longer.

EPILOGUE

JUST AFTER THE LIBERATION, William Christian Bullitt took leave from the French First Army in southern France to fly to Paris. When he mounted the balcony of his old embassy to survey the Place de la Concorde, Parisians let out a cheer and burst into applause. His sense of humour forced him to admit they probably mistook him for General Eisenhower, who was about his height and just as bald. Bullitt soon rejoined his unit, and an accident during the battle for Alsace permanently injured his back. Ignoring the pain, he fought beside the French to Baden Baden in Germany. On 8 May 1945, a day after the Germans surrendered, he attended the ratification ceremony. France awarded him the Croix de Guerre and the Legion of Honour. Bullitt died of cancer at the American Hospital of Paris on 15 February 1967.

Bullitt's counsellor at the Paris embassy, Robert Murphy, remained in the foreign service after the war. He became ambassador to Belgium and Japan and was President Eisenhower's personal representative to Lebanon during its civil war of 1958. Although he retired from his post as under secretary for political affairs in October 1959, he became an unofficial adviser to Presidents John Kennedy, Lyndon Johnson and Richard Nixon. In his 1964 memoirs, *Diplomat among Warriors*, he omitted all mention of Charles Bedaux. Murphy died in January 1978.

Charles Bedaux was buried at the Mount Auburn Cemetery for Christian Scientists on Halcyon Lake in Cambridge, Massachusetts. Isabella Waite attended his funeral and interment, lamenting that her employer's death denied him the opportunity to exonerate himself in a public trial. His defenders, including engineer Marcel Grolleau, insisted he committed suicide to avoid giving testimony that would jeopardize the lives of his wife, Fern, and his friends in the Resistance. The new French government investigated Bedaux's wartime activities in 1944 and, finding evidence that he had sabotaged German factory production in France and protected Jewish property, awarded him a knighthood of the Legion of Honour. The citation specifically commended him for 'economic contributions to the well-being of France'. After the war, the city of Tours named the street which runs near the avenue Winston Churchill the avenue Charles Bedaux. In the United States, sixty-five years after Bedaux's death, the FBI continued to withhold many of its documents on Bedaux from the US National Archives and from other public scrutiny. Fern Lombard Bedaux died at the Château de Candé in 1974.

Shortly after the liberation, some of Sylvia Beach's former 'bunnies' returned to Paris. T. S. Eliot, Cyril Connolly and Stephen Spender crossed the English Channel to visit their favourite bookseller. Eliot gave her soap and Chinese tea, both as scarce as they had been during the occupation. She moved into the fourth floor apartment where she had hidden her books and mementos from the Germans. Adrienne gave Sylvia lunch every day in her kitchen, as she had during the war. In October 1944, Sylvia wrote to her sister Holly, 'We eat quantities of soup as there is no meat – no milk – no eggs – no butter – no chocolate. There ain't no hot water, nor light nor coal.' Life in the first years of liberation under the Free French administration was nearly as bleak as it had been under the Germans. Adrienne's spirits flagged, as Sylvia told Holly: 'She is sad, has lost her father and now her mother is dying.' Adrienne suffered from increasingly painful rheumatism and was diagnosed with Ménière's syndrome of the inner ear. Sylvia found her, as she had found her own mother in 1927, in a coma from a barbiturate overdose on 19 June 1950. Her closest friend and former lover died the next evening.

In an article on resistance literature that Sylvia wrote for the *Paris Herald Tribune* in January 1945, the editors noted that Shakespeare and Company was 'closed for the time being'. It never reopened, and the site became an antique shop. Sylvia joined the board of the American Library, her old rival, in 1950, and gave it 5,000 volumes from her

American literature collection. Her translation of Henri Michaux's *Barbare en Asie* earned her the Denise Clarouin Award. Other honours followed, including an exhibition of her memorabilia in 1959, *The Twenties: American Writers in Paris and Their Friends*. On Blooms-day, 16 June 1962, she dedicated the Martello Tower near Dublin as a centre of Joycean studies. Four months later, she died at home, four floors above her great nursery of Franco-American letters, at 12 rue de l'Odéon. She was 75.

In 1964, an American bookseller in Paris rechristened his eccentric Le Mistral shop on the Left Bank of the Seine facing Notre Dame 'Shakespeare and Company' – a name he called 'a novel in three words'. George Whitman had come to Paris in 1947 and met Sylvia during a reading in his shop by the British author Lawrence Durrell. He was too shy to ask her permission to borrow her shop's name for his own, so he waited until her death to pay the homage. He called his daughter, to whom he entrusted responsibility for the shop in 2005, Sylvia Beach Whitman.

On Sunday, 27 August 1944, Aldebert de Chambrun received an urgent call from the concierge at his son René's house in the Place du Palais Bourbon. *Résistants* were about to kill the family's cook, Elie Ruel. Aldebert went straight there. A few minutes later, one of René's neighbours called Clara to come as well. Clara talked her way through a checkpoint of the Forces Françaises de l'Intérieure (FFI), whom Clara and their other detractors called the 'Fifis', to enter the square. She saw her 72-year-old husband standing between a terrified Elie Ruel and a firing squad. The general warned the armed men, 'You will have to shoot me first.' Clara walked over to her husband. Someone brought her a chair. She sat down, and the situation seemed to calm sufficiently for Aldebert to search for an officer. 'I must say,' Clara wrote of the Fifi captain Aldebert found, 'he looked as foolish as the others when he found himself face to face with the General under whose command he had been at Fez.'

The captain asked Aldebert what Ruel's alleged crime was. Alde-bert answered, 'The same offense as mine: loyalism. He is superior to me, though, in that he is a very good cook, without whose services my wife and I will be deprived of our evening soup and noodles.' The captain dismissed the firing squad. Clara and Aldebert spent nights at René and Josée's to protect the place. The old count and countess left René's house early each day for work at the American Library and the American Hospital. Before dawn on 9 September, Aldebert heard unusual noises outside and told Clara, 'The Fifis seem to be coming here. You had better disappear.' She went into the bathroom, but not before a band of armed men broke in. One pointed a submachine gun at her while she changed out of her nightgown. As they were led outside, a local policeman saw them and called for help. Seven more gendarmes appeared on the scene and persuaded the Fifis to bring Aldebert and Clara to the Prefecture of Police rather than to their own headquarters in rue du Helder. This probably saved the count and countess from the mobs and revolutionary courts that were executing suspected collaborators.

At the Prefecture of Police, the count and countess were held in what Clara called 'filthy conditions'. A sympathetic woman jailer allowed them to receive food from a local café in the tiny cell where they spent the night. Elisabeth Comte of the American Hospital lobbied hard for their release. At the American Embassy, diplomats told her they could not become involved. Miss Comte went to Aldebert's brother, Charles, a respected diplomat with credibility among the Gaullists for his opposition to the Nazis. He called de Gaulle's office to declare he 'would hold de Gaulle's chief of staff personally responsible' if his brother and Clara were not released at once. Miss Comte took Aldebert and Clara in a hospital car that evening from the Prefecture to their house in the rue de Vaugirard, which had been looted in their absence.

In the months that followed, Aldebert and Clara were gradually eased out of their jobs at the hospital and the library. Post-liberation correspondence by the boards of both institutions referred obliquely to the 'Chambrun situation'. Rather than pay them tribute for having saved Paris's two main American institutions from the Nazis, the governors curried favour with the Gaullists by distancing themselves from a couple who had been too close to Pierre Laval and Maréchal Pétain.

When the passions of the *épuration*, or purge, that followed liberation eased, René and Josée de Chambrun came out of hiding. *Personae non gratae* with the new French government and the US Embassy, they spent the rest of their lives exonerating her father Pierre Laval's wartime legacy and published many books on his career. Along with Aldebert, they were with the 80-year-old Clara at her bedside when she died at home in Paris on 1 June 1954. Aldebert died a year later.

During the liberation of Paris, Sumner Jackson was working fourteen hours a day on a forge at the Neuengamme concentration camp near Hamburg. His middle finger became infected and had to be amputated by a fellow prisoner, a Czech surgeon. His 17-year-old son Phillip laboured in the kitchen from midnight to two o'clock each afternoon. A spilled vat of boiling water inflicted third degree burns on his foot. But father and son survived better than most of the inmates, who died of exhaustion or were murdered by the German guards. Some time in the spring of 1945, Sumner was reassigned from factory work to the camp infirmary.

In the eight months prior to April 1945, as Germany was falling to the Allies, Phillip estimated that the Germans murdered 35,000 prisoners. On 21 April, the British army reached the outskirts of Neuengamme. The Nazis herded its remaining inmates into cattle trucks for the train journey to Lübeck. Ten days later, most of the prisoners were put aboard three ships in the harbour. Sumner and Phillip boarded the 6,000-ton cargo carrier *Thielbeck*. On 10 May, Phillip wrote a letter to his 'Dear Friends' that told what happened next:

On the morning of May 3rd, the English, who were close by on the shore, ordered the ships to enter into the port, as they believed the ships carried troops or runaway Germans. The 'Adlon' returned to port. The two others were ordered by the S.S. on board to remain in the shoals. At 3 p.m. after having been given warning we were sunk. First the 'Cap [d'] Ancona,' then the 'Thielbeck' on which we both were, my father and self, [hit] by rocket carrying Typhoons. The Cap [d'] Ancona was set on fire by the projectiles. Fortunately I was on deck and was not hit by the projectiles. I waited 5 minutes in hopes of seeing my father. I could not see him. I then jumped into the sea.

After the RAF bombed the ships, Phillip splashed through the cold sea to climb into a lifeboat. The Germans threw him overboard when they realized he was a prisoner rather than a sailor. He and another 200 men swam towards the beach. 'The first 150 who landed on the shore,' Phillip wrote, 'were shot by the S.S.' The rest then swam in the opposite direction. Once ashore, Phillip could not find Sumner. It was only later that a French prisoner told him he had seen his father 'about a hundred yards from the ship "swimming with a plank," already in difficulties'.

Dr Sumner Jackson was never seen again, and his body was not recovered. The brave American partisan, who refused all compromise with the Nazis from the day they occupied Paris, died three days after Hitler killed himself in Berlin and five days before Germany surrendered. The RAF did not conduct an inquiry to discover why its pilots had attacked three shiploads of Allied prisoners in the Bay of Lübeck. Of the estimated 7,000 inmates aboard the *Thielbeck*, only 200 survived.

Phillip Jackson, believing his mother had already died in a concentration camp, volunteered for the British army. Toquette, however, had survived many months in the Ravensbrück camp, although badly disabled from starvation and exhaustion, to be repatriated to Sweden through the efforts of Count Folke Bernadotte. She and Phillip were reunited in Paris two months after the German surrender. On 18 July, Toquette wrote to Sumner's sister Freda, 'I want you to know that I never ceased to be in love with Sumner for whom I had forever a great admiration and respect. He had such big qualities.'

ENDNOTES

PART ONE: 14 JUNE 1940

Chapter One: The American Mayor of Paris

p. 9 Two million people Henri Michel, *Paris Allemand*, Paris: Albin Michel, 1981, p. 29.

p. 9 'The only living' Robert Murphy, *Diplomat among Warriors: Secret Decisions that Changed the World*, New York: Doubleday and Company, 1964, p. 55.

p. 10 'We in the embassy felt' *Ibid.*, p. 53.

p. 10 The exiled American Ambassador Herbert Lottman, *The Fall of Paris: June 1940*, London: Sinclair-Stevenson, 1992, p. 250.

p. 11 'The few people who remained' Murphy, *Diplomat among Warriors*, p. 53.

p. 11 'Contrary to rumors' Letter from Admiral Roscoe Hillenkoetter, quoted in Orville H. Bullitt (ed.), *For the President: Personal and Secret, Correspondence Between Franklin D. Roosevelt and William C. Bullitt*, Boston: Houghton Mifflin, 1972, p. 469.

p. 11 Robert Murphy, rather than let Murphy, *Diplomat among Warriors*, p. 53.

p. 12 'Most Americans Staying' *New York Times*, 19 May 1940, p. 1.

p. 12 'They showed us' 'U.S. Flier Returns, Bitter at France', *New York Times*, 3 August 1940, p. 10.

p. 13 The embassy issued more 'U.S. Property in France Has Light War Toll', *Chicago Daily Tribune*, 16 July 1940, p. 9.

p. 13 'The American Church will' 'The American Church in Paris', *Sunday Bulletin*, 9 June 1940, p. 2, from the Archives of the American Church, 63–65 Quai d'Orsay, not catalogued.

p. 13 'No American ambassador' Bullitt to Roosevelt, 30 May 1940, in Bullitt (ed.), *For the President*, p. 441.

p. 14 'But our government' Will Brownell and Richard N. Billings, *So Close to Greatness: A Biography of William C. Bullitt*, New York: Macmillan, 1987, p. 94.

p. 14 'This isn't a treaty' *Ibid.*

p. 14 Ernest Hemingway, who had left *Ibid.*, p. 203.

p. 15 'the French Army' 'Salient Excerpts from the White Book Issued by the German Foreign Office', *New York Times*, 30 March 1940, p. 4.

p. 15 He had even arranged 'Chemidlin's Last Ride', *Time*, 6 February 1939. The secret programme to train French pilots on the latest American warplanes became public when a Douglas Aircraft light bomber crashed and one of those injured turned out to be Captain Paul Chemidlin of the French army. The Senate Military Affairs Committee then discovered that, after the US army had turned down Bullitt's request to train the French, he persuaded the army to arrange the test flights anyway. *Time* magazine correctly described Roosevelt's intervention as 'not a spy story but a new chapter in U.S. foreign policy'.

p. 15 'This Embassy is' Bullitt to Hull, 11 June 1940, in Bullitt (ed.), *For the President*, p. 466.

p. 15 Gallup published its latest Norman Moss, *Nineteen Weeks: Britain, America and the Fateful Summer of 1940*, London: Aurum Press, 2004, p. 124.

p. 15 'I have talked with' Bullitt (ed.), *For the President*, p. 462.

p. 16 'As I said to you' *Ibid.*, p. 466.

p. 16 'I propose to send' *Ibid.*, p. 467.

p. 16 His communications, like everyone Cable from Bullitt to Franklin Roosevelt, 12 June 1940, in *ibid.*, p. 467.

p. 16 'Paris has been declared' Cable from Chargé d'Affaires in Germany to Secretary of State, 13 June 1940, in *ibid.*, p. 471.

p. 17 'Delegates till 5 a.m.' Gerald Walter, *Paris under the Occupation*, New York: Orion Press, 1960, p. 18.

p. 17 Dentz acquiesced, sending Lottman, *The Fall of Paris*, pp. 337–40. Lottman's account of the surrender is one of the most thorough and reliable. See also John Williams, *The Ides of May: The Defeat of France, May–June 1940*, London: Constable, 1968, pp. 316–20.

p. 17 Some Germans did not Williams, *The Ides of May*, p. 37.

p. 18 'That doesn't matter' William Smith Gardner, 'The Oldest Negro in Paris', *Ebony*, vol. 8, no. 2, February 1952, pp. 65–72.

p. 18 General Bogislav von Studnitz, commander Roger Langeron, *Paris, juin 1940*, Paris: Flammarion, 1946, p. 42.

p. 18 'were born with monocles' Michel, *Paris Allemand*, p. 59.

p. 19 'the moment had arrived' Murphy, *Diplomat among Warriors*, p. 56.

p. 19 'You are Americans ... The whole city' *Ibid.*, pp. 56–7.

p. 19 Inside the Crillon's gilt *Ibid.*, p. 57.

p. 19 'as if we were' *Ibid.*, pp. 57–8.

p. 20 Von Studnitz gave ... 'brushed aside this' *Ibid.*, p. 58.

p. 20 **The war he added** ... 'none of us' *Ibid.*, p. 58.

p. 20 **'although it was only 10.30'** Admiral Roscoe H. Hillenkoetter letter to Orville H. Bullitt, reproduced in Bullitt (ed.), *For the President*, p. 469.

p. 20 **Von Studnitz invited** Hillenkoetter letter in *Ibid.*, p. 470.

p. 20 **'Colonel Fuller was'** Quentin Reynolds, *The Wounded Don't Cry*, London: Cassell and Compay, 1941, p. 40.

p. 20 **'Never ... We're confident'** Virginia Cowles, *Looking for Trouble*, London: Hamish Hamilton, 1941, pp. 374–5.

p. 20 **'His hands trembled'** Clare Boothe, 'Europe in the Spring: An American Playwright Reports on a Continent's Last Days of Freedom', *Life*, 25 July 1940, p. 80.

p. 21 **Back in his office** ... 'nice fellas' Murphy, *Diplomat among Warriors*, p. 59. Murphy wrote that Mitchell came to Paris with Buffalo Bill's Wild West Show and remained when it went bankrupt. The show opened in Paris in 1889 as part of the World Exposition, and it did not go bankrupt until long after its return to the United States.

p. 21 **Von Studnitz, recalled ... Fuller and Hillenkoetter** Hillenkoetter letter in Bullitt (ed.), *For the President*, p. 470.

p. 22 **'The general wanted'** Lottman, *The Fall of Paris*, p. 361

p. 22 **From an upper window** Author's interview with Mme Colette Faus, Paris, 22 January 2007.

p. 22 **'On that day'** Philip W. Whitcomb, testimony in *France during the German Occupation, 1940–1944: A Collection of 292 Statements on the Government of Maréchal Pétain and Pierre Laval*, translated from the French by Philip W. Whitcomb, Palo Alto, CA: The Hoover Institution, Stanford University, vol. III, 1957, p. 1606.

p. 23 **The triumphalism of** Roger Manville and Heinrich Fraenkel, *The July Plot: The Attempt on Hitler's Life in July 1944*, London: The Bodley Head, 1964, p. 63.

p. 23 **Martial parades established** Early that morning, the French writer Paul Léautaud was leaving his house in the Paris suburbs when he saw the wife of the local mayor at her door. He wrote in his diary, 'She tells me that the radio has announced that Paris is under the protection of the American ambassador. I say, "We're doing well. The American ambassador in front of the German army! That should prevent us from being bumped off. The American ambassador will come: Look here! He's dead!" As usual, I mimed what I said. I made her laugh, her and her children.' See Paul Léautaud, *Journal littéraire*, vol. XIII, February 1940–June 1941, Paris: Mercure de France, 1962, p. 81.

Chapter Two: The Bookseller

p. 24 As the first German Adrienne Monnier, *Trois agendas d'Adrienne Monnier*, Texte établi et annoté par Maurice Saillet, Paris: published 'par ses amis', 1960, p. 37. Sylvia's autobiography, written twenty years later, disagrees with Adrienne Monnier's diary on Sylvia's whereabouts when the Germans marched in. In *Shakespeare and Company* (London: Faber and Faber, 1960, p. 218), Sylvia wrote that she was in the office of a doctor friend, Thérèse Bertrand-Fontaine, when she saw refugees leaving Paris and German soldiers marching in after them. This is more likely a recollection that compressed distinct events, because all of Paris's refugees had left at least one day before the Germans entered the city. I have relied on Adrienne's diary, which was written at the time.

p. 24 'endless procession of' Beach, *Shakespeare and Company*, p. 218.

p. 24 'Those boots always' Niall Sheridan, interview with Sylvia Beach, *Sylvia Beach: Self-Portrait*, documentary film on Radio Telefis Eireann (RTE), Dublin, 1962.

p. 25 ' I never left Paris' Noel Riley Fitch, *Sylvia Beach and the Lost Generation: A History of Literary Paris in the Twenties and Thirties*, New York: W. W. Norton and Company, 1983, p. 401.

p. 26 Alice B. Toklas called *Ibid.*, p. 100.

p. 26 'these two extraordinary' Janet Flanner, 'The Infinite Pleasure: Sylvia Beach', *Janet Flanner's World: Uncollected Writings 1932–1975*, London: Secker and Warburg, 1980, p. 310.

p. 27 'DAMN the right bank' Fitch, *Sylvia Beach and the Lost Generation*, p. 61.

p. 28 'loved to browse' William L. Shirer, *Twentieth Century Journey: Memoir of a Life and the Times*, vol. I: *The Start, 1904–1930*, Boston: Little Brown, 1984, p. 241.

p. 28 'Probably I was' Sylvia Beach wrote this in an unpublished draft of her memoirs, *Shakespeare and Company*. Quoted in Fitch, *Sylvia Beach and the Lost Generation*, p. 78.

p. 28 'the intrepid, unselfish' Flanner, 'The Infinite Pleasure: Sylvia Beach', p. 309.

p. 29 'probably the best known' Fitch, *Sylvia Beach and the Lost Generation*, p. 41.

p. 29 'their club, mail drop' Flanner, 'The Infinite Pleasure: Sylvia Beach', p. 310.

p. 30 'But something must' Fitch, *Sylvia Beach and the Lost Generation*, p. 355.

p. 31 'He was beginning' 'Hemingway Curses, Kisses, Reads', *Paris Herald Tribune*, 14 March 1937.

p. 31 A year later Fitch, *Sylvia Beach and the Lost Generation*, p. 386. The award is also listed in Sylvia's entry in *Americans in France: A Directory, 1939–1940*, Paris: American Chamber of Commerce in France, 1940, p. 72.

p. 32 'Loud noise of planes … we should live' Monnier, *Trois agendas de Adrienne Monnier*, p. 36.

p. 32 'she could not be' Beach, *Shakespeare and Company*, p. 213.

p. 32 'did try to get away' *Ibid.*, pp. 217–18ff.

p. 32 'fell right between' Monnier, *Trois Agendas de Adrienne Monnier*, p. 29.

p. 32 Adrienne kissed the spot Fitch, *Sylvia Beach and the Lost Generation*, p. 398.

p. 33 'I still had some' Arthur Koestler, *The Scum of the Earth*, London: Cape, 1941, reprinted London: Eland Books, 1991, p. 103.

p. 33 'For a few days' Arthur Koestler, *Arrow in the Blue*, vol. II, *The Invisible Writing*, London: Collins with Hamish Hamilton, 1954, p. 420.

p. 33 The president of International PEN Emmanuelle Loyer, *Paris à New York: Intellectuels et artistes français en exil 1940–1947*, Paris: Bernard Grasset, 2005.

p. 33 'It is impossible' 'Celebrities Forced to Flee France Arrive Here by Way of Lisbon', *New York Times*,16 July 1940, p. 1.

p. 33 Two American diplomats Fitch, *Sylvia Beach and the Lost Generation*, p. 400.

p. 33 'From the day the Jews' Adrienne Monnier, 'On Anti-Semitism', *La Gazette des Amis des Livres*, Paris, December 1938, reprinted in Adrienne Monnier, *The Very Rich Hours of Adrienne Monnier: An Intimate Portrait of the Literary and Artistic Life in Paris Between the Wars*, translated by Richard McDougall, New York: Charles Scribner's Sons, 1976, p. 378.

p. 33 Sylvia had sold artists' prints Fitch, *Sylvia Beach and the Lost Generation*, p. 383.

p. 34 'What if the Germans' Monnier, *Trois agendas d'Adrienne Monnier*, p. 38. There is an excellent translation of Adrienne's occupation diary in *The Very Rich Hours of Adrienne Monnier*, pp. 391–402.

p. 35 'I was amazed' Robert Murphy, *Diplomat among Warriors: Secret Decisions that Changed the World*, New York: Doubleday and Company, 1964, pp. 59–60. Murphy added, 'I reflected ruefully that the United States Government might have practiced to advantage some of that German foresight. In our own early ventures in military government, Washington's neglect of this phase of waging war created unnecessary difficulties for General Eisenhower, and especially for me as his political adviser.' That was twenty years before the US occupation of Vietnam and forty before its occupation of Iraq.

p. 35 'The German soldiers' Roger Langeron, *Paris, juin 1940*, Paris: Flammarion, 1946, p. 45.

p. 35 The Germans honoured Telegram of 4 July 1940 from Bullitt to Department of State, in Orville H. Bullitt (ed.), *For the President, Personal and Secret: Correspondence between Franklin Delano Roosevelt and William C. Bullitt*, Boston: Houghton Mifflin, 1972, p. 478.

p. 35 Married to an aristocrat David Pryce-Jones, *Paris in the Third Reich: A History of the German Occupation, 1940–1944*, London: Collins, 1981, p. 24.

p. 35 Another American loss 'U.S. Property in France Has Light War Toll', *Chicago Daily Tribune*, 16 July 1940, p. 9.

p. 35 'So these are Bullitt's' Murphy, *Diplomat among Warriors*, p. 60.

p. 36 In the evening, Bullitt Langeron, *Paris, juin 1940*, p. 54.

p. 36 'If order is maintained' *Ibid.*, p. 46.

Chapter Three: The Countess from Ohio

p. 37 The American Embassy beat The embassy left the Hôtel Bristol on 1 December 1940. See Dorothy Reeder, 'The American Library in Paris: September 1939–June 1941, CONFIDENTIAL', Report to the American Library Association, 19 July 1941, American Library Association Archives, University of Illinois at Urbana-Champaign, p. 9.

p. 38 'promised to remain' Clara Longworth de Chambrun, *Shadows Lengthen: The Story of My Life*, New York: Charles Scribner's Sons, 1949, p. 101.

p. 38 'Was it really' Dorothy Reeder: 'The American Library in Paris: September 1939–June 1941, Confidential'.

p. 38 'theory that, should' Longworth de Chambrun, *Shadows Lengthen*, p. 99.

p. 38 'My temperamental dislike' *Ibid.*, p. 99.

p. 38 Pierre, who as the eldest *Americans in France: A Directory, 1939–1940*, Paris: American Chamber of Commerce in France, 1940, p. 83: the Marquis de Chambrun listed his residences as 19 avenue Rapp, Paris 7, and the Château l'Empery-Carrières, Lozère.

p. 39 'My husband argued' Longworth de Chambrun, *Shadows Lengthen*, p. 99.

p. 39 'There were trucks' *Ibid.*, pp. 103–4.

p. 39 'I recall the silhouettes' *Ibid.*, p. 105.

p. 40 'an excited servant ... compromised by giving ... all thought of self' *Ibid.*, p. 109.

p. 40 'By birth and education' *Ibid.*, p. 3.

p. 41 *Impressions of Lincoln and the Civil War* Adolphe de Chambrun, *Impressions of Lincoln and the Civil War: A Foreigner's Account,* translated by General Aldebert de Chambrun, New York: Random House, 1952.

p. 41 **recounted his friendship** Chambrun declined, because his Catholicism would not let him attend the theatre on Good Friday.

p. 41 **'never considered the ... Like all his family'** Clara Longworth de Chambrun, *Shadows Like Myself*, New York: Charles Scribner's Sons, 1936, p. 93.

p. 42 **She perfected her French** Clara became a close friend of Aldebert's older sister, Thérèse, who was married to Count Savorgnan de Brazza, the Italian-born French explorer for whom Brazzaville in West Africa was named. She was close to others in the same aristocratic circle. See Longworth de Chambrun, *Shadows Like Myself*, p. 29.

p. 42 **The award was presented** Pétain's full name was Henri-Philippe-Bénoni-Omer Pétain, but he was usually called Philippe Pétain.

p. 43 **'But there is an end'** Longworth de Chambrun, *Shadows Like Myself*, p. 243.

p. 43 **'the appearance of General'** *Ibid.*, p. 277.

p. 43 **It was said that American** Colonel Charles E. Stanton, in a speech at Lafayette's tomb in the Picpus Cemetery on 4 July 1917, said, 'Lafayette, we are here!' See 'Immortal War Slogans', *New York Times*, 11 January 1942, p. 25.

p. 43 **'In the spring of 1925'** Longworth de Chambrun, *Shadows Like Myself*, p. 327.

p. 43 **The French Academy awarded** Mary Niles Mack, 'Between Two Worlds: The American Library in Paris during the War, Occupation and Liberation (1939–1945)', *Library Trends*, Winter 2007, University of Illinois at Urbana-Champaign, p. 7.

p. 44 **Two years later** Yves Pourcher, *Pierre Laval vu par sa fille d'après ses carnet's intimes*, Paris, Le Cherche-Midi, 2002, p. 105. See also 'Miss Laval is Bride; Becomes U.S. Citizen', *Chicago Daily Tribune*, 20 August 1935, p. 17.

p. 44 **'Swarthy as a Greek'** 'Man of the Year', *Time*, 4 January 1932.

p. 44 **In October 1931** *Time* commented on Laval's meeting with President Herbert Hoover at the White House: 'President Hoover is well known to dislike almost all Frenchmen. He and Premier Laval had high words which they called "free and frank". Smoking U.S. cigarettes at the furious rate of 80 per day, the didactic Frenchman in striped trousers, black jacket, white tie and suede-topped buttoned shoes wagged his short forefinger at the President in high-laced shoes and conservative business suit, making hotly such points as that France will not stand for having another Moratorium [on German war reparations payments to France] thrust forward from the U.S. "suddenly and brutally".' See *Ibid.*

p. 44 **Friends said that** Interview with Thierry Bertmann, godson of René de Chambrun's close American friend, Seymour Weller, Paris, March 2006.

p. 45 **'There was too much of it'** Longworth de Chambrun, *Shadows Lengthen*, p. 109.

p. 45 **'a wild scheme'** *Ibid.*

p. 45 **Although Clara favoured … René founded the** *Ibid.*, p. 53.

p. 45 **'she had referred'** Vincent Sheean, *Between the Thunder and the Sun*, New York: Random House, 1943, p. 67.

p. 46 **'There we found'** General Aldebert de Chambrun, 'Financial Crisis in 1935; Attempted Assassination at Versailles', in *France during the German Occupation, 1940–1944: A Collection of 292 Statements on the Government of Maréchal Pétain and Pierre Laval*, translated from the French by Philip W. Whitcomb, Palo Alto, CA: The Hoover Institution, Stanford University, vol. III, 1957, p. 1558.

p. 46 **'The sights on the road'** Longworth de Chambrun, *Shadows Lengthen*, p. 110.

p. 46 **'Madame de Polignac'** *Ibid.*, p. 111.

p. 46 **'No gas Madame' … 'There is if you heat it.'** *Ibid.*, pp. 111–12.

p. 47 **'Having explored … he was in fact'** Clara Longworth de Chambrun, *Shadows Like Myself*, p. 113.

p. 48 **'And then, just as'** René de Chambrun, *I Saw France Fall*, New York: William Morrow and Company, 1940, pp. 155–6.

p. 48 **'It is historically interesting'** Longworth de Chambrun, *Shadows Lengthen*, p. 98.

p. 48 **'That any man'** *Ibid.*, p. 107.

p. 48 **'nothing would have been left'** Longworth de Chambrun, *Shadows Like Myself*, p. 114.

p. 49 **'the very symbol'** *Ibid.*, p. 116.

p. 49 **'Both of them were'** Clara Longworth de Chambrun (Document No. 167) in *France During the German Occupation, 1940–1944*, vol. III, 1957, p. 1362.

p. 49 **'Our three weeks there'** Longworth de Chambrun, *Shadows Lengthen*, p. 113.

Chapter Four: All Blood Runs Red

p. 50 **'I said good-bye'** From Bullard's unpublished memoir, 'All Blood Runs Red', reproduced in P. J. Carisella and James W. Ryan, *The Black Swallow of Death*, Boston: Marlborough House, 1972, p. 236.

p. 50 **'I had a stroke'** Quoted *ibid.*, p. 238.

p. 50 **'During the bombardments … lay cut in half'** *Ibid.*, p. 239.

p. 51 **'This near lynching'** Craig Lloyd, *Eugene Bullard: Black Expatriate in*

Jazz-Age Paris, Athens, GA and London: University of Georgia Press, 2000, p. 12.

p. 51 **'there never was any name-calling'** Carisella and Ryan, *The Black Swallow of Death*, p. 70.

p. 52 **'I was always'** *Ibid.*, p. 156.

p. 52 **'a certain person in Paris'** *Ibid.*

p. 53 **The squadrons in which** Lloyd, *Eugene Bullard*, p. 58.

p. 53 **He was also the only black** A subsequent investigation by the US air force found that the US Army had initially recommended Bullard 'for transfer to the [US] Air Service as a sergeant rather than receive a commission'. William C. Hemidahl, Chief, Reference Division, Center of Air Force History, 'Memorandum for AF/DPP, From: Center for Air Force History, Subject: Application for Correction of Military Records – Bullard, Eugene J.', 3 August 1994, p. 1. All other American flyers were granted immediate American officers' commissions. Major General Michael McGinty, the director of Air Force Personnel Programs, concluded in 1994 that 'Eugene Bullard was not granted entry into the American Air Service because of his race.' Michael McGinty, Major General, USAF, 'Memorandum for SAF/MIBR, From: HQ USAF/DPP, 1040 Air Force Pentagon, Subject: Application for Correction of Military Records (DD Form 149) – Bullard, Eugene J., 123-45-6789', 8 August 1994. No African-American pilot was commissioned until 1943, and that was in a racially segregated squadron.

p. 54 **'If someone needed'** Quoted in Lloyd, *Eugene Bullard*, p. 103.

p. 55 **Bullard opened another** William Shack, *Harlem in Montmartre*, Berkeley, CA and London: University of California Press, 2001, p. 109.

p. 55 **'Like most American men'** Carisella and Ryan, *The Black Swallow of Death*, p. 229.

p. 55 **Fluent in German, French** Lloyd, *Eugene Bullard*, p. 111.

p. 55 **'Of course, they figured'** Carisella and Ryan, *The Black Swallow of Death*, p. 231.

p. 56 **'Bullard, I didn't know'** *Ibid.*, p. 233.

p. 56 **Trumpeter Arthur Briggs** Rudolph Dunbar, 'Trumpet Player Briggs Freed After Four Years in Camp near Paris', *Chicago Daily Defender*, 23 September 1945, p. 3.

p. 57 **'Major Bader assigned'** Carisella and Ryan, *The Black Swallow of Death*, p. 241.

p. 58 **'to take advantage'** Letter from Roger Bader, Galeries Saint-Michel, boulevard Saint-Michel, Paris V, 20 September 1947.

p. 58 **Bullard walked and hitch-hiked** Lloyd, *Eugene Bullard*, pp. 118–20.

p. 58 **'By the time ... I made such good time ... Better get out of that'** Carisella and Ryan, *The Black Swallow of Death*, pp. 237–43.

p. 59 **'I told him I had never'** *Ibid.*

p. 59 **'Columbus, Georgia, October 9, 1894'** Bullard gave his year of birth as 1894 in his memoirs (see *ibid.*, p. 244), but another biographer, Craig Lloyd, who did thorough documentary research, wrote that the date was 9 October 1895, as given in the family's Bible (see Craig Lloyd, *Eugene Bullard*, p. 8). He may have added a year to his age in 1914 to join the Foreign Legion.

p. 59 **On 12 July, Bullard left** 'Americans Report Nazis Fill Spain', *New York Times*, 19 July 1940, p. 10.

p. 59 **'My bicycle had vanished'** Carisella and Ryan, *The Black Swallow of Death*, p. 246.

Chapter Five: Le Millionnaire américain

p. 60 **'We wandered like'** Gaston Bedaux, *La Vie ardente de Charles Bedaux*, Paris: privately published, 3 June 1959, p. 68.

p. 60 **'didn't want to believe me'** *Ibid.*

p. 60 **As the Germans deployed** *Ibid.*

p. 60 **Ambassador Bullitt and Counsellor Murphy** 'Embassy Refuge Picked', *New York Times*, 3 December 1939, p. 5.

p. 61 **Bedaux, who granted a lease** Bedaux, *La Vie ardente de Charles Bedaux*. A copy of the uncashed cheque is reproduced in an appendix.

p. 61 **The dining table seated** Janet Flanner, 'Annals of Collaboration: Equivalism I', *The New Yorker*, 22 September 1945, p. 40.

p. 61 **'The chateau has one'** 'Embassy Refuge Picked', *New York Times*, 3 December 1939, p. 5.

p. 61 **Hagerman, an amateur artist'** 'Le Château de Candé ou le premier "Americain Présence Post" en France', *Echos des USA*, publication of the American Embassy, Paris, no. 8, March–April 2007, p. 2.

p. 61 **By early June 1940** Janet Flanner, 'Annals of Collaboration: Equivalism I', *The New Yorker*, 22 September 1945, p. 29.

p. 62 **Fullerton found Bedaux** Jim Christy, *The Price of Power: A Biography of Charles Eugene Bedaux*, New York: Doubleday and Company, 1984, p. 214.

p. 62 **'slothful and unbridled'** Janet Flanner, 'Annals of Collaboration: Equivalism II', *The New Yorker*, 6 October 1945, p. 40.

p. 62 **Bedaux, who believed** George Ungar, *The Champagne Safari*, documentary film, Canada, 1995, at 1:04:00.

p. 62 **'I can be of more'** Christy, *The Price of Power*, p. 214.

p. 62 **'She grumbled that'** Quentin Reynolds, *The Wounded Don't Cry*, London: Cassell and Company, p. 70.

p. 63 **'We were a bit'** *Ibid.*

p. 63 'No one woke' *Ibid.*, p. 71.

p. 63 When a German battalion Roster of the American Field Service Volunteers, French Units, 1939–1940.

p. 63 'There were quite' Peter Muir, *War without Music*, New York: Charles Scribner's Sons, 1940, p. 249.

p. 64 He finally found *Ibid.*, p. 262.

p. 64 'we had better start' 'Americans Report Nazis Fill Spain', *New York Times,* 19 July 1940, p. 10.

p. 64 'It was then' Muir, *War without Music*, p. 252.

p. 64 'On our arrival' Carisella and Ryan, *The Black Swallow of Death*, pp. 247–8.

p. 65 At Charles Bedaux's luxurious Robert Gildea, *Marianne in Chains: In Search of the German Occupation of France, 1940–45*, London: Macmillan, 2002, p. 43.

p. 65 The German army was encircling *Ibid.*, p. 46.

p. 65 The hospital dispatched Christy, *The Price of Power.*, p. 214.

Chapter Six: The Yankee Doctor

p. 66 Back in Paris … By the time Bullitt Dr Charles Bove with Dana Lee Thomas, *Paris: A Surgeon's Story*, New York: Little, Brown and Company, 1956, p. 223. Dr Bove's account differs slightly from the majority of historians'. He wrote that de Martel took an overdose of Luminal and turned on the gas jets 'to make doubly certain that he would be dead on the day the Germans entered Paris'. De Martel's suicide did not come as a shock. Bove found his colleague 'so deep in melancholy that nothing could arouse him'. Before the German advance on Paris, Bove wrote, 'Martel had always been one of the jolliest members of staff. He was a debonair dresser with perpetually smiling eyes and a tongue that was always ready to burst into a humorous sally. He was the eternal playboy who had refused to surrender to his years. But now he had become a man transformed. For days he had scarcely spoken a word to us, and then only on business.'

On 10 June, the writer André Maurois had a worrying conversation with de Martel:

'As for me', he had said to us, 'my mind is made up: the moment I learn that they are in the city I shall kill myself.'

And then he explained to us at length that most people do not know how to kill themselves, and bungle the job, but that a surgeon holds the revolver as precisely as he holds a scalpel and always hits a vital spot. Then, half-seriously, he added: 'If you, too, have no desire to survive our misfortunes, I offer you my services …'

At ten o'clock in the evening, when I was already on the 'plane bound for England, the sound of the telephone interrupted my wife, who was sadly selecting the few objects she could take with her. It was Thierry de Martel.

'I wanted to find out', he said, 'whether you and your husband were still in Paris.'

'André has been sent on a mission to London', she replied, 'and, as for me, I am leaving tomorrow at dawn.'

'I am going to leave too', he said in a strange tone, 'but for a much longer voyage ...'

... 'You can still do so much good', she said. 'Your patients, your assistants, your nurses, all of them need you ...'

'I cannot go on living', Martel said. 'My only son was killed in the last war. Until now I have tried to believe that he died to save France. And now here is France, lost in her turn. Everything I have lived for is going to disappear. I cannot go on.'

(From André Maurois, *Why France Fell*, translated from the French by Denver Lindley, London: The Bodley Head, 1941, pp. 115–16.)

p. 66 'disgustingly stupid novels' Adrienne Monnier, *The Very Rich Hours of Adrienne Monnier: An Intimate Portrait of the Literary and Artistic Life in Paris between the Wars*, translated by Richard McDougall, New York: Charles Scribner's Sons, 1976, p. 522.

p. 67 'Do not cry!' Quoted in Charles Robertson, *An American Poet in Paris: Pauline Avery Crawford and the Herald Tribune*, Columbia and London: University of Missouri Press, 2001, p. 32. See also Pauline Avery Crawford, *The Enchanted Isle*, unpublished manuscript, Smith College Archives.

p. 67 'one attempt to ... His gaze wandered' Bove, *Paris*, p. 223.

p. 67 'I know ... We Americans' *Ibid.*, p. 222.

p. 67 'There is a kind' Paul Léautaud, *Journal littéraire*, vol. XIII, February 1940–June 1941, Paris, *Mercure de France*, 1962, p. 174.

p. 68 Thomas Kernan, the American editor Thomas Kernan, *Paris on Berlin Time*, Philadelphia and New York: J. P. Lippincott Company, 1941, p. 162.

p. 68 'In him we lost' Maurois, *Why France Fell*, p. 117. When Maurois reached London, Charles de Gaulle asked him to condemn Maréchal Pétain on a BBC radio transmission to France. Maurois could not comply, because Pétain had defended him years before against anti-Semites in the Académie Française. See Emmanuel Loyer, *Paris à New York: Intellectuels et artistes français en exil, 1940–1947*, Paris: Grasset, 2005, p. 113.

p. 68 'The surgeon, who was at the end' 'Mort du Docteur de Martel', *Le Matin*, 18 June 1940, from the Archives of the American Hospital of Paris, File: 'The Second World War'.

p. 69 'He wore only' Clemence Bock, *Souvenirs sur le Docteur Jackson*, quoted in Hal Vaughan, *Doctor to the Resistance: The Heroic Story of an American Surgeon and His Family in Occupied France*, Washington: Brassey's, 2004, p. 19.

p. 69 Captain Sumner Jackson transferred General Services Administration, Statement of Service, Date: 19 April 1965, Massachusetts General Hospital Archives, File: Dr. Sumner Jackson. The document shows that Jackson was commissioned a first lieutenant of the US Medical Reserve Corps on 23 July 1917. See also, in the same file, Headquarters, United States Army Cantonment, Camp Devens, Massachusetts Special Orders No. 221, 12 September 1919, Discharge Papers, when Jackson was honourably discharged as a captain.

p. 70 When Jackson left the army Vaughan, *Doctor to the Resistance*, p. 15.

p. 70 'This hospital is a little' Bove, *Paris*, p. 32.

p. 71 The little hospital that admitted American Hospital entry in Alfred M. Brace (ed.), *Americans in France: A Directory, 1926*, Paris: American Chamber of Commerce in France, 1927, p. 32.

p. 71 Dr Bove removed his appendix Bove, *Paris*, p. 60.

p. 71 James Joyce was made Noel Riley Fitch, *Sylvia Beach and the Lost Generation: A History of Literary Paris in the Twenties and Thirties*, New York: W. W. Norton, 1983, p. 141.

p. 71 'The permanent American ... break into that' Eric Sevareid, *Not So Wild a Dream*, New York: Alfred A. Knopf, 1946, p. 95.

p. 72 'Dean [Frederick Warren] Beekman' *Ibid.*, p. 96.

p. 72 His entry in *Americans in France: A Directory, 1939–1940*, Paris: American Chamber of Commerce in France, 1940, p. 126.

p. 73 'selected a building' 'American Hospital to Open New Angoulême Hospital', *New York Herald Tribune*, 8 June 1940.

p. 73 French General Lannois came 'The American Hospital of Paris in the Second World War', an official history prepared by the hospital staff, printed in France, 1940, p. 13, American Hospital of Paris Archives, File: German Occupation by Kathleen Keating and Various Other Histories, 1940–1944.

p. 73 With the general Vaughan, *Doctor to the Resistance*, pp. 36–7.

p. 73 'When the Allies, pushed Bove, *Paris*, pp. 218–19.

p. 74 'It's only a matter' *Ibid.*, p. 220. Vaughan, *Doctor to the Resistance*, p. 37.

p. 75 'At the end of May' 'Ambulances from America', *Time*, 3 June 1940.

p. 76 One American ambulance driver 'Driver of American Ambulance Hit by German Shell Missing', *New York Herald Tribune*, 7 May 1940, p. 1.

p. 76 'I received a telegram' Letter to the editor, *Life*, 24 June 1940, p. 4.

p. 76 At least two American drivers 'Ambulances from America', *Time*, 3 June 1940.

p. 76 'Coster was in the Colonel's office' Muir, *War without Music*, pp. 69–70.

p. 76 'with the knowledge ... At noon I gave up' *Ibid.*, p. 90.

p. 76 ' Lovering Hill, commander' 'Search for Drivers of Ambulance Fails', *New York Times*, 26 May 1940, p. 29.

p. 77 The French government awarded George Rock, *History of the American Field Service, 1920–1955*, New York: American Field Service Publication, 1956, p. 7.

p. 77 'I walked into ... He turned his gun' Donald Q. Coster, 'Behind German Lines', *Reader's Digest*, 3 November 1940 (pp. 115–25), p. 117.

p. 77 'There ... we were ...You may may have seen' *Ibid.*, p. 117.

p. 78 'The general ... Beautiful to watch' *Ibid.*, p. 123.

p. 78 'In the fraction ... Ah – we never see' *Ibid.*, p. 120.

p. 79 'We hurried to the *Kommandant*' *Ibid.*, p. 123.

p. 79 'We were stopped three' *Ibid.*, p. 125.

p. 79 'one of the American ambulance' George Kennan, *Sketches from a Life*, New York: Pantheon Books, 1989, p. 70 (diary entry for 2 July 1940, Paris–Brussels).

p. 79 'Refugees were laboriously ... Her dress was torn' *Ibid.*, pp. 71–2 (same diary date).

p. 80 'At the hotel the ambulance' *Ibid.*, p. 73 (same diary date). The next-door neighbour may have been Dorothy Reeder, who was then residing at the Bristol.

p. 80 'Was there not some Greek' *Ibid.*, p. 74 (diary entry for 3 July 1940).

p. 80 'This explained why King' Coster, 'Behind German Lines', *Reader's Digest*, 3 November 1940 (pp. 115–25), p. 125.

p. 81 Until the false identity Donald Coster interview with Kathleen Keating, 'The American Hospital in Paris During the German Occupation', 19 May 1981, 14-page typescript, p. 6, American Hospital of Paris Archives, File: German Occupation by Kathleen Keating and Various Other Histories, 1940–1944.

p. 81 'The Germans permitted Dr. Jackson' Dr Morris Sanders, 'The Mission of Dr. Sumner Jackson', *The News of Massachusetts General Hospital*, vol. 24, no. 5, June–July 1965, p. 6.

p. 81 'With the Occupation of Paris' Quoted in Vaughan, *Doctor to the Resistance*, p. 60.

p. 81 'An impressive line of ambulances' Otto Gresser, 'History of the American Hospital of Paris', 28 September 1978, 14-page typescript, p. 4, Archives of the American Hospital of Paris, File: History by Otto Gresser.

p. 82 He blamed what he called Quoted in an interview with Phillip Jackson, in Vaughan, *Doctor to the Resistance*, p. 48.

p. 82 'Too much praise cannot be' 'The American Hospital in Paris in the Second World War', printed in France, 1940, p. 31, Archives of the American Hospital of Paris, File: German Occupation by Kathleen Keating and Various Other Histories, 1940–1944.

p. 82 Dr Thierry de Martel left a nephew 'Drue Tartière, Back from Paris, Tells of Hiding Flyers from Foe', *New York Herald Tribune*, 7 January 1945, p. 6.

p. 82 'for I had grown weary' Drue Tartière with M. R. Werner, *The House near Paris: An American Woman's Story of Traffic in Patriots*, New York: Simon and Schuster, 1946, p. 9.

p. 83 German radio announced *Ibid.*, p. 18.

p. 83 'grandmothers holding dead babies' *Ibid.*, p. 12.

p. 83 'we realized that the so-called' *Ibid.*, p. 13.

p. 83 'Lingerie is on the next floor' Brian Moynahan, *The French Century*, London: Flammarion, 2007, p. 271.

p. 83 'The day was stifling' Drue Tartière, *The House near Paris*, p. 16.

p. 84 'In Tours, there was even greater' *Ibid.*, p. 17.

p. 84 'From the Bordeaux radio station' *Ibid.*, pp. 18–19.

p. 84 'a boy was arranging ... I had stood next to him' *Ibid.*, p. 4.

p. 85 'old Citroën with a motor' A. J. Liebling, *The Road Back to Paris*, London: Michael Joseph, 1944, p. 85. See also 'War Babies', *Time*, 17 June 1940.

p. 85 'We had our *café au lait*' Liebling, *The Road Back to Paris*, pp. 90–91.

p. 85 Many Frenchmen had already Antoine de Saint-Exupéry, *Wartime Writings, 1939–1944*, New York: Harcourt, Brace, Jovanovich, 1986, pp. xiv and 52.

p. 86 'The voice spoke of resistance' Liebling, *The Road Back to Paris*, p. 137.

p. 86 'Within three years ... the last bare-knuckle' *Ibid.*, p. 98.

PART TWO: 1940

Chapter Seven: Bookshop Row

p. 89 Sylvia Beach and Adrienne Monnier Adrienne Monnier, *Trois agendas d'Adrienne Monnier, Texte établie et annoté par Maurice Saillet*, Paris: published 'par ses amis', 1960, p. 38.

p. 89 'Sylvia, who left' *Ibid.*, pp. 39–40.

p. 90 'Fouquet's open ... another orchestra' *Ibid.*, pp. 40–41.

p. 90 'open with terrace ... No, only when' *Ibid.*, pp. 42–3.

p. 90 'ravishing, books in profusion ... Nothing at the market' *Ibid.*, pp. 44–8.

p. 91 'This morning, saw' *Ibid.*, p. 48.

p. 91 'We often have' Adrienne Monnier, 'A Letter to Friends in the Free Zone', originally published in *Le Figaro Littéraire*, February 1942, in Adrienne Monnier, *The Very Rich Hours of Adrienne Monnier: An Intimate Portrait of the Literary and Artistic Life in Paris between the Wars*, translated with introduction and commentaries by Richard McDougall, New York: Charles Scribner's Sons, 1976, p. 404.

p. 91 'Parisians who survived' Sylvia Beach, *Shakespeare and Company*, London: Faber and Faber, 1960, p. 218.

p. 92 Eleanor Beach had originally ... 'The cinema for my sister' Sylvia Beach Papers, Princeton University Library, Box 14. Miscellaneous note.

p. 92 'She was not pretty' Katherine Anne Porter, 'Paris: A Little Incident in the rue de l'Odéon', *Ladies Home Journal*, August 1964 (pp. 54–5), p. 54.

p. 92 'Cyprian was so beautiful ... Among my sister's admirers' Beach, *Shakespeare and Company*, pp. 22–3.

p. 93 The poet Léon-Paul Lafargue Cyprian was born in 1893, six years after Sylvia. She was named Eleanor after her mother, but she changed it to Cyprian. Her stage name was Cyprian Gilles. Her other Paris films were *The Fortune Teller* (1920), *L'Aiglonne* (1921) and *Amie d'enfance* (1922).

p. 93 An unexpected tragedy further Noel Riley Fitch, *Sylvia Beach and the Lost Generation: A History of Literary Paris in the Twenties and Thirties*, New York: W. W. Norton and Company, 1983, pp. 260–61.

p. 93 'It's pleasant to think' Letter from Sylvia Beach to Holly Beach Dennis, 9 January 1940, Sylvia Beach Papers, Princeton University Library, CO108, Box 20, Folder 8. Majority Style Folder.

p. 94 'If only I could' Letter from Sylvia Beach to Rev. Sylvester Beach, 10 April 1940, Sylvia Beach Papers, Princeton University Library, CO108, Box 20, Folder 7.

p. 94 'Of course ... we can't' Letter from Holly Beach Dennis to Sylvia Beach, 20 May 1940, Sylvia Beach Papers, Princeton University, CO108, Box 14, Folder 18.

p. 94 'very glad to read ... Are you still' Letter from Carlotta Welles Briggs to Sylvia Beach, 25 August 1940, Sylvia Beach Papers, Princeton University Library, CO108, Box 58, Folder 2.

p. 94 A mutual friend Don and Petie Kladstrup, *Wine and War*, New York: Broadway Books, 2001, p. 106.

p. 95 'But the really unpleasant' Letter from Gertrude de Gallaix to Sylvia Beach, 2 September 1940, Sylvia Beach Papers, Princeton University Library, CO108, Box 14, Folder 18.

p. 95 'The most dangerous time' *Ibid.*

p. 96 In the American beauty's suite In this coterie of writers and would-be writers, the Germans were more anti-Nazi than the French. Jünger was on the fringes of the July Plot to kill Hitler, and Heller had grave misgivings about occupying France. Jouhandeau, Drieu La Rochelle and the other Frenchmen praised Hitler and derided the Jews.

p. 96 'stupified to be shaking' C. Mauriac, *Bergène ô tour Eiffel*, Paris: B. Grasset, 1985, pp. 222–5.

p. 96 'She was beautiful, great' Gerhard Heller, *Un Allemand à Paris*, Paris: Editions du Seuil, 1981, p. 62.

p. 96 'Among the collaborationists' Silas P., 'Letter from France II (July)', *Horizon*, vol. 4, no. 23, November 1942, p. 351.

p. 97 'He was there when [Paul] Valéry' Adrienne Monnier, 'Benoist-Méchin', in Monnier, *The Very Rich Hours of Adrienne Monnier*, pp. 133–4.

p. 97 She did not write what became In Laval's government of 18 April 1942, Jacques Benoist-Méchain was promoted to 'secrétariat d'Etat chargé de la main d'oeuvre française en Allemagne'. In September, he assumed the new post of 'secrétariat général à la Police' under René Bousquet and stood down in January 1944.

Chapter Eight: Americans at Vichy

p. 98 Miss Morgan, who had returned 'Five Women Sail to Assist Allies', *New York Times*, 3 March 1940, p. 3.

p. 98 'About that time ... Finno-hysteria broke out' Polly Peabody, *Occupied Territory*, London: The Cresset Press, 1941, p. 3.

p. 98 The American-Scandinavian Field Hospital's 'Hospital Formed to Help Finland', *New York Times*, 11 February 1940, p. 28. The group's headquarters were at 340 Park Avenue, and among the sponsors were Prince Carl, chief of the Swedish Red Cross, former President Herbert Hoover, Mrs Frederic Guest and Mrs Winston Guest.

p. 98 'the Black Eagle of Harlem' Peabody, *Occupied Territory*, p. 7. (I met 'Colonel' Julian in Beirut in 1975, when he announced an offer to restore Emperor Haile Selasse to his throne in Ethiopia. He may actually have come to Lebanon to sell arms to one faction or another in the nascent civil war. The adventures of this flamboyant character had already been recorded in Peter Nugent's *The Black Eagle of Harlem*, New York: Bantam Books, 1972.)

p. 99 'At each station' Peabody, *Occupied Territory*, p. 104.

p. 99 'Hell, we'll be just ... I turned on him' *Ibid.*, pp. 105–6.

p. 99 '"Where is everybody"' *Ibid.*, pp. 110–11.

p. 99 'The people were' *Ibid.*, p. 114.

p. 100 'the Mayor had not waited' *Ibid.*, p. 115.

p. 100 'Stepping into the street' *Ibid.*, pp. 117–18.

p. 100 'During the first few days' *Ibid.*, p. 119.

p. 101 'a French duchess' *Ibid.*, p. 122.

p. 101 The American Embassy made its 'Office Memorandum, American Consul Walter W. Orebaugh, to S. Pinckney Tuck, Chargé d'Affaires ad interim, Vichy', 31 October 1942, Enclosure: List of Properties, US National Archives, College Park, Maryland, General Records of the State Department, Decimal File Box 1168, 351.115/136.

p. 101 'They made up their minds' Clara Longworth de Chambrun, *Shadows Lengthen: The Story of My Life*, New York: Charles Scribner's Sons, 1949, p. 129.

p. 101 Ambassador Bullitt had left Orville Bullitt (ed.), *For the President, Personal and Secret: Correspondence Between Franklin D. Roosevelt and William C. Bullitt*, Boston: Houghton Mifflin, 1972, p. 476. Will Brownell and Richard N. Billings, *So Close to Greatness: A Biography of William C. Bullitt*, New York; Macmillan, 1987, pp. 261–2.

p. 101 Bullitt caught up with Paul Saurin, 'The Allied Landing in North Africa', in *France During the German Occupation, 1940–1944: A Collection of 292 Statements on the Government of Maréchal Pétain and Pierre Laval*, Translated from the French by Philip W. Whitcomb, Palo Alto, CA: The Hoover Institution, Stanford University, vol. II, 1957, p. 600. Saurin, parliamentary deputy for Oran, met Bullitt and Murphy at the Hôtel de Charlannes just after their arrival.

p. 101 'seemed to have lost' Longworth de Chambrun, *Shadows Lengthen*, p. 129.

p. 102 The Americans tended See Robert O. Paxton, *Vichy France: Old Guard and New Order, 1940–1944*, New York: W. W. Norton and Company (also London: Barrie and Jenkins), 1972, pp. 60–63. Part of the thesis of Paxton's excellent book is that the Vichy initiatives seeking collaboration with Germany were supported by Pétain,

Admiral Darlan and a majority of ministers, rather than by Laval alone.

p. 102 **Pétain not only cut** Paxton, *Vichy France*, p. 56. Laval was reported to have said to Pétain when he ordered the attack on the British, 'You have just lost one war. Do you want to lose another?'

p. 102 **The dissenter was** 'Lone Dissenting Senator In France Is a U.S. Citizen', *New York Times*, 10 July 1940, p. 4.

p. 102 **'During that morning'** Peabody, *Occupied Territory*, p. 119.

p. 103 **'the single example of courage'** Bullitt (ed.), *For the President*, pp. 490–91.

p. 104 **'*Vive la République*'** *Ibid.*, p. 491. Brownell and Billings, *So Close to Greatness*, p. 262. See also William L. Shirer, *The Collapse of the Third Republic: An Inquiry into the Fall of France in 1940*, New York: Simon and Schuster, 1969, p. 942. Shirer wrote that the voice was that of Senator Astier. He added, 'The Third Republic was dead. It had committed suicide.'

p. 104 **'The last scene'** Bullitt (ed.), *For the President*.

p. 104 **'Say there, Aldebert'** Yves Pourcher, *Pierre Laval vu par sa fille d'après ses carnets intimes*, Paris: Le Cherche-Midi, 2002, p. 235. This story comes from a diary of Josée Laval de Chambrun. The diaries are held by the Fondation Josée et René de Chambrun in René and Josée's former house at 6-bis Place du Palais Bourbon, Paris 75007. The directors of the foundation allowed me to read, but not to copy, Josée's diaries for the occupation years. Many of the entries, however, are reproduced in Pourcher's book. The directors did permit me to read and copy René and Josée de Chambrun's letters and other documents.

p. 104 **'I was introduced'** Peabody, *Occupied Territory*, p. 122.

p. 104 **'I am going to … Of all the people'** *Ibid.*, p. 123.

p. 105 **'Without suspecting that'** Longworth de Chambrun, *Shadows Lengthen*, p. 132.

p. 105 **'A row of high screens** *Ibid.*, p. 128.

p. 105 **'What a kowtowing'** *Ibid.*

p. 105 **'Of course not'** Brownell and Billings, *So Close to Greatness*, p. 262.

p. 105 **'In those first weeks … I think most'** Robert Murphy, *Diplomat among Warriors*, New York: Doubleday and Company, 1964, p. 71.

p. 106 **'The old soldier … The Marshal was then** *Ibid.*, pp. 72–3.

p. 107 **'The president wants'** René de Chambrun, *Mission and Betrayal, 1940–1945: Working with Franklin Roosevelt to Help Save Britain and Europe*, Stanford, CA: Hoover Institution Press, 1992, p. 66.

p. 107 **'Radiograms reporting the advance'** Letter from René de Chambrun to New York, recipient's name blocked out by the FBI, 31 May 1945, from FBI files supplied under Freedom of Information Act, unnumbered file, FOIPA No. 1088544-001. See also de Chambrun, *Mission and*

Betrayal, pp. 67–8. René de Chambrun, *I Saw France Fall: Will She Rise Again?*, New York: William Morrow and Company, 1940, p. 199.

p. 108 'I maintain that' Chambrun, *Mission and Betrayal*, p. 69.

p. 108 Alice had once caught 'Two for Cissy', *Time*, 2 August 1937.

p. 109 'You have been able' René de Chambrun, *Pierre Laval: Traitor or Patriot?*, New York: Charles Scribner's Sons, 1984, p. 62.

p. 109 Aware of food shortages de Chambrun, *Mission and Betrayal*, p. 115.

p. 110 'refreshed and ready' 'Black Week', *Time*, 24 June 1940.

p. 110 'France will remain firmly' de Chambrun, *Pierre Laval*, p. 63.

p. 111 'The president has' *Ibid.*, p. 64.

p. 111 'René de Chambrun' 'Concrete Guy', *Time*, 21 October 1940.

p. 111 'like his mother' Longworth de Chambrun, *Shadows Lengthen*, p. 137.

p. 112 'He is a plausible' British Embassy, Washington, Telegram from Mr Butler (Washington), No. 2675, Registry Number C 12267/7407/17, Foreign Office Files p. 211, British National Archives, Kew.

p. 112 'we don't like' *Ibid.*

Chapter Nine: Back to Paris

p. 113 'It was late' Polly Peabody, *Occupied Territory*, London: The Cresset Press, 1941, pp. 151–2.

p. 113 'put both fists ... This was my' *Ibid.*, p. 155.

p. 114 'My old lady' Clara Longworth de Chambrun, *Shadows Lengthen: The Story of My Life*, New York: Charles Scribner's Sons, 1949, p. 139.

p. 114 'a German official ... The use of the' *Ibid.*, p. 139.

p. 115 'During those first' *Ibid.*, p. 142.

p. 115 'young, attractive ... a grand sense' 'Life in Paris, Special Wednesday Reportage', First Library Broadcast, Paris-Mondiale, 21 February 1940, in the Archives of the American Library of Paris, Box 20, File K.5 (American Library Clippings, 1939–1940).

p. 116 'pasted U.S. seals' Dorothy Reeder, 'The American Library in Paris: September 1939–June 1941, CONFIDENTIAL', Report to the American Library Association, 19 July 1941, American Library Association Archives, University of Illinois at Urbana-Champaign, p. 9.

p. 116 'It is a funny point' *Ibid.*, p. 10.

p. 116 The occupation meant *Ibid.*, p. 12.

p. 116 'a stiff Prussian-looking' Longworth de Chambrun, *Shadows Lengthen*, p. 144.

p. 117 'held each other' *Ibid.*

p. 117 'You will necessarily ... No, my dear young' Longworth de Chambrun, *Shadows Lengthen*, pp. 144–5.

Endnotes

p. 117 Works by Ernest Hemingway 'L'Histoire de la Librairie Américaine de Paris', Account written by Dorothy Reeder during the occupation in Paris, beginning, 'When the war broke out ...', p. 1, American Library in Paris Archives, Box 20, File K.26. See also, in same file, Milton E. Lord, 'A Report upon the American Library in Paris: Findings and Recommendations', p. 1. See also Edgar Ansel Mowrer, 'Nazis Forcing Own Culture on French People', *Chicago Daily News*, 16 October 1940, p. 1: the Bernhard List 'includes 143 items on four pages ... Four other Americans appear on the Bernhard list: the newspapermen, Louis Fischer and H. R. Knickerbocker, Prof. Calvin B. Hoover, and Leon G. Turrou, formerly of the F.B.I.' Mowrer added, 'The American Lending Library in Paris was also visited but upon the librarian's promise to respect German wishes, nothing was taken away.'

p. 117 'for purposes of study' *Ibid.*

p. 117 'No Jews are' Longworth de Chambrun, *Shadows Lengthen*, p. 145.

p. 117 'My simple solution' *Ibid.*

p. 118 'GREETINGS BEST WISHES' American Library of Paris Archives, Box 20, File K5.2 War Years (September–November 1940).

p. 118 'We are now open' American Library of Paris Archives, Box 9, File E.3, Letter from Dorothy Reeder to Mr Michel Gunn, Rockefeller Foundation, 49 West 49th Street, New York, 19 September 1940. The letter is sparing with information, perhaps because it would have to pass the German censor. She added, 'The Comtesse and the General are back.'

p. 118 'Few people came' 'L'Histoire de la Librairie Américaine de Paris', Account written by Dorothy Reeder during the occupation in Paris, beginning, 'When the war broke out ...', p. 1, American Library in Paris Archives, Box 20, File K.26.

p. 118 'It is enough to say' *Ibid.*

p. 119 'I want particularly' American Library of Paris Archives, Box 20, File K5.2 War Years (September–November 1940).

p. 119 'Dr. Gros has' American Library of Paris Archives, Box 9, File E.3, Letter from Dorothy Reeder to Mr Michel Gunn, Rockefeller Foundation, 49 West 49th Street, New York, 19 September 1940.

Chapter Ten: In Love with Love

p. 121 'a Mephistophelean little' *Time*, 15 November 1937.

p. 121 'He reminded himself' Janet Flanner, 'Annals of Collaboration: Equivalism I', *The New Yorker*, 22 September 1945, p. 29.

p. 121 'Franco-American' Bedaux His biographers differ on his date of birth. Jim Christy, in *The Price of Power: A Biography of Charles Eugene Bedaux*, New York: Doubleday and Company, 1984, on p. 3

gives it as 10 October 1886. George Ungar's film biography, *The Champagne Safari*, Canada, 1995, said it was 26 May 1886. Bedaux's passport renewal form of 1941 also states that he was born on 10 October 1886. It is reproduced in C. M. Hardwick, *Time Study in Treason: Charles E. Bedaux, Patriot or Collaborator*, Chelmsford, Essex: Peter Horsnell, publisher, undated, probably 1990, p. 7.

p. 121 **'a real Horatio'** 'Wally's Host – A Tale of Sandhog to Millionaire', *Chicago Daily Tribune*, 31 March 1937, p. 6.

p. 121 **When a woman** Christy, *The Price of Power*, p. 15.

p. 122 **Arriving aged 19** Ibid., p. 21. Ungar, *The Champagne Safari*.

p. 122 **'I soon found'** *Liberty* magazine, 1930, quoted in Christy, *The Price of Power*, pp. 25–6.

p. 122 **American labour unions ... 'proper use of'** 'Bedaux Arrested in Deal with Foe', *New York Times*, 14 January 1943, pp. 1 and 3.

p. 122 **In 1936, Charlie Chaplin** See Internet Movie Data Base, *Modern Times*.

p. 123 **'Let us be the missionary'** Ungar, *The Champagne Safari*, Bedaux speech at 18 minutes 40 seconds.

p. 123 **'stripped of its'** 'Mr. Bedaux's Friends', *Time*, 15 November 1937.

p. 123 **'the most completely'** Ibid.

p. 123 **Among them was 'Colonel'** Christy, *The Price of Power*, p. 63.

p. 123 **The next year, his first** Janet Flanner, 'Annals of Collaboration: Equivalism I', *The New Yorker*, 22 September 1945, p. 29.

p. 124 **He claimed later** Ibid., p. 34.

p. 124 **'Men, women, children ... worldly, boldly battered'** Ibid., pp. 30 and 29.

p. 124 **In 1924, Bedaux** Christy, *The Price of Power*, p. 62. 'Parisys Silenced?', *Time*, 15 February 1926.

p. 124 **The Bedauxs, who had no** Ungar, *The Champagne Safari*. The film includes footage of the Bedauxs that Charles commissioned to record his 1934 expedition.

p. 125 **Bedaux loved inventing** Christy, *The Price of Power*, p. 61.

p. 125 **'A man loves'** Janet Flanner, 'Annals of Collaboration: Equivalism III', *The New Yorker*, 13 October 1945, p. 48.

p. 125 **Within ten years** Yves Levant and Marc Nikitin, 'Should Charles Eugene Bedaux be Revisited?', Paper presented to the Eighteenth Annual Conference of the Business Research Unit, Cardiff Business School, Cardiff, Wales, 14–15 September 2006, p. 11. See also Janet Flanner, 'Annals of Collaboration: Equivalism I', *The New Yorker*, 22 September 1945, p. 29.

p. 125 **The young counts** Franz Joseph was Emperor of Austria and King of Hungary from 1848 to 1916.

p. 125 **Friederich met Bedaux** Author's correspondence with von Ledebur's family in Vienna, June 2008.

p. 125 He approached a German Janet Flanner, 'Annals of Collaboration: Equivalism II', *The New Yorker*, 6 October 1945, p. 32.

p. 125 Through him, Bedaux became *Ibid.*

p. 125 Bedaux commissioned her *Ibid.*

p. 126 'My wife and I believe' 'Wally's Host – A Tale of Sandhog to Millionaire', *Chicago Daily Tribune*, 31 March 1937, p. 6.

p. 127 'my wife and I' Christy, *The Price of Power*, p. 146.

p. 127 'She was so much finer' Janet Flanner, 'Annals of Collaboration: Equivalism I', *The New Yorker*, 22 September 1945, p. 40.

p. 127 'unceasing affection … knew how to help' Gaston Bedaux, *La Vie ardente de Charles Bedaux*, Paris: privately published, 3 June 1959, p. 88.

p. 127 Bedaux's wedding present Janet Flanner, 'Annals of Collaboration: Equivalism II', *The New Yorker*, 6 October 1945, p. 32; and Christy, *The Price of Power*, p. 59.

p. 127 Friedrich von Ledebur, who met Federal Bureau of Investigation interview with Frederick Ledebur, Telemeter, 21 January 1944, US Department of Justice Communications Section, from FBI files supplied under Freedom of Information Act, unnumbered file, pp. 64692, 64693 and 64694. FOIPA No. 1088544-001. (All records released by the FBI are from RG65, Records of the Federal Bureau of Investigation, World War II, FBI Headquarters Files, 100-49901 Sections 1–2, Charles Bedaux (FOIPA), Box number 113.) FBI agents questioned Ledebur in Ventura, California, on 20 January 1944.

p. 128 Subsequently, the duke Fritz Wiedemann had been a captain in the 16th Bavarian Regiment, commanding Corporal Adolf Hitler. He became Hitler's adjutant in 1934 and was close enough to the dictator to be able to criticize him from time to time. However, in 1938, after the savagery of the Kristallnacht pogroms in Germany, Hitler dismissed Wiedemann and Dr Hjalmar Schacht, who had criticized the thugs responsible. Wiedemann was assigned, along with his mistress, the half-Jewish Princess Stefanie von Hohenlohe, as German Consul-General in San Francisco. See John Toland, *Adolf Hitler*, New York: Doubleday and Company, 1976, p. 509.

p. 128 Watson had enjoyed a private Edwin Black, *IBM and the Holocaust: The Strategic Alliance between Nazi Germany and America's Most Powerful Corporation*, New York: Crown Publishers, 2001, pp. 132–3.

p. 128 'the slightest concern' 'Mr. Bedaux's Friends', *Time*, 15 November 1937.

p. 129 Bedaux suffered what was This story is told, in differing details, in Christy, *The Price of Power*, pp. 167–83; Janet Flanner, 'Annals of Collaboration: Equivalism II', *The New Yorker*, 6 October 1945, p. 34; and Martin Allen, *Hidden Agenda*, London: Macmillan, 2000, pp. 86–98. Gaston Bedaux's privately printed biography of his brother, *La Vie ardente de Charles E. Bedaux*, on p. 61, refers to the incident briefly: 'Unhappily, from the other side of the ocean, for reasons that I shall ignore, an angry reception had been prepared.' Charles told his brother that, from that day, 'his life was constantly in danger'.

p. 130 **Bedaux went to Britain** Christy, *The Price of Power*, p. 206.

p. 130 **When Bedaux discovered** Janet Flanner, 'Annals of Collaboration: Equivalism II', *The New Yorker*, 6 October 1945, p. 36.

p. 130 **At the end of June** 'U.S. Property in France Has Light War Toll', *Chicago Daily Tribune*, 16 July 1940, p. 6.

p. 131 **The Bedaux Company's Dutch headquarters** Federal Bureau of Investigation interview with Frederick Ledebur, Telemeter, 21 January 1944, U.S. Department of Justice Communications Section, from F.B.I. files supplied under Freedom of Information Act, unnumbered file, pp. 64692, 64693 and 64694. FOIPA No. 1088544-001.

p. 132 **An excellent horseman** Christy, *The Price of Power*, p. 202. Friedrich von Ledebur later worked in films as a coordinator of horse stunts and an actor. He appeared in Alfred Hitchcock's 1946 *Notorious* and played Queequeg in John Huston's *Moby-Dick* in 1956. Also in *Moby-Dick* was his English ex-wife, Iris Tree, the daughter of Sir Herbert Beerbohm Tree. His last film role was as Admiral Aulent in Fellini's *Ginger and Fred* in 1976. See Internet Movie Database at www.imdb.com/name/nmo496428/. He died, aged 86, in 1986.

p. 132 **Abetz was married** W. Sternfeld, 'Ambassador Abetz', *Contemporary Review*, London, August 1942, p. 86. See also 'There It Goes?', *Newsweek*, 4 January 1943, p. 38. *Newsweek* wrote, 'Handsome, elegant, speaking perfect French, Abetz penetrated the most exclusive circles.'

p. 132 **'Bedaux was more dynamic'** Christy, *The Price of Power*, p. 217.

p. 133 **'This millionaire, French'** Bernard Ullmann, *Lisette de Brinon, ma mère: Une Juive dans la tourment de la Collaboration*, Paris: Editions Complexe, 2004, p. 96.r

p. 133 **He invited Bedaux** Ungar, *The Champagne Safari*, at 1:02:30. See also Christy, *The Price of Power*, p. 216.

p. 133 **The friendship that** Janet Flanner, 'Annals of Collaboration: Equivalism I', *The New Yorker*, 22 September 1945, p. 31.

p. 134 **'He is a man drafted'** Christy, *The Price of Power*, p. 216.

p. 134 **'During this preliminary'** Pierre Laval, *The Unpublished Diary of Pierre Laval*, with an introduction by Josée Laval, Countess R. de Chambrun, London: Falcon Press, 1948, p. 71.

p. 134 **Medicus supplied Bedaux** Henri Michel, *Paris Allemand*, Paris: Albin Michel, 1981, p. 46.

p. 134 Dr Franz Medicus was a regular Janet Flanner, 'Annals of Collaboration: Equivalism III', *The New Yorker*, 13 October 1945, p. 32.

p. 134 Before the war, de Brinon Alexander Werth, *France: 1940–1944*, London: Robert Hale Ltd, 1956, p. 126. Werth gives a thorough account of de Brinon's career on pp. 126–30. See also William Shirer, *The Collapse of the Third Republic: An Inquiry into the Fall of France in 1940*, New York: Simon and Schuster, 1969, p. 385n.

p. 135 The Germans declared Ullmann, *Lisette de Brinon, ma mère*, pp. 44 and 108.

p. 135 Bedaux gave Pierre-Jérôme In the confused world of ideological commitments of that time, Pierre-Jérôme was attracted to groups that his openly fascist stepfather admired. His brother wrote, 'As an adolescent in the 1930s, he adhered to the youth movements of the extreme right that flourished in the Latin Quarter without realizing that hate or contempt for Jews was in integral part of their doctrine.' See *Ibid.*, p. 16. Pierre-Jérôme had enlisted in the army in 1939 and was among the cadets at Saumur who resisted the German advance. Bernard wrote that his brother took provisional employment in a prefecture in the Basses-Pyrénées soon after the beginning of the occupation. See *Ibid.*, p. 113. Bedaux's son, Charles Emile, told his father's biographer Jim Christy that Charles Eugene employed de Brinon's stepson in his French company. Author's correspondence with Jim Christy, July 2008.

p. 135 His wife's absence Ullmann, *Lisette de Brinon, ma mère*, p. 124. Lisette knew of the affair and was jealous of Mittre.

p. 135 For her part, Lisette Werth, *France: 1940–1944*, p. 126.

Chapter Eleven: A French Prisoner with the Americans

p. 136 'the flowers, the walkways' André Guillon, 'Testimony of a French PoW on His Time at the American Hospital of Paris', 13-page typescript in French, p. 1, American Hospital of Paris Archives, File: André Guillon. (My translation.)

p. 136 'neutrality that we ... There were no sentries' *Ibid.*, p. 2.

p. 137 Later, it was revealed Note: Coster went to North Africa as one of the vice-consuls in the spy network that Robert Murphy had established under the Murphy–Weygand Agreement ostensibly to monitor American relief shipments. Afterwards, he took part in the Normandy landings as an intelligence officer. After the war, he had a career with the CIA in Vietnam and Algeria.

p. 137 'I remember Dr Jackson ... this ethnic group ... The nurses imposed ... I went out regularly' Guillon, 'Testimony of a French PoW on His Time at the American Hospital of Paris', p. 5.

p. 138 **'He was taken to'** 'U.S. Hospital Aid Expanded in Paris', *New York Times*, 29 June 1940, p. 22.

Chapter Twelve: American Grandees

p. 139 **Dean Jay and his wife** *Americans in France: A Directory, 1939–1940*, Paris: American Chamber of Commerce in France, 1940, p. 126. Jackson lived and maintained a medical practice at 11 avenue Foch, just up the hill from the Jays.

p. 139 **Mr Post had been** 'Reshuffle', *Time*, 23 December 1935.

p. 140 **'At present ... we have'** 'Minutes of a Special Meeting of the Board of Governors of the American Hospital of Paris', 26 July 1940, American Hospital of Paris Archives, File: Bound book: Minutes of the American Hospital of Paris, 1940.

p. 140 **The Count de Chambrun** René de Chambrun, *Sorti du Rang*, Paris: Atelier Marcel Jullian, 1980, p. 224. Gresser was from Thurgovie and Comte from Vaud.

p. 140 **'should endeavor to slow'** 'Minutes of a Special Meeting of the Board of Governors of the American Hospital of Paris', 22 August 1940, American Hospital of Paris Archives, File: Bound book: Minutes of the American Hospital of Paris, 1940.

p. 141 **'in the event of'** 'Minutes of a Regular Meeting of the Board of Governors of the American Hospital of Paris', 19 September 1940, American Hospital of Paris Archives, File: Correspondence and Reports, 1941, and Minutes, 19 September 1940 to 7 November 1941.

p. 141 **The last item of business** The 31-page report was published two months later under the title 'The American Hospital of Paris in the Second World War', and was used for publicity and fund raising in the United States. American Hospital of Paris Archives, File: German Occupation by Kathleen Keating and Various Other Histories, 1940–1944. The report stated on p. 9, 'Too much praise cannot be given to Dr. Sumner Jackson, who has been a member of the Attending Staff since 1925 and who accepted the professional supervision of the wounded for the period of the war.'

p. 142 **'sevices or municipal'** 'Minutes of a Regular Meeting of the Board of Governors of the American Hospital of Paris', 21 November 1940, American Hospital of Paris Archives, File: Bound book: Minutes of the American Hospital of Paris, 1940.

p. 142 **'The Winter 1940–1941'** Otto Gresser, 'History of the American Hospital of Paris', 28 September 1978, 14-page typescript, p. 5, Archives of the American Hospital of Paris, File: History by Otto Gresser.

p. 142 'Then I noticed' Interview with Otto Gresser in Kathleen Keating, German Ocupation and Various Other Histories, p. 9.

p. 143 'After more questions' *Ibid.*

p. 143 With no gas for cooking Otto Gresser, 'Histoire de l'Hôpital Américain – 4ème Partie', *American Hospital of Paris Newsletter*, vol. 3, no. 11, March 1975, Paris, p. 4.

Chapter Thirteen: Polly's Paris

p. 144 'Thus we sailed' Polly Peabody, *Occupied Territory*, London: The Cresset Press, 1941, p. 177.

p. 144 'The room was full' *Ibid.*, pp. 179–80.

p. 145 'The curfew hour' *Ibid.*, pp. 180–81. Polly's idiosyncratic punctuation is in the original.

p. 145 'We cannot dance' *Ibid.*, p. 181.

p. 145 'A new hope' *Ibid.*, p. 185.

p. 145 'At the camps ... In any event' *Ibid.*, p. 187.

p. 146 'they either hadn't heard' *Ibid.*, p. 194.

p. 146 'With no more work' *Ibid.*, p. 197.

p. 146 'The first of October ... You can't have him' *Ibid.*, p. 203.

p. 147 'One day in September ... The following days' Thomas Kernan, *Paris on Berlin Time*, Philadelphia and New York: J. P. Lippincott Company, 1941, pp. 182–4.

p. 147 'The newspaper *France*' Peabody, *Occupied Territory*, p. 205.

p. 148 'pedestrians hooted and' *Ibid.*, p. 210.

p. 148 Polly and the journalist ... 'The cyclist rode' *Ibid.*, pp. 210–11.

Chapter Fourteen: Rugged Individualists

p. 150 'The Germans were ... This is probably' Janet Flanner, 'Annals of Collaboration: Equivalism II', *The New Yorker*, 6 October 1945, p. 36.

p. 150 Yet Bedaux endangered his wealth Gaston Bedaux, *La Vie ardente de Charles Bedaux*, privately published, Paris, 3 June 1959, p. 71.

p. 150 He did the same for Alexandra Martin Allen, *Hidden Agenda: How the Duke of Windsor Betrayed the Allies*, London: Macmillan, 2000, p. 58.

p. 150 Bedaux also helped Christy, *The Price of Power*, p. 217.

p. 151 'He must be speaking' Clara Longworth de Chambrun, *Shadows Lengthen: The Story of My Life*, New York: Charles Scribner's Sons, 1949, p. 153.

p. 151 In the meantime, Hitler Four months earlier, Franco had asked the British Ambassador in Madrid, Sir Samuel Hoare, 'Why do you not end the war now? You can never win it.' See Peter Collier, *1940: The World in Flames*, London: Hamish Hamilton, 1979, p. 153. The Battle of Britain, which the Luftwaffe was losing to British fighters, changed his mind about the British: 'They'll fight and go on fighting: and if they are driven out of Britain, they'll carry on the fight from Canada: they'll get the Americans to come in with them. Germany has not won the war.' See John Toland, *Adolf Hitler*, New York: Doubleday and Company, 1976, p. 636.

p. 152 **'the two million French'** Toland, *Adolf Hitler*, p. 639.

p. 152 **'This collaboration must'** *Ibid.*, p. 640.

p. 152 **At the same time** Herbert Lottman, *Pétain: Hero or Traitor, The Untold Story*, New York: William Morrow and Company, 1985, p. 215.

p. 152 **'careful notes'** Pierre Laval, *The Unpublished Diary of Pierre Laval*, with an introduction by Josée Laval, Countess R. de Chambrun, London: Falcon Press, 1948, p. 75.

p. 152 **'I was placed to the right ... his differences with ... Laval was happy ... So long as I have'** Gaston Bedaux, *La Vie ardente de Charles Bedaux*, Paris, privately published, 3 June 1959, p. 72.

p. 153 **When Laval criticized** *Ibid.*, p. 73.

p. 153 **'a lively intelligence'** *Ibid.*

p. 153 **At this time, according** Christy, *The Price of Power*, pp. 220–21.

p. 153 **'With unconcealed pride'** Adrienne Monnier, 'Lust', in Adrienne Monnier, *The Very Rich Hours of Adrienne Monnier*, translated by Richard McDougall, New York: Charles Scribner's Sons, p. 169. Laure Murat in *Passage de l'Odéon: Sylvia Beach, Adrienne Monnier et la vie littéraire à Paris dans l'entre-deux-guerres*, Paris: Fayard, 2003, p. 34, wrote that Valéry's first reading of '*Mon Faust*' took place in Adrienne's flat on 1 March 1941, for the silver anniversary of Adrienne's bookshop.

p. 153 **'the feminine character ... an ingenuous intellectual'** *Ibid.*, pp. 170–72.

p. 154 **Carlotta sent her a cheque** Letter from Carlotta Briggs to Sylvia Beach, 17 October 1940, Sylvia Beach Papers, Princeton University Library, CO108, Box 58, Folder 2.

p. 154 **'In case she is'** Letter from Carlotta Briggs to Sylvia Beach, 2 November 1940, Sylvia Beach Papers, Princeton University Library, CO108, Box 58, Folder 2.

p. 154 **'I told you'** Holly Beach Dennis to Sylvia Beach, 13 November 1940, Sylvia Beach Papers, Princeton University Library, CO108, Box 14, Folder 18.

p. 155 **'The greatest blessing'** Noel Riley Fitch, *Sylvia Beach and the Lost Generation: A History of Literary Paris in the Twenties and Thirties*, New York: W. W. Norton, 1983, p. 401.

p. 155 **'happily till the very'** *Ibid.*, p. 402.

p. 155 'He told me between' André Guillon, 'Testimony of a French PoW on His Time at the American Hospital of Paris', 13-page typescript in French, p. 7, American Hospital of Paris Archives, File: André Guillon. (My translation.)

p. 155 'I found myself' *Ibid.*

p. 156 'How the Americans' *Ibid.*, p. 8.

p. 156 'The American doctor' *Ibid.*, p. 9.

p. 156 'Operating by day' Otto Gresser, 'History of the American Hospital – Part III', *American Hospital of Paris Newsletter*, vol. 2, no. 10, November 1974, Paris, p. 3.

p. 156 General Huntziger and his wife *Le Journal Officiel de l'Etat Français* of 19 November 1941 recorded that four other hospital employees had been granted the Médaille d'Honneur du Service de Santé, Medal of Honour of the Health Service: volunteer driver Gertrude Hamilton, an American; Marie Thion de la Chaume, French director of ambulance services; and Else Rye, the chief night nurse, Danish.

p. 157 'I read them' André Guillon, 'Testimony of a French PoW on His Time at the American Hospital of Paris', p. 12.

p. 157 'She had the grace' *Ibid.*, p. 11.

p. 157 'He was alone' 'Personnel Reste à L'Hôpital le 14 Juin 1940', p. 5, American Hospital of Paris Archives, File: Testimony of a Wounded French PoW on his time at A.H.P, 1940, and Personnel, 1940. Mlle Svetchine is the only nurse listed whose name is Russian and begins with an S.

p. 157 'You undress ... There was obviously' Guillon, 'Testimony of a French PoW on His Time at the American Hospital of Paris', p. 12.

p. 158 Mademoiselle D. was probably 'U.S. Acts on Clerk Jailed by Gestapo', *New York Times*, 7 December 1940, p. 2.

Chapter Fifteen: Germany's Confidential American Agent

p. 159 On 12 December Herbert Lottman, *Pétain: Hero or Traitor, The Untold Story*, New York: William Morrow, 1985, p. 227.

p. 159 *L'Aiglon,* or 'the little eagle' 'The Dead Eaglet', *Time*, 23 December 1940.

p. 159 Laval warned Abetz Yves Pourcher, *Pierre Laval: Vu par sa fille d'après ses carnets intimes*, Paris: Le Cherche-Midi, 2002, p. 207. Herbert Lottman, a reliable historian, writes in *Pétain: Hero or Traitor*, p. 227, that Laval drove from Paris to Vichy with Fernand de Brinon, without giving a source.

p. 160 'I had scarcely entered' Pierre Laval, *The Unpublished Diary of Pierre Laval*, with an introduction by Josée Laval, Countess R. de Chambrun, London: Falcon Press, 1948, p. 82.

p. 160 **At the Hôtel du Parc** Fernand de Brinon, *Mémoires*, Paris: La P. Internationale, 1949, pp. 52–4. See also Yves Pourcher, *Pierre Laval*, p. 210, quoting Josée Laval's diary. Historian Herbert Lottman explained, 'If Action Française [the extreme rightist, Catholic and monarchist group founded by Charles Maurras], a major influence in the cabinet, was anti-Semitic and anti-Freemason, even a certain degree anti-British, it was above all anti-German.' See Herbert Lottman, *Pétain: Hero or Traitor*, p. 233.

p. 160 **'a palace revolution'** Pourcher, *Pierre Laval*, p. 209.

p. 160 **Pétain announced his** René de Chambrun, *Pierre Laval: Traitor or Patriot?*, New York: Charles Scribner's Sons, 1984, p. 59.

p. 160 **He sent Hitler** David Irving, *Hitler's War and the War Path, 1933–1945*, London: Focal Point, 1991, p. 333.

p. 160 **'This is a heavy … Even if we now'** Ulrich von Hassell, *The von Hassell Diaries: 1938–1944*, London: Hamish Hamilton, 1948, p. 150.

p. 161 **Hitler accepted Ribbentrop's** Lottman, *Pétain: Hero or Traitor?*, p. 231.

p. 161 **On Sunday, 15 December** Ian Ousby, *Occupation: The Ordeal of France, 1940–1944*, London: Pimlico, 1999, p. 117.

p. 161 **The ceremony was** 'The Dead Eaglet', *Time*, 23 December 1940.

p. 161 **'I saw for the first time'** Pourcher, *Pierre Laval*, p. 212, quoting Josée Laval de Chambrun's diary.

p. 161 **'The people from … where he is safe'** Pourcher, *Pierre Laval*, p. 213.

p. 161 **'I spent the saddest'** de Chambrun, *Pierre Laval: Traitor or Patriot?*, p. 65.

p. 161 **Worse came the next** Jim Christy, in *The Price of Power: A Biography of Charles Eugene Bedaux*, New York: Doubleday and Company, 1984, p. 222, writes that 'on December 15, Joseph von Ledebur left for the Russian front'. There would be no Russian front until Germany's invasion of the Soviet Union in June 1941.

p. 162 **On Tuesday morning, 17 December** Pourcher, *Pierre Laval*, p. 213. Josée Laval in her diary for 20 December 1940 reports seeing Lisette de Brinon in Vichy with a friend named Fernande. Bernard Ullmann, *Lisette de Brinon, ma mère: Une Juive dans la tourmente de la Collaboration*, Paris: Editions Complexe, 2004, pp. 116–18.

p. 162 **'We played no'** Robert Murphy, *Diplomat among Warriors*, New York: Doubleday and Company, 1964, p. 88.

p. 163 **'You are worth a thousand men'** Christy, *The Price of Power*, p. 224.

p. 163 **'The beautiful palace'** von Hassell, *The von Hassell Diaries: 1938–1944*, p. 153.

p. 164 **This may have been to** Irving, *Hitler's War and the War Path*, p. 38. This office, Irving writes, had the monopoly of wiretapping from April

1933. Its printed reports on brown paper were called the 'Brown Pages', and were distributed to senior Nazis in locked dispatch boxes. On p. 39, Irving writes that the conversations of Julius Streicher, Unity Mitford, Princess Stephanie von Hohenlohe, her lover Fritz Wiedemann and other 'fringe actors' were routinely monitored.

p. 164 'I like to look at you' Janet Flanner, 'Annals of Collaboration – Equivalism II', *The New Yorker*, 6 October 1945, p. 36.

p. 164 Still out of earshot Raymond Aron, *The Vichy Regime: 1940–44*, New York: Macmillan, 1958, p. 267.

p. 164 'We would rather' Janet Flanner, 'Annals of Collaboration: Equivalism II', *The New Yorker*, 6 October 1945, p. 39; and Christy, *The Price of Power*, p. 225.

p. 165 The Germans had seized *Ibid.*, p. 123: 'we were reduced to three million tons of coal when 39½ millions represented our minimum needs'.

p. 165 'The last time I saw Paris' 'The Last Time I Saw Paris', *Time*, 23 December 1940. Music and lyrics copyright Chappell and Company, New York, 1940.

PART THREE: 1941

Chapter Sixteen: The Coldest Winter

p. 169 'Charles was amused' Gaston Bedaux, *La vie ardente de Charles Eugene Bedaux*, privately published, Paris, June 1959, p. 74.

p. 170 De Gaulle asked him to Milton Viorst, *Hostile Allies: FDR and De Gaulle*, New York: Macmillan, 1965, p. 60.

p. 170 'I consider this' Jim Christy, *The Price of Power: A Biography of Charles Eugene Bedaux*, New York: Doubleday and Company, 1984, p. 226.

p. 170 'Weygand and his' Viorst, *Hostile Allies*, p. 60.

p. 171 'To demonstrate his' Robert Murphy, *Diplomat among Warriors*, New York: Doubleday and Company, 1964, p. 107.

p. 171 Weygand called Bedaux Janet Flanner, 'Annals of Collaboration: Equivalism II', *The New Yorker*, 6 October 1945, p. 39.

p. 171 With Medicus's support Janet Flanner, 'Annals of Collaboration: Equivalism II', *The New Yorker*, 6 October 1945, p. 39.

p. 172 'Bunny gave me' Yves Pourcher, *Pierre Laval vu par sa fille d'après ses carnets intimes*, Paris: Le Cherche-Midi, 2002, p. 218.

p. 173 The American Hospital's board 'Minutes of a Special Meeting of the Board of Governors of the American Hospital of Paris', 13 February 1941,

Archives of the American Hospital of Paris, File: Correspondence and Reports, 1941, and Minutes, 19 September 1940 to 7 November 1941.

p. 173 'Another hospital year ... I report with' 'Report of the First Vice-President, March 20th, 1941', Archives of the American Hospital of Paris, File: Correspondence and Reports, 1941, and Minutes, 19 September 1940 to 7 November 1941.

Chapter Seventeen: Time to Go?

p. 174 'had a higher opinion' Fleet Admiral William D. Leahy, *I Was There: The Personal Story of the Chief of Staff to Presidents Roosevelt and Truman Based on his Notes and Diaries Made at the Time*, London: Victor Gollancz, 1950, p. 42.

p. 174 'Please tell her not' Clara Longworth de Chambrun, *Shadows Lengthen: The Story of My Life*, New York: Charles Scribner's Sons, 1949, p. 165.

p. 174 'Why should the United States' 'American Wife of French General Sees No Reason U.S. Should Fight', *Cincinnati Times-Star*, 3 October 1939, p. 1.

p. 175 'Extreme politeness was ... A considerable number' Longworth de Chambrun, *Shadows Lengthen*, p. 150.

p. 175 On 15 April, the hospital's Report of General Aldebert de Chambrun, Managing Director of the American Hospital of Paris, to the Board of Directors, 9 December 1944, p. 1, American Hospital of Paris Archives, American Hospital Reports: 1940–1944.

p. 175 'the same formula' Longworth de Chambrun, *Shadows Lengthen*, p. 166.

p. 175 Officially, the American Hospital Dorothy Lagard, *American Hospital of Paris: A Century of Adventure, 1906–2006*, Paris: Le Cherche-Midi, 2006, p. 51. (This is the official history of the hospital.) See also 'Proposal to affiliate to French Red Cross', at Meeting of the Board of Governors of the American Hospital of Paris, 4 April 1941, p. 2, American Hospital of Paris Archives, File: Correspondence and Reports 1941, and Minutes, 19 September 1940 to 7 November 1941.

p. 176 'a cable was sent' Letter from E. A. Sumner to Dr John Marshall, Rockefeller Foundation, 5 May 1941, American Library of Paris Archives, Box 9, File E.3.

p. 177 'When our popular directress' Longworth de Chambrun, *Shadows Lengthen*, p. 167.

p. 177 'Accordingly, here I was' *Ibid.*

p. 177 'overcoats, mufflers and gloves' 'Our Library in Paris', *New York Times*, 21 June 1945.

p. 177 'the individual designated' Longworth de Chambrun, *Shadows Lengthen*, p. 168.

p. 178 **When Maynard Barnes** 'Embassy in Paris Gets a Phone Call', *New York Times*, 26 August 1944, p. 5. 'Caffery Thanks Aids Who Held U.S. Embassy', *New York Herald Tribune*, 11 January 1945, p. 4. Mme Blanchard was assisted in maintaining the empty embassy by Pierre Bizet, the guardian; Georges Rivière, electrician; and Antoine Mertens, who took care of the ambassador's residence in the avenue d'Iéna.

p. 178 **After reporting to Ambassador Leahy** Leahy, *I Was There*, p. 42. Leahy wrote, 'The Germans had ordered our Embassy office in Paris to be closed, and Maynard Barnes, who had been in charge there since Bullitt's departure after the Armistice, arrived in Vichy *en route* to the United States. I tried to search his mind, but found only that he had a higher opinion of Laval than prevailed generally. I got a fairly unfavorable opinion of Barnes, because he did not seem to be in full agreement with what the President was trying to do.'

p. 178 **Close sailed to the United States** Cable from Allan Arragon, Morgan and Cie., Châtel-Guyon, Puy de Dôme, to Nelson Dean Jay, New York, 7 May 1941, American Hospital of Paris Archives, File: Correspondence, 1940–1945.

p. 178 'After the departure' Longworth de Chambrun, *Shadows Lengthen*, p. 165.

p. 178 'accumulated and buried' Leahy, *I Was There*, p. 41.

Chapter Eighteen: *New Perils in Paris*

p. 180 'I traveled to Vichy ... stressed how greatly' René de Chambrun, *Pierre Laval: Traitor or Patriot?*, New York: Charles Scribner's Sons, 1984, p. 68. See also Ralph Heinzen, 'Laval and the United States, Laval and Communism, Scuttling of the Fleet – Montoire', testimony in *France during the German Occupation, 1940–1944: A Collection of 292 Statements on the Government of Maréchal Pétain and Pierre Laval*, translated from the French by Philip W. Whitcomb, Palo Alto, CA: The Hoover Institution, Stanford University, vol. III, 1957, pp. 1601–3, for full details of the interview.

p. 180 'I have just received' Letter from Sumner W. Jackson to Edward B. Close, 3 June 1941, American Hospital of Paris Archives, File: Correspondence and Reports, 1941.

p. 181 **Keeping his War Risk** '*Bulletin d'Entrée*', American Hospital of Paris document, 1 June 1940, Massachusetts General Hospital Archives, File: Sumner Jackson.

p. 181 'JAY MORGAN BANK' Telegram from General de Chambrun to Nelson Dean Jay, 18 June 1940, American Hospital of Paris Archives, File: Correspondence and Reports, 1941.

p. 181 'practically all of the' Letter from William Nelson Cromwell to Nelson Dean Jay, 20 June 1941, American Hospital of Paris Archives, File: Correspondence, 1940–1945.

p. 181 'June deficit francs' Morgan and Cie, Cable, 9 July 1941, 41/8882 to [Nelson Dean] Jay, American Hospital of Paris Archives, File: Correspondence, 1940–1945.

p. 182 'Since the hospital' Letter from Max Shoop, Sullivan and Cromwell, to Nelson Dean Jay, J. P. Morgan and Company, 10 July 1941, American Hospital of Paris Archives, File: Correspondence, 1940–1945.

p. 182 'His breathing was' 'Financial Crisis in 1935, Attempted Assassination at Versailles', Statement of General Aldebert de Chambrun, *France During the German Occupation, 1940–1944*, vol. III, p. 1560.

p. 182 'He always paid' 'Memories of Laval, His Rescue of an Englishwoman', Statement by Countess Clara Longworth de Chambrun, *Ibid.*, p. 1362.

p. 183 'The car has left' René de Chambrun, *Pierre Laval: Traitor or Patriot?*, New York: Charles Scribner's Sons, 1984, p. 69.

p. 183 'I don't know' 'Financial Crisis in 1935, Attempted Assassination at Versailles', Statement of General Aldebert de Chambrun, p. 1560.

p. 183 'a tough 21-year-old' 'Terrorism Cuts Both Ways', *Time*, 8 September 1941.

p. 184 'I had taken a vow' Yves Pourcher, *Pierre Laval vu par sa fille, d'après ses carnets intimes*, Paris: Le Cherche-Midi, pp. 228–9.

p. 184 'a haven for French' 'Our Library in Paris', *New York Times*, 21 June 1945.

p. 184 On Memorial Day 'Services Curtailed in Occupied France', *New York Times*, 31 May 1941, p. 1.

p. 185 'We surely were' Robert Murphy, *Diplomat among Warriors*, New York: Doubleday and Company, 1964, p. 109.

p. 185 One of the twelve Coster and some of the other vice-consuls spoke French, but none could speak Arabic. Lack of linguistic expertise in the field would be a recurring motif in OSS operations, as in those of its successor, the Central Intelligence Agency. Another theme that emerged early was the agency's propensity for staging coups. Donovan almost immediately became involved in a misguided coup d'état attempt, when he set aside a secret fund of $50,000 to overthrow the Arab bey of Algiers and replace him with another chieftain who was pro-Allied. Murphy wrote, 'Nothing would have enraged our French colleagues more than this kind of monkey business, or been more ruinous to our chances of obtaining the support of French military forces. As for fifty thousand dollars! Our whole operation in Africa had not cost that much over a period of many months.' Murphy, *Diplomat among Warriors*, p. 110. Donovan was saved from folly by the US naval attaché in Tangier, Marine Colonel William A. Eddy. Murphy wrote that Eddy 'had grown up in the Middle East and was fluent in Arabic ... and no American knew more about Arabs or about power politics in Africa'.

p. 185 'I did not know ... I soon found' Fleet Admiral William D. Leahy, *I Was There: The Personal Story of the Chief of Staff to Presidents Roosevelt and Truman Based on his Notes and Diaries Made at the Time*, London: Victor Gollancz, 1950, p. 32.

p. 185 'found both the ... Gift books are distributed ... Since General de Chambrun' Ralph Heinzen, dispatch of 16 September 1941, United Press, Paris via Air Mail, original typescript, p. 3, American Hospital of Paris Archives, File: Newspaper cuttings.

p. 186 Aldebert and Clara de Chambrun 'Nazis Give Notice', *New York Times*, 22 May 1941, p. 1. The paper reported, 'There are approximately 2,000 [Americans] there.'

p. 187 'We have already' ... An order for Memorandum from General de Chambrun to Messrs Nelson Dean Jay and Edward B. Close, 6 November 1941, American Hospital of Paris Archives, File: Correspondence and Reports, 1941, and Minutes, 19 September 1940 to 7 November 1941.

Chapter Nineteen: Utopia in Les Landes

p. 188 'Distribution of products' Charles Emile Bedaux, 'The American-Radical, Equivalism: The Revolt of the Consumer', reprinted in *The Price of Power: A Biography of Charles Eugene Bedaux*, New York: Doubleday and Company, 1984, p. 301.

p. 189 In 1939, Bedaux Janet Flanner, 'Annals of Collaboration: Equivalism II', *The New Yorker*, 6 October 1945, p. 35.

p. 189 Hitler had since dismissed John Toland, *Adolf Hitler*, New York: Doubleday and Company, 1976, p. 508. Schacht's criticism ceased when he was told that, far from being an unofficial pogrom, *Kristallnacht* had been contrived by Hitler and his subordinates.

p. 189 'Monsieur, are you' Janet Flanner, 'Annals of Collaboration: Equivalism II', *The New Yorker*, 6 October 1945, p. 35.

p. 189 As Schacht continued *Ibid.*

p. 190 'This war will not' Christy, *The Price of Power*, p. 203. Gaston Bedaux, *La Vie ardente de Charles Bedaux*, privately published, Paris,

3 June 1959, p. 67; Gaston recalled that his brother said the same thing, but to the Prefect of Beauvais, M. Bussière.

p. 190 'He understood nothing' Christy, *The Price of Power*, p. 220.

p. 190 Bedaux asked for authorization Roquefort cheese is made in Roquefort-sur-Soulzon in Aveyron.

p. 190 Roquefort lay inland Janet Flanner, 'Annals of Collaboration: Equivalism II', *The New Yorker*, 6 October 1945, p. 42.

p. 191 The Bedaux model Jim Christy's and Janet Flanner's assessments of Roquefort disagree. Christy wrote that Bedaux created 'a prosperous, peaceful society, a haven of reason in a world gone mad' (*The Price of Power*, p. 231). Flanner held that the brier business was not run on an equivalist basis at all and that the whole scheme died quickly ('Annals of Collaboration: Equivalism II', p. 42). Yves Levant and Marc Nikitin went to Roquefort in 2004 to see what memories remained of the Bedaux experiment. They met five people who had worked at the paper mill. 'They all remember the visit of the Bedaux engineers and the coming of C. E. Bedaux himself, as well as the setting up of the Bedaux pay system in the paper mill of Roquefort ... On the other hand, none of these workers remembers any social project ... It is therefore highly likely for us that the social aspect of his work had been for C. E. Bedaux but an alibi aimed at finding favour in the eyes of his close friends and of posterity' (Yves Levant and Marc Nikitin, 'Should Charles Eugene Bedaux be Revisited?', Paper presented to the Eighteenth Annual Conference of the Business Research Unit, Cardiff Business School, Cardiff, Wales, 14–15 September 2006, pp. 22–3).

p. 191 'sold lock, stock' Christy, *The Price of Power*, p. 237.

p. 192 'the little nine-hole' Robert Murphy, *Diplomat among Warriors: Secret Decisions that Changed the World*, New York: Doubleday and Company, 1964, p. 180.

p. 192 'the roster of' Christy, *The Price of Power*, p. 238.

p. 192 'let it be known' 'Paraphrase of Telegram, From: Vichy (Paris), To: The Secretary of State, 29 September 1941', File Number 100-49901, Section Number 1, Serials 1–100, Subject: Charles E. Bedaux, US National Archives, College Park, Maryland.

Chapter Twenty: To Resist, to Collaborate or to Endure

p. 193 'There were a few' Sylvia Beach, *Shakespeare and Company*, London: Faber and Faber, 1960, p. 218.

p. 193 'young friend Violaine' Letter from Sylvia Beach to Rev. Sylvester Beach, 27 February 1940, Sylvia Beach Papers, Princeton University Library, CO108, Box 20, Folder 7.

p. 194 **'very pure, truly'** Paul Valéry, 'Discours sur Henri Bergson', 9 January 1941, Reproduced at http://www.uqac.uquebec.ca/zone30/ Classiques_des_sciences_sociales/index.html.

p. 194 **At Shakespeare and Company** Françoise Bernheim was born on 24 July 1912.

p. 194 **'I wasn't on good'** Sylvia Beach, Interview with Niall Sheridan, *Self Portraits: Sylvia Beach*, documentary film on Radio Telefis Eireann (RTE), Dublin, 1962.

p. 195 **While Rome burns ... soon after the 15th'** Letter from Sylvia Beach to Carlotta Welles Briggs, 14 August 1941, Sylvia Beach Papers, Princeton University Library, CO108, Box 58, Folder 16.

p. 195 **'Food is missing'** Letter from Sylvia Beach to Adrienne Monnier, 25 August 1941, Sylvia Beach Papers, Princeton University Library, CO108, Box 58, Folder 16. Original in French. My translation.

p. 196 **The last letter** Letter from Holly Beach Dennis to the Secretary of State, 21 October 1942, Sylvia Beach Papers, Princeton University Library, CO108, Box 14, Folder 18. Holly wrote that the last letter she had received from Sylvia was in June 1940, but she must have meant June 1941. There are many letters in the Beach Papers at Princeton and the Harry Ransom Center at the University of Texas, Austin, between the two sisters up to that date and one from Sylvia to Carlotta Briggs written on 14 August 1941.

p. 196 **A parcel of clothing** 'Nazis Give Notice', *New York Times*, 22 May 1941, p. 1. The paper wrote that the US Post Office stopped accepting parcels for France, 'because the British censors were seizing all packages as contraband'.

p. 196 **George Antheil, Ernest Hemingway** Noel Riley Fitch, *Sylvia Beach and the Lost Generation: A History of Literary Paris in the Twenties and Thirties*, New York: W. W. Norton and Company, 1983, p. 404.

p. 196 **At one of Candé's** Janet Flanner, 'Annals of Collaboration: Equivalism II', *The New Yorker*, 6 October 1945, p. 44.

p. 197 **'I advanced the philosophy'** Jim Christy, *The Price of Power: A Biography of Charles Eugene Bedaux*, New York: Doubleday and Company, 1984, p. 235.

p. 197 **'My idea was'** *Ibid.*, p. 236.

p. 198 **Janet Flanner wrote** Janet Flanner, 'Annals of Collaboration: Equivalism II', *The New Yorker*, 6 October 1945, p. 44.

p. 199 **'Many people in Germany'** Christy, *The Price of Power*, pp. 239–40.

p. 199 **His activities came** 'Memorandum for Mr. Tamm, Federal Bureau of Investigation', from H. E. Kreisker, Commander, USNR, Office of Naval Intelligence, Washington, 15 December 1941, United States National

Archives, College Park, Maryland, File 100-49901, Section Number 1, Serials 1–100.

p. 199 'The Paris stock market' Gerhard Heller, *Un Allemand à Paris*, Paris: Editions du Seuil, 1981, p. 64.

p. 200 'let it be known' 'Paraphrase of Telegram, From: Vichy (Paris): To: The Secretary of State; Date September 29, 1941', United States National Archives, College Park, Maryland, File 100-49901, Section Number 1, Serials 1–100.

p. 200 'Mrs. Rogers stated' 'COMMENTS ON THE ALLEGED CURRENT ACTIVITIES OF MR CHARLES BEDAUX IN OCCUPIED FRANCE', Department of State, Division of European Affairs, 24 November 1941, United States National Archives, College Park, Maryland, File 100-49901, Section Number 1, Serials 1–100.

p. 200 'in Rome, Italy ... He is a man' *Ibid.*, p. 2 of the memorandum.

p. 201 'Dear Mr. Hagerman ... He wishes to return' Letter from Charles E. Bedaux to W. E. Hagerman, Esq., 6 December 1941, United States National Archives, College Park, Maryland, File 100-49901, Section Number 1, Serials 1–100, Number 65167.

p. 203 They went to Les Landes Cable from W. E. Hagerman, to Secretary of State, 16 January 1942, Confidential, 'Whereabouts of Charles E. Bedaux, a naturalized American citizen', File Number 130– Bedaux, C.E., Document 100-49901-08, US National Archives, College Park, Maryland. Hagerman received Bedaux's letter on 31 December 1941.

Chapter Twenty-one: Enemy Aliens

p. 204 'was permitted to' *Ibid.* The *New York Times* reported that Jackson came from Germantown, Pennsylvania, although he was from Maine. Pennsylvania had been his last workplace in the United States.

p. 204 Ninety-five of the internees Beate Husser, *Le Camp de Royallieu à Compiègne: Etude historique*, Paris: Fondation pour la Mémoire de la Déportation, September 2001.

p. 204 The men were installed *Ibid.*, p. 48.

p. 204 'He came to tell me' Letter from René de Chambrun to New York, recipient's name blocked out by the FBI, 31 May 1945, Federal Bureau of Investigation Archives, File provided under a Freedom of Information Act request and unnumbered. FOIPA No. 1088544-001.

p. 205 One week after the Nazis '3 Americans Taken from Paris', *New York Times*, 24 December 1941, p. 3.

p. 205 A distinguished, 70-year-old Noel Riley Fitch, *Sylvia Beach and the Lost Generation: A History of Literary Paris in the Twenties and Thirties*, New York: W. W. Norton and Company, 1983, p. 404.

p. 205 'My German customers' Sylvia Beach, *Shakespeare and Company*, Faber and Faber, London, 1960, p. 219.

p. 206 At Christmas, Sylvia Sylvia Beach Notebook, Christmas presents, 1940–1945, Sylvia Beach Papers, Princeton University Library, CO108, Box 22, Folder 6.

p. 206 '"Well," I said ... He came back' Interview by Niall Sheridan with Sylvia Beach, *Self Portraits: Sylvia Beach*, documentary film on Radio Telefis Eireann (RTE), Dublin, 1962.

p. 207 'You ask me how' Adrienne Monnier, 'A Letter to Friends in the Free Zone', originally published in *Le Figaro Littéraire*, February 1942, in Adrienne Monnier, *The Very Rich Hours of Adrienne Monnier: An Intimate Portrait of the Literary and Artistic Life in Paris between the Wars*, translated with introduction and commentaries by Richard McDougall, New York: Charles Scribner's Sons, 1976, p. 407.

p. 207 'After escaping from' Sylvia Beach, 'Inturned', in Jackson Mathews and Maurice Saillet, *Sylvia Beach (1887–1962)*, Paris: Mercure de France, 1963, p. 136.

p. 207 'succeeded in stiring up' Clara Longworth de Chambrun, *Shadows Lengthen: The Story of My Life*, New York: Charles Scribner's Sons, 1949, p. 175.

p. 208 As soon as the United States David H. Stevens, Rockefeller Foundation, letter to Edward A. Sumner, 16 December 1941, American Library of Paris Archives, Box 9, File E.3, 1941.

p. 208 'the Library is being ... keep an open mind' Edward A. Sumner, letter to the Rockefeller Foundation, 19 December 1941, American Library of Paris Archives, Box 9, File E.3, 1941.

p. 208 'might become a tool' Mary Niles Mack, 'Between Two Worlds: The American Library in Paris during the War, Occupation and Liberation (1939–1945)', University of California at Los Angeles Department of Information Studies, p. 24.

p. 208 Clara was assisted *Ibid.*, p. 25.

p. 209 'The hospital feast' Longworth de Chambrun, *Shadows Lengthen*, p. 175.

p. 209 'we encouraged one another' *Ibid.*, p. 166.

PART FOUR: 1942

Chapter Twenty-two: First Round-up

p. 213 In mid-January, the Germans 'Vichy Curbs Americans', *New York Times*, 14 January 1942, p. 6.

p. 213 'no women yet interned' 'AMERICAN INTERESTS, OCCUPIED FRANCE, RUSH', Telegram from Huddle, US Embassy, Berne, to Secretary of State, 9 February 1942, US National Archives, College Park, Maryland, RG 389, Box 2141, Compiègne (2).

p. 213 'should be considered' *Ibid.*

p. 213 'The German authorities' 'Nazis Ease Plight of Seized Americans', United Press report, Vichy, *New York Times*, 29 January 1942, p. 6. There was only one American hospital in Paris, and enemy alien internees were not hostages under international law.

p. 213 'consider this information ... They are not allowed' Enclosure No. 2 to Dispatch No. 749, 2 February 1942, Letter from S. Pinckney Tuck, Counsellor of Embassy, to the Secretary of State, US National Archives, College Park, Maryland, RG 389, Entry 460A, Box 2141, File: Addresses, France, American Prisoner of War Information Bureau Records Branch.

p. 214 'At the same time' *Ibid.*

p. 214 The Vichy authorities 'Three U.S. Banks Licensed in France', *New York Times*, 31 January 1942, p. 25.

p. 215 'Institutions such as the' '200 Americans in Paris Said to Be Nazi Hostages', *New York Times*, 29 January 1942, p. 1, continued on p. 8.

p. 215 The American Chamber of Commerce 'American Places to Reopen in Paris', *New York Times*, 31 August 1944, p. 4.

p. 215 'These patients were' Otto Gresser interview in Kathleen Keating, 'The American Hospital in Paris during the German Occupation', 19 May 1981, 14-page typescript, p. 7, American Hospital of Paris Archives, File: German Occupation by Kathleen Keating and Various Other Histories, 1940–1944.

p. 215 Many of the 340 men 'American Freed in Paris', *New York Times*, 9 February 1942, p. 4.

p. 215 Dr Morris Sanders was 'Nazis Free U.S. Doctor, Morris Sanders Back at Work at Paris Hospital', *New York Times*, 2 May 1942, p. 2.

p. 215 'no other interference' Otto Gresser, 'History of the American Hospital of Paris', 14-page typescript, p. 6, American Hospital of Paris Archives, File: History by Otto Gresser.

p. 216 A proposal came in January Max Wallace, *The American Axis*, New York: St Martin's Press, 2003, p. 94.

p 216 'should be humanely' Quoted in *Ibid.*, p. 98.

p. 216 'It's the Nazis' Quoted in *Ibid.*, p. 244.

p. 216 'From this time on' General Aldebert de Chambrun, Managing Governor, Letter to the Board of Directors of the American Hospital of Paris, 9 December 1944, pp. 2–3, American Hospital of Paris Archives, File: Report, 1940–1944.

Endnotes

p. 217 'There were so few' Sylvia Beach, *Shakespeare and Company*, London: Faber and Faber, 1960, p. 219.

p. 217 'the Gestapo kept' Interview with Sylvia Beach by Niall Sheridan, *Self Portraits: Sylvia Beach*, documentary film on Radio Telefis Eireann (RTE), Dublin, 1962.

p. 217 'Hardest to put up' Adrienne Monnier, 'A Letter to Friends in the Free Zone', originally published in *Le Figaro Littéraire*, February 1942, in Adrienne Monnier, *The Very Rich Hours of Adrienne Monnier: An Intimate Portrait of the Literary and Artistic Life in Paris between the Wars*, translated with introduction and commentaries by Richard McDougall, New York: Charles Scribner's Sons, 1976, p. 404.

p. 217 'I shared the strange' Sylvia Beach, 'Inturned', in Jackson Mathews and Maurice Saillet, *Sylvia Beach (1887–1962)*, Paris: Mercure de France, 1963, pp. 136–7.

p. 217 'An average bottle' 'U.S. Films Appear in Paris Secretly', *New York Times*, 27 April 1942, p. 6.

p. 217 'Even the electricity' Ninetta Jucker, *Curfew in Paris: A Record of the German Occupation*, London: The Hogarth Press, 1960, p. 175.

p. 218 'No one who has' *Ibid.*

p. 219 In February 1942, Rittmeister Janet Flanner, 'Annals of Collaboration: Equivalism II', *The New Yorker*, 6 October 1945, p. 45. Flanner wrote of Ledebur's new posting, 'That simplified everything.'

p. 219 'I was therefore authorized' Gaston Bedaux, *La vie ardente de Charles Bedaux*, privately published, Paris, 3 June 1959, p. 49.

p. 219 'Charles told me' *Ibid.*, p. 104.

p. 219 'In 1941 ... he adopted' *Ibid.*, p. 79.

p. 220 'This idea crystallized' *Ibid.*

p. 220 'One day, my brother' *Ibid.*, pp. 79–80.

p. 221 'My dear Frederic ... My friend returned to see me' Enclosure, Foreign Travel Control, 'Memorandum for Mr. J. Edgar Hoover, Director, Federal Bureau of Investigation', 10 January 1944, Federal Bureau of Investigation Archives, File provided under a Freedom of Information Act request and unnumbered. FOIPA No. 1088544-001. (Note: of 109 pages reviewed by the FBI, only 83 pages were declassified for release. Most of those released had long passages blocked out.) Bedaux's letter was read by British Censorship, which gave a copy to the FBI. Mrs Waite received the letter and showed it to Ledebur.

p. 221 Frederic, as Friedrich called Federal Bureau of Investigation, Form Number 1, NY File Number 66-6045, 14 October 1942, Federal Bureau of Investigation Archives, File provided under a Freedom of Information Act request and unnumbered. FOIPA No. 1088544-001.

p. 222 'written on a typewriter' Agent E. P. Coffey, 'Memorandum for Mr. Tracy', 26 August 1942, Federal Bureau of Investigation Archives, File provided under a Freedom of Information Act request and unnumbered. FOIPA No. 1088544-001.

p. 222 'Our overwhelming superiority' 'France Bombed with U.S. Leaflets Giving Goals of War Production', *New York Times*, 6 February 1942, p. 6. Vidkun Quisling was the Nazi-imposed prime minister of Norway.

p. 223 'The U.S. is polite' 'U.S. Rejects Vichy's Explanation of Its Working With the Nazis', *Life*, 16 March 1942, p. 29.

Chapter Twenty-three: The Vichy Web

p. 224 'His father-in-law' René de Chambrun, *Pierre Laval: Traitor or Patriot?*, New York: Charles Scribner's Sons, 1984, p. 71.

p. 224 Monahan was on the board of governors 'Minutes of the Special Meeting of the Board of Governors of the American Hospital of Paris Held on April 4th, 1941', p. 2, in American Hospital of Paris Archives, File: Correspondence and Reports 1941, and Minutes, 19 September 1940 to 7 November 1941.

p. 225 'Laval knew how' Chambrun, *Pierre Laval: Patriot or Traitor?*, p. 72.

p. 226 'My father-in-law and I' *Ibid.*, p. 73. Georges Féat, a naval captain in Pétain's military cabinet, confirmed de Chambrun's version of events in his testimony for the Hoover Institution Collection. See 'Laval's Return in 1942', *France During the German Occupation, 1940–1944: A Collection of 292 Statements on the Government of Maréchal Pétain and Pierre Laval*, translated from the French by Philip W. Whitcomb, Palo Alto, CA: The Hoover Institution, Stanford University, 1957, vol. III, pp. 1564–5. However, in the French edition of the same volume, *La Vie de la France sous L'Occupation (1940–1944)*, Paris: Librarie Plon for Institut Hoover, 1957, pp. 1694–7, Féat stated that the impulse for the meeting came from Laval, who had met Marshal Hermann Goering in Paris in March 1942. Goering warned Laval, according to Féat, that Germany was going to take direct control of France.

p. 226 'Ralph Heinzen, of the United Press' Fleet Admiral William D. Leahy, *I Was There: The Personal Story of the Chief of Staff to Presidents Roosevelt and Truman Based on his Notes and Diaries Made at the Time*, London: Victor Gollancz, 1950, p. 109.

p. 226 On 1 April 1942, Josée From the diaries of Josée de Chambrun, in Yves Pourcher, *Pierre Laval vu par sa fille d'après ses carnets intimes*, Paris: Le Cherche-Midi, 2002, pp. 241–2. Josée's dates conflict with those given by René in his *Pierre Laval: Patriot or Traitor?*, pp. 72–3.

René wrote that he went to Vichy two days after 31 March, when Monahan contacted him. However, the date of the meeting between Pétain and Laval was 25 March, so it is more probable that Monahan contacted René some time before. Josée's diary dates with the references to her birthday, their stay at Château de Candé and Easter in Biarritz were made at the time. René's account was written forty years later.

p. 227 In Paris, Josée From the diaries of Josée de Chambrun, Pourcher, *Pierre Laval vu par sa fille d'après ses carnets intimes*, p. 242.

p. 227 A few days later *Ibid.*, p. 243.

p. 228 They went instead to Major-General Robert Gildea, *Marianne in Chains: In Search of the German Occupation of France, 1940–1944*, New York: Macmillan, 2002, p. 265.

p. 228 Oberg was the protégé Maurice Larkin, *France since the Popular Front: Government and People, 1936–1996*, Oxford: Clarendon Press, 1998, p. 98.

p. 228 'They all must go' H. R. Kenward, *Occupied France: Collaboration and Resistance, 1940–1944*, Oxford: Blackwell, 1985, p. 63. See also Marcel Ophuls's1971 documentary film, *Le Chagrin et la pitié*, in which Ophuls questioned René de Chambrun about Laval's refusal to spare the children.

p. 228 The Vélodrome d'Hiver was Robert O. Paxton, *Vichy France: Old Guard and New Order, 1940–1944*, New York: W. W. Norton, 1972, pp. 181–2. On p. 183, Paxton wrote, 'In the end, some 60,000–65,000 Jews were deported from France, mostly foreigners who had relied upon traditional French hospitality. Perhaps 6,000 French citizens also took that gruesome journey. Some 2,800 of the deportees got back.'

p. 229 'One. All close male' Gérard Walter, *Paris under the Occupation*, translated from the French by Tony White, New York: Orion Books, 1960, p. 188.

p. 229 Oberg hunted down 'Sparing the Butcher's Life', *Time*, 5 May 1958.

p. 229 'let it be known' Walter, *Paris under the Occupation*, p. 140.

p. 229 The star had a practical purpose *Ibid.*, p. 147. (Walter reproduced General Oberg's list of seventeen types of public space forbidden to Jews.)

p. 230 'as I went about' Sylvia Beach, *Shakespeare and Company*, London: Faber and Faber, 1960, p. 219.

p. 230 When Sylvia, Françoise and an American Noel Riley Fitch, *Sylvia Beach and the Lost Generation: A History of Literary Paris in the Twenties and Thirties*, New York: W. W. Norton and Company, 1983, p. 402.

p. 230 '"They dare …" he yelled' Sylvia Beach, 'French Literature Went Underground', *New York Herald Tribune*, Paris edition, 4 January 1945, p. 2.

p. 231 'Papa adores these' Fitch, *Sylvia Beach and the Lost Generation*, p. 403.

p. 231 'The morale in the camp ... From the hygienic' 'Camp for Interned Americans at Compiègne: Visited June 16, 1942, by Drs. Schirmer and J. de Morsier', from the Special Division, Department of State to the War Department, US National Archives, College Park, Maryland, RG 389, Entry 460A, Box 2142, General Subject File, 1942–1946, Camp Reports: France.

p. 231 'There are no air' 'Confidential, Report No. 1 – Compiègne', from Fred O. Auckenthaler and Dr Alfred Castelberg, from the Special Division of the Department of State to the War Department, Information Bureau, US National Archives, College Park, Maryland, RG 389, Box 2141, Compiègne (2).

p. 231 'British planes last' 'Camp Reported Hit', *New York Times*, 25 June 1942, p. 6.

p. 232 'four Americans were' '4 U.S. Internees Killed', *New York Times*, 26 July 1942, p. 4.

p. 232 'German planes, in reprisal' 'Paraphrase of Telegram Received, From: Bern; To: Secretary of State; Dated: August 4, 1942, 2 p.m.; Number 3586', From the Special Division of the Department of State to the War Department (PMG), 19 August 1942, US National Archives, College Park, Maryland, RG 389, Box 2141, Compiègne (2).

p. 232 'foreign airplane which ... since that occurence' *Ibid.*

p. 232 'Some of the internees' 'Confidential, Date of Visit: July 25th, 1942', From the Special Division of the Department of State to the War Department (Information Bureau), 3 September 1942, US National Archives, College Park, Maryland, RG 389, Box 2141, Compiègne (2).

p. 233 Almost as soon as Laval Sarah Fishman, 'Grand Delusions: The Unintended Consequences of Vichy France's Prisoner of War Propaganda', *Journal of Contemporary History*, vol. 26, no. 21, April 1991, p. 233. (Article is on pp. 229–54.)

p. 233 In June, Laval *Ibid.*, p. 239.

p. 233 Laval reached an accord *Ibid.*, p. 237.

p. 234 On 24 August 1942 'Black List', *Life*, 24 August 1942, p. 86.

p. 234 'My estimate of Charles' S. Pinckney Tuck, Vichy, to Secretary of State, 'Subject: Conversation with Mr. Charles Bedaux', 25 July 1942, US National Archives, College Park, Maryland, File and box numbers unknown.

p. 234 'Germany had been' Clara Longworth de Chambrun, *Shadows Lengthen: The Story of My Life*, New York: Charles Scribner's Sons, 1949, p. 169.

p. 235 'confronted by an officer ... I guarantee that ... I gave my word' *Ibid.*, p. 169–70.

p. 235 'seated at a tiny' *Ibid.*, p. 105. The yellow star decree was issued on 1 June 1942. See Walter, *Paris under the Occupation*, p. 144.

p. 235 'I met them walking' Longworth de Chambrun, *Shadows Lengthen*, p. 105.

p. 235 The library staff still Gérard Walter wrote that of 200,000 Jews, about half of them French nationals, in Paris before the German invasion, many had not been able to return after the June 1940 exodus. (In Greater Paris, the total had been about 300,000, according to most sources.) The Germans deported 5,000 foreign Jews in May 1941. 'In fact, the check made in November, 1941, established the number of Jews in Paris as 92,864 aged over fifteen, and 17,728 children between the ages of six and fifteen.' Walter, *Paris under the Occupation*, p. 138.

p. 236 'Without actually raising' Longworth de Chambrun, *Shadows Lengthen*, p. 170.

p. 236 'which being a few blocks' *Ibid.*, p. 173.

p. 236 'There was a deafening ... What had happened' *Ibid.*

p. 237 The culprit, 21-year-old Larry Collins and Dominique Lapierre, *Is Paris Burning?*, New York: Simon and Schuster, 1965, p. 279.

p. 237 On 20 October 1941 Fleet Admiral William D. Leahy, *I Was There: The Personal Story of the Chief of Staff to Presidents Roosevelt and Truman Based on His Notes and Diaries Made at the Time*, London: Victor Gollancz, 1950, p. 65.

p. 237 'Everyone on the platform' 'A Letter from Paris', *The Nation*, 10 January 1942, p. 39.

p. 237 After the killing Walter, *Paris under the Occupation*, p. 167.

p. 237 'harder and harder' Longworth de Chambrun, *Shadows Lengthen*, p. 174.

p. 237 'Général de Chambrun received' *Ibid.*

p. 238 In Princeton, New Jersey Sylvia Beach Notebook, Christmas presents, 1940–1945, Sylvia Beach Papers, Princeton University Library, CO108, Box 20, Unnumbered folder. The folder includes Holly's letter to Secretary of State Cordell Hull stating her doubts about the letters, but there is no reply from Hull. The handwriting in the letter allegedly written by Françoise Bernheim bears some resemblance to authentic letters by Françoise, which may imply that she was forced by the Germans to write the letter. Sylvia did not refer to the letters in her subsequent writing about the occupation.

Chapter Twenty-four: The Second Round-up

p. 239 'Before leaving ... I was given' Clemence Bock diary, quoted in Hal Vaughan, *Doctor to the Resistance: The Heroic Story of an American Surgeon and His Family in Occupied France*, Washington: Brassey's, 2004, p. 54.

p. 240 'and the English ... That evening we were at' *Ibid.*

p. 240 While Dr Jackson Janet Flanner, 'Annals of Collaboration: Equivalism III', *The New Yorker*, 13 October 1945, p. 34.

p. 241 The French driver Jim Christy, *The Price of Power: A Biography of Charles Eugene Bedaux*, New York: Doubleday and Company, 1984, p. 252.

p. 241 On 28 September, the French 'Embassy in Vichy Gets Arrest Data', *New York Times*, 29 September 1942, p. 7.

p. 241 'On the grounds of' 'Paraphrase of Telegram Received, From: (Paris) Vichy; To: Secretary of State, Washington, D.C.', 28 September 1942, Re: Arrests of Americans in Paris, US National Archives, College Park, Maryland, RG 389, Entry 460A, Box 2142, General Subject File, 1942–1946, Camp Reports: France.

p. 242 'circular letters urging' 'Embassy in Vichy Gets Arrest Data', *New York Times*, 29 September 1942, p. 7.

p. 242 'The new arrivals' Donald A. Lowrie, Enclosure No. 1 to No. 3721, dated 3 November 1942, from the American Legation, Berne, US National Archives, College Park, Maryland, RG 389, Box 2141, Compiègne (2).

p. 242 'that there was a fine ... The kitchen was' 'Report on Visit by Messrs. Auguste Senaud and Hemming Andermo to the American Internment Camp at Compiègne, October 16, 1942', Enclosure No. 1 to Despatch No. 3822 dated 16 November 1942, from American Legation, Berne, US National Archives, College Park, Maryland, RG 389, Box 2141, Compiègne (2).

p. 243 'The visit was passionate' Gaston Bedaux, *La vie ardente de Charles Bedaux*, Paris: privately published, 3 June 1959, p. 74.

p. 243 'My brother ... spoke to me' *Ibid.*, p. 75.

p. 243 'undertake a study' Robert Murphy to the Secretary of State, 'Interview with Mr. Charles E. Bedaux', 30 October 1942, Document Number 851T.OO/52, US National Archives, College Park, Maryland.

p. 243 'You are comfortably lodged' *Ibid.*

p. 244 He witnessed guards beating Hal Vaughan, *Doctor to the Resistance*, p. 56.

p. 244 'The Boches continued ... came to get me' Clemence Bock diary, quoted in *Ibid.*, pp. 54–5.

p. 244 'Several Americans Released' 'Several Americans Released in France, Dr. Jackson of Hospital at Neuilly Is Among Those Freed', *New York Times*, 3 October 1942, p. 6. The paper added that another released detainee was Mrs Charles Bedaux, 'but her French-born husband is still interned at St. Denis'. Bedaux was by then at Compiègne.

p. 245 He sent ambulances Hal Vaughan, *Doctor to the Resistance*, p. 62.

p. 245 Through trusted friends Goélette-Frégate's nomenclature was distinctly nautical. *Goélette* is French for schooner, *frégate* is frigate; and a *chaloupe* is a rowing boat. *Saint-Jacques* is a scallop. Although they helped *résistants* and Allied soldiers to go by sea from Spain and Portugal to England, all their operations were on land in France.

p. 245 Charles Bedaux, meanwhile, turned Robert Murphy to the Secretary of State, 'Interview with Mr. Charles E. Bedaux', 30 October 1942, Document Number 851T.OO/52, US National Archives, College Park, Maryland. Box and Serial Numbers unknown.

Chapter Twenty-five: 'Inturned'

p. 246 'the Gestapo would come' Interview with Sylvia Beach by Niall Sheridan, *Self Portraits: Sylvia Beach*, documentary film on Radio Telefis Eireann (RTE), Dublin, 1962.

p. 246 'I must pack up' Sylvia Beach, 'Inturned', in Jackson Mathews and Maurice Saillet, *Sylvia Beach (1887–1962)*, Paris: Mercure de France, 1963, p. 137.

p. 247 'dressed as though' Sylvia Beach, *Shakespeare and Company*, London: Faber and Faber, 1960, p. 137.

p. 247 'Caroline Dudley had been' Craig Lloyd, *Eugene Bullard: Black Expatriate in Jazz-Age Paris*, Athens, GA and London: University of Georgia Press, 2000, pp. 100–102.

p. 247 She was taking care of Gertrude Stein Donald Gallup (ed.), *The Flowers of Friendship: Letters Written to Gertrude Stein*, New York: Alfred A. Knopf, 1953, pp. 370–71.

p. 247 'After they had ... we were the only' Lansing Warren, '1,400 Americans Seized in France', *New York Times*, 30 September 1942, p. 1.

p. 247 'The arrests began' 'Report of the Swiss Consulate at Paris Regarding the Internment of American Citizens at Vittel', Enclosure No.1 to Despatch No. 3652 of 26 October 1942, from American Legation, Berne, US National Archives, College Park, Maryland, RG 389, Box 2142.

p. 248 'in a minute garden' Sylvia Beach, 'Inturned', p. 138.

p. 248 'A crowd was gathered' Drue Tartière, *The House near Paris*, New York: Simon and Schuster, 1946, p. 103.

p. 248 'On Sunday visitors' Donald A. Lowrie, YMCA representative, 'Report on Camps at Vittel and Compiègne', 29 October 1942, Enclosure No. 1 to Despatch No. 3732 dated 3 November 1942 from the American Legation, Berne, US National Archives, College Park, Maryland, RG389, Box 2142. The accounts of the internees, like Sylvia Beach and Drue Tartière, contradict those of the observers from the Red Cross and the YMCA on one important point. The women wrote that they were held in the monkey cage, and the observers' reports said they were held in the Salle des Fleurs or the restaurant of the zoo. The observers, however, appear not to have seen the women until they were sent to Vittel.

p. 248 'The first person' Tartière, *The House near Paris*, p. 104.

p. 249 'our lovely ... Noel Murphy' *Ibid.*, pp. 104–5.

p. 250 'My attention was' *Ibid.*, p. 105.

p. 250 'There were Americans' Beach, 'Inturned', p. 138.

p. 250 'busy trying to make' *Ibid.*, p. 138.

p. 250 'Sick women were lying ... did not seem' Tartière, *The House near Paris*, p. 105.

p. 251 'All night long' Interview with Sylvia Beach by Niall Sheridan, *Self Portraits: Sylvia Beach*, film documentary on Radio Telefis Eireann (RTE), Dublin, 1962.

p. 251 'As they were putting' Tartière, *The House near Paris*, pp. 104–5.

p. 251 'group of French collaborationists' *Ibid.*, p. 105.

p. 251 'Mrs. Charles Bedaux' 'Several Americans Released in France', United Press, Vichy, *New York Times*, 3 October 1942, p. 6.

p. 251 On Monday morning, 28 September 'Report of the Swiss Consulate at Paris Regarding the Internment of American Citizens at Vittel', Enclosure No. 1 to Despatch No. 3652 of 26 October 1942, from American Legation, Berne, US National Archives, College Park, Maryland, RG389, Box 2142.

p. 252 'I'm going to get' Tartière, *The House near Paris*, p. 108.

p. 253 'to a remote railway' Beach, 'Inturned', pp. 138–9.

p. 253 'took pleasure in throwing' Tartière, *The House near Paris*, p. 111.

p. 254 'As we marched along' *Ibid.*

p. 254 'The haste with which' 'Report of the Swiss Consulate at Paris Regarding the Internment of American Citizens at Vittel', Enclosure No.1 to Despatch No. 3652 of 26 October 1942, from American Legation, Berne, US National Archives, College Park, Maryland, RG 389, Box 2142.

p. 254 'While awaiting the opening' *Ibid.*

p. 254 Frontstalag 194 already Report of Red Cross delegates Rudolph Iselin and Dr Hans Wehrle, Vittel, 22 and 23 July 1942, p. 1, US National Archives, College Park, Maryland. RG 389, Box 2142.

p. 255 'paper, envelopes, flashlights ... There's nothing in there' Tartière, *The House near Paris*, p. 113.

p. 255 She looked terribly ... our big room' *Ibid.*, p. 114.

p. 256 'the Giraff' Readers should, by now, be accustomed to Sylvia Beach's idiosyncratic spelling (and punctuation).

p. 256 'All the previous reports' Donald A. Lowrie, YMCA representative, 'Report on Camps at Vittel and Compiègne', 29 October 1942, Enclosure No. 1 to Despatch No. 3732 dated 3 November 1942 from the American Legation, Berne, US National Archives, College Park, Maryland, RG 389, Box 2142.

p. 257 'tea, coffee, butter ... a dozen eggs' Tartière, *The House near Paris*, p. 116.

p. 257 'fattened up considerably' Beach, 'Inturned', p. 141.

p. 257 'We American internees' *Ibid.*, p. 142.

p. 257 'For the first few weeks' Ninetta Jucker, *Curfew in Paris: A Record of the German Occupation*, London: The Hogarth Press, 1960, pp. 158–9. See also pp. 159–64 on American women at Vittel.

p. 258 'antagonisms cropped up ... The Englishwomen hissed' Tartière, *The House near Paris*, p. 138.

p. 258 'beautiful fruit ... Set me free' Letter from Sylvia Beach to Adrienne Monnier, 15 October 1942, in French, translation mine, Maurice Saillet Collection, Harry Ransom Humanities Research Center, University of Texas at Austin, Series II, Box 2, File 6.

p. 258 'A can of condensed milk' Beach, 'Inturned', p. 143.

p. 258 In October 1942, Dr Edmond Gros 'Dr. Gros, Headed Neuilly Hospital', *New York Times*, 18 October 1942, Obituaries.

p. 259 'There is no one' Red Cross cable from N. D. Jay and E. B. Close to Mrs Edmund L. Gros, 20 October 1942, American Hospital of Paris Archives, File: Correspondence, 1940–1945.

p. 259 'English, Canadian or Free' Letter from Eugene J. Bullard to Army Information Office, Washington, DC, 22 September 1941, US National Archives, College Park, Maryland, RG 59, Box 5027, Document 842.2221.222 PS/PLS.

p. 260 'Your extended sojourn' Carisella and Ryan, *The Black Swallow of Death*, Boston: Marlborough House, 1972, p. 250.

Chapter Twenty-six: Uniting Africa

p. 261 'The German authorities ... the required raw materials' Gaston Bedaux, *La vie ardente de Charles Bedaux*, Paris: privately published, 3 June 1959, p. 81.

p. 261 **Dr Franz Medicus's Department** Janet Flanner, 'Annals of Collaboration: Equivalism III', *The New Yorker*, 13 October 1945, p. 34.

p. 262 **'This peanut scheme'** *Ibid.*, p. 32.

p. 262 **'When I put myself'** *Ibid.*, p. 34.

p. 263 **'The bewildered man'** Robert Murphy, *Diplomat among Warriors: Secret Decisions that Changed the World*, New York: Doubleday and Company, 1964, p. 121.

p. 264 **'I explained how seriously'** *Ibid.*, p. 123.

p. 265 **'Mr. Bedaux's release'** Robert Murphy, Memorandum to the Secretary of State, 'Subject: Interview with Mr. Charles E. Bedaux, Strictly Confidential', 30 October 1942, Document Number 851T.00/52, US National Archives, College Park, Maryland.

p. 265 **'had been definitely abandoned ... According to this plan'** *Ibid.*

p. 266 **'a leading member'** 'The Dangerous Middle', *Time*, 27 June 1955.

p. 266 **'sleek Jacques Lemaigre-Dubreuil'** 'Despair on the Even', *Time*, 12 June 1944.

p. 266 **A few days after this interview** Janet Flanner, 'Annals of Collaboration: Equivalism III', *The New Yorker*, 13 October 1945, p. 35. Jim Christy, *The Price of Power: A Biography of Charles Eugene Bedaux*, New York: Doubleday and Company, 1984, p. 257.

p. 266 **'Here opinions are divided'** *Ibid.*, p. 257.

p. 267 **'I am on the right side'** Federal Bureau of Investigation interview with Frederick Ledebur, Telemeter, 21 January 1944, US Department of Justice Communications Section, from FBI files supplied under Freedom of Information Act, unnumbered file, pp. 64692, 64693 and 64694. FOIPA No. 1088544-001.

p. 267 **'The last word'** Bedaux, *La vie ardente de Charles Bedaux*, p. 85.

Chapter Twenty-seven: Americans Go to War

p. 268 **'He treated me politely'** Drue Tartière with M. R. Werner, *The House near Paris: An American Woman's Story of Traffic in Patriots*, New York: Simon and Schuster, 1946, pp. 121–2.

p. 268 **Jean Fraysse, Drue's friend ... 'I can understand'** *Ibid.*, pp. 124–5.

p. 269 **'Darlin', it's awfully nice'** *Ibid.*, p. 127.

p. 269 **'Have a *crise*'** *Ibid.*, p. 145.

p. 270 **Von Weber came into my room ... 'I was thoroughly scared'** *Ibid.*, pp. 130–32.

p. 271 **'I think it's a disgrace'** *Ibid.*, p. 133.

p. 271 **'So, for two hours'** Robert Murphy, *Diplomat among Warriors: Secret Decisions that Changed the World*, New York: Doubleday and Company, 1964, p. 146.

p. 271 'seized the telegraph ... After a resistence' A. J. Liebling, *The Road Back to Paris*, London: Michael Joseph, 1944, pp. 197–8.

p. 271 **Charles Bedaux was ... the German officer** Janet Flanner, 'Annals of Collaboration: Equivalism III', *The New Yorker*, 13 October 1945, p. 35.

p. 272 **'By that time'** Murphy, *Diplomat among Warriors*, p. 154.

p. 272 **'Only a few hours'** *Ibid.*, p. 154.

p. 273 **'I am sending word ... Dr. Lévy and Dr. Pigache'** Tartière, *The House near Paris*, p. 134.

Chapter Twenty-eight: Murphy Forgets a Friend

p. 275 **'knocked on my door ... not knowing whether'** Keeler Faus, Diary, Sunday, 8 November 1942. (Faus's meticulous daily diaries for the years 1940 to 1944 were made available to me by his wife, Mme Colette Faus, in Paris.)

p. 276 **'The night before the Germans'** Margaret Collins Weitz, *Sisters in the Resistance: How Women Fought to Free France, 1940–1945*, New York: John Wiley and Sons, 1995, p. 198.

p. 276 **'one goon had'** Adam Nossiter, *The Algeria Hotel: France, Memory and the Second World War*, Boston: Houghton Mifflin, 2001, p. 163.

p. 276 **'a German stuck the point'** Keeler Faus, Diary, Wednesday, 11 November 1942.

p. 277 **'not retard French'** Jim Christy, *The Price of Power: A Biography of Charles Eugene Bedaux*, New York: Doubleday and Company, 1984, p. 268.

p. 277 **'I am carrying out'** John MacVane, 'Department of Amplification', letter to the editor, *The New Yorker*, 3 November 1945, pp. 80–81.

p. 278 **'Carrying through the study'** Christy, *The Price of Power*, p. 270.

p. 278 **'It is almost impossible'** A. J. Liebling, *The Road Back to Paris*, London: Michael Joseph, 1944, p. 198.

p. 279 **The New York Metropolitan ... 'the Fighting French'** 'Photo of the Week', *Life*, 7 December 1942, pp. 40–41.

Chapter Twenty-nine: Alone at Vittel

p. 280 **'His eyes filled'** Drue Tartière with M. R. Werner, *The House near Paris: An American Woman's Story of Traffic in Patriots*, New York: Simon and Schuster, 1946, p. 139.

p. 280 **Noel Murphy and Sarah Watson** The Foyer International des Etudiantes had been founded by Mrs John Jacob Hoff, an American who had been president of the Detroit YWCA. She gave it to the University of Paris. See 'Mrs. Labouchere, A Welfare Worker', *New York Times*, 14 April 1943, p. 23.

p. 280 A Hungarian priest with Drue Tartière said a Hungarian priest had arranged Miss Watson's release, and Sylvia Beach wrote that the person responsible was the rector of the University of Paris.

p. 280 'Suddenly, on Christmas … Ours [the Hôtel Central]' Sylvia Beach, 'Inturned', in Jackson Mathews and Maurice Saillet, *Sylvia Beach (1887–1962)*, Paris: Mercure de France, 1963, p. 140.

p. 281 *Dis à notre ami* Letter from Sylvia Beach to Adrienne Monnier, 30 December 1942, Maurice Saillet Collection, Harry Ransom Humanities Research Center, University of Texas at Austin, Box 3, Folder 2 (Vittel).

p. 281 Wilkinson had assured Letter from Tudor Wilkinson to Adrienne Monnier, 7 November 1942, Maurice Saillet Collection, Harry Ransom Humanities Research Center, University of Texas at Austin, Box 3, Folder 3.

p. 281 Christmas at Vittel 'Report on a Visit to the British and American Camp, Vittel, on Monday, January 4th, 1943, by Mr. August Senaud, War Prisoners' Aid of the YMCA, Paris Office', p. 2, US National Archives, College Park, Maryland, RG 389, Box 2142, Camp Reports: France, File: Vittel Vosges (Frontstalag 194).

p. 282 'Every day I went' Sylvia Beach, 'Inturned', p. 141.

Chapter Thirty: The Bedaux Dossier

p. 283 'From acquaintances in' Edmond Taylor, *Awakening from History*, Boston: Gambit, 1969, pp. 327–8.

p. 284 'Charles Bedaux, the stretch-out' Commander Harry C. Butcher, 'Diary – Butcher (November 30, 1942–January 7, 1943) (2)', Dwight D. Eisenhower Presidential Papers, 1916–1952, Dwight D. Eisenhower Library, Abilene, Kansas, Principal File, Box 166. (Ellipses in the original.)

p. 284 'I tried to broadcast' John MacVane, 'Department of Amplification', letter to the editor, *The New Yorker*, 3 November 1945, pp. 80–81.

p. 285 'German, Italian, French' Percy E. Foxworth to Director, FBI, 18 February 1942, Serial 100-49901-5, US National Archives, College Park, Maryland.

p. 285 Bedaux's name 'Paraphrase of Telegraph, Vichy (Paris) to Secretary of State, September 29, 1941, Subject: Charles E. Bedaux', File Number 100-49901, Section Number 1, Serials 1–100, US National Archives, College Park, Maryland.

p. 285 'no futher action' P. E. Foxworth, Assistant Director, New York, to Director, Washington, 29 April 1942, 100-49901-6X, US National Archives, College Park, Maryland. Foxworth enclosed a verbatim copy of a report on Marie Claude Carpenter, 'formerly secretary to Henri Bidaux'. This gossip included her answer to a question in New York about 'Bidaux's'

current activities. 'Working for the Germans, of course,' was the laconic
reply. The conversation further revealed that at that particular moment
Bidaux [sic] was 'working for the Germans in Spain'. If he wanted to close
the file at that time, his enclosure was bound to keep it open.

p. 286 'where they frequented ... Mr. Bedaux's brother' Worthing E.
Hagerman, Lisbon, 'Memorandum to Secretary of State, Whereabouts of
Charles E. Bedaux, a naturalized American citizen', 9 June 1942, 100-
49901-8, US National Archives, College Park, Maryland.

p. 286 'It is also requested' J. Edgar Hoover to Special Agent in Charge,
New York, 1 August 1942, FBI Files, unnumbered, released under
Freedom of Information Act, FOIPA No. 1088544-001.

p. 286 'He is reported' N. L. Pieper, FBI, San Francisco, to Director, FBI,
2 September 1942, FBI Files, unnumbered, released under Freedom of
Information Act. FOIPA No. 1088544-001.

p. 287 'Fred Ledebur is alleged' G. R. Levy, FBI, New York, 'Memorandum
for Mr. Ladd, Re: Frederic Ledebur, Espionage – G', 31 July 1942, FBI
Files, unnumbered, released under Freedom of Information Act. FOIPA
No. 1088544-001.

p. 287 'Will you please forward' Wendell Berge, Assistant Attorney
General, 'Memorandum for the Director, FBI, Re: Charles E. Bedaux',
16 October 1942, FBI Files, unnumbered, released under Freedom of
Information Act. FOIPA No. 1088544-001.

PART FIVE: 1943

Chapter Thirty-one: Murphy versus Bedaux

p. 291 'there are six documents' John Edgar Hoover, Director, FBI,
'Memorandum for Mr. Tolson, Mr. Tamm, Mr. Ladd', Document 100-
49901-[illegible], Federal Bureau of Investigation Archives, file
provided under a Freedom of Information Act request. FOIPA No.
1088544-001.

p. 292 'inquire of General Eisenhower' John Edgar Hoover, Director, FBI,
'Memorandum for the Attorney General', 4 January 1943, Federal
Bureau of Investigation Archives, unnumbered file provided under a
Freedom of Information Act request and unnumbered. FOIPA No.
1088544-001. (The FBI and Department of Defense declined to supply
the author with the War Department's file on Bedaux that Ladd had
attached to the memorandum.)

p. 292 'lodged comfortably in a villa' Gaston Bedaux, *La Vie ardente de
Charles Bedaux*, Paris: privately published, 3 June 1959, p. 85.

p. 292 **'I have had photostatic'** D. M. Ladd, 'Memorandum for the Director', 10 January 1943, Federal Bureau of Investigation Archives, file provided under a Freedom of Information Act request and unnumbered. FOIPA No. 1088544-001.

p. 293 **'Mr. Foxworth attempted'** G. O. Burton, 'Memorandum for Mr. D. M. Ladd', Federal Bureau of Investigation Archives, File 100-49901-30 provided under a Freedom of Information Act request. FOIPA No. 1088544-001.

p. 293 **'Charles E. Bedaux, friend'** 'Bedaux Arrested in Deals with Foe', *New York Times*, 14 January 1943, p. 1. See also 'Windsors' Host Held as Trader with the Enemy', *Chicago Daily Tribune*, 14 January 1943, p. 5.

p. 293 **'quite disappointing'** D. M. Ladd, 'Memorandum for Mr. Tamm', 14 January 1943, Federal Bureau of Investigation Archives, File No. 100-49901-22 provided under a Freedom of Information Act request. FOIPA No. 1088544-001.

p. 293 **Someone, probably in the State** 'Too Many Systems', *Time*, 25 January 1943. *Time* wrote, 'Unofficially it was said he had tried to buy up the North African orange crop for the Nazis. Bedaux's record would indicate that his zest for chasing dollars had involved him more deeply.'

p. 294 **'a man who loves danger'** 'Bedaux Arrested in Deals with Foe', *New York Times*, 14 January 1943, p. 5.

p. 294 **'sadness and disheartenment'** Bedaux, *La Vie ardente de Charles Bedaux*, p. 103.

Chapter Thirty-two: Sylvia's War

p. 298 **'After receiving your'** Letter from Tudor Wilkinson to Adrienne Monnier, 7 November 1942, Maurice Saillet Collection, Harry Ransom Humanities Research Center, University of Texas at Austin, Box 3, Folder 3.

p. 298 **'I stood there in shock'** Mary Berg (Miriam Wattenberg), *The Diary of Mary Berg: Growing Up in the Warsaw Ghetto* (originally published in English as *Warsaw Ghetto: A Diary*, New York: L. B. Fischer, 1945), translation from the Polish by Susan Glass, Oxford: Oneworld, 2006, p. xxviii.

p. 299 **'While we are waiting'** *Ibid.*, p. 210.

p. 299 **'Not a trace of the snow'** *Ibid.*, p. 213.

p. 299 **'When I told them'** *Ibid.*, p. 214.

p. 299 **'His wife and child ... It seems that the Germans'** *Ibid.*, p. 234.

p. 300 **'A problem which concerns'** 'Report on Visit to the Internment Camp of Vittel by Mrs. Andermo and Messrs. Senaud and Andermo on

February 8, 1943', US National Archives, College Park, Maryland, RG 389, Box 2142, File: Vittel Vosges (Frontstalag 194), Camp Reports: France.

p. 300 'Resistance was overcome' Sylvia Beach, 'Inturned', in Jackson Mathews and Maurice Saillet, *Sylvia Beach (1887–1962)*, Paris: Mercure de France, 1963, p. 143.

p. 300 'There is no more wonderful ... The Internees try' Berg, *The Diary of Mary Berg*, p. 216.

p. 300 'The relations between them ... The Nazis gave the' *Ibid.*, p. 218.

p. 300 Sylvia's detention allowed Letter from Holly Beach Dennis to Sylvia Beach, 28 January 1945, in which Holly wrote, 'I have heard from you three times since June 1940: your letter from camp of October 1942, which reached me in March 1943; your letter of October 1944 (mailed in Washington), which I received on October 10th and your post card of October 16th, 1944.' Sylvia Beach Collection, CO108, Box 14, Folder 18, Princeton University Library.

p. 301 'And what if my dear' Sylvia Beach, 'Inturned', p. 143.

p. 301 'I came back to Paris' Interview with Sylvia Beach by Niall Sheridan, *Self Portraits: Sylvia Beach*, documentary film for Radio Telefis Eireann (RTE), Dublin, 1962.

p. 301 'Miss Sarah Watson undertook' Sylvia Beach, *Shakespeare and Company*, London: Faber and Faber, 1960, p. 220.

p. 302 'nobody let on' Interview with Sylvia Beach by Niall Sheridan, *Self Portraits: Sylvia Beach*, documentary film for Radio Telefis Eireann (RTE), Dublin, 1962.

p. 302 'active in bringing out' Sylvia Beach, 'French Literature Went Underground', *New York Herald Tribune*, Paris edition, 4 January 1945, p. 2.

p. 302 '*Ce volume, publié*' Beach, *Shakespeare and Company*, p. 221. 'Midnight Editions', *Time*, 25 September 1944.

p. 303 'Sylvia has been to see' Handwritten letter from Adrienne Monnier to Maurice Saillet, 30 March 1943, 6 pages (this passage is on p. 6), Maurice Saillet Collection, Harry Ransom Humanities Research Center, University of Texas at Austin, Box 3, Folder 3. Original in French. My translation.

p. 303 'to keep them from' Drue Tartière, with M. R. Werner, *The House near Paris: An American Woman's Story of Traffic in Patriots*, New York: Simon and Schuster, 1944, p. 206.

Chapter Thirty-three: German Agents?

p. 304 'The society charged' 'De Chambrun Criticized', *New York Times*, 7 March 1943.

p. 304 'restore the dignity' Michael R. Marrus and Robert O. Paxton, *Vichy France and the Jews*, New York: Basic Books, 1981, p. 312.

p. 304 For a time, Vichy *Ibid*., pp. 310–15.

p. 305 'organizing a series' Cable from the Ministry of Economic Warfare to W. Simpson, HM Embassy, Buenos Aires, Argentina, 23 July 1943, R.700/924/2, British National Archives, Kew.

p. 305 No evidence emerged Secret cable from F. W. McCombe, British Embassy, Washington, DC, 30 November 1943, to H. S. Gregory, Trading with the Enemy Department, 24 Kingsway, London WC2, Number: TED.275, British National Archives, Kew: 'By a very roundabout process I learn that you have asked Censorship to include the two Polignacs [Guy and Gladys de Polignac], René de Chambrun etc., in the Special Watch List, presumably as part of the chase which involves Laval, the Bank of Worms and Eastern Provinces Administration Ltd.'

p. 305 Although his arrest made Gaston Bedaux, *La Vie ardente de Charles Bedaux*, Paris: privately published, 3 June 1959, p. 85.

p. 305 United Press correspondent Geoffrey Warner, *Pierre Laval and the Eclipse of France*, New York: Macmillan, 1968, p. 359. Warner relied mainly on documents from German military intelligence, the Abwehr, that survived the war.

p. 306 'The Germans are going' Fleet Admiral William D. Leahy, *I Was There: The Personal Story of the Chief of Staff to Presidents Roosevelt and Truman Based on his Notes and Diaries Made at the Time*, London: Victor Gollancz, 1950, pp. 73–4.

p. 307 'Dr Keller was a repulsive' André Enfière, 'Edouard Herriot et Pierre Laval', testimony in *La Vie de la France sous L'Occupation (1940–1944)*, vol. II, Paris: Librairie Plon, 1957, p. 1067.

p. 307 'I must admit that' *Ibid*., pp. 1067–8.

p. 308 'No indication subject ... Acquaintances characterize subject' FBI Form Number 1, 'Title: Frederic Ledebur', 8 April 1943, Federal Bureau of Investigation Archives, file provided under a Freedom of Information Act request and unnumbered. FOIPA No. 1088544-001.

p. 309 'Did Watchdog, who was' 'Minutes of the Working Committee, Hemisphere Intelligence Conference, Wednesday, March 24, 1943, New York City', Federal Bureau of Investigation Archives, file provided under a Freedom of Information Act request and unnumbered. FOIPA No. 1088544-001.

p. 309 'Charles Eugene Bedaux' The FBI refused to provide the transcript of that interview and other documents sixty years later, despite repeated Freedom of Information appeals.

Chapter Thirty-four: A Hospital at War

p. 310 On 4 April 1943 '133 Flying Fortresses Raid Paris Plant After R.A.F. Hammers at Essen; U.S. Units Gain Six Miles in Tunisia', *New York Times*, 5 April 1943, p. 1.

p. 311 'German propaganda was' Ninetta Jucker, *Curfew in Paris: A Record of the German Occupation*, London: The Hogarth Press, 1960, p. 75.

p. 311 'reached its crucial point' General Aldebert de Chambrun, Managing Governor, Letter to the Board of Directors of the American Hospital of Paris, 9 December 1944, p. 4, American Hospital of Paris Archives, File: Report, 1940–1944.

p. 311 'He was suffering' Jucker, *Curfew in Paris*, pp. 168–9.

p. 312 'The problem was solved' Clara Longworth de Chambrun, *Shadows Lengthen: The Story of My Life*, New York: Charles Scribner's Sons, 1949, p. 174.

p. 312 Otto Gresser recalled Otto Gresser, 'Histoire de l'Hôpital Américain – 5ème Partie', *American Hospital of Paris Newsletter*, vol. III, no. 11, March 1975, p. 4.

p. 312 'So ... we did some' Otto Gresser interview in Kathleen Keating, 'The American Hospital in Paris during the German Occupation', 19 May 1981, 14-page typescript, p. 7, American Hospital of Paris Archives, File: German Occupation by Kathleen Keating and Various Other Histories, 1940–1944, p. 10. See also Otto Gresser, 'History of the American Hospital of Paris', 28 September 1978, 14-page typescript, p. 5, Archives of the American Hospital of Paris, File: History by Otto Gresser: 'Fearing a possible shortage of water in case of bombardment, after digging in the middle of the garden, an underground Seine was discovered ready to be used in case of emergency.' The well was not needed.

p. 312 René Rocher, the French Rocher, who had also had a successful career as an actor, was one of a series of temporary directors during the war. They were all filling in for the Odéon's longstanding Jewish director, Paul Abram, who was dismissed when the Germans occupied Paris in 1940. He resumed the directorship in 1945.

p. 312 '*The Life and Death*' Longworth de Chambrun, *Shadows Lengthen*, p. 176.

p. 312 'The play is short' *Ibid.*, p. 177. The book actually states, 'The play is short, demanded no cuts, and could *not* be produced even during the brief playing-time which was allowed, for curtains had to be down and lights extinguished by ten-fifty.' I have removed 'not', which appears to be a typographical error.

p. 313 'How can we begin' *Ibid.*, p. 177.

p. 313 *King John* opened Yves Pourcher, *Pierre Laval vu par sa fille d'après ses carnets intimes*, Paris, Le Cherche-Midi, 2002, p. 286.

p. 313 A week later, someone Gérard Walter, *Paris Under the Occupation*, translated from French by Tony White, New York: Orion Press, 1960, p. 191.

Chapter Thirty-five: The Adolescent Spy

p. 314 German U-boats trawled My father, Commander Charles Glass, Jr, took part in the convoys and recalled German torpedoes sinking ships around his. One U-boat torpedo missed his ship by a few feet.

p. 314 A picturesque town 'British Photograph Bombing of the Nazi U-Boat Hideout at St. Nazaire', *Life*, 11 May 1942, pp. 30–31.

p. 314 During one raid 'U.S. Raid Blasts St. Nazaire; 6 Bombers Lost in Battle', *New York Times*, 17 February 1943, p. 1.

p. 314 'the toughest target' 'Saint Nazaire Raided; Clouds Curb Blow', *New York Times*, 3 May 1943, p. 5.

p. 315 In Paris, R went Hal Vaughan, *Doctor to the Resistance: The Heroic Story of an American Surgeon and His Family in Occupied France*, Washington: Brassey's, 2004, pp. 71–6, based on lengthy interviews with Phillip Jackson.

Chapter Thirty-six: Clara under Suspicion

p. 318 'new and peculiar ... in case we' Clara Longworth de Chambrun, *Shadows Lengthen: The Story of My Life*, New York: Charles Scribner's Sons, 1949, p. 186.

p. 318 When Clara and Hilda walked 'News of the American Library', *Library Journal*, December 1944, p. 1068. See also 'Milton Lord Reports from Paris', *Library Journal*, July 1945, pp. 622–4.

p. 319 'If they have been circulated' Longworth de Chambrun, *Shadows Lengthen*, p. 187.

p. 319 'Madame, I am very' *Ibid.* (Italics in original.)

p. 319 To avoid further German 'News of the American Library', *Library Journal*, December 1944, p. 1068.

p. 320 After three years Longworth de Chambrun, *Shadows Lengthen*, pp. 189–90.

p. 320 But, in New York, expatriate 'French Add a "Little Bit of Paris" to Old New York for Bastille Day', *New York Times*, 15 July 1943, p. 13.

p. 321 **'Portrait of an American'** Quoted in Vaughan, *Doctor to the Resistance*, p. 91.

p. 321 **Sumner was operating** *Ibid.*, pp. 79–80. Phillip Jackson recounted the story to Vaughan in Paris in 2002.

p. 323 **'a nice place … Everything, bed and linens'** After-action report, quoted in *Ibid.*, p. 93.

p. 323 **'I suppose my mother'** *Ibid.*, p. 94.

p. 324 **In late October** Frank Griffiths, *Winged Hours*, London: William Kimber, 1981, p. 123.

p. 324 **Spanish police arrested Joe** *Ibid.*, p. 178.

p. 324 **Back in England** Of the seven other B-17 crew who survived, two were captured and the other five received help from the Resistance to escape to Spain.

Chapter Thirty-seven: Calumnies

p. 325 **Her son and his wife** Château Haut-Brion had belonged to American banker Clarence Dillon since 1935. Weller was Dillon's cousin. Aldebert de Chambrun had alerted Dillon to the sale of Haut-Brion, and Pierre Laval was Weller's sponsor for French citizenship. Dillon was a mentor to René de Chambrun during his time in New York.

p. 325 **René rarely missed** From the diary of Josée de Chambrun, in Yves Pourcher, *Pierre Laval vu par sa fille d'après ses carnets intimes*, Paris: Le Cherche-Midi, 2002, pp. 302–4.

p. 326 **'brought to America'** Paul Wohl, 'Laval's Personal Fortune Reported Safe in US', *New York Herald Tribune*, 5 December 1943, p. 1.

p. 326 **No proof was offered** When Laval was tried for treason in 1945, financial impropriety was not among the many charges against him. His biographers do not mention them.

p. 326 **René admitted that** René de Chambrun, *Mission and Betrayal, 1940–1945: Working with Franklin Roosevelt to Help Save Britain and France*, Palo Alto, CA: Hoover Institution Press, 1992, p. 66.

p. 326 **'At present he is attached … The Paris building'** Paul Wohl, 'Laval's Personal Fortune Reported Safe in US', *New York Herald Tribune*, 5 December 1943, p. 1.

p. 327 **The most likely source** The British, who circulated anti-de Chambrun rumours throughout the war, may have found in Paul Wohl a vulnerable conduit for disinformation. Wohl was born in Berlin in 1901, and he had moved to the United States in 1938 as a correspondent for the Czech press. In 1941, the *Christian Science Monitor* hired him, although he also wrote for other papers, including the *New York Herald Tribune*.

The US did not intern him as an enemy alien, although it could have. He was unmarried and kept forty-seven turtles at his apartment in Greenwich Village. See his obituary, 'Paul Wohl, Journalist, Dead; Wrote About Political Affairs', *New York Times*, 4 April 1985.

p. 327 'instructing that they be' D. M. Ladd, FBI Washington, 'Memorandum for Mr. E. A. Tamm', 12 January 1943, Document 100-49901-29, US National Archives, College Park, Maryland.

p. 327 'My own Charles darling' The translations of the three letters with a covering letter from the Adjutant General's office to the Justice Department are reproduced in C. M. Hardwick, *Time Study in Treason: Charles E. Bedaux, Patriot or Collaborator*, Chelmsford, Essex: Peter Horsnell, 1990, pp. 61–3.

p. 329 'an invaluable, meticulous' Janet Flanner, 'Annals of Collaboration: Equivalism III', *The New Yorker*, 13 October 1945, p. 35.

p. 329 'code telegrams; business' *Ibid.*, p. 36.

p. 330 'Coming home from' Clara Longworth de Chambrun, *Shadows Lengthen: The Story of My Life*, New York: Charles Scribner's Sons, 1949, pp. 175–6.

PART SIX: 1944

Chapter Thirty-eight: The Trial of Citizen Bedaux

p. 335 'extremely straightforward person' FBI Form Number 1, Title: Changed, Frederic Ledebur, Mrs. Isabella Cameron Waite, File No. 65-6045 KJH, 25 February 1943, New York.

p. 335 But Bedaux, despite Gaston Bedaux, *La Vie ardente de Charles Bedaux*, Paris: privately published, 3 June 1959, p. 89.

p. 336 'I will be here' Jim Christy, *The Price of Power: A Biography of Charles Eugene Bedaux*, New York: Doubleday and Company, 1984, p. 282.

p. 336 'What assurance do' *Ibid.*, p. 280.

p. 337 'he showed an ebullience' Janet Flanner, 'Annals of Collaboration: Equivalism III', *The New Yorker*, 13 October 1945, p. 39.

p. 337 'that [Frederic] Ledebur' J. Edgar Hoover, FBI cable to SAC, San Francisco, 18 January 1944, from FBI files supplied under Freedom of Information Act, unnumbered file. FOIPA No. 1088544-001.

p. 337 'OUR WASHINGTON ATTORNEY' FBI File Number 65-3349, 'Title: Frederick George Ledebur, Espionage G[erman]', 12 typewritten pages, from FBI files supplied under Freedom of Information Act, FOIPA No. 1088544-001.

p. 338 'in the event BEDAUX' *Ibid.*

p. 338 'I received your ... It was always' Gaston Bedaux, *La Vie ardente de Charles Bedaux*, p. 110. (The letter is reproduced in its entirety in French, but wartime restrictions meant that Gaston's card and Charles's letter would have taken circuitous routes through neutral countries to reach their destinations.)

p. 338 'Well, one of these days' Christy, *The Price of Power*, p. 283.

p. 339 'Dear friend, I cannot' *Ibid.*, p. 295.

p. 340 'is seriously ill' 'Charles Bedaux Seriously Ill in Miami Hospital', Associated Press, Miami, 17 February 1944, in *Chicago Daily Tribune*, 18 February 1944, p. 7.

Chapter Thirty-nine: The Underground Railway

p. 341 'Just have news' Copy of Incoming Cablegram, Max Shoop to Nelson Dean Jay, 9 February 1944, American Hospital of Paris Archives, File: Correspondence, 1940–1945.

p. 341 **Miss M. Thevoz, former chief** The official list of *Personnel reste à l'Hôpital le 14 Juin 1940* refers to Mlle M. Thevoz, *Directrice des Infirmières*, directress of nurses. Archives of the American Hospital of Paris, File: Personnel, 1940.

p. 341 'understand Shoop's reference' Letter from N. D. Jay to Leslie Allen, 23 Wall Street, New York, NY, 14 February 1944, American Hospital of Paris Archives, File: Correspondence, 1940–1945.

p. 341 'Please say that none' Second letter from N. D. Jay to Leslie Allen, 23 Wall Street, New York, NY, 14 February, American Hospital of Paris Archives, File: Correspondence, 1940–1945. It is not clear why Jay wrote two letters to Leslie Allen, giving the same information in different words, on the same day.

p. 341 **The board attributed** Neal H. Petersen (ed.), *From Hitler's Doorstep: The Wartime Intelligence Reports of Allen Dulles, 1942–1945*, University Park, PA: Pennsylvania State University Press, 1996, p. 544. Shoop's former partner in the Paris office of Sullivan and Cromwell, Philippe Monod, was OSS Agent 405 with the code name Martel. Monod, a Frenchman, represented the combined Resistance body, *Forces Françaises Combattantes de la Metropole* (FFCM), with Allen Dulles in Switzerland (*ibid.*, p. 53). Shoop, who liaised between the OSS and the Resistance, had known Dr Jackson in Paris. He and Monod should have had details of Dr Jackson's escape network.

p. 342 'about starvation and the family's' 'Tracing Noted Surgeon', *Boston Herald*, 5 September 1944, in Massachusetts General Hospital Archives, File: Sumner Jackson.

p. 342 'He was drawn' Diary of Clemence Bock, p. 9, quoted in Hal Vaughan, *Doctor to the Resistance: The Heroic Story of an American Surgeon and His Family in Occupied France*, Washington: Brassey's, 2004, p. 108.

p. 342 'He from time to time' Otto Gresser interview, Kathleen Keating, 'The American Hospital in Paris During the German Occupation', 14-page typescript, p. 6, American Hospital of Paris Archives, File: German Occupation by Kathleen Keating and Various Other Histories, 1940–1944.

p. 343 'Nothing, of course, could' Alice-Leone Moats, *No Passport for Paris*, New York: G. P. Putnam's Sons, 1945, p. 172.

p. 343 'were directly connected … Usually the men' *Ibid.*, p. 193.

p. 344 'Not daring to knock … "Gee", one of the boys' *Ibid.*, pp. 195–6.

p. 344 Jane and Rosemary told Alice-Leone … 'It was safe' *Ibid.*, p. 199.

p. 345 Rosemary prepared Carlow *Ibid.*, p. 200.

p. 346 'You will always be followed … Once they have grilled' *Ibid.*, p. 180.

p. 346 In February 1944, Drue Drue Tartière with M. R. Werner, *The House near Paris: An American Woman's Story of Traffic in Patriots*, New York: Simon and Schuster, 1944, pp. 235–6.

Chapter Forty: Conspiracies

p. 347 'Charles E. Bedaux was' 'Bedaux Legendary As Mystery Man', *New York Times*, 20 February 1944, p. 28.

p. 347 'consider whether he should' 'Bedaux Ends Life as He Faces Trial on Treason Count', *New York Times*, 20 February 1944, p. 1.

p. 347 'Bedaux submitted a list' Edwin A. Lahey, 'Bedaux and His Friends', *New Republic*, 6 March 1944, p. 308. (Full article: pp. 307–8.)

p. 348 'They subjected investigators' 'Dead Men Don't Blab', *The Nation*, no. 158, 11 March 1944, p. 297.

p. 348 'I had been so used' Gaston Bedaux, *La Vie ardente de Charles Bedaux*, Paris: privately published, 3 June 1959, p. 88.

p. 349 'Perhaps I would not' Edmond Taylor, *Awakening from History*, Boston: Gambit, 1969, p. 328.

Chapter Forty-one: Springtime in Paris

p. 350 'They have come from America' Mary Berg (Miriam Wattenberg), *The Diary of Mary Berg: Growing Up in the Warsaw Ghetto* (originally published in English as *Warsaw Ghetto: A Diary*, New York: L. B. Fischer,1945), translation from the Polish by Susan Glass, Oxford: Oneworld, 2006, p. 245.

p. 350 On board the *Gripsholm* '128 Still Aboard Liner Gripsholm', *New York Times*, 17 March 1944, p. 5.

p. 351 'boarded by an official' Frank S. Adams, '35 Soldiers, Ill but Happy, First to Leave *Gripsholm*', *New York Times*, 16 March 1944, p. 1.

p. 351 One passenger was ... 'The Paris air' 'Paris Ghost City, Repatriate Says', *New York Times*, 17 March 1944, p. 4.

p. 352 'Life in Paris' Clara Longworth de Chambrun, *Shadows Lengthen: The Story of My Life*, New York: Charles Scribner's Sons, 1949, p. 181.

p. 353 'Those who listened ... We could not then' *Ibid.*, p. 182.

p. 353 'the fallen houses ... as he did' *Ibid.*, p. 183.

p. 353 'It was an ironical' *Ibid.*, p. 181.

p. 354 'The quarter presented ... People in this' Alice-Leone Moats, *No Passport for Paris*, New York: G. P. Putnam's Sons, 1945, pp. 237–8.

p. 355 On 9 April, she and René Yves Pourcher, *Pierre Laval vu par sa fille d'après ses carnets intimes*, Paris, Le Cherche-Midi, 2002, p. 315.

p. 355 'I am not unhappy' Julian Jackson, *France: The Dark Years 1940–1944*, Oxford: Oxford University Press, 2001, p. 310.

p. 355 Josée de Chambrun, one of the most Pourcher, *Pierre Laval vu par sa fille d'après ses carnets intimes*, p. 312.

p. 355 Moreover ... they even consented' Longworth de Chambrun, *Shadows Lengthen*, p. 183.

p. 356 'I hesitated a moment' *Ibid.*

p. 356 'During this ceremony' Longworth de Chambrun, *Shadows Lengthen*, pp. 184–5.

p. 357 'I imagine that ... tracked it down' Alice-Leone Moats, *No Passport for Paris*, pp. 217 and 222.

Chapter Forty-two: The Maquis to Arms!

p. 359 'From German sources' Neal H. Petersen (ed.), *From Hitler's Doorstep: The Wartime Intelligence Reports of Allen Dulles, 1942–1945*, University Park, PA: Pennsylvania State University Press, 1996, p. 37.

p. 359 Help came from an unexpected Larry Collins and Dominique Lapierre, *Is Paris Burning?*, New York: Simon and Schuster, 1965, pp. 190–91n.

p. 360 While in Niort *Ibid.*

p. 360 Posch-Pastor adopted the alias Hal Vaughan, *Doctor to the Resistance: The Heroic Story of an American Surgeon and His Family in Occupied France*, Washington: Brassey's, 2004, p. 105.

p. 361 'The lawyer was quite' Alice-Leone Moats, *No Passport for Paris*, New York: G. P. Putnam's Sons, 1945, p. 243.

p. 361 'We all admire' *Ibid.*, p. 244.

p. 361 That night, Alice-Leone Moats *Ibid.*, p. 274.

Chapter Forty-three: Résistants *Unmasked*

p. 363 'all general meetings' Telegram 48-52 to London, 3 July 1943, from Allen Dulles, in Neal H. Petersen (ed.), *From Hitler's Doorstep: The Wartime Intelligence Reports of Allen Dulles, 1942–1945*, University Park, PA: Pennsylvania State University Press, 1996, p. 77.

p. 364 'compromising letters addressed' Incoming Telegram, [US Minister to Switzerland Leland] Harrison to Secretary of State, 7 August 1944, RG 59, Decimal File 1940–44, Box 1160, Document 351.1121 Jackson, Sumner W./8-744, US National Archives, College Park, Maryland.

p. 364 Hints that something was wrong Hal Vaughan, *Doctor to the Resistance: The Heroic Story of an American Surgeon and His Family in Occupied France*, Washington: Brassey's, 2004, p. 105, p. 109.

p. 366 'We were all arrested' Handwritten letter from Charlotte (Toquette) Jackson to her sister-in-law, Mrs Clifford (Freda) Swensen, 18 May 1945, Massachusetts General Hospital Archives, File: Sumner Jackson.

p. 366 'Today is the day ... My courage is' Letter from Charlotte (Toquette) Jackson to her sister, Alice (Tat) Barrelet de Ricou, 31 May 1944, quoted in Vaughan, *Ibid.*, p. 112.

p. 367 'We had spent 8 days' Phillip Jackson, handwritten letter, 'Dear Friends', 10 May 1945, from Neustadt, Holstein, Germany, Massachusetts General Hospital Archives, File: Sumner Jackson.

p. 367 'We were then separated' *Ibid.*

p. 367 'As I was an' Interview with Phillip Jackson, May 2000, Paris, in Vaughan, *Doctor to the Resistance*, p. 114.

p. 368 'informed U.S. Legation' Letter via airmail pouch from Minister, American Legation, Berne, to Secretary of State, 8 June 1944, Document 351.1121, Jackson, Sumner W./6-2944, US National Archives, College Park, Maryland.

p. 368 'Swiss Legation Vichy' Incoming Telegraph, Harrison to Secretary of State, 13 July 1944, RG 59, Decimal File, 1940–44, Document 351.1121 Jackson, Sumner W./7-1344, US National Archives, College Park, Maryland.

p. 368 'On June 27, 1944' 'Memorandum for the American Embassy in Paris', Enclosure No. 1 to Despatch No. 1148 from American Embassy, Paris, 27 February 1945, 13 July 1944, RG 59, Decimal File, 1940–44, Document 351.1121 Jackson, Sumner W./3-545, US National Archives, College Park, Maryland.

p. 368 'At the same time' *Ibid.*

p. 369 **'We are not in the war'** 'The Unliberated – The France Still in Chains Writhed with Hope and Hate', *Time*, 19 June 1944.

p. 369 **The Resistance did** 'Patriots Cut Rails From Paris South', *New York Times*, 11 August 1944, p. 3.

p. 369 **'The star of hope'** Clara Longworth de Chambrun, *Shadows Lengthen: The Story of My Life*, New York: Charles Scribner's Sons, 1949, p. 212.

p. 370 **Paris, as its supply** Dominiqe Lapierre, 'August 1944, When Allied Flags Began to Appear in Paris Windows', *International Herald Tribune*, Paris, 22 August 1994.

Chapter Forty-four: Via Dolorosa

p. 371 **'One fine day'** Phillip Jackson, handwritten letter, 'Dear Friends', 10 May 1945, from Neustadt, Holstein, Germany, Massachusetts General Hospital Archives, File: Sumner Jackson. See also State Department typed transcript of the same letter, RG 59, Decimal File, 1945–49, Box 1710, Document 351.1121 Jackson, Sumner W./5-2445. On p. 367 Phillip is quoted that he spent 16 days in the Gestrapo prison, however, in this quote it is 14 days.

p. 371 **'finally had been'** 'Memorandum for the American Embassy in Paris', Enclosure No. 1 to Despatch No. 1148 from American Embassy, Paris, 27 February 1945, 13 July 1944, RG 59, Decimal File, 1940–44, Box 5280, Document 351.1121 Jackson, Sumner W./3-545, US National Archives, College Park, Maryland.

p. 371 **'Inquiry of Swiss Foreign'** Incoming Telegram, Harrison to Secretary of State, 28 August 1944, RG 59, Decimal File, 1940–44, Document 351.1121 Jackson, Sumner W./8-2844, US National Archives, College Park, Maryland.

p. 372 **'Journey by bus'** Phillip Jackson, handwritten letter, 'Dear Friends', 10 May 1945, from Neustadt, Holstein, Germany, Massachusetts General Hospital Archives, File: Sumner Jackson. See also State Department typed transcript of the same letter, RG 59, Decimal File, 1945–49, Box 1710, Document 351.1121 Jackson, Sumner W./5-2445.

p. 372 **When he and Phillip** 'Paragraph of a Cable Received', from Leland Harrison, US Minister to Switzerland, to Secretary of State, 2 June 1944, Cable number 3504, RG 389: Records of the Provost Marshal General, American POW Information Bureau, General Subject File, 1942–1946, File: Vittel Vosges (Frontstalag 194), US National Archives, College Park, Maryland. Harrison wrote that the Germans moved the camp because 'black market operations were indulged in by certain elements at Compiègne for quite a while'.

p. 372 'Red Cross parcels' Phillip Jackson, handwritten letter, 'Dear Friends', 10 May 1945, from Neustadt, Holstein, Germany, Massachusetts General Hospital Archives, File: Sumner Jackson. See also State Department typed transcript of the same letter, RG 59, Decimal File, 1945–49, Box 1710, Document 351.1121 Jackson, Sumner W./5-2445.

p. 372 'We were escorted' *Ibid.*

Chapter Forty-five: Schwarze Kapelle

p. 374 'Hitler's dead' Roger Manville and Heinrich Fraenkel, *The July Plot: The Attempt on Hitler's Life in July 1944*, London: The Bodley Head, 1964, p. 130.

p. 375 'the nightmare of a shadowy' Edmond Taylor, *Awakening from History*, Boston: Gambit, 1969, p. 328.

Chapter Forty-six: Slaves of the Reich

p. 376 'Nobody knew why ... A man of' George Martelli with Michel Hollard, *The Man Who Saved London: The Story of Michel Hollard, D.S.O., Croix de Guerre*, London: Companion Book Club, 1960, pp. 235–6.

Chapter Forty-seven: One Family Now

p. 379 'Kindly make it clear' Neal H. Petersen (ed.), *From Hitler's Doorstep: The Wartime Intelligence Reports of Allen Dulles, 1942–1945*, University Park, PA: Pennsylvania State University Press, 1996, p. 334.

p. 379 Enfière informed Laval Hubert Cole, *Laval: A Biography*, London: Heinemann, 1963, p. 262.

p. 379 On the morning of Larry Collins and Dominique Lapierre, *Is Paris Burning?*, New York: Simon and Schuster, 1965, p. 75.

p. 379 Laval was having dinner Pierre Laval, *The Unpublished Diary of Pierre Laval*, London: Falcon Press, 1948, p. 172.

p. 380 'A notice of arrest' *Ibid.*, p. 175.

p. 380 'President Herriot and you' René de Chambrun, *Sorti du rang*, Paris: Atelier Marcel Jullian, 1980, p. 237.

p. 380 'it was a marvelous summer day' Josée Laval de Chambrun, 'The Last Luncheon with Pierre Laval', in René de Chambrun, *Pierre Laval: Traitor or Patriot?*, New York: Charles Scribner's Sons, 1984, Exhibit I, p. 193. See also Josée Laval de Chambrun, in 'A Luncheon on 17 August 1944', *France During the German Occupation, 1940–1944: A*

Collection of 292 *Statements on the Government of Maréchal Pétain and Pierre Laval,* translated from the French by Philip W. Whitcomb, vol. II, Palo Alto, CA: The Hoover Institution, Stanford University, 1957, pp. 1022–5.

p. 380 'Abetz looked very much embarrassed … anecdotes and reminiscences' de Chambrun, *pp.* 194–5.

p. 381 René followed his wife *Ibid., Sorti du rang,* p. 239.

p. 381 'There is a side' de Chambrun, *Pierre Laval: Traitor or Patriot?,* p. 110. Seymour Weller was the cousin of Clarence Dillon, who bought Château Haut-Brion in 1935 at the suggestion of Aldebert de Chambrun. René had been sponsored by Dillon in New York and was a regular guest at his house in Far Hills, New Jersey, before the war.

p. 381 The American was his friend Seymour Weller's cousin, Joan de Mouchy, told the author in 2006 that, when a German officer warned him he was about to be interned, he would check into the American Hospital for a supposed operation. Weller was the cousin of Joan's grandfather, Clarence Dillon, who owned the Château de Haut-Brion vineyards. Pierre Laval sponsored Weller for French citizenship in 1939.

p. 382 'I hurried to Matignon … She knew that I' Clara Longworth de Chambrun, *Shadows Lengthen: The Story of My Life,* New York: Charles Scribner's Sons, 1949, p. 216.

p. 382 'in whose hands' Laval, *The Unpublished Diary of Pierre Laval,* p. 175.

p. 382 'The German police' Longworth de Chambrun, *Shadows Lengthen,* p. 217. Laval wrote that, in fact, three of his ministers managed to disappear: Cathala, Grasset and Chassaigne (Pierre Laval, *The Unpublished Diary of Pierre Laval,* p. 175).

p. 382 The three Chambruns Collins and Lapierre, *Is Paris Burning?,* p. 93.

p. 383 'I was in love with the daughter' Yves Pourcher, *Pierre Laval vu par sa fille d'après ses carnets intimes,* Paris: Le Cherche-Midi, p. 70.

p. 383 The Federal Reserve chief Sylvia Jukes Morris, *Rage for Fame: The Ascent of Clare Boothe Luce,* New York: Random House, 1997. On p. 17, the author wrote that Clara and Aldebert had dinner in Washington with Eugene and Agnes Meyer in 1932 just before Meyer bought the *Washington Post.* René was living in New York at the time. The author added, 'Not many years before, Alice's [Roosevelt's] husband, Nicholas, Speaker of the House, had been surprised in flagrante delicto with Cissy [Patterson] on a bathroom floor.'

p. 383 There was also an aversion Clara confessed that, when her cousin Margaret married Pierre de Chambrun in 1895, 'I could not disguise from myself that I felt badly about Margaret's marriage, just as two years before I had taken her conversion [to Catholicism] rather hard, not that my own Protestantism was at all of a militant character, for we had all been brought up in the atmosphere of tolerance which is one of the best characteristics of Cincinnati' (Clara Longworth de Chambrun, *Shadows Like Myself*, New York: Charles Scribner's Sons, 1936, p. 29). For Clara, tolerance won out when she married Pierre's brother, the Catholic Aldebert, six years later. For René to marry a woman of German-Jewish background, though, may have been less acceptable. René's reluctance to stray beyond family bounds explained, in part, his loyalty to a father-in-law whom the Allies believed incarnated French submission to Germany. Eugene Meyer bought the *Washington Post* at a bankruptcy sale in 1933, and in 1939 Florence Meyer married Austrian character actor Oscar Homulka. Her younger sister, Katharine, married Philip Graham and later became publisher of the *Washington Post*.

p. 384 'We had risked spending' René de Chambrun, *Sorti du rang*, p. 239.

p. 384 'Come now! Good' Will Brownell and Richard N. Billings, *So Close to Greatness: A Biography of William C. Bullitt*, New York: Macmillan, 1987, p. 302.

p. 384 *Ibid.*, p. 304.

Chapter Forty-eight: The Paris Front

p. 385–6 'Heartbroken as I was ... Inside the gardens' Clara Longworth de Chambrun, *Shadows Lengthen: The Story of My Life*, New York: Charles Scribner's Sons, 1949, pp. 219–20.

p. 386 'Whatever happens ... the Führer' Larry Collins and Dominique Lapierre, *Is Paris Burning?*, New York: Simon and Schuster, 1965, p. 141.

p. 387 'Amateurish barricades sprang' de Chambrun, *Shadows Lengthen*, p. 224.

p. 387 'The children engaged' Sylvia Beach, *Shakespeare and Company*, London: Faber and Faber, 1960, pp. 222–3.

p. 388 'We heard that "'they'" *Ibid.*, p. 223.

p. 388 The area commander General Aldebert de Chambrun to the Board of Directors of the American Hospital of Paris, 9 December 1944, p. 5 (of a 7 page typescript), in Archives of the American Hospital of Paris, File: American Hospital Report: 1940–1944. Otto Gresser, the hospital's superintendent of administrative services during the occupation, wrote that the Germans in Neuilly had '18 guns, 5 tanks, 60 trucks and a large supply of munitions'.

p. 389 'I ask you to consider' René de Chambrun, *Sorti du rang*, Paris: Atelier Marcel Jullian, 1980, p. 229.

p. 389 On the morning of 19 August Collins and Lapierre, *Is Paris Burning?*, p. 113.

p. 389 'a fortress capable' de Chambrun, *Sorti du rang*, p. 230.

p. 390 'It is impossible' *Ibid.*, p. 229.

p. 390 'Strange spectacle that' *Ibid.*

p. 390 **The French and German soldiers** Interview with Otto Gresser, in Kathleen Keating, 'The American Hospital of Paris During the German Occupation', May 1981, 14-page typescript, Archives of the American Hospital of Paris, File: The German Occupation by Kathleen Keating and Various Other Histories.

p. 391 'many persons of extremely' Longworth de Chambrun, *Shadows Lengthen*, p. 221.

p. 391 'I recognized her' *Ibid.*, p. 221.

p. 392 **Clara had promised ... 'arrived safely at home'** *Ibid.*, p. 223.

Chapter Forty-nine: Tout Mourir

p. 393 **The Nazis had sent** Telegram sent (Secretary of State Cordell) Hull to American Embassy London, 14 September 1944, RG 59, Decimal File 1940–1944, Box 1160, Document 351.1121, Jackson, Sumner W./9-1444, US National Archives, College Park, Maryland.

p. 393 **The others were Lucienne** Catherine Rothman-Le Dret, *L'Amérique déportée: Virginia d'Albert-Lake de la Résistance à Ravensbrück*, Nancy: Presses Universitaires de Nancy, 1994, pp. 17 and 41.

p. 393 **Toquette's sister, Tat** Letter from Julia Barrelet de Ricou, American wife of Toquette's brother, to Mrs Franklin Roosevelt, 1 November 1944, RG 59, Decimal File 1940–1944, Box 1160, Document 351.1121, Jackson, Sumner W./9-664.

p. 394 'I am full of hope' Larry Collins and Dominique Lapierre, *Is Paris Burning?*, New York: Simon and Schuster, 1965, p. 62.

p. 394 'his gigantic size ... *Nicht Messe*' Maisie Renault, *La Grande Misère*, Paris: Chavane, 1948, pp. 19–20.

p. 394 'Since this morning' From the journal of Virginia d'Albert-Lake, quoted in Rothman-Le Dret, *L'Amérique déportée*, p. 96.

p. 394 'They pitied us' Virginia d'Albert-Lake, *An American Heroine in the French Resistance: The Diary and Memoir of Virginia d'Albert-Lake*, New York: Fordham University Press, 2006, p. 144. See also Rothman-Le Dret, *L'Amérique déportée*, p. 97.

p. 394 **The trains taking** Renault, *La Grande Misère*, p. 21.

p. 396 **His French Second Armoured** Collins and Lapierre, *Is Paris Burning?*, pp. 61–2n.

p. 396 'It is highly desirable' John Lichfield, 'Liberation of Paris: The Hidden Truth', *Independent*, London, 31 January 2007. See also Olivier Wieviorka, *Histoire du débarquement en Normandie*, Paris: Seuil, 2007.

p. 397 'This guerilla warfare ... was credibly informed' Clara Longworth de Chambrun, *Shadows Lengthen: The Story of My Life*, New York: Charles Scribner's Sons, 1949, pp. 224–5.

p. 398 **Clara did not know** Collins and Lapierre, *Is Paris Burning?*, pp. 249 and 279.

p. 398 'He came on his bicycle ... and, before Joyce' Sylvia Beach, *Shakespeare and Company*, London: Faber and Faber, 1960, p. 102.

p. 399 'Cannon is roaring' Longworth de Chambrun, *Shadows Lengthen*, p. 225.

p. 399 'The hospital found ... I am, General' René de Chambrun, *Sorti du rang*, Paris: Atelier Marcel Jullian, 1980, pp. 230–31.

p. 399 'I asked why he' Longworth de Chambrun, *Shadows Lengthen*, p. 226. There are accounts of the battle at Neuilly from Aldebert, Clara and René de Chambrun, as well as from Otto Gresser. They conflict on a few dates and times, as well as the exact statements made by the principals. My account emphasizes the points on which they agree and, where they do not, relies on the eyewitnesses, Aldebert and Gresser, more than the two who were told about it, Clara and René. Their versions agree, however, on the main points.

p. 399 'The French have to receive' de Chambun, *Sorti du rang*, p. 231.

p. 400 'More wounded have ... I did not need' Longworth de Chambrun, *Shadows Lengthen*, p. 226.

p. 400 **Leclerc, she believed** Clara was not alone in thinking the Resistance were ruffians. A Free French lieutenant, who ordered his MP not to allow Ernest Hemingway to get ahead of a regular armed column, added, 'And none of that guerrilla rabble either.' See Ernest Hemingway, 'How We Came to Paris', *Collier's*, 7 October 1944, p. 65. Despite the fact that the Resistance was providing the Allies with minute by minute intelligence on the location of German tanks and defences, many of the regular officers distrusted them.

p. 401 'What you hear is' Another version of this incident was that von Cholitz was asked by a secretary why the bells were ringing. He is said to have replied, 'They are ringing for us, my little girl. They are ringing because the Allies are coming into Paris. Why else do you suppose they would be ringing?' Collins and La pierne, *op. cit.*, p. 258.

p. 401 'went to the roof' Otto Gresser interview with Kathleen Keating, 'The American Hospital in Paris during the German Occupation', 19 May 1981, 14-page typescript, p. 11, American Hospital of Paris Archives, File: German Occupation by Kathleen Keating and Various Other Histories, 1940–1944.

p. 402 **On schedule, a command car ... 'Stack arms'** Longworth de Chambrun, *Shadows Lengthen*, p. 226.

p. 402 The 'fanatic' Major Goetz de Chambrun, *Sorti du rang*, p. 233.

p. 402 'we met within three' Otto Gresser, 'History of the American
Hospital', 14-page typescript, 28 September 1978, American Hospital of
Paris Archives, unnumbered blue file: 'Miscellaneous materials'.

p. 402 'Telegraph exact location' Telegram, Hull to Harrison, Berne,
25 August 1944, RG 59, Decimal file 1945–1949, Box 1710, Document
351.1121, Jackson, Sumner W./8-744, US National Archives, College
Park, Maryland.

PART SEVEN: 24–26 AUGUST 1944

Chapter Fifty: Liberating the Rooftops

p. 407 'It was Saturday' Adrienne Monnier, 'Americans in Paris', in *The
Very Rich Hours of Adrienne Monnier: An Intimate Portrait of the
Literary and Artistic Life in Paris Between the Wars*, translated by
Richard McDougall, New York: Charles Scribner's Sons, 1976, p. 416.

p. 407 'The way back' *Ibid.*

p. 408 'Sylvia ran down' *Ibid.*, p. 416. Hemingway did not write of his
reunion with Sylvia Beach in his *Collier's* articles about the liberation of
Paris, but Sylvia and Adrienne did. Most of their accounts are in
Adrienne's 'Americans in Paris' and in Sylvia's *Shakespeare and
Company*, London: Faber and Faber, 1960, pp. 223–4. Sylvia discussed it
with Niall Sheridan for the documentary film *Self Portraits: Sylvia Beach*,
Radio Telefis Eireann (RTE), Dublin, 1962. She was in Dublin for the
dedication of the Martello Tower, where the first chapter of *Ulysses*
opens, on 16 June 1962, the fifty-eighth anniversary of Bloomsday.

p. 408 'I flew downstairs' *Shakespeare and Company*, p. 220.

p. 408 'War correspondents are' Ernest Hemingway, 'Battle for Paris',
Collier's, 30 September 1944, p. 83.

p. 408 'I couldn't say' Ernest Hemingway, 'How We Came to Paris',
Collier's, 7 October 1944, p. 17.

p. 408 'For the moment' Monnier, 'Americans in Paris', p. 417.

p. 409 'invited them to come' *Ibid.*

p. 409 'We went up to Adrienne's' *Shakespeare and Company*, p. 220.

p. 409 'Hadn't I, Adrienne' Adrienne Monnier, 'Americans in Paris', p. 417.

p. 409 'He brought his men' Interview by Niall Sheridan with Sylvia Beach,
Self Portraits: Sylvia Beach, documentary film for Radio Telefis Eireann
(RTE), Dublin, 1962.

p. 410 When Hemingway brought Beach, *Shakespeare and Company*,
p. 224: 'We heard firing for the last time in the rue de l'Odéon.
Hemingway and his men came down again and rode off in their jeeps –
"to liberate", according to Hemingway, "the cellar of the Ritz".'

p. 410 At the American Embassy 'Caffery Thanks Aids Who Held U.S. Embassy', *New York Herald Tribune*, Paris, 11 January 1945, p. 4.

Chapter Fifty-one: Libération, *not Liberation*

p. 412 Anderson folded his newspaper William Smith Gardner, 'The Oldest Negro in Paris', *Ebony*, vol. 8, no. 2, February 1952, pp. 65–72. Charles Anderson, then 91, told Gardner he had courted Eugénie Delmar for a year and a half before they married in 1922. She took him afterwards to meet her family in Calais. 'They have never once even *mentioned* the fact that I'm a Negro,' Anderson said. Anderson supplemented his income from de Brosse by teaching chess, English and music. Although a good musician who lived in Montmartre, he did not frequent its American black jazz clubs before the war. This may have been because he neither drank nor smoked and was devoted to his wife.

Epilogue

p. 414 'We eat quantities ... She is sad' Letter from Sylvia Beach to Holly Beach Dennis, 4 October 1944, Sylvia Beach Papers, Princeton University, CO108, Box 20, Unnumbered folder.

p. 414 'closed for the time being' Sylvia Beach, 'French Literature Went Underground', *Paris Herald Tribune*, 4 January 1945, p. 2.

p. 415 'I must say' Longworth de Chambrun, *Shadows Lengthen: The Story of My Life*, New York: Charles Scribner's Sons, 1949, p. 233.

p. 416 At the Prefecture ... Miss Comte took Aldebert Eric Hawkins, 'Elder Chambruns Questioned in Paris Collaborationist Purge', *New York Herald Tribune*, 11 September 1944.

p. 416 'Chambrun situation' Letter from Edward A. Sumner to Dr David H. Stevens, Rockefeller Foundation, 12 March 1945, American Library of Paris Archives, File: Correspondence.

p. 416 Rather than pay 'American Library in Paris Intact', *Library Journal*, vol. 70, no. 1, February 1945, p. 111.

p. 417 Along with Aldebert 'Member of Pioneer Family Dies in France', *Cincinnati Times Star*, 2 June 1945. 'Mme. De Chambrun Dies in Paris at 80', *New York Times*, 2 June 1945, p. 31.

p. 417 'On the morning' Letter from Phillip Jackson, 8–10 May 1945, written at Neustadt, Holstein, Germany, in Massachusetts General Hospital Archives, Dr Sumner Jackson file.

p. 418 'I want you to know Letter from Charlotte Jackson to Freda Swensen, 18 July 1945, Massachusetts General Hospital Archives, Dr Sumner Jackson file.

ACKNOWLEDGEMENTS

Fluctura nec mergitur.
(It wavers but does not sink.)

Official motto of Paris

LARRY COLLINS, whose offer to be a mentor of this book was quickly accepted, deserves special thanks. If he had lived long enough to go over the manuscript with the master's red pencil, it would have been infinitely improved. No one wrote a better book on Paris at the conclusion of the German occupation than his and Dominique Lapierre's *Is Paris Burning?* It is my regret that I must thank him posthumously for his good will and inspiration.

I must offer exceptional thanks to Priscilla Rattazzi and Stanley and Lisa Weiss, without whose friendship and support this book would not have been completed. If I were not dedicating this book to my father, who read the early chapters just before he died, it would be dedicated to them.

In France, I owe much to the Duc and Duchesse de Mouchy, Joan and Philippe, for advice, kindness, hospitality and insights into Franco-American life now and during the war. I must also thank my old friends Jonathan and Geneviève Randal, Julian Nundy, Elizabeth Lennard and Ermanno Corrado for unfailing support and more of their time than they needed to give. I am grateful as well for valuable help from Sarah Kefi, Anna Elliot, Lee Hunnewell, Luke Burnap, Thierry Bertmann, Colette Faus, Michael Neal, Caroline Huot, Rowan Fraser, Sophie Grivet of the René and Josée de Chambrun Foundation, Adele Witt and the rest of the American Library of Paris staff, Rebecca Allaigre of the American Hospital of Paris, Frances

Bommart of the American Cathedral, Werner Paravicini of the Institut Historique Allemand, Don and Petie Kladstrup, Madame Claude du Granrut, William Pfaff and Sylvia Beach Whitman of the revived Shakespeare and Company Bookshop.

In Britain, I am grateful to Allan Massie, David Sievewright, Charles and April Fawcett, Edward Venning, Carol Anderson, Laura Cooper of the Royal Institute for International Affairs, Amanda Court and the other staff members of the London Library, the archivists at the National Archives in Kew Gardens and the Travel Bookshop in Notting Hill. My debt to Vera Tussing for rendering German documents into impeccable English is considerable.

In the United States, my profound thanks must go to one of the world's finest researchers, who should soon be producing books of her own, Cora Currier. My gratitude extends to Nancy Smith and Susan Boone of the Sophie Smith Collection at the Smith College Library, Chris and Jennifer Isham, Mary Kathryn Cox, Mrs Mary Alice Burke, Elaine Krikorian, Svetlana Katz, Giselle Remy Brachter of the Craig Lloyd/Eugene Bullard Collection at the Columbia State University Archives, Ayuna Haruun of the *Chicago Defender*, Rob Warden, Douglas Spitzer, Dolores Kennedy, Pegeen Bassett, Elizabeth L. Garver of the Harry Ransom Humanities Research Center at the University of Texas at Austin, Mary Miller of the American Library Association Archives at the University of Illinois, the staffs of the New York Public Library and the Library of Congress, John Taylor and his fellow archivists at the National Archives at College Park, Maryland, Martha Stone and Jeff Mifflin of Massachusetts General Hospital and John F. Fox, Jr, historian at the Federal Bureau of Investigation.

Jim Christy, who wrote a biography of Charles Bedaux (*The Price of Power*), and Hal Vaughan, biographer of Sumner Jackson (*Doctor to the Resistance*), were exceptionally kind in pointing me towards documents I needed and only they knew about. I owe them favours that I look forward to repaying.

Natasha Grenfell, Laure Boulay and Jasper Guinness exceeded the usual parameters of friendship to grant me congenial surroundings and their delightful company in houses far from the distractions of my confused life. I am beholden as well to Alessandro and Michelle Corsini (and their eight children) for weekends in their Porto Ercole house to revise this book in the garden that inspired Puccini to write 'Turandot'. My gratitude to them is unbounded but, now, not unstated.

I would also like to mention my children Julia, Edward, George, Hester and Beatrix, and my godchildren, Mia Ross, Laura Gilmour, Charlie Cockburn and Max McCullin, for no other reason than that they are my children and godchildren.

It is usual for writers to show appreciation to their publishers and agents, but this utterance of gratitude is more than pro forma. My lawyers in New York, Steve Sheppard and Michael Kennedy, my New York agent, Tina Bennett, my London agent, Georgina Capel, Ann Godoff of Penguin, Martin Redfern, Michael Upchurch, Minna Fry, Taressa Brennan, Judith House and Richard Johnson of HarperCollins and France Roque of Editions Saint-Simon gave me time, encouragement and sympathy that moved our professional connections into the realm of friendship.

My final acknowledgement must go to the Café Flore, Café La Palette, Café de Tournon (haunt of my literary hero, Joseph Roth) and Bar du Marché in Paris, Caffè Appia Antica and Camilloni a Sant-Eustachio in Rome and the Coffee Plant and the Café Oporto in London, all of whose staffs supplied me with the coffee, ash trays and writing tables that I needed to put this story on paper. No one was better provided with space in which to puzzle out a tale that took a long time to decipher and longer still to tell.

SELECT BIBLIOGRAPHY

Books

Allen, Martin. *Hidden Agenda: How the Duke of Windsor Betrayed the Allies*. London: Macmillan, 2000.

Americans in France: A Directory, 1939–1940. Paris: American Chamber of Commerce in France, 1940.

Aubrac, Lucie. *Outwitting the Gestapo*, translated by Konrad Bieber. Lincoln: University of Nebraska Press, 1985.

Beach, Sylvia. *Shakespeare and Company*. London: Faber and Faber, 1960.

Bedaux, Gaston. *La Vie ardente de Charles Bedaux*. Paris: privately published, 3 June 1959.

Berg, Mary (Miriam Wattenberg). *The Diary of Mary Berg: Growing Up in the Warsaw Ghetto* (originally published in English as *Warsaw Ghetto: A Diary*, 1945). Oxford: translation from Polish by Susan Glass, Oneworld, 2006.

Black, Edwin. *IBM and the Holocaust: The Strategic Alliance Between Nazi Germany and America's Most Powerful Corporation*. New York: Crown Publishers, 2001.

Bove, Dr Charles with Thomas, Dana Lee. *Paris: A Surgeon's Story*. New York: Little, Brown and Company, 1956.

Brownell, Will and Billings, Richard N. *So Close to Greatness: A Biography of William C. Bullitt*. New York: Macmillan, 1987.

Bullitt, Orville (ed.). *For the President, Personal and Secret: Correspondence Between Franklin D. Roosevelt and William C. Bullitt*. Boston: Houghton Mifflin, 1972.

Carisella, P. J. and Ryan, James W. *The Black Swallow of Death*. Boston: Marlborough House, 1972.

Christy, Jim. *The Price of Power: A Biography of Charles Eugene Bedaux*. New York: Doubleday and Company, 1984.

Cole, Hubert. *Laval: A Biography*. London: Heinemann, 1963.

Collier, Peter. *1940: The World in Flames*. London: Hamish Hamilton, 1979.

Collins, Larry and Lapierre, Dominique. *Is Paris Burning?* New York: Simon and Schuster, 1965.

Cowles, Virginia. *Looking for Trouble.* London: Hamish Hamilton, 1941.

d'Albert-Lake, Virginia. *An American Heroine in the French Resistance: The Diary and Memoir of Virginia d'Albert-Lake*, ed. Judy Barrett Litoff. New York: Fordham University Press, 2006.

de Brinon, Fernand. *Mémoires.* Paris: La P. Internationale, 1949.

de Chambrun, Adolphe. *Impressions of Lincoln and the Civil War: A Foreigner's Account*, trans. General Adlebert de Chambrun. New York: Random House, 1952.

de Chambrun, René. *Mission and Betrayal, I Saw France Fall: Will She Rise Again?* New York: William Morrow and Company, 1940.

de Chambrun, René. *Sorti du rang.* Paris: Atelier Marcel Jullian, 1980.

de Chambrun, René. *Pierre Laval: Traitor or Patriot?* New York: Charles Scribner's Sons, 1984.

de Chambrun, René. *Mission and Betrayal, 1940–1945: Working with Franklin Roosevelt to Help Save Britain and Europe.* Stanford, CA: Hoover Institution Press, 1992.

de Saint-Exupéry, Antoine. *Wartime Writings, 1939–1944.* New York: Harcourt, Brace, Jovanovich, 1986.

Fabre, Marc-André. *Dans les prisons de Vichy.* Paris: Albin Michel, 1995.

Fitch, Noel Riley. *Sylvia Beach and the Lost Generation: A History of Literary Paris in the Twenties and Thirties.* New York: W. W. Norton and Company, 1983.

Flanner, Janet. *Janet Flanner's World: Uncollected Writings 1932–1975.* London: Secker and Warburg, 1980.

France During the German Occupation, 1940–1944: A Collection of 292 Statements on the Government of Maréchal Pétain and Pierre Laval, trans. from French by Philip W. Whitcomb. Palo Alto, CA: The Hoover Institution, Stanford University, three volumes, 1957. French edition *La Vie de la France sous L'Occupation (1940–1944).* Paris: Librarie Plon for Institut Hoover, 1957.

Gallup, Donald (ed.). *The Flowers of Friendship: Letters Written to Gertrude Stein.* New York: Alfred A. Knopf, 1953.

Gildea, Robert. *Marianne in Chains: In Search of the German Occupation of France, 1940–1945.* New York: Macmillan, 2002.

Gilliam, Florence. *France: A Tribute by an America Woman.* New York: E. P. Dutton and Company, 1945.

Griffiths, Frank. *Winged Hours.* London: William Kimber, 1981.

Hardwick, C. M. *Time Study in Treason: Charles E. Bedaux, Patriot or Collaborator*, Chelmsford: Peter Horsnell, undated ... probably 1990.

Heller, Gerhard. *Un Allemand à Paris.* Paris: Editions du Seuil, 1981.

Select Bibliography

Husser, Beate. *Le Camp de Royallieu à Compiègne: Etude historique*. Paris: Fondation pour la Mémoire de la Déportation, September 2001.

Irving, David. *Hitler's War and the War Path, 1933–1945*. London: Focal Point, 1991.

Jackson, Julian. *France: The Dark Years 1940–1944*. Oxford: Oxford University Press, 2001.

Jucker, Ninetta. *Curfew in Paris: A Record of the German Occupation*. London: The Hogarth Press, 1960.

Kennan, George. *Sketches from a Life*. New York: Pantheon Books, 1989.

Kenward, H. R. *Occupied France: Collaboration and Resistance, 1940–1944*. Oxford: Blackwell, 1985.

Kernan, Thomas. *Paris on Berlin Time*. Philadelphia and New York: J. P. Lippincott Company, 1941.

Kladstrup, Don and Petie. *Wine and War*. New York: Broadway Books, 2001.

Koestler, Arthur. *The Scum of the Earth*. London: Cape, 1941. Reprinted Eland Books, 1991.

Koestler, Arthur. *The Invisible Writing*, vol. II of *Arrow in the Blue*, London: Collins with Hamish Hamilton, 1954.

Lagard, Dorothy. *American Hospital of Paris: A Century of Adventure, 1906–2006*. Paris: Le Cherche-Midi, 2006.

Langeron, Roger. *Paris, juin 1940*. Paris: Flammarion, 1946.

Larkin, Maurice. *France since the Popular Front: Government and People, 1936–1996*. Oxford: Clarendon Press, 1998.

Laval, Pierre. *The Unpublished Diary of Pierre Laval*, introduction Josée Laval, Countess R. de Chambrun. London: Falcon Press, 1948.

Leahy, Fleet Admiral William D. *I Was There: The Personal Story of the Chief of Staff to Presidents Roosevelt and Truman Based on his Notes and Diaries Made at the Time*. London: Victor Gollancz, 1950.

Léautaud, Paul. *Journal littéraire*, Paris: Mercure de France, vol. XIII, Feb. 1940–June 1941, 1962 and vol. XV, Nov. 1942–June 1944, 1963.

Liebling, A. J. *The Road Back to Paris*. London: Michael Joseph, 1944.

Lloyd, Craig. *Eugene Bullard: Black Expatriate in Jazz-Age Paris*. Athens, GA and London: University of Georgia Press, 2000.

Longworth de Chambrun, Clara. *Shadows Like Myself*. New York: Charles Scribner's Sons, 1936.

Longworth de Chambrun, Clara. *Shadows Lengthen: The Story of My Life*. New York: Charles Scribner's Sons, 1949.

Lottman, Herbert. *Pétain: Hero or Traitor: The Untold Story*. New York: William Morrow and Company, 1985.

Lottman, Herbert. *The Fall of Paris: June 1940*. London: Sinclair-Stevenson, 1992.

Loyer, Emmanuelle. *Paris à New York: Intellectuels et artistes français en exil 1940–1947*. Paris: Bernard Grasset, 2005.

Manville, Roger and Fraenkel, Heinrich. *The July Plot: The Attempt on Hitler's Life in July 1944*. London: The Bodley Head, 1964.

Marrus, Michael R. and Paxton, Robert O. *Vichy France and the Jews*. New York: Basic Books, 1981.

Martelli George with Hollard, Michel. *The Man Who Saved London: The Story of Michel Hollard, D.S.O., Croix de Guerre*. London: Companion Book Club, 1960.

Maurois, André. *Why France Fell*, trans. from French by Denver Lindley. London: The Bodley Head, 1941.

Michel, Henri. *Paris Allemand*. Paris: Albin Michel, 1981.

Moats, Alice-Leone. *No Passport for Paris*. New York: G. P. Putnam's Sons, 1945.

Monnier, Adrienne. *Trois agendas d'Adrienne Monnier*, texte établi et annoté par Maurice Saillet. Paris: published 'par ses amis', 1960.

Monnier, Adrienne. *The Very Rich Hours of Adrienne Monnier: An Intimate Portrait of the Literary and Artistic Life in Paris between the Wars*, trans. with introduction and commentary Richard McDougall. New York: Charles Scribner's Sons, 1976.

Moss, Norman. *Nineteen Weeks: Britain, America and the Fateful Summer of 1940*. London: Aurum Press, 2004.

Moynahan, Brian. *The French Century*. London: Flammarion, 2007.

Muir, Peter. *War without Music*. New York: Charles Scribner's Sons, 1940.

Murphy, Robert. *Diplomat among Warriors: Secret Decisions that Changed the World*. New York: Doubleday and Company, 1964.

Nugent, Peter. *The Black Eagle of Harlem*. New York: Bantam Books, 1972.

Ousby, Ian. *Occupation: The Ordeal of France, 1940–1944*. London: Pimlico, 1999.

Paxton, Robert O. *Vichy France: Old Guard and New Order, 1940–1944*. New York: W. W. Norton and Company (also London: Barrie & Jenkins), 1972.

Peabody, Polly. *Occupied Territory*. London: The Cresset Press, 1941.

Petersen, Neal H. (ed.), *From Hitler's Doorstep: The Wartime Intelligence Reports of Allen Dulles, 1942–1945*. University Park: Pennsylvania State University Press, 1996.

Pourcher, Yves. *Pierre Laval vu par sa fille d'après ses carnets intimes*. Paris: Le Cherche-Midi, 2002.

Pryce-Jones, David. *Paris in the Third Reich: A History of the German Occupation, 1940–1944*. London: Collins, 1981.

Renault, Maisie. *La Grande misère*. Paris: Chavane, 1948.

Reynolds, Quentin. *The Wounded Don't Cry*. London: Cassell and Company, 1941.

Robertson, Charles. *An American Poet in Paris: Pauline Avery Crawford and the Herald Tribune*. Columbia: University of Missouri Press, 2001.

Rock, George. *History of the American Field Service, 1920–1955*. New York: American Field Service Publication, undated.

Rothman-Le Dret, Catherine. *L'Amérique déportée: Virginia d'Albert-Lake de la Résistance à Ravensbrück*. Nancy: Presses Universitaires de Nancy, 1994.

Sevareid, Eric. *Not So Wild a Dream*. New York: Alfred A. Knopf, 1946.

Shack, William. *Harlem in Montmartre*. Berkeley: University of California Press, 2001.

Sheean, Vincent. *Between the Thunder and the Sun*. New York: Random House, 1943.

Shirer, William. *The Collapse of the Third Republic: An Inquiry into the Fall of France in 1940*. New York: Simon and Schuster, 1969.

Shirer, William L. *Twentieth Century Journey: Memoir of a Life and the Times*, vol. I: *The Start, 1904–1930*. Boston: Little Brown and Company, 1984.

Tartière, Drue with Werner, M. R. *The House near Paris: An American Woman's Story of Traffic in Patriots*. New York: Simon and Schuster, 1946.

Taylor, Edmond. *Awakening from History*. Boston: Gambit, 1969.

Toland, John. *Adolf Hitler*. New York: Doubleday and Company, 1976.

Ullmann, Bernard. *Lisette de Brinon, ma mère: Une Juive dans la tourment de la Collaboration*. Paris: Editions Complexe, 2004.

Vaughan, Hal. *Doctor to the Resistance: The Heroic Story of an American Surgeon and His Family in Occupied France*. Washington: Brassey's, 2004.

Viorst, Milton. *Hostile Allies: FDR and De Gaulle*. New York: Macmillan, 1965.

von Hassell, Ambassador Ulrich. *The von Hassell Diaries: 1938–1944*. London: Hamish Hamilton, 1948.

Wallace, Max. *The American Axis*. New York: St Martin's Press, 2003.

Walter, Gérard. *Paris under the Occupation*. New York: Orion Press, 1960.

Warner, Geoffrey. *Pierre Laval and the Eclipse of France*, New York: Macmillan, 1968.

Werth, Alexander. *France: 1940–1944*. London: Robert Hale Ltd, 1956.

Wieviorka, Olivier. *Histoire du débarquement en Normandie*. Paris: Seuil, 2007.

Williams, John. *The Ides of May: The Defeat of France, May–June, 1940*. London: Constable, 1968.

Film

Ophuls, Marcel. *Le Chagrin et la pitié*, France, 1971.
Sheridan, Niall. *Self-Portraits: Sylvia Beach*, documentary film on Radio
 Telefis Eireann (RTE), Dublin, 1962.
Ungar, George. *The Champagne Safari*, Canada, 1995.

INDEX